P9-EGL-752

# Sydney &
# New South Wales

Justine Vaisutis

Lindsay Brown, Jocelyn Harewood, Wendy Kramer,
Charles Rawlings-Way, Penny Watson

# Destination New South Wales

New South Wales is a work of beauty, several millennia in the making. Lunar landscapes in the south's 'big empty' and volcanoes out west are tempered by emerald rainforests in the north and a come-hither coastline skirting the east.

It's Australia's most eclectic state, and one of great contrasts. It's for nomads to spend a day in the outback devoid of civilisation, and for social butterflies to ham it up with Sydney's millions. It's for caravanning families to exhaust the Central Coast, and for ski bunnies to hit Mt Kosciuszko's slopes. It's for New Age neophytes to indulge in Byron Bay, and for gemstone addicts to fossick in New England.

Mighty rivers quench its dusty pockets and mighty mountains touch the sky. In the north of the Great Dividing Range, the misty rainforests of Washpool National Park are World Heritage–listed. Walkers traverse wildflowers in the Northwest's Warrumbungles or the hazy Blue Mountains, and divers swim with dolphins in the South Coast's Jervis Bay. Surfers conquer breaks up north and gastronomes conquer appetites in the prolific wineries and restaurants. For every traveller the road is easy. This is a state where the tourist infrastructure enables you to hit the beach in the morning, the bush in the afternoon and the bars by sundown.

New South Wales is the country's most populous state, and also the cheekiest. That laconic antipodean wit is thick in this neck of the woods – you'll find it in Sydney's gay bars, rural pubs, Darling River cruises and beachside cafés. But it's cut with genuine charm and convivial locals, who'll do their damnedest to enhance your trip.

MTMEDIA

# Sydney

HOLGER LEUE

Hit Sydney's pulsating nightlife (p95)

DENNIS JONES

Carve up the surf on Sydney's northern beaches (p64)

*Opposite:*
Take in the sights of glorious Sydney Harbour (p52)

*Previous page:*
The dramatic Perry Dunes (p293), Wentworth

Check out the spectacular 360-degree views from the Sydney Tower (p58)

HOLGER LEUE

# Highlights

ANDREW BAIN

Take a hike in the scenic Budawang
National Park (p304)

OLIVER STREWE

Visit the renowned wineries of the Hunter Valley
(p140)

Crowds flock to beautiful Bondi Beach (p61), Sydney

GARETH MCCORMACK

JOHN BANAGAN

Go skiing at the popular Thredbo snowfields (p297)

Find out how big country music is in Tamworth (p215)

PATRICK HORTON

Wander among the Walls of China (p273) in the remote Mungo National Park

CHERYL FORBES

Spot some kangaroos (p35) in NSW's idyllic national parks

MARK NEWMAN

Enjoy the breathtaking view of the Three Sisters (p123), Blue Mountains

ROSS BARNET

Relax and unwind in stunning Byron Bay (p186)

CLAVER CARROLL

# Contents

# Regional Map Contents

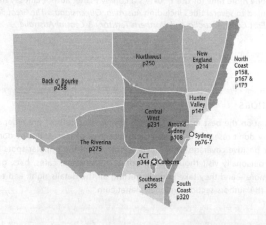

# The Authors

## JUSTINE VAISUTIS
### Coordinating Author & North Coast

Justine's love affair with the New South Wales coast began when she was barely old enough to fit into swimmers. Once she got the appropriate attire sorted she graduated to spending entire summers on a bodyboard on the South Coast. It compensated for the winter chills of her Canberran childhood. She has since lived in Sydney and traversed the coastline from Eden to Tweed Heads on several occasions. This is her second time round on Lonely Planet's *New South Wales* guide, having previously explored Around Sydney. For this edition she pottered about the North Coast, noodling for the best markets, pubs, treks and, of course, bodyboard-beaches. She also wore her swimmers.

### My Favourite Trip

My favourite trip would last about two months. It starts with a tent and a car in Jervis Bay and climbs slowly to Sydney for pub sessions, museums and downtime with mates. Then it continues through the Central Coast, where I'd temporarily hang the boots in Terrigal for the beach and more mateship. I'd hit the vino in the Hunter and the surf at Seal Rocks before hiding out in Dorrigo and Bellingen for a while. But time waits for no beach bum, so I'd find my way to the coast again and amble up to Yamba and then Byron for Middle Eastern brekkies and exotic massages. Last stop would be Brunswick Heads, where I'd spend my remaining days in its fabulous pub.

## LINDSAY BROWN
### Australian Capital Territory

Lindsay hails from Wollongong and has fractured memories of school excursions to Canberra to see how government worked and how planned cities were supposed to work. A lot has changed in and around the national capital and he enjoyed the challenge of negotiating the circuits and roundabouts one more time for this book. As a Lonely Planet author Lindsay has contributed to several titles including *Australia*, *Queensland & The Great Barrier Reef*, *East Coast Australia* and *Northern Territory & Central Australia*.

---

### LONELY PLANET AUTHORS

Why is our travel information the best in the world? It's simple: our authors are independent, dedicated travellers. They don't research using just the internet or phone, and they don't take freebies in exchange for positive coverage. They travel widely, to all the popular spots and off the beaten track. They personally visit thousands of hotels, restaurants, cafés, bars, galleries, palaces, museums and more – and they take pride in getting all the details right, and telling it how it is. For more, see the authors section on lonelyplanet.com.

## JOCELYN HAREWOOD          Central West, Back o' Bourke & The Riverina

Jocelyn was fascinated to see how much the Riverina had changed since she used to holiday there twenty-odd years ago, but Back o' Bourke was the big adventure – just as her dad taught her, helped by Ion L Idriess' books. Central West weaved its own magic throughout her childhood as her three brothers were always heading off to Bathurst for motor racing, and the whole family was into star-gazing. It was a thrill to finally check out all the activities on offer up that way.

## WENDY KRAMER                        Hunter Valley, New England & Northwest

Whether boot-scooting in Tamworth or chitchatting with opal miners in Lightning Ridge, this little lady feels completely comfortable wherever she may travel – particularly in the Hunter Valley where she has fond memories of playing between the oak barrels at the old Saxonvale Winery as a child (but not-so-fond memories of being clobbered in the head by a stray gumboot during a gumboot-throwing competition at the winery). However, she loves the beach and the love of her life is Newcastle, so it's little surprise Wendy quit her job and bought a unit there while researching this book. Life is short and the world is wide, but Newcastle is home.

## CHARLES RAWLINGS-WAY                            Sydney & Around Sydney

Growing up a shy, unkempt Tasmanian, Charles harboured a secret lust for Sydney's dangerous curves. When he finally mustered the nerve to ask for a date, her cool bars and warm beaches washed over him like a tide – lust turned into love and inescapable fascination.

A lapsed architect, underrated rock guitarist and optimistic home renovator, Charles greased the production cogs at Lonely Planet's HQ for many years before becoming a freelance travel writer in 2005. He regularly flees Melbourne's calmer cultures for a walk on Sydney's wild side, and to visit his mum. In between paragraphs, Charles keeps one eye on his next adventure and the other on fellow LP wordsmith Meg Worby.

## PENNY WATSON                                  Southeast & South Coast

Penny Watson is a journalist of 12 years and full-time travel writer who splits her time between Melbourne and Seville, Spain. She grew up in Albury and spent much of her early years road-tripping in the surrounding small towns and countryside and swimming in the Murray River. With half her family now residing in Sydney, Penny has become ever adept at making the Melbourne–Albury–Sydney round trip more interesting. 'A good country pub can work wonders,' she says, 'as can a secluded beach where it's just you, the view and the big blue.'

## CONTRIBUTING AUTHORS

**Michael Cathcart** teaches history at the Australian Centre, the University of Melbourne. He is well known as a broadcaster on ABC Radio National and presented the ABC TV series *Rewind*. He is also noted as the man who abridged Australia's best-known historian, Manning Clark, by turning his six-volume classic, *A History of Australia*, into one handy book.

**Dr Tim Flannery** is one of Australia's leading thinkers and writers. An internationally acclaimed scientist, explorer and conservationist, he was the recipient of the prestigious Australian of the Year award in 2007. He is a leading member of the Wentworth Group of Concerned Scientists, which reports independently to government on sustainability issues. Former director of the South Australian Museum, Tim is chairman of the South Australian Premier's Science Council and Sustainability Roundtable. He takes up a position at Sydney's Macquarie University in mid-2007.

**Dr David Millar** is a travel medicine specialist, diving doctor and lecturer in wilderness medicine who graduated in Hobart, Tasmania. He has worked in all states of Australia (except the Northern Territory) and as an expedition doctor with the Maritime Museum of Western Australia, accompanying a variety of expeditions around Australia, including the *Pandora* wreck in Far North Queensland and Rowley Shoals off the northwest coast. David is currently a medical director with the Travel Doctor in Auckland.

# Getting Started

New South Wales (NSW) is a dream destination for travellers seeking low-fuss, low-maintenance, low-stress fun. The excellent infrastructure and resources mean you can decide you need a holiday on a Tuesday night and be halfway to your destination by Wednesday morning. All budgets are catered for and pre-planning is a concept relegated to school holidays.

## WHEN TO GO

Truth be told, any time is a good time to be *somewhere* in NSW. Australia's seasons are the antithesis of those in Europe and the USA. Summer starts in December (when the weather and longer daylight hours are perfect for swimming and other outdoor activities), autumn in March, winter in June and spring in September. The climate in NSW varies depending on the location, but the rule of thumb is that the further north you go the warmer and more humid it'll be. It's also hotter and drier the further west you go.

Sydney is lovely for much of the year. The temperature rarely falls below 10°C except overnight in winter, and although temperatures can hit 40°C during summer, the average summer maximum is 25°C. The average monthly rainfall ranges from 75mm to 130mm. Much the same can be said for the climate on the coast, although the swimming season starts earlier by a month or more towards Byron Bay.

See Climate (p370) for more information.

Canberra is cold in winter and scorching in summer, so spring and autumn are the best times to visit the Australian Capital Territory (ACT).

Inland, it gets hot soon after winter and just keeps getting hotter the further you get from the coast and highlands. The outback regularly stays above 40°C.

This temperature variation equates to varying high seasons throughout the state. Along the coast, summer and school and public holidays equals high season. During the Christmas period in particular you'll find yourself competing with hordes of determined Aussie holidaymakers – see Holidays (p376) for more information.

In the southeast snowfields, July to October encompasses high season. Similarly winter is the best (and high) season to visit the Back O' Bourke.

Regardless of where you are, expect spontaneous price rises during the respective high season for everything from accommodation to petrol.

## COSTS

NSW is an affordable destination by 'first world' standards, but how much you should budget for depends on what kind of traveller you are. Accommodation will be your greatest expense, followed by transport and food on a fairly even par. Hiring a car, seeing the sights, staying in hotels or motels and enjoying the fabulous food and grog will cost you $110 to $160 per person per day. In Sydney you can push that figure up by $50 or so, but in less-touristed areas like the west, you can reduce it by the same figure.

Travellers with a demanding brood in tow will find there are many inexpensive ways to keep kids satisfied, including beach and park visits, camping grounds and motels equipped with pools and games rooms, junior-sized restaurant meals and youth/family concessions for attractions. For more information on travelling with children see p370.

Backpackers and budget travellers can still take in the sights on $60 to $100 per day, by camping or staying in hostels or pubs, self-catering whenever possible and taking the bus.

**LONELY PLANET INDEX**

| | |
|---|---|
| 1L petrol | $1.15-1.40 |
| 1L bottle water | $3 |
| Stubby of VB | $4 |
| Souvenir T-shirt | $25 |

## TRAVEL LITERATURE

NSW has been the setting for some of Australian literature's most inspiring, thought-provoking and just plain entertaining works.

Katrina M Schlunke's *Bluff Rock – Autobiography of a Massacre* examines the early relationship between indigenous and non-indigenous Australians, centring on the tragic story of Bluff Rock where an alleged massacre of Aborigines occurred in the 1840s.

Acclaimed novelist Peter Carey gives his own account of his home town in *30 Days in Sydney*, a quirky, goofy and highly readable tale from behind the venetian blinds.

*The Secret River* by Kate Grenville follows an ex-convict who stakes his claim around the Hawkesbury River in the 19th century. It vividly explores issues of identity, belonging and ownership in colonial and contemporary Australia.

The Pilliga Scrub is the focus of *A Million Wild Acres* by Eric Rolls. The book looks at how settlers, failed farms and dead koalas combined to propagate the vast forest of today.

*Safety* by Tegan Bennett is a tale of non-nuclear love, truth and frailty on the banks of the Parramatta River.

Coined a contemporary fairy tale, Murray Bail's *Eucalyptus* is the story of a widower raising his daughter on a property in western NSW. It is a celebration of the enigmatic Australian bush and the quirky Australian psyche.

*Determined* is an autobiographical account of Stephen Aracic's journey from Yugoslavia during WWII to Australia and his ensuing love affair with the black opals of Lightning Ridge.

*Secret Men's Business* by Allan Duffy of Broken Hill is a book of bush ballads and politically incorrect verse. It's a poignant reminder of how different life is in the outback, and of the great range of personalities and local characters you'll meet out there.

## INTERNET RESOURCES

**Citysearch.com** (www.citysearch.com.au) Events, dining, arts, bars and music listings for Sydney.
**Lonely Planet** (www.lonelyplanet.com) Destination summaries, accommodation and flight bookings, links to related sites, Bluelists and invaluable advice from travellers on the Thorn Tree.
**NSW National Parks & Wildlife Service** (www.nationalparks.nsw.gov.au) Official site with reams of information on over 600 parks and reserves.

---

**HOW MUCH?**

Coffee $3-3.50

Schooner/midi of beer $4/2.50

Surfboard hire $30-50

Meat pie $3.50

---

### DON'T LEAVE HOME WITHOUT...

- *ABC Travellers Guide* for the frequency of every ABC radio station across NSW
- Comfy sneakers or hiking boots for beach, bush and mountain walks
- Sunscreen, sunglasses and a hat to deflect ultrafierce UV rays (p402)
- A beanie for the Blue Mountains (p119) or the Southeast snowfields (p295)
- Good maps for outback meanders and good sherry for cold, quiet outback nights (p257)
- Extra-pungent insect repellent to ward off merciless flies and mosquitoes (p372)
- A towel and bathers/togs/swimmers/swimming costume/cossie/trunks/speedos/budgie smugglers...for the beach
- Valid travel licence, ID card or passport and visa if required (p380)
- An enhanced tolerance to alcohol plus your favourite hangover cure, especially if spending lots of time in Sydney (p95)

## TOP FIVES

### Must-See Movies

One of the best places to do your essential trip preparation is on a comfy couch with your eyeballs pleasurably glued to the small screen. Head down to your local video store to pick up these Australian flicks with a New South Wales bent. See p32 for reviews of some of these and other locally produced films.

- *Lantana* (2001) Directed by Ray Lawrence
- *Jindabyne* (2006) Directed by Ray Lawrence
- *Oyster Farmer* (2004) Directed by Anna Reeves
- *Two Hands* (1999) Directed by Gregor Jordan
- *The Dish* (2000) Directed by Rob Sitch

### Eco-Experiences

Eco-tourism is a growing concept in NSW and there are numerous ways you can minimise your environmental footprint while you explore the landscape. We recommend the following five ways to tread lightly:

- Natural Wanders (p64) Kayaking in Sydney Harbour
- Tread Lightly Eco Tours (p125) Bushwalks in the Blue Mountains
- Mountain Bike Tours (p190) Mountain biking in the North Coast hinterland
- Mountain Trails (p175) Eco-friendly 4WD tours near Coffs Harbour
- Paperbark Camp (p329) Eco-friendly and very swish camping in Jervis Bay

### Festivals & Events

Australians will seize on just about any opportunity for a celebration – due as much to good-humoured exuberance and an enjoyment of the arts and sport, as any excuse to consume vast amounts of food, wine and beer. These are our top five reasons to get festive – other events are listed on p374, and throughout this book.

- Sydney to Hobart Yacht Race (p69) December to January
- Country Music Festival, Tamworth (p215) January
- Sydney Gay & Lesbian Mardi Gras (p71) February
- Surfest (p144) March
- East Coast International Blues & Roots Music Festival (p190) September

**Sydney Morning Herald** (www.smh.com.au) Site for Sydney's best paper, with plenty of news about what's happening in Sydney and NSW.
**Tourism New South Wales** (www.visitnsw.com.au) Vast amounts of information on accommodation, activities and much more.

# Itineraries

## CLASSIC ROUTES

**THE BLUE MOUNTAIN RUN**     One week/Parramatta to Bells Line of Road

Start in Sydney's mini-me CBD **Parramatta** (p111). Potter through the historic buildings here but then be on your way – the mountains await.

Stop in **Glenbrook** (p121), at the base of the mountains, for Aboriginal hand stencils and the Norman Lindsay Gallery, and get camera happy as you pass Jamison Valley and Wentworth Falls. Spend your first night in gracious **Leura** (p122). Admire the vivid gardens and jaw-dropping views, and cosy up in a boutique B&B for the night.

Next day, continue west to the Blue Mountains' big smoke – **Katoomba** (p123). Bask in the bohemian milieu, relish the gourmet food and mosey through the galleries. Base yourself here for a few nights to explore the national park.

Hit the road again and shift north to **Blackheath** (p127), for some of the mountains' best lookouts. Spend a night in unadulterated **Mt Victoria** (p129) and catch the iconic Mount Vic Flicks. Detour further west to see the troglodytic **Jenolan Caves** (p129) before winding your way back east via **Bells Line of Road** (p130).

This western loop around the dramatic Blue Mountains covers around 300km by road. To best enjoy the scenery and towns of the mountains give yourself a week.

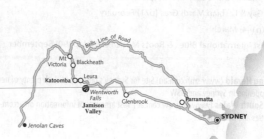

SOUTH
PACIFIC
OCEAN

# THE LONG COASTAL HAUL          One month/Eden to Tweed Heads

Start your coastal adventure in the state's southern pocket – **Eden** (p341) is a good place to base yourself for national park adventures and your foray into the Tasman Sea. Ambling ever so slightly, stay a while in **Merimbula's** (p339) scenic inlet for spectacular diving, or **Narooma** (p334) for river cruises, good surfing and Montague Island's wildlife.

Next, park yourself in **Murramarang National Park** (p332) for fabulous beach-side camping and beautiful surf beaches. Pop into **Ulladulla** (p330) and tackle the climb to Pigeon House Mountain if you're brave. Otherwise continue north to Jervis Bay for wreck dives, dolphin cruises and diminished crowds in **Huskisson** (p328).

Continue north to gorgeous **Berry** (p325) for B&B bliss and wineries. In **Sydney** (p50) you'll need a few days to explore the big smoke. But the beaches, reserves and Sunday afternoons of **Newcastle** (p142) beckon.

Swing by **Port Stephens** (p158) and get lost in the shimmering dunes of Stockton Bight, then meander through the stunning **Myall Lakes National Park** (p160) before hiding out in **Seal Rocks** (p161). Dose up on good food, good wine and good views in pretty **Port Macquarie** (p163) and then go bush with the birdlife and camp in **Hat Head National Park** (p168).

Detour a little to **Bellingen** (p171) for fabulous food and boutique B&Bs and then exhaust yourself rafting, horse riding, surfing and jumping out of planes in **Coffs Harbour** (p174).

Stop in **Yamba** (p182) and **Angourie** (p183) to escape the crowds and make the most of the jaw-dropping views and outstanding seafood. Wind things up with a recovery week in **Byron Bay** (p186), but be sure to visit the fabulous pub at **Brunswick Heads** (p194) and the scenic beaches of **Tweed Heads** (p194).

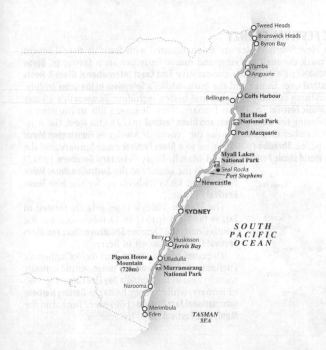

This classic run takes in NSW's 1400km shoreline. The landscape and climate shift markedly as you climb and the route takes in everything from national park camping to the glitz of Sydney. Allow at least a month to fully enjoy this road trip.

# TAILORED TRIPS

## THE GROG-GLUTTON'S JUNKET

There are more grapes than we know what to do with in New South Wales, and your help is urgently needed to consume them.

While still in control of your faculties, you'd best start in the obvious location – the Hunter Valley. Start in the '**Lower**' (p149) where you'll find old favourites like Wyndham Estate and Lindemans, plus gourmet cheeses and olives to stop the wobbles. Then, pacing yourself mind, make your way north to the '**Upper**' (p153) and indulge in spicy cab savs and shiraz. Once you've got the vino goggles fastened, you can venture out west to the wineries of **Mudgee** (p235) for a night with the poet and stunning views with Simon. Or if that's too far, stop in **Wagga Wagga** (p276) for award-winning drops and a barbie, or in **Leeton** (p283) for tastings. **Griffith** (p283) has the goods in this neck of the woods though – big names like McWilliam's Hanwood Estate mingle with boutique lovelies.

On the South Coast, **Berry** (p325) and **Nowra** (p328) have slick and fancy wineries, but it's worth making the painless trek to Bermagui for the glorious **Mimosa Cottages & Wines** (p337).

Up north, the wineries accompany their vino with award-winning food around **Port Macquarie** (p163).

## MUSIC FESTIVAL FRENZY

Folk in New South Wales are so enamoured with festivals they'll invent one to mark the mail arriving, and music festivities are a favourite. **Byron Bay's festivals** (p190) include the massive **East Coast International Blues & Roots Music Festival** over Easter and the indie-addict's **Splendour in the Grass** in July. But everything country is bigger and better, including Tamworth's 10-day **Country Music Festival** (p215) in January. Tiny Bellingen fills to bursting in August during the **Bellingen Jazz and Blues Festival** (p172). Out west, the Australian Chamber Orchestra wows the crowds at Mudgee's **Huntington Music Festival** (p236). **Thredbo** (p298) hums to a **Blues Festival** every January and the **Thredbo World Music Festival** in mid-March. Every February **Goulburn** (p312) croons to the sounds of the **Australian Blues Music Festival** and kicks its heels up for the **Irish Music Festival** in June.

The Hunter Valley's vineyards are treated to **Jazz in the Vines** (p151) in October, and on the South Coast, the October **Shoalhaven Jazz and Blues Festival** (p326) kicks off in Berry.

The cities give it a good burl too – Canberra's Parliament House features noise people actually want to hear at the **Australia Day Live Concert** (p356) in January, while Sydney hosts the **Darling Harbour International Jazz Festival** (p69) every June, and the **Manly Jazz Festival** (p69) in October.

# Snapshot

Drop some caves in New South Wales (NSW) at the moment and you'll pick up lively debates covering culture, the environment and all manner of sociopolitical issues. Of course, you may have to wade past talk of the eternal quest to make that disposable income stretch further. At present you need to be on the better side of middle class or prepared to sacrifice your child's education (or, indeed, having a child) if you want to drive a car or add bananas to your Weet-Bix. While there seems to be reasonable explanation for both – the war in Iraq for the former, and Cyclone Larry decimating North Queensland's banana plantations for the latter – most folk find it a stretch for the government to raise interest rates as a result of these two items.

Given NSW's ever-fragile ecology, environmental issues get plenty of airplay and water shortages rate highly. Foreign visitors to the state may be surprised to see billboards reminding residents to shower less, flush less and abandon all thoughts of a green lawn. But dam levels in most urban areas are close to critical and Sydney is consuming water faster than it can sustain supply. Bushfires now commence their summer scourge as early as mid-spring, heightening the need for better water management. In the state's dry west and outback, folk lament the lack of rain, how we need rain, when it last rained and when, please, is it going to rain. Road conditions run a close second out there, but inevitably the conversation simply turns to what the roads will be like when it rains.

Climate change has found its way into the vernacular and although people feel a need to stem the rising temperatures, they don't feel a need for it to hurt their hip pocket. The jury is out on whether nuclear energy is good, bad or just plain ugly. Similarly, there's a great deal of chat around Narooma and Batemans Bay about the proposed Batemans Marine Park, which, if approved, would stretch all the way from Wallaga Lake in the south to Bawley Point in the north. The idea's solid, but locals need to know whether it will hinder commercial fishing and other recreational activities. The good news is that plans to open a new Marine Discovery Centre in Eden (see p341) have been met with firm support from locals, who recognise the lucrative benefits of ecotourism.

In the social corner we have an ongoing discussion about immigration (see p29 for more on why) and whether NSW can sustain multicultural harmony. Most of the population would be appalled at the very thought that it can't, but one off race riots in Sydney and misinformation about how to identify a 'typical terrorist' demonstrate pockets of tension. For some, the cultural shift that comes with the influx of new identities has been too swift, prompting attempts to distinguish between what is 'Australian' or, more importantly, what is 'un-Australian'. For the most part it seems that 'un-Australian' can be attached to any activity other than beer, football or Australian Idol.

The cost of housing and Sydney's subsequent urban spread in all directions continues to set tongues wagging. Real estate remains the state capital's obsession, now and forever. However, Canberran homeowners are now able to report with pride that their property prices are just about on par. Given the Australian dream to own a house and a dog (see p29) it's not surprising that new homeowners are simply moving further afield.

In the Hunter Valley (p140), bumper crops have become the viticulturist's lament, and overproduction of wine is a big issue. Medium-sized wineries agonise about how to crack the export market while stockpiles of scrummy reds gather dust in their cellars. There is even talk of ripping out the grapes… What is the world coming to?!

Meanwhile tour operators lament the devastating impact of public-liability insurance. Increased premiums are wreaking havoc on small companies, who are also feeling the pinch due to petrol prices, which brings us full circle. For the most part, however, you'll find that folk in NSW consider all these issues secondary to the firm belief that they live on the luckiest plot on earth.

# History Michael Cathcart

## TWO WORLDS MEET

On the beaches and rocky outcrops of Sydney Harbour, the Eora people and their neighbours hunted and fished for thousands of years. In fact, someone travelling around the harbour in Aboriginal times would have encountered several different peoples. Each group maintained its own distinct set of spiritual beliefs, or 'Dreaming'. And each spoke their own language – these included Dharug, Dharawal, Gundungurra and Kurringgai. This linguistic diversity existed across New South Wales (NSW) – indeed, across the entire continent.

The Aborigines' world was challenged on 19 April 1770, when Lieutenant James Cook of the British Navy climbed onto the deck of his ship *Endeavour* and saw a miraculous sight. In the gentle light of dawn, a vast uncharted country of wooded hills and gentle valleys had appeared across the ocean.

Ten days later, he dropped anchor in a bay and went ashore, where he was met warily by the local people. The ship's scientists were so excited by the unfamiliar plants they found there that Cook named the place 'Botany Bay'. But the Aborigines were alarmed by the intrusion. As Cook noted in his journal, 'All they seemed to want was for us to be gone.'

Michael Cathcart teaches history at the Australian Centre, the University of Melbourne. He is well known as a broadcaster on ABC Radio National and presented the ABC TV series *Rewind*.

## A COLONY OF THIEVES

But in 1788, the English were back to stay. They numbered 751 ragtag convicts and children, and around 250 soldiers, officials and their wives. This motley 'First Fleet' was under the command of a diligent naval captain named Arthur Phillip. Unimpressed by Cook's marshy Botany Bay, Phillip was delighted to discover a magnificent harbour just a few miles up the coast. There, on a small cove, in the land of the Eora people, Phillip established a British penal settlement. He renamed the place after the British Home Secretary, Lord Sydney. The date of the landing was 26 January 1788, an occasion remembered each year with a public holiday known as 'Australia Day'.

For more on the indigenous history of Sydney see www.cityofsydney.nsw.gov.au/barani and www.gadigal.org.au.

The fact that a national holiday commemorates the arrival of a party of prisoners may seem inglorious – but it helps explain both the egalitarianism and the sense of irony that sometimes accompany expressions of nationalism in Australia.

Robert Hughes' bestseller, *The Fatal Shore* (1987), depicts convict Australia as a terrifying 'Gulag' where Britain tormented rebels, vagrants and criminals. But other historians point out that powerful men in London saw transportation as a scheme for giving prisoners a new and useful life. Indeed, with Phillip's encouragement, many convicts soon earned their 'ticket of leave', a kind of parole that gave them their freedom throughout the colony and the right to seek work on their own behalf.

But the convict system could be savage. Women (who were outnumbered five to one) lived under constant threat of sexual exploitation. Female convicts who offended their gaolers languished in the depressing 'female factories'. As the Eora people saw, to their horror, male convict re-offenders were cruelly flogged or even hanged. (Just six weeks after the landing, Phillip hanged a 17-year-old boy named John Barrett on the shores of Sydney Cove, for stealing food.)

The most vivid eyewitness account of the First Fleet is *1788* by Watkin Tench (edited by Tim Flannery).

The British government had instructed Governor Phillip to treat the local Aborigines 'with amity and kindness'. But he could do nothing to stop the

For the counter-
argument to Hughes'
The Fatal Shore, see The
Europeans in Australia:
A History, Volume 1 by
Alan Atkinson (1998).

lethal impact of European diseases, including syphilis, smallpox and the 'flu, on the local populations. Alcohol and the poor British diet also took their toll. His attempts to befriend Aborigines, notably an adventurous man named Bennelong, ended sadly, with Bennelong himself dying of alcoholism and loneliness. The Sydney Opera House stands on a tongue of land that bears his name, Bennelong Point.

## MACQUARIE

By the early 1800s, Sydney was a bustling port. A space in the bush had been cleared for vegetable gardens, new houses, warehouses and streets – and windmills seemed to occupy the top of every hill. But Phillip's plans to create a vigorous new society in Australia had come adrift. His successors at Government House had lost control to a caste of corrupt, self-serving military officers. Members of this infamous 'Rum Corps' were busily enriching themselves by controlling trade and land, and treating the convicts as their own private labour force. But in 1809 they met their match when the British government dispatched Governor Lachlan Macquarie to restore the rule of law.

An autocratic British governor may seem an unlikely hero for Australians. In fact, Macquarie transformed Sydney into a well-planned colony graced with fine civic architecture. Many of his buildings, including several designed by the convict-architect Francis Greenway, survive to this day – notably the Hyde Park Barracks in Sydney's Macquarie St, where you can see Macquarie's name painted on the façade (see Macquarie Street Area, p57, and Windsor, p117).

Macquarie was a man of progressive and civic-minded social attitudes. He championed the cause of convicts who had served their time (the 'Emancipists'), promoting many of them to significant public offices and welcoming them to his circle at Government House. This policy outraged the 'Exclusives' – those members of the wealthy classes who maintained rigid British manners and accents, and old-world notions of class.

The early history of the
city is well told at the
Museum of Sydney. Visit
www.hht.net.au
/museums/mos/main for
more information.

By then, many of the white children in the colony were speaking with a new, assertively Australian accent. Distinctively Australian attitudes and manners were taking shape in the streets of Sydney. In fact, the convicts of Sydney gave white Australians an important part of their mythology. For generations afterwards, Australians disowned any suggestion that there was a 'convict stain' on the pages of their own family history. Yet, there was also a deep sympathy for the convicts. Throughout the 20th century, school children learned how Britain's Industrial Revolution had been brutal to the poor and the working class, and how convicts were often transported to Australia for such crimes as 'stealing a loaf of bread' to feed their starving children. It is a powerful image – and one that convinced generations of colonists that Australia might just prove to be a fairer place than the old country that had dealt so harshly with its underclass.

## FRONTIER

The colonists were partitioned from the inland by the formidable cliffs and canyons of the 'Blue Mountains'. While some simple folk thought China lay on the other side, the sheep graziers and cattlemen dreamt of rolling farmlands in the mysterious hinterland. In 1813, when Sydney was in the grip of a drought, three graziers found a route across the barrier and discovered that the great Aboriginal territories beyond were indeed rich in grasslands.

This discovery unleashed the ambitions of the so-called 'squatters'. These were men of capital who took their flocks ever deeper into the Aboriginal territories in search of pastures and water. In many areas, Aborigines fought against the advance, and history remembers leaders of the Aboriginal resistance such as Pemulwuy and Mosquito. At the same time, the government was anxious to monitor the activities of the squatters on the frontier, and determined to enforce the principle that the government – and no-one else – actually owned the land. To assert its authority, it dispatched expeditions of explorers, including John Oxley, Charles Sturt and Thomas Mitchell, to discover what mysteries and resources lay in the Aboriginal territories.

The Blue Mountains are part of an elevation that runs the length of eastern Australia, known, rather grandly, as the Great Dividing Range. The rivers on the gentle, western side of the range flow inland, and the early explorers were tantalised by the mystery of where they went. As they pondered this 'riddle of the rivers', some predicted they would find a mighty Mississippi-type river, which would become the highway for Australian development. A few believed there was a wide inland sea – a sort of Sea of Galilee – in the heart of the country. But the inland journeys of the explorers and squatters often took them into increasingly dry and arid territory. The comparison with the United States was harsh. In America, the explorers had discovered a bountiful land, which they interpreted as an expression of God's blessing – a sign of white America's 'manifest destiny'. The Australians' journey westward was, by contrast, a journey into disappointment.

Nevertheless, the sheep flourished, and the government filled its coffers by leasing the Aboriginal territories to the squatters. The colony's income was boosted by the discovery of massive goldfields at Ophir (near Orange, p238) in 1851. The possibility of instant wealth attracted a flood of youthful miners from Europe, America and China.

## DEMOCRACY & GROWTH

At the same time, the colonists' agitation for a more democratic form of government reached sympathetic ears in London, and the colonists began to debate the constitution under which a parliament should operate. But the squatters were uneasy. They were now the de facto aristocracy of the colony and were determined to hang onto their political power. This division between the urban democrats and landed conservatives was reflected in the structure of the new Parliament of New South Wales, which adopted a radical form of manhood suffrage in the lower house, while the practice of appointing the upper chamber allowed it to function as the conservative 'squatters house'.

Australia was developing an export economy based on primary production. The sheep industry expanded into the west of the state in the 1890s with the discovery of massive reserves of artesian water. At the same time, wheat, dairying and sugar were developing as major industries. NSW became an exporter of brown coal, and mining fed the smelters and industries that were developing in Newcastle and Wollongong to the immediate north and south, respectively, of Sydney.

The rapid expansion of the NSW economy since 1788 had created a continual demand for labour. Whereas England and Ireland were burdened with the misery and poverty of a 'surplus population', Australian colonists were actively encouraging migration. This single fact gave the workforce a bargaining power undreamt of in Britain. Good wages, social mobility and increasingly strong unions fed the belief that Australia might become 'the working man's paradise'. Employers, on the other hand, notably the squatters, were anxious to keep wage costs low, and the appeal of cheap Asian or Islander labour was irresistible.

For information on the history and attractions of the Blue Mountains see www.bluemts.com.au.

The classic work on frontier violence is Henry Reynolds' *The Other Side of the Frontier* (1986). In the bitter 'history wars', Keith Windschuttle's self-published *The Fabrication of Aboriginal History* (2002) has fuelled right-wing scepticism about the extent of such violence.

You can visit charming Parliament House (known as 'the Bear Pit'). See details and lots of historical information at www.parliament.nsw.gov.au.

## NATIONALISM

Against this background, popular Sydney magazine the *Bulletin* (founded in 1880) began to champion a version of Australian nationalism that was working class, male, white and republican. Known as 'the bushman's bible', the *Bulletin* popularised a view of the archetypal Australian as a laconic, unintellectual but resourceful bushman who was independent, contemptuous of authority and loyal to his mates. Of all the *Bulletin* writers, two in particular have an enduring place in the Australian imagination. Henry Lawson was a Sydney socialist with a flair for revolutionary verse and comic short stories. Lawson visited the outback of northern NSW during a merciless drought, and returned to the city convinced that the bush was a zone of silence, stoic mateship and human comedy based on hopelessness. 'Banjo' Paterson, on the other hand, was a bushman to his very soul. He celebrated the wide spaces of Australia as 'sunlit' and 'glorious', most notably in his classic ballad, 'Clancy of the Overflow', and in Australia's most famous poem, 'The Man from Snowy River'.

Read 'The Man from Snowy River' and other works by 'Banjo' Paterson at http://whitewolf .newcastle.edu.au/words /authors.html.

## LABOUR IN ACTION

During the 1890s, a cruel depression brought the curse of unemployment and hunger to cities and towns throughout NSW. But the working people – particularly the unionised shearers, timber cutters and waterside workers – were fierce in their resistance to bosses who attempted to cut their wages or replace them with cheaper nonunionised workers. As the colony threatened to become a powder keg of industrial violence, the Labor Party was formed to give a legitimate political voice to the demands of the workers. At the same time, various states responded to the suffering and unrest by using the law to protect the wages and living standards of the poorest workers, setting a pattern that was to endure in Australia for the next 100 years.

For more on writers and painters of the colonial bush legend see www .cultureandrecreation .gov.au/articles/bush.

## FEDERATION & WAR

On 1 January 1901, NSW and the other colonies federated to form the nation of Australia. This was not a declaration of independence. This new Australia was a dominion of the British Empire. It was as citizens of the Empire that thousands of Australian men volunteered to fight in the Australian Imperial Force when WWI broke out in 1914. They fought in Turkey, Sinai and Europe – notably on the Somme. More than 200,000 of them were killed or wounded over the four terrible years of the war. Today, in every city and town across the state, you will see war memorials that commemorate their service. The Returned Services League (RSL) was formed in the immediate aftermath of the war to represent the aspirations and interests of the ex-soldiers. A visitor to NSW is certain, somewhere along the way, to encounter one of the enormous RSL clubs, which began as the League's meeting halls. With the legalisation of poker machines in 1956, these clubs began to swell into the gaudy gambling, dining and entertainment centres that today provide a major alternative to the local pub – especially in regional parts of the state.

The most accessible version of the Anzac legend is Peter Weir's epic Australian film, *Gallipoli* (1981). The cast includes a young Mel Gibson.

## A DIVIDED SOCIETY

By 1929, the promise that the soldiers would return to a land fit for heroes had proved, for many, to be a cruel lie. That year, the cold wind of the Great Depression blew through the farms and factories of the state. Around one in five Australian breadwinners was out of work. Poverty and hunger divided the unemployed from the majority of the population who continued to work and put dinner on the table.

The politics of the period were dominated by the inflammatory rhetoric and policies of 'Big' Jack Lang, the larger-than-life Labor premier of NSW. The federal government and all the states had borrowed heavily from London, to pay for the war and to finance social projects such as roads and hospitals. Lang announced that he would default on his loan repayments. Rather than line the pockets of international bankers, he said, he would feed the hungry of NSW. This defiant rhetoric divided the state. Supporters hailed Lang as a 'new Lenin'. But the mass of middle-Australians saw him as a demagogue whose policies would ruin Australia's financial credibility. Normally sober conservatives began to form paramilitary groups, preparing to meet the revolution they believed Lang was inciting.

In the midst of this bitterness, the great Sydney Harbour Bridge was rising like a steel rainbow in the heart of the city, uniting its northern and southern regions. The bridge became a great symbol of hope and accomplishment, and Lang was determined to bask in its glory when the day came for its opening in 1932. But as the crowds waited expectantly, he was beaten to the ribbon by a member of the paramilitary New Guard. A horseman named Francis De Groot cut the ceremonial ribbon with a sabre and declared the bridge open, in the name of the decent citizens of NSW. Weeks later, Lang was forced to an election, and soundly defeated.

For more on this famous, little-understood man see Andrew Moore's brilliant *Francis De Groot: Irish Fascist Australian Legend* (2005).

## WAR & NEW HORIZONS

In 1939 Australians were once again fighting a war alongside the British, this time against Hitler in WWII. But the military situation changed radically in December 1941 when the Japanese bombed the American Fleet at Hawaii's Pearl Harbor. The Japanese swept through Southeast Asia and, within weeks, were threatening Australia. It was not the British, but the Americans, who came to Australia's aid. As thousands of Australian soldiers were taken prisoner and suffered in the brutal Japanese POW camps, Sydney was among the Australian cities that opened its arms to US servicemen. This experience laid the foundations for the US–Australia alliance that remains so strong, and so bitterly controversial, today.

After the war, Australia was convinced it had to increase its population if it were to fend off another Asian attack – a conviction that was made all the stronger by the rise of communist China. The government embarked on a massive immigration program, attracting migrants from Britain and mainland Europe. These 'new Australians' made a huge impact on NSW, especially in the irrigation farms of the Riverina, in the building of the great Snowy Mountains hydro-electric scheme, in the large industrial centres and in Sydney itself. No-one anticipated how profoundly these newcomers would transform the country. By the 1970s, Australia had abolished its old policies of racial discrimination and declared itself to be a multicultural country.

## TODAY

Sydney is now a confident world city. The pace of life is fast. The cost of living is high. And people keep coming. In 2000, Sydney welcomed the new millennium by hosting a spectacularly successful Olympic Games, during which fans and athletes flooded into the harbour city from all over the world.

Today, Australia is a wealthy country with a vigorous economy. New free-market policies have stripped away the sense of job security most Australians once regarded as their birthright. In a globalised economy, Australian workers have lost their protection against the cheap labour of Asia and the demands of the workplace are becoming more and more overwhelming.

For a fascinating exploration of the relationship between Australia and Japan see the Australian War Memorial's project at http://ajrp.awm.gov .au/AJRP/AJRP2.nsf.

At the same time, Australians are once again debating their attitudes to race and cultural diversity. Ugly race riots on Sydney's Cronulla Beach in 2005 laid bare the tensions between some old and new Australians. Prime Minister John Howard prefers to emphasise unity over diversity, having no truck with the ideas of a pluralist or multicultural society. But the voices of tolerance and diversity remain strong in Australia. The country's immigration policies attract immigrants from all over the world, particularly from Asia. And the general friendliness of Australians – and their openness to travellers – is evidence that many Australians still maintain a profound and enduring culture of goodwill and good sense.

# The Culture

## REGIONAL IDENTITY

Australia has an ancient past and culture, enriched by at least 50,000 years of Aboriginal heritage, but its modern identity is still in its infancy, and New South Wales (NSW) is where it all began. This is a country whose recent past, present and future is tied inexorably to the trials and tribulations of immigration. The British were the most influential participants in this process. For them, the seminal times of the colony of NSW were characterised by extreme hardship, resentment at being sent so far with so little, and an incalculable sense of loss of loved ones and homes left behind. For pioneers pushing beyond Sydney's adolescent urban limits, the struggle against nature and tyranny intensified. To cope, they forged a culture based on the principles of a 'fair go' and congratulatory back slaps for challenges to authority, and told stories of the Aussie 'battler' that were passed down through generations. Mateship became a code that transcended official law.

Although visitors to NSW will still encounter this sense of anti-establishment, decades of prosperity have watered it down to larrikin cheek. But the struggle to forge a new existence in an alien landscape is still palpable, owing to Australia's consistent relationship with immigration. Waves of newcomers have brought their own stories, cultures and myths to meld with those already in place. Many migrants have come with a huge sense of hope and expectancy, to start life afresh. Many have arrived as refugees, and their ordeals and courage add to the ethos of the colonial 'battler'.

Colonial history has been revisited through art, literature and cinema. There's also a long-overdue acknowledgment that the original Aboriginal inhabitants of this country are fundamental to a true definition of Australian culture today. Australians enjoy a sophisticated, modern society with immense variety, a global focus, if not a regional one, and a sense of optimism even though it's tempered by world events.

Although there's some truth in the stereotypes that Australians are open-minded, down-to-earth, big-hearted, laconic, larrikin-minded, egalitarian and honest, these definitions are largely one dimensional. Australian culture is much richer for its indigenous heritage and multicultural mix. While on your travels here, you may hear 'g'day' from an Akubra-wearing, laconic, whiskery, bush larrikin, his voice will be but one among many. This exciting time of redefinition for multicultural Australia will throw unexpected people and experiences in your path. It's a young culture melding with the oldest culture in the world; and the incredibly rich opportunities are only starting to be realised.

*The Lady Bushranger: The Life of Elizabeth Jessie Hickman* (by Pat Studdy-Clift) relays the circus career, cattle duffing (stealing) and fugitive life of a female bushranger in and around Wollemi National Park.

Crikey (www.crikey.com .au) is an unforgiving indie news service that peels back the layers of truth commercial media won't go near.

## LIFESTYLE

Australians have been sold to the world as outdoorsy, sporty, Fosters-guzzling, croc-wrestling folk. In reality, most have never wrestled a small lizard and would drink Fosters only as a last resort. This is particularly true in NSW, where the beer is fine (see p46).

But the Australian dream to own an overgrown house on a quarter-acre block is rife in NSW. The average home is middle class and inside it you'll find a married heterosexual couple, though it is becoming increasingly likely they will be de facto, or in their second marriage. Gay marriage is not sanctioned by law in Australia, but most urban Australians are open-minded about homosexuality, especially in the gay mecca, Sydney. The more remote the location however, the less accepting you'll find this attitude.

Similarly, sexism is not tolerated in urban areas, but women may experience varying degrees (mostly in the form of appreciative glances and throw-away comments) in rural and remote areas.

*Kings in Grass Houses* (by Mary Durack) details the great overland trek of the Duracks and Costellos in 1876. Having escaped the potato famine in Ireland, they drove cattle from Goulburn to the Kimberleys in WA.

'Mum and Dad' will have married around the age of 30, and are now proud parents to a whopping mortgage and 1.7 kids, probably called Jack, Lachlan, Olivia or Charlotte (Kylie's been bumped out of the top ten). The average weekly gross income for the household will be $1200; more in Sydney, where salaries and the cost of living are higher.

Our typical family drags a caravan off to the beach every holiday, and on weekends they watch sport, go to the movies or head to the shops. And our couple likes a few quiet ones up the pub, though despite the long-held reputation that Australians are boozers, recent figures show they drink less than Brits. Today wine is the number-one drink of choice.

Around 55% of women and 70% of men will be employed. Though the glass ceiling is becoming a thing of the past, the average male income is about a third higher than the average female income.

## ECONOMY

*The Birth of Sydney* (by Tim Flannery) follows the growth of Australia's largest city – from conception, to crime to cosmopolitan chaos. Voices chiming in include indigenous people, European immigrants and Charles Darwin.

NSW has a robust and growing economy. Any road trip along the coast will reveal an ever-increasing suburban sprawl as Sydney struggles to contain its property boom. This has been augmented by the federal government handing out a grant to all first home owners and the NSW government's absorption of some property taxes. Generally, people in NSW are in a frenzy of making money and spending it just as quickly. This manic consumption, along with an inordinately high addiction to credit-card debt, prompts frequent interest rate hikes to slow the pace of spending and inflation. The result is a fairly stable Aussie dollar – see p15 for more information about the cost of travelling in NSW.

## POPULATION

NSW is Australia's most populace state and a third of the country lives here. Sydney alone boasts more than 4 million residents – two thirds of the state's population.

The remaining third lives largely in coastal areas. The least populated areas are inland, where many of the small towns experience little or negative growth. Regions like the NSW far west have one of the lowest population

---

### WEIRD AND WONDERFUL NSW

It's weird, it's wonderful and it's oh so NSW. There is a bevy of oddities in this state to keep the eccentric entertained.

Haven't found your unique talent yet? Perhaps you need to test your cherry-pip-spitting skills at Young's Cherry Festival (p247). Alternatively head to **Stroud** (p155) for a brick-throwing competition, and if that proves too taxing any (male) mug has a shot at the title at the beard-growing competition at Beardies Festival in **Glen Innes** (p223).

Elvis has left the building – we know because he rocks up to Parkes (p243) every year for the Elvis Revival Festival.

Tired of losing money on the nags? Maybe have a flutter at the National Guinea Pig Races in **Grenfell** (p246), the sheep races in **Hay** (p288) or the goat races in **Lightning Ridge** (p256).

Not to be outdone, the town folk of **Nundle** (p226) dress up as Chinese people for the Go for Gold Festival, and in **Eden** (p341), locals form teams to run back and forth with buckets of seawater to keep a mock whale alive during the Whale Festival. But no town has it sorted like **Nimbin** (p200), which celebrates – the annual Mardi Grass festival with the hemp olympix and a massive scoob-fest.

densities in the world. As employment opportunities become increasingly centralised in urban areas, this trend looks set to continue.

Like the rest of Australia, NSW is multicultural. A quarter of its residents were born overseas, many arriving from Italy and Greece after WWII, but recent immigrants hail from New Zealand, the UK, China, Vietnam, Africa, the Pacific, the Middle East and India among many other places. Some 2.1% of the NSW population identify as being of Aboriginal origin.

Almost half of Australia's recent population growth is due to immigration, with NSW attracting the majority (38%) of newcomers.

## SPORT

In NSW, National Rugby League (NRL) games (www.nrl.com.au) are the spectator sport of choice. NRL players represent their states (NSW or Queensland) in the annual State of Origin series. To see one of these games is to acquire a terrifying appreciation of Newton's law of motion: a force travelling in one direction can only be stopped with the application of an equal and opposite force.

Historically, rugby union was an amateur sport played by the upper class, and its century-long rivalry with professional rugby league was the closest thing sport had to a clash of ideologies. In 1995, however, rugby turned professional and union is now mainstream.

The Wallabies is the national team. Apart from the Rugby World Cup, Bledisloe Cup matches against New Zealand are the most anticipated fixtures and form part of the Tri-Nations tournament that also includes South Africa.

Australia's state funding of professional sports is among the highest proportionally in the world.

Slowly but surely, Sydneysiders are also warming to Australian Football League (AFL) games, thanks in no small part to the Sydney Swans who won the Grand Final in 2005 and were runners up in 2006.

And then there's cricket. Anyone remotely familiar with this sport will know how seriously Australians take it. Having dominated the international stage for around 15 years, the Australians were knocked unceremoniously off their perch by England during the 2005 Ashes series. Shane Warne, the world's most successful bowler, and one of Australia's deadliest weapons, sought vengeance by conquering as many fair maidens from the mother country as possible.

For many Australians, the thought of watching an entire test match (five days) is tantamount to watching carpet grow. But the cricket is as much about beer, food, and sunshine as it is about winning. You will see cricket grounds throughout NSW, attracting local clubs and spectators of varying skills and professionalism.

## ARTS

NSW has a thriving arts scene anchored by the big money of Sydney. Towns up and down the coast and in the mountains also attract their share of artists and as you explore the state, you'll encounter many fine galleries and studios. Australia's most famous annual arts event, the Archibald Prize, debuted in 1921 at the National Art Gallery of New South Wales (now the Art Gallery of New South Wales). Now a nationwide obsession, it celebrates the best of Australian portrait artists, as well as landscapes, photography and murals.

Look for the CD All You Mob, a compilation of indigenous sounds assembled in Sydney. Notable is the song 'Down River' in which young Aborigines rap about their lives.

Sydney, by virtue of its population and stature, has a thriving music scene. Much of the action is around rock and pop. Local performers of note include long-time favourites the Whitlams, whose Sydney-centric material has managed to translate into popularity Australia-wide, and the rowdy punk energy of Frenzal Rhomb, whose live appeal to thrashing teenagers has to be seen to be believed. Grunge rockers-turned orchestral maestros Silverchair hail from Newcastle. Grinspoon, one of the country's most successful acts, formed in

Check out www.sydney
festival.org.au, the
website for the Sydney
Festival, held annually in
January.

Lismore in 1995. Other acts are the hard-to-define Machine Gun Fellatio; the
talented Gelbison; Bondi-based noise-merchants Cog; and the most-hyped
local act of the new millennium, the Vines. You can pretty much find any
other musical genre you can imagine in and around the city.

Elsewhere in NSW, you'll likely hear a lot of traditional rock with a lot of
country and western as well (local popularity of the latter is proportional
to the dryness of the landscape). Each year Tamworth's festival (p215)
draws hundreds of thousands. Aboriginal artists often merge their traditional music with rock, hip-hop and other styles. Look for Yothu Yindi or
Christine Anu.

## Cinema

Most people need little introduction to Australia's vibrant movie industry,
one of the first established in the world and playground for screen great Errol
Flynn. A host of talent has followed in his footsteps, including the likes of
Nicole Kidman, Naomi Watts, Russell Crowe (born in New Zealand, but
who's trifling over details?), Cate Blanchett, Heath Ledger, Toni Collette
and Rachel Griffiths.

In the decade from
1996–2006, Australians
won 13 Academy Awards
for acting, cinema-
tography, art design,
animation, costume
design, sound and visual
effects.

Construction of Fox Studios Australia in Sydney cemented the already
healthy industry, which in addition to producing its own films has become a
location of choice for many American productions drawn by Sydney's talent
pool and – depending on exchange rates – relatively low costs. Big-budget
extravaganzas, financed with overseas money and made for the overseas
market, include *The Matrix* trilogy (featuring numerous Sydney skyscrap-
ers) *Star Wars* Episodes I, II and III, *Mission Impossible 2* and *Superman
Returns*. Sydneysider Baz Luhrmann's *Moulin Rouge* was also made there,
and starred 'our' Nicole.

Films from the 1990s such as *Strictly Ballroom, Muriel's Wedding*, and *The
Adventures of Priscilla, Queen of the Desert* consolidated Australia's reputation as a producer of quirky comedies about local misfits. In recent years
most films made for an Australian audience have abandoned the worn-out
ocker stereotypes and started to explore the country's diversity. Indigenous
stories have found a mainstream voice on the big screen, with films such as
*The Tracker, Rabbit Proof Fence, Australian Rules* and *Ten Canoes* – illustrations of a nation starting to come to terms with its racist past and present.
Cultural and gender stereotypes continue to erode in a genre of intimate
dramas exploring the human dimension, such as *Somersault, Jindabyne,
Japanese Story*, and *Head On*, the latter featuring a gay Greek-Australian
as the lead character. By staying relevant to contemporary Australians, the
industry continues to survive and thrive.

The website for the NSW
Film and Television Office,
www.fto.nsw.gov.au,
gives you the lowdown
on what's being shot and
where in the state.

Notable Australian films in or about NSW:

**Lantana** (2001, director Ray Lawrence) Touted as a 'mystery for grown-ups', this is an extraordinary ensemble piece and deeply moving meditation on life, love, truth and grief.

**Looking for Alibrandi** (2000, director Kate Woods) A charming story of what it's like to grow up
Italian in modern Sydney.

**Little Fish** (2005, director Rowan Woods) The story of a former heroin addict struggling to escape her
past, backdropped by the wider cultural issues surrounding Sydney's 'Little Saigon' – Cabramatta.

**Muriel's Wedding** (1994, director PJ Hogan) Life in suburban NSW is less than dull for Muriel.
Things pick up after a tropical holiday, a name change and more.

**Somersault** (2004, director Cate Shortland) A grittier coming-of-age story, touching on peer
pressure and the marked difference between sex and love.

**The Dish** (2000, director Rob Sitch) Australia's role in the *Apollo 11* moon mission is explored in
this warm-hearted film set in the satellite station at Parkes (p243).

**The Man Who Sued God** (2001, director Mark Joffe) A dry comedy with a philosophical twist,
filmed in Bermagui (p337).

**The Year My Voice Broke** (1987, director John Duigan) A classic look at NSW country life in 1962 Braidwood (p303). A coming-of-age story based on the triangular relationship of three adolescents learning to deal with the perceptions and prejudices of their townsfolk.
**Two Hands** (1999, director Gregor Jordan) A humorous look at Sydney's surprisingly daggy criminal underworld.

## Literature

In the late 19th century, an Australian literary flavour began to develop through the Bulletin School (named after the magazine of the same name that is still available in Sydney), with authors such as Henry Lawson (1867–1922), AB 'Banjo' Patterson (1864–1941) and Miles Franklin (1879–1954), whose novel *My Brilliant Career* (1901) caused a sensation, especially when it was revealed that Miles was a woman.

The aftereffects of the Bulletin School's romantic vernacular tradition lasted many years, and it wasn't until the 1970s (a time of renewed interest in Australian writing) that images of the bush, Australian ideas of mateship and the chauvinism of Australian culture were fully questioned by readers and writers and a new voice began to make itself heard. This voice was more urban, and reflected the concerns of an increasingly confident Australia. Questions about the past were asked and assumed literary styles were found wanting; a uniquely Australian voice began to emerge. A rather quirky strain of 'magic realism' can be found in many recent Australian novels – an interesting quality, given the reputation of Australians for straightforwardness.

Australian writers of international stature include: Patrick White (winner of the Nobel Prize in Literature 1973), Thomas Keneally (Booker Prize-winner 1982), Peter Carey (Booker Prize-winner 1988 and 2001), David Malouf (International Impac Dublin Literary Award 1996), Murray Bail (Commonwealth Writers Prize 1999), Tim Winton (Miles Franklin Award-winner 1992), and Kate Grenville (Orange Prize 2001).

Here are just a few excellent books with NSW settings:

**Matthew Flinders' Cat** (Bryce Courtenay) A tale of unfortunate hardships and unlikely friendships in Sydney's very unsavoury underworld.
**The Bodysurfers** (Robert Drewe) Seductive stories from the northern beaches.
**The Harp in the South** (Ruth Park) Accounts of an impoverished family's life in Surry Hills when the suburb was a crowded slum. In the 1980s this book was turned into a popular TV miniseries.
**The Idea of Perfection** (Kate Grenville) Ideas and cultures clash when a Sydney museum curator goes to rural NSW to save an old bridge and meets a reticent engineer charged with destroying it.
**The Showgirl & the Brumby** (Lucy Lehman) Modern-day rural life in NSW is the focus of this novel about two girls and dreams lived and refused. Perfect context for your drives through fields of cotton and sheep.
**Voss** (Patrick White) Written in 1957, this novel contrasts the harsh and unforgiving outback with colonial life in Sydney. In the 1980s *Voss* was transformed into an opera, with a libretto by David Malouf.

*Australia, An Ecotraveler's Guide* (by Hannah Robinson) steers travellers to the country's best wildlife haunts and national parks, with hundreds of photos and descriptive information on birds, mammals and other creatures.

# Environment

'Renewable energy, sustainable agriculture and water use lie at the heart of the changes Australians must make – from farms, to suburbs, to the city centre.' Tim Flannery

## THE LAND

There are four main geographical areas of New South Wales (NSW).

In *The Weather Makers*, Tim Flannery argues passionately for the urgent need to address – NOW – the implications of a global climate change that is damaging all life on earth and endangering our very survival. It's an accessible read.

The strip of land between the sea and the Great Dividing Range runs from Tweed Heads on the Queensland border to Cape Howe on the Victorian border. The coast is lined with superb beaches and there are many bays, lakes and meandering estuaries.

The Great Dividing Range runs like a spine along the length of Australia's East Coast. In the south of NSW, the range rears up to form the Snowy Mountains, with Australia's highest peak, Mt Kosciuszko (2228m). The enormous Kosciuszko National Park (p295) protects much of the Snowy Mountains, or 'Snowies'. The eastern side of the range tends to form a steep escarpment and is mostly heavily forested. Most of the ancient range's peaks have been worn down to a series of plateaus or tablelands, the largest ones being the New England tableland, the Blue Mountains, the Southern Highlands and the Monaro tableland. Short and swift rivers rise in the Great Dividing Range and flow east to the sea. In the north of the state, these eastward-flowing rivers have large coastal deltas and are mighty watercourses.

NSW has three United Nations World Heritage Sites (http://whc.unesco .org/heritage.htm): the Central Eastern Rainforest Reserves (p196), the Blue Mountains (p119) and Willandra Lakes (p287).

The western side of the Great Dividing Range is less steep than the eastern and dwindles into a series of foothills and valleys, which provide some of the most fertile farmland in the country. Also rising in the Great Dividing Range, but meandering westward across the dry plains to reach the sea in South Australia, are the Darling and the Murray Rivers, and their significant tributaries such as the Lachlan and the Murrumbidgee. These rivers have often changed their sluggish courses, and the Murray-Darling Basin takes in nearly all of the state west of the Great Dividing Range. The plains are riddled with creeks, swamps and lakes.

The western plains begin about 300km inland, and from here westward the state is almost entirely flat. On the western edge of NSW, Broken Hill (p266) sits at the end of a long, low range that juts into the state from South Australia (SA) and is rich with minerals. North of the Darling River, which cuts diagonally across the plains, the country takes on the red soil of the outback.

## WILDLIFE

Most of Australia's many unusual types of wildlife can be abundant in NSW. The one real notable missing star is the deadly box jellyfish – so no loss there. Native animals you're most likely to see in the wild are wallabies and kangaroos, possums and koalas. However, there's a huge range of small, mainly nocturnal, animals going about their business unobserved.

Australia's most distinctive fauna are the marsupials and monotremes. Marsupials such as kangaroos and koalas give birth to partially developed young, which they suckle in a pouch. Monotremes – platypuses and echidnas – lay eggs but also suckle their young. Over 700 species of plants and animals are listed as endangered under the *NSW Threatened Species Conservation Act*.

## Animals

### BIRDS

The only bird larger than the Australian emu is the African ostrich, also flightless. The emu is a shaggy-feathered bird with an often curious nature. After the female emu lays the eggs, the male hatches them and raises the young. Emus are common in the Riverina (p287) and the far west (p257).

There's an amazing variety of parrots and cockatoos. The common pink and grey galahs are noisy, although the sulphur-crested cockatoos are even louder. Rainbow lorikeets have brilliant colour schemes and in some parks accept a free feed from visitors.

A member of the kingfisher family, the kookaburra is heard as much as it is seen – you can't miss its loud, cackling laugh, usually at dawn and sunset. Kookaburras are common near the coast, particularly in the southeast.

The lyrebird, found in moist forest areas, is famous for its vocal abilities and its beauty. Lyrebirds are highly skilled mimics that copy segments of other birds' songs to create unique hybrid compositions. During the courting season, with his colourful fernlike tail feathers spread like a fan, the male puts on a sensational song-and-dance routine to impress potential partners.

The black-and-white magpie (no relation to the European bird of the same name) has a distinctive and beautiful warbling call.

### DINGOES

Australia's native dog, the dingo is thought to have arrived in Australia around 6000 years ago. It was domesticated by the Aborigines, but after the Europeans arrived and Aborigines could no longer hunt freely, the dingo again became 'wild'. By preying on sheep (but mainly rabbits, rats and mice), dingoes earned the wrath of graziers. These sensitive, intelligent dogs are legally considered to be vermin. Some are still found in the high country.

### KANGAROOS

The extraordinary breeding cycle of the kangaroo is well adapted to Australia's harsh, unpredictable environment.

The young kangaroo, or joey, just millimetres long at birth, claws its way unaided to the mother's pouch where it attaches itself to a nipple that expands inside its mouth. A day or two later the mother mates again, but the new embryo doesn't begin to develop until the first joey has left the pouch permanently.

At this point the mother produces two types of milk – one formula to feed the joey at heel, the other for the baby in her pouch. If environmental conditions are right, the mother then mates again. If food or water is scarce, however, the breeding cycle is interrupted until conditions improve.

As well as many species of wallabies (some endangered), there are two main species of kangaroos in NSW: the grey kangaroo and the majestic red kangaroo, which is common in the far west and can stand 2m tall. The no-nonsense reds have been known to disembowel dogs that bother them.

Kangaroos have an affinity for golf courses. You can spot them in more natural settings in national parks such as Murramarang National Park (p332) and Blue Mountains National Park (p119).

### KOALAS

Distantly related to the wombat, koalas are found along the eastern seaboard and inland in places like Gunnedah (p252). Their cuddly appearance belies an irritable nature, and they'll scratch and bite if sufficiently provoked. However, most of the time they resemble an inert fur bag asleep in high branches of trees.

Graham Pizzey and Frank Knight's *Field Guide to Birds of Australia* (edited by Peter Menkhorst, seventh edition 2003) is an indispensable guide for bird-watchers, and anyone else even peripherally interested in Australia's feathered tribes. Knight's illustrations are both beautiful and helpful in identification.

Koalas initially carry their babies in pouches, but later the larger young cling to their mothers' backs. They feed only on the leaves of certain types of eucalypt (found mainly in the forests of the Great Dividing Range) and are particularly sensitive to changes to their habitat.

### PLATYPUSES & ECHIDNAS

The platypus and the echidna are the only living representatives of the monotremes, the most primitive group of mammals. Both lay eggs, as reptiles do, but have mammary glands and suckle their young.

The amphibious platypus has a duck-like bill, webbed feet and a beaverlike body. Males have poisonous spurs on their hind feet. The platypus is able to sense electric currents in the water and uses this ability to track its prey. Platypuses are shy creatures, but they occur in many rivers. Bombala, in the state's southeast, is a good place for platypus-spotting.

The echidna is a spiny anteater that hides from predators by digging vertically into the ground and covering itself with dirt, or by rolling itself into a ball and raising its sharp quills.

### POSSUMS

There's a wide range of possums – they seem to have adapted to all sorts of conditions, including those of the city, where you'll find them in parks, especially around dusk. Some large species are found in suburban roofs; they eat cultivated plants and food scraps.

### REPTILES

There are many species of snake in NSW, all protected. Many are poisonous, some deadly, but few are aggressive and they'll usually get out of your way before you realise that they're there. See Dangers & Annoyances (p371) for ways to avoid being bitten and what to do in the unlikely event that you are.

There's a wide variety of lizards, from tiny skinks to prehistoric-looking goannas which can grow up to 2.5m long, although most species in NSW are much smaller. Goannas can run very fast and when threatened use their big claws to climb the nearest tree – or perhaps the nearest leg!

Bluetongue lizards are slow-moving and stumpy. Their even slower and stumpier relations, shinglebacks, are common in the outback.

### WOMBATS

The wombat is a slow, solid, powerfully built marsupial with a broad head and short, stumpy legs. These fairly placid, easily tamed creatures are legally killed by farmers, who object to the damage done to paddocks by wombats digging large burrows and tunnelling under fences. Like other nocturnal animals, they tend to lumber across roads at night and are difficult to see.

### ENDANGERED SPECIES

The yellow-footed rock wallaby was thought to be extinct until a group was found in western NSW in the 1960s. National parks were created to protect them and local farmers agreed to protect them on their properties. But the wallabies can't compete with feral goats for food and shelter and their numbers are decreasing. They can still be seen in Mutawintji National Park (p266) northeast of Broken Hill.

### INTRODUCED SPECIES

The Acclimatisation Society was a bunch of do-gooders in the Victorian era who devoted themselves to 'improving' the countries of the British Empire by introducing plants and animals. On the whole, their work was disastrous.

The wedge-tailed eagle is found in NSW's open wooded areas. Its wingspan of 2.5m makes it the largest bird of prey in Australia.

The official take on environmental issues comes from the Australian Government Department of Environment and Heritage, see www.deh.gov.au.

The Australian Conservation Foundation (ACF) is the largest nongovernment organisation involved in protecting the environment, see www.acfonline.org.au.

Exotic animals thriving in NSW include rabbits, cats (big, bad feral versions of the domestic moggie), pigs (now bristly black razorbacks with long tusks) and goats. In the Snowy Mountains and towards the Queensland border you might see wild horses (brumbies). These have all been disastrous for native animals, as predators and as competitors for food and water.

Probably the biggest change to the ecosystem has been caused by sheep. To make room for sheep, the bush was cleared and the plains planted with exotic grasses. Many small marsupials became extinct.

## Plants

Australia has a huge diversity of plant species – more than Europe and Asia combined.

The eucalyptus – often called the gum tree – is everywhere except in the deepest rainforests and the most arid regions. Of the 700 species of the genus *Eucalyptus*, 95% occur naturally in Australia.

Gum trees vary in form and height. Species commonly found in NSW include the tall, straight river red gum; the stunted, twisted snow gum with its colourful trunk striations; the spotted gum common on the coast; and the scribbly gum, which has scribbly insect tracks on its bark. Eucalyptus oil is distilled from certain types of gum trees and used for pharmaceutical and perfumed products.

Around 600 species of wattle are found in Australia. Most species flower during late winter and spring, when the country is ablaze with the bright yellow flowers and the reason for the choice of green and gold as the national colours is obvious. The golden wattle is Australia's floral emblem.

### INTRODUCED SPECIES

The majestic Norfolk Island pine, naturally enough a native of Norfolk Island, lines the foreshores of many coastal towns in NSW. There are many other introduced species – most, such as oaks and willows, brought in by homesick settlers to replicate their homeland. One of the most outstanding introduced trees in NSW is the jacaranda. In spring and summer, its vivid mauve or blue flowers bring a splash of colour to many towns around the coast and the ranges.

Some introduced plants have also caused major problems by choking out native flora and pastures. Noxious weeds such as Paterson's curse can be found growing wild in many parts of the state.

## NATIONAL PARKS

There are close to 200 national parks and protected areas in NSW, covering about four million hectares and protecting environments as diverse as the peaks of the Snowy Mountains, the subtropical rainforest of the Border Ranges and the vast arid plains of the outback. Some parks include designated wilderness areas that offer outstanding remote-area walking.

The **National Parks & Wildlife Service** (NPWS; ☎ 1300 361 967; www.nationalparks.nsw.gov .au) does a good job, and many national parks have visitors centres where you can learn about the area, as well as camp sites and other walking tracks. Where there isn't a visitors centre, visit the nearest NPWS office for information. Bush camping (ie heading into the bush and camping where you please) is allowed in many national parks, but not all – check before you go.

There are car entry fees for 44 of the more popular national parks: generally around $3 to $11 per car ($16 to $27 per car per day, depending on the time of year, for Kosciuszko National Park, p295). Camping fees are about $3 to $10 per person, and sometimes free for bush camping with limited facilities.

The Climate Project is a programme which trains ordinary citizens (in the US, Australia and the UK, so far) to become Climate Change Messengers who present the information delivered by Al Gore in the documentary, *An Inconvenient Truth*. For more, go to www .theclimateproject.org.

The Wilderness Society focuses on protection of wilderness and forests, visit www.wilderness .org.au.

Almost two million hectares of park land is protected wilderness area, close to 2% of NSW. Such areas are considered largely untouched by modern human activity.

**ENVIRONMENTAL CHALLENGES**  *Tim Flannery*

The European colonisation of Australia, commencing in 1788, heralded a period of catastrophic environmental upheaval, with the result that Australians today are struggling with some of the most severe environmental problems to be found anywhere. It may seem strange that a population of just 20 million, living in a continent the size of the USA minus Alaska, could inflict such damage on its environment, but Australia's long isolation, its fragile soils and difficult climate have made it particularly vulnerable to human-induced change.

Damage to Australia's environment has been inflicted in several ways, the most important being the introduction of pest species, destruction of forests, overstocking rangelands, inappropriate agriculture and interference with water flows. Beginning with the escape of domestic cats into the Australian bush shortly after 1788, a plethora of vermin – from foxes to wild camels and cane toads – has run wild in Australia, causing extinctions in the native fauna. One out of every 10 native mammals living in Australia prior to European colonisation is now extinct, and many more are highly endangered. Extinctions have also affected native plants, birds and amphibians.

The destruction of forests has also had a profound effect. Most of Australia's rainforests have suffered clearing, while conservationists fight with loggers over the fate of the last unprotected stands of 'old growth'. Many Australian rangelands have been chronically overstocked for more than a century, the result being extreme vulnerability of both soils and rural economies to Australia's drought and flood cycle, as well as extinction of many native species. The development of agriculture has involved land clearance and the provision of irrigation, and here again the effect has been profound. Clearing of the diverse and spectacular plant communities of the Western Australian wheatbelt began just a century ago, yet today up to one-third of that country is degraded by salination of the soils. Between 70kg and 120kg of salt lies below every square metre of the region, and clearing of native vegetation has allowed water to penetrate deep into the soil, dissolving the salt crystals and carrying brine towards the surface.

In terms of financial value, just 1.5% of Australia's land surface provides over 95% of agricultural yield, and much of this land lies in the irrigated regions of the Murray-Darling Basin. This is Australia's agricultural heartland, yet it too is under severe threat from salting of soils and rivers. Irrigation water penetrates into the sediments laid down in an ancient sea, carrying salt into the catchments and fields. If nothing is done, the lower Murray River will become too salty to drink in a decade or two, threatening the water supply of Adelaide, a city of over a million people.

Despite the enormity of the biological crisis engulfing Australia, governments and the community have been slow to respond. It was in the 1980s that coordinated action began to take place, but not until the '90s that major steps were taken. The establishment of Landcare (an organisation enabling people to effectively address local environmental issues; www.landcare australia.com.au) and the expenditure of $2.5 billion through the National Heritage Trust Fund have been important national initiatives. Yet so difficult are some of the issues the nation faces that, as yet, little has been achieved in terms of halting the destructive processes. Individuals are also banding together to help. Groups such as the Australian Bush Heritage Fund (www .bushheritage.asn.au) and the Australian Wildlife Conservancy (AWC; www.australianwildlife.org) allow people to donate funds and time to the conservation of native species. Some such groups have been spectacularly successful; the AWC, for example, already manages many endangered species over its 1.3 million acre holdings.

So severe are Australia's problems that it will take a revolution before they can be overcome, for sustainable practices need to be implemented in every arena of life – from farms to suburbs and city centres. Renewable energy, sustainable agriculture and water use lie at the heart of these changes, and Australians are only now developing the road-map to sustainability that they so desperately need if they are to have a long-term future on the continent.

*Tim Flannery is one of Australia's leading thinkers and writers. Formerly director of the South Australian Museum, Tim is chairman of the South Australian Premier's Science Council and Sustainability Roundtable. He was the recipient of the prestigious Australian of the Year award in 2007.*

The NPWS is also responsible for some other reserves. State recreation areas often contain bushland, but the quality of the forest might not be as good as in national parks. Many are centred on lakes or large dams where water sports are popular, so they can be crowded in summer. There's often commercial accommodation (usually a caravan park), and bush camping is usually not permitted. There are exceptions to this, however, and this book will identify where camping is possible in the beautiful wilderness of NSW.

Nature reserves are generally smaller reserves, usually with day-use facilities, protecting specific ecosystems.

Historic sites protect areas of historical significance, such as the ghost town of Hill End (p234) near Bathurst and Aboriginal rock-art sites.

## STATE FORESTS

State forests, used for timber harvesting, conservation purposes and public recreation, cover around three million hectares. Bush camping (free) is allowed in most state forests, as are trail bikes, 4WDs, horses and pets. Often there are designated walking tracks.

Brochures and maps are available from the **State Forests Information Centre** ( ☎ 02-9980 4100; www.forest.nsw.gov.au). These forests are administered by State Forests of NSW, which has regional offices and forest centres around the state.

> If you're going to visit a lot of national parks in NSW, consider an annual pass to cover the cost of entering the 44 parks that charge daily vehicle entry fees. There are four options ranging from $22 for any one designated park (excluding Kosciuszko National Park) to $190 for access to all parks.

---

### TRAVEL WIDELY, TREAD LIGHTLY, GIVE SUSTAINABLY – THE LONELY PLANET FOUNDATION

The Lonely Planet Foundation proudly supports nimble nonprofit institutions working for change in the world. Each year the foundation donates 5% of Lonely Planet company profits to projects selected by staff and authors. Our partners range from Kabissa, which provides small nonprofits across Africa with access to technology, to the Foundation for Developing Cambodian Orphans, which supports girls at risk of falling victim to sex traffickers.

Our nonprofit partners are linked by a grass-roots approach to the areas of health, education or sustainable tourism. Many – such as Louis Sarno who works with BaAka (Pygmy) children in the forested areas of Central African Republic – choose to focus on women and children as one of the most effective ways to support the whole community. Louis is determined to give options to children who are discriminated against by the majority Bantu population.

Sometimes foundation assistance is as simple as restoring a local ruin like the Minaret of Jam in Afghanistan; this incredible monument now draws intrepid tourists to the area and its restoration has greatly improved options for local people.

Just as travel is often about learning to see with new eyes, so many of the groups we work with aim to change the way people see themselves and the future for their children and communities.

# New South Wales Outdoors

Boasting a beguiling landscape and a diverse terrain and climate, New South Wales (NSW) is an activity-addict's playground. The variety of pursuits will tempt even **hardened** exercise phobes to get a little more intimate with the beaches, rocks, wilderness trails, mountains, slopes and hills. Below is a handful of what's on offer, but for more information see Activities, p369.

Local professionals can set you up with equipment and training. Climbing Australia has excellent info on rock climbing in NSW. See www.climbing.com.au.

## ABSEILING & ROCK CLIMBING

There is fantastic rock climbing and abseiling in the Blue Mountains, especially around Katoomba (p123). Climbing Bald Rock (p225), the largest granite rock in the southern hemisphere, is a challenge that rewards with great views.

In the Southeast, there are abseiling tours in the Bungonia State Conservation Area (p312).

## CANOEING, KAYAKING & RAFTING

There's lovely canoeing by day or night on the Bellingen River (p171) and in Oxley Wild Rivers National Park (p218), although you need your own gear for the latter. Further north you can go ocean kayaking with dolphin- and whale-spotting thrown in around Ballina (p185) and in the Cape Byron Marine Park (p189). Adrenalin junkies can get stuck into white-water rafting on the Nymboida River near Coffs Harbour (p175)

## BUSHWALKING

NSW's national parks hold discovery walks and tours with an eco-bent for kids during school holidays. Click onto www .nationalparks.nsw.gov. au or call ☎ 1300 361 967 for details.

Encompassing 1400km of coastline and a smorgasbord of landscapes, NSW is riddled with stunning bushwalks with a variety of standards, lengths and terrains to suit all levels of experience. In most instances sturdy walking shoes, plenty of water as well as a hat and sunscreen are mandatory.

In Sydney, try the jaw-droppingly beautiful Bondi to Coogee Walk (p66) with ocean views and Aboriginal rock carvings, or the Manly Scenic Walkway (p66), which takes in vast harbour views and rugged bushland.

Near Sydney, Katoomba (p125) is the best spot to base yourself for mustdo walks in the Blue Mountains, which you can do solo or on a tour (p125). Experienced hikers can tackle Royal National Park's 28km Coastal Walking Trail (p109), and picnicking day-trippers can take in short trails through Ku-ring-gai Chase National Park (p112).

The hiking and walking in and around Barrington Tops National Park (p156), a World Heritage site in the Hunter Valley, is superb. There are

---

**PUBLIC LIABILITY**

The huge cost of public-liability insurance in Australia has forced the closure or scaling back of numerous tours and organised outdoor activities such as horse riding and rock climbing, and threatened the viability of many small businesses.

The exorbitant insurance costs faced by small businesses and volunteer organisations have been blamed on a vast range of issues: the collapse of several major Australian insurance companies; insurance industry greed; some ridiculously high legal payouts awarded to people for minor incidents; a growing culture of litigation; low safety standards by some outfits; and ambulance-chasing lawyers seeking the biggest possible compensation.

Federal, state and territory representatives have met several times to discuss the problem, but at the time of writing many businesses were feeling the strain and more may have gone to the wall by the time you read this book.

## NSW NATIONAL PARKS

NSW has over 600 national parks and reserves that capture its rich diversity of landscapes and wildlife. From the outback's lunar plains and dunes to the moss-cloaked northern rainforests, these conservation areas provide exquisite playgrounds for nature lovers. For comprehensive listings, grab a copy of the free *NSW National Parks Guide*, available from National Parks & Wildlife Service (NPWS) offices and many visitors centres.

Having trekked, climbed, driven and camped through as many of the parks as possible, our authors reckon this list is the best of the best.

- **Kosciuszko National Park** (p295) NSW's largest national park; Australia's highest mountain. Serene camping spots, wildlife, overland bushwalks, glacial lakes and year-round activities.
- **Dharug National Park** (p116) Wilderness area on the north bank of the Hawkesbury River; home to the Dharug people and 10,000 year-old rock carvings.
- **Dorrigo National Park** (p173) World Heritage–listed rainforest, walking tracks for all fitness levels, waterfalls and astonishing views.
- **Morton National Park** (p134 and p331) Unruly wilderness, towering sandstone cliffs, wildflowers, divine waterfalls, and panoramic views from the summit of Pigeon House Mountain.
- **Mt Kaputar National Park** (p254) Exquisite ecologies that shift elaborately with the drive to the summit of a 21 million year-old volcano; bushwalking, rock climbing, mountain-biking and camping.
- **Mungo National Park** (p273) Remote and beautiful park encompassing the Willandra Lakes World Heritage area, shimmering sand dunes, moon-landscapes and camping.
- **Nightcap National Park** (p199) Diverse subtropical rainforest, endangered wildlife, ambling to difficult walks, emerald forests, dramatic lookouts and steep waterfalls.
- **Royal National Park** (p109) The world's oldest national park, with vertiginous cliffs, secluded beaches, lush rainforest and isolated seaside communities.
- **Sydney Harbour National Park** (p52) Scattered pockets of harbourside bushland, magical walking tracks, Aboriginal engravings, quirky islands and historical sights.
- **Warrumbungle National Park** (p252) Remnant volcanic landforms shaped by the Warrumbungle eruption some 17 million years ago. Excellent walking, serene camping and cosy cabins.

## Responsible Travel

As with all conservation areas, the best way to maintain their health is to tread lightly and limit your footprint as much as possible. Keep the following in mind whenever you're in a national park:

- Always take out what you took in – don't burn, bury or leave any rubbish behind.
- Never veer off walking tracks, even if it's muddy or dusty.
- Only camp in designated areas.
- If cooking, use a fuel stove, they're quicker cleaner and better for the bush.
- Respect traditional Aboriginal owners by leaving the area as you found it – don't take artefacts as 'souvenirs' with you.

Bushfires are a very real danger in NSW. As a general rule in national parks (and beyond), always check fire restrictions before lighting a fire, only use fires for cooking, only light fires in the fireplaces provided and keep fires small to conserve wood. Listen to local radio for news of total fire bans or contact the nearest NPWS office if you're unsure of what is permitted. See p372 for more on bushfires.

In many of the outback national parks, it's prohibited to drive after heavy rains due to the damage tyres cause to the roads. You risk hefty fines or getting stuck in the middle of nowhere (a far worse scenario) if you tempt fate.

---

**CONSIDERATIONS FOR RESPONSIBLE BUSHWALKING**

Please consider the following when hiking, to help preserve the ecology and beauty of Australia.

- Do not urinate or defecate within 100m (320ft) of any water sources. Doing so can lead to the transmission of serious diseases and pollutes precious water supplies.

- Use biodegradable detergents and wash at least 50m (160ft) from any water sources.

- Avoid cutting wood for fires in popular bushwalking areas as this can cause rapid deforestation. Use a stove that runs on kerosene, methylated spirits or some other liquid fuel, rather than stoves powered by disposable butane gas canisters.

- Hillsides and mountain slopes are prone to erosion; it's important to stick to existing tracks.

---

numerous walks in Kosciuszko National Park (p295), including the 21km glacial lakes walk or an 18km trek to the summit of Australia's highest mountain. On the South Coast, you can feast your eyes on sublime views from the top of Pigeon House Mountain (p331), but the climb is not for the faint of heart.

In the North Coast hinterland you can take your pick of 7km to 10km walks in the World Heritage–listed Dorrigo National Park (p173) or spend a couple of dawn hours scaling the heights of Mt Warning (p210).

In the northwest, there are many good walks around Warrumbungle National Park (p252).

Longer routes include the 250km Great North Walk (p138) from Sydney to Newcastle, which can be walked in sections, or covered in a two-week trek. Alternatively you could follow in the footsteps of historic explorers on the 440km Hume and Hovell Walking Track (p309), which passes beautiful high country between Yass and Albury.

*Lonely Planet's Walking in Australia provides detailed information about bushwalking.*

## MOUNTAIN-BIKING & CYCLING

Those who cycle for fun have access to great cycling routes and touring country for day, weekend or even multi-week trips, while very experienced pedallers can consider trips through the outback or a tour of the coast. Sydney (p64) has a recreational bike-path system, peaceful (and car-less) tracks through Centennial Park, and an abundance of bike-hire places. Canberra (p354) has one of the best cycle-path networks in Australia and tracks lead all the way to the Murrumbidgee River. There are bike hire, information and tour companies based here.

Longer-distance rides in NSW are limited only by your endurance and imagination. In the Southeast, Tumut State Forest (p309) is becoming increasingly popular with avid mountain bikers and has constructed tracks. Nearby, serious cyclists can challenge themselves on the Cannonball Run near Thredbo – see p300.

*Outdoor stockists are good sources of bushwalking information. Alternatively, the Confederation of Bushwalking Clubs NSW maintains a large website (www.bushwalking.org. au) with lots of useful information.*

There are also opportunities to mountain-bike through national park bushland in Botany Bay National Park (p109) and Royal National Park (p109). There's more rugged mountain-biking in the Blue Mountains National Park (p119), and the *Cycle the Hunter* brochure details suggested circuits throughout the Hunter Valley.

On the North Coast, Ballina (p185) is known for its ambling cycling paths and there are plenty of hire outfits in town. Mountain-biking tours are an eco-friendly way to explore the nearby hinterland with outfits like Mountain Bike Tours (p190).

The northwest and west to the outback are notable for their open roads. In the more moderate months, you can enjoy long-distance rural rides on roads relatively untravelled. Bike hire in Sydney, Canberra and main urban and tourist centres will set you back around $20 to $50 per day. See the Transport chapter p387 for information about bike purchase and hire, and about road regulations.

Some good cycling organisations include the following.

**Bicycling Australia** ( ☎ 02-4274 4884; www.bicyclingaustralia.com) National organisation with advice, forums, destination suggestions and bike-related classifieds.

**Bicycle Federation of Australia** ( ☎ 02 6249 6761; www.bfa.asn.au) Australia's national cycling organisation.

**Bicycle New South Wales** ( ☎ 02-9218 5400; www.bicyclensw.org.au; Level 5, 822 George St, Sydney) Excellent organisation; a stop by the office for advice, maps and books is worthwhile.

**Pedal Power ACT** (www.pedalpower.org.au)

Bicycles Network Australia (www.bicycles .net.au) is an excellent omnibus website for cyclists, listing information about second-hand sales, hire, cycling destinations and news.

## SAILING & CRUISES

Sydney Harbour is one of the world's great – and most photogenic – sailing locations. There are plenty of sailing schools offering lessons and cruises; Darling Harbour and Rushcutters Bay are good spots to head. Notable schools include **Eastsail Sailing School** (www.eastsail.com.au) and **Sydney by Sail** (www.sydneybysail .com.au). Prices vary from $95 for beginner lessons to $475 for yachtmaster courses. See p65 for more information.

Of course if you're just interested in the sailing experience without the effort there are plenty of Sydney Harbour cruises to choose from, ranging from cocktail cruises with **Matilda Cruises** (www.matilda.com.au) to hop-on hop-off ferries. See p68 for details.

Just north of Sydney you can charter a boat to meander through the waterways of Ku-ring-gai Chase National Park (p112) or coast up the mighty Hawkesbury from Brooklyn (p114). The Central Coast offers some beautiful sailing opportunities and there are good charter outfits and cruises in Terrigal and The Entrance; see p139. Climbing even further north you can rent a boat to cruise Port Macquarie's pretty marina (p165) or hire anything from a tinnie to a catamaran in Ballina (p185). There's great fishing to be done right up north and you can cast a line on a fishing charter from Tweed Heads (p195).

On the South Coast you can hire runabouts or take a cruise from Batemans Bay (p332).

Elsewhere in NSW, the best places for charters, lessons and information are the local sailing clubs.

Sydney Boat Share (www .sydneyboatshare.com .au) is a boat share organisation for avid sailors keen to own their own boat without the spare dosh.

## SKIING & SNOWBOARDING

NSW has an enthusiastic but short ski season running from about mid-June to early September. Snowfalls are unpredictable, but hotspots like Thredbo have snowmaking machines to cover for Mother Nature.

The aptly named Snowy Mountains in and around Kosciuszko National Park (p295) hold the top places to ski: resorts such as Charlotte Pass, Perisher Blue, Selwyn and Thredbo, which tend to get crowded on weekends. During winter heavy penalties apply if drivers don't carry snow chains – even if there's no snow.

Cross-country skiing is popular and most resorts offer lessons and hire out equipment. Kosciuszko National Park includes some of the country's best trails, and often old cattle-herders' huts are the only form of accommodation, apart from your tent.

The Skiing Australia website (www.skiing australia.org.au) has links to major resorts and race clubs.

## SURFING

In Australia, surfing isn't just an activity, it's a spiritual pursuit. Folk start young and by their teens, spend whole summers searching out the next new swell. Practically any coastal town in NSW will have good surf nearby.

Click onto www
.wannasurf.com.au for a
full roundup of the best
waves in NSW.

Board hire will set you back around $40 per day. If you're planning to learn from scratch, a few lessons are mandatory. They'll equip you with the basic moves, but far more importantly you'll learn how to identify dangerous rips and swells – a skill which could save your life. You'll also learn some important surf etiquette – a skill which could save your dignity.

Sydney hotspots include Bondi, Tamarama and Cronulla in the south, and Manly, Palm Beach and Curl Curl in the north. There are ample schools and board hire; see p65. The Central Coast has less-crowded beaches than Sydney, and is a good spot to learn – see the 'Watertainment' boxed text on p139 for instructors. Terrigal, Avoca and Umina beaches have the best waves, although you should be careful of strong currents at these places.

Experienced surfers can test their mettle on the Acids Reef Break at Wollongong's North Beach (p323), but there are also kinder breaks here and at Wollongong City Beach. The South Coast also has some good swells, particularly around Narooma at Potato Point and Mystery Bay – see p335.

For more surfing informa-
tion, news, surf cams and
photos, look up www
.coastalwatch.com.

The North Coast is peppered with surfing secrets and mythical breaks. In Newcastle there are surf schools and competition-attracting breaks at Bar Beach, Dixon Park Beach and Merewether (p142). Crescent Head (p167) has kept the legacy of the longboard alive owing to the perfectly suited swell of Little Nobby's Junction. Diggers Beach is the best for surf at Coffs Harbour (p175) and the strong rips at Angourie (p183) lure hardened surfers. But the most celebrated waves tumble further north. Lennox Head (p186) has a peeling right hander, which obliges experienced surfers and kite-surfers. Byron Bay's roots are surfing and the peeling rights of Clarks Beach (p187) are suitable for most levels. Byron is also home to a number of excellent surf schools including **Mojosurf Adventures** (www.mojosurf.com.au) and **Samudra** (www.samudra.com.au), which offer five-day camps combined with yoga.

## WILDLIFE-WATCHING

Migrating southern right and humpback whales pass close to Australia's southern coast between the Antarctic and warmer waters, and whale-watching cruises allow you to get close to these magnificent creatures. Good spots are Eden (p341) on the South Coast, and further north in Port Macquarie (p165), Coffs Harbour (p175) and Ballina (p185).

Lonely Planet's *Watching
Wildlife: Australia* is a
great companion for
spotting and identifying
wildlife in any pocket of
NSW wilderness.

Dolphins can be seen year-round at many places along the coast, such as Jervis Bay (p328), Port Stephens (p158) and Byron Bay (p189).

Montague Island (p335), on the South Coast, is a nature reserve home to penguins, fur seals and sea birds. For the warm and fuzzy variety, you'll find plenty of wallabies, kangaroos and possums in the Blue Mountains, hundreds of tame kangaroos in Pambula (p341) and roving koalas in Port Macquarie (p163).

# Food & Drink

Born in convict poverty and raised on a diet heavily influenced by Great Britain, Australian cuisine has come a long way. This is now one of the most dynamic places in the world to have a meal, thanks to immigration and a dining public willing to give anything new, and better, a go. Sydney can claim to be a dining destination worthy of touring gourmands from New York to Paris. More importantly real people, including travellers, will feel the effects of New South Wales' (NSW) ever-blossoming food culture.

The influx of immigrants (and their cuisine) has found locals trying (and liking) everything from lassi to laksa. This passionate minority has led to a rise in dining standards, better availability of produce and a frenetic buzz about food in general. It's no wonder Australian chefs, cookbooks and food writers are so sought-after overseas.

We've even coined our own phrase, Modern Australian (Mod Oz), to describe our cuisine. If it's a melange of East and West, it's Modern Australian. If it's not authentically French or Italian, it's Modern Australian. Mod Oz is our attempt to classify the unclassifiable.

Seafood co-ops along the NSW coast are a great option for fresh seafood – gorge on a five-star diet on a one star budget.

## STAPLES & SPECIALITIES

Nothing compares to Australia's seafood, harnessed from some of the purest waters you'll find anywhere, and usually cooked with care. Oyster connoisseurs salivate over Sydney's rock oysters, and those found further south in Pambula and Merimbula. Rock lobsters are fantastic and fantastically expensive, and mud crabs, despite the name, are a sweet delicacy. Another odd-sounding delicacy are 'bugs' – like shovel-nosed lobsters without a lobster's price tag. Yabbies (freshwater crayfish) can be found throughout the region.

Prawns are incredible, particularly sweet school prawns or the eastern king (Yamba) prawns found along northern NSW. Add to that countless wild fish species and you've got one of the greatest bounties on earth.

Almost everything grown from the land was introduced to Australia. The sheer size and diversity of climates in Australia means that there's an enormous variety of produce on offer in NSW.

Heart and Soul by celebrated Australian chef Kylie Kwong lists the author's favourite Mod-Oz recipes based on her experience working in some of NSW's finest restaurants with Australia's top chefs.

Most Australians stick to cereal and toast for breakfast, indulging perhaps in a slap up bacon-and-egg-feast on weekends. For lunch they still devour sandwiches, although the humble ham-and-cheese-on-white has relinquished its reign to focaccias, pita wraps, and toasted Turkish bread combos filled with everything from tandoori chicken to organic tofu (or ham and cheese). At night, Australians eat anything and everything. On weekends, particularly in urban areas, you'll also find many folk indulging

---

### ORGANIC REVOLUTION

NSW, particularly the North Coast, is an increasing producer of organic food – that is food that has been grown or produced without the use of pesticides or chemicals. The health benefits are obvious – you get to enjoy your tomatoes, carrots and apples without fear of swallowing dozens of potentially harmful pesticides with them. But organically grown food is also of huge benefit to the environ-ment. It saves soil and water from years of pesticide contamination, and eliminates the need for hazardous waste disposal. In addition, most organic farms are small and independently owned, so the money you spend goes straight back to self-sustainable, environmentally friendly projects. And lastly, there's the taste – after you've tasted your first organic tomato there's just no going back.

in a long pub lunch or *yum cha* (the classic southern Chinese dumpling feast).

## DRINKS

You're in the right country if you're after a drink. Once a nation of tea-and beer-swillers, Oz is now turning its attention to coffee and wine. You're probably not far from a wine region right now.

The closest region to Sydney, the Hunter Valley, first had vines planted in the 1830s, and is noted for big-bodied reds such as shiraz. Further inland, there are vineyards at Canberra, Cowra, Orange and Mudgee.

Plenty of good wine comes from big producers with economies of scale on their side, but the most interesting wines are usually made by small vignerons where you pay a premium – but the gamble means the payoff, in terms of flavour, is often greater. Much of the cost of wine (nearly 42%) is due to a high taxing program courtesy of the Australian government.

Beer, for years, has been of the bland, chilled-so-you-can-barely-taste-it variety. Now microbrewers and boutique breweries are filtering through – see the boxed text Liquid Gold below for hot tips.

In terms of coffee, Australia is leaping ahead, with Italian-style espresso machines in virtually every café. As well, boutique roasters are all the rage and, in urban areas, the qualified *barista* (coffee maker) can be found virtually everywhere.

## CELEBRATIONS

Celebrating in the Australian manner often includes equal amounts of food and alcohol. A birthday could well be a barbecue (barbie) of steak (or prawns), washed down with a beverage or two. Weddings are usually big slap-up dinners.

Many regions of NSW hold food festivals. There are harvest festivals in wine regions, and various communities, such as the town of Orange (p239) hold annual events. Look for weekly markets like the Byron Farmers Market (p193) where a variety of producers – many organic – sell an array of interesting produce and foods.

For many an event, especially in the warmer months, many Australians fill the car with an Esky (a portable, insulated ice chest to keep everything cool), tables, chairs, a cricket set or a footy, and head off for a barbie by the lake/river/beach. If there's a 'total fire ban' (which, increasingly, occurs each

*Quaff* (2007) by Peter Forrestal is the quintessential guide to the best wines available in Australia for under $15 a bottle, including over 400 local and imported labels.

An annual publication with lots of useful information on many readily available wines is the *Penguin Good Australian Wine Guide*, by Huon Hooke and Ralph Kyte-Powell.

---

### LIQUID GOLD

Given that beer consumption is a recognised pastime in Australia (and in some areas it's a competitive sport), it's surprising that the choice of local brews remained so limited for so long. But the country has entered the age of the microbrewery, and these gems of industry are turning the watery schooner of draught on its head.

A microbrewery is defined as a brewery that produces under 15,000 barrels of beer annually, a production rate that enables the breweries to focus on taste and quality. Any beer drinker worth their wheat would be mad to miss the following microbreweries:

- **Wig & Pen** (p360) A range of 10 beers brewed on-site, including superb ales.
- **Potters Hotel & Brewery** (p148) Kolsch, lager, bock and ginger beer with bite.
- **Five Islands Brewing Company** (p324) Nine draughts including 'Parkyns Shark Oil' (an Indian Pale Ale) to the 'Bulli Black' (dark ale brewed with chocolate).
- **Malt Shovel Brewery** (Map p86; ☎ 8594 0200; www.malt-shovel.com.au; 99 Pyrmont Bridge, Camperdown, Sydney) Brews the renowned James Squire series.

**COFFEE CULTURE**

Australians love their coffee and whether you hanker for a short mach, soy latte, skinny cap, double espresso or flat white, you'll find *baristas* willing to prove their worth just about anywhere. Our authors reckon there are a few standouts worthy of a mention though:

- **Argent St Café & Restaurant** (p271)
- **Bar Coluzzi** (p96)
- **Classique Café Restaurant** (p282)
- **Estobar** (p145)
- **My Café** (p359)
- **Simon's Coffee Lounge** (p117)
- **Succulent Cafe** (p192)
- **Ziegler's** (p233)

summer), the food is precooked and the barbie becomes more of a picnic, but the essence remains the same.

## WHERE TO EAT & DRINK

Typically, a restaurant meal in Australia is a relaxed affair. It may take 15 minutes to order, another 15 before the first course arrives, and maybe half an hour between entrées and mains. The upside of this is that outside of Sydney (where time and a table is money), any table you've booked in a restaurant is yours for the night, unless you're told otherwise. So sit, linger and live life in the slow lane.

A competitively priced place to eat is in a club or pub that offers a counter meal. This is where you order your meal (usually staples such as a fisherman's basket, steak or chicken parma) at the kitchen, take a number, and wait until it's called out or displayed on a screen. Plenty of clubs have now revolutionised the system using technology so you may get a table 'beeper' to notify you. Many pubs now have dedicated 'steak nights', where you can tuck into a T-bone or porterhouse for around $10.

Solo diners find that cafés and noodle bars are welcoming, good fine dining restaurants often treat you like a star, but sadly, some midrange places may still make you feel a little ill at ease.

One of the most interesting features of the dining scene is the Bring Your Own (BYO), a restaurant that allows you to bring your own alcohol. If the restaurant also sells alcohol, the BYO bit is usually limited to bottled wine only and a corkage charge is added to your bill. The cost is either per person or per bottle, and ranges from nothing to $15 per bottle in fancy places. Some fine restaurants may not allow BYO at all.

Most restaurants open at noon for lunch and from 6pm or 7pm for dinner. Locals usually eat lunch shortly after noon, and dinner bookings are usually made for 7.30pm or 8pm, though in the major cities some restaurants stay open past 10pm.

### Quick Eats

There's not a huge culture of street vending in NSW, though you may find a pie or coffee cart in some places. In Sydney and other urban and well-touristed spots like Wollongong, Newcastle and Byron Bay, quick eats are easy to find, most commonly in the form of sushi shops, Indian, Thai or Vietnamese takeaways, kebab shops or sandwich bars. In rural areas options

Bill Granger, the undisputed king of breakfast in Sydney, specialises in low-fuss, maximum-taste dishes. You can too with one of his cookbooks; *Bills Sydney Food* (2001), *Bills Food* (2002) and *Simply Bill* (2005).

A Tim Tam Shooter is where the two diagonally opposite corners of this rectangular chocolate biscuit are nibbled off, and a hot drink (tea is the true aficionado's favourite) is sucked through the fast-melting biscuit as if through a straw.

www.eatlocal.com.au is a
nifty website for reviews,
photos, and sometimes
even menus for restau-
rants in the Hunter Valley
and Central Coast.

are generally limited to a milk bar, which serves traditional hamburgers (with bacon, egg, pineapple and beetroot if you want) and that Aussie icon – the small-town bakery. It may sound humble, but these pride themselves on their homemade pies, sausage rolls, pasties, sweet slices and, of course, just-baked bread. Fish and chips is still hugely popular, most often eaten at the beach on a Friday night. American-style fast food is also (unfortunately) abundant in urban areas.

Pizza has become one of the most popular fast foods; most home-delivered pizzas are American-style (thick and with lots of toppings) rather than Italian-style. That said, wood-fired, thin Neapolitan-style pizza is often available, even in country towns. In Sydney, Roman-style pizza (buy it by the slice) is becoming more popular, but you can't usually buy American-style pizza in anything but whole rounds.

## VEGETARIANS & VEGANS

In NSW's cities vegetarians will be well catered for. Cafés seem to always have vegetarian options, and even the best restaurants may have complete vegetarian menus. Take care with risotto and soups, though, as meat stock is often used. Vegans will find the going much tougher, but there are usually dishes that are vegan-adaptable at restaurants. The Australian Vegetarian Society's useful website (www.veg-soc.org) lists vegetarian-friendly places to eat throughout NSW.

The Sydney Morning
Herald puts out an annual
restaurant guide, the
Good Food Guide, that
rates over 400 restaurants
in NSW.

## EATING WITH KIDS

Dining with children in NSW is relatively easy. Avoid the flashiest places and children are generally welcomed, particularly at Chinese, Greek or Italian restaurants. Kids are usually welcome at cafés; bistros and clubs often see families dining early. Many fine-dining restaurants don't welcome small children. Most places that do welcome children don't have separate kids menus, and those that do usually offer everything straight from the deep fryer – such as crumbed chicken and chips. It is better to find something on the menu (say a pasta or salad) and have the kitchen adapt it slightly to your children's needs.

The best news for travelling families, weather permitting, is that there are plenty of free or coin-operated barbecues in parks. Beware of weekends and public holidays when fierce battles can erupt over who is next in line for the barbie. For more on travelling with children, see p370.

---

### AUTHORS' RECOMMENDATIONS

The team of authors who wrote this edition also have an eclectic list of favourite places for a bite in NSW:

- **Wildrice** (p93) in Sydney
- **Papadino's Pizzeria** (p131) in Lithgow
- **Balcony Bar & Restaurant** (p192) in Byron Bay
- **Cipriani** (p359) in Canberra
- **Betty & Muriel's** (p280) in Junee
- **Broken Earth Café & Restaurant** (p271) in Broken Hill
- **Selkirks** (p239) in Orange
- **Red Grapevine Restaurant & Bar** (p221) in Armidale
- **Pelicans** (p335) in Narooma
- **Silo** (p145) in Newcastle

**BILLS & TIPPING**

The total at the bottom of a restaurant bill is all you really need to pay. It should include Goods and Services Tax (GST), as should menu prices, and there is no 'optional' service charge added. Waiters are paid a reasonable salary, so they don't rely on tips to survive. Often, though, especially in cities, people tip a little in a café, while the tip for excellent service can go as high as 15% in whizz-bang establishments.

## HABITS & CUSTOMS

At the table, it's good manners to use British knife and fork skills, keeping the fork in the left hand, tines down, and the knife in the right (though you can be forgiven for using your fork like a shovel). Talking with your mouth full is considered uncouth, and fingers should only be used for food that can't be tackled any other way.

If you're lucky enough to be invited over for dinner at someone's house, always take a gift such as a bottle of wine, flowers or a box of chocolates.

'Shouting' is a revered custom where people rotate paying for a round of drinks. Just don't leave before it's your turn to buy! At a toast, everyone should touch glasses and look at one another.

Australians like to linger a bit over coffee. They like to linger a really long time while drinking beer. And they tend to take quite a bit of time if they're out to dinner.

In NSW, smoking is banned in restaurants, cafés and other eateries where food is consumed indoors, including pubs, so sit outside if you love to puff.

*Australians consume more than 206,000 tonnes of seafood per year.*

## COOKING COURSES

Many good cooking classes are run by food stores such as **Simon Johnson's** (☎ 1800 655 522, 02-8244 8288; www.simonjohnson.com) *Talk Eat Drink* series in Sydney. Others are run by markets, such as the **Sydney Seafood School** (☎ 02-9004 1111; www.sydneyfishmarket.com.au).

Some longer courses for the inspired include the following.

**Elise Pascoe Cooking School** (☎ 02-4236 1666; www.cookingschool.com.au; Jamberoo Valley) Food writer and renowned cook Elise Pascoe runs mostly weekend cooking classes in a stunning setting two hours south of Sydney.

**Le Cordon Bleu** (☎ 1800 064 802, www.lecordonbleu.com.au; Sydney) The original must do French cooking course, from 10 weeks to five years (part-time).

**Nan Tien Buddhist Temple** (p321) Vegetarian cooking classes seasoned with t'ai chi and meditation.

*The Australian Food & Wine website, run by two food writers who trained as chefs, has information on cooking schools, restaurants, cook books plus plenty of their own Modern Australian recipes. They'll email a monthly newsletter, too, www .campionandcurtis.com.*

## EAT YOUR WORDS

Some essential culinary lingo:

**barbie** – a barbecue, where (traditionally) smoke and overcooked meat are matched with lashings of coleslaw, potato salad and beer

**Esky** – a portable, insulated ice chest to hold your tinnies, before you pop them in your tinny holder. May be carried onto your *tinny*, too.

**middy** – a mid-sized glass of beer

**nummits** – delicious, can be an adjective or noun

**pav** – pavlova; the meringue dessert topped with cream, passionfruit and kiwifruit or other fresh fruit

**sanger/sando/sambo** – a sandwich

**schooner** – a big glass of beer; but not as big as a pint

**snags** – (aka surprise bags); sausages

**Tim Tam** – a commercial chocolate biscuit that lies close to the heart of most Australians

**tinny** – usually refers to a can of beer; also a small boat you go fishing in

# Sydney

At the heart of Sydney – Australia's oldest, largest and most diverse city – is the outrageously good-looking Sydney Harbour. Like a psychedelic supermodel, the city curves and sways through this glamorous maze of sandstone headlands, lazy bays and legendary surf beaches. The Sydney experience is essentially physical – dunk yourself in the Bondi surf, sail under the Harbour Bridge on a yacht, jog along the Coogee cliff tops or rampage through Centennial Park on horseback. Everybody seems to be outside – the beaches are swarming, street cafés buzz and the harbour blooms with sails.

Jealous as hell, the rest of Australia stereotypes Sydney as more body-beautiful than bookish, more *carpe diem* than museum – a narcissistic 'Sin City' fixated on sunglasses, salons and soy lattes. Sure, there's a lot of blonde dye in Bondi, but the genetic legacy of the British and Irish convicts who built Sydney is more evident in gutsy self-belief than anything mirror-worthy.

Sydney is no less complex socially than it is on the map. An edgy multiculturalism ignites the food scene and fuels the nocturnal life – you'll lose yourself in the restaurants, bars and clubs just as easily as on the streets. Aboriginal heritage makes an impact through art; you'll see many urban galleries celebrating indigenous culture.

Whether it's the launching pad or the final fling of your New South Wales adventure, your Sydney days will be active and engaging, your nights indulgent and intense. The rest of Australia is in denial – Sydney is as good as it gets.

## HIGHLIGHTS

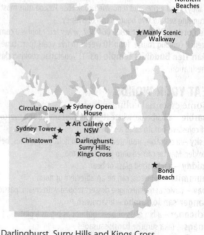

- Carve up the surf at **Bondi Beach** (p61) or the **Northern Beaches** (p64)
- Enjoy fresh seafood, divine Australian wine and harbour hubbub at a **Circular Quay restaurant** (p91)
- Catch a show and ogle the architecture at the **Sydney Opera House** (p54)
- Check out the stunning indigenous art at the **Art Gallery of New South Wales** (p59)
- Engage your senses: sights, sounds, smells, tastes and textures in **Chinatown** (p56)
- Forget you're in the middle of a huge city on the bushy **Manly Scenic Walkway** (p66)
- Soar up **Sydney Tower** (p58) for jaw-dropping 360-degree views
- Get wobbly at the **bars and pubs** (p95) around Darlinghurst, Surry Hills and Kings Cross

Map labels: Northern Beaches; Manly Scenic Walkway; Circular Quay; Sydney Opera House; Sydney Tower; Art Gallery of NSW; Chinatown; Darlinghurst; Surry Hills; Kings Cross; Bondi Beach

| ■ TELEPHONE CODE: 02 | ■ POPULATION: 4,444,500 | ■ AREA: 12,407 SQ KM |

# HISTORY

The Sydney region is the ancestral home of the Eora people (the Ku-ring-gai, Birrabirragal and Cadi tribes) who possessed an intimate understanding of environmental sustainability, spoke three distinct languages and maintained sophisticated sacred and artistic cultures. In 1788 Captain Arthur Phillip established Australia's first European settlement at Sydney Cove, today's Circular Quay. In a typically ugly pattern of European colonisation, the Eora were stripped of legal rights to their land and were systematically incarcerated, killed or driven away by force – many more succumbed to introduced European diseases.

Early Sydney bumbled through near starvation and rum-fuelled political turmoil, but things didn't boom until the 1850s gold rush put a rocket under the economy. Sydney's population doubled in a decade.

In the 20th century, post-WWII immigrants from the UK, Ireland and the Mediterranean brought spirit and prosperity to Sydney. American GIs swarmed into Sydney during the Vietnam War, changing the city's face yet again. Hosting the 2000 Olympic Games thrust Sydney into the global limelight, and the city wasn't shy about stepping onto the stage.

Simmering racial tensions exploded into mob violence on Sydney's southern beaches in late 2005 – an ugly development that remains unresolvedly snagged in the city's social conscience.

# ORIENTATION

Central Sydney grips Sydney Harbour (Port Jackson) in a passionate embrace, while Greater Sydney covers more than 1200 sq km from Botany Bay to the south, the Blue Mountains to the west and Pittwater to the north. The harbour runs east–west, dividing the city in two – the Sydney Harbour Bridge and Harbour Tunnel connect the south and north shores. The city centre and most of the action are south of the harbour. Sydney's Kingsford Smith Airport is 10km south of the city centre, jutting into Botany Bay

The Central Business District (CBD) is long and narrow, stretching from The Rocks and Circular Quay in the north to Central Station in the south, bounded by Darling Harbour and Chinatown to the west, and funky inner-city suburbs Darlinghurst, Surry Hills, Kings Cross and Paddington to the east.

Further east are the affluent Eastern Suburbs, reaching from Woollahra to Watsons Bay. To the southeast is Bondi, Sydney's quintessential ocean suburb. The Eastern Beaches track south from here: Tamarama, Bronte, Coogee, Maroubra and Cronulla.

The Inner West includes the rejuvenated once-were-warehouse suburbs Ultimo and Pyrmont, bohemian Glebe, picture-perfect Balmain, Italian-flavoured Leichhardt and grungy Newtown.

The suburbs north of the bridge are known as the North Shore, the jewel of which is affable, beachy Manly. The magnificent Northern Beaches stretch north from here – 30km of sandy suburbs, rocky headlands and iconic surf beaches.

## Maps

Lonely Planet's *Sydney City Map* has detailed coverage of central Sydney and the Blue Mountains. If you're driving around the city, a *Sydney UBD* street directory (around $35) is invaluable.

**Department of Lands** (Map pp78-9; ☎ 9236 7720; www.lands.nsw.gov.au; 1 Prince Albert Rd; ☺ 9am-5pm Mon-Fri) Topographic map heaven.

**Map World** (Map pp78-9; ☎ 9261 3601; www.map world.com.au; 280 Pitt St; ☺ 9am-5.30pm Mon-Fri, 10am-3.45pm Sat) Maps, atlases, GPS and travel guides.

# INFORMATION
## Bookshops

**Ariel** (Map p84; ☎ 9332 4581; www.arielbooks.com.au; 42 Oxford St, Paddington ☺ 9am-midnight) Art, film, fashion, design and travel guides.

**Dymocks** (Map pp78-9; ☎ 9235 0155; www.dymocks .com.au; 424-28 George St; ☺ 9am-6.30pm Mon-Fri, to 6pm Sat, 10am-5pm Sun) Mainstream titles, stationery and a café.

**Gleebooks** (Map p86; ☎ 9660 2333; www.gleebooks .com.au; 49 Glebe Point Rd, Glebe; ☺ 9am-9pm) Sydney's best bookshop – politics, arts and fiction.

**Kinokuniya** (Map pp78-9; ☎ 9262 7996; www.kino kuniya.com; Level 2, The Galeries Victoria, 500 George St; ☺ 10am-7pm Mon-Sat, to 6pm Sun) Over 300,000 titles – Sydney's biggest bookshop.

**Travel Bookshop** (Map pp78-9; ☎ 9261 8200; www .travelbooks.com.au; 175 Liverpool St; ☺ 9am-6pm Mon-Fri, 10am-5pm Sat) Crammed with, you guessed it, travel books.

## Emergency

**Lifeline** ( ☎ 13 11 14; www.lifeline.com.au) Over-the-phone counselling services, including suicide prevention.

**SYDNEY**

**National Roads & Motorists Association** (NRMA; Map pp78-9; ☎ 13 21 32; www.nrma.com.au; 74-6 King St; ☺ 9am-5pm Mon-Fri) Car insurance and roadside service.

**Police** ( ☎ 000) Central Sydney (Map pp78-9; 192 Day St, Sydney); Kings Cross (1-15 Elizabeth Bay Rd, Kings Cross); The Rocks (132 George St, The Rocks)

**Rape Crisis Centre** ( ☎ 9515 6111, 1800 424 017)

## Internet Access

**Global Gossip** Bondi (37 Hall St, Bondi); Central Station (760 George St, Sydney); City Centre (415 Pitt St, Sydney); Kings Cross (Map p82; ☎ 9326 9777; 61 Darlinghurst Rd, Kings Cross; per hr $2; ☺ 9am-midnight) Traveller-friendly chain.

**Internet World** (Map pp78-9; ☎ 9262 9700; 369 Pitt St, Sydney; per hr $2; ☺ 24hr) Fast servers and commercial FM beneath medicinal fluoro light.

## Medical Services

**Kings Cross Travellers Clinic** (Map p82; ☎ 9358 3066; www.travellersclinic.com.au; 13 Springfield Ave, Kings Cross; ☺ 9am-1pm & 2-6pm Mon-Fri, 10am-noon Sat) General medical, dive medicals and morning-after pill scripts; bookings advised.

**St Vincent's Hospital** (Map p82; ☎ 8382 7111; wwwsvh.stvincents.com.au; cnr Victoria & Burton Sts, Darlinghurst; ☺ 24hr emergency)

**Sydney Hospital & Sydney Eye Hospital** (Map pp78-9; ☎ 9382 7111; www.sesahs.nsw.gov.au/syd hosp; 8 Macquarie St, Sydney; ☺ 24hr emergency)

**Travel Doctor** (Map pp78-9; ☎ 9221 7133; www .traveldoctor.com.au; Level 7, 428 George St, Sydney; ☺ 9am-5pm Mon-Wed & Fri, to 8pm Thu, 9am-12.30pm Sat) Travel shots and medical advice.

## Money

There are plenty of ATMs throughout Sydney; both **American Express** (Map pp78-9; ☎ 1300 139 060; 105 Pitt St, Sydney; ☺ 8.30am-5pm Mon-Fri) and **Travelex** (Map pp78-9; ☎ 9231 2523; 175 Pitt St, Sydney; ☺ 9am-5pm Mon-Fri, 10am-2pm Sat) have city branches. Seven-day exchange bureaus include:

**Central Station** (Map pp78-9; Coach Terminal; ☺ 9am-4pm)

**Circular Quay** (Map pp78-9; Wharf 6; ☺ 8am-9.30pm)

**Kings Cross** (Map p82; cnr Springfield Ave & Darlinghurst Rd; ☺ 8am-midnight)

## Post

Stamps are sold at post offices, Australia Post retail outlets in most suburbs and most newsagencies.

**General Post Office** (GPO; Map pp78-9; ☎ 13 13 18; www.auspost.com.au; 1 Martin Place; ☺ 8.15am-5.30pm Mon-Fri, 10am-2pm Sat)

**Poste Restante Service** (Map pp78-9; ☎ 13 13 18; www.auspost.com.au; 310 George St; ☺ 8.15am-5.30pm Mon-Fri, 10am-2pm Sat) Bring identification to collect mail.

## Tourist Information

**City Host Information Kiosks** (Map pp78-9; ☺ 9am-5pm winter, 10am-6pm summer) Circular Quay (cnr Pitt & Alfred Sts); Martin Place (btwn Elizabeth & Castlereagh Sts); Town Hall (cnr Druitt & George Sts)

**Sydney Visitor Centres** The Rocks (Map pp78-9; ☎ 9240 8788; www.sydneyvisitorcentre.com; cnr Argyle & Playfair Sts; ☺ 9.30am-5.30pm); Darling Harbour (Map pp78-9; ☎ 9240 8788; www.sydneyvisitorcentre.com; 33 Wheat Rd; ☺ 9.30am-5.30pm) Super comprehensive; also acts as an accommodation agency.

**Tourism NSW** Sydney ( ☎ 13 20 77; www.visitnsw.com .au; ☺ 9am-5pm Mon-Fri); Airport ( ☎ 9667 6050; International Arrivals, Terminal 1; ☺ 5am-11pm) State-wide accommodation and travel advice.

**Tourist Information Service** ( ☎ 9669 5111; ☺ 7am-10pm) Sydney-centric information and accommodation.

**Travellers' Information Service** (Map pp78-9; ☎ 9281 9366; sydneycoach@optusnet.com.au; Sydney Coach Terminal, Eddy Ave; ☺ 6am-10.30pm) Helpful, busy office handling accommodation bookings, coach tickets, public transport information and maps.

# SIGHTS
## Sydney Harbour

Stretching 20km inland to the mouth of the Parramatta River, Sydney Harbour (aka Port Jackson) is Sydney's shimmering soul, its beaches, coves, bays, islands and waterside parks providing crucial relief from the ordeals of urban life. Crisscrossed by ferries and carpeted by weekend yachts, it's both the city's playground and a major port.

Forming the gateway to the harbour are **North Head** (Map pp76-7) and **South Head** (Map pp76-7). **Watsons Bay** (Map pp76-7) nestles on South Head's harbour side, fostering a salty cottage atmosphere. The **harbour beaches** are generally sheltered, calm coves with little of the frenzied foam of the ocean beaches. On the south shore is **Camp Cove** (Map pp76-7), a photogenic swimming beach where Arthur Phillip first landed, and the shark-netted **Shark Bay** (Map pp76-7). On the North Shore (Map pp76-7) try **Manly Cove**, **Reef Beach**, **Clontarf**, **China-mans Beach** and **Balmoral**.

### SYDNEY HARBOUR NATIONAL PARK

This park protects scattered pockets of harbourside bushland with magical walking tracks (see Manly Scenic Walkway, p66), lookouts, Aboriginal engravings and historic sites. Its southern side incorporates South Head and Nielsen Park; on the North Shore it includes North Head, Dobroyd Head, Middle Head and Ashton Park.

Five harbour islands are also part of the Sydney Harbour National Park: **Clark Island** (Map pp76–7) off Darling Point, **Shark Island** (Map pp76–7) off Rose Bay, **Rodd Island** (Map pp76–7) in Iron Cove, **Goat Island** (Map pp78–9), once a hellish convict gulag, and the small fortified **Fort Denison** (Map pp76–7) off Mrs Macquaries Point. Nicknamed 'Pinchgut' for its meagre rations, Fort Denison once isolated recalcitrant convicts. Paranoid fears of a Russian invasion during the mid-19th-century Crimean War led to its fortification.

Except for Goat Island, which is currently off-limits, the harbour islands are open for marooning. The National Parks and Wildlife Service (NPWS) runs 2½-hour **Fort Denison tours** (adult/concession/family $22/18/72; ⊗ 11.45am Mon-Fri, 11.30am & 2.30pm Sat & Sun) – book at the Sydney Harbour National Park Information Centre at Cadman's Cottage (p54). You'll have to organise your own transport to Rodd and Clark Islands (eg water taxi; p105) which incurs a $5 landing fee, also payable at Cadman's Cottage. **Matilda Rocket Express** (Map pp78-9; ☎ 9264 7377; www.matilda.com.au; adult/concession/family $16/15/53; ⊗ 10.30am, 11.45am, 1.45pm & 3.30pm) rockets you to Shark Island from Circular Quay. The Harbour Trust runs tours to **Cockatoo Island** (Map pp76-7; ☎ 8969 2199; adult/concession/family $25/15/75; ⊗ 10.30am & 1.30pm Sat, 10am & 2pm Sun), the harbour's largest island.

---

**SYDNEY IN...**

**Two Days**
Immerse yourself in history with a ramble through the **Rocks** (p54) to Sydney Cove, continuing past the **Sydney Opera House** (p54) to the chilled-out lawns of the **Royal Botanic Gardens** (p59). Grab a cab to **Bondi Beach** (p61) and hurl yourself into the Pacific, then take in an evening **Opera House show** (p99).

Kick-start your heart on the second day with a **BridgeClimb** (p68) over Sydney Harbour Bridge. Hang with the masters at the **Art Gallery of New South Wales** (p59) or ship yourself out onto the harbour: ride the ferry to **Taronga Zoo** (p62), or to **Manly** (p62) for a surf. Chow down in **Chinatown** (p56) then hit some **Darlinghurst bars** (p95) for a jazzy nightcap.

**Four Days**
Sleep late, then wield your credit card with abandonment at Paddington's **Oxford St boutiques** (p102). Check out the **Sydney Aquarium** (p57) or scale **Sydney Tower** (p58) in the afternoon. Complete the day at a **Darling Harbour eatery** (p92), then cool your boots in the boardwalk bars.

Start day four with a bracing Bondi swim, eat a cruisy, open-air Sydney breakfast then tackle the awesome **Bondi to Coogee Clifftop Trail** (p66). Bus it back into town then head to **Surry Hills** (p92) for dinner and drinks.

**One Week**
Cultivate a taste for old-time Sydney refinement with a visit to **Vaucluse House** (p61) or **Elizabeth Bay House** (p60), then undo your high-brow aspirations with a trashy night-on-the-tiles in **Kings Cross** (p59). The next day, a shimmering harbour ferry ride to **Watsons Bay Hotel** (p97) transports you to beer-garden heaven.

Sydney's **weekend markets** (p103) are varied, entertaining and crowded: load up on recycled fashion, multicultural eats and tacky Australiana for the folks back home.

Rock-out to some nocturnal **live music** or cut the rug at some Sydney **clubs**. If all that clash and throb isn't your scene, a day trip to the **Northern Beaches** (p64) will rejuvenate your spirits.

Dinner with a view is essential on your final night – treat yourself to some top-notch **Mod Oz cuisine** at Circular Quay (p91) with icon-festooned views of the Opera House and Sydney Harbour Bridge.

SYDNEY

## Sydney Opera House

'The sun did not know how beautiful its light was until it was reflected off this building.' So said famous architect Louis Kahn, aghast with admiration for the **Sydney Opera House** (Map pp70-9; ☎ 9250 7111; www.sydneyoperahouse.com; Bennelong Pt, Circular Quay E). Danish architect Jørn Utzon's competition-winning 1956 design is Australia's most recognisable icon and essential sight. It's mused to have drawn inspiration from orange segments, snails, palm fronds and Mayan temples, and poetically likened to a 'nun's scrum' and the sexual congress of turtles. It's architecturally orgasmic from any angle, but the ferry view approaching Circular Quay is hard to beat.

The predicted four-year construction started in 1959, and after a tumultuous tirade of ego clashes, technical difficulties and delays, the Opera House finally opened in 1973. The 67m-high roof features 27,230 tonnes of Swedish tiles (1,056,000 of them). Two thousand four hundred annual events cost over $40 million to run and keep the Concert Hall organ's 10,500 pipes humming.

There are four main auditoriums for dance, concerts, opera and theatre events, plus the left-of-centre Studio for emerging artists. The acoustics are superb, the internal aesthetics like the belly of a whale. Most events sell out quickly, but 'partial view' tickets are often available on short notice. There's also an Exhibition Hall and an artsy-craftsy Sunday Market on the concourse. The bimonthly *Events Diary* details forthcoming performances and is available free inside. The Kids At The House programme features kids' music, dance and drama including the Babies' Proms Orchestra (orchestral nursery rhyme and picture-book accompaniment) and introductory ballet with Australian Ballet dancers.

Get your tickets at the **box office** ( ☎ 9250 7777; ⏰ 9am-8.30pm Mon-Sat, 2hrs pre-show Sun). Kids under five aren't admitted to most performances, so check before you book.

Opera House **tours** ( ☎ 9250 7250; adult/concession $23/16; ⏰ 1hr tours 9am-5pm) take you from 'front of house' to backstage. Due to rehearsals, not every tour can visit every theatre , but you're more likely to see everything if you arrive early. Let them know in advance if you require wheelchair access.

Disabled access to the theatres is pretty good, but some areas require staff assistance; call ☎ 9250 7250 for details. Public transport to Circular Quay is the best way to get here, but if you're driving there's a **car park** ( ☎ 9247 7599; enter via Macquarie St; nightly rate $25; ⏰ 6.30am-1.00am) under the building.

## The Rocks

The site of Sydney's first European settlement, the Rocks, has evolved unrecognisably from its squalid, overcrowded origins. Residents once sloshed through open sewers and alleyways festered with disease, prostitution and drunken lawlessness. Sailors, whalers and rapscallions boozed and brawled shamelessly in countless harbourside pubs.

The Rocks remained a commercial and maritime hub until shipping services left Circular Quay in the late 1800s. A bubonic plague outbreak in 1900 continued the decline. Construction of the Harbour Bridge in the '20s brought further demolition, entire streets disappearing under the bridge's southern approach.

It wasn't until the 1970s that The Rocks' cultural and architectural heritage was recognised. The ensuing redevelopment has saved a lot of old buildings but has turned the area into a sanitised, 'olde worlde' tourist trap. Kitsch cafés and tourist shops hocking stuffed koalas and Opera House key rings now prevail.

**Cadman's Cottage** (Map pp78-9; ☎ 9247 5033; www.nationalparks.nsw.gov.au; 110 George St; ⏰ 9.30am-4.30pm Mon-Fri, 10am-4.30pm Sat & Sun), built on a buried beach, is Sydney's oldest house (1816). Namesake John Cadman was government coxswain. Water police detained criminals here in the 1840s; it was later converted into a home for retired sea captains. Further along George St is the weekend **Rocks Market** (p103).

The excellent new **Rocks Discovery Museum** (Map pp78-9; ☎ 1800 067 676; www.rocksdiscovery museum.com; 2-8 Kendall La; admission free; ⏰ 10am-5pm) digs deep into artefact-soaked Rocks history and provides a sensitive insight into the lives of the Cadigal people, The Rocks' original inhabitants.

Beyond the **Argyle Cut** (Map pp78-9), an impressive tunnel excavated by convicts, is Millers Point, a relaxed district of early colonial homes. **Argyle Place** (Map pp78-9) is an English-style village green on which any Australian has the legal right to graze livestock. Overlooking it is **Garrison Church** (Map pp78-9), Australia's oldest church

(1848). Nearby the Lord Nelson Brewery Hotel and the **Hero of Waterloo Hotel** (Map pp78–9) jostle for supreme respect as Australia's oldest pub.

The 1850s, copper-domed, Italianate **Sydney Observatory** (Map pp78-9; ☎ 9217 0485; www.sydney observatory.com.au; Watson Rd; admission free; ☻ 10am–5pm) sits atop Observatory Park. Inside there's a **3-D Space Theatre** (adult/child/family $6/4/16; ☻ 2.30pm & 3.30pm Mon-Fri, 11am, noon, 2.30pm & 3.30pm Sat & Sun) and an interactive Australian astronomy exhibition. Squint at galaxies far, far away during Night Viewings (tickets for adult/child/family cost $15/12/40); bookings are required. In the old military hospital building nearby, the **SH Ervin Gallery** (Map pp78-9; ☎ 9258 0173; www.nsw.nationaltrust.org.au/ervin.html; Watson Rd; adult/child $6/4 ☻ 11am-5pm Tue-Sun) exhibits Australian art, including the annual *Salon des Refusés* collection of alternative Archibald Prize entries.

The wharves around Dawes Point are rapidly emerging from prolonged decay. Walsh Bay's Pier 4 houses the renowned Sydney Theatre Company (p101), Bangarra Dance Company, **Australian Theatre for Young People** (ATYP; Map pp78-9) and Sydney Dance Company. The impressive Sydney Theatre (p101) is across the road.

## Sydney Harbour Bridge

Whether they're driving over it, climbing up it, rollerblading across it or sailing under it, Sydneysiders adore their bridge. Dubbed the 'old coat hanger', it's a spookily big object – moving around Sydney you'll catch sight of it in the corner of your eye and get a fright! The bridge links the CBD with the North Sydney business district, spanning the harbour at one of its narrowest points. Completed in 1932 at a cost of $20 million, the city took 60 years to pay it off.

The best way to experience the bridge is on foot – don't expect much of a view crossing by car or train. Staircases climb up to the bridge from both shores leading to a footpath running the length of the eastern side. A cycle way wheels along the western side. You can climb the southeastern pylon to the **Pylon Lookout** (Map pp78-9; ☎ 9240 1100; www.pylonlookout.com.au; adult/concession $8/3; ☻ 10am-5pm), or ascend the great arc on a BridgeClimb (p68).

## Circular Quay

Circular Quay, built around Sydney Cove, is Sydney's public transport hub, with ferry quays, bus stops, a train station and the **Overseas Passenger Terminal**. (Map pp78–9). European settlement grew around the Tank Stream, which now trickles underground into the harbour near Wharf 6. For many years Circular Quay was also Sydney's port, but these days it's more of a recreational space, with harbour walkways, grassy verges, outstanding restaurants, fisherfolk and buskers of unpredictable merit.

Emerging phoenix-like from extensive renovations, the cavernous 1885 **Customs House** (Map pp78-9; ☎ 9242 8555; www.cityofsydney.nsw.gov /library; 31 Alfred St; admission free; ☻ 8am-midnight Mon-Fri, 10am-midnight Sat, noon-5pm Sun; library 10am-7pm Mon-Fri, 11am-4pm Sat & Sun) houses the Customs House Library. Under the glass floor of the foyer is a geeky (but undeniably impressive) 1:500 model of Sydney. If you feel like a stylish lunch with a view, take the elevator up to Café Sydney on the top floor ( ☎ 9251 8683).

### MUSEUM OF CONTEMPORARY ART

Always challenging, the **MCA** (Map pp78-9; ☎ 9245 2400; www.mca.com.au; 140 George St; admission free; ☻ 10am-5pm) fronts Circular Quay West in a stately Art Deco building and has been raising even the most open-minded Sydney eyebrows since 1991. Its constantly changing, controversial exhibitions from Australia and overseas range from incredibly hip to in-your-face, sexually explicit and profoundly disturbing.

## Macquarie Place Area

Narrow lanes lead south from Circular Quay towards the city centre. At the corner of Loftus and Bridge Sts is **Macquarie Place,** (Map pp78–9) a leafy public square proudly displaying a cannon and anchor from the First Fleet flagship, HMS *Sirius*, and an 1818 obelisk etched with road distances to various points in the nascent colony.

Inside the old Water Police Station (1858) nearby, the **Justice & Police Museum** (Map pp78-9; ☎ 9252 1144; www.hht.net.au; cnr Albert & Phillip Sts; adult/child/family $8/4/17 ☻ 10am-5pm Sat & Sun, daily in Jan) zooms in on disreputable activities, with exhibits of confiscated weapons, butt-ugly mugshots and forensic evidence from Sydney's most heinous crimes.

### MUSEUM OF SYDNEY

This thoroughly engaging **museum** (Map pp78-9; ☎ 9251 5988; www.hht.net.au; cnr Bridge & Phillip Sts;

**DISCOUNT SYDNEY SIGHTSEEING**

The Historic Houses Trust's **Ticket Through Time** ( ☎ 8239 2288; www.hht.net.au/visit/admission_prices; adult/child/family $30/15/60) gets you into all 11 of the HHT's houses and museums in the Sydney area, including Vaucluse House (p61), Government House (p59), Elizabeth Bay House (p60), Justice & Police Museum (p55), Museum of Sydney (p55) and Hyde Park Barracks Museum (p58). Visit four or more of these and you'll save yourself some hard-earned cash.

Alternatively, the **See Sydney & Beyond Card** ( ☎ 1300 661 711; www.seesydneycard.com) offers admission to a wide range of Sydney's attractions including sightseeing tours, harbour cruises, museums, historic buildings and wildlife parks. Prices for one/two/three/seven-day cards are adult $65/119/149/209, child $45/65/79/139. The two/three/seven-day cards are also available with public transport included for adult $159/205/275, child $85/109/175. Cards are available online or at the Sydney Visitor Centres (p52).

adult/child/family $10/5/20 ( ⌚ 9.30am-5pm) is east of Macquarie Place, on the site of Sydney's first (and infamously pungent) Government House (1788). The city's early history (including pre-1788) comes to life here through whispers, arguments, gossip, artefacts and state-of-the-art installations. There's also a damn fine café on-site.

## City Centre

Central Sydney stretches from Circular Quay in the north to Central Station in the south. The business hub is towards the northern end, but the southern end is being redeveloped, gradually shifting the city's focus. For a lofty city view, take a trip up Sydney Tower (p58).

Sydney lacks a true civic centre, but **Martin Place** (Map pp78–9) comes close. This grand pedestrian mall extends from Macquarie St to George St, lined by monumental financial buildings and the Victorian colonnaded General Post Office. There's a cenotaph commemorating Australia's war dead, an amphitheatre for lunchtime entertainment and plenty of places to sit and watch the crowds. Security guards fight a losing battle against the skateboarders on weekends.

Sydney's 1874 **Town Hall** (Map pp78–9) is a few blocks south of here on the corner of George and Druitt Sts. The elaborate chamber room and concert hall inside match the fabulously ornate exterior. Next door, the Anglican **St Andrew's Cathedral** (Map pp78–9), built around the same time, is Australia's oldest cathedral. Next to St Andrew's, taking up an entire city block, the high-Victorian Queen Victoria Building (p103) is Sydney's most sumptuous shopping complex. Running a close second is the entirely over-the-top

Strand Arcade (p103) between Pitt St Mall and George St.

There are 45-minute group and self-guided tours of the lavish **State Theatre** (Map pp78-9; ☎ 9373 6862; www.statetheatre.com.au; 49 Market St; adult/child $12/8; ⌚ 11.30am-3pm Mon-Fri), built in 1929. Even a quick peek at the glittering foyer is worthwhile.

Breathing life into the city's lacklustre southwestern zone are Sydney's teensy Spanish Quarter (Map pp78–9) and thriving **Chinatown** (Map pp78–9), a tight nest of restaurants, shops and aroma-filled alleyways around Dixon St. Chinatown goes berserk during Chinese New Year in late January/early February – streets throng with sideshows, digitally accompanied musicians and stalls selling everything from good-luck tokens to black-sesame ice-cream burgers (seeing jaunty, fire-breathing paper dragons after eating these is not a hallucinogenic effect).

## Darling Harbour

This rambling, purpose-built, waterfront tourist park lining Cockle Bay on the city's western edge was once industrial docklands with factories, warehouses and shipyards. These days, the official spiel promotes more leisurely industry: 'Darling Harbour – Play It Your Way!'

Dotted between an architectural spoil of flyovers, fountains, sculptures and sailcloth are some great museums and sights, a plethora of harbour cruise outlets and the overrated Harbourside Shopping Centre. The snazzy **Cockle Bay Wharf** (Map pp78–9) and **King Street Wharf** (Map pp78–9) precincts contain a dangerous array of cafés, bars and restaurants for when you're all museumed-out. Don't forget the harbour itself – below the flocks of tourists and belligerent ibises, it remains unflappably calm.

A stroll across **Pyrmont Bridge** (Map pp78–9), the world's first electric swing bridge, leads you into Pyrmont, home of the Sydney Fish Market (right) and the playground of bigger fish, **Star City Casino** (Map pp78–9; ☎ 9657 8694; www.starcity.com.au; 80 Pyrmont St, Pyrmont; 24hr).

Darling Harbour and Pyrmont are serviced by ferry, Monorail, Metro Light Rail (MLR) and the Sydney Explorer bus. A dinky **people-mover train** (adult/child $3.50/2.50; 10am-6pm) connects the sights; the visitors centre (p52) is underneath the highway, next to the Imax cinema. The free Darling Harbour Jazz Festival happens in June.

### SYDNEY AQUARIUM

Visitors wander goggle-eyed through underwater glass tubes at this ever-popular **aquarium** (Map pp78-9; ☎ 8251 7800; www.sydneyaquarium.com.au; Aquarium Pier; adult/child/family $27/14/65; 9am-10pm; last admission 9pm), celebrating the richness of Australian marine life. Three 'oceanariums' are moored in the harbour: sharks, rays and humungous fish in one; Sydney Harbour marine life and seals in the other two. Don't miss the Van Gogh colours of the Great Barrier Reef exhibit, platypuses and crocodiles at the Southern and Northern Rivers exhibits, and the fairy penguins in the Southern Oceans section. Arrive early to beat the crowds and fully appreciate the piped indigestive whale music.

### AUSTRALIAN NATIONAL MARITIME MUSEUM

Beneath an Utzon-like roof, this thematic **museum** (Map pp78-9; ☎ 9298 3777; www.anmm.gov.au; 2 Murray St; admission free, special exhibits adult/child/family from $10/6/20; 9.30am-5pm) examines Australia's inextricable relationship with the sea. Exhibitions range from Aboriginal canoes to surf culture and the Navy. You can almost taste the salt… There's good disabled access to the museum, but not to the boats moored out the front. Regular guided tours are available.

### POWERHOUSE MUSEUM

This hip and progressive **museum** (Map pp78-9; ☎ 9217 0100; www.powerhousemuseum.com; 500 Harris St, Ultimo; standard exhibits adult/child/family $10/5/25, additional costs for special exhibits; 10am-5pm) whirrs away inside the former power station for Sydney's defunct tram network. High-voltage interactive demonstrations wow school groups with the lowdown on how lightning strikes, magnets grab and engines growl. Decorative arts, social history and eclectic exhibitions also get the hands on treatment.

### CHINESE GARDEN OF FRIENDSHIP

Built according to the balanced principles of Yin and Yang, these **gardens** (Map pp78-9; ☎ 9281 6863; www.chinesegarden.com.au; adult/child/family $6/3/15; 9.30am-5pm) are an oasis of tranquillity in the otherwise hectic Darling Harbour. Designed by architects from Guangzhou (Sydney's sister city) for Australia's 1988 bicentenary, the garden interweaves pavilions, waterfalls, lakes and paths. Savour some tea and cake at the Chinese Teahouse by the lotus pond.

### SYDNEY FISH MARKET

With over 15 million kilograms of seafood shipped through here annually, this cavernous, multicultural **fish market** (Map p86; ☎ 9004 1122; www.sydneyfishmarket.com.au; cnr Pyrmont Bridge Rd & Bank St, Pyrmont; 7am-4pm) is the place to introduce yourself to a bewildering array of still-thrashing sub-sea Sydneysiders. Chefs, locals and overfed seagulls haggle over mud crabs, Balmain bugs, lobsters, oysters, mullet, rainbow trout and fat slabs of salmon. There are plenty of fishy restaurants, a deli, wine centre, sushi bar, oyster bar, even a florist. Arrive early to check out the early morning auctions or take a behind the scenes **Auction Tour** ($20; 7-8.30am Thu) – reservations aren't required, but wear closed-toe shoes. You can also book yourself in for regular seafood cooking classes at the **Sydney Seafood School** ( ☎ 9004 1111; classes from $75), or just wander around and enjoy the stinky piscatorial action. The Fish Market is west of Darling Harbour on Blackwattle Bay; the MLR stops outside.

## Macquarie Street Area

A crop of early public buildings graces Macquarie St, defining the city's edge from Hyde Park to the Opera House. Many of these buildings were commissioned by Lachlan Macquarie, the first NSW governor to have a vision of Sydney beyond its convict origins. He enlisted convict architect Francis Greenway to help realise his plans.

Two Greenway gems front onto Queens Square at Hyde Park's northern end: **St James Church** (Map pp78-9), Sydney's oldest church, built in 1819, and the **Hyde Park Barracks**

**Museum** (Map pp78-9; ☎ 8239 2311; www.hht.net.au; adult/child/family $10/5/20; ☺ 9.30am-5pm), also built in 1819. The barracks functioned as convict quarters for Anglo-Irish sinners (1819–48), an immigrant depot (1848–86) and government courts (1887–1979) before its current incarnation – a window into everyday convict life.

Further down Macquarie St are the deep verandas, formal colonnades and ochre tones of the twin 1816 **Mint** (Map pp78-9; ☎ 8239 2288; www.hht.net.au; admission free; ☺ 9am-5pm Mon-Fri) and **Parliament House** (Map pp78-9; ☎ 9230 2111; www .parliament.nsw.gov.au; admission free; ☺ 9am-5pm Mon-Fri) buildings, originally wings of the infamous Rum Hospital, which was built by two Sydney merchants in 1816 in return for a monopoly on the rum trade. You can watch the elected representatives outdo each other when parliament sits, or take a guided tour (call for bookings and times). Wheelchair access is available by prior arrangement.

Next to Parliament House, the **State Library of NSW** (Map pp78-9; ☎ 9273 1414; www.sl.nsw.gov.au; ☺ 9am-6pm Mon-Fri, 11am-5pm Sat & Sun) holds over five million tomes, the smallest being a tablet-sized *Lord's Prayer*, and hosts innovative exhibitions in its **galleries** ( ☺ 9am-5pm Mon-Fri, 11am-5pm Sat & Sun). Disabled access is excellent.

At the top of Bridge St, the Sydney Conservatorium of Music (see p99 for musical recital details) was the Greenway-designed stables and servants' quarters for Macquarie's planned Government House. Macquarie was usurped as governor before the house was finished, partly because of the project's extravagance.

Built between 1837 and 1845, the Gothic Revival **Government House** (Map pp78-9; ☎ 9931 5222; www.hht.net.au; admission free; ☺ 10am-3pm Fri-Sun, grounds to 4pm daily, 45min tours from 10.30am) is just off Macquarie St in the Royal Botanic Gardens. Unless there's an official event happening, you can tour through the fussy furnishings.

### AUSTRALIAN MUSEUM

Not far from Macquarie St, this **natural history museum** (Map pp78-9; ☎ 9320 6000; www.amonline .net.au; 6-8 College St; standard exhibits adult/child/family $10/5/20, additional costs for special exhibits; ☺ 9.30am-5pm) was established just 40 years after the First Fleet dropped anchor. There are excellent

---

### THE BEST VIEWS IN TOWN

Sydney is geographically befuddling – a birds-eye view is the best way to understand the land. The **Harbour Bridge** is the obvious vantage point: climb up to the **Pylon Lookout** (p55) or take the **BridgeClimb** (p68).

The **Sydney Tower** (Map pp78-9; ☎ 9333 9222; www.sydneytoweroztrek.com.au; 100 Market St; adult/child $23.50/14; ☺ 9am-10.30pm) is about as high as Sydneysiders get without wings or drugs – the 360-degree 250m-high views to the Blue Mountains, Botany Bay, the harbour and the Pacific are unbeatable. Feeling brave? Fulfil your Luke Skywalker fantasies on a **Skywalk** ( ☎ 9333 9200; www .skywalk.com.au; adult/child $129/95; ☺ 9am-10pm) – don a spiffy 'skysuit', shackle yourself to the safety rail and step onto two glass-floored outdoor platforms, 260m above the street. There are two excellent **revolving restaurants** here, after your walk sit and spin above the twinkling harbour city.

On a more terrestrial level, pack a picnic and check out the panoramas from **Mrs Macquaries Point** at the end of the Royal Botanic Gardens, or from **Observatory Hill** in Millers Point. On the North Shore, **Blues Point Reserve** and **Bradleys Head** are a couple of tasty vantage points. Near Kings Cross, the northern end of Victoria St in **Potts Point** opens out to the cityscape and its classic icons; it's a pretty spot, especially at night.

Sydney's stupendous setting also offers some kickin' combinations of vistas and victuals. If you're looking to impress someone, try these classy restaurants with sassy views:

- **Bondi Social** (Map p87; ☎ 9365 1788; 1st fl, 38 Campbell Pde, Bondi; mains $10-26; ☺ lunch Fri-Sun, dinner daily) Mod Oz, cocktails and famous beach views.
- **Forty One** (Map pp78-9; ☎ 9221 2500; 42nd fl, Chifley Tower, 2 Chifley Sq; mains from $39; ☺ lunch Tue-Fri, dinner Mon-Sat) Luxury dining; harbour sights and lights.
- **Summit** (Map pp78-9; ☎ 9247 9777; 47th fl, Australia Sq, 264 George St; mains $32-39; ☺ lunch Sun-Fri, dinner daily) Revolving vistas, great food and retro-cool interiors.
- **Wharf** (Map pp78-9; ☎ 9250 1761; Pier 4, Hickson Rd, Walsh Bay; mains $27-35; ☺ lunch & dinner Mon-Sat) Picture-postcard views, sexy staff and magical Mod Oz.

Aboriginal and native wildlife exhibitions, self-guided tours and indigenous performances on Sundays (call for times). Kids get busy in the Skeleton and Search & Discover Galleries. There's excellent wheelchair access.

## Art Gallery of New South Wales

The **gallery** (Map pp78-9; ☎ 9225 1744; www.artgallery .nsw.gov.au; Art Gallery Rd, The Domain; admission free, varied costs for touring exhibitions; ⏲ 10am-5pm Thu-Tue, to 9pm Wed, free guided tours 1pm) plays a prominent and gregarious role in Sydney society. Highlights include outstanding permanent displays of 19th- and 20th-century Australian art, Aboriginal art, 15th- to 19th-century European and Asian art, and blockbuster international exhibitions. The controversial, much-discussed Archibald Prize exhibits here annually – portraits of the famous and not-so-famous bringing out the art critic in everyone.

Kids swarm to GalleryKids Sunday programme (workshops, performances and guided tours with costumed actors). There are also concerts, screenings, courses, celebrity talks and programmes for the deaf and visually impaired. Wheelchair access is good.

## Royal Botanic Gardens

The **Royal Botanic Gardens** (RBG; Map pp78-9; ☎ 9231 8111; www.rbgsyd.nsw.gov.au; Mrs Macquaries Rd; admission free; ⏲ 7am-sunset) were established in 1816 as the colony's vegetable patch. The attitude here is relaxed – signs say, 'Please walk on the grass. We also invite you to smell the roses, hug the trees, talk to the birds and picnic on the lawns'. Take a **free guided walk** ( ⏲ 10.30am daily & 1pm Mon-Fri), or **Aboriginal Heritage Tour** ( ☎ 9231 8134; $20 per person; ⏲ 2pm Fri), both departing the Gardens Shop. A trackless train does a circuit if you've outdone yourself.

Highlights include the rose garden, the South Pacific plant collection, the prickly arid garden, the glass pyramid at the **Tropical Centre** (adult/child $4.20/2.20; ⏲ 10am-4pm) and a sinister, swooping bat colony (a murder of bats?). Management periodically tries to oust the bats (they destroy the vegetation), but they just keep hanging around. Actually, calling them bats is a misnomer – they're grey-headed flying foxes (*Pteropus policephalus*).

Most RBG paths are wheelchair accessible.

## Other Parks & Gardens

The **Domain** (Map pp78-9) is the large grassy area linking the RBG and Hyde Park, pre-

served by Governor Phillip in 1788 for public recreation. The Art Gallery of New South Wales (left) is here, and the lawns host free summer concerts and Carols by Candlelight every Christmas. The unfailingly eccentric **Speakers' Corner** ( ⏲ noon-4pm Sun) transpires in front of the art gallery – religious zealots, nutters, political extremists, homophobes, hippies and academics express their earnest opinions.

On the eastern edge of the city centre is the formal **Hyde Park** (Map pp78-9), originally the colony's racetrack and cricket pitch. Swan around the grand avenue of trees, fountains and giant chessboard or check out the **Anzac Memorial** (Map pp78-9; ☎ 9267 7668; www.rslnsw .com.au; admission free; ⏲ 9am-5pm). The interior dome is studded with one star for each of the 120,000 NSW citizens who served in WWI. The pines near the entrance grew from seeds gathered at Gallipoli.

A Gothic megalith, **St Mary's Cathedral** (Map pp78-9; ☎ 9220 0400; www.sydney.catholic.org.au; cnr College St & St Marys Rd; admission free; ⏲ 6.45am-6.30pm Sun-Fri, from 9am Sat) overlooks Hyde Park from the east. The first service was held here in 1833, but the massive spires weren't finished until 2000.

On the other side of Hyde Park, the **Great Synagogue** (Map pp78-9; ☎ 9267 2477; www.great synagogue.org.au; 187a Elizabeth St; adult/child $5/3; ⏲ tours noon Tue & Thu) dates from 1878. Tours include the AM Rosenblum Museum's artefacts and a video presentation on Jewish beliefs, traditions and history in Australia. Notice is required for wheelchair access.

Sydney's biggest park is **Centennial Park** (Map p84), a grassy 220-hectare expanse filled with folks walking, kicking balls around, cycling, rollerblading, horseriding (p65) and relaxing under trees with their noses buried in books.

**Moore Park** (Map p84) abuts Centennial Park and contains sports pitches, a public golf course, Fox Film Studios, the Entertainment Quarter, Aussie Stadium and the Sydney Cricket Ground (SCG). **Sportspace Tours** ( ☎ 1300 724 737; www.sydneycricketground.com.au; adult/ child/family $25/15/60; ⏲ 10am & 1pm Mon-Fri, 10am Sat) runs 1½-hour behind-the-scenes SCG and Aussie Stadium tours.

## Kings Cross

Riding high above the CBD under the big Coca-Cola sign (as much a Sydney icon as

LA's Hollywood sign), 'The Cross' is a bizarre, densely populated dichotomy of good and evil. Strip joints, tacky tourist shops and backpacker hostels bang heads with classy restaurants, funky bars and gorgeous guesthouses. The Cross retains a sleazy, cannibalistic aura, but the vague sense of menace is more imaginary than real. Sometimes the razzle-dazzle has a sideshow appeal; sometimes walking up Darlinghurst Rd promotes pity. Either way, it's never boring.

In the early 19th century, Kings Cross was mostly grand estates. Terrace houses sprung up in the 1840s; a wine-stained bohemian element moved in during the 1930s. The suburb's reputation for vice congealed during the Vietnam War, when American sailors flooded The Cross with a tide of bawdy debauchery.

The gracious tree-lined streets of neighbouring **Potts Point** (Map p82) and **Elizabeth Bay** (Map p82) feature well-preserved Victorian, Edwardian and Art Deco houses and flats. Built between 1835 and 1839, the neoclassical **Elizabeth Bay House** (Map p82; ☎ 9356 3022; www.hht .net.au; 7 Onslow Ave, Elizabeth Bay; adult/chid/family $8/4/17; ⓨ 10am-4.30pm Tue-Sun) was the finest house in the colony. Horrendous 20th-century apartments encircle it, but the exquisite oval salon and stairwell are timeless architectural delights.

Probably the only word in the world with eight 'o's, **Woolloomooloo** (Map p82), down McElhone Stairs (Map p82) from The Cross, was once a slum full of drunks, sailors, and drunk sailors. Things are begrudgingly less pugilistic these days – the pubs are relaxed and the wharf (Map p82) contains some brilliant restaurants. The infamously lowbrow Harry's Café de Wheels (p93) remains. Gulp down a late-night pie and mash.

It's a 15-minute walk to The Cross from the city, or jump on a train. The buses 323-7, 324-5 and 333 from the city also pass through here.

## Inner East

The spirited backbone of the Inner East is **Oxford Street** (Map p84), a long string of shops, cafés, bars and clubs that exudes a flamboyance largely attributable to Sydney's gay community. The Sydney Gay & Lesbian Mardi Gras (p69) gyrates through here every February. **Taylor Square** (Map p84) is gay Sydney's decadent nucleus.

Oxford St runs all the way from Hyde Park to Centennial Park, continuing to Bondi Junction.

Confusingly, street numbers recommence east of South Dowling St, the Darlinghurst–Paddington border. Bus 378 from Railway Square and buses 380, 389 and L82 from Circular Quay run the length of Oxford St.

Wedged between Oxford and William Sts, **Darlinghurst** (see the Darlin' It Hurts boxed text, opposite) is home to the **Sydney Jewish Museum** (Map p82; ☎ 9360 7999; www.sydneyjewishmuseum .com.au; 148 Darlinghurst Rd; adult/child/family $10/7/22; ⓨ 10am-4pm Sun-Thu, to 2pm Fri, closed Jewish holidays), with evocative, powerful exhibits on Australian Jewish history and the Holocaust.

South of Darlinghurst is **Surry Hills** (Map p84), home to a raffish mishmash of inner-city groovers and a swag of good pubs. Once the undisputed centre of Sydney's rag trade and print media, many of its warehouses have been converted to slick apartments. Preserved as a temple to rock 'n' roll artistry, the **Brett Whiteley Studio** (Map p84; ☎ 9225 1881; www.brettwhiteley.org; 2 Raper St; adult/concession $7/5; ⓨ 10am-4pm Sat & Sun) exhibits some of Whiteley's most raucous paintings. Get in early for weekend discussions, performances, readings and workshops. Surry Hills is a short walk east of Central Station or south from Oxford St. Catch buses 301, 302 or 303 from Circular Quay.

Next door to Surry Hills, **Paddington** (Map p84), aka 'Paddo', is an elegant suburb of restored terrace houses on steep leafy streets. Paddington was built for aspiring Victorian artisans, but the lemminglike rush to the outer suburbs after WWII turned it into Australia's worst slum. Renewed passion for Victorian architecture (and the realisation that the outer suburbs were unspeakably boring) fuelled Paddington's 1960s resurgence. By the '90s, real estate was out of reach for all but the lucky and the loaded.

The **Victoria Barracks** (Map p84; ☎ 9339 3170; cnr Oxford St & Greens Rd; tour free, museum adult/child $2/1; ⓨ tour 10am Thu, museum 10am-4pm Thu & Sun, closed Dec-Feb) are a tightly-managed malarial vision from the peak of the British Empire. Thursday's tours of the Georgian buildings take in a flag-raising ceremony, marching band (subject to availability) and the paraphernalia-packed war museum.

The best time to explore Paddington's streets and hibiscus-lined laneways is on Saturdays when the Paddington Market (p103) is pumping. Join the meandering throngs for a foot massage, tarot reading or funky shirt to wear clubbing that night.

Near Moore Park, much of the former Sydney Showgrounds has been converted into the private Fox Studios and the **Entertainment Quarter** (Map p84; ☎ 9383 4333; www.entertainmentquarter.com.au; ☻ 10am-late), which some claim is only a 'quarter entertaining'. Jokes aside, the cinemas, bowling alley, shops, bars and restaurants aren't a bad way to spend an afternoon.

### Eastern Suburbs

Handsome **Rushcutters Bay** (Map p82) is a five-minute walk east of Kings Cross; its harbourside park is a great spot for cooped-up travellers to stretch their legs. The Eastern Suburbs extend east from here – a shimmering, conservative conglomeration of Range Rovers, skinny models and mortgage madness. The harbour-hugging New South Head Rd passes through **Double Bay** (Map p84) and **Rose Bay** (Map pp76–7) then climbs east into **Vaucluse** (Map pp76–7) .

An imposing, turreted specimen of Gothic Australiana, **Vaucluse House** (Map pp76-7; ☎ 9388 7922; www.hht.net.au; Wentworth Rd, Vaucluse; adult/child/family $8/4/17; ☻ 10am-4.30pm Tue-Sun) is Sydney's last remaining 19th-century harbourside estate. Explorer and political sabre-rattler William Charles Wentworth lived here from 1828 to 1862. The Bondi Explorer bus (p68) stops outside.

At the entrance to Sydney Harbour is **Watsons Bay** (Map pp76–7), a snug community with restored fisherman's cottages, a palm-lined park and a couple of nautical churches. From here, follow the harbour around curio-infested South Head, which has awesome views across the harbour entrance to North and Middle Head. On Watson Bay's ocean-side is the **Gap** (Map pp76–7) – an epic cliff top lookout where sunrises, sunsets, canoo-

dling and suicide leaps transpire with similar frequency.

Buses 324 and 325 from Circular Quay service the Eastern Suburbs via Kings Cross. Grab a seat on the left heading east to snare the best views.

### Eastern Beaches

Definitively Sydney, **Bondi** (Map p87) is one of the world's great beaches – ocean and land collide, the Pacific arrives in great foaming swells, and all people are equal, as democratic as sand. It's the closest ocean beach to the city centre, has consistently good (though crowded) waves and is great for a rough 'n' tumble swim. The suburb itself has a unique atmosphere due to its mix of old Jewish and other European communities, dyed-in-the-wool Aussies, New Zealanders who never went home, working travellers and the *seriously* good-looking.

Most of the pubs, bars and restaurants are set back from the beach along Campbell Pde (Map p87) and Hall St (Map p87). Nearby is Sunday's Bondi Markets (p103), and there are some Eora **Aboriginal rock engravings** (Map p87) north of the beach near the cliffs at the Bondi Golf Club – the name 'Bondi' derives from an Aboriginal word for the sound of the surf.

Catch bus 380, 389, L82 from the city or 381 from Bondi Junction to get to the Bondi. Tracking south from here along the majestic **Bondi to Coogee Clifftop Trail** (p66) are **Tamarama**, **Bronte**, **Clovelly** and **Coogee** beaches. **Maroubra** and **Cronulla** are further south again. For details see the Sydney's Best Beaches boxed text (p63).

### Inner West

West of the centre is the higgledy-piggledy peninsula suburb **Balmain** (Map pp76–7). Once a notoriously rough dockyard neighbourhood, it has been turned into an arty, upper-crust area of restored Victoriana flush with pubs and cafés. Don't miss the Saturday **market** (p103). Catch a ferry from Circular Quay, buses 432–4 from Railway Sq or 441–2 from the Queen Victoria Building (QVB).

Southwest of the city, bohemian **Glebe** (Map p86) nudges up to the University of Sydney. Here you'll find a backstreet Buddhist temple, decent accommodation and countless students cruising café-lined Glebe Point Rd (aromatherapy and crystals galore). Saturday's **market** (p103) overruns Glebe Public School. Glebe is a smoggy 10-minute walk from Central Station along Broadway, or cross Darling Harbour's Pyrmont Bridge then follow Pyrmont Bridge Rd (20 minutes). Buses 431–4 from Millers Point run via George St along Glebe Point Rd. The MLR also services Glebe.

South of Sydney Uni is **Newtown** (Map p86), a melting-pot of social and sexual subcultures, students and home renovators. King St, its relentlessly urban main drag, is full of funky clothes stores, bookshops and cafés. Slowly moving upmarket, Newtown retains an irrepressible dose of grunge and a rockin' live-music scene. Take the train, or buses 422–3, 426 or 428 from Circular Quay to King St.

Southwest of Glebe is predominantly Italian **Leichhardt** (Map pp76–7), increasingly popular with students and yuppies. Norton St is the place for pizza, pasta and slick Mediterranean style. Bus 413 from Wynyard, or 435–8 or 440 from Circular Quay service Leichhardt.

## North Shore

On the northern side of the Harbour Bridge is **North Sydney** (Map pp76–7), a high-rise office centre with little to tempt the traveller. **McMahons Point** (Map pp76–7) is a low-key, forgotten suburb below the western side of the bridge. There's a row of cheery alfresco cafés on Blues Point Rd, running down to Blues Point Reserve on Lavender Bay. At the end of Kirribilli Point, just east of the bridge, are **Admiralty House** (Map pp76–7) and **Kirribilli House** (Map pp76–7), the Sydney residences of the Governor General and Prime Minister respectively.

On the eastern shore of Lavender Bay is **Luna Park** (Map pp76–7; ☎ 9922 6644; www.luna parksydney.com; 1 Olympic Pl, Milsons Point; admission free, multi-ride passes from $18; ⏰ 10am-10pm Sun-Thu, 10am-

midnight Fri & Sat), with its sinister chip-toothed clown entry. It has been periodically closed by noise police in recent decades, but for the moment the Ferris Wheel, Rotor, Flying Saucer and Tumble Bug still offer varying degrees of nerve-wracking and nausea.

East of here are the upmarket suburbs **Neutral Bay** (Map pp76–7), **Cremorne** (Map pp76–7) and **Mosman** (Map pp76–7), all with coves and harbourside parks perfect for picnics. Ferries from Circular Quay service these suburbs. On the northern side of Mosman is improbably pretty **Balmoral** (Map pp76–7), facing Manly across Middle Harbour. See the Sydney's Best Beaches boxed text for details (opposite).

## Taronga Zoo

Haven't spotted any kangaroos bouncing down George St yet? **Taronga Zoo** (Map pp76-7; ☎ 9969 2777; www.zoo.nsw.gov.au; Bradleys Head Rd, Mosman; adult/child/family $30/16.50/79; ⏰ 9am-5pm) houses 4000 kangaroos, koalas, platypuses and similarly hirsute Australians. Feeding sessions and keeper talks happen throughout the day, and **twilight concerts** take place in February and March. Zoo ferries depart Circular Quay's Wharf 2, half-hourly from 7.15am on weekdays, 8.45am Saturday and Sunday. The zoo is really steep, so if you arrive by ferry, take the **Sky Safari** cable car (included in admission) or bus 238 to the top entrance and work your way downhill. The **ZooPass** (p106) includes return ferry rides, Sky Safari and admission. The nightly **Roar & Snore** ( ☎ 9978 4791; adult/child $156/105) is an overnight family experience with a night-time safari, barbecue dinner and tents under the stars. Breakfast and behind-the-scenes tours arrive with the dawn.

## Manly

Laid-back Manly clings to a narrow isthmus between ocean and harbour beaches near North Head. Surrounded by stuffy harbour enclaves, Manly's shaggy surfers, dusty labourers and relaxed locals are refreshing company. The **Manly Visitors Information Centre** (Map p88; ☎ 9976 1430; www.manlytourism.com; Manly Wharf forecourt; ⏰ 9am-5pm Mon-Fri, 10am-5pm Sat & Sun) has lots of local info and free pamphlets on the 10km **Manly Scenic Walkway** (p66).

The **Corso** (Map p88) connects Manly's ocean and harbour beaches – surf shops, burger joints, juice bars and lousy cappuccino cafés proliferate. A footpath follows the ocean

## SYDNEY'S BEST BEACHES

Sydney's sensational beaches teem with weekend life, but Sydneysiders also swim before, after or instead of going to work. Most beaches are clean, easily accessible and are patrolled by surf lifesavers. Shark patrols operate during summer. Many beaches are topless; a couple are nude – feel free to do as locals do! See below, and also **Bondi** (p61), **Manly** (opposite) and **Northern Beaches** (p64):

**Avalon** (Map p108) Caught in a sandy '70s time warp, Avalon is the mythical Australian beach you always dreamed of but could never find. The surf's consistent; the relaxed back streets are lined with sleepy cafés and second-hand bookshops. To get here, catch bus L88, 190 or L90 from Wynyard.

**Balmoral** (Map pp76–7) Split in two by an unfeasibly picturesque rocky outcrop, Balmoral is popular with picnicking North Shore families. Swimmers, kayakers and windsurfers migrate to the shark-netted southern end. Catch bus 175 from Wynyard then 275 from Spit Junction.

**Bronte** (Map p87) Norfolk Island pines and sandstone headlands encircle the bowl-shaped park behind Bronte, a small family-oriented beach that can get wild and seaweedy. The rock pool is perfect, as are the beachy cafés along the once exceedingly uncool shopping strip. Catch bus 378 from Railway Sq.

**Camp Cove** (Map pp76–7) When Phillip realised Botany Bay just didn't cut it, he sailed north into Sydney Harbour, his boots sinking into Camp Cove's sand on 21 January 1788. It's a gorgeous golden harbour beach frequented by families and topless beach babes. Catch the ferry to Watsons Bay, or bus L82 or 324–5 from Circular Quay.

**Clovelly** (Map p87) The concrete terrace skirting along skinny Clovelly bay makes it more pool than beach, but the swell still surges in. A friendly beloved grouper fish lived here for many years until he was speared by a tourist, but there are still groupers to be seen underwater. Bring your snorkel, but don't go killing anything... Catch bus 339.

**Coogee** (Map p87) Coogee is an Aboriginal word for rotting seaweed, but don't let that deter you. The beach is wide and handsome – room enough for frisbee-throwing backpackers, grommets and groovers alike as low-flying airliners buzz the beach. Catch bus 353 from Bondi Junction, or bus 372–4 or 313–4 from Circular Quay.

**Cronulla** (Map p108) Cronulla's *looong* surf beach stretches beyond the dunes to the Botany Bay refineries. It's an edgy place with dingy fish-and-chip shops and insomnious teens, the ragged sense of impending 'something' erupting into racial violence in 2005. The '70s cult novel *Puberty Blues* captured the local teen scene. Catch the train to Cronulla.

**Dee Why** (Map p108) Distorted from *diwai*, an Aboriginal name for a local bird, Dee Why is a no-fuss family beach fronted by chunky apartments, some good cafés and ubiquitous surf shops. Grommets hit the waves and mums hit the rock pool. Catch bus L85, L88, 190 or L90 from Wynyard.

**Lady Bay** (Map pp76–7) This diminutive, mainly gay nudist beach sits at the bottom of a cliff, on top of which (somewhat ironically) is a Royal Australian Navy facility. To get here, follow the cliff-top walking track from (somewhat ironically) Camp Cove. Catch the ferry to Watsons Bay, or bus L82 or 324–5 from Circular Quay.

**Maroubra** (Map p108) Maroubra rivals Bondi for size and swell, but its suburban location provides immunity from Bondi's more hectic trappings. The notorious 'Bra Boys' gang remains entrenched in the community psyche, but don't let them keep you out of the surf. Catch buses 376–7, 396 or X77 from Circular Quay, 395 from Railway Sq, or X96 from Elizabeth St.

**Palm Beach** (Map p108) The northernmost of the Northern Beaches, Palm Beach is a meniscus of bliss. Barrenjoey Lighthouse overlooks free-roaming nudists at the northern end; enduring Australian TV soap *Home & Away* films its treacle-sweet episodes at the sheltered southern end. Catch bus L90 or 190 from Wynyard, or 193 from Avalon.

**Shark Bay** (Map pp76–7) Despite the name, there's really nothing to worry about – a shark net protects swimmers from becoming something's lunch. It's a family scene, with harbour views and the shady, vaguely spooky-looking Nielsen Park as a backdrop. Catch bus 325 from Circular Quay.

**Tamarama** (Map p87) Fully deserving its nickname 'Glamarama', Tamarama's deep, sexy gulch attracts the generically gorgeous. Signs say, 'No frisbees, no kites, no ball games'. No fun. Still, if you feel at home here, you're probably not into those kinds of things anyway... Catch bus 361 from Bondi Junction.

shoreline around a small headland to tiny **Fairy Bower Beach** (Map p88) and the picturesque **Shelly Beach** (Map p88) . On the harbour side, the refurbished **Manly Wharf** (Map p88) offers cafés, pubs and restaurants. West of here is **Oceanworld** (Map p88; ☎ 8251 7879; www.oceanworld .com.au; W Esplanade; adult/child/family $18/10/44; ☒ 10am-5.30pm), a daggy-looking '80s aquarium with underwater transparent tubes through which you become alarmingly intimate with 10ft sharks. Not the place to come if you're on the way to Manly Beach for a surf... Next door, the beachy **Manly Art Gallery & Museum** (Map p88; ☎ 9949 1776; www .manly.nsw.gov.au; adult/child $3.60/1.20; ☒ 10am-5pm Tue-Sun) focuses on Manly's relationship with the beach.

North Head Scenic Dr provides stunning ocean, harbour and city views. Along this route, the **Manly Quarantine Station** (Map p88; ☎ 9247 5033; www.nationalparks.nsw.gov.au; adult/child $11/7.70; ☒ 1.15pm Thu & Sun, bookings essential) is located, where isolated epidemic-disease carriers dwelt between 1832 and 1984. Ghosts of the dead linger; take the adults-only **Ghost Tour** ($27.50; ☒ 7.30pm Wed & Fri-Sun) or **Kids' Ghost Walk** ($13.30; ☒ 6pm Fri).

To get to Manly, catch the ferry or JetCat, bus 169 or E69 from Wynyard, or 151 from the QVB.

### Northern Beaches

Sydney's **Northern Beaches** (Map pp76-7; www .sydneynorthernbeaches.com.au) make a low-key, sandy day trip. Extending north from Manly, they form a continuous 30km stretch of laidback 'burbs, craggy headlands, fish and chip shops and over twenty beaches, finishing at **Palm Beach**. Along the way are **Freshwater**, **Curl Curl**, **Dee Why**, **Collaroy**, **Narrabeen** and **Warriewood** beaches. More spectacular are **Whale**, **Avalon** and **Bilgola** beaches, all with dramatic, plummeting headlands. Buses 136 and 139 run from Manly to Dee Why and Curl Curl respectively. Bus L90 runs from Wynyard to Palm Beach. See also the Sydney's Best Beaches boxed text (p63).

## ACTIVITIES
### Canoeing & Kayaking

Sydney Harbour is the obvious choice for kayaking, but bear in mind that the harbour is both big and busy, especially if you're a novice. Contact the **New South Wales Canoeing Association** (Map pp78-9; ☎ 9660 4597; www.nswcanoe .org.au; Wentworth Park Complex, Wattle St, Ultimo) for canoe course and hire information.

Kayak harbour tours conducted by **Natural Wanders** (Map pp76-7; ☎ 9899 1001; www.kayaksydney .com; per person incl brunch $110; ☒ 9am 1pm) leave from Lavender Bay Wharf, pass under the bridge to secluded North Shore bays. Bookings are essential; there is an over-15-years-old age limit.

### Cycling

Sydney's topography, humidity and drivers can make for a frustrating cycling experience. Centennial Park is popular for pedalling – less traffic, long paths. **Bicycle NSW** (Map p84; ☎ 9281 4099; www.bicyclensw.org.au; Level 5, 822 George St) publishes *Cycling Around Sydney*, which details city routes and paths.

#### CYCLE HIRE

Many cycle-hire shops also have weekly rates; many require a hefty deposit (about $500) and/or credit card details.

**Cheeky Monkey Cycles** (Map pp78-9; ☎ 9212 4460; www.cheekymonkey.com.au; 456 Pitt St; per day $35; ☒ 8.30am-6.30pm Mon-Sat) Touring specialists with good-quality gear.

**Inner City Cycles** (Map p86; ☎ 9660 6605; www.inner citycycles.com.au; 151 Glebe Point Rd, Glebe; per day $33; ☒ 9.30am-6pm Mon-Wed & Fri, to 7pm Thu, 9am-4pm Sat, 11am-3pm Sun).

**Wooly's Wheels** (Map p84; ☎ 9331 2671; www .woolyswheels.com; 82 Oxford St, Paddington; per day $39; ☒ 9am-6pm Mon-Fri, to 8pm Thu, to 4pm Sat & Sun) Quality wheels on Centennial Park's doorstep.

### Diving

Sydney's best shore dives are Gordons Bay, north of Coogee; Shark Point, Clovelly; and Ship Rock, Cronulla. Popular boat dive sites are Wedding Cake Island off Coogee, Sydney Heads, and off Royal National Park.

**Dive Centre Bondi** (Map p87; ☎ 9369 3855; www .divebondi.com.au; 192 Bondi Rd, Bondi; ☒ 8.30am-6pm Mon-Fri, from 7.30am Sat & Sun) Four-day PADI courses from $350; shore & boat dives.

**Dive Centre Manly** (Map p88; ☎ 9977 4355; www .divesydney.com.au; 10 Belgrave St, Manly; ☒ 8.30am-7pm Mon-Fri, from 7.45am Sat & Sun) Learn-to-dive courses from $345; guided shore dives, weekend boat dives and half-day introductory sessions.

### Golf

There are more than 80 golf courses in the metropolitan area, though most are members-only. Book to play on public courses (especially on weekends).

**Bondi Golf Club** (Map p87; ☎ 9130 1981; www.bondi golf.com.au; 5 Military Rd, North Bondi; 18 holes $18.50; ⊗ 7am-sunset Mon-Fri, 12.30pm-sunset Sat & Sun) Spectacular cliff-top public course (9-hole, par 28).

**Moore Park Golf Course** (Map p84; ☎ 9663 1064, www.mooreparkgolf.com.au; cnr Anzac Pde & Cleveland St; 18 holes Mon-Fri $45, Sat & Sun $50; ⊗ 6am-10pm) The CBD's closest public course (18-hole, par 70).

## Horse Riding

The **Centennial Parklands Equestrian Centre** (Map p84; ☎ 9332 2809; www.cp.nsw.gov.au; Lang Rd, Paddington; per hr incl equipment $60; ⊗ 9am-5pm) conducts one-hour, 3.6km horse rides around treelined Centennial Park, Sydney's favourite urban green space. Several stables conduct rides include the following ones; equine familiarity not required.

**Centennial Stables** ( ☎ 9360 5650; www.centennial stables.com.au)

**Eastside Riding Academy** ( ☎ 9360 7521; www.east sideriding.com.au)

**Moore Park Stables** ( ☎ 9360 8747; www.moorepark stables.com.au)

## In-line Skating

The Bondi and Manly beach promenades and Centennial Park's pathways are superb for skating.

**Manly Blades** (Map p88; ☎ 9976 3833; www.manly blades.com.au; 2/49 North Steyne, Manly; hire per hr from $15; ⊗ 9am-6pm) Top-of-the-range blades, skateboards and safety gear, right across from the beach. Private lessons $50 per hour.

**Rollerblading Sydney** (Map pp76-7; ☎ 0411 872 022; www.rollerbladingsydney.com.au; Milsons Point Train Station; ½hr per person $50-99; ⊗ 8am-6pm Sat & Sun, 7-9pm Mon-Fri) Your reassuring instructor sends you barrelling across Sydney Harbour Bridge with lessons, quality skates and protective gear.

## Sailing

Sydney has dozens of yacht clubs and sailing schools. Even if you're not a serious sea salt, an introductory lesson is a super way to see the harbour.

**Eastsail Sailing School** (Map pp76-7; ☎ 9327 1166; www.eastsail.com.au; d'Albora Marina, New Beach Rd, Rushcutters Bay; cruises per person from $95; ⊗ 9am-6pm) A sociable outfit with a flotilla of boats. Hoist the mainsail on a morning or afternoon yacht cruise; introductory 'Yachtmaster' courses from $475.

**Sydney by Sail** (Map pp78-9; ☎ 9280 1110; www .sydneybysail.com.au; Festival Pontoon, National Maritime

Museum, Darling Harbour; tour $130, course $425; ⊗ 9am-5pm) Daily harbour sailing tours and comprehensive introductory weekend sailing courses – 12 hours on the water will ensure you're shipshape.

## Surfing

On the South Shore, get tubed at Bondi, Tamarama, Coogee, Maroubra and Cronulla. On the North Shore, there are a dozen gnarly surf beaches between Manly and Palm Beach, including Curl Curl, Dee Why, Narrabeen, Mona Vale and Newport.

**Aloha Surf** (Map p88; ☎ 9977 3777; alohasurfmanly@ hotmail.com; 44 Pittwater Rd, Manly; board hire half-/full-day $20/40; ⊗ 9am-6pm) Longboards, shortboards, bodyboards: try your luck at Manly Beach.

**Let's Go Surfing** (Map p87; ☎ 9365 1800; www.lets gosurfing.com.au; 128 Ramsgate Ave, Bondi; 2hr lesson incl board & wetsuit adult/child $75/39; ⊗ 9am-7pm) Small-group lessons in the North Bondi swell. Board and wetsuit hire (no lesson) $30 for two hours. Also at Maroubra.

**Manly Surf School** (Map p88; ☎ 9977 6977; www .manlysurfschool.com; North Steyne Surf Club, Manly; lessons per hr incl board & wetsuit adult/child $50/40; ⊗ 9am-6pm) Small-group surf lessons in the Manly shore-breaks. Also at Palm Beach and Collaroy.

## Swimming

There are 100-plus public swimming pools in Sydney and many beaches have protected rock pools. Harbour beaches offer sheltered and shark-netted (but sometimes soupy) swimming, but nothing beats (or cures a hangover faster than) Pacific Ocean waves. Always swim within the flagged lifeguard-patrolled areas, and never underestimate the surf.

Outdoor city pools include these ones.

**Andrew 'Boy' Charlton Pool** (Map pp78-9; ☎ 9358 6686; www.abcpool.org; 1C Mrs Macquaries Rd, The Domain; adult/child $5.20/3.60; ⊗ 6am-8pm Sep-Apr) A 50m outdoor saltwater pool named after the 1924 Olympian; five-star amenities and harbour-view café.

**Dawn Fraser Baths** (Map pp76-7; ☎ 9555 1903; Elkington Park, Glassop St, Balmain; adult/child $3.40/2; ⊗ 7.15am-6.15pm Oct-Nov & Mar-Apr, 6.45am-7pm Dec-Feb) These magnificently restored late-Victorian baths (1884) picturesquely protect swimmers from underwater undesirables.

**North Sydney Olympic Pool** (Map pp76-7; ☎ 9955 2309; www.northsydney.nsw.gov.au; Alfred St South, Milsons Point; adult/child $4.90/2.40; ⊗ 5.30am-9pm Mon-Fri, 7am-7pm Sat & Sun) Next to Luna Park, right on the harbour.

## Tennis

There are hundreds of public tennis courts in Sydney. **Tennis NSW** ( ☎ 1800 153 040; www.tennisnsw .com.au) lobs up information.

**Millers Point Tennis Court** (Map pp78-9; ☎ 9256 2222; Kent St, The Rocks; per hr $25; ☸ 8am-10.30pm) A hard court cut into a leafy sandstone nook.

**Parklands Tennis Centre** (Map p84; ☎ 9662 7033; www.parklandssportscentre.citysearch.com.au; cnr Anzac Pde & Lang Rd, Moore Park; per hr from $16.50; ☸ 9am-10pm) Faux-grass and hard courts.

## WALKING TOURS
### Bondi to Coogee Clifftop Trail

This beautiful coastal walk leads south from Bondi Beach along the clifftops to Coogee via Clovelly, Tamarama and Bronte beaches, interweaving panoramic views, swimming spots and foody delights.

Begin at the Eora **Aboriginal rock engravings** (1) between the tower and the cliffs at Bondi Golf Club. Some decades ago they were bizarrely 're-grooved' by the well-meaning but insensitive local council. March south along Military Rd, left into Ramsgate Ave and taste the sea spray at the **lookout** (2). The trail then runs along the rocks to the beach – if the surf's humungous, stay high and dry on Ramsgate Ave. Have a quick dip then rummage through Sunday's funky **Bondi Beach Market** (3; p103), or stick your head into **Bondi Pavilion** (4) for an exhibition or performance.

Grab a bite, a bikini or some surfboard wax on **Campbell Parade** (5) then promenade along the beach to Notts Ave and the glistening **Bondi Icebergs** (6; p94) pool and restaurant. Step onto the cliff path at the end of Notts Ave – the blustery sandstone cliffs and grinding Pacific Ocean couldn't be more spectacular (watch for dolphins, whales and surfers). Slide past sexpot **Tamarama Beach** (7; p63) to **Bronte Beach** (8; p63) where beachy cafés will bolster you.

Continue past the **Bronte Baths** (9) through the sun-bleached **Waverley Cemetery** (10) where writer Henry Lawson and cricketer Victor Trumper are among the subterranean. Duck into the sunbaked **Clovelly Bowling Club** (11) for a beer or a game of bowls, then breeze past the cockatoos, banksias and canoodling lovers in Burrows Park and Bundock Park to **Clovelly Beach** (12; p63).

Follow the footpath up through the car park, along Cliffbrook Pde then down the steps to the upturned dinghies lining **Gor-**

**WALK FACTS**

**Start** bus 380 or 389 from Circular Quay to North Bondi
**Finish** bus 372–4 or 313–4 from Coogee to Circular Quay
**Distance** 5km
**Duration** 2-3 hours

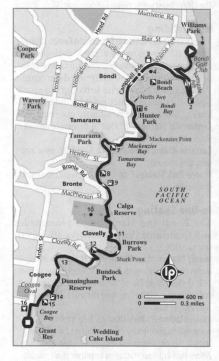

**dons Bay** (13). The trail continues through Dunningham Reserve to **Giles Baths** (14), then lands you smack-bang on glorious **Coogee Beach** (15; p63). Swagger into the **Coogee Bay Hotel** (16; p97) and toast your efforts with a cold lager.

## Manly Scenic Walkway

This epic walk tracks west from Manly around North and Middle Harbour, past waterside mansions, harbour viewpoints and through rugged Sydney Harbour National Park (wear sturdy shoes!). Take water and grab a snack before you leave Manly. At times you'll feel completely isolated in bushland – it's easy to forget you're right in the middle of Sydney!

Check the surf at **Manly Beach (1)** then cruise down The Corso to **Oceanworld (2; p64)** on West Esplanade. Scan the view through The Heads from **Fairlight (3)** and the yachts tugging on their moorings near **Forty Baskets Beach (4)**. Cackling kookaburras mock you as you enter the **Sydney Harbour National Park (5)** and approach **Reef Beach (6)**. The track becomes steep, sandy and rocky further into the park – look for wildflowers, fat goannas sunning themselves and spiders in bottlebrush trees. The views from **Dobroyd Head (7)** are unforgettable. Check out the **deserted 1930s sea shanties (8)** at the base of Crater Cove cliff, and **Aboriginal rock carvings (9)** on an unsigned ledge left of the track before the **Grotto Point Lighthouse (10)**.

> **WALK FACTS**
>
> **Start** ferry to Manly, bus 151 from the QVB, or 169 or E69 from Wynyard
> **Finish** bus 151, 169 or E69 from The Spit to the city
> **Distance** 10km
> **Duration** 4 hours

turnoff. Quiet, calm **Castle Rock Beach (11)** is at the western end of the national park.

There aren't any cafés or eateries en route, so fortify yourself at Manly before your walk, or pack a picnic and hit the tables at Tania Park or **Clontarf Beach (12)**. Bus it back into the city from the southern end of the **Spit Bridge (13)**.

## SYDNEY FOR CHILDREN

Organised ankle-biter activities ramp up during school holidays (December/January, April, July and September) – check www.sydney forkids.com.au and the free *Sydney's Child* and *Kid Friendly* magazines for listings. Otherwise, Sydney Aquarium (p57), Taronga Zoo (p62), Oceanworld (p64) and Luna Park (p62) are sure-fire entertainers. The Sunday GalleryKids programme at the Art Gallery of New South Wales (p59) includes dance, stories, magic, cartoons, Aboriginal performance, costumed tour guides and exhibition-specific events.

Darling Harbour is great for kids – there's a playground, paddleboat pond and a cutesy Thomas the Tank Engine-esque people mover (p57) looping around the bay (or they can

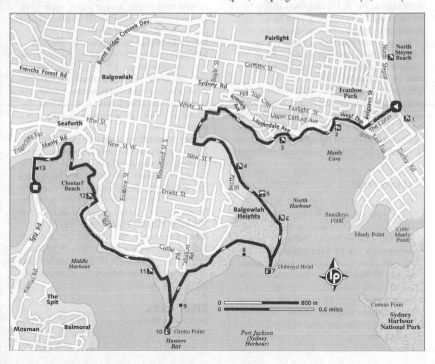

just feed the seagulls). **Lollipops Playland** (Map p84; ☎ 9331 0811; www.lollipopsplayland.com.au; Shop 201 Bent St, Entertainment Quarter, Lang Rd, Moore Park; child under-1 free, child over-1 $12; adult $5; ☒ 9.30am-6pm) is a multistorey, exploratory funhouse with ball pits, mazes, tunnels and nets. There's also two outdoor, state-of-the-art playgrounds built on bouncy matting for spills 'n' thrills. Nearby are Centennial Park horse rides (p65). At Manly Quarantine Station, the Kids' Ghost Walk (p64) is a spooky good time. If all else fails, take them to the beach!

# TOURS
## Harbour Cruises
Here are just a few of the many ferry, catamaran and sailing cruises available on Sydney Harbour:

**Captain Cook Cruises** (Map pp78-9; ☎ 9206 1111; www.captaincook.com.au; Wharf 6, Circular Quay; adult/child/family $25/12/55; ☒ 9.30am-5.30pm) CCC run hop-on hop-off Explorer Cruises. Dodging windsurfers, ferries, 18ft skiffs and a menagerie of harbour craft, they scoot between Shark Island, Watsons Bay, Taronga Zoo & Darling Harbour. Ask about lunch and dinner cruises.

**Matilda Cruises** (Map pp78-9; ☎ 9264 7377; www.matilda.com.au; Pier 26, Aquarium Wharf, Darling Harbour; adult/child/family $29/25/75; ☒ 9.30am-5.30pm) Matilda's proud armada of catamarans, yachts and ferries will float you out onto the water and zoom you 'round Sydney's main harbour sights on a one-hour Rocket Tour. Full-day sailing adventures and luxurious cocktail dinner cruises are also available.

**Sydney Ferries** (Map pp78-9; ☎ 9246 8300, 13 15 00; www.sydneyferries.nsw.gov.au; Wharf 4, Circular Quay; adult/child/family from $15/9/45; ☒ 8am daily, 1pm Mon-Fri, 12.30pm Sat & Sun, 8pm Mon-Sat) If anyone's got the credentials to show you Sydney Harbour, it's Sydney Ferries. One-hour to 2½-hour morning, afternoon and evening harbour-sights-and-lights cruises are available, chugging around on Sydney Harbour's cherished old ferries.

## City Bus Tours
**Bondi Explorer** ( ☎ 13 15 00; www.sydneypass info; adult/child $39/19, from driver & Bus TransitShops; ☒ every 30min 8.45am-4.15pm) The blue STA Bondi Explorer bus does a two-hour, 19-stop loop of the inner city and Eastern Suburbs from Circular Quay to Kings Cross, Double Bay, Rose Bay, Vaucluse, Watsons Bay, the Gap, Bondi Beach and Coogee, returning to the city along Oxford St.

**Sydney Explorer** ( ☎ 13 15 00; www.sydneypass .info; adult/child $39/19, from driver & Bus TransitShops; ☒ every 20min 8.40am-5.20pm) The red STA Sydney Explorer bus follows a two-hour, 26-stop hop-on hop-off loop from Circular Quay through Kings Cross, Chinatown, Darling Harbour and The Rocks, with pithy on-board commentary and discounted entry to attractions.

## Walking Tours
**BridgeClimb** (Map pp78-9; ☎ 8274 7777; www .bridgeclimb.com; 5 Cumberland St, The Rocks; adult $169-296, child $100-195; ☒ 3½hr tours around the clock) Once only painters and daredevils scaled the Harbour Bridge – now anyone can! Make your way through the departure lounge and extensive training session, don your headset, umbilical cord and dandy grey jumpsuit (Elvis would be so proud) and up you go. Go to the toilet *before* you start the climb.

**Sydney Aboriginal Discoveries** ( ☎ 9680 3098, 0405-289 016; www.sydneyaustour.com.au/Abordiscover. html; tour per person $65-180; ☒ 2-4hr tours daily) This outfit runs several different tours focusing on Aboriginal culture and history, including indigenous landmarks and sacred sites, a tasty feast of native Australian foods and a Dreamtime cruise. Call for details on tours, departure points and times.

**Sydney Architecture Walks** (Map pp78-9; ☎ 8239 2211; www.sydneyarchitecture.org; tours depart Museum of Sydney, cnr Bridge & Phillip Sts; adult/concession $25/20; ☒ 2hr walks, rain or shine) These bright young archi-buffs run four themed walking tours: Sydney Opera House, Public Art, Harbour Features & Buildings and Urban Patterns of Sydney. Call for bookings and departure times.

**The Rocks Walking Tours** (Map pp78-9; ☎ 9247 6678; www.rockswalkingtours.com.au; 23 Playfair St, The Rocks; adult/child/family $20/11/51; ☒ 10.30am, 12.30pm, & 2.30pm Mon-Fri, 11.30am & 2pm Sat & Sun) Ninety-minute tours of the historic Rocks area that both entertain and exercise.

## Other Tours
**Bonza Bike Tours** (Map pp78-9; ☎ 9331 1127; www .bonzabiketours.com; tours depart Portobello Caffé, Circular Quay E; adult/child $70/50; ☒ 10.30am &

2.30pm Oct-Mar, 10.30am & 1.30pm Apr-Sep) These bonza bike boffins run daily 3½-hour 'Sydney Classic' bike tours – they make a great introduction to the harbour city, trundling past the Opera House, Hyde Park, Darling Harbour, Chinatown, Sydney Tower and the Royal Botanic Gardens.

**Harbour Jet** (Map pp78-9; ☎ 1300 887 373; www .harbourjet.com; Shop 113a, Level 1 Harbourside, Darling Harbour; adult/child/family from $60/40/180; ☼ 9am-7pm) The Harbour Jet boats rocket you around the harbour in an untamed, white-knuckle, sea-spray ride of 270-degree spins, fishtails and 75km/h power-stops that'll test how long it has been since you had breakfast.

**Maureen Fry** (☎ 9660 7157; www.ozemail.com .au/~mpfry; 2hr tours per person from $18) The omniscient Maureen runs introductory tours to Sydney, from The Rocks to Macquarie St to Paddington. Mainly for groups; individuals by arrangement.

**Whale Watching Sydney** (Map pp78-9; ☎ 9583 1199; www.whalewatchingsydney.net; Eastern Pontoon, Circular Quay; 3hr tours adult/child/family $80/45/205; ☼ 9am & 1pm May-Nov) Humpback and Southern Wright whales habitually shunt up and down the Sydney coastline, sometimes venturing into the harbour. WWS runs seasonal tours with a 98% sighting success rate!

## FESTIVALS & EVENTS
### January
**Sydney Festival** (www.sydneyfestival.org.au) This massive event floods the city with art in January, including free outdoor concerts in the Domain.

**Australia Day** (26 January) Regattas, barbecues and fireworks.

**Chinese New Year** (January/February) Dragon-boat races, food stalls, fireworks, acrobats, buskers, Chinatown parade.

**Flickerfest** (www.flickerfest.com.au) International short-film festival at Bondi Pavilion.

### February
**Tropfest** (www.tropfest.com.au) The world's largest short-film festival. Custom-made seven-minute films incorporate a compulsory surprise prop (bubble, hook, kiss etc) and are judged by an international megastar like Salma Hayek or Gabriel Byrne.

**Sydney Gay & Lesbian Mardi Gras** (www.mardigras .org.au) In late February, the highlight of this world-famous festival is the over-the-top, sequined Oxford St parade, culminating in a bacchanalian party at the Entertainment Quarter.

### March/April
**Royal Easter Show** (www.eastershow.com.au) Twelve days at Homebush: animals, agriculture and plenty to entertain the kids.

**Women's Festival** (www.internationalwomensday.com) Celebrations coinciding with International Women's Day.
**Sydney Cup** (www.ajc.com.au) Australia's second-most popular horse race; at Royal Randwick.

### May
**Sydney Writers' Festival** (www.swf.org.au) Celebrates literary Sydney, with guest authors, talks and forums.
**Australian Fashion Week** (www.mafw.org.au) Early May at Circular Quay.

### June
**Sydney Film Festival** (www.sydneyfilmfestival.org) A 14-day orgy of cinema at the State Theatre and Dendy cinemas.
**Sydney Biennale** (www.biennaleofsydney.com.au) International arts festival held in even-numbered years at the Art Gallery of New South Wales and city venues.
**Darling Harbour International Jazz Festival** (www .darlingharbour.com) Free jazzy jamboree.

### July
**Yulefest** (www.katoomba-nsw.com/yulefest.html) Blue Mountains businesses celebrate a maladjusted southern-hemisphere Christmas.

### August
**City to Surf Run** (www.city2surf.sunherald.com.au) Held on the second Sunday in August, 50,000 fools run 14km from Hyde Park to Bondi Beach.

### September
**Royal Botanic Gardens Spring Festival** (www.rbg syd.nsw.gov.au) Spring is celebrated with concerts, plant markets and a plethora of pollen.
**Festival of the Winds** (www.waverley.nsw.gov .au/info/pavilion/fotw) A multicultural kite-flying festival at Bondi Beach.
**Rugby League Grand Final** (www.nrl.com.au) The two best teams in the National Rugby League decide who's better.

### October
**Manly Jazz Festival** (www.manly.nsw.gov.au/manly jazz) Labour Day weekend; three days of bebop and za ba de da.

### November
**Sculpture by the Sea** (www.sculpturebythesea.com) Mid-November; the clifftop trail between Bondi and Bronte transforms into a sculpture garden.

### December
**Christmas Day** (25 December) Backpackers descend on Bondi Beach, much to the consternation of overworked lifesavers.

**Sydney to Hobart Yacht Race** (www.rolexsydney hobart.com; 26 December) Sydney Harbour teems with onlookers for the start of this gruelling ocean race.

**New Year's Eve** (31 December) The Rocks, Kings Cross and Bondi Beach heave with alcohol-sodden celebrations; fireworks displays over the harbour.

## SLEEPING

Sydney's well of accommodation seems to never run dry, with everything from budget hostels to cosy B&Bs, comfortable motels, authentic Aussie pubs and deluxe harbour-view hotels. Between November and February, prices (especially at beachside hotels) jump by as much as 40%. Conversely, when tumbleweeds blow through foyers in the slower winter months, you can often strike a bargain. Many city hotels cater primarily to business travellers, so their weekend rates may be lower. Predictably, a view can play a big part in determining the price of a Sydney room. Booking through an accommodation agency like Tourism NSW (p52) can sometimes land you a discount.

Read up on Sydney's neighbourhoods before deciding where to stay: party people should head for Kings Cross, Darlinghurst, Paddington or Bondi; shoppers, gourmands and highlight hunters should shoot for The Rocks, CBD, Darling Harbour or Chinatown. If you want to keep things low-key, try Glebe, Potts Point, Surry Hills or Manly.

In this chapter, a budget room is classified as up to $50/100 for a single/double. Midrange doubles cost between $101 and $200; top-end doubles start at $200 a night. Serviced apartments usually sleep more than two people – good value for groups and families.

### City Centre, The Rocks & Circular Quay

#### BUDGET

**Base Backpackers Wanderers on Kent** (Map pp78-9; ☎ 9267 7718; www.basebackpackers.com; 477 Kent St; dm $26-32; s & d $90; 🌐 🖳 ) Strangely deserted during the day (everyone's out enjoying themselves), Sydney's Base Backpackers branch livens up at night when things get downright raucous at the bar. Stay in the sanitary girls-only 'sanctuary' ($34) or risk boy-contamination in the dorms. Some rooms are shoeboxes – caveat emptor.

**Y Hotel** (Map pp78-9; ☎ 9264 2451; www.yhotel .com.au; 5-11 Wentworth Ave; dm $35, s/d/tr/f from $75/90/110/175; 🅿 🌐 🖳 🕭 ) Standards here are high – simple, spotless rooms with TV, phone, fridge and

air-con plus an adjoining café downstairs. The city centre is just beyond Hyde Park across the road and Oxford St is a wiggle away. Busy as a woodpecker during Mardi Gras. Child-friendly; good wheelchair access.

**Grand Hotel** (Map pp78-9; ☎ 9232 3755; www .merivale.com; 30 Hunter St; s/d/tr $80/90/110; 🌐 ) One of Sydney's oldest hotels, the Grand's lower floors pulsate with pokies, pool tables and beery hordes. Keep going up and you'll find neat rooms with TVs and fridges. Shared bathrooms can be a drag, but for these prices in this location, you won't hear anyone complaining.

#### MIDRANGE

**Mercantile Hotel** (Map pp78-9; ☎ 9247 3570; www .mercantilehotel.citysearch.com.au; 25 George St, The Rocks; d from $110) The Mercantile's green-tiled exterior hints at the Irish sympathies emanating from the bar. Upstairs the basic, renovated, pub-style rooms take a less partisan approach with neutral colours and shared bathrooms. Four suites have spas ($140); avoid near St Patrick's Day.

**Lord Nelson Brewery Hotel** (Map pp78-9; ☎ 9251 4044; www.lordnelson.com.au; 19 Kent St, Millers Pt; d $120-180; 🌐 ) Built in 1841, this boutique sandstone pub has its own brewery (try a pint of 'Nelson's Blood'), and is just far enough from The Rocks' tourist throng. Rooms are elegantly colonial (stripy sheets and dormer windows), most with private bathrooms.

**Australian Hotel** (Map pp78-9; ☎ 9247 2229; www .australianheritagehotel.com; 100 Cumberland St, The Rocks; d $125) Despite the shared bathrooms, this pub accommodation scores points for snug communal rooms, 24-hour harbour-view roof terrace, complimentary glasses of port and the patriotic bar downstairs (96 Australian beers!).

**Palisade Hotel** (Map pp78-9; ☎ 9247 2272; www .palisadehotel.com.au; 35 Bettington St, Millers Pt; d/tw $125/130) Standing in Gothic isolation atop Millers Point, this old-time, nicotine-stained dock workers' pub has dodged kitsch Rocks-style makeovers and remains a great place for a beer and a cheap night's sleep. Basic, shared-facility rooms are weary but have magnificent harbour views.

**Russell** (Map pp78-9; ☎ 9241 3543; www.therussell.com .au; 143a George St, The Rocks; d incl breakfast from $140, with bathroom $235; 🌐 ) Traditionally decorated rooms (Laura Ashley, you have a lot to answer for), lounge areas with fireplaces, library and

## GAY & LESBIAN SYDNEY

Gay is the new straight in Sydney; gay and lesbian culture forming a vocal, vital part of Sydney's social fabric. **Taylor Square** (Map p84) on Oxford St Is the centre of arguably the second-largest gay community in the world; Newtown is home to Sydney's lesbian scene. Gay beachlife focuses on Lady Bay (p63) and Tamarama (p63). Also check out Red Leaf Pool on New South Head Rd, Double Bay, and Andrew 'Boy' Charlton Pool (p65). For men, tans, moustaches and heavy pecs are the 'classic' look; the lesbian scene is a bit more inclusive. Despite broad acceptance, a homophobic streak still taints some community sectors and 'gay bashing' isn't unknown. For the record, in NSW male homosexual sex is legal over the age of 18; for women it's over 16.

Sydney's famous **Gay & Lesbian Mardi Gras** ( ☎ 9568 8600; www.mardigras.org.au) started in 1978 as a political march commemorating New York's Stonewall riots, and evolved into a month-long arts festival which culminates in a fleshy street parade on the last Saturday in February. Gyms empty out, solariums cool down and 'Back, Sack & Crack' wax emporiums tally their profits. The rampant 200-float parade begins on Elizabeth St around 7.30pm and cavorts the length of Oxford St. Around 700,000 spectators line the streets – find a balcony or cordon off a pavement patch before it starts. Tickets to the post-parade **Mardi Gras Party** sell out by mid-January. They're usually only available to Mardi Gras members, though interstate and overseas visitors receive temporary membership.

Free gay media incudes *SX, Sydney Star Observer* and *Lesbians on the Loose*. For counselling and referral call the **Gay & Lesbian Counselling Service of NSW** ( ☎ 8594 9596; www.glcsnsw.org .au). **Gay & Lesbian Tourism Australia** (www.galta.com.au) has a wealth of information about gay and lesbian travel in Oz.

Go for a wander along the city end of Oxford St, or try the following popular faves on for size.

**ARQ** (Map p84; ☎ 9380 8700; www.arqsydney.com.au; 16 Flinders St, Darlinghurst; Thu/Fri/Sat/Sun free/$10/20/5; ☻ 9pm-6am Thu & Fri, 10pm-9am Sat, 9pm-9am Sun) If Noah had to fill his bilge with groovy, gay clubbers, he'd head here with a big net and some tranquillisers. This flash megaclub has a cocktail bar, recovery room and two dance floors with hi-energy house music, drag shows and a hyperactive smoke machine.

**Exchange Hotel** (Map pp78-9; ☎ 9331 2956; www.qbar.com.au; 34-44 Oxford St, Darlinghurst; Q Bar/Phoenix/ Exchange free-$20/5-10/free; ☻ Q Bar & Phoenix 10pm-late, Exchange 10pm-4am Mon-Fri, 9am-6am Sat & Sun) Q Bar upstairs pumps hot house nightly; Phoenix club downstairs is the sticky, sexy, claustrophobic home to an alternative gay crowd. Sandwiched in between, the Exchange is a regulation beery pub.

**Imperial Hotel** (Map p86; ☎ 9519 9899; www.theimperialhotel.com.au; 35 Erskineville Rd, Erskineville; admission free; ☻ 3pm-midnight, to 2.30am Thu, to 6am Fri & Sat) The Art Deco Imperial's drag shows inspired *Priscilla, Queen of the Desert* (the opening scene was filmed here). Any drag queen worth her sheen has played the Cabaret Room, while the Cellar Bar, Public Bar and Priscilla Lounge heave with chesty pool boys and raging house.

**Midnight Shift** (Map p84; ☎ 9360 4319; www.themidnightshift.com; 85 Oxford St, Darlinghurst; video bar free, club $10-20; ☻ video bar noon-late Mon-Fri, from 3pm Sun, club 11pm-late Fri & Sat) Sydney's perennial good-time boy palace packs in everyone from beefcakes to drags. The grog is cheap, the patrons messy, Kylie rules and mankind chalks its collective cue by the pool tables. Pick up a 'Pick up Card' at the bar to help with introductions ('I'm easy…but it looks like you're hard…').

**Newtown Hotel** (Map p86; ☎ 9517 1728; www.newtownhotel.com; 174 King St, Newtown; admission free; ☻ 11am-midnight Mon-Fri, 10am-midnight Sat, to 10pm Sun) The Newtown does a heady G&L trade with folks who just want to go to the local boozer and have a few laughs. Musical stimulation is provided by sensationally sequined drag acts.

**Oxford Hotel** (Map p84; ☎ 9331 3467; 134 Oxford St, Taylor Sq, Darlinghurst; admission free; ☻ downstairs 24hr, Gilligans 5pm-late, Ginger's 6pm-late Wed-Sat) Big and crimson, the ever-lovin' Oxford is a Taylor Sq beacon. Downstairs it's beer-swilling and mannish. First-floor Gilligan's serves luxe cocktails; top-floor Ginger's has indulgent lounge service. After-dance party crowds heave and sway.

**Sol's Deck Bar** (Map p84; ☎ 9360 8868; www.solsdeckbar.net.au; 191 Oxford St, Darlinghurst; admission free Mon-Wed, $5 Thu-Sun; ☻ restaurant 11am-late, bar 8pm-late) When you drag your bones out of bed at whatever pm, boot it down to Sol's for a beer, some tapas and a perv over Taylor Sq. The cocktail bar fires up later on with resident DJs. Lipstick ladies love Friday night's 'Bitch' session.

a rooftop garden just minutes from Circular Quay make the Russell a solid choice. Rooms have fresh flowers; families do what families do in the four-bed suite.

**Bed & Breakfast Sydney Harbour** (Map pp78-9; ☎ 9247 1130; www.bedandbreakfastsydney.com; 142 Cumberland St, The Rocks; s/d from $130/155; ⊡ 🖳 ) This 100-year-old guesthouse boldly claims to be the 'World's best-located B&B' – with The Rocks and the city on your doorstep, it's difficult to argue. Rooms with private bathrooms manage to capture an Australian flavour without straying into twee territory. Smaller shared-bathroom rooms are also available.

**Hyde Park Inn** (Map pp78-9; ☎ 9264 6001; www .hydeparkinn.com.au; 271 Elizabeth St; s/d/f incl breakfast from $140/155/190; P 🖾 🖳 ) Dating back to the late '60s, this place invests little in aesthetics but a lot in generous room sizes and friendliness. All rooms have kitchenettes, the best of them have Hyde Park views. We're assured the 1986 apricot colour scheme is about to meet its maker.

**Vibe Hotel** (Map pp78-9; ☎ 9282 0987; www.vibe hotels.com.au; 111 Goulburn St; d from $185; P 🖾 🖳 🖳 ) Vibe's management ran the renovators' broom through every corner of this old-stager hotel, creating an utterly funky establishment. Lime, purple and black colours course through foyers; rooms feature maximal mirrors, stripy retro bed linen and cool abstract art. Good weekend rates.

**TOP END**

**Blacket** (Map pp78-9; ☎ 9279 3030; www.theblacket .com; 70 King St; d from $225 🖾 🖳 ) Alluringly calm, Blacket's uber-stylish suites blend 'escape' with lashings of contemporary cool. Loft suites – all white, caramel and grey – sleep four and have spa, separate lounge, kitchenette and gadgetry (cable TV, CD players and wi-fi). Frequent online specials.

**Hilton** (Map pp78-9; ☎ 9266 2000; www.sydney .hilton.com; 488 George St; d from $270; P 🖾 🖳 🖳 ) Try to contain your glee as you waltz into the refurbished Hilton. Cooler-than-cool rooms feature black timber bedheads, flat-screen TVs, DVD player and internet telephony. Superchef Luke Mangan runs the restaurant; Zeta bar (p95) lures beautiful people. Business facilities are state of the art.

**Establishment** (Map pp78-9; ☎ 9240 3100; www.es tablishmenthotel.com; 5 Bridge La; d from $290; 🖾 🖳 ) So hip it hurts, Establishment is the secret hideaway for superstars and squillionaires (not so secret now, eh?) with the snazziest interiors in town – exquisite furnishings, indulgent bathrooms and high-tech services proliferate. Clubs, bars and restaurants on-site.

## Central Station, Chinatown & Darling Harbour

**BUDGET**

**Wake Up!** (Map pp78-9; ☎ 9288 7888; www.wakeup .com.au; 509 Pitt St; dm from $24, d & tw from $88; 🖾 🖳 ) Backpackers sleep soundly in this converted 1900 department store on top of Sydney's busiest intersection. It's a convivial, colourful, professionally-run hostel with a tour desk, 24-hour check-in, sunny café, bar and no excuse for neglecting your inner party-animal.

**Railway Square YHA** (Map pp78-9; ☎ 9281 9666; www .yha.com.au; 8 Lee St; dm $27-33, d $78-88; 🖳 🖳 ) Adjoining Central Station, this hostel's main building is an historic 1904 train shed – some of the dorms are inside New South Wales' old 'red rattler' train carriages. Facilities lean to the functional side of fancy, but are better than you'd expect for these prices. The more expensive doubles have bathrooms.

**Sydney Central YHA** (Map pp78-9; ☎ 9218 9000; www .yha.com.au; 11 Rawson Pl; dm from $29, d & tw from $86; P 🖾 🖳 🖳 ) Near Central Station this 1913 heritage-listed monolith has been renovated to within an inch of its life. Rooms are brightly painted and the kitchens are great, but the highlight is sitting in the rooftop pool making faces at the Department of Commerce workers in the office tower across the street.

**MIDRANGE**

**Pensione Hotel** (Map pp78-9; ☎ 9265 8888; www .pensione.com.au; 631-635 George St; s/d/f $100/115/250; 🖾 🖳 ) This tastefully reworked post office (derelict for 40 years!) features smart, neutrally shaded rooms with air-con, TV, fridge and good security. Mark Rothko prints and a wooden staircase warm the simple, restrained surrounds. Aim for a rear room – George St traffic grumbles in the night.

**Capitol Square Hotel** (Map pp78-9; ☎ 9211 8633; www.rydges.com/capitolsquare; cnr George & Campbell Sts; d from $110; P 🖾 ) Entirely convenient near both Chinatown and Darling Harbour, with double-glazed widows to keep out the noise. Tidy en suite rooms strive for a plush, mildly regal atmosphere. Wheelchair access available; frequent internet deals.

**Vulcan Hotel** (Map p84; ☎ 9211 3283; www.vulcan hotel.com.au; 500 Wattle St, Ultimo; s/d from $100/130; P 🖾 )

Vulcan was a watering hole well into the '90s before the lousy pub rooms were converted into boutique budget accommodation. Discrete international staff direct you to minimalist grey-and-white en suite rooms, complete with TV and mini-bar. No sign of Dr Spock here...

**Aaron's Hotel** (Map pp78-9; ☎ 9281 5555; www.aarons hotel.com.au; 37 Ultimo Rd, Chinatown; s/d from $110/130; ✉ 🖵) Aaron doesn't actually exist – he was invented to secure top-of-the-page 'Aa' listing in the *Yellow Pages*. The cunning plan seems to have worked – Aaron's brilliantly located, clean, light-filled rooms are always full. Kid-friendly; wheelchair accessible.

**Glasgow Arms Hotel** (Map pp78-9; ☎ 9211 2354; www.glasgowarmshotel.com.au; 527 Harris St, Ultimo; s/d $120/135; ✉) Scoot your way across the road from the Powerhouse Museum, through the bar, beyond the poker machines and upstairs to the Glasgow Arms' traditionally decorated, no-frills pub-style rooms. The balcony rooms on William Henry St are the pick of the bunch.

**Metro Hotel Sydney Central** (Map pp78-9; ☎ 9283 8088; www.metrohospitalitygroup.com; 431 Pitt St; d from $135; P ✉ 🖵 ✇) Centrally located, the courteous Metro has a brassy lobby, a business centre and serviceable rooms with classy touches (Brett Whiteley prints), plus a rooftop pool if you feel like ignoring the city below. Deluxe rooms are stylish; standard rooms aren't.

## Kings Cross, Potts Point & Woolloomooloo

### BUDGET

**Original Backpackers** (Map p82; ☎ 9356 3232; www.originalbackpackers.com.au; 160-162 Victoria St, Kings Cross; dm/s/d $25/55/65; 🖵) A hostel for almost 25 years, this may well be Sydney's original backpackers. It's a rambling 176-bed affair in two character-filled Victorian houses, with friendly staff, decent bathrooms, good security and gas cooking. The social scene is lively and inclusive without being debauched.

**Highfield Private Hotel** (Map p82; ☎ 9326 9539; www.highfieldhotel.com; 166 Victoria St, Kings Cross; dm/s/d incl breakfast $25/60/70) Clean and serviceable without igniting anyone's interior-design passions, Highfield is a reliable independent option, with simple rooms (shared bathrooms) and solid 24-hour security. Top floor rooms are the sunniest.

**Woodduck Harbour City Backpackers** (Map pp78-9; ☎ 1800 882 922; www.harbourcitybackpackers.com

.au; 50 Sir John Young Cres, Woolloomooloo; dm $20 15; d & tw from $70; 🖵) Friendly and funky, this Woolloomooloo hostel has been getting great feedback from travellers, mostly for its awesome roof terrace which floats you up into the city lights. It's a huge place with 250 beds, but the ceilings are high and rooms airy – you'll never feel like you're stuffed into someone else's backpack.

**Eva's Backpackers** (Map p82; ☎ 9358 2185; www.evasbackpackers.com.au; 6-8 Orwell St, Potts Point; dm $25, d & tw $60; 🖵) Eva's is a perennial backpackers favourite, probably because it's far enough out of the Kings Cross fray to maintain some composure and dignity. Smile-free staff have a bit too much composure at times, but it's clean, secure and there's an ace rooftop barbecue area and sociable kitchen/dining room.

**Pink House** (Map p82; ☎ 9358 1689, 1800 806 385; www.pinkhouse.com.au; 6-8 Barncleuth Sq, Kings Cross; dm $26, d & tw incl breakfast from $65; 🖵) Yep, it's a pink house. The relentless colour attack continues inside through spritely communal areas, across creaky floorboards into robustly furnished dorms. There are three leafy patios where hungover guests nod off in the shade. Free barbecues are a hit.

**O'Malley's Hotel** (Map p82; ☎ 9357 2211; www.omalleyshotel.com.au; 228 William St, Kings Cross; s/d/tr incl breakfast $70/80/90) This jocular Irish pub has traditionally decorated, well-furnished rooms with private bathrooms upstairs that are surprisingly quiet, given the William St location and nightly twiddle-dee-dee live music downstairs. Harbour-view rooms are winners.

**Royal Sovereign Hotel** (Map p82; ☎ 9331 3672; www.darlobar.com.au; cnr Liverpool St & Darlinghurst Rd, Darlinghurst; d from $80) Directly above the boozy Darlo Bar (BYO carplugs), these small, nifty rooms put you in the thick of the action at a bargain price. Olive/cream/grey colour schemes scream, 'I was hip five years ago', but communal bathrooms are immaculate.

### MIDRANGE

**Bernly Private Hotel** (Map p82; ☎ 9358 3122; www.bernlyprivatehotel.com.au; 15 Springfield Ave, Kings Cross; dm/s/d/f incl breakfast from $15/45/60/130; 🖵) The larger-than-it-looks backstreet Bernly has simple shared-facility rooms with 24-hour reception and a rooftop garden. There's also a crop of 'executive' doubles with private bathrooms ($100 per night). The location is potentially a bit dodgy, but the greatest risk probably comes from dodging dog poo.

**Maisonette Hotel** (Map p82; ☎ 9357 3878; maisonettehotel@bigpond.com; 31 Challis Ave, Potts Point; s/d from $60/100) This friendly place above the Challis Ave caffeine cauldron is top value, offering small, bright rooms with kitchenettes, TVs and spick-and-span bathrooms. Ask about lower rates for longer stays.

**Hotel 59** (Map p82; ☎ 9360 5900; www.hotel59.com .au; 59 Bayswater Rd, Kings Cross; s/d/tr from $90/100/135; ✖) Hotel 59 is good bang for your buck on the quiet part of Bayswater Rd, with nouveau-Med rooms and smiley staff who go out of their way not to get in your way. The café downstairs does whopping cooked breakfasts ($5 to $11) for those barbarous Kings Cross hangovers.

**Macleay** (Map p82; ☎ 9357 7755; www.themacleay .com; 28 Macleay St, Potts Point; d $115-135, tw/tr $130-150; ⓟ ✖ ⬛) The upper floors of these serviceable serviced apartments have harbour panoramas. Rooms are mired in an '80s design quagmire (shame, Ken Done, shame…), and when the laundry's running, the hallways smell like an oven full of wet socks, but the location, price and friendliness-factor win through.

**Crest Hotel** (Map p82; ☎ 9358 2755; www.cresthotel .com.au; 111 Darlinghurst Rd, Kings Cross; d $130-150; ⓟ ✖) With the definitive Kings Cross location, the Crest caters to business bods, visiting Koreans (there's an amazing Ginseng Bathhouse on-site) and boozy boys'-nights-out that last for days. The rooms are comfy but could be anywhere in the world if you don't have a harbour view.

**Victoria Court Hotel** (Map p82; ☎ 9357 3200; www .victoriacourt.com.au; 122 Victoria St, Potts Point; d from $150; ⓟ ✖) The Victoria is a sweetly run guesthouse filling a pair of three-storey 1881 brick terrace houses with 22 rooms with private bathrooms, all with TVs and plenty of over-the-top Victoriana (floral quilts, chandeliers, paintings of fruit etc). Still, it's clean, secure and tastily located.

**Mariners Court** (Map p82; ☎ 9358 3888; www .marinerscourt.com.au; 44-50 McElhone St, Woolloomooloo; d/tr/f from $155/175/200; ⓟ ⬛ ♿) A tucked-away treasure, this ship-shape port in a storm won't be the flashest place you'll stay in Sydney, but it offers that rare combination of location, price and roominess. All rooms have courtyards or balconies, some with leafy outlooks. Good wheelchair access.

**Simpsons of Potts Point** (Map p82; ☎ 9356 2199; www.simpsonspottspoint.com; 8 Challis Ave, Potts Point; s/d

from $155/175; ⓟ ✖ ⬛) An 1892 red-brick politician's palace, Simpsons has been dutifully converted into a quiet, refined B&B. The 14 spacious rooms with private bathrooms feature fireplaces, balconies and antique prints. The lounge has a piano if you want to mingle or tinkle.

**TOP END**

**Regents Court** (Map p82; ☎ 9358 1533; www.regent scourt.com.au; 18 Springfield Ave, Potts Point; d $240-275; ⓟ ✖ ⬛) Boutique, Art Deco Regents Court is big on personal service and mid-century furnishings. Handsome, spacious rooms with private bathrooms have impeccably stocked kitchenettes. Michael Hutchence once roamed the roof terrace with its Potts Point pot plants and barbecue.

**BLUE Sydney** (Map p82; ☎ 9331 9000; www.tajhotels .com/Sydney; 6 Cowper Wharf Rd, Woolloomooloo; d from $405; ⓟ ✖ ⬛ ♿) The hotel rooms in Woolloomooloo's redeveloped wharf may be a bit poky, but boutique sensibilities are redemptive. Hobnob with bigwigs and biz-kids at the Water Bar, relax at the day spa, cruise the wharf restaurants or sneak a peep at Russell Crowe's end-of-pier pad.

## Darlinghurst & Surry Hills
### MIDRANGE

**Hotel Altamont** (Map p82; ☎ 9360 6000; www.altamont .com.au; 207 Darlinghurst Rd, Darlinghurst; d incl breakfast from $100; ⓟ ✖ ⬛ ♿) Altamont flagged the end of '60s peace and love, but here in Darlinghurst the good times continue unabated. Spiffy-looking doubles with private bathrooms feel as though they should cost more than they do, staff and communal areas are welcoming (especially the terrace), and it's tantalisingly close to The Cross.

**City Crown Motel** (Map p84; ☎ 9331 2433; www .citycrownmotel.com.au; 289 Crown St, Surry Hills; d from $100; ⓟ ✖ ⬛) In an awesome Surry Hills location, this unfailingly busy motel has plush new carpet throughout, clean, simple rooms (none particularly spacious), and an on-site café serving mean caffeine. Prices skyrocket 50% during Mardi Gras.

**Cambridge Park Inn** (Map p84; ☎ 9212 1111; www .cambridgeinn.com.au; 212 Riley St, Surry Hills; d $145-170; ⓟ ✖ ⬛ ♿) The embodiment of what famous architect Robin Boyd called the 'Great Australian Ugliness', this hotel ain't pretty. On the plus side it's superbly located, personable for its size and has a heated pool, spa, sauna and super views from the upper floors. Beauty is only skin deep.

## TOP END

**Kirketon** (Map p82; ☎ 9332 2011; www.kirketon.com.au; 229 Darlinghurst Rd, Darlinghurst; d from $220; P ⬚ ⬚ ) The Kirketon's designer rooms are as impeccably turned out as its brash young clientele. Stylishly sparse suites are jazzed up with ritzy toiletries, bright wall colours, retro furnishings, Lindt chocolates, mohair throw rugs and plush bathrobes. The staff are just as good-looking.

**Medusa** (Map p82; ☎ 9331 1000; www.medusa.com.au; 267 Darlinghurst Rd, Darlinghurst; d from $270; ⬚ ⬚ ) Medusa the seducer's shocking-pink exterior hints at the witty, luscious décor inside. Small colour-saturated suites with enormous beds, mod-con bathrooms and regal furnishings open onto a tranquil courtyard and reflection pool; meditation will minimise the chances of your hair turning into snakes. If it does, Medusa is very pet-friendly.

## Paddington & Woollahra
### MIDRANGE

**Hughenden** (Map p84; ☎ 9363 4863; www.hughendenhotel.com.au; 14 Queen St, Woollahra; s/d incl breakfast from $130/150; P ⬚ ) A quirky Italianate guesthouse located a stone's throw from Paddington, the SCG and Centennial Park. Rooms feature antique bric-a-brac flourishes; some have balconies. For your distraction there's Sunday high tea, poetry readings and Sir Victor the nocturnal pianist.

**Sullivans Hotel** (Map p84; ☎ 9361 0211; www.sullivans.com.au; 21 Oxford St, Paddington; d $145-160; P ⬚ ⬚ ⬚ ) Popular with gay travellers, this well-managed 64-room motel in 'Paddinghurst' has tidy rooms which, aside from the contemporary bathrooms, feel surprisingly un-hip. Still, the location's great, and the brick-paved central courtyard has a solar-heated pool and dribbling fountain.

## Eastern Suburbs
### MIDRANGE

**Savoy Hotel** (Map pp76-7; ☎ 9326 1411; www.savoyhotel.com.au; 41 Knox St, Double Bay; d $120-150, f $190-260; P ⬚ ) Sitting pretty among the generically good-looking in Double Bay's coffee strip, the Savoy's rooms offer unexpected amounts of individual character. Atrium-view rooms are the cheapest; strive for an executive balcony suite looking towards the harbour.

## TOP END

**Doyles Palace Hotel** (Map pp76-7; ☎ 9337 5444; www.doyles.com.au; 1 Military Rd, Watsons Bay; d $145-420; P ⬚ ) In one of Sydney's most beautiful spots, this is really a plush-o-rama top-end hotel, but they have excellent midrange rooms and good winter rates too. Reservations, and fish and chips at Doyles on the Beach (p93) are essential.

## Glebe
### BUDGET

**Glebe Point YHA** (Map p86; ☎ 9692 8418; www.yha.com.au; 262-264 Glebe Point Rd; dm $25-29, s/d $60/70; ⬚ ) An incredible hulk of a hostel with colourful, basic rooms and shared bathrooms. The main lure is the party-people rooftop with its barbecue nights, speed-dating extravaganzas and salsa showdowns. Kitchens and bathrooms are reliable in a YHA kind of way.

**Alishan International Guest House** (Map p86; ☎ 9566 4048; www.alishan.com.au; 100 Glebe Point Rd; dm $25, s/d from $55/77; P ⬚ ) In a substantial, quiet, 111-year-old house in the centre of Glebe, the Alishan (an area of Taiwan, don't you know?), is clean, quiet and well run, with multilingual staff, spacey communal areas, gas cooking and a disabled-access room.

**Wattle Guest House** (Map p86; ☎ 9552 4997; www.wattlehouse.com.au; 44 Hereford St; dm/s/d incl breakfast $30/75/80; P ) Readers have bombarded us with glowing reports of the Wattle – they must be doing something right! It's a super-tidy 1877 Victorian house with shared bathrooms and affable management, not far from Glebe Point Rd. Sorry, no kids.

### MIDRANGE

**Hotel Unilodge** (Map p86; ☎ 9338 5000; www.unilodgehotel.com.au; cnr Broadway & Bay St; s/d/tr $120/160/180; P ⬚ ⬚ ) The rooms inside this former Grace Bros department store lack the 'wow' factor, but are good value. Impressive facilities include a business centre, indoor lap pool, pool table, gym, magical roof terrace and efficient staff nattering away to each other on walkie-talkies.

**Tricketts Bed & Breakfast** (Map p86; ☎ 9552 1141; www.tricketts.com.au; 270 Glebe Point Rd; s $150, d $180-200; P ⬚ ) Inside this preciously restored 1880s merchant's mansion, seven large rooms with private bathrooms are decked out with antiques and Persian rugs. The garden is a verdant wonderland and there's a kitchen, ballroom, billiard table and barbecue. No under-12s.

(Continued on page 89)

A B C D

1 Eastwood

Chesterfield Rd
Eastwood
Midson Rd
Vimiera Rd
Terry Rd
Marsfield
Waterloo Rd
Talavera Rd
Abuklea Rd
Agincourt Rd
Herring Rd
Kent Rd
North Rd
Lovell Rd

Lane Cove
National Park

Lady Game Dr

Grosvenor Rd
Lindfield

Chelmsford Ave
Roseville

Chatswood
Archer St
Victoria Ave

Denistone East
Denistone
Chatham Rd
Shaftsbury Rd
Esg pde
Bridge Rd
Quarry Rd
North Ryde
Coxs Rd
Blenheim Rd
Chatswood West

Artarmon
Artarmon Rd
Hampden Rd
Herbert St
Dalley St

2 West Ryde
Adelaide St
Station St
Belmore St
Anzac Ave
Parkes St
Buffalo Rd
Pittwater Rd
Twin Rd
Badajoz Rd
East Ryde
Ryde
Cressy Rd

Lane Cove North
Lane Cove West

St Leonards

Andrew St

Putney
Mitchell St
Pellisier Rd
Morrison Rd
Manning St
Hunters Hill
Longueville Rd
Kenneth St
Lane Cove
Greenwich

Homebush Bay
Rhodes
Hilly St
Parramatta River
Gladesville
Tarban
Alexandra St
Woolwich Rd
The Point Rd
Riverview
Longueville
Greenwich Rd

Balls Head Bay
Berrys Bay

3 Olympic Park Railway Station
Concord West
Concord
Majors Bay Rd
Nullah Rd
Abbotsford
Great North Rd
Chiswick
Drummoyne
Spectacle Island
Snapper Island
Cockatoo Island
Birchgrove
Mort Bay
Snails Bay
Goat Island

Homebush
Western Mwy
Homebush West
Pomeroy St
Burwood Rd
Crane St
Lyons Rd W
Henley Marine Dr
Five Dock
Rodd Point
Rodd Island
Lilyfield
Russell Lea
Hampden Rd
Elkington Park
3
Balmain
Darling St
Beattie St
Rozelle
White Bay
Johnstons Bay
Anzac Bridge
Pyrmont

4 Barker Rd
Redmyre Rd
Wentworth Rd
Homebush Rd
Shaftsbury Rd
Burwood
Croydon Rd
Bland St
Boomerang St
Haberfield
Leichhardt
Allen St
Norton St
Balmain Rd
Catherine St
Nelson St
Rozelle Bay
Blackwattle Bay
Bridge Rd
St Johns Rd
Glebe
Bay St

Strathfield
Ashfield
Croydon
18
Italian Forum
Annandale
The University of Sydney

Strathfield South
Cosgrove Rd
Enfield
Prospect Rd
Summer Hill
Ashbury
Petersham
Salisbury Rd
Camperdown
Newtown

5 Belfield
Ninth Ave
Campsie
Canterbury
Dulwich Hill
Wardell Rd
Addison Rd
Stanmore
See Glebe & Newtown Map (p86)
Mitchell Rd
Hunter St

Lakemba St
Haldon St
Hurlstone Park
Marrickville Rd
Livingstone Rd
Marrickville

Alexandria

6 Roselands
Belmore
Homer St
Earlwood
Hannam St
Kingsgrove
Bardwell Park
Cooks River
Kingsford Smith Sydney Airport
1
St Peters
Tempe
Coward St
Mascot
Botany

0 — 2 km
0 — 1.0 miles

**INFORMATION**
Tourism NSW (Airport Branch)......1 D6

**SIGHTS & ACTIVITIES**
Admiralty House..............................2 E3
Dawn Fraser Baths...........................3 D3
EastSail Sailing School....................4 F4
Kirribilli House.................................5 F3
Luna Park........................................6 E3
Natural Wonders.............................7 E3
North Sydney Olympic Pool..............8 E3
Rollerblading Sydney.......................9 E3
Sydney Flying Squadron.................10 E3
Taronga Zoo..................................11 F3
Vaucluse House.............................12 G3

**SLEEPING**
Balmain Lodge...............................13 D3
Doyles Palace Hotel.......................14 G3
Glenferrie Lodge............................15 E3
Lane Cove River Tourist Park..........16 C1
Savoy Hotel...................................17 F4

**EATING**
Aqua Dining...............................(see 8)
Bathers' Pavilion Café....................18 F2
Doyles on the Beach..................(see 14)
Grappa..........................................19 C4
Kazbah..........................................20 D3

**DRINKING**
London Hotel.................................21 D4
Watson's Bay Hotel....................(see 14)

**ENTERTAINMENT**
Performance Space.........................22 E5

**SHOPPING**
Balmain Market.............................23 D4
Westfield Bondi Junction................24 F5
Zimmerman Swim.......................(see 24)

Sydney Harbour (or Jackson)

Kirribilli Point

Mrs Macquaries Point
Mrs Macquaries Rd

Woolloomooloo Bay

Finger Wharf

Cooper Wharf Rdwy

See Kings Cross Map (p82)

Lincoln Cres

Farm Cove

Bennelong Point

Sydney Opera House

Royal Botanic Gardens

Conservatorium Rd

Shakespeare Pl

Hospital Rd

Art Gallery Rd

Sydney Harbour Tunnel

Sydney Cove

Circular Quay East

Circular Quay

Cahill Exp

Macquarie St

Phillip La

Bent St

Martin Place

Phillip St

Campbells Cove

The Rocks

George St

Alfred St

Loftus St

Young St

Bridge St

Pitt St

O'Connell St

Hunter St

Castlereagh St

Sydney Harbour Bridge

Dawes Point

Lower Fort St

Bridfield Hwy

Cumberland St

Gloucester St

Harrington St

Essex St

Grosvenor St

Bond St

Curtin Pl

Martin Pl

George St

Walsh Bay

Wharf Theatre (Pier 4 & 5)

Windmill St

Argyle Pl

Observatory Hill

Upper Fort St

Trinity Ave

Jamison St

Margaret St

Wynyard

York St

York La

Sussex La

Erskine St

Sussex St

Kent St

Jenkins St

High La

High St

Hickson Rd

Towns Pl

Dalgety Rd

Rhodens St

Millers Point

Goat Island

Simmons Point

Clifton
Gallimore Ave
Darling St
Luckes Ave
Weston St
Paul St
Pearson St
Johnston St
Hosking St
Balmain East
William St

Peacock Point

Johnstons Bay

See Glebe & Newtown Map (p86)

Darling Point

Pyrmont Bay Wharf

Pyrmont Bay

Darling Island Rd

Star City

Pirrama St

Pyrmont

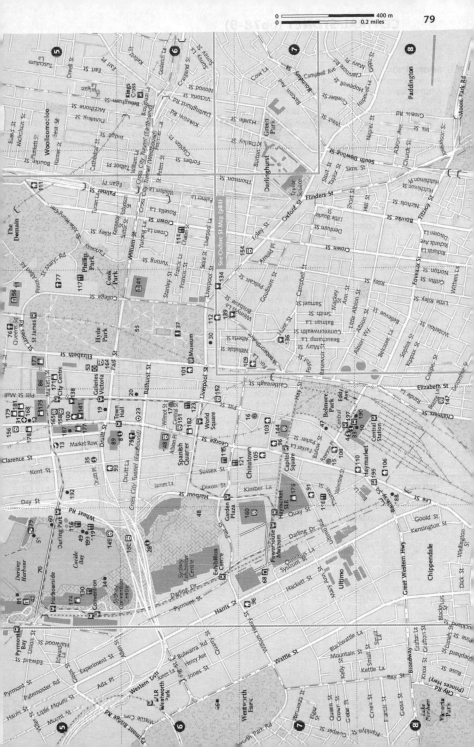

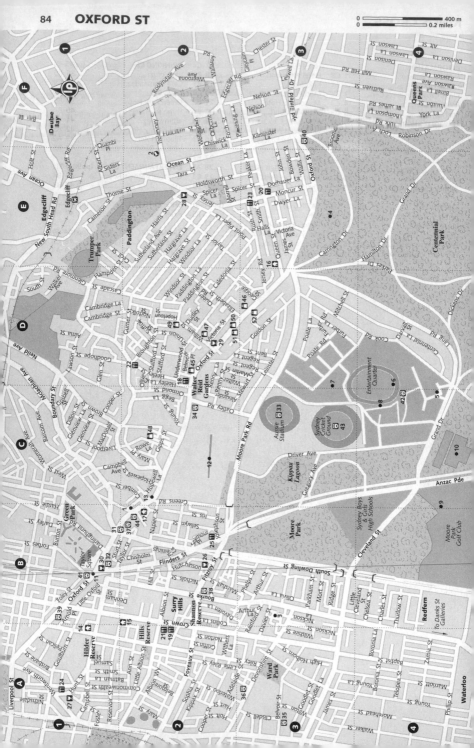

**INFORMATION**
Ariel..........................................1 B2
German Consulate.....................2 E2

**SIGHTS & ACTIVITIES** (pp52–66)
Brett Whiteley Studio..................3 B3
Centennial Park..........................4 E3
Centennial Parklands Equestrian
Centre......................................5 C4
Entertainment Quarter................6 D4
Fox Studios.................................7 C3
Lollipops Playland.......................8 C4
Moore Park Golf Club..................9 C4
Parklands Tennis Centre.............10 C4
Taylor Square............................11 B1
Victoria Barracks.......................12 C2
Woolys Wheels.........................13 C2

**SLEEPING** (pp70–91)
Cambridge Park Inn...................14 A1
City Crown Motel.......................15 B2
Hughenden..............................16 E3
Sullivans Hotel..........................17 B2

**EATING** (pp91–5)
Arthurs Pizza............................18 D2
Bills Surry Hills..........................19 A2
Bills Woollahra..........................20 E3
Billy Kwong...............................21 A2
Gusto.......................................22 D2
Jones the Grocer........................23 E3
Longrain...................................24 A1
Wildrice...................................25 B2

**DRINKING** (pp95–8)
Cricketers Arms Hotel.................26 B2
Hollywood Hotel........................27 A1
Lord Dudley Hotel......................28 E2
Paddington Inn..........................29 D2
Sol's Deck Bar...........................30 E1

**ENTERTAINMENT** (pp98–101)
Academy Twin Cinema................31 B1
ARQ.........................................32 B1
Aussie Stadium..........................33 C3
Chauvel Cinema........................34 C2
Company B................................35 A3
Gaelic Club...............................36 A3
Goodbar...................................37 B2
Hopetoun Hotel.........................38 B2
Midnight Shift...........................39 B1

Moonlight Cinema......................40 F3
Oxford Hotel.............................41 B1
Sydney Comedy Store.................42 C4
Sydney Cricket Ground................43 C3
Verona Cinema..........................44 B2

**SHOPPING** (pp101–4)
Bracewell..................................45 D2
Calibre.....................................46 D3
Collette Dinnigan.......................47 D2
Hogarth Galleries Aboriginal Art
Centre.....................................48 C2
Leona Edmiston.........................49 D2
Morrissey..................................50 D2
Paddington Market....................51 D2
Scanlan & Theodore...................52 D3

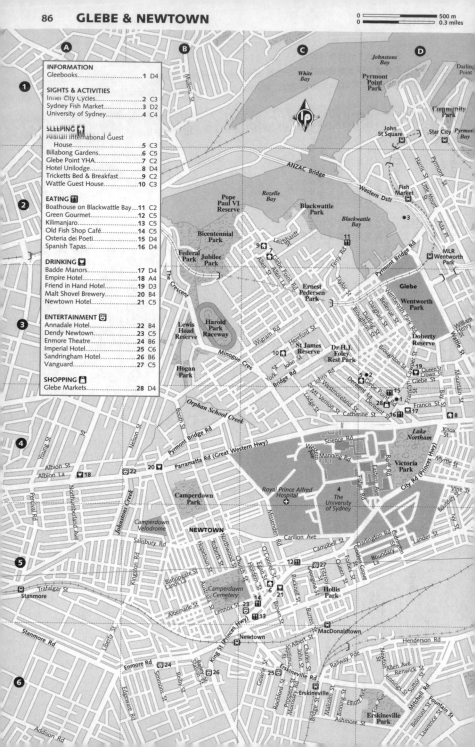

INFORMATION
Gleebooks..................................1  D4

SIGHTS & ACTIVITIES
Inner City Cycles........................2  C3
Sydney Fish Market......................3  D2
University of Sydney.....................4  C4

SLEEPING
Alishan International Guest
 House.....................................5  C3
Billabong Gardens.......................6  C5
Glebe Point YHA.........................7  C2
Hotel Unilodge...........................8  D4
Tricketts Bed & Breakfast..............9  C2
Wattle Guest House....................10  C3

EATING
Boathouse on Blackwattle Bay....11  C2
Green Gourmet..........................12  C5
Kilimanjaro..............................13  C5
Old Fish Shop Café.....................14  C5
Osteria dei Poeti.......................15  D4
Spanish Tapas..........................16  D4

DRINKING
Badde Manors..........................17  D4
Empire Hotel............................18  A4
Friend in Hand Hotel...................19  D3
Malt Shovel Brewery...................20  B4
Newtown Hotel.........................21  C5

ENTERTAINMENT
Annadale Hotel..........................22  B4
Dendy Newtown.........................23  C5
Enmore Theatre.........................24  B6
Imperial Hotel...........................25  C6
Sandringham Hotel.....................26  B6
Vanguard................................27  C5

SHOPPING
Glebe Markets...........................28  D4

0 ——— 600 m
0 ——— 0.4 miles

(Continued from page 75)

## Newtown
### BUDGET
**Billabong Gardens** (Map p86; ☎ 9550 3236; www.billa bonggardens.com.au; 5-11 Egan St; dm/s $25/49, d $66-80; Ⓟ Ⓠ Ⓡ) This enduring motel/hostel offers a broader experience than most backpacker joints, with travellers, touring rock bands and urbanites of all persuasions lobbing up on the doorstep. Rooms come with or without bathrooms, encircling a central solar-heated pool.

## Balmain
### BUDGET
**Balmain Lodge** (Map pp76-7; ☎ 9810 3700; fax 9810 1500; 415 Darling St; s/d $80; Ⓟ) Rotating around a ferny courtyard on Balmain's Darling St backbone, the no-fuss, shared-facility rooms here have kitchenettes, TV and DVD and not much chutzpah. But you're not here to sit in your room, are you? Balmain has enough pubs, cafés and restaurants to keep you entertained for weeks. Two disabled access rooms; kid-free zone.

## Bondi
### BUDGET
**Bondi Sands** (Map p87; ☎ 1800 026 634; www.bondi sands.com; 252 Campbell Pde; dm/d incl breakfast from $20/50; Ⓠ) Just 60m from the sand, Bondi Sands was on a highway to hell before the new owners steered it back from the brink. Rooms are simple and clean with shared bathrooms; a few have stunning views – ask for No 7, 8, 17 or 18. If you miss out, head for the roof terrace.

**Bondi Beachouse YHA** (Map p87; ☎ 9365 2088; www.bondibeachouse.com.au; 63 Fletcher St; dm/s/d/f from $22/70/80/110; Ⓟ Ⓠ) A short stroll from the beach, Bondi Beachouse has clued-up staff, a pool table, TV rooms, barbecue, free play stuff (surfboards, snorkels, etc) and Tamarama Beach views from the rooftop spa. It's a friendly, clean, sunnyside-up kinda joint. Bus 380 from Circular Quay stops nearby.

**Indy's Surfside Bondi** (Map p87; ☎ 9365 4900, www .surfsidebackpackers.com.au; 35a Hall St; dm/d $25/65; Ⓠ) Not for the mild-mannered, beer-stained Indy's is Bondi Party Central, with enormous psychedelic surf murals, big-screen TVs and frenetic communal areas smelling vaguely of illicit herbs. Security is tight, preventing the whole street from crashing the party.

**Sinclairs of Bondi** (Map p87; ☎ 9338 9911; www .sinclairsbondi.com.au; 11 Bennett St; dm $28; s $50-80; d & tw

incl breakfast $66-90; t $110-127, Ⓟ Ⓠ) High on the hill above Bondi Beach, this austere-looking house has 25 rooms with varying bed configurations to suit you or your bus of merry pranksters. It's clean, quiet and low-key; stay elsewhere if you're in party mode.

### MIDRANGE
**Beach Road Hotel** (Map p87; ☎ 9130 7247; brh bondi@bigpond.com; 71 Beach Rd; s/d $70/85; Ⓧ) This chipper hotel is part of a big, boxy pub two blocks back from the beach. Nautical décor surfs through the bars, eateries and nightclub to the rooms, which are clean and bright with TV and decent bathrooms. Lose yourself (or any number of people) in the massive beds. Things get rowdy after dark (good or bad, it's up to you).

**Hotel Bondi** (Map p87; ☎ 9130 3271; www.hotelbondi .com.au; 178 Campbell Pde; s/d/tr from $50/100/130; Ⓟ Ⓧ) Let it all hang out at the landmark 'Pink Palace' on Bondi Beach. Small, tidy rooms have wardrobe-sized private bathrooms and faux-colonial furnishings, and sometimes aren't far enough from the drunken hordes downstairs. Still, if you have a beach view, you'll be laughing.

**Bondi Beach B&B** (Map p87; ☎ 9365 6522; www .bondibeach-bnb.com.au; 110 Roscoe St; s/d/tw/f incl breakfast $100/150/150/250; Ⓟ) Owners Nadia and Michael go all-out to make this place feel like your own home (only cleaner, and more Mediterranean). You're close to all the good stuff in Bondi, but you can also find a park. Ask about room-only rates and low season discounts.

### TOP END
**Ravesi's** (Map p87; ☎ 9365 4422; www.ravesis.com.au; 118 Campbell Pde; d $125-295, ste $245-450; Ⓧ Ⓠ) Ravesi's fits into the Bondi scene like a briefcase on a beach, but the shaggy, salty surfset don't seem to mind the suits necking Euro beers at the bar. Upstairs, the 16 chocolate-and-cream rooms are sophisticated, many with balconies and ocean views.

## Coogee
### BUDGET
**Wizard of Oz Backpackers** (Map p87; ☎ 9315 7876; www.wizardofoz.com.au; 172 Coogee Bay Rd; dm $22-44; Ⓠ) In a refurbished California bungalow a few hundred metres up the yellow brick road from the beach, this laid-back place is painted out in a muted, undersea palette, perhaps in an effort to subdue Coogee's incessant party

vibe. Dorms house four to 14 slumberers; communal areas (centring around the barbecue and big-screen TV) are lively.

**Grand Pacific Private Hotel** (Map p87; ☎ 9665 6301; fax 9665 6203; cnr Beach & Carr Sts; s/d/tr with shared bathrooms from $35/45/65) In *no* way is this place anywhere near grand, but oddly charming in a decaying, down-at-heel, Charles Bukowski kind of way. And the beachside location is sensational! Grab that person you're having a dirty affair with (having bumped off their spouse) and hole up for a seedy seaside weekend straight from a true-crime novel.

**Coogee Beachside Accommodation** (Map p87; ☎ 9315 8511; www.sydneybeachside.com.au; 178 Coogee Bay Rd; d & tw $75) Run by the folks from Wizard of Oz up the road, Beachside offers simple, clean doubles and twins with tidy shared bathrooms in a converted house. If you're in Sydney for a while, they also have one-, two- and three-bed apartments for longer stays.

### MIDRANGE

**Coogee Bay Boutique Hotel** (Map p87; ☎ 9665 0000; 9 Vicar St; d $100-250, P 😣 ) Above the impossibly effervescent Coogee Bay Hotel are casual, old-school pub rooms, plus fancier, spacious suites in a newer wing on Vicar St. All rooms have private bathrooms, fridge and TV – bring earplugs for the older rooms if you don't want to lip-synch to the bands downstairs.

**ourpick Dive Hotel** (Map p87; ☎ 9665 5538; www .divehotel.com.au; 234 Arden St; d & tw incl breakfast $150-220; 🖳 ) Dive into Coogee for this impeccable beachside midranger, about as far from being a dive as it is from the city. Plush purple and green carpets, huge comfy beds, TVs and private bathrooms in every room, 50m to the beach – the bus ride from town is a small price to pay.

## Manly
### BUDGET

**Manly Backpackers** (Map p88; ☎ 9977 3411, 1800 662 500; www.manlybackpackers.com.au; 24 Raglan St; dm/d/apt $34/80/180; P 🖳 ) Manly's most reliable budget option, this converted ambulance station is a complex upstairs/downstairs affair with plenty of beds, boozy nocturnal activities, international staff and enormous kitchens. The best rooms open onto balconies; studio apartments (in a separate building) are perfect for small groups. Winter rates plummet.

**Manly Beach House** (Map p88; ☎ 9977 7050; www .manlybeachhouse.com.au; 179 Pittwater Rd; s/d/tr $50/60/70;

(P 🖳 ) Readers recommend this homely, mega-friendly, good-value option, a four-minute walk from the beach. Polite management prides itself on making sure you're comfortable and have all the requisite local info. Shared facilities are clean and serviceable.

### MIDRANGE

**101 Addison Road** (Map p88; ☎ 9977 6216; www.bb -manly.com; 101 Addison Rd; s/d $100/150) Behind a huge frangipanni tree, this quaint four-star B&B has two romantic rooms and snug communal areas. If it's not beach weather, plunk on the grand piano ivories, shuffle some rooks and knights around or have a twang on the guitar. There are only two rooms, so book ahead.

**Manly Paradise** (Map p88; ☎ 9977 5799; www.manly paradise.com.au; 54 North Steyne; motel d $110-165, apt $220-400; P 😣 😣 ) Feel the salt on your skin at these comfortable apartments sleeping five, with balconies overlooking Manly's ocean beach. There's a heated rooftop pool, spa, sauna, half-court tennis and cable TV. Grab an '80s-style motel room (plenty of plastic and peach) if you're feeling more 'road'.

**Periwinkle Guest House** (Map p88; ☎ 9977 4668; www.periwinkle.citysearch.com.au; 18-19 E Esplanade; s/d incl breakfast $135/165; P ) This lavishly restored Victorian manor faces the sunset across Manly Cove. Twelve rooms with private bathrooms are elegant and well appointed, and there's a stylish, cosy kitchen. If your wallet can stand the heat, avoid the ground floor rooms facing the courtyard which can get a bit stuffy.

### TOP END

**Manly Pacific** (Map p88; ☎ 9977 7666; www.accorhotels .com.au; 55 North Steyne; d from $190; P 😣 🖳 😣 ) Right on Manly's ocean beach, this dapper mid-rise hotel is 15 minutes by JetCat from Circular Quay and a million miles from the city's withering hustle. Check the surf from oceanfront balconies, or hit the rooftop pool if you don't want sand in your laptop.

## North Shore
### BUDGET

**Collaroy Beachhouse YHA** (Map p108; ☎ 9981 1177; www .sydneybeachouse.com.au; 4 Collaroy St, Collaroy; dm $20-39, d & tw $54-80, f $84-130; P 🖳 😣 ) If you're around the Northern Beaches, the new owners at this clean, airy hostel will make you feel at home. There are free surfboards, bikes and snorkelling gear, and a rooftop pool. Pizza, barbecue and movie nights keep things happening.

## CAMPING IT UP

If you're sleeping in your campervan or camping, there are depressingly few places close to central Sydney where you can park or pitch for the night. If the surf's up, the enthusiastically managed **Sydney Lakeside Holiday Park** (Map p108; ☎ 9913 7845; www.sydneylakeside.com.au; Lake Park Rd, Narrabeen; unpowered/powered sites per 2 people $45/50, cabins from $140; P ⚒ ▣ ) is a beachy option, 26km north of Sydney. If another night on the sleeping mat doesn't appeal, they have dozens of air-conditioned cabins.

Also on the North Shore, **Lane Cove River Tourist Park** (Map pp76-7; ☎ 9888 9133; www.lcrtp .com; Plassey Rd, North Ryde; unpowered/powered sites per 2 people $30/36, cabins from $125; P ⚒ ▣ ⚒ ) is closer to the city (10km out) with 150 caravan sites, plus cabins. Cool off in the pool when city temperatures swelter.

Around 15km south of the city, **Grand Pines Tourist Park** (Map p108; ☎ 9529 7329; www.thegrandpines .com.au; 289 The Grand Pde, Sans Souci; powered sites per 2 people $40, cabins from $69; P ▣ ) doesn't have tent sites, but you can park your campervan or bunk down in a cabin or on-site caravan.

**Glenferrie Lodge** (Map pp76-7; ☎ 9955 1685, 1800 121 011; www.glenferrielodge.com; 12a Carabella St, Kirribilli; dm/s/d/f incl breakfast $40/79/99/159; ▣ ) Outside this barrel-chested 1880s house is a ridiculous sculpture that someone unearthed in their backyard. Ignore it (and the equally ridiculous prime minister down the street) and head inside where clean rooms, spotless shared bathrooms and helpful management await. Close to Milsons Point train station and Kirribilli ferry pier.

## EATING

Other Australian cities hate to admit it, but Sydney – with its multicultural melange, abundant fresh produce and geographic assets – has won the food trifecta. Adelaide may have the great wines, Melbourne the café culture and Hobart the seafood, but Sydney has it all, and right on Sydney Harbour.

Start the day with a strong espresso and a plate of inner-city ricotta hotcakes, then chow into the fresh catch of the day at a waterfront restaurant for lunch. Rise above it all with a glittering harbour view and a bold Mod-Oz dinner, wolf down a pie and sauce at the footy or after a night on the tiles, or spend the wee hours lingering over a chandelier-and-laminate supper in a Chinatown food den.

At the top end, celebrity chefs plate up mini-masterpieces for wealthy corporate crowds. Those on tighter budgets need not despair – thousands of cafés, bistros and restaurants offer innovative, quality meals at moderate prices. When all else fails, go for the great Aussie fish and chips by the beach.

## City Centre, The Rocks & Circular Quay

**Bodhi** (Map pp78-9; ☎ 9360 2523; Cook & Phillip Park, 2-4 College St; yum cha $5-8, mains $6-18; ☺ lunch daily, dinner Tue-Sun) Bodhi scores high for its cool design and leafy disposition. Quick-fire waiters bounce off stainless-steel minimalism inside and slatted wooden tables and umbrellas outside. Have a swim at the pool next door before daily *yum cha*, a relaxed and value-for-money affair. The barbecue buns rule.

**Mother Chu's Vegetarian Kitchen** (Map pp78-9; ☎ 9283 2828; 367 Pitt St; mains $8-15; ☺ lunch & dinner Mon-Sat) Shimmering in plastique splendour beneath the monorail, Mother Chu's blends vegetarian Taiwanese, Japanese and Chinese influences to ensure the perfect tofu or claypot hit. There's not much going on in terms of ambience, but the veg-lovers don't seem to mind.

**Sailors Thai Canteen** (Map pp78-9; ☎ 9251 2466; 106 George St; mains $16-26; ☺ lunch-8pm) Wedge yourself into a gap between arts-community operators, politicians and media manoeuvrers at Sailors' long communal zinc-topped table and order the Chang Mai chicken curry. The balcony tables fill up fast, but fortune might be smiling on you.

**One Alfred Street** (Map pp78-9; ☎ 9241 4636; 1 Alfred St; mains around $17; ☺ breakfast, lunch & dinner) An unexpected gem among the morass of Circular Quay fast-food joints, One Alfred Street serves up classics like slow-cooked Wagyu beef with potato and parsnip flakes, and quality fish and chips. Also great for a morning caffeine fix or a lazy afternoon vino (Antipodean wines only!).

**Quay** (Map pp78-9; ☎ 9251 5600; Level 3, Overseas Passenger Terminal, Circular Quay W; mains $33-54; ☺ lunch

Tue-Fri, dinner daily) With iconic Sydney on view, sitting on the balcony next to the teary, streamer-hurling non-embarkers at the passenger terminal is surreal. Equally euphoric is Quay's stylish service, outstanding wine list and Peter Gilmore's cooking (try the poached quail with truffle custard).

**Guillaume at Bennelong** (Map pp78-9; ☎ 9241 1999; Sydney Opera House; mains $35-42; ☺ lunch Thu & Fri, dinner Mon-Sat) Turn the old 'dinner-and-show' cliché into something meaningful at the Sydney Opera House. Snuggle into a banquette and enjoy acclaimed chef Guillaume Brahimi's masterful cuisine. His basil-infused tuna with mustard seed and soy vinaigrette has fans hollering operatically all over town.

**Aria** (Map pp78-9; ☎ 9252 2555; 1 Macquarie St; mains $44-52; ☺ lunch Mon-Fri, dinner daily) Aria is the star in Sydney's fine-dining firmament, an award-winning combination of chef Matthew Moran's stellar dishes, awesome Opera House views (is there a sexier building?) and faultless service. The mouth-watering lamb rack is hard to overlook. Pre- and after-theatre supper menu available.

**Rockpool** (Map pp78-9; ☎ 9252 1888; 107 George St, The Rocks; mains $49-60; ☺ dinner Tue-Sat) Behind an unassuming green façade, Rockpool is arguably Sydney's best restaurant (oh, how they argue…). Chef Neil Perry's modern seafood creations continue to wow the critics – expect crafty, contemporary cuisine with Asian influences, faultless service and an alluring wine list. Order Perry's signature stir-fried mud crab omelette.

## Chinatown & Darling Harbour

**Chinese Noodle Restaurant** (Map pp78-9; ☎ 9281 9051; Shop 7, Prince Centre, 8 Quay St, Chinatown (entry from Thomas St); mains $7-12; ☺ lunch & dinner) It's sweaty, shoulder-to-shoulder eating beneath wreaths of plastic grapes in this busy noodle nook, the stringy fare made fresh daily. The combination dish looks like spaghetti bolognaise on steroids – masses of thick wheat noodles, pork, shredded cucumber and lashings of chilli and black vinegar.

**BBQ King** (Map pp78-9; ☎ 9267 2433; 18-20 Goulburn St, Chinatown; mains $10-30; ☺ lunch & dinner) Low on ambience but big on flavour, the King serves up royal portions of roast duck, suckling pig and other Cantonese staples. You might need a Tsing Tao or three to stay sane amidst the mildly obnoxious chaos. Take-away bald glazed ducks next door; open late.

**Blackbird** (Map pp78-9; ☎ 9283 7385; Balcony, Cockle Bay Wharf, Darling Harbour; mains $12-20 ☺ breakfast, lunch & dinner) This place veritably thrums from the minute it opens its doors for breakfast. Funky young staff cruise the cool interior delivering hearty bowls of pasta, New York–style pizzas from the hot-stone oven and fat triangles of cake. Perfect to fuel up before or after a big night out.

**Chinta Ria, Temple of Love** (Map pp78-9; ☎ 9264 3211; L2 Cockle Bay Wharf, Darling Harbour; mains $15-26; ☺ lunch Mon-Sat, dinner daily) Swirling choreographically around an enormous concrete Buddha, Chinta Ria's temple-in-the-round offers zingy Malaysian hawker-style food at reasonable prices. Go with a rabble of friends for Hokkien noodles, sambal prawns, seafood laksa, super-slippery fried *kuay teow* and flaky roti bread.

**Golden Century** (Map pp78-9; ☎ 9212 3901; 393-99 Sussex St, Chinatown; mains $15-50; ☺ lunch & dinner) Open until 4am, this frenetic restaurant cooks crustaceans straight from the fish tanks displaying your nervous-looking dinner, forming a window-wall to the street. Splash out on the whole lobster cooked in ginger and shallots: from-tank-to-net-to-kitchen-to-table.

**Zaaffran** (Map pp78-9; ☎ 9211 8900; 2nd fl, 345 Harbourside, Darling Harbour; mains $18-34; ☺ lunch & dinner) In a city with a gazillion cheap Indian joints, Zaaffran stands out. Authentic and innovative curries are served up in front of awesome views across Darling Harbour's sparkle and sheen. Book a balcony seat and launch into the beef vindaloo. Good vegetarian selection too.

## Darlinghurst, Surry Hills & East Sydney

**Bar Reggio** (Map pp78-9; ☎ 9332 1129; 135 Crown St, East Sydney; mains $10-15; ☺ lunch & dinner Mon-Sat) Blink and you'll miss this classic, dimly-lit little Italian diner in East Sydney's 'Little Italy' district. The walls are plastered with Ferrari flags and Rome murals; the menu board in the window has been there so long the lettering has started to flake off. Pasta, pizza, meat and fish dishes have stood the test of time. Closed Sundays (church!).

**Onde** (Map p82; ☎ 9331 8749; 345 Liverpool St, Darlinghurst; mains $18-26; ☺ dinner) Culturally enriching, palate-pleasing and great value – no wonder Onde is always packed. Some Darlinghursters eat here three times a week for the great service, adventurous wine list and trad faves like duck terrine, lamb tenderloin and buttermilk berry pudding. No bookings.

**Longrain** (Map p84; ☎ 9280 2888; 85 Commonwealth St, Surry Hills; mains $18-36; ☟ lunch Mon-Fri, dinner Mon-Sat) Longrain makes serving dozens of louche city diners looks easy. Inside a century-old, wedge-shaped printing-press building, urbanites slurp down delicacies such as red venison and snakebean curry and fish dishes deserving of their own church. Cocktails at the bar afterwards; no reservations.

**bills** (Map p82; ☎ 9360 9631; 433 Liverpool St, Darlinghurst; mains $19-25; ☟ lunch & dinner Mon-Sat) Sydney adores Bill Granger's sunny eatery with its newspaper-strewn communal table. Dishes such as sweetcorn fritters with roast tomato, spinach and bacon are equally adorable. Also at Surry Hills (Map p84; ☎ 9360 4762; 359 Crown St), and Woollahra (Map p84; ☎ 9328 7997; 118 Queen St).

**Billy Kwong** (Map p84; ☎ 9332 3300; 3/355 Crown St, Surry Hills; mains $19-42; ☟ dinner) Chef Kylie Kwong's novel take on Chinese cuisine soon explains why this hip eating house is always so busy. You can't go wrong with staples like spicy, diced, fried green beans with hoisin and garlic, or a generous serve of Kylie's signature dish, the crispy-skin duck with plum sauce.

**our pick** **Wildrice** (Map p84; ☎ 8354 0088; Shop 1, 160 Flinders St, Darlinghurst; mains $20-28; ☟ dinner Mon-Sat) In Darlinghurst's obscure southern reaches, Wildrice is a glorious exaltation of modern Thai cooking. Rice arrives in moulded conical mounds, which you smother with red chicken-breast curry and grilled sweet-chilli scampi. Coriander by the bushel; absolutely sensational.

## Kings Cross, Potts Point & Woolloomooloo

**Harry's Café de Wheels** (Map p82; ☎ 9357 3074; Cowper Wharf Rd, Woolloomooloo; mains $5-10; ☟ breakfast, lunch & dinner) For over 50 years, cab drivers, sailors and boozed-up nocturnals have slurred orders for pea-and-pie floaters over Harry's famous counter. Sit on a milk crate overlooking the hulking Woolloomooloo warships and inhale a 'Tiger' (pie, peas, mashed potatoes and gravy). Deadly.

**Fratelli Paradiso** (Map p82; ☎ 9357 1744; 12 Challis Ave, Potts Point; mains $12-25; ☟ breakfast & lunch daily, dinner Mon-Fri) This stylish bistro-bakery has them queuing at the door. The intimate, mod room showcases seasonal Italian dishes cooked with Mediterranean zing. Lots of busy black-clad waiters, lots of Italian chatter, lots of oversized sunglasses – somehow Rome doesn't seem so far away...

**Hugo's Bar Pizza** (Map p82; ☎ 9357 4018; 33 Bayswater Rd, Kings Cross; mains $18-24; ☟ dinner) Punchy little brother of Hugo's Lounge upstairs, this indoor/outdoor neighbourhood nook has been wowing pizza fans with its delicious discs and home-style Italian fare. The marble-fronted bar and sunken velvet lounge are luxurious, but the menu won't break the bank.

## Paddington, Woollahra & Eastern Suburbs

**Gusto** (Map p84; ☎ 9361 5640; 2a Heely St, Five Ways, Paddington; mains $6-14; ☟ breakfast, lunch & dinner) Busy to the point of embarrassment for neighbouring businesses, Gusto does things with gusto. Egg-ham-and-tomato-breakfast rolls nourish skinny actresses on the footpath tables; the deli doles out cheeses, pesto, hams and olives with enthused abandon.

**Jones the Grocer** (Map p84; ☎ 9362 1222; 68 Moncur St, Woollahra; mains $10-15; ☟ breakfast & lunch) Bob the Builder, Jones the Grocer – some things just make sense. JTG offers high-end groceries, cookbooks and gourmet goodies galore. Munch into a caramel slice with a serious coffee at the café, then double wrap some double brie and hotfoot it to Centennial Park for a picnic.

**Arthur's Pizza** (Map p84; ☎ 9332 2220; 260 Oxford St, Paddington; mains $10-25; ☟ lunch Sat & Sun, dinner daily) For some reason Arthur's sign was originally installed upside down. We liked it that way, but in a fit of reverse rebellion it's been turned rightside up. Don't let this abject conformity deter you from Arthur's pizzas, which continue to rebel. Try the 'Zorro' (olives, ricotta, red onion, spinach and semidried tomato).

**Doyles on the Beach** (Map pp76-7; ☎ 9337 2007; 11 Marine Pde, Watsons Bay; mains $29-51; ☟ lunch & dinner) King of Sydney seafood for so long, you might think Doyles is resting on its laurels. Nevertheless, it ain't your average fish-and-chipper, and catching the harbour ferry to Watsons Bay for a seafood lunch is a quintessential Sydney experience.

## Glebe

**Osteria dei Poeti** (Map p86; ☎ 9571 8955; 73 Glebe Point Rd; mains $17-28; ☟ lunch Fri & Sat, dinner Mon-Sat) Fostering 'benign benevolence' through stomach satisfaction, the talkative 'Tavern of Poets' serves unpretentious, home-style Italian that's poetic enough to be beyond most domestic kitchens. If the occasional poetry readings are overly florid, head for the deck outside.

Spanish Tapas (Map p86; ☎ 9571 9005; 26 Glebe Point Rd; tapas $10-14, mains $20-23; ☒ lunch Thu-Sat, dinner daily) This is a good-time restaurant: shared tapas plates, spirited music, raucous diners and waiters who say, 'Yezz, we jave a table foil yu!' Cheap jugs of sangria dissolve party resistance and fire you up for flamenco-dancing displays.

Boathouse on Blackwattle Bay (Map p86; ☎ 9518 9011; Ferry Rd, Glebe; mains $39-43; ☒ lunch & dinner Tue-Sun) The best restaurant in Glebe, and one of the best seafood restaurants in Sydney. Offerings range from oysters so fresh you'd think you shucked them yourself to a snapper pie that'll go straight to the top of your favourite dish list. Anzac Bridge views; reservations essential.

## Newtown

Kilimanjaro (Map p86; ☎ 9557 4565; 280 King St; mains $10-13; ☒ lunch Wed-Sun, dinner daily) Its cosy tables, carved-wooden bowls, saffron aromas and cheery atmosphere will raise your appetite high above the Serengeti. Authentic dishes, such as the Yassa (chicken on the bone marinated in spicy tomato sauce) are utterly filling.

Green Gourmet (Map p86; ☎ 9519 5330; 115 King St; mains $13-15; ☒ lunch & dinner) This is a self-serve, pay-per-kilo, kind-to-animals eatery, plating up Chinese-Malaysian vegetarian at affordable prices. On weekends, grab a few morsels of cruelty-free *yum cha* and wash it down with one of the excellent teas on offer. Alcohol-free too.

## Balmain

Kazbah (Map pp76-7; ☎ 6555 7067; 37a Darling St; mains $33-35; ☒ breakfast & lunch Sat & Sun, dinner Wed-Sat) Rock the Kazbah for weekend brunch (bookings essential), or a peppy dinner with the windows folded out to the hot summer street. Generous serves feature plenty of eggplant, tahini, hummus and cumin; leave room for the Turkish delight icecream with blueberries and currant vodka.

## Leichhardt

Bar Italia (Map pp76-7; ☎ 9560 9981; 169-71 Norton St; mains $14-24; ☒ breakfast, lunch & dinner) This enduringly popular restaurant serves fabulous pasta and famous *gelato*, the essential accessory for a Norton St *passeggiata* (stroll). A wisteria-hung courtyard, Italian soccer posters, good honest food and a little red wine make for an authentic experience. Don't expect slick Italian design – the pleasure is in the food.

Grappa (Map pp76-7; ☎ 9560 6090, Shop 1, 267-277 Norton St; mains $30-40; ☒ lunch Tue-Fri & Sun, dinner daily) Grappa's open kitchen, snazzy bar and cream-leather seats provide the setting for rich, succulent dishes (such as baked snapper in rock-salt crust) and bounteous wood-fired pizzas. If it's warm, sit outside on the terrace, sip chianti (or some grappa) and think of Tuscany. Ahhh, Tuscany…

## Bondi

Gertrude & Alice (Map p87; ☎ 9130 5155; 40 Hall St; mains $10-15; ☒ breakfast, lunch & dinner) This second-hand bookshop/café is so un-Bondi – there's not a model or surfer in sight! Students and academics hang out reading, sipping chai tea and acting like Americans in Paris. Join them for a mezze platter and theological discussion around communal tables in shambolic book-lined rooms.

Gelbison (Map p87; ☎ 9130 4042; 10 Lamrock Ave; mains $10-18; ☒ dinner) Legendary enough for a local rock band to name themselves after it, never-changing Gelbison entertains families, backpackers, locals and visiting movie stars (is Gelbison an anagram of Mel Gibson?) with great-value pizza and pasta. Sit with the surfers over a steaming bowl of prawn-and-mushroom fettuccine or a 'magic boot' pizza.

Sean's Panaroma (Map p87; ☎ 9365 4924; 270 Campbell Pde; mains $24-35; ☒ lunch Sat & Sun, dinner Wed-Sat) One of Sydney's more romantic dinner spots, with ocean vistas, creative dishes, friendly staff and celebrity attendees. Sean Moran's restless menu lets you eat with the seasons. Suckling pig roasted with cabbage, pear, sweet potato and anise is a winter night's feast. In summer, succumb to seafood.

North Bondi Italian Food (Map p87; ☎ 9300 4400; 118-20 Ramsgate Ave; mains $26-29; ☒ lunch Wed-Sun, dinner daily) Expansive windows float your eyes beyond the terrace to the sighing North Bondi swell. You won't hear any sighs inside (it's all hard surfaces and conversations) but the pasta, seafood, soups and salads engage your other senses. Try the generous wild boar *papardelle*. Wines by the glass.

Bondi Icebergs (Map p87; ☎ 9365 9000; 1 Notts Ave; mains $35-75; ☒ lunch & dinner Tue-Sun) Poised above the famous swimming pool, Icebergs' views sweep across the Bondi Beach arc to the sea. Jacketed, bow-tied waiters deliver fresh seafood and steaks cooked with élan. The wine list is superb, and the bar, overlooking the Campbell Pde lights, is never boring for a beer.

## Coogee & Bronte

**Siam Spice** (Map p87; ☎ 9665 5077; 215 Coogee Bay Rd, Coogee; mains $10-20; ☺ lunch & dinner) Sydney and cheap Thai are synonymous, but the food here sidesteps the cliché by virtue of sheer quality. Surrounded by Southeast Asian décor, adorable dishes like chunky beef *massaman* curry and grilled king prawns with aromatic salad and chilli jam will spice up your life.

**Swell** (Map p87; ☎ 9386 5001; 465 Bronte Rd, Bronte; mains $11-28; ☺ breakfast, lunch & dinner) Pull up a pew next to Anthony LaPaglia for seaside Swell's spanking day-turns-to-night menu. Greet the day with poached eggs, pumpkin, feta and spinach, linger into lunch with a snazzy steak sandwich and return at dinnertime for the salt-and-pepper squid.

**Barzura** (Map p87; ☎ 9665 5546; 64 Carr St, Coogee; mains $17-26; ☺ breakfast, lunch & dinner) Frequented by retired Australian cricketers in dark sunglasses, Barzura's views have to be the best of any café in Sydney (if not the country!). The sunbaked stretch north along Coogee beach to Bondi is a stunner, as are deliciously uncomplicated salads, pides, pasta dishes and generous breakfasts, all served with a smile.

## North Shore & Manly

**Bathers' Pavilion Café** (Map pp76-7; ☎ 9969 5050; 4 The Esplanade, Balmoral; mains $21-32; ☺ breakfast, lunch & dinner) Romantic Spanish Mission–style architecture, sweeping harbour views and outstanding Mod-Oz food collide at one of Sydney's most timeless eateries. You might want to dine with the snooty Balmoral set at the restaurant next door for far less democratic prices. Then again, you might not...

**Bower Restaurant** (Map p88; ☎ 9977 5451; cnr Marine Pde & Bower La, Manly; mains $24-30; ☺ breakfast & lunch daily, dinner Thu) Follow the foreshore path east from Manly's ocean beach to this little white food room, within spray's breath of tiny Fairy Bower beach. The 'Big Bower Breakfast' ($17) is a knockout, Mod Oz mains are delicious, it's BYO, and they're not afraid to let Olivia Newton John wail from the stereo.

**Le Kiosk** (Map p88; ☎ 9977 4122; 1 Marine Pde, Shelly Beach, Manly; mains $29-37; ☺ lunch daily, dinner Fri-Sun) 'Le Kiosk' sounds ugly but defines romance – a little sandstone cottage, subtle lighting, open fireplace and the lull of lapping waves. The

food proves a worthy paramour, swoon over snapper fillet with sautéed calamari, bacon, chilli and cauliflower. Solid vegetarian options too.

**Aqua Dining** (Map pp76-7; ☎ 9964 9998; cnr Paul & Northcliff Sts, Milsons Point; mains $35-38; ☺ lunch & dinner) Perched above the North Sydney Olympic Pool, Aqua Dining's muted mushroom hues play second-fiddle to bridge and harbour views, while the service is superior – that rare mix of courteous, knowledgeable (the wine list beggars belief) and amiable. Yell enthusiastically for the saddle of lamb.

# DRINKING

Pubs are a crucial part of the Sydney social scene, varying from the traditional (elaborate 19th-century affairs with pressed tin ceilings, or cavernous Art Deco joints with tiled walls), to the modern and minimalist. Bars are generally more stylish and urbane, often with a dress code (oh-so smart casual).

There are some rambling old pubs in The Rocks, but determining just how old they are is an inexact science. Things get rowdy here on weekends and St Patrick's Day (17 March). For more stylish surrounds and long cocktail lists, join the after-work booze hounds in the city and Circular Quay. Unless otherwise specified, admission to the bars and pubs below is free.

Twenty-four-hour-party people head for Darlinghurst and Kings Cross – its trashy main drag, Darlinghurst Rd, has plenty of drinking (and stripping) options, though there are some stylish speakeasies around here too. Glitzy fashionistas populate Paddington's pubs; students and artists drink in Surry Hills. The inner west is great for a low-key schooner – Balmain, Glebe and Newtown have plenty of decent boozers.

Wide-awake caffeine strips include Darlinghurst Rd and Victoria St in Darlinghurst, Newtown's King Street and Glebe Point Rd.

## Bars

### CITY CENTRE

**Zeta** (Map pp78-9; ☎ 9265 6070; 4th fl, Hilton Hotel, 488 George St; ☺ 5pm-2am Mon-Fri, to 3.30am Sat) Ride the Hilton escalators up to Zeta, which captivates a chic young city crew with its white vinyl lounges, discrete curtained booths (what *was* Snoop Dog smoking in there?) and enormous gas inferno. Sip grilled fruit cocktails and eyeball the QVB dome from the terrace.

**Tank Stream Bar** (Map pp78–9; ☎ 9240 3109; 1 Tank Stream Way; ☼ 4pm-midnight Mon-Fri, from noon Fri) After-work suits and secretaries get high and heady poised over Sydney's original water supply. The Tank Stream runs thick with bottled beer, wine and cocktails, and the corporate mob can't get enough. Neither could Robbie Williams.

**Establishment** (Map pp78–9; ☎ 9240 3000; 252 George St; ☼ 11am-late Mon-Fri, 6pm-late Sat) Establishment's cashed-up crush proves the art of swilling cocktails after a hard, city day is not lost. Sit at the majestic marble bar, in the swish courtyard or be absorbed by a leather lounge as stock-brokers scribble their phone numbers on the backs of coasters for flirty city chicks.

**Bar Europa** (Map pp78–9; ☎ 9232 3377; Basement, 82 Elizabeth St; ☼ 4pm-late Tue-Fri, 8pm-late Sat) Basement vibe, subtle lighting and three debonair rooms divided by sexy screens cement Europa's rep-utation as an intimate, clubby hideaway for inner-city professionals. Sip a Sydneysider Sour as DJs play laid-back funk, sigh, and wonder what he/she is doing now…

### KINGS CROSS & DARLINGHURST

**Victoria Room** (Map p82; ☎ 9357 4488; Level 1, 235 Vic-toria St, Darlinghurst; ☼ 6pm-midnight Tue-Thu, to 2am Fri & Sat, 2pm-midnight Sun) Plush chesterfields, Art Nouveau wallpaper, dark-wood panelling and bamboo screens – the Victoria Room is the spoilt love child of a 1920s Bombay gin pal-ace and a Hong Kong opium den. Don your white linen suit and panama hat and order a Raspberry Debonair.

**Jimmy Lik's** (Map p82; ☎ 8354 1400; 186 Victoria St, Potts Point; ☼ 5pm-midnight) Understated and sub-tle, Jimmy's is very cool, with benches almost as long as the cocktail list (try a Thai-hewn Mekong Mary with chilli *nam jim*). Jimmy's Thai restaurant is next door – there's usually a wait for a seat, but with tasty bar snacks available, who's in a hurry?

**Hugo's Lounge** (Map p82; ☎ 9357 4411; Level 1, 33 Bays-water Rd, Kings Cross; admission $10 Fri, Sat & Sun; ☼ 6.30pm-2am Thu, to 3am Fri-Sun) Upper-crust interiors attract a glossy crowd: media celebs conducting histri-onic conversations in between mobile-phone calls. If it feels like a CD launch you weren't invited to, head to Hugo's Bar Pizza (p93) downstairs for some tasty respite.

### SURRY HILLS

**Mars Lounge** (Map pp78–9; ☎ 9267 6440; 16 Wentworth Ave; ☼ 5pm-midnight Tue, Wed & Sun, to 3am Thu-Sat) Red leather booths; disco-ball reflections catching in the corner of your eye – Mars is *sooo* money. Sip a cocktail and try to stay focussed as you watch the bar staff in action, most of whom seem to be auditioning for a gig in a Justin Timberlake video.

## Cafés

**Bar Coluzzi** (Map p82; ☎ 9380 5420; 322 Victoria St, Darlin-ghurst; ☼ 5am-7pm) Legendary Coluzzi has been infusing Darlinghurst with caffeine for 50 years. The food is fine, but come for the spoon-standing-up-straight-in-the-cup coffee.

**Old Fish Shop Café** (Map p86; ☎ 9519 4295; 239a King St; ☼ 6am-7pm) In a converted fish shop (no prizes for figuring that out), this is Newtown's tattooed, dreadlocked, caffeine-hungry hub. Friendly pierced staff will fix you a double shot as you put your feet up on the cushions in the window and watch the Newtown freak show pass onwards to oblivion.

**Badde Manors** (Map p86; ☎ 9660 3797; 37 Glebe Point Rd; ☼ 8am-midnight Mon-Thu, to 1am Fri & Sat, 9am-mid-night Sun) The feeling's eclectically old-world, but Badde Manors is a new-age kinda café, with cool, composed service – no sign of the alleged bad manners. Dogs sleep blissfully outside, dreaming of the Portuguese custard tarts and steaming lattes behind the glass.

**Café Hernandez** (Map p82; ☎ 9331 2343; 60 Kings Cross Rd, Kings Cross; ☼ 24hr) With some of the best coffee in Sydney, old-school Hernandez has been keeping taxi drivers and arty students awake since the '60s. When it's 3am and the joint's jumping, you'd be forgiven for thinking you're in Madrid. Reconsider your third cup – there's no bathroom.

## Pubs

### THE ROCKS

**Australian Hotel** (Map pp78–9; ☎ 9247 2229; 100 Cumber-land St, The Rocks; ☼ 11.30am-midnight Mon-Sat, to 10pm Sun) This laid-back, good-humoured hotel has an astounding 96 Australian brews on offer. Try to think of four more to hit the century as you wobble through the list. The pub food borders on gourmet, and you can also sleep upstairs if you've had a few too many (p70).

**Lord Nelson Brewery Hotel** (Map pp78–9; ☎ 9251 4044; 19 Kent St, Millers Point Rocks; ☼ 11am-11pm Mon-Sat, noon-10pm Sun) Built in 1841, the 'Nello' claims to be Sydney's oldest pub (or is it the Hero of Waterloo down the road?) The on-site brewery cooks up six robust stouts and ales (don't try them all at once), and there's decent midrange accommodation upstairs (p70).

## WOOLLOOMOOLOO

**Old Fitzroy Hotel** (Map p82; ☎ 9356 3848; 129 Dowling St, Woolloomooloo; ❤ 11am-midnight Mon-Sat, 3-10pm Sun) Is it a pub? A theatre? A bistro? Actually it's all three. Grab a bowl of laksa, assess the acting talent of tomorrow and wash it all down with a beer ($33 the lot). The outdoor deck is unbeatable on a steamy summer night.

**Tilbury Hotel** (Map pp78-9; ☎ 9368 1955; 12-18 Nicholson St, Woolloomooloo; ❤ 8am-midnight Mon-Fri, from 9am Sat, from 10am Sun) Once the dank domain of burly sailors and salty ne'er-do-wells, the Tilbury now sparkles on Sydney's social scene. Yuppies, yachties, suits, gays and straights populate the light, bright interiors, packing the bistro and beer garden on weekends.

## DARLINGHURST & SURRY HILLS

**Darlo Bar** (Map p82; ☎ 9331 3672; 306 Liverpool St, Darlinghurst; ❤ 10am-midnight Mon-Sat, noon-midnight Sun) Occupying its own tiny block, the Darlo's triangular retro room is a magnet for thirsty urban bohemians with something to read or a hankering for pinball or pool. It's pretty much a neighbourhood pub, but it's a very interesting neighbourhood.

**Cricketers Arms** (Map p84; ☎ 9331 3301; 106 Fitzroy St, Surry Hills; ❤ noon-midnight Mon-Sat, noon-10pm Sun) The polysexual Cricketers with its cruisy, cosy vibe is a favourite haunt of arts students, locals, gays and turntable boffins. It's ace for a beer anytime, and there's tapas on tap and open fires for those rare times Sydney that actually gets cold.

**Hollywood Hotel** (Map p84; ☎ 9281 2765; 2 Foster St, Surry Hills; ❤ 11am-midnight Mon-Wed, to 3am Thu-Sat) An inner-city prow-shaped Art Deco gem, the Hollywood hasn't felt the need to buff itself up to a superficial sheen. A mixed (dare we say, bohemian) crowd of Surry Hillbillies gets down to serious beer business. Live jazz Monday to Thursday from 8pm.

**Green Park Hotel** (Map p82; ☎ 9380 5311; 360 Victoria St, Darlinghurst; ❤ 10am-2am Mon-Fri, noon-2am Sat & Sun) The ever-rockin' Green Park has pool tables, a beer garden with funky Dr Seuss lighting and a huge central bar teeming with travellers, gays and pierced locals. Bowie and Queen rule the jukebox.

## PADDINGTON & WOOLLAHRA

**Paddington Inn** (Map p84; ☎ 9380 5277; 338 Oxford St, Paddington; ❤ noon-midnight Sun-Thu, to 1am Fri & Sat) The Paddo's exterior makes stylised use of peeling paint – inside it's all organically

shaped wall nooks, stainless-steel stools and mildly sinister lighting. Good-looking locals elbow around the pool table; the restaurant serves upmarket pub grub.

**Lord Dudley Hotel** (Map p84; ☎ 9327 5399; 236 Jersey Rd, Woollahra; ❤ 11am-11pm Mon-Wed, to midnight Thu-Sat, noon-10pm Sun) Packed with poncy, scarf-wearing MG drivers and block-shouldered Rugby Union types, the Lord Dudley is as close as Sydney gets to an English pub. Dark woody walls; quality beers by the pint.

## BALMAIN & GLEBE

**London Hotel** (Map pp76-7; ☎ 9555 1377; 234 Darling St, Balmain; ❤ 11am-midnight Mon-Sat, noon-10pm Sun) The watery Harbour Bridge views from the London's long balcony above the street are quintessentially Sydney (about as far from London as you can get). There's a great range of Oz beers on tap, plus a few quality Euro interlopers (Heineken, Hoegaarden et al), jovial punters and non-stop rugby on the telly.

**Friend in Hand** (Map p86; ☎ 9660 2326; 58 Cowper St, Glebe; ❤ 10am-late) This place has changed the rules of what's supposed to happen in an Australian pub. Sure, you can drink all the beer you want, but don't be surprised when the eating competitions, water-pistol fights, crab racing, cheesy Joel/John piano men and hula-hoop spin-offs cut into your drinking time.

## BONDI & COOGEE

**Coogee Bay Hotel** (Map p87; ☎ 9665 0000; cnr Coogee Bay Rd & Arden St, Coogee; ❤ 9am-3am Thu-Sat, to midnight Sun, to 1am Mon-Wed) The rambling, rowdy Coogee Bay complex has live music at the legendary Selinas, a beer garden, open-mic nights, comedy, cocktail lounge, sports bar, bistro and bottle shop. Sit on a stool in the window overlooking the beach, sip a cold one and wait for the perfect sunset.

**Beach Road Hotel** (Map p87; ☎ 9130 7247; 71 Beach Rd, Bondi; ❤ 10am-2.30am Mon-Fri, 9am-12.30am Sat, 10am-10pm Sun) Weekends at this big, yellow, boxy pub are a boisterous multilevel alcoholiday, with Bondi types (bronzed, buff and brooding) and woozy out-of-towners playing pool, drinking beer and digging live bands and DJs. Sleep off your hangover upstairs (p89).

## EASTERN SUBURBS

**Watsons Bay Hotel** (Map pp76-7; ☎ 9337 4299; 10 Marine Pde, Watsons Bay; ❤ 10am-midnight) Surrounded by two pricey seafood restaurants (both called Doyles) and a boutique hotel (also called

Doyles), you'll be pleased to know that Doyles' superlative harbour views can also be enjoyed with a jug of beer and a seat on the terrace. Avoid weekends when it's packed to the gills.

### MANLY

**Manly Wharf Hotel** (Map p88; ☎ 9977 1266; E Esplanade; ◷ 11.30am-midnight Mon-Sat, 11am-10pm Sun) On the harbour side of Manly, the fabulously well-designed Manly Wharf Hotel is perfect for sunny afternoon beers. Tuck away a few middys after a salty day combating the surf then pour yourself onto the ferry.

## ENTERTAINMENT

After dark, things get busy in Sydney's bars, clubs, outdoor cinemas, sports stadiums and live-music pubs. Sydney's jazz and blues circuit is healthy and innovative. The live rock scene is reclaiming patrons so rudely stolen by clubs in the '90s.

Cinema listings can be found in Sydney's daily newspapers. Pick up the Metro section in Friday's *Sydney Morning Herald* for comprehensive entertainment listings. Free weekly street magazines such as *Drum Media*, *3D World* and *The Brag* specialise in gig and club information. Tickets for most shows can be purchased directly from venues or the following distributors:

**Moshtix** (Map pp78-9; ☎ 9209 4614; www.moshtix .com.au; Red Eye Records, 370 Pitt St; ◷ 9am-6pm Mon-Fri, to 9pm Thu, to 5pm Sat, 11am-5pm Sun) Servicing alternative music venues.

**Ticketek** (Map pp78-9; ☎ 13 28 49; www.ticketek .com.au; 195 Elizabeth St; ◷ 9am-5pm Mon-Wed, to 7pm Thu & Fri, to 4pm Sat)

**Ticketmaster** (Map pp78-9; ☎ 13 61 00; www.ticket master.com.au; State Theatre, 49 Market St; ◷ 9am-5pm Mon-Fri)

## Cinemas

**Academy Twin Cinema** (Map p84; ☎ 9331 3457; www .palacecinemas.com.au; 3a Oxford St, Paddington; tickets adult/ child $15/12; ◷ 11am-9.30pm) Arthouse enthusiasts roll up for Academy's broad selection of independent Australian and international releases and annual Italian, Mardi Gras, French and Spanish film festivals (in February, March, April and May respectively).

**Verona Cinema** (Map p84; ☎ 9360 6099; www.palace cinemas.com.au; 17 Oxford St, Paddington; tickets adult/child $15/12; ◷ 11am-9.30pm) Just down the road from the affiliated Academy Twin (above), the Verona also has a café and bar, so you can sit, sip and dissect the good (usually non-mainstream) flick you've just seen.

**Dendy Opera Quays** (Map pp78-9; ☎ 9247 3800; www .dendy.com.au; Shop 9, 2 Circular Quay E; tickets adult/child $14/10.50; ◷ 10.30am-9.45pm) When the harbour glare and squawking seagulls get too much, duck into the dark folds of this plush cinema, screening first-run, independent world films, augmented by friendly attendants, a café and bar. Also at Newtown (Map p86; ☎ 9550 5699; 261-3 King St).

**Chauvel Cinema** (Map p84; ☎ 9361 5398; www.chauvel cinema.net.au; cnr Oxford St & Oatley Rd, Paddington; tickets adult/concession $12/10; ◷ 1pm-midnight Mon-Fri, from 11am Sat & Sun) Inside the historic Paddington Town Hall, the recently revamped Chauvel's mission statement is to offer distinct and alternative cinema experiences and to foster Sydney's film culture.

**Govinda's Movie Room** (Map p82; ☎ 9380 5155; www.govindas.com.au; 112 Darlinghurst Rd; Darlinghurst; dinner & movie $22; ◷ 6-11pm) The Hare Krishna Govinda's is an all-you-can-gobble vegetarian smorgasbord, including admission to the mainstream movie-room upstairs.

**IMAX** (Map pp78-9; ☎ 9281 3300; www.imax.com .au; Southern Promenade, Darling Harbour; tickets adult/child

---

### SYDNEY OUTDOOR CINEMA

What better way to enjoy a balmy summer evening than to bring a rug, a picnic and a mate, and watch a film on a huge outdoor screen! **Moonlight Cinema** (Map p84; ☎ 1300 551 908; www .moonlight.com.au; Centennial Park, Oxford St (Woollahra Gate); tickets adult/concession $15/13; ◷ dusk, late Nov-early Mar) screens classics like *Breakfast at Tiffany's* and *A Clockwork Orange*. Buy tickets online, by phone or at the gate from 7pm (subject to availability).

**Open Air Cinema** (Map pp78-9; ☎ 1300 366 649; www.stgeorge.com.au/openair; Mrs Macquaries Point, Royal Botanic Gardens; tickets adult/concession $18/17; ◷ box office 6.30pm, screenings 8.30pm Jan-Feb) has a three-storey screen with surround-sound, harbour sunsets and swanky food and wine. **Bondi Open Air Cinema** (Map p87; ☎ 9209 4614; www.bondiopenair.com.au; Bondi Pavilion, Bondi) is similar but saltier. Bookings essential for both venues.

$18/14; 10am-10pm) It's big bucks for a 45-minute movie, but everything about IMAX is big. The eight-storey screen shimmers with a selection of kid-friendly documentaries (sharks, Mars, haunted castles etc), many in 3-D, that win over reluctant adults as well. Size matters.

**George St Cinemas** (Map pp78-9; 9273 7431; www.greaterunion.com.au; 505 George St; tickets adult/child $14.80/11.30; 9.30am-midnight) With more cinemas than seems feasible, this big-screen behemoth combines three huge complexes in an orgy of popcorn-fuelled populist cinematography.

## Clubs

**Slipp Inn** (Map pp78-9; 8297 7000; 111 Sussex St; admission free-$15; noon-4am Thu & Fri, 6pm-4am Sat) Slip in to this warren of moody rooms and bump hips with the cool kids (can you believe Crown Prince Frederik of Denmark met his Tasmanian missus here?). Resident and international selectors serve up old-school funk, Latin, breaks, tech and house. Refuel on pizza and Thai.

**GoodBar** (Map p84; 9360 6759; 11a Oxford St, Paddington; admission $10-15; 9pm-3am Wed, Fri & Sat) Looking for Mr Goodbar? If he's hiding in this tiny club, it won't take you long to flush him out. No luck? Console yourself with funk, soul, reggae and hip-hop among the taut Paddington bods who make it past the face police on the door.

**Home** (Map pp78-9; 9266 0600; Cockle Bay Wharf, Darling Harbour; admission $25; 11pm-6am Fri, 9pm-6am Sat) Welcome to the pleasuredome: a three-level, 2000-capacity timber-and-glass 'prow' that's home to a huge dance floor, countless bars, outdoor balconies and sonics that make other clubs sound like transistor radios. Top-name international DJs spin house; live bands amp it up.

**Tank** (Map pp78-9; 9240 3007; 3 Bridge La; admission $15-25; 10.30pm-6am Fri & Sat) They've got a VIP room here – the question is, are you 'I' enough? Muster tank-loads of glamour and buckets of chutzpah and crash the party. Otherwise, mingle with *waaay*-too-young clean-shaven stockbrokers and their waif girlfriends in this world-class, underground club.

**Yu** (Map p82; 9358 6511; 171 Victoria St, Potts Point; admission $10-20; 10pm-6am Fri-Sun) Debut the glam new Eastern-Suburbs you at Yu. Sydney's best house DJs and vocal MCs (MC Fro) spin hip-hop, nu-skool, vocal and funky house in three rooms divided by sliding video

screens. Sunday's 'After Hours' session kicks til you can't take no mo'.

**Cave** (Map pp78-9; 9566 4755; Star City Casino, Pirrama Rd, Pyrmont; admission $10-25; 9pm-3am Wed & Thu, to 5am Fri-Sun) This flashy fleshpot at Star City Casino fills with clubbers who like their sounds state-of-the-art, dynamic and all lit up. The dress code zooms in on labels and sex appeal, attracting J-Lo wannabes and the gamblers who know when to hold 'em.

## Live Music
### CLASSICAL

**City Recital Hall** (Map pp78-9; 8256 2222; www.cityrecitalhall.com; 2-12 Angel Pl; tickets free-$60; box office 9am-5pm Mon-Fri) Classically configured, this custom-built 1200-seat venue boasts near-perfect acoustics. Catch top-flight companies like Musica Viva, the Australian Brandenburg and Chamber Orchestras, the Sydney Symphony and touring international ensembles, soloists and opera singers.

**Sydney Conservatorium of Music** (Map pp78-9; 9351 1222; www.music.usyd.edu.au; cnr Macquarie & Bridge Sts; tickets free-$25; box office 9am-5pm Mon-Fri) 'The Con' has a history of bulbous building costs: the $145 million spent a few years ago refurbished its five live venues. The annual student/teacher performance programme includes choral, jazz, opera and chamber recitals, and free lunchtime and 'Cocktail Hour' concerts.

**Sydney Opera House** (Map pp78-9; 9250 7777; www.sydneyoperahouse.com; Bennelong Pt, Circular Quay E; ticket prices vary with shows; box office 9am-8.30pm Mon-Sat, 2hrs pre-show Sun) As well as theatre and dance, the Opera House (p54) regularly hosts classy classicists.

**Australian Chamber Orchestra** ( 8274 3800; www.aco.com.au)

**Musica Viva** ( 8694 6666; www.mva.org.au)

**Opera Australia** ( 9699 1099; www.opera-australia.org.au)

**Sydney Philharmonic Choirs** ( 9251 2024; www.sydneyphilharmonia.com.au)

**Sydney Symphony** ( 8251 4600; www.sydneysymphony.com)

### JAZZ & BLUES

**Basement** (Map pp78-9; 9251 2797; www.thebasement.com.au; 29 Reiby Pl, Circular Quay; tickets from $15; noon-1.30am Mon-Thu, to 2.30am Fri, 7.30pm-3am Sat, 7pm-1am Sun) Sydney's premier jazz venue presents big touring acts (Taj Mahal) and big local talent (Vince Jones, Mia Dyson). A broad musical mandate also sees funk, blues and soul bands performing plus the odd spoken-word gig. Book a table by the stage.

**Empire Hotel** (Map p86; ☎ 9557 1701; www.empire live.com.au; cnr Parramatta Rd & Johnston St, Annandale; tickets free-$20; ☺ 9am-3pm Mon-Sat, 10am-midnight Sun) The Empire's 300-capacity bar gets down 'n' dirty with Sydney's best blues and roots. Local bands with loyal followings play free gigs; listen out for international artists and regular metal, ska, rockabilly, country-and-western and swing dancing nights!

**Wine Banq** (Map pp78-9; ☎ 9222 1919; www.wine banq.com.au; 53 Martin Pl; tickets from $10; ☺ noon-late Tue-Fri, 6pm-late Sat) Carved out of an architect's book of dreams, this is the sexiest jazz room in Sydney. A brilliant wine list adds to the appeal. Past performers include Wynton Marsalis, James Morrison and Harry Connick Jr.

**Soup Plus** (Map pp78-9; ☎ 9299 7728; www.soupplus .com.au; cnr Margaret & Clarence Sts; tickets Mon-Thu $10-12, dinner & show Fri & Sat $35; ☺ 7.30pm Mon-Fri (live music), from 8.30pm Sat) Ditching its sweaty, low-altitude George St cellar for slick new digs was risky, but Soup Plus continues to lure city jazzniks with jazz, swing, big-band and a parade of vocal stylists. Raucous office groups shake the boss off their backs most nights.

## ROCK

**Annandale Hotel** (Map p86; ☎ 9550 1078; www.an nandalehotel.com; cnr Parramatta Rd & Nelson St, Annandale; tickets free-$30; ☺ 11am-midnight Tue-Sat, to 10pm Sun, to 11pm Mon) The Annandale survived the live-music morgue in the '90s and now spearheads Sydney's rock revival, coughing up nightly alt-rock, metal, punk and electronica. Afr00ed punters traverse the sticky carpet between sets by Jet, the Dandy Warhols and Eskimo Joe. 'F*£k this, I'm going to the Annandale!'

**Gaelic Club** (Map pp78-9; ☎ 9211 1687; www.the gaelicclub.com.au; 64 Devonshire St, Surry Hills; tickets $10-30; ☺ varies with shows) Get your earwax blasted out at the Gaelic courtesy of iconic internationals like The Darkness and The Strokes, or homegrown sonic assailants like Wolfmother and Silverchair. It's a mid-size, split-level, multi-purpose affair – much beer and moshing.

**Hopetoun Hotel** (Map p84; ☎ 9361 5257; www .hopetounhotel.com.au; 416 Bourke St, Surry Hills; tickets free-$15; ☺ noon-midnight Mon-Sat, to 10pm Sun) Once the uncontested crucible for new Sydney rock bands, the diminutive 'Hoey' is still a launching pad for garage bands on the boil.

**Enmore Theatre** (Map p86; ☎ 9550 3666; www .enmoretheatre.com.au; 130 Enmore Rd, Newtown; tickets $20-60; ☺ box office 9am-6pm Mon-Fri, 10am-4pm Sat) Originally a vaudeville playhouse, the elegantly wasted Enmore now hosts alt-rockers like Queens of the Stone Age, Lou Reed and PJ Harvey. The 1600-capacity theatre feels like an old-time movie hall, with café, wooden floors, lounge areas and balconies.

**Metro** (Map pp78-9; ☎ 9287 2000; www.metrotheatre .com.au; 624 George St; tickets $25-65; ☺ box office 10am-7pm Mon-Fri, noon-7pm Sat) Big-name indie acts grace the Metro's stage, like The Eels and well-chosen local rockers like The Butterfly Effect. International DJs lend weight to the cause. Theatre-style tiers, air-con, super sound and visibility: r-o-c-k ROCK!

**Sandringham Hotel** (Map p86; ☎ 9557 1254; fax 9517 9325; 387 King St, Newtown; tickets $8-12; ☺ 11am-midnight Mon-Sat, to 10pm Sun) We were nervous the Sando's renovations would spell the end of live music here, but thankfully you can still get rocked from Tuesday to Sunday for not much money. Acoustic acts upstairs; Goth-metal night Sunday.

**Vanguard** (Map p86; ☎ 9557 7992; www.thevanguard .com.au; 42 King St, Newtown; dinner & show per person from $36, general admission $10-40; ☺ dinner from 7pm, music from 8pm) This place aspires to be freethinking, intellectual, and artistic. The intimate 1920s-themed band room satisfies these criteria; occasional Russell Crowe gigs do not… Most seats are reserved for dinner-and-show punters.

**Sydney Entertainment Centre** (Map pp78-9; ☎ 9320 4200; www.sydentcent.com.au; 35 Harbour St, Haymarket; ticket prices vary with shows; ☺ box office 9am-5pm Mon-Fri) Sydney's largest indoor venue holds 12,000 howling rock fans, recent acts including Coldplay, Snoop Dog, the Black Eyed Peas and Jamiroquai. Like most monster venues, the sound quality leaves a little to be desired.

## Spectator Sports

Like to watch? On any given Sydney weekend there'll be all manner of balls being hurled, kicked and batted around, plus sailing on the harbour. Sydneysiders are excruciatingly passionate about the **National Rugby League** (NRL; www.nrl.com.au; tickets from Ticketek $20-40), the season transpiring at suburban stadiums and Aussie Stadium (opposite), with September finals. The fever-inducing NSW vs. Queensland State of Origin series is played annually.

From March to September, 2005's premiership-winning Sydney Swans play in the **Australian Football League** (AFL; www.afl.com.au; tickets from Ticketmaster $20-40) at the Sydney Cricket Ground and Telstra Stadium (below).

The **National Basketball League** (NBL; www.nbl.com .au; tickets from Ticketmaster $10-60) season runs from April to November, the Sydney Kings playing at the Sydney Entertainment Centre (below).

The **cricket** (www.cricinfo.com) season runs from October to March, the Sydney Cricket Ground hosting interstate Pura Cup matches and sellout international Test and World Series Cup matches.

**Tennis NSW** ( ☎ 9763 7644; www.tennisnsw.com.au) has info on local tournaments and the Medibank International tournament at the Sydney International Tennis Centre (below) in the second week of January.

Out on the harbour, the 18ft-skiff racing season runs from September to March. The **Sydney Flying Squadron** (Map pp76-7; ☎ 9955 8350; www.sydneyflyingsquadron.com.au; 76 McDougall St, Milsons Point; adult/child $15/5.50; ☯ 2-4.30pm Sat, Sep-Apr) conducts viewings.

Sydney's big-ticket sports venues include the following.

**Aussie Stadium** (Map p84; ☎ 9360 6601; www .aussiestadium.com; Driver Ave, Moore Park)

**Sydney Cricket Ground** (Map p84; ☎ 9360 6601; www.sydneycricketground.com.au; Driver Ave, Moore Park)

**Sydney Entertainment Centre** (opposite)

**Sydney International Tennis Centre** (Map p108; ☎ 8746 0777; www.sydneytennis.com.au; Rod Laver Dr, Olympic park, Homebush)

**Telstra Stadium** (Map p108; ☎ 8765 2000; www .telstrastadium.com.au; Olympic Blvd, Homebush Bay)

## Theatre & Comedy

**Company B** (Map p84; ☎ 9699 3444; www.belvoir.com .au; Belvoir Street Theatre, 25 Belvoir St, Surry Hills; tickets from adult/concession $48/30; ☯ box office 9.30am-6pm Mon-Sat, to 7.30pm Wed Sat, 2.30-7.30pm Sun) Artistic director Neil Armfield is the darling of the Sydney theatre world. Cinema stars like Geoffrey Rush clamour to perform his adventurous, modern interpretations in the recently refurbished Belvoir St Theatre.

**Sydney Comedy Store** (Map p84; ☎ 9357 1419; www .comedystore.com.au; Entertainment Quarter, Lang Rd, Moore Park; tickets $15-30; ☯ box office 10am-6pm Mon, to midnight Tue-Sat) This purpose-built comedy hall lures big-time Australian, overseas (US, Irish etc) and Edinburgh stand-ups and nurtures new talent with open-mic and 'New Comics' nights.

**Sydney Theatre** (Map pp78-9; ☎ 9250 1999; www .sydneytheatre.org.au; 22 Hickson Rd, Walsh Bay; tickets $69-130; ☯ box office 9am-8.30pm Mon-Fri, from 11am Sat) Opening in 2004 with a name it seems odd no-one thought of before, the resplendent Sydney Theatre at the base of Observatory Hill puts 850 bums on seats for specialist drama and dance.

**Sydney Theatre Company** (STC; Map pp78-9; ☎ 9250 1777; www.sydneytheatre.com.au; Wharf Theatre, Pier 4, 5 Hickson Rd, Walsh Bay; tickets $20-130; ☯ box office 9am-8.30pm, from 11am Sat) Working in tandem with the Sydney Theatre across the road, the STC is Sydney's premier theatre company. Major Australian actors (Barry Otto, Deborah Mailman) perform works by Alan Bennett, David Williamson and Shakespeare. Ask about $20 'Student Rush' tickets. In late 2006 Cate Blanchett and hubbie Andrew Upton joined the company as joint artistic directors.

Major theatres hosting West End and Broadway musicals, opera and concerts (tickets from $50 to $150) include:

**Capitol Theatre** (Map pp78-9; ☎ 9320 5000; www .capitoltheatre.com.au; 13 Campbell St, Haymarket; ☯ box office 9am-5pm Mon-Fri)

**Lyric Theatre** (Map pp78-9; ☎ 9657 8500; www .lyrictheatre.com.au; Star City Casino, 80 Pyrmont St, Pyrmont; ☯ box office 9am-5pm Mon-Sat, from 11am Sun)

**State Theatre** (Map pp78-9; ☎ 9373 6852; www .statetheatre.com.au; 49 Market St; ☯ box office 9am-5pm Mon-Fri, to 8pm performance nights)

**Theatre Royal** (Map pp78-9; ☎ 9224 8444; www .mlccentre.com.au; MLC Centre, 108 King St; ☯ box office Mon-Fri, 11am-8pm Sat, 1-8pm Sun)

## SHOPPING

Sydneysiders treat shopping as a recreational activity rather than a necessity. Shopping in central Sydney is fast and furious – the CBD brims with department, chain and international fashion stores around **Pitt St Mall** (Map pp78-9). Much more chilled-out are inner-city shopping strips in Paddington, Glebe and Newtown – long, sinuous swathes of boutiques, cafés and bookshops. Paddington is designer heaven; for antiques head to Queen St, Woollahra. For music and retro fashion try Crown St, Surry Hills. There's a cluster of outdoor shops around the corner of Kent and Bathurst Sts in the city, while The Rocks oozes 'Australiana' (tacky souvenirs). Late-night shopping is on Thursday night – most stores stay open until 9pm.

The Sydney visual arts scene is edgy and competitive. If you have a free afternoon, swan around the **art galleries** (Glenmore Rd, Five Ways, Goodhope St, Gurner St) in Paddington's back streets or head to Waterloo's **Danks St** (Map p84) where a progressive crop of galleries has taken root.

## Aboriginal Art

**Artery** (Map p82; ☎ 9380 8234; Shop 2, 221 Darlinghurst Rd, Darlinghurst) More art retail than art gallery, Artery deliberately steers away from the glitzy Sydney gallery scene, sourcing its contemporary, original selections from up-and-coming Central Australian artists. Prices are realistic and affordable, modern indigenous jewellery, hand-woven baskets and gorgeous canvasses starting at $25.

**Gannon House** (Map pp78-9; ☎ 9251 4474; 45 Argyle St, The Rocks) Purchasing works directly from Aboriginal communities, Gannon House (named after colonial builder Michael Gannon) takes an umbrella approach to its exhibits, jumbling Aboriginal artefacts, paintings and didgeridoos with contemporary white Australian abstract art. The results are disarmingly harmonious.

**Gavala** (Map pp78-9; ☎ 9212 7232; Shop 131, 1st fl, Harbourside Shopping Centre, Darling Harbour) Gavala sells only authentic indigenous products that are licensed, authorised or purchased directly from artists and communities, or both. It's 100% Aboriginal-owned, stirring up an outback vibe with a mind-boggling collation of paintings, boomerangs, didgeridoos, artefacts, books, clothing and CDs.

**Hogarth Galleries** (Map p84; ☎ 9360 6839; 7 Walker La, Paddington) A cultural beacon in an obscure Paddington laneway, Hogarth Galleries has

been supporting and promoting Aboriginal art since 1972. Honouring established artists and sourcing up-and-comers, Hogarth exhibits contemporary dot paintings, basketry, framed prints, fabrics, spears and didgeridoos.

## Australiana

**Australian Wine Centre** (Map pp78-9; ☎ 9247 2755; Shop 3, Goldfields House, 1 Alfred St, Circular Quay) This basement store is packed with quality Australian wine, beer and spirits. Pick up some Yellowglen for a bubbly night or organise a shipment of Ninth Island Pinot Noir back home. Healthy wallets can access Cuban cigars and a swaggering range of Penfold's Grange wines.

**Flame Opals** (Map pp78-9; ☎ 9247 3446; 119 George St, The Rocks) If you've been seduced by shimmering opals, this is the place to consummate the relationship. Prices range from about $20 to 'If you have to ask, you can't afford it…'. There's a tax-free concession for overseas customers.

**RM Williams** (Map pp78-9; ☎ 9262 2228; 389 George St) Urban cowboys and country folk can't get enough of this hard-wearing outback gear. It's the kind of stuff prime ministers don when they want to seem sincere about something, whilst referring to it as 'clobber'. Favourites include oilskin jackets, Akubra hats, moleskin jeans and leather work boots.

**Strand Hatters** (Map pp78-9; ☎ 9231 6884; Shop 8, Strand Arcade, 412 George St) Got a cold/wet head? Strand Hatters will cover your crown with a classically Australian Akubra bush hat (made from rabbit felt). Staff block and steam hats to customers' cranial requirements (crocodile-teeth hatbands cost extra).

## Clothes

**Calibre** (Map p84; ☎ 9380 5993; 398 Oxford St, Paddington) Hip, high-calibre Calibre fills the wardrobes of Sydney's power players with schmick suits in seasonal fabrics and colours, plus brand-name sunnies, shoes, ties and briefcases. Gordon Gecko eat your heart out.

**Leona Edmiston** (Map p84; ☎ 9331 7033; 88 William St, Paddington) With two new stores in LA, Leona Edmiston clearly knows a thing a or two about dresses. Her designs have been described as exuberantly feminine, flirtatious and fun, cut from the best cottons, silks and jerseys. Colours range from luscious, sophisticated reds to pinstripes and polka dots.

---

### BUYING INDIGENOUS ART

Most of Sydney's amazing indigenous art comes from elsewhere in Australia. To ensure you're not perpetuating a non-indigenous cash-in on Aboriginal art's popularity, make sure you're buying from an authentic dealer selling original art, and if the gallery doesn't pay their artists upfront, ask exactly how much of your money will make it back to the artist or community. Another good test is to request some biographical info on the artists – if the vendor can't produce it, keep walking.

**Scanlan & Theodore** (Map p84; ☎ 9380 9388; 122 Oxford St, Paddington) Regularly topping with-it gals' lists of favourite designers, Scanlan & Theodore excel in beautifully-made pieces for the evening or the office, with fabrics you just can't help but fondle.

**Zimmerman Swim** (Map pp76-7; ☎ 9387 5111; Shop 3048, Westfield Shopping Centre, 500 Oxford St, Bondi Junction) Half of Bondi's boobs and bums are clad in Zimmerman swimwear – they understand that Sydneysiders spend a lot of time in the surf, but still want to look sexy.

Some other divine designers to check out include these ones.

**Alannah Hill** (Map pp78-9; ☎ 9221 1251; Level 1, Strand Arcade, 412 George St) Feather boas, fishnet stockings and diaphanous cocktail dresses.

**Bracewell** (Map p84; ☎ 9331 5844; 274 Oxford St, Paddington) Structured and sassy; Mavi and Sass & Bide jeans.

**Collette Dinnigan** (Map p84; ☎ 9360 6691; 33 William St, Paddington) Flouncy beaded dresses popular with Hollywood's Aussie gals.

**Morrissey** (Map p84; ☎ 9380 4722; 372 Oxford St, Paddington) Sexy, high-heeled style – bring your gold credit card.

**Wayne Cooper** (Map pp78-9; ☎ 9221 5292; 1st fl, Strand Arcade, 412 George St) Release your inner vixen in devilish gear.

## Markets

**Balmain Market** (Map pp76-7; ☎ 0418 765 736; cnr Darling St & Curtis Rd, Balmain; ☀ 8.30am-4pm Sat) Milling around the shady grounds of St Andrews Congregational, stalls selling arts, crafts, books, clothing, jewellery, plants and fruit and veg jumble together like socks in a drawer. The church itself is open if you want a Middle Eastern snack or need to consult St Andy about a prospective purchase.

**Bondi Markets** (Map p87; ☎ 9315 8988; Bondi Beach Public School, cnr Campbell Pde & Warners Ave, Bondi; ☀ 9am-4pm Sun) 'Remember the days of the old school yard? We used to laugh a lot…' The kids are at the beach on Sundays while their school fills up with Bondi funksters rummaging through funky second-hand clothes and books, hippy beads and earrings, aromatherapy oils, candles, old Cat Stevens records…

**Glebe Markets** (Map p86; ☎ 4237 7499; Glebe Public School, cnr Glebe Point Rd & Derby Pl, Glebe; ☀ 9am-4pm Sat) Sydney's dreadlocked, shoeless, inner-city contingent beats a hazy course to this crowded market. Once massaged, fuelled on lentil burgers and swathed in funky retro gear, they retreat to the lawns, pass the peace pipe and chill out to an African drum soundtrack.

**Paddington Market** (Map p84; ☎ 9331 2923; St John's Church, 395 Oxford St, Paddington; ☀ 10am-4pm Sat) Sydney's most-attended weekend market congregates around Paddington Uniting Church, offering up everything from vintage clothes and hip fashions to jewellery, books, massage and palmistry. Parking is a misery – take public transport.

**Paddy's Markets** (Map pp78-9; ☎ 1300 361 589; cnr Hay & Thomas Sts, Haymarket; ☀ 9am-5pm Thu-Sun) Paddy's is the Sydney equivalent of Istanbul's Grand Bazaar, but swap the incense, hookahs and carpets for mobile phone covers, Eminem T shirts and cheap sneakers. There are over 1000 stalls in this capitalist cavern – pick up a VB singlet for uncle Bruce or just wander the aisles in awe.

**Rocks Market** (Map pp78-9; ☎ 9240 8717; George St, The Rocks near Sydney Harbour Bridge; ☀ 10am-5pm Sat & Sun) Under a long white canopy, the 150 stalls here are a little on the tacky side of the tracks (fossils, opals, faux-Aboriginal etc) but are still worth a gander.

## Shopping Centres & Department Stores

**David Jones** (Map pp78-9; ☎ 9266 5544; cnr Market & Castlereagh Sts) In two enormous city buildings, DJs is Sydney's premier department store. The Market St store has menswear, electrical and a highbrow food court; Castlereagh St has women's and children's wear and a friendly concierge to point you in the right direction.

**Myer** (Map pp78-9; ☎ 9238 9111; cnr George & Market Sts) Formerly the dowdy Grace Bros, Myer has made a concerted effort to liven things up a bit. Over seven floors, there's everything from hip fashions (Wayne Cooper, Seduce, Chloe) to big-name cosmetics (Chanel, Lancôme, Clinique), plus lingerie, sunglasses and a café.

**Queen Victoria Building** (QVB; Map pp78-9; ☎ 9265 6869; 455 George St) The QVB is a magnificent high-Victorian masterpiece occupying an entire city block. Yeah, sure, the 200 speciality shops are great, but check out the wrought-iron balconies, stained-glass shopfronts, mosaic floors, tinkling baby grand and hyper-kitsch animated Royal Clock (featuring the Battle of Hastings and hourly beheading of King Charles I).

**Strand Arcade** (Map pp78-9; ☎ 9232 4199; 412 George St & 193-5 Pitt St Mall) Constructed in 1891 in a squeezy space between George and Pitt Sts, the Strand Arcade rivals the QVB for ornateness. Three floors of designer fashions, Australiana and old-world coffee shops will make your shortcut through here considerably longer.

**Westfield Bondi Junction** (Map pp76-7; ☎ 9947 8000; 500 Oxford St, Bondi Junction) This slick new mall claims to be the biggest in Oz; definitely the biggest in Sydney. With more than 300 shops over six shiny levels, it's brought style and chutzpah to slovenly Bondi Junction: David Jones, Myer, street fashion, jewellery, books, music, cinemas and valet parking.

**World Square** (Map pp78-9; ☎ 9262 7926; cnr George & Liverpool Sts) The old Anthony Horden & Sons department store on this site was demolished in the '80s, but it's taken 20 years for World Square to emerge in its place. City-slickers have been rewarded for their patience with coffee shops, sushi bars, shoe shops and a huge Rebel Sport outlet with every conceivable bat and ball.

## GETTING THERE & AWAY
### Air
Sydney's **Kingsford Smith Airport** (Map pp76-7; ☎ 9667 9111; www.sydneyairport.com.au) is Australia's busiest, so don't be surprised if there are delays. It's only 10km south of the city centre, making access easy, but this also means that flights cease between 11pm and 5am due to noise regulations. The T1 (international) and T2 and T3 (domestic) terminals are a 4km, $5 bus or train ride apart.

You can fly into Sydney from all the usual international points and from within Australia. Both **Qantas** ( ☎ 13 13 13; www.qantas.com.au) and **Virgin** ( ☎ 13 67 89; www.virginblue.com.au) have frequent flights to other capital cities. Smaller Qantas-affiliated airlines fly to smaller Oz destinations.

### Bus
All private interstate and regional bus travellers arrive at **Sydney Coach Terminal** (Map pp78-9; ☎ 9281 9366; Central Station, Eddy Ave; ☽ 6am-10.30pm). The government's CountryLink rail network is also complemented by coaches. Most buses stop in the suburbs on the way in and out of Sydney. If you hold a VIP or YHA discount card, shop around the major bus companies with offices here:

**Firefly** ( ☎ 1300 730 740; www.fireflyexpress.com.au)
**Greyhound** ( ☎ 13 14 99; www.greyhound.com.au)
**Murrays** ( ☎ 13 22 51; www.murrays.com.au)

### Train
Sydney's main rail terminus for **CountryLink** interstate and regional services is **Central Station** (Map pp78-9; ☎ 13 22 32; www.countrylink.info; Eddy Ave; ☽ staffed ticket booths 6am-10pm, ticket machines 24hr). Call for information, reservations and arrival/departure times. CountryLink discounts often nudge 40% on economy fares – sometimes cheaper than buses!

## GETTING AROUND
For bus, ferry and train information, timetables and fare deals, call the Sydney Transit Authority's **Transport Infoline** (STA; ☎ 13 15 00) or check www.131500.com.au.

### To/From the Airport
#### BUS
Bookings are essential for the following services.
**Kingsford Smith Transport** ( ☎ 9666 9988; single/return $10/18; ☽ 5am-11pm) Connecting the airport and central Sydney hotels.
**Manly Airport Bus** ( ☎ 0500 505 800; single/return $30/63; ☽ 5am-11pm) A door-to-door service to/from Manly.

#### TAXI
A ride to/from Circular Quay should cost from $25 to $35; to/from Central Station from $20 to $30.

#### TRAIN
**Airport Link** ( ☎ 13 15 00; www.airportlink.com.au; single/return from Central Station to domestic terminal $12/18, to international terminal $13/19; ☽ every 10-15min, 5am-midnight daily) runs from city train stations; return fares are cheaper after 9am and on weekends. A one-way trip takes about 15 minutes.

### Boat
#### FERRY
Sydney transport's most civilised option – harbour ferries, JetCats (to Manly) and RiverCats (to Parramatta) – depart Circular Quay. Most ferries operate from 6am to midnight; those servicing tourist attractions operate shorter hours. The Circular Quay **Ferry Information Office** (Map pp78-9; ☎ 9207 3170; www.sydneyferries.info; ☽ 7am-5.45pm Mon-Sat, 8am-5.45pm Sun) has details. Many ferries have connecting bus services.

A one-way inner-harbour ride on a regular ferry costs adult/concession $5/3. A one-way ride to Manly on the JetCat costs $8 (no concession, 15 minutes, half-hourly). A one-way RiverCat ride to Parramatta costs adult/concession $8/4 (50 minutes, hourly).

### WATER TAXI

Water taxis ply dedicated shuttle routes; rides to/from other harbour venues can be booked.

**Yellow Water Taxis** (Map pp78-9; ☎ 9555 9778; www
.yellowwatertaxis.com.au; ☯ 7am-midnight) Circular Quay to Darling Harbour adult/child $13/8; 40-minute Harbour Tours adult/child $25/15.

**Watertours** (Map pp78-9; ☎ 9211 7730; www
.watertours.com.au; ☯ 9.30am-11pm) Opera House to Darling Harbour adult/child $15/10; one hour Harbour and Nightlights Tours adult/child $30/20.

## Bus

Sydney buses run almost everywhere. Bondi, Coogee and parts of the North Shore are serviced only by bus. Nightrider buses operate skeletally after regular services cease around midnight.

The main city bus stops are Circular Quay, Wynyard Park (York St) and Railway Sq. Buy tickets from newsagencies, Bus TransitShops and on buses. Pay the driver as you enter, or dunk prepaid tickets in ticket machines by the door. Fares start at $1.70; most trips are under $3.50. There are **Bus TransitShops** at Circular Quay (Map pp78-9; www.sydneybuses.info; cnr Alfred & Loftus Sts; ☯ 7am-7pm Mon-Fri, 8.30am-5pm Sat & Sun), Wynyard Station (Map pp78-9; Carrington St), Railway Sq (Map pp78-9; George St), and the Queen Victoria Building (Map pp78-9; York St).

Bus routes starting with an X indicate limited-stop express routes; those with an L have limited stops. Most buses depart the city on George or Castlereagh Sts, ploughing down George or Elizabeth Sts on the way back in.

## Car & Motorcycle

### BUYING OR SELLING A CAR

The second-hand car industry is a minefield of mistrust and dodgy wheelers-and-dealers, but with a bit of research you can still land a decent deal. Parramatta Rd is lined with used-car lots, and the *Trading Post* (www
.tradingpost.com.au), a weekly rag available at newsagents, lists second-hand vehicles.

Always read the fine print when buying or selling a car. Some dealers will sell you a car with an undertaking to buy it back at an agreed price – don't accept verbal guarantees, get it in writing. The **Register of Encumbered Vehicles** (REVS; ☎ 13 32 20; www.revs.nsw.gov.au) is a

government organisation that can check to ensure the car you're buying is fully paid-up and owned by the seller.

Before you buy any vehicle, regardless of the vendor, we strongly recommend you have it checked by a competent mechanic – we've heard horror stories from readers whose trusty steeds have proved to be not-so-trusty. The National Roads & Motorists Association (NRMA; p52) organises inspections and provides 24-hour emergency roadside assistance for members, with reciprocal arrangements with motoring organisations overseas and interstate.

Companies who specialise in buying and selling cars to/from travellers include:

**Kings Cross Car Market** (Map p82; ☎ 1800 808 188; www.carmarket.com.au; car park Level 2, cnr Ward Ave & Elizabeth Bay Rd, Kings Cross; ☯ 9am-5pm Sun-Thu, 9am-4pm Fri & Sat) Park your machine in the car park and wait for a buyer. Potentially hit-and-miss, but always busy.

**Travellers Autobarn** (Map pp78-9; ☎ 1800 674 374; www.travellers-autobarn.com.au; 177 William St, Kings Cross; ☯ 9am-6pm Mon-Sat, 10.30am-3pm Sun) Guaranteed buyback, warranties and insurance available.

### RENTAL

Expect to pay around $70 per day for a zippy small car. Rates sometimes include insurance and unlimited kilometres; some companies require you to be over 25 years old. At the time of writing petrol cost around $1.45 per litre, and was steadily rising.

If you're looking to hire a campervan, **Wicked Campers** (Map p108; ☎ 1800 246 869; www
.wickedcampers.com.au; 5 Tenterden Rd, Botany; ☯ 9am-4pm Mon-Fri, 9am-noon Sat) rents out spectacularly painted vehicles with room in the back where you can sleep. The following stalwarts also have vans (and regular cars) at their airport and city branches.

**Avis** ( ☎ 13 63 33, www.avis.com.au)
**Budget** ( ☎ 13 27 27; www.budget.com.au)
**Europcar** ( ☎ 1300 131 390; www.europcar.com.au)
**Hertz** ( ☎ 13 30 39; www.hertz.com.au)
**Thrifty** ( ☎ 1300 367 227; www.thrifty.com.au)

The *Yellow Pages* lists many other car-hire companies, some specialising in renting clapped-out wrecks at rock-bottom prices – read the fine print!

**Bikescape** (Map p86; ☎ 1300 736 869; www.bike
scape.com.au; 183 Parramatta Rd, Annandale; per day from $80; ☯ 9am-5.30pm Mon-Fri, 9-10am & 4-5pm Sat) rents out well-serviced, low mileage motorcycles and scooters. The savvy staff can also organise tours.

## ROAD TOLLS

There's a $3 southbound toll on the Sydney Harbour Bridge and Tunnel. If you're heading from the North Shore to the Eastern Suburbs, it's easier to take the tunnel. There's a $4 northbound toll on the Eastern Distributor; the infamous Cross City Tunnel costs $3.50 one-way. Sydney's main motorways (M1, M2, M4, M5 and M7) are also tolled ($2.20 to $3.80). There are cash booths at toll gates, but the whole system will soon be electronic – check www .rta.nsw.gov.au for the latest info.

## Fare Deals

The **SydneyPass** (www.sydneypass.info) offers three, five or seven days unlimited travel over a week on STA buses, ferries and the rail network's Red TravelPass zone (inner suburbs). Passes include the Airport Express, Sydney and Bondi Explorer buses, JetCats, RiverCats and STA-run harbour cruises. They cost adult/child/family $100/55/275 (three days), $145/70/360 (five days) and $165/80/410 (seven days). Buy passes from STA, train stations, Bus TransitShops, the Sydney Visitor Centre at The Rocks (p52) or Airport Express and Explorer bus drivers.

**TravelPasses** offer unlimited rail, bus and ferry rides at cheap weekly rates. There are various colour-coded grades offering combinations of distance and service. A weekly Red TravelPass (inner suburbs) available at train stations, STA offices, Bus TransitShops and newsagents costs adult/concession $33/17.

If you're just catching buses, a **TravelTen** ticket from newsagents and Bus TransitShops offers 10 discounted bus trips. There are various colour codes for different distances; a Red TravelTen ticket (inner suburbs) costs adult/concession $30/15. **FerryTen** tickets from the Circular Quay ticket office are also good value – 10 inner-harbour rides for adult/concession $33/17. **DayTripper** tickets letting you ride most inner-suburban trains, buses and ferries cost adult/concession $16/8.

Several transport-plus-entry tickets available from the Circular Quay Ferry Information Office (p104) work out cheaper than catching a return ferry and paying entry separately. These include the **ZooPass** (adult/child/concession $39/21/34) and the **AquariumPass** (adult/child/family $33/17/81).

## Monorail & Metro Light Rail (MLR)

The privately operated **Metro Monorail** ( ☎ 9285 5600; www.metromonorail.com.au; single circuit $5, day pass adult/family $9/22; ☺ every 4min, 7am-10pm Mon-Thu, to midnight Fri & Sat, 8am-10pm Sun) is a lugubrious elevated worm circling around Darling Harbour and the city. The full loop takes about 14 minutes.

Also privately run, the future click **Metro Light Rail** (MLR; ☎ 9285 5600; www.metrolightrail.com .au; Zone 1 adult/concession $3/2, Zone 1 & 2 adult/concession $4/3, day pass adult/concession $9/7; ☺ 24hr, every 15min 6am-midnight, every 30min midnight-6am) glides between Central Station and Pyrmont via Chinatown and Darling Harbour. The Zone 2 service beyond Pyrmont to Lilyfield stops at 11pm Sunday to Thursday, midnight Friday and Saturday. Purchase tickets on board.

Note that the SydneyPass (left) isn't valid on the Monorail or MLR.

## Taxi

Taxis and cab ranks proliferate in Sydney. Flag fall is $2.80, then it's $1.62 per kilometre (plus 20% from 10pm to 6am). The waiting charge is 68c per minute. Passengers must pay bridge, tunnel and road tolls (even if you don't incur them 'outbound', the returning driver will incur them 'inbound').

Major taxi companies that offer phone bookings ($1.40 fee) include these ones.
**Arrow Taxis** ( ☎ 13 22 11)
**Legion** ( ☎ 13 14 51)
**Premier Cabs** ( ☎ 13 10 17)
**Taxis Combined** ( ☎ 8332 8888)

## Train

Sydney's vast suburban rail network is the deft way to get around. Lines radiate from the underground City Circle (seven city-centre stations), but don't service the Northern and Southern Beaches, Balmain or Glebe. All suburban trains stop at Central Station, and usually one or more of the other City Circle stations too.

Trains run from around 5am to midnight. On weekends and after 9am on weekdays you can buy an off-peak return ticket, valid until 4am the next day, for little more than a standard one-way fare.

Twenty-four-hour ticket machines occupy most stations but humans are usually available too if you'd rather talk to something that'll listen. If you have to change trains, buy a ticket to your ultimate destination, but don't exit the transfer station en route or your ticket will be invalid.

For train information, visit the **CityRail Information Booth** (Map pp78-9; ☎ 13 15 00; www.131500 .com.au; Wharf 5, Circular Quay; ☺ 9.05am-4.50pm).

# Around Sydney

Sydney's suburbs spread over a broad coastal plain like spilt honey, hemmed in by rugged country on three sides and the Pacific Ocean on the other. The area sustains Australia's largest concentration of people, the urban melange thinning as the kilometres stretch inland. Beyond the city, bushwalking tracks, cycling paths, scenic train routes and roads connect a small-town smorgasbord, interspersed with gorgeous waterways, uncrowded beaches and magical national parks.

The proximity of these delights to Sydney means that public transport is often a viable option – you can cover a lot of ground on day trips, with or without your own wheels. To the west, the wooded foothills of the Great Dividing Range rise to the lofty Blue Mountains, with their heaven-sent scenery and quirky villages. To the south, Royal National Park harbours lost-to-the-world beaches, rainforest pockets and precipitous cliff-scapes. Inland, fertile soils support the rural settlements of Macarthur Country and historic Macquarie towns, extending south to the dignified Southern Highlands.

Occupying a hefty chunk of Sydney's north, Ku-ring-gai Chase National Park's dense bushland and sandstone outcrops are cut by shimmering inlets. Further north, the landscape is defined by the meandering brown snake of the Hawkesbury River, with its ferry crossings, oyster farms and sleepy towns. Beyond here are the inland lakes and surf-centric communities of the Central Coast.

## HIGHLIGHTS

- Hole up in a **Blue Mountains** (p119) pub or Art Deco café as ethereal mists descend

- Stumble across isolated coves, empty beaches and thick native bush in **Royal National Park** (p109)

- Traverse the rippling reaches of the **Hawkesbury River** (p114) on a houseboat

- Look for lyrebirds and Aboriginal rock engravings in **Ku-ring-gai Chase** (p112) and **Brisbane Water National Parks** (p136)

- Soak up the colonial history with some tea and cake in the **Southern Highlands** (p131)

- Ride a RiverCat along the length of Sydney Harbour to historic **Parramatta** (p111)

- Fall off the edge of the Southern Highlands into the quintessentially Australian **Kangaroo Valley** (p135)

- Carve up the surf at the beaches along the **Central Coast** (p136)

# AROUND SYDNEY

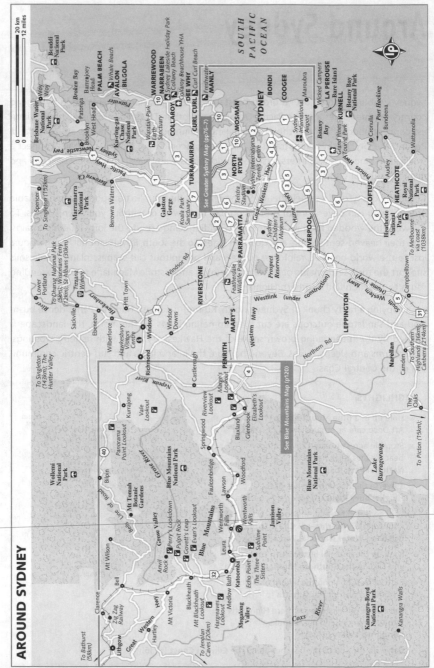

# GREATER SYDNEY

The teeming, smoggy metropolis of Sydney is tempered by natural beauty on its fringes. Heading west, the Great Western Hwy (M4) leaves a trail of development in its wake, but the expansive Ku-ring-gai Chase and Royal National Parks stem suburban proliferation along the coast. The scattering of small towns and wide-open spaces following the Hume Hwy south are devoid of frenetic activity but rich in history.

## BOTANY BAY

Perpetuated by sea shanties, it's a common misconception among Sydney first-timers that the city is built on Botany Bay. It's true that Captain James Cook's Australian landfall was here (his naturalist Joseph Banks named it Botany Bay after the many botanical specimens he found), but Sydney grew around Port Jackson's more reliable water source 15km to the north. The white beaches, craggy landscape and native bush that confronted Cook when he stepped ashore still dominate Botany Bay's coastal verges, but digging deeper exposes south Sydney's smoke-stacked industrial heartland. Despite the refineries, Botany Bay has scenic stretches and holds a special, endearing place in Australian history.

Beyond the oil tankers, industrial subdivisions and business parks, **Botany Bay National Park** (cars $7, pedestrians & cyclists free; ☟ 7am-7.30pm, to 5.30pm Jun-Aug) occupies both headlands of the bay – 458 hectares of bushland and coastal walking tracks, picnic areas and an 8km cycle track. Cook's monument-marked landing place is on the southern side of the park in trailer-trashy Kurnell. The **Discovery Centre** ( ☎ 02-9668 9111; www.nationalparks.nsw.gov.au; Cape Solander Dr, Kurnell; admission free; ☟ 11am-3pm Mon-Fri, 10am-4.30pm Sat & Sun) conveys the impact of European arrival and has information on the surrounding wetlands. There's also material exploring Cook's life and expeditions. The entry fee for cars applies only on the southern headland – pedestrian access is free. Most of the walking tracks begin close to the park entrance, so you might as well park outside. To get here via public transport, catch the train to Cronulla (p111) then **Crowthers Buslink** ( ☎ 02-9523 4047; www.buslink.net.au) bus 987 from Cronulla train station 10km away (one-way adult/child $4/2, 20 minutes, hourly 8am to 5pm).

**La Perouse** is on Botany Bay's northern headland, at the spot where the French explorer of the same name arrived in 1788. He turned up just six days after Cook's First Fleet arrived (much sooner than expected) and gave Mother England a decent scare. Anglo-Franco relations were apparently conducted without the usual disdain, La Perouse and his men camping at Botany Bay for a few weeks before sailing off into the Pacific, never to be seen again. It wasn't until 1826 that the wrecks of their ships were discovered on a reef near Vanikoro in the Solomon Islands. There's a monument at La Perouse, built in 1828 by French sailors, to commemorate the explorer. You can also visit the fabulous **La Perouse Museum & Visitors Centre** ( ☎ 02-9311 3379; www.environment.nsw.gov.au; Cable Station, Anzac Pde, La Perouse; adult/child/family $6/3/13; ☟ 10am-4pm Wed-Sun) housed inside the old cable station (1882). The centre has relics from La Perouse's many expeditions, plus changing exhibitions on local history and environment.

About 50m offshore at La Perouse is the strange **Bare Island** ( ☎ 02-9247 5033; www.nationalparks.nsw.gov.au; tours adult/concession/family $8/6/22; ☟ 1.30 & 2.30pm Sat & Sun Oct-Feb, Sun only Mar-Sep), a decaying, grass-tussocked concrete fort built in 1885 to discourage a feared Russian invasion. A 45-minute guided tour is the only way to access the island.

### Getting There & Away

Buses 394 and L94 run from Circular Quay to La Perouse (one-way adult/child $5/3, 45 minutes, every 20 minutes).

## ROYAL NATIONAL PARK

The traditional land of the Dharawal people, the 16,500-hectare **Royal National Park** (cars $11, pedestrians & cyclists free; ☟ main roads 24hr, beach roads sunrise-8.30pm) was established in 1879, making it the oldest national park in the world. The park features vertiginous cliffs, secluded beaches, coastal scrub, lush rainforest, isolated seaside communities and raucous flocks of huge yellow-tailed black cockatoos.

The national park begins at Port Hacking, 30km south of Sydney, and stretches 20km further south. The park's main road detours to **Bundeena**, a small town on Port Hacking – a world away from Sydney's clash and throb. There's not a lot to do here beyond swimming at Horderns Beach and walking the **Bundeena-Malanbar Heritage Walk** (coastal views and Aboriginal sites).

## ROYAL NATIONAL PARK

The sandstone plateau at the northern end of the park is an ocean of low scrub, the fuel for three voracious bushfires in recent years. The most serious one (1994) destroyed 95% of the park; more diligent prevention measures have been implemented since. You'll find taller forest trees in river valleys and at the park's southern boundary on the edge of the Illawarra Escarpment. In late winter and early spring the park is carpeted with wild flowers.

Further into the park is **Wattamolla Beach** and lagoon, which is great for a swim, and **Garie Beach**, great for a surf. **Era**, **South Era** and **Burning Palms** Beaches also have good surf, but **Marley Beach** can be risky (Little Marley is safer). You can also swim in the upper

reaches of Kangaroo Creek but not the Hacking River.

There are some super picnic sites, walks and cycling tracks in the park. A walking and cycling track follows the Hacking River south from Audley; others pass tranquil, freshwater swimming holes. If you have time, the spectacular two-day, 28km **coastal walking trail** skirts the park's eastern boundary and is highly recommended.

The **visitors centre** ( ☎ 02-9542 0648; www.national parks.nsw.gov.au; Farnell Rd, Audley; ☯ 9am-4pm) can assist with camping permits, maps and bushwalking details. You can hire exercise accoutrements at the **Audley Boat Shed** ( ☎ 02-528 9867; Farnell Rd, Audley; ☯ 9am-5pm), including rowboats, canoes and kayaks ($16/30 per hour/day), aqua bikes ($12 per 30 minutes) and bicycles ($14/30 per hour/day).

## Sleeping & Eating

**Garie Beach YHA** ( ☎ 02-9261 1111; Garie Beach, Royal National Park; dm $14) There's no phone or electricity at this mega-basic, 12-bunk hostel and you have to lug in all your food, but it's close to one of the best surf beaches in NSW and is utterly secluded. Book via the **YHA Membership & Travel Centre** (Map pp78-9; ☎ 02-9261 1111; www.yha.com.au; 422 Kent St, Sydney; ☼ 9am-5pm Mon-Fri, 10am-2pm Sat) or the Cronulla Beach YHA, both of which have the key. It's a 15-minute walk from Garie Beach car park, 3½ hours from Otford train station, or 6½ hours from Bundeena.

**Cronulla Beach YHA** ( ☎ 02-9527 7772; www.cronulla beachyha.com; L1, 40 Kingsway, Cronulla; dm/d/f $28/75/95; ▣ ) The two gregarious brothers who run this comfy hostel know Cronulla intimately. Their cheerful vibe rubs off on guests and it's a top spot to hone your surfing skills or hook up with fellow coastal trail walkers. En suite doubles approach motel quality; there's good wheelchair access; the pool table, videos, body boards and linen are free.

**Beachhaven Bed & Breakfast** ( ☎ 02-9544 1333; www.beachhavenbnb.com.au; 13 Bundeena Dr, Bundeena; d incl breakfast $250-275; ▨ ▣ ) Beachhaven B&B looks a bit naff in a faux-Tudor kind of way, but has two lavish suites right on heavenly Horderns Beach. There's a barbecue, lawns to loll around on and a beautiful beach-view deck, just begging for time-wastage.

There's a drive-in **camp site** (adult/child $8/4) at Bonnie Vale near Bundeena. If you're walking, you can camp along the coastal trail and at Uloola on the western side of the park; grab a permit ($3 per person per night) from the visitors centre.

**Passionfruit Café** ( ☎ 02-9527 6555; 48 Brighton St, Bundeena; mains $5-20; ☼ breakfast & lunch daily, dinner Fri-Tue) Passionfruit's owners expertly disguise their top-quality cooking as fast-food, managing to fool even the crustiest of local yokels. The homemade lasagne, cakes and pizzas are winners; the Big Bundeena Brekky ($10) will set your day on a steady course.

**Café Manna** ( ☎ 02-9523 9555; 4/22 Brighton St, Bundeena; mains $10-15; ☼ breakfast & lunch) Unexpectedly classy Manna serves fabulous salads, gourmet kebabs and pies, toasted sandwiches and decent coffee – after several dirty days on the coastal walking track, manna from heaven indeed.

## Getting There & Away

From Sydney, take the Princes Hwy south and turn off south of Loftus to the park's northern end – it's about a 45-minute drive from the city. If you're driving north from Wollongong, don't miss the famous 665m sea-bridge section of Lawrence Hargrave Dr between Clifton and Coalcliff, dangling out over the cliffs (p323).

If you're cycling, catch a **CityRail** ( ☎ 13 15 00; www.131500.com.au) train to Cronulla from Central Station (one-way adult/concession $5/3, one hour, half-hourly), then ferry across (see next). Alternatively, Loftus, Engadine, Heathcote, Waterfall and Otford train stations are on the park boundary, with trails leading into the park. Loftus is closest to the visitors centre (6km).

The most scenic route into the park is to take the train to Cronulla then the **Cronulla National Park Ferries'** ( ☎ 02-9523 2990; www.cronullaferries. com.au; Cronulla Wharf) boat to Bundeena (one-way adult/concession $5/3, 30 minutes, hourly). Cronulla Wharf is off Tonkin St just below the train station. This outfit also runs **Port Hacking Scenic Cruises** through the summer (adult/child/family $18/13/50, three-hour cruise, 10.30am Monday to Saturday, 10.30am and 2pm Sunday) with reduced winter services.

# PARRAMATTA

☎ 02 / pop 152,600

Twenty-four kilometres west of Sydney, Parramatta, a Darug Aboriginal name meaning 'the place where eels lie down', was Australia's second European settlement. Sydney's sandy soils were lousy for growing carrots – Parramatta's river plains were chosen instead.

During the 1980s, the local rugby league team, the **Parramatta Eels**, was unbeatable, its acid-wash-clad, mullet-proud fans perpetuating Sydneysiders' view of Parramatta as little more than a lowbrow shopping-mall 'burb full of neanderthals. A rash of horrendous architectural disservices helped add to this perception, but with the '80s dead and buried, Parramatta has got on with the task of establishing itself as Sydney's second CBD, injecting a healthy dose of culture and a nascent style of its own.

Modernity aside, Parramatta retains a small-town vibe and a clutch of precious colonial buildings. The utterly helpful **Parramatta Heritage Centre** ( ☎ 8839 3311; www.parracity.nsw.gov .au; 346A Church St; ☼ 9am-5pm) can steer you towards the city's attractions.

## WILDLIFE PARKS

Several wildlife parks on Sydney's fringes let you get close to Australia's iconic wildlife.

**Koala Park Sanctuary** (Map p108; ☎ 02-9484 3141; www.koalapark.com; 84 Castle Hill Rd, West Pennant Hills; adult/child $19/9; ⏰ 9am-5pm, koala presentations 10.20am, 11.45am, 2pm & 3pm) Koala Park is a 4.5-hectare forest – as much a sanctuary for visitors as it is for the little grey tourist-magnets. Cuddle the cute critters at koala presentations while kangaroos, wombats, echidnas, dingoes and native birds watch nonplussed from the sidelines. Via public transport, take the train to Pennant Hills then catch Hills bus 631, 632 or 633 (adult/child $3/2, 10 minutes).

**Featherdale Wildlife Park** (Map p108; ☎ 02-9622 1644; www.featherdale.com.au; 217 Kildare Rd, Doonside; adult/child/family $19/10/55; ⏰ 9am-5pm) Featherdale's bushy park houses 2000 native Australians, eating, sleeping, shagging, defecating and generally being beastly. Hand-feed kangaroos, wallabies and emus, slither with reptiles, stroke soporific koalas or kill some time with a Tasmanian devil (no, they don't spin around like tornados). Excellent wheelchair access. It's a 40-minute drive from the city, or take the train to Blacktown then Busways bus 725 (adult/child $2/1, 10 minutes).

**Waratah Park Earth Sanctuary** (Map p108; ☎ 02-9986 1788; www.waratahpark.com.au; 13 Namba Rd, Duffys Forest; adult/child $17/11; ⏰ 10am-9pm, reduced winter hrs) This place was once the backdrop for the iconic '60s Australian TV show *Skippy the Bush Kangaroo*. The new owners demolished the grim old cages and constructed this rambling free-range wildlife park. Mammals such as kangaroos, bandicoots, potoroos and wallabies come out to play on evening spotlight tours (80% of Australia's wildlife is nocturnal). Entry via bookings only. It's a 30-minute drive from the city.

## Sights

**Old Government House** ( ☎ 9635 8149; www.nsw.national trust.org.au; Parramatta Park; adult/concession/family $8/5/18; ⏰ 1hr tours 10am-4.30pm Mon-Fri, 10.30am-4.30pm Sat & Sun), established in 1799, was Parramatta's first farm and housed successive NSW governors until the 1850s. It's now a preciously maintained museum. Nearby on O'Connell St, between Argyle St and Campbell St, the open, paper-dry lawns of **St John's Cemetery** ( ☎ 9686 6861; ⏰ sunrise-sunset) comprise Australia's oldest cemetery (1870), the resting place of many an early settler.

**Elizabeth Farm** ( ☎ 9635 9488; www.hht.nsw.gov.au; 70 Alice St; adult/concession/family $8/4/17; ⏰ 10am-5pm) contains part of Australia's oldest surviving European home (1793), built by renegade pastoralist/rum trader John Macarthur. It's now a hands-on museum – recline on the furniture and thumb voyeuristically through Elizabeth Macarthur's letters.

Not far away, **Hambledon Cottage** ( ☎ 9635 6924; cnr Hassall St & Gregory Pl; adult/child $4/3; ⏰ 11am-4pm Wed, Thu, Sat & Sun), built in 1824 for the Macarthurs' daughter's governess, was later used as weekend lodgings and almost became a car park in the 1980s.

An 1880s colonial bungalow, **Experiment Farm Cottage** ( ☎ 9635 5655; 9 Ruse St; adult/concession/family $6/4/14; ⏰ 10.30am-3.30pm Mon-Fri, 11am-3.30pm Sat & Sun) was built by Governor Phillip in 1791 for emancipist farmer James Ruse as an experiment to see how long it would take him to wean himself from government supplies. Ruse subsequently became Australia's first private farmer; his life is depicted in the musty cellar museum.

## Getting There & Away

By car, follow Parramatta Rd west from the city and onto the tolled Western Motorway (M4; $2) at Strathfield. It's a 45-minute drive.

**CityRail** ( ☎ 13 15 00; www.131500.com.au) trains run from Sydney's Central Station to Parramatta (one-way adult/child $4/2, 30 minutes, half-hourly). You can also get here on the **RiverCat** ( ☎ 13 15 00; www.131500.com.au) from Circular Quay (one-way adult/child $8/4, 50 minutes, hourly) – Sydney Harbour thins into the lazy, waterlily-laden Parramatta River, which measures just 25m across.

## KU-RING-GAI CHASE NATIONAL PARK

This 15,000-hectare **national park** (per car $11; ⏰ sunrise-sunset), 24km north of the city centre, borders the southern edge of Broken Bay and the western shore of Pittwater. On display is that classic Sydney cocktail of bushland, sandstone outcrops and water vistas, plus walking tracks, horse-riding trails, picnic areas and Aboriginal rock engravings.

Staffed by friendly (if a little doddery) volunteers, the **Kalkari visitors centre** ( ☎ 02-9472

9300; www.nationalparks.nsw.gov.au; Ku-ring-gai Chase Rd; (☿) 9am-5pm) runs guided tours. It's about 2.5km into the park from the Mt Colah entrance. The road descends from Kalkari to the **Bobbin Head picnic area** and **Bobbin Head Information Centre** ( ☎ 02-9472 8949; www.nationalparks.nsw.gov.au; Bobbin Head Rd; ☿ 10am-4pm) at the old Bobbin Head Inn on Cowan Creek, then climbs to the Turramurra entrance.

Elevated park sections offer **glorious water views** over Cowan Creek, Broken Bay and Pittwater. The view from West Head across Pittwater to Barrenjoey Lighthouse on Barrenjoey Head (an annexe of the national park) is also a winner.

Normally elusive **lyrebirds** are conspicuous at West Head during their May-to-July mating season; West Head Rd also offers access to **Aboriginal engravings and handprints**. From the Resolute picnic area it's 100m to some faint ochre handprints at **Red Hands Cave** (not to be confused with the Blue Mountains cave of the same name). Another 500m along Resolute Track is an engraving site. A 3km loop from here takes in Resolute Beach and another engraving site. The Basin Track makes an easy stroll to some well-preserved engravings; the Echidna Track off West Head Rd has boardwalk access to engravings. There's also a mangrove boardwalk from the Bobbin Head car park.

A sailing trip around Scotland Island, Broken Bay and Pittwater is the perfect way to see the park – contact **Halvorsen** ( ☎ 02-9457 9011;

AROUND SYDNEY

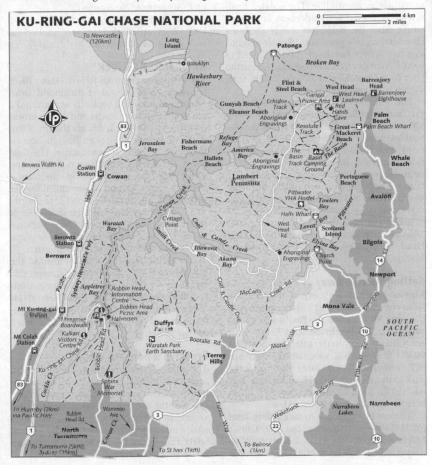

**KU-RING-GAI CHASE NATIONAL PARK**

www.halvorsenmarina.com.au; ☉ 8am-5pm) at Bobbin Head for information on where to charter or hire a boat. Sharks in Broken Bay make for a risky swim, but there's a netted area at The Basin if you simply must cool off.

**Barrenjoey Head**, the knobbly northern end of Palm Beach, is also part of Ku-ring-gai Chase National Park. Take a 30-minute tour of **Barrenjoey Lighthouse** ( ☎ 02-9472 9300; www .nationalparks.nsw.gov.au; adult/child $3/2; ☉ 11am-3pm Sun) for sensational views of the area.

## Sleeping & Eating

**Pittwater YHA Hostel** ( ☎ 02-9999 5748; www.yha.com .au; Ku-ring-gai Chase National Park; dm $28, d & tw $66) Proud of their outstanding Pittwater views and idyllic location, the staff here are almost as friendly as the wildlife. The isolated bush setting is a must for wilderness fans, who won't mind the basic but comfy facilities (the kitchen is a good'un). Splash around in a two-person kayak (per hour $15); BYO food. Bookings essential. To get here, take the ferry from Church Point to Halls Wharf, then stomp 10 minutes up the hill.

The only place you can camp in Ku-ring-gai Chase is the **Basin Camping Ground** ( ☎ 02-9974 1011; www.basincampground.com.au; Ku-ring-gai Chase National Park; per night adult/child $10/5), a 2.8km walk from West Head Rd or a ferry or water-taxi ride from Palm Beach. The site sits on an improbably scenic sandy spit jutting into Pittwater. There are basic amenities, but bring your own food and cooking equipment. Bookings essential.

Inside the park there are takeaway **cafés** (mains $5-15; ☉ breakfast & lunch) at the Bobbin Head Information Centre and Halvorsen Marina.

## Getting There & Away

Ku-ring-gai Chase is about a 45-minute drive from the city, with four road entrances to the park: Mt Colah on the Pacific Hwy; Turramurra in the southwest; and Terrey Hills and Church Point in the southeast. **Shorelink Buses** ( ☎ 02-9457 8888; www.shorelink.com.au) bus 577 runs from Turramurra Station to the park entrance on Bobbin Head Rd (one-way adult/child $4/2, 20 minutes, hourly). From here it's about 3km to Bobbin Head.

Another bus option is to take **Sydney Buses** ( ☎ 13 15 00; www.131500.com.au) bus 190, L90 or L88 from Wynyard Park in the city to Warringah Mall, Dee Why or Mona Vale then bus 156 to Church Point. Ask for a ticket for the entire journey (one-way adult/child $6/3, one hour 30 minutes, hourly).

The **Palm Beach Ferry Service** ( ☎ 02-9974 2411; www.palmbeachferry.com.au) shunts between Palm Beach Wharf in Pittwater and The Basin (one-way adult/concession $12/6, 15 minutes, hourly). **Palm Beach & Hawkesbury River Cruises** ( ☎ 02-9974 2159, 0414 466 635; www.sydney sceniccruises.com) operates a there-and-back ferry from Palm Beach to Bobbin Head, via Patonga (return adult/child $35/20, four hours 30 minutes, 11am Monday to Friday, 9am, 11am and 3.45pm Saturday and Sunday). Call for bookings. **Church Point Water Taxis** ( ☎ 0428 238 190) operates services on demand between Church Point Ferry Wharf and Palm Beach ($55 for up to six people, 20 minutes).

To get to Palm Beach, take bus 190 or L90 from Wynyard Park (one-way adult/child $6/3, one hour 30 minutes, half-hourly).

# HAWKESBURY RIVER

The slow-roaming, smoky Hawkesbury River begins as a wet sliver near Richmond, from where it ribbons and moils its way around a series of rainy river towns and bushy promontories. By the time it reaches the sea, 30km north of Sydney at Broken Bay, its beautiful bulk dominates the landscape. The final 20km stretch is dotted with coves, beaches and picnic spots, the river spreading into inlets at Berowra Creek, Cowan Water and Pittwater to the south, and Brisbane Water to the north. The Hawkesbury also links the shorelines of Marramarra and Ku-ring-gai Chase National Parks in the south and Dharug, Brisbane Water and Bouddi National Parks to the north.

The fertile farming country around the Hawkesbury sustains vineyards, vegetable farms, flower acreages and alpaca studs. Contact **Hawkesbury Harvest** ( ☎ 02-4570 1250, 0415 244 477; www.hawkesburyharvest.com.au) for information on wine and farm trails and seasonal work opportunities.

## Brooklyn & Berowra Waters

The small oyster-farming town of **Brooklyn** squats on the Hawkesbury where it departs its thickly wooded banks and swells into the open space of the estuary. Tattooed locals stomp around in gumboots and beanies, their lives settled into a measured pace revolving around boats, fishing and fishing boats. Things liven up on summer weekends.

The **Riverboat Postman** ( ☎ 02-9985 7566; fax 02-9985 7658; Brooklyn Wharf, Brooklyn; adult/child/family $45/25/115; ☯ 9.30am-1.15pm Mon-Fri) is Australia's last operating mail boat and a decidedly old-school way to get a feel for the river. It chugs 40km up the Hawkesbury as far as Marlow, near Spencer, with additional 'coffee cruises' in summer. Combine the two experiences on an all-day cruise (adult/child/family $60/40/150); call for times and bookings. The 8.16am train from Sydney's Central Station gets you to Brooklyn's Hawkesbury River Station in time to meet the morning boat. You may have to change at Hornsby.

For an authentic taste of the local preoccupation, take a **Crab 'N' Oyster Cruise** ( ☎ 02-9985 9237; www.crab-n-oystercruises.com.au; Brooklyn Wharf, Brooklyn; per person $84; ☯ 11.30am-2pm) up the river – shuck some oysters, haul in crab traps then cook and eat the fruits of your labour. It also runs 1½-hour morning and afternoon tea cruises ($66 per person) departing 9am and 3.30pm respectively. Two days advance booking required.

If you don't have time for a cruise, you can slither down some sensationally snotty local oysters at **Joshua's Seafood Bar Café** ( ☎ 02-9985 7877; 5 Bridge St, Brooklyn; 12 oysters $8-15; ☯ breakfast & lunch Thu-Sun, dinner Wed-Sun). It also has a takeaway kiosk on the wharf.

Further upstream, a narrow forested waterway diverts from the Hawkesbury and peters down to the chilled-out river town **Berowra Waters** where a handful of businesses, boatsheds and residences cluster around the free, 24-hour ferry across Berowra Creek. If you feel like exploring, rev the river in an outboard dinghy from the **Berowra Waters Marina** ( ☎ 02-9456 3200; fax 02-9456 4244; 199 Bay Rd, Berowra Waters; half-day $70; ☯ 8.30am-5.30pm Mon-Fri, from 7.30am Sat & Sun). In the same complex, the **Fish Café** ( ☎ 02-9456 4665; 199 Bay Rd, Berowra Waters; mains $10-17; ☯ breakfast & lunch daily, dinner Wed-Sun) serves various fishy delights plus salads, steaks and burgers with a serene river outlook.

If you want to stay the night in the area, the **Hawkesbury River Accommodation Booking Service** ( ☎ 02-9987 7090; www.hawkesburyriverrealestate.com.au; 2/5 Bridge St, Brooklyn; ☯ 9am-5pm Mon-Fri, to 4pm Sat, 10am-3pm Sun) has the lowdown on local accommodation options (excluding houseboats; see boxed text p116).

Berowra Waters is 5km west of the Sydney–Newcastle Fwy – take the Berowra turn-off. The road hairpins down to the township

through jagged sandstone terraces (lousy for caravans). The Brooklyn turn-off is further north, just before the freeway crosses the Hawkesbury. An alternative (and just as curvy) route to Berowra Waters is the road through the Galston Gorge, north of Hornsby in Sydney's northeast.

**CityRail** ( ☎ 13 15 00; www.131500.com.au) trains run from Sydney's Central Station to Berowra (one-way adult/child $6/3, 45 minutes, roughly hourly) and on to Brooklyn's Hawkesbury River Station (one-way adult/child $7/4, one hour). Berowra Station is a solid 6km trudge from Berowra Waters. **Hawkesbury Cruises** ( ☎ 02-9985 9900; www.hawkesburycruises.com.au) runs water taxis on demand to anywhere along the river.

## Wisemans Ferry & Around

The sedentary riverside hamlet of **Wisemans Ferry** (Map p137) spills over a bow of the Hawkesbury River where it slides east towards Brooklyn. Access from the south is via the direct Old Northern Rd. A more camera-conducive route is from the east, via Old Wisemans Ferry Rd, wedged between Dharug National Park and the river. Two free 24-hour ferries connect the Wisemans Ferry river banks. Note that swimming in the Hawkesbury between Wisemans Ferry and Windsor during summer is sometimes ill-advised due to blue-green algae. Call the **Environment Protection Authority** (EPA; ☎ 13 15 55) pollution line for updates.

The town's social hub is the historic sandstone **Wisemans Ferry Inn** ( ☎ 02-4566 4301;

---

**DON'T PAY THE FERRYMAN**

As the Hawkesbury River curls abstractly across the plains, roads (on far more linear trajectories) invariably bump into it. Dating back to 1827, a curious culture of free, 24-hour, winch-driven ferries has evolved to shunt vehicles across the water. Your car is guided onto the punts by burly, bearded, fluoro-clad ferrymen, who lock safety-gates into position then shunt you to the other side, sliding into the opposite riverbank with a satisfying shudder. You'll find ferries at Berowra Waters, Wisemans Ferry, Lower Portland and Sackville. Turn off your headlights if you're waiting for the ferry at night so you don't blind the approaching skipper.

fax 02-4566 4780; Old Northern Rd, Wisemans Ferry; d & tw $66, f $75), which has six basic pub rooms with shared bathrooms, smudged with '70s décor. The pub downstairs buzzes with country singers, smokers and lingerie barmaids, the bistro (mains $12-25; open lunch and dinner) serves hefty country plates of steak, pasta and seafood.

If bawdy pub revelry doesn't float your boat, the exotically named **Del Rio Riverside Resort** ( ☎ 02-4566 4330; www.delrioresort.com.au; Chaseling Rd, Webbs Creek, Wisemans Ferry; unpowered/powered sites per 2 people $30/33; cabins from $100; ⊠ ⊇ ) is a rambling caravan park on the opposite side of the river, with loads of activities (swimming pool, nine-hole golf course, tennis courts, movie screenings, bushwalks etc), roomy sites, cabins ranging from ho-hum to home-away-from-home and a restaurant (mains $16-27; open lunch Saturday and Sunday, dinner daily). Follow the signs 2.5km from the Webbs Creek ferry crossing at Wisemans Ferry.

Largely unsealed roads on both sides of the Macdonald River run north from Wisemans Ferry to tiny **St Albans** (Map p137) in Darkinjung tribal country. It's a photo-worthy drive, with rocky, wattle-dappled bush on one side and soft river ripples on the other.

**Settlers Arms Inn** ( ☎ 02-4568 2111; www.settlersarms.com.au; 1 Wharf St, St Albans; d from $130; ⊇ ) is the town's heart and soul, a noble sandstone pub dating back to 1836. If you want to stay the night, book an en-suite cabin behind the pub.

The Inn's chunky old **bar** ( ☎ 02-4568 2111; mains $13-25; ☉ lunch daily, dinner Fri-Sun) feels like a bushrangers' den, with English-style ales on tap, a thigh-warming winter hearth and

fabulous pies, soups, steak sandwiches and antipastos from the kitchen. Summer daytrippers pack the beer garden and timber tables out the front.

On the hill behind the pub (behind the totem poles), **St Albans Gallery** ( ☎ 02-4568 2286; stalbansgallery@myisp.net.au; ☉ 11am-5pm Fri-Sun) has quirky exhibitions of local jewellery, glass, painting, sculpture and indigenous art. Have a coffee and some homemade cake on the balcony after you've had a browse.

## National Parks

Before the 1789 introduction of smallpox decimated 90% of their society, **Dharug National Park** (Map p137) was home to the Dharuk people (also spelled Dharug or Darug). It's a 14,000-hectare wilderness on the north bank of the Hawkesbury River, noted for its rock carvings dating back nearly 10,000 years. Forming the western boundary of the park is the dilapidated **Old Great North Rd**, built by convicts in the 1820s to link Sydney and Newcastle. There's drive-in camping in the park 8km east of Wisemans Ferry at **Mill Creek camp site** (per night adult/child $5/3), and free walk-in camping 12km north of Wisemans Ferry at **Ten Mile Hollow camp site** on Old Great North Rd. Book through the Gosford NPWS Office (p136).

On the south side of the Hawkesbury is the 11,760-hectare **Marramarra National Park** (Map p137), with vehicle access from Old Northern Rd about 20km south of Wisemans Ferry. There's free bush-camping on the river at **Gentlemans Halt camp site**, a 10km walk from the road, and at **Marramarra Creek camp site**, a

---

### HAWKESBURY HOUSEBOATS

Stressed-out Sydneysiders love to switch off their mobile phones, pack the kids in the back of the SUV and flee to the Hawkesbury for a relaxed weekend of fishing, chardonnay sipping and houseboat cruising. Houseboat hire rates skyrocket during summer and school holidays, but most outfits offer affordable low-season, midweek and long-term rental specials. As a rough guide, a two-/four-/six-berth boat for three nights costs from $600/750/1000 between May and September, prices doubling during summer.

Most companies base themselves at Brooklyn; here are some of the main players:

- **Able Hawkesbury River Houseboats** ( ☎ 1800 024 979; www.hawkesburyhouseboats.com.au; 3008 River Rd, Wiseman's Ferry)

- **Brooklyn Marina** ( ☎ 02-9985 7722; www.brooklynmarina.com.au; 45 Brooklyn Rd, Brooklyn)

- **Holidays Afloat** ( ☎ 02-9985 7368; www.holidaysafloat.com.au; 65 Brooklyn Rd, Brooklyn)

- **Ripples Houseboats** ( ☎ 02-9985 5555; www.ripples.com.au; 87 Brooklyn Rd, Brooklyn)

4km walk from the road. Contact the **NPWS Office** ( ☎ 02-9472 8949; www.nationalparks.nsw.gov.au) in Ku-ring-gai Chase National Park for bookings and information.

## MACQUARIE TOWNS

The river flats of the upper Hawkesbury River, in the lee of the Blue Mountains, offered the young colony of NSW rich agricultural land for much-needed food. It was here that Governor Lachlan Macquarie established the five 'Macquarie Towns' – Pitt Town, Castlereagh, Windsor, Richmond and Wilberforce. Today the latter three make an interesting triangular meander, particularly en route to the Blue Mountains on the Bells Line of Road (p130).

### Windsor

☎ 02

Windsor, founded in 1810 on the banks of the Hawkesbury River, was the main Macquarie Town and retains a crop of gracefully proportioned colonial buildings. The town seems to have shrugged off rural slow-pokery and stagnation and feels surprisingly lively and artsy.

The **Hawkesbury Historical Museum** ( ☎ 4577 2310; www.windsor-nsw.com.au; 7 Thompson Sq; adult/child $3/1; ◷ 11am-3pm Fri-Wed), in the 1843 Daniel O'Connell Inn, has a collection of exhibits portraying pioneering life in the region. There's also a room devoted to the Royal Australian Air Force (RAAF), and plenty of tourist paraphernalia.

If you're architecturally inclined, have a wander around the lantern-topped, convict-built **St Matthew's Church** ( ☎ 4577 3193; fax 4577 3193; Moses St; ◷ 10am-3pm, services 8am, 10am & 5.30pm Sun), erected in 1820 and designed by convict architect Francis Greenway. Another Greenway special is the elegant 1822 **Windsor Courthouse** ( ☎ 4577 5023; fax 4587 7272; cnr Court & Pitt Sts), still a functional courthouse.

The shambling **Macquarie Arms Hotel** ( ☎ 4577 2206; fax 4577 3465; 99 George St; ◷ 10am-midnight) proclaims itself the oldest pub in Australia (1815), though there are a few 'oldest pubs' around. History hasn't gone to its head and it's still very much a small-town pub, with a sunny beer garden, a decent bistro (mains $13-24, open lunch and dinner) and rows of shiny Harleys parked out the front.

On Sundays you can satiate your crafty Australiana cravings, pick up a pot of homemade jam or contemplate a career in busking at the **Windsor Mall Craft Markets** ( ☎ 4572

7348; www.windsormallcraftmarkets.com.au; Windsor Mall, George St btw Fitzgerald & Baker Sts; ◷ 9am-4pm Sun). After the market, pluck up the courage for a lantern-lit **Windsor Ghost Tour** ( ☎ /fax 4577 6882; per person $25; ◷ 7-9.15pm) that night. Tours start and end at the Macquarie Arms and include a light supper. Bookings essential; no under-10s (too spooky).

The spanking new **Hawkesbury Regional Gallery** ( ☎ 4560 4441; www.hawkesbury.com.au; L1, Deerubbin Centre, 300 George St; admission free; ◷ 10am-4pm Mon & Wed-Fri, to 3pm Sat & Sun) has become Windsor's cultural centre, with art exhibitions, literary launches, film screenings and kids' events. It's worth a look if only for the snazzy architecture.

If you're in Windsor on a Sunday, the **Hawkesbury Paddlewheeler** ( ☎ 4575 1171; www .paddlewheeler.com.au; Windsor Bridge Wharf; per person $30; ◷ 12.30-2.30pm Sun) splashes up and down the river on its octogenarian-friendly Lunch & Jazz cruise.

There are a couple of serviceable (if unspectacular) motels in town if you feel like staying the night:

**Windsor Motel** ( ☎ 4577 3626; www.windsormotorinn .com; 54 George St; d from $90; ⚇ ) Clean and tidy motel anonymity.

**Windsor Terrace Motel** ( ☎ 4577 5999; www.windsor terracemotel.com; 47 George St; d from $110; ⚇ ) Overlooking the river.

If the pub isn't your style, you can get a reliable coffee at **Simon's Coffee Lounge** ( ☎ 4577 2208; 1/100 George St, Windsor Mall; mains $6-14; ◷ breakfast & lunch) or a cheerily meat-centric meal at **Cookies Bar & Grill** ( ☎ 4577 5422; 22 Fitzgerald St; mains $17-25; ◷ lunch & dinner).

Driving from Sydney, the direct route to Windsor is Windsor Rd (Route 40), the northwestern continuation of Parramatta's Church St (you'll have to sidestep the Church St Mall). West of Parramatta, Northern Rd climbs north from Penrith on the Great Western Hwy. **CityRail** ( ☎ 13 15 00; www.131500.com.au) trains run from Sydney's Central Station to Windsor (one-way adult/child $7/4, one hour 10 minutes, roughly hourly); you might need to change at Blacktown.

### Wilberforce & Around

Wee Wilberforce, 6km north of Windsor, is an agricultural river-flat town without much going for it, and no-one around to tell you otherwise. If you're looking for somewhere to eat or sleep, head for Windsor.

Picnickers and taxidermists might want to swing by the **Butterfly Farm** ( ☎ 02-4575 1955; www.butterflyfarm.com.au; 446 Wilberforce Rd, Wilberforce; adult/child $6/3; �½ 10am-5pm), where you can barbecue the innards of your hamper then work it off in the swimming pool (adult/child $4/3). The river beaches on the property draw marauding water-skiers; the museum features glass-fronted cases of wing-pinned butterflies and an interesting collation of old bottles, boots and tin cans. **Westbus** ( ☎ 02-9890 0000; www.westbus.com.au) buses 668 and 669 run from Windsor Station to Wilberforce (one-way adult/child $3/2; 15 minutes, infrequently).

The immaculately restored 1809 **Ebenezer Church** ( ☎ 02-4579 9491; 78 Coromandel Rd, Ebenezer; �½ 10am-3.30pm, service 8.30am Sun), 5km north of Wilberforce (turn right off Singleton Rd), is said (in hushed, reverent whispers) to be the oldest church in Australia, its Sunday pews still filling. The adjoining cemetery is littered with skewed pioneer graves gradually succumbing to gravity. Continue your reflection next door at the **Schoolmaster's House** ( ☎ 02-4579 9350; 78 Coromandel Rd, Ebenezer; �½ 10am-3.30pm), another 'Australia's oldest', which has a little local history museum and serves Devonshire tea on a grapevine-shaded terrace. Just down the road from here, the **Shallow Rock Reach Walking Trail** follows the Hawkesbury riverbank for 1.2km (one hour return), passing tall remnant river forest, open woodlands, lookouts, picnic spots and guffawing kookaburras.

Established in 1887, the Tuscanesque sandstone **Tizzana Winery** ( ☎ 02-4579 1150; www.tizzana.com.au; 518 Tizzana Rd, near Ebenezer, r incl breakfast $175-220; �½ noon-6pm Sat & Sun; ▨ ) has cellar-door sales of its own wines and perky drops from other local vineyards. Then check in to the superb five-star accommodation upstairs (think shutters, open fires, Persian rugs, big bathrooms, bigger beds). One of the rooms here has its own veranda and courtyard, ideal for knocking off the rest of the red.

## Richmond
☎ 02

Founded in 1810, Richmond is a substantial country town with some fine Georgian and Victorian buildings, but it lacks Windsor's touch of class – there are more tractor, water-tank and chainsaw vendors here than anything else.

Architectural relics of interest include the 1878 **courthouse** and **police station** ( ☎ 4578 0731;

fax 4578 0732; cnr Market & Windsor St) and, around the corner on Market St, the quasi-Gothic **St Andrew's Church** ( ☎ 4578 3820; �½ services 8.30am, 9.45am & 6pm Sun), dating from 1845. The similarly historic **St Peter's Church** ( ☎ 4578 1205; www.richmondanglican.com.au; 384 Windsor St; �½ services 8am, 10am & 7pm Sun), built in 1841, is at the western end of town. The cedar pews inside are stoically impressive; the oldest pioneer tombstone in the cemetery dates from 1809. More recent is the appealingly paint-peeling **Regent Cinema** ( ☎ 4578 1800; www.richmondregent.com.au; 149 Windsor St; adult/concession $10/8; �½ 10am-11pm), which oozes Art Deco charm and screens recent releases.

Oddly stranded halfway between Richmond and Windsor, the **Hawkesbury visitors centre** ( ☎ 4578 0233; www.hawkesburytourism.com.au; Bicentennial Park, Ham Common, Windsor Rd, Clarendon; �½ 9am-5pm), near the RAAF base, is the Hawkesbury region's main information centre, also handling accommodation bookings. Richmond's **NPWS Office** ( ☎ 4588 5247; www.nationalparks.nsw.gov.au; Bowmans Cottage, 370 Windsor St; �½ 9am-12.30pm & 1.30-4.30pm Mon-Fri) is inside a heritage-listed 1817 weatherboard cottage, providing information and permits for the area's national parks.

Richmond's most reliable sleeping option is the **Best Western Colonial Motel** ( ☎ 4578 1166; www.colonialmotel.com.au; 161 March St; d from $100; ▨ ), offering a particularly clean version of the usual motel fare.

If you're hungry, duck into **Madisons Bar & Brasserie** ( ☎ 4588 5808; cnr Windsor & Paget Sts; mains $14-20; �½ breakfast Sun, lunch & dinner daily), a stylish mustard-and-rust-coloured Georgian house on the main street. Steaks, roasts, hearty soups and the odd seafood dish are on the menu, with outdoor summer tables and an open fire in winter.

**CityRail** ( ☎ 13 15 00; www.131500.com.au) trains run from Sydney's Central Station to Richmond (one-way adult/child $7/4, one hour 20 minutes, roughly hourly); you might need to change at Blacktown.

## MACARTHUR COUNTRY

The Hume Hwy (South Western Motorway) follows a rising corridor southwest from Sydney, with the jagged Blue Mountains National Park to the west and the coastal escarpment to the east. This is cleared, rolling sheep country containing some of the state's oldest towns, though Liverpool and Campbelltown have been subsumed by Sydney's ever-expanding suburban girth You can still catch a rural eyeful by dodging the motorway and taking Northern Rd between Penrith and Narellan (just north of Camden).

## Camden
☎ 02

About 50km southwest of Sydney, Camden is an old-fashioned, rootsy, church-going country town with the kind of main street Bruce Springsteen likes to sing about. There's a whiff of agriculture in the air, the town's gardens and historical sites bravely holding off the encroaching big-house-on-a-small-block suburbia. In the 1830s, John and Elizabeth Macarthur ran vaguely Frankensteinian sheep-breeding experiments here, the beginnings of Australia's wool industry.

**John Oxley Cottage** ( ☎ 4658 1370; www.camden .nsw.gov.au; Camden Valley Way, Elderslie; ☒ 9.30am-4pm), 3km north of the town's centre, was built in the 1890s as a workman's cottage. Under the new roofing iron are the original roof shingles, under which the visitors centre has local information. Pick up a copy of the *Camden Heritage Walk* pamphlet documenting the town's historic sites.

Newly renovated **Camden Historical Society Museum** ( ☎ 4655 3400; 40 John St; admission free; ☒ 11am-4pm Thu-Sun) has opened its doors to reveal 'working country town' displays capturing Camden's growth and history.

East of Camden, off Narellan Rd, the **Mount Annan Botanic Garden** ( ☎ 4648 2477; www.rbgsyd.nsw .gov.au; Mt Annan Dr, Mt Annan; adult/child/family $4/2/9; ☒ 10am-6pm Oct-Mar, to 4pm Apr-Sep), the native-plant branch of Sydney's Royal Botanic Gardens, claims to be the largest botanic garden in the southern hemisphere. With 4000 species on 1000 acres strewn with 400 lazy kangaroos and wallaroos, its claim seems entirely plausible.

For a bird's-eye inspection of Camden's surrounds, **Balloon Aloft** ( ☎ 1800 020 568; www .balloonaloft.com; 144 Wine Country Dr, North Rothbury; adult/child $295/180) runs hour-long hot-air balloon flights, mushrooming into the dawn from Camden airport (champagne breakfast afterwards). Call for bookings and times.

Not far from John Oxley Cottage, the **Poplar Caravan Park** ( ☎ /fax 4658 0485; 21 Macarthur Rd, Elderslie; unpowered & powered sites per 2 people $22, cabins from $80) has plenty of tent-pitching space and the usual cabin fodder. Whether or not the surrounding trees are poplars is debatable.

Debate it over a beer and a country pub meal at the **Argyle Inn** ( ☎ 4655 8189; 75 Argyle St; mains $18-27; ☒ lunch & dinner), a terracotta-roofed family pub on Camden's main street (look for the plough and harrow above the awning).

If you're driving to Camden, take the F5 Fwy south from Sydney and follow the signs. Alternatively, take a **CityRail** ( ☎ 13 15 00; www.131500.com.au) train from Sydney's Central Station to Campbelltown (one-way adult/child $7/4, one hour, half-hourly), then **Busways** ( ☎ 4368 2277; www.131500.com.au) bus 895 or 896 (one-way adult/child $5/3, 25 minutes, half-hourly) into Camden.

## Picton
☎ 02

Originally called Stonequarry, Picton – smaller, less trafficked and better looking than Camden – is entirely detour worthy. It's coal rather than stone that's mined under the hills these days, causing a subsidence problem or two for some local houses. Still standing are the National Trust–listed buildings on upper **Menangle St**.

Inside the old post office, the **Wollondilly visitors centre** ( ☎ 4677 3962; www.stonequarry.com.au; cnr Argyle & Menangle Sts; ☒ 9am-5pm) has racks of tourist brochures, including one detailing the Historic Picton Walking Tour. If you're tired after your walk, recover in a spa room at the **White Waratah Retreat** ( ☎ 4677 2121; www.whitewaratah retreat.com.au; 1665 Remembrance Dr; d from $110; ☒ ), a motel dressed in retreat's clothing.

In the morning, the cheerily mainstream **Cutting Edge Café** ( ☎ 4677 0699; 3/135 Argyle St; mains $8-15; ☒ breakfast & lunch Wed-Mon) serves big cooked breakfasts, city-standard coffee and surprisingly worldly mains like *mussaman chicken* curry and grilled Cajun barramundi fillets.

From Camden, drive about 20km south to Picton along Remembrance Dr. **CityRail** ( ☎ 13 15 00; www.131500.com.au) trains run to Picton from Sydney's Central Station (one-way adult/child $9/5, one hour 30 minutes, roughly hourly).

# BLUE MOUNTAINS

For more than a century the Blue Mountains have been luring Sydneysiders up from the sweltering plains with promises of cool-climate relief and naughty fireside weekends. Sweetening the invitation are astounding scenery, fabulous bushwalks and more gorges, gumtrees and gourmet restaurants

# BLUE MOUNTAINS

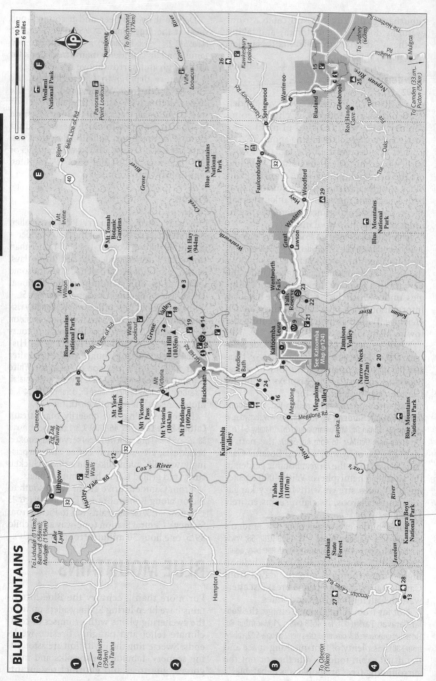

than seems viable. The purple haze that gives the mountains their name comes from a fine mist of oil exuded by eucalyptus trees.

The foothills begin 65km inland from Sydney, rising to a 1100m-high sandstone plateau riddled with valleys eroded into the stone over thousands of years. In 1813, Wentworth, Blaxland and Lawson were the first Europeans to traverse the mountains. Today's Great Western Hwy follows their route through the laid-back towns of Blaxland, Lawson and Wentworth Falls. Katoomba is the 'King of the Mountain', with Art Deco cafés, an edgy arts scene and active pub life.

There are three national parks in the area, the most accessible of which is the **Blue Mountains National Park**, protecting large tracts of forest north and south of the Great Western Hwy. Absorb the park's eye-popping scenery at the numerous drive-up lookouts, or get amongst the greenery on established bushwalking tracks. Southwest of here is **Kanangra Boyd National Park**, accessible from Oberon or Jenolan Caves. Launch into a bushwalk, descend into limestone caverns or check out the amazing Kanangra Walls Plateau encircled by sheer

cliffs. **Wollemi National Park**, north of Bells Line of Road, is the state's largest forested wilderness area (nearly 500,000 hectares) with rugged bushwalking and native critters aplenty.

Entry to these parks is free unless you enter the Blue Mountains National Park at Bruce Rd, Glenbrook ($7 per car, walkers free).

## GLENBROOK TO WENTWORTH FALLS

From Marge's Lookout and Elizabeth's Lookout, near Glenbrook, there are super views back to Sydney. The section of the Blue Mountains National Park south of Glenbrook contains **Red Hands Cave**, an old Aboriginal shelter with hand stencils on the walls. It's an easy, 7km return walk southwest of the Glenbrook NPWS centre (closed at the time of writing) on Great Western Hwy.

Celebrated artist, author and *bon vivant* Norman Lindsay, famed for his saucy artworks, lived in Faulconbridge from 1912 until his death in 1969. His home and studio is now the **Norman Lindsay Gallery & Museum** ( ☎ 02-4751 1067; www.hermes.net.au/nlg; 14 Norman Lindsay Cres, Faulconbridge; adult/child $9/6; ☉ 10am-4pm) with a significant collection of his paintings, watercolours, drawings and sculptures. There's a fabulous café on site too.

A brick-and-iron barn sprouting from the bush 8km northeast of Springwood, the eco-friendly **Hawkesbury Heights YHA** ( ☎ 02-4754 5621; www.yha.com.au; 840 Hawkesbury Rd, Hawkesbury Heights; adult/child $24/12) has solar power and sensational valley views. Inside, beneath tree-trunk structural framing, are comfortable rooms, a wood heater, a huge kitchen and an amazing sandstone-slab table. Sleeps 12 in twin or double rooms; reservations essential. Unless you have wheels, it's a sweaty hike from Springwood.

As you head into Wentworth Falls, you'll get your first real taste of Blue Mountains scenery: views to the south open out across the majestic **Jamison Valley**. **Wentworth Falls** themselves launch a plume of fraying droplets over a 300m drop – check them out from **Falls Reserve**. This is also the starting point for a network of walking tracks, which delve into the sublime **Valley of the Waters**, with waterfalls, gorges, woodlands and rainforests.

**Camp sites** are accessible by road at **Euroka Clearing** (vehicle/adult/child $7/6/3) near Glenbrook, and **Murphys Glen** near Woodford. Check track/road condition updates and collect permits for Euroka Clearing at the Richmond **NPWS Office** (p118).

# LEURA

☎ 02 / pop 4000

Leura is a gracious, affluent town fashioned around undulating streets, unparalleled gardens and sweeping Victorian verandas. Art Deco houses mingle with contemporary architecture and the suburban streets ooze style. The **Mall**, the tree-lined main street, offers rows of country craft stores and cafés for the daily tourist influx.

## Information

**Leura Visitors Gateway** ( ☎ 4784 2881; www.bmgst.com; 121 The Mall; ☽ 9am-5pm) Run by knowledgeable, enthusiastic staff, this centre books accommodation and door-to-door Blue Mountains and Jenolan Caves tours and has a local art gallery next door.

## Sights & Activities

**Leuralla Toy & Railway Museum** ( ☎ 4784 1169; www.toyandrailwaymuseum.com.au; 36 Olympian Pde; adult/child $12/6; ☽ 10am-5pm) is an Art Deco mansion set amid five misty hectares of handsome English gardens. The house is a memorial to HV 'Doc' Evatt, a former Australian Labor Party leader and the first UN president. Kids love the model-railway and toy museum (everything from Barbie to Bob the Builder).

Designed in the 1930s by famous Danish landscaper Paul Sorensen, **Everglades Gardens** ( ☎ 4784 1938; www.evergladesgardens.info; 37 Everglades Ave; adult/child $6/2; ☽ 10am-5pm Oct-Mar, to 4pm Apr-Sep) is a National Trust property and Leura's horticultural heartland. Fountains, waterfalls, terraced lawns, freestone walls, a museum, art gallery and tearooms – a must for green thumbs.

**Sublime Point** is a dramatic clifftop lookout south of Leura. On sunny days the clouds shadow-dance across the vast blue valley below. Further north is **Gordon Falls Reserve**, an idyllic picnic spot. From here you can trek the Prince Henry Cliff Track, or take the Cliff Drive 4km west past Leura Cascades to Katoomba's Echo Point.

## Festivals

Finding it easy being green, the **Leura Gardens Festival** ( ☎ 4757 2539; www.leuragardensfestival.com.au) happens in the first week of October.

## Sleeping & Eating

**Woodford of Leura** ( ☎ 4784 2240; www.leura.com; 48 Woodford St; d from $185) From the Hobbitesque

Gothic entrance to the fittings in the pristine bathrooms, this stylish B&B is genteel all over. Beyond the stunning garden (another Paul Sorensen extravaganza), period furniture jostles around a log fire. Standard rooms, stylish suites and long-stay discounts are available. It's about 1km from the town centre.

**Post Office Restaurant** ( ☎ 4784 3976; 148 The Mall; mains $28-30; ☽ lunch & dinner) You guessed it, it's an old post office. By day the ambient eatery serves fresh café fare; by night the cuisine is positively cultivated – even fussy palates swoon over fresh pastas and smoked, braised meat and fish dishes. Shimmying, black-clad service and moody music top it all off.

Other recommendations:

**Leura House** ( ☎ 4784 2035; www.leurahouse.com.au; 7 Britain St; s/d from $129/158) A grand Victorian home on Leura's highest point (room 11 has views to Sydney). Indulgent rooms, spacious common areas and balconies.

**Loaves and the Dishes** ( ☎ 4784 3600; 180a The Mall; mains $10-15; ☽ breakfast & lunch) Wholesome, hearty deli goodies in a curvy corner Deco café.

## Getting There & Around

The direct route to the Blue Mountains from Sydney is via Parramatta Rd, detouring onto the tolled Western Motorway (M4; $2) at Strathfield. (

**CityRail** ( ☎ 13 15 00; www.131500.com.au) runs from Sydney's Central Station to Leura (adult/child $12/6, two hours, hourly). The **Blue Mountains Bus Co** ( ☎ 4751 1077; www.mountainlink.com.au) runs from Valley Heights (near Springwood) to Mt Victoria, stopping pretty much everywhere in between, including Leura (one-way adult/child $8/4, 45 minutes, five daily Monday to Friday, three Saturday).

You can hire a car in Valley Heights from **RediCAR** ( ☎ 4751 8920; www.redicar.com.au; 42 Great

---

### CLIMATIC CONFUSION

Be prepared for a climatic shift as you assail the Blue Mountains – swelter in Coogee, shiver in Katoomba. The mountains are promoted as a cool-climate attraction, but visit any time: summer days are hazy perfection; autumn fogs make Katoomba an eerily atmospheric place. Despite the chill, winter days can be sunny, and down in the sheltered valleys, insects buzz in warm, windless bliss. Winter snows sometimes dapple the highest peaks.

Western Hwy, Valley Heights; (🕑) 9am-5pm Mon-Fri, to noon Sat) from $69 per day.

## KATOOMBA
🕿 02 / pop 18,000

Swirling otherworldly mists, steep streets lined with Art Deco buildings, astonishing valley views and a quirky miscellany of brilliant restaurants, buskers, artists, galleries, homeless people, bawdy pubs and classy hotels – Katoomba manages to be bohemian and bourgeois, embracing and menacing, all at once. Locals are beautifully dissolute – lots of people seem to be smoking, wearing a beanie or growing a beard. A vague sniff of 'herb' wafts between cafés and camping supply shops.

## Orientation

Katoomba's grid layout hurdles the Great Western Hwy. Almost everything visitors will need or want lies south of the highway – the main drag is Katoomba St, running south from the train station. Echo Point and the Three Sisters are at the southern end of town, where the Jamison Valley's dramatic plunge truncates the soft urban sprawl.

## Information

### INTERNET ACCESS
**Katoomba Book Exchange** ( 🕿 4782 9997; katbook exchange@telstra.com; 32 Katoomba St; per 30min/1hr $4/7; (🕑) 10am-6pm Tue-Sat, noon-6pm Sun & Mon) The first 15 minutes are free if you order a coffee.

### MEDICAL SERVICES
**Blue Mountains District Hospital** ( 🕿 4784 6500; fax 4784 6730; cnr Woodlands Rd & Great Western Hwy; (🕑) 24hr emergency)
**Katoomba Medical Centre** ( 🕿 4782 2222; fax 4782 3635; 143 Katoomba St; (🕑) 8.30am-6.30pm Mon-Fri, to noon Sat) Doctors by appointment.

### MONEY & POST
There are numerous banks and ATMs on Katoomba St. The post office is behind the shopping centre, between Katoomba and Park Sts.

### TOURIST INFORMATION
**Blue Mountains Accommodation Booking Service** ( 🕿 4782 2857; www.bluemountainsbudget.com; 157 Lurline St; (🕑) 10.30am-5.30pm) Free accommodation booking service.
**Echo Point visitors centre** ( 🕿 4782 9865, 1300 653 408; www.australiabluemountains.com.au; Echo Point; (🕑) 9am-5pm) Sizable centre with can-do staff.

## Sights

At the southern end of town (about 2km from the train station), Katoomba's big-ticket drawcard is **Echo Point**. A series of sensational viewing platforms transports your gaze out over the Jamison Valley, white-winged cockatoos squabbling below you in the forest canopy. The impressive **Three Sisters** rock formation towers over the scene. The story goes that the Three Sisters were turned to stone by a sorcerer to protect them from the unwanted advances of three young men, but the sorcerer died before he could turn them back into humans. Bummer… Warning: Echo Point draws vast, serenity-spoiling tourist gaggles, their idling buses farting fumes into the mountain air – arrive early before they do.

To the west of town is **Scenic World** ( 🕿 4782 2699; www.scenicworld.com.au; cnr Cliff Dr & Violet St; $16/8 return; (🕑) 9am-5pm). If you can stomach the megaplex vibe and blaring *Raiders of the Lost Ark* theme, ride the 1880s railway down the 52-degree incline to the valley floor. Wander the 2.5km forest boardwalk or the 12km-return track to the **Ruined Castle** rock formation (Map p120), then catch the cablecar back up the slope. It also has a glass-floored **Scenic Skyway** cablecar floating out across the valley.

Just west of Katoomba, intrepid trio Wentworth, Blaxland and Lawson notched the **Explorers' Tree** to mark their trail. This sad, bushfire-ravaged stump has been amputated, gored by termites and filled with concrete, earning it the title *Eucalyptus concretus*.

## Activities

### ABSEILING, CANYONING & ROCK CLIMBING
The Blue Mountains seems custom-made for climbing, hiking and cycling; several companies offer all of the above. Prices below indicate easy or beginner grades; more advanced equals more dollars.
**Australian School of Mountaineering** ( 🕿 4782 2014; www.asmguides.com; 166 Katoomba St; (🕑) 9am-4.30pm) Full-day abseiling or canyoning ($145), rock climbing ($165), and two-day bush survival courses ($325). YHA member discount.
**Blue Mountains Adventure Company** ( 🕿 4782 1271; www.bmac.com.au; L1, 84a Bathurst Rd; (🕑) 9am-5pm) Abseiling (from $135), canyoning (from $155) and rock climbing (from $165) adventures.
**Explore The Blue Mountains** ( 🕿 4780 0000; www.explorethebluemountains.com; 1 Katoomba St; (🕑) 9am-5pm) Half-day abseiling ($135 including lunch), canyoning ($169 including lunch) and two-hour horse-riding trips

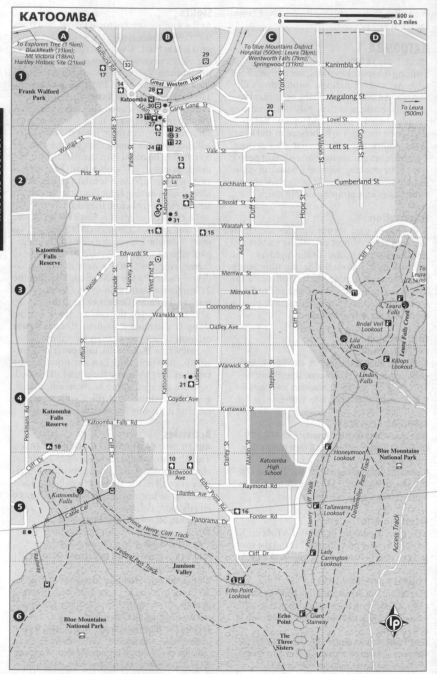

($85), which include a 'Stockman Experience' (billy tea, damper and whip cracking).

**High'n'Wild Mountain Adventures** ( ☎ 4782 6224; www.high-n-wild.com.au; 3/5 Katoomba St; ☯ 9am-5pm) Half-/full-day abseiling (from $90/135), climbing ($109/169) and full-day canyoning ($150). YHA member discount.

### BUSHWALKING

Unless the weather is dire, a mountain bushwalk is mandatory. Head for Jamison Valley, south of Katoomba, or Grose Valley, northeast of Katoomba and east of Blackheath. The area south of Glenbrook is also worthwhile.

The Echo Point visitors centre (p123) has information on short and day walks; the Blue Mountains Heritage Centre in Blackheath (p128) supplies longer walk details. It's rough, broken country and even experienced walkers get lost – get reliable information, walk with a friend and tell someone where you're headed. Take plenty of water or boil/treat what you collect (many local waterways are polluted). Mountain weather changes quickly, so bring warm clothes in all seasons.

Guided bushwalking or bushcraft tours can be arranged through several of the activity companies listed. Rates range from $45 to $150 per day, depending on the difficulty.

## Tours

Departing Sydney, the reader-recommended **Oztrails** ( ☎ 9387 8390, 0411 288 805; www.oztrails.com .au; day tours $85) wheels small groups around the Blue Mountains sights, finishing with a ferry ride back to Circular Quay on the Parramatta River. **HQ Tours** ( ☎ 9666 8433; www.hqtours.com.au) runs backpacker-friendly Blue Mountains tours, also departing Sydney. Its Eco-scenic day trip (per person $79) includes three hours of guided bushwalking around the main sights.

Overnight tours (per person $239) visit the Jenolan Caves and include dorm accommodation at Katoomba YHA.

**Fantastic Aussie Tours** ( ☎ 4782 1866, 1300 300 915; www.fantastic-aussie-tours.com.au; 283 Main St; adult/child $63/43; ☯ tours 11.15am-5.15pm daily, office 9am-5pm) operates coach tours to the Jenolan Caves and runs the double-decker **Blue Mountains Explorer Bus** ( ☎ 4782 4807; www.explorerbus.com.au; 283 Main St; adult/child $32/16; ☯ 9.45am-5.15pm), a hop-on hop-off service on an hourly Katoomba/Leura loop, stopping at 30 attractions. Tickets last all day. Another hop-on hop-off service taking in the same sights is **Trolley Tours** ( ☎ 4782 7999, 1800 801 577; www.trolleytours.com.au; 285 Main St; adult/child $15/12; ☯ 9.15am-5pm Mon-Fri, 9.45am-3.45pm Sat & Sun). It's a bus not so cunningly disguised as a trolley, with piped commentary. You can get a weekly ticket (adult/child $21/18) and go on a tour to Jenolan Caves (from $48).

**Tread Lightly Eco Tours** ( ☎ 4788 1229; www.treadlightly .com.au; 2hr/day tours $35/185) gives you encounters with local flora and fauna in remote mountain areas on guided bushwalks and 4WD tours. The emphasis is on ecosensitive interpretation of the land. Tours run daily on demand.

Also recommended:
**Blue Mountains Walkabout Tours** ( ☎ 0408 443 822; www.bluemountainswalkabout.com; day tours per person $95) Indigenous heritage tours with Aboriginal guides, departing Faulconbridge Station.
**Cool Safaris** ( ☎ 4735 3977, 0438 353 162; www.cool safaris.com.au; half-/full-day tours per person $95/175) 4WD tours with a native wildlife and Aboriginal art focus.

## Festivals & Events

Every year between June and August, chilly Blue Mountains towns cheer themselves up with **Yulefest** ( ☎ 4782 9865, 1300 653 408; www.yulefest .com.au), an out-of-kilter Christmas celebration.

Festivities reach a pagan peak at Katoomba's **Winter Magic Festival** on 21 June, with a street parade, market stalls and general frivolity to welcome the winter solstice.

## Sleeping

### BUDGET

**Katoomba Mountain Lodge** ( ☎ 4782 3933; www.ka toombamountainlodge.com.au; 31 Lurline St; dm/s/d from $18/42/58; 🖳 ) This place gets a good rap from readers – hysterically uncool wallpaper and naff timber panelling are the price you'll pay for the best-value rooms in town. It's a cheerily run 90-year-old house right in the middle of town, with astounding views from some of the top floor rooms.

**No 14** ( ☎ 4782 7104; www.bluemts.com.au/no14; 14 Lovel St; dm $22, d without/with bathroom $59/66) Lowkey with hippy overtones, this colourful hostel feels like a cheery share-house. There are plenty of nooks and crannies to find some breathing space if you need it, and polished floorboards make a pleasant change from festering carpets. Dorms have three beds; atticstyle doubles are comfy and private.

**Central Blue Mountains Backpackers** ( ☎ 4782 9630, 1800 287 370; www.centralblue.com.au; 144 Bathurst Rd; dm/s/d/f from $22/50/65/120; 🖳 🖳 ) Opened in 2005, this gargantuan hostel near the station has an industrial-sized kitchen, excellent security and clean rooms, but feels nondescript in a nursing home kind of way. The fact that it used to be a nursing home may explain this.

**Blue Mountains YHA** ( ☎ 4782 1416; www.yha.com. au; 207 Katoomba St; dm/d/f from $24/73/116; 🖳 ) The austere Art Deco exterior of this much-lauded hostel belies its cavernous, sparkling innards. Dorms and family rooms are spotlessly bright; common areas have more beanbags than bums. Highlights include a pinball machine, pool tables, open fires, a giant chess set, central heating, barbecues and curry nights. Hard to fault.

Some alternatives include:

**Flying Fox** ( ☎ 4782 4226, 1800 624 226; www.the flyingfox.com.au; 190 Bathurst Rd; unpowered sites per 2 people/dm/d $24/22/60; 🖳 ) Small, laid-back hostel in a 105-year-old house, with upbeat staff, good security and a chilled-out vibe.

**Katoomba Falls Caravan Park** ( ☎ 4782 1835; www .bmcc.nsw.gov.au; Katoomba Falls Rd; unpowered/powered sites per 2 people $25/32, cabins from $75) Gets mixed reviews from travellers, but the only Katoomba camping option.

### MIDRANGE

**Clarendon Guesthouse** ( ☎ 4782 1322; www.clarendon guesthouse.com.au; 68 Lurline St; s without/with bathroom from $45/65, d from $90/170) 🖳 motel only; 🖳 🖳 ) The rambling old Clarendon is light on ceremony and heavy on character. Original rooms (with shared bathrooms) are charmingly old-school; the newer motel extension is snazzier than its exterior suggests. Convivial vibes snake their way up the stairs from the atmospheric band room (opposite).

**Cecil Guesthouse** ( ☎ 4782 1411; www.ourguest.com .au/cecil.html; 108 Katoomba St; s without/with bathroom $75/80, d $84/106) Rakishly dilapidated in a Fawlty Towers kind of way, old Cecil has creaky floorboards, unrenovated walls and kooky lounge rooms – put character before ritz and you won't be disappointed. The dining room does breakfast and dinner, and there's a tennis court if you're feeling Federer.

**Shelton-Lea** ( ☎ 4782 9883; www.sheltonlea.com; 159 Lurline St; r with bathroom incl breakfast $110-170) Moss, mustard and maroon colours with a splash of Art Deco make this B&B a stylish choice. Three bedrooms each have their own sitting areas, plus classy touches like old radios and lead-lighting by the kilo. Way romantic.

There are three affordable, ship-shape motels close to Echo Point. Their décor is nothing to write home about, but who writes letters these days?

**Echo Point Motor Inn** ( ☎ 4782 2088, 1800 024 879; www.echopointmotel.com; 18 Echo Point Rd; s/d/f from $80/90/130) Affable hosts; rooms with or without views.

**3 Explorers Motel** ( ☎ 4782 1733; fax 4782 1146; 197 Lurline St; s/d/f from $79/90/155; 🖳 🖳 ) Floral print proliferation; NRMA, RAC and AAA member discounts.

**3 Sisters Motel** ( ☎ 4782 2911; www.threesistersmotel .com.au; 348 Katoomba St; s $65-95, d $90-120; 🖳 ) Funky retro neon sign; serviceable rooms with less funk.

### TOP END

**Carrington Hotel** ( ☎ 4782 1111; www.thecarrington.com .au; 15-47 Katoomba St; d incl breakfast $190-485) Katoomba's social and architectural high-water mark, the Carrington has been accommodating road-weary travellers since 1880. Every inch has been refurbished, but its historical character remains intact. The rooms are truly indulgent; the dining room and ballroom are utterly opulent.

## Eating

**Paragon Café** ( ☎ 4782 2928; 65 Katoomba St; mains $10-20; ⏱ breakfast & lunch) The heritage-listed 1916

Paragon is Katoomba's undisputed Art Deco masterpiece. Sampling coffee and chocolates in the salubrious surrounds is a compulsory Blue Mountains experience.

**Savoy** ( ☎ 4782 3845; 26-28 Katoomba St; mains $11-19; ☻ breakfast, lunch & dinner) The Savoy has booths (we love booths), and is perfect for day-time pastas, burgers, focaccias and salads. At night the lights lower and the menu lifts – progressive dishes like pan-seared barramundi with lime and chilli, and kangaroo sirloin with roast zucchini, garlic and red wine jus bring smiles to faces.

**Niagara** ( ☎ 4782 4001; 92 Bathurst Rd; mains $13-26; ☻ lunch & dinner) High ceilings with ornate cornices, oversized tiles underfoot and large wooden booths embellish this gay-/family-/vegetarian-friendly diner. The food is fab too: gourmet burgers, pastas and salads with a twist during the day, scrumptious steaks and fish at night. Monthly dinner-and-show Cabaret Nights ($55) are sequin-soaked spectaculars.

**IsoBar Café** ( ☎ 4782 4063; 40 Katoomba St; mains $17-23; ☻ breakfast, lunch & dinner) Despite the hackneyed IsoBar name, this café hums with chilled vibes, ambient tunes and moody lighting – as funky as Katoomba gets. Tasty staples include Turkish toasties, burgers, stir-fries and salads.

**Solitary** ( ☎ 4782 1164; 90 Cliff Dr; mains $26-33; ☻ lunch Sat & sun, dinner Wed Sun) To-die for views, sublime food and inescapable romance are Solitary's stock in trade – not the place for solitary dining. Mains like venison and juniper sausages, and scallop and Moreton Bay bug ravioli are inventive; desserts are downright sexy. Excellent service; reservations are essential.

## Entertainment

**Clarendon Band Room** ( ☎ 4782 1322; www.clarendonguesthouse.com.au; 68 Lurline St; admission $15-50; ☻ live music Thu-Sun nights) When Australia's finest musicians are in town (which is often enough), they usually strut their stuff at the Clarendon Guesthouse band room. Dinner-and-show tickets cost $30 extra.

**Hotel Gearin** ( ☎ 4782 4395; www.gearinhotel.com; 273 Great Western Hwy; admission free; ☻ 7am-2am Mon-Thu, to 3am Sat & Sun, 10am-10pm Sun) Gear up for a night at the Gearin, Katoomba's best watering hole. It's owned by actor Jack Thompson – a good enough excuse for a beer, a $5 steak or a game of pool.

**Carrington Bar** ( ☎ 4782 1111; www.thecarrington .com.au; 10-16 Katoomba St; admission free; ☻ 9.30am-1.30am Mon-Thu, to 4.30am Fri & Sat, to 11pm Sun) The lowbrow wing of the upper-crust hotel, this is the place for shooters, schooners, pool tables and Guns 'N' Roses ricocheting off the jukebox. There's a nightclub upstairs on Saturday nights (admission $5).

**TrisElies** ( ☎ 4782 4026; www.triselies.com.au; 287 Bathurst Rd; admission free or $15 depending; ☻ 8pm-3am Thu-Sun) Jazz, reggae, DJs and ska in a blood-red-painted bunker at the top of the town.

**Edge Cinema** ( ☎ 4782 8900; www.edgecinema.com .au; 225 Great Western Hwy; adult/child $13/9; ☻ 10am-late) The Edge screens current mainstream flicks plus a 40-minute Blue Mountains documentary called *The Edge* on a giant screen (adult/child $15/10). Tuesday is discount day (aka Cheap-ass Tuesday) – $9 for most films.

## Getting There & Around

**CityRail** ( ☎ 13 15 00; www.131500.com.au) runs to Katoomba from Sydney's Central Station (one-way adult/child $12/6, two hours, hourly).

The **Blue Mountains Bus Co** ( ☎ 4751 1077; www .mountainlink.com.au) services Katoomba en route from Mt Victoria to the north (one-way adult/child $7/4, 40 minutes, four daily Monday to Friday) and Springwood to the east (one-way adult/child $9/5, one hour, seven daily Monday to Saturday). The **Blue Mountains Explorer Bus** (p125) and **Trolley Tours** (p125) trace circuitous routes through Katoomba and Leura.

**Velo Nova** ( ☎ 4782 2800; www.velonova.com.au; 182 Katoomba St; half-/full-day $28/50; ☻ 9am-5pm Mon & Wed-Sat, 9.30am-4.30pm Sun) rents out hi-tech, 24-speed, all-terrain mountain bikes. Saturday morning group rides run along Cliff Drive, finishing up with a café coffee.

If it's late and you've got a few beer-soaked notes left, call **Katoomba-Leura-Wentworth Falls Taxis** ( ☎ 4783 1311).

## BLACKHEATH & AROUND

The crowds and commercial frenzy fizzle considerably 10km north of Katoomba in neat, petite Blackheath (Map p120). The town still measures up in the accommodation, food and scenery stakes, though, and it's an excellent base for visiting the Grose and Megalong Valleys.

East of town are lookouts at **Govett's Leap**, **Bridal Veil Falls** (the highest in the Blue Mountains) and **Evans Lookout**. To the northeast, via Hat Hill Rd, are **Pulpit Rock**, **Perry's Lookdown** and **Anvil Rock**. There are steep walks into the Grose Valley from Govett's Leap; Perry's Lookdown is the start of the shortest route (five hours one-way) to the magical **Blue Gum Forest**. From Evans Lookout there are tracks to Govett's leap (1½ hours one-way) and to Junction Rock continuing to the Blue Gum Forest (six hours one-way).

To the west and southwest lie the Kanimbla and Megalong Valleys, with spectacular views from **Hargrave's Lookout**. Register your walk and get trail condition updates from the **Blue Mountains Heritage Centre** ( ☎ 02-4787 8877; www.nationalparks.nsw.gov.au; Govett's Leap Rd; ⊗ 9am-4.30pm).

**CityRail** ( ☎ 13 15 00; www.131500.com.au) runs to Blackheath from Sydney's Central Station (one-way adult/child $13/7, two hours 15 minutes, hourly).

The **Blue Mountains Bus Co** ( ☎ 02-4751 1077; www.mountainlink.com.au) services Blackheath, Govett's Leap Rd, Evans Lookout Rd and Hat Hill Rd en route from Mt Victoria to the north (one-way adult/child $6/3, 15 minutes, four daily Monday to Friday) and Katoomba to the south (one-way adult/child $7/4, 25 minutes, 12 daily Monday to Friday, four Saturday, two Sunday). Buses take you to within 1km of Govett's Leap, but Perry's Lookdown and Evans Lookout are 6km and 4km walks, respectively, from the bus stops.

## Sleeping & Eating

**Gardners Inn** ( ☎ 02-4787 8347; www.gardnersinn.com; 255 Great Western Hwy; s/d incl breakfast $45/80) Across from Blackheath Station, this is the oldest hotel (1832) in the Blue Mountains; the basic pub rooms upstairs hark back to days of yore. Downstairs the swishy bistro (mains $16-20, lunch and dinner) serves pub nosh on the gourmet side of the tracks. Wine tastings 6pm to 8pm Friday nights.

**Jemby-Rinjah Eco Lodge** ( ☎ 02-4787 7622; www.jembyrinjahlodge.com.au; 336 Evans Lookout Rd; standard/deluxe cabins from $150/199) In a sequestered bush setting, these ecocabins are lodged so deeply in the bottlebrush you'll have to bump into one to find it. One- and two-bedroom vertical-weatherboard cabins are jauntily designed; the deluxe models have Japanese plunge-style spas.

**Blackheath Caravan Park** ( ☎ /fax 02-4787 8101; Prince Edward St; unpowered/powered sites per 2 people $23/28, cabins from $45) This small park does the simple things well without setting the mountains ablaze with personality: decent

camp sites, serviceable facilities, good-value cabins.

There are free camp sites at Perry's Lookdown, which has a car park and is a convenient base for walks into the Grose Valley and at Acacia Flat, near the Blue Gum Forest in the Grose Valley. It's a steep descent from Govett's Leap or Perry's Lookdown (pack lightly).

**Café Memento** ( ☎ 02-4787 5123; cnr Wentworth & Govett's Leap Rd; mains $5-15; ⊗ breakfast & lunch Thu-Tue) Injecting Blackheath with a world view and a social conscience, colourful Café Memento serves organic breakfasts, wraps, soups, cakes and burgers. Political inclinations aside, the food is great and there's a sunny patio.

**Vulcan's** ( ☎ 02-4787 6899; 33 Govett's Leap Rd; mains $32; ⊗ lunch & dinner Fri-Sun) Arguably the Blue Mountains' best restaurant, this cosmopolitan, urbane eatery serves food erupting with flavour in a lava-coloured room. The kitchen takes centre stage. Bookings are essential.

Other recommendations:

**Altitude Delicatessen** ( ☎ 02-4787 6199; 20 Govett's Leap Rd; mains $5-12; ⊗ breakfast & lunch) Zingy deli sandwiches, filos, antipastos, coffee and window seats.

**Blackheath Motor Inn** ( ☎ 02-4787 8788; www.blackheathmotorinn.com.au; 281 Great Western Hwy; d from $80; ⊗ ) Clean, snug motel rooms with funky '60s chalet style. Where's Britt Eckland when you need her?

## MEGALONG VALLEY

Unless you walk in or take Katoomba's Scenic Railway, the only way you'll see a Blue Mountains gorge from the inside is in the Megalong Valley. This is straw-coloured rural Australia, a real departure from the quasi-suburbs strung along the ridgeline. An amazingly well-surfaced road snakes down from Blackheath through pockets of rainforest. The 600m **Coachwood Glen Nature Trail**, 2km before Werribee, features dripping fern dells, stands of mountain ash and sun-stained sandstone cliffs.

The **Megalong Australian Heritage Centre** ( ☎ 02-4787 8188; www.megalong.cc; Megalong Rd; admission adult/child/family $8/5/20; ⊗ 9am-5pm) is a display farm agri-heaven for little tackers – visitors can feed and pat sheep, ducks, ponies and alpacas. There's guided horseriding (one/two hours per person $45/85), plus farm shows and activities during school holidays.

The **Farm Accommodation** (unpowered sites per 2 people/dm $24/20, d incl breakfast $85, 4-bed cottages from $195) comprises basic dorm beds, B&B guesthouse rooms and two self-contained cottages.

**Werribee Trail Rides** ( ☎ 02-4787 9171; www.aust ralianbluehorserides.com.au; Megalong Rd; 30min/2hr rides $30/78; ☼ 10am-5pm) offers horse-riding packages to suit everyone. See the area pioneer-style by adding your weight to a two-day/one-night 'Pub Crawl' ride!

## MT VICTORIA

☎ 02 / pop 870

With its remote, unadulterated village vibe, National Trust–classified Mt Victoria was once more influential than Katoomba. At 1043m, it's the highest town in the mountains – crisp air, solitude, towering foliage and historic buildings are what you're here for.

Nothing is far from the train station, where the **Mt Victoria Museum** ( ☎ 4787 1210; Mt Victoria Railway Station; adult/child $3/50c; ☼ 2-5pm Sat & Sun) is chock-full of quirky Australiana. Gawk at convict relics, old farm equipment, maps, photos, portraits, taxidermy and Ned Kelly's sister's bed. Other interesting buildings include the 1914 **Victoria & Albert Guesthouse**, the 1849 **Toll Bar Cottage** and the 1874 **St Peters Church**.

Inside an old public hall, **Mount Vic Flicks** ( ☎ 4787 1577; www.bluemts.com.au/mountvic; Hartley Ave; adult/child $9/7; ☼ noon-10.30pm Fri-Sun, from 10am Thu) is cinema 'the way it used to be', with ushers, a piano player and door prizes. Mainstream and art-house releases shimmer across the screen; Thursday morning tickets are $6!

Off the highway at **Mt York** is a surreal gathering of monuments, plaques and structures commemorating Wentworth, Blaxland and Lawson's 1813 mountain crossing.

**CityRail** ( ☎ 13 15 00; www.131500.com.au) runs to Mt Victoria from Sydney's Central Station (one-way adult/child $14/7, two hours 30 minutes, hourly). The **Blue Mountains Bus Co** ( ☎ 4751 1077; www.mountainlink.com.au) runs to Mt Victoria from Katoomba (one-way adult/ child $6/3, 15 minutes, four daily Monday to Friday).

### Sleeping & Eating

**Hotel Imperial** ( ☎ 4787 1878; www.hotelimperial.com.au; 1 Station St; dm $25, d without/with bathroom incl breakfast from $129/139) This grand, castellated old dame is the best pub in the area, by a mountain mile. Downstairs rooms are budget and basic; upstairs they're grand and gracious. The bar has live music and log fires, there's a stellar beer garden, and the kitchen (mains $16-24; open breakfast, lunch and dinner) cooks solid pub grub.

**Manor House** ( ☎ 4787 1369; www.themanorhouse .com.au, Montgomery St; d incl breakfast $155-230) Each of the 13 en-suite rooms in this vintage guesthouse has a dash of heritage; perhaps a Victorian wardrobe, Art Deco fittings, or a veranda. The restaurant (mains $24; open lunch and dinner by arrangement; bookings essential) has a small but inventive menu; try the pesto and artichoke lasagne.

## HARTLEY HISTORIC SITE

In the 1830s the Victoria Pass route (through Mt Victoria) made travelling inland from the coast a helluva lot easier. However, the moral and physical discomforts associated with being hailed up by bushrangers soon became an issue. To counter the problem, a police post was established at Hartley, 11km northwest of Mt Victoria, the village flourishing until the railway bypassed it in 1887. Now deserted, this tiny, sandstone ghost town still has a curious crop of historic buildings.

The **NPWS Information Centre** ( ☎ 02-6355 2117; www.nationalparks.nsw.gov.au; ☼ 10am-1pm & 2-4.20pm) is in the old **Farmer's Inn** (1845) near **St Bernards Church** (1848). You can explore Hartley for free or take a guided tour of the 1837 **Greek Revival Courthouse** (tours per person $6; ☼ hourly 10am-3pm).

**Collits Inn** ( ☎ 02-6355 2072; www.collitsinn.com.au; Hartley Vale Rd; tw/d from $155/185, cottage from $260) is a sumptuously renovated 1823 inn with elegant guestrooms and a self-contained cottage.

Even if you're not stopping overnight call into the Inn's **restaurant** ( ☎ 02-6355 2072; 2-/3-course meal $65/75; ☼ lunch Fri-Sun, dinner Thu-Sun) because the munificent French-influenced cooking is worth the detour. Reservations essential. Follow the signs off the Great Western Hwy 5km east of Hartley.

## JENOLAN CAVES

Southwest of Katoomba on the western fringe of Kanangra Boyd National Park, the troglodytic **Jenolan Caves** ( ☎ 02-6359 3911; www.jenolancaves .org.au; Jenolan Caves Rd; admission with tour adult/child/family from $17/12/44; ☼ 9.30am-5.30pm; P $5) is one of the most extensive and complex limestone cave systems in the world. Named *Binoomea*, or 'Dark Places', by the Gundungurra tribe, the caves took shape 400 million years ago.

You must take a tour to see them, various tour packages traversing a surreal 10-cave warren. More comprehensive tours include the 2½-hour ghost ($32, 8pm Saturday) and adventure ($58, 1.15pm daily) tours.

---

**DETOUR: BELLS LINE OF ROAD**

The Great Western Hwy barrels straight through the Blue Mountains, but if you have time the spectacular 90km **Bells Line of Road** is far more rewarding. Named after Archibald Bell Jnr, the 19-year-old who discovered the route in 1023, the road was constructed by convicts in 1841, navigating a pass between Richmond and Lithgow. It's far quieter than the highway and offers bountiful views from the mountains' eastern slopes, orchards and roadside apple carts around Bilpin, and lofty scenery all the way to Lithgow.

To get here, head northwest from Sydney on Windsor Rd then take Richmond Rd west, which becomes Bells Line of Road beyond Richmond.

Between Bilpin and Bell, **Mt Tomah Botanic Gardens** ( ☎ 02-4567 2154; www.rbgsyd.nsw.gov .au; Bells Line of Road, Bilpin; adult/child/family $4/2/9; ☽ 10am-4pm Apr-Sep, to 5pm Oct-Mar) is the cool-climate annexe of Sydney's Royal Botanic Gardens. Native plants cuddle up to exotic species including magnificent rhododendron displays. Many areas are wheelchair accessible; a people-mover circles on the hour.

**Mt Wilson** (www.mountwilson.info) is 8km north of Bells Line of Road. Like Katoomba, this town was settled by Anglophiles, but unlike Katoomba with its guesthouses and cool cafés, Mt Wilson is all hedgerows, European trees and mansions with big gates and driveways. About 1km from the village is the **Cathedral of Ferns**, a wet rainforest remnant with tree ferns and native doves exploding from the foliage – an almost unbearably serene 10-minute stroll.

One for the trainspotters, the **Zig Zag Railway** ( ☎ 02-6355 2955; www.zigzagrailway.com.au; Clarence Station, Bells Line of Road; adult/child/family $20/10/50; ☽ 11am, 1pm & 3pm daily), 10km east of Lithgow, was designed to bring the Great Western Railway tracks down from the mountains to Lithgow, gently zigzagging down the precipice. It's a 1½-hour return train ride.

---

**Classical concerts** ( ☎ 1300 763 311; www.georgcello .com; adult/child $38/20; ☽ 4pm Sat twice monthly) in the caves are a sonic revelation. Book ahead for all tours, as they sell-out quickly. See p125 for tour details from Sydney and Katoomba.

The caves are 30km from the Great Western Hwy. The narrow Jenolan Caves Rd becomes a one-way system between 11.45am and 1.15pm daily, running clockwise from the caves out through Oberon.

The 42km **Six Foot Track** from Katoomba to the Jenolan Caves is a fairly challenging three-day hike (two days if you're hyperactive or un-encumbered). Built as a bridle track to compete with the railways, 'Six Foot' refers to its width – wide enough for two horses to pass. Consult the Echo Point visitors centre in Katoomba (p123) before you attempt anything.

Most accommodation is affiliated with caves management, including **Jenolan Caves Cottages** ( ☎ 02-6359 3911; www.jenolancaves.org.au; Jenolan Caves Rd; cottages sleeping 6-8 people $90-125, Bellbird Cottage $145-180) about 8km north of the caves – four comfortable, self-contained cottages and the beautifully renovated 1930s Bellbird Cottage, all with bushy views.

Looking like something Jack Nicholson might take a Shining to, the fabulously eerie **Jenolan Caves House** ( ☎ 02-6359 3322; www.jeno lancaves.house.com.au; Jenolan Caves Rd; dm $25, motel d $95-185, guestroom d $65-295) caters to all wallets and tastes. Gatehouse dorms sleep six, Mountain Lodge motel doubles are modern, Caves House guestrooms range from traditional to opulent. The **restaurant** (mains $25-28; ☽ breakfast & dinner) serves trad English fare.

## LITHGOW

☎ 02 / pop 21,000

In the western foothills of the Blue Mountains, Lithgow is famous for producing a whole lot of coal and Marjorie Jackson – aka 'The Lithgow Flash' – the 100m and 200m gold medallist at the 1952 Helsinki Olympics. It's a sombre, agrarian working town with as many pubs as employment offices (a lot of both), but makes a handy base for mountain biking or fishing in the surrounding hills. The mega-helpful lantern-shaped **visitors centre** ( ☎ 6353 1859; www .tourism.lithgow.com; cnr Cooerwull Rd & Great Western Hwy; ☽ 9am-5pm) books accommodation and has free *Mountain Bike Riding in Lithgow* and *Lithgow Region Fishing Guide* pamphlets.

### Sleeping & Eating

**Lithgow Valley Motel** ( ☎ 6351 2334; www.lithgowval leymotel.com.au; 45 Cooerwull Rd; s/d from $55/66) About 3km from the town centre; the bedspreads here are the brightest things in Lithgow, filling great-value, clean, old-style motel rooms with splendour.

**Lithgow Tourist & Van Park** ( ☎ 6351 4350; www.lithgowcaravanpark.com.au; 58 Cooerwull Rd; unpowered/powered sites per 2 people $16/21, cabins from $50) Across the road from the Lithgow Valley Motel, the main selling points here are loads of open space, effervescent birdlife and the odd sheep promenading around the adjoining paddocks.

**Papadino's Pizzeria** ( ☎ 6353 1455; 65 Main St; mains $12-22; ⏰ lunch Tue-Fri, dinner Tue-Sun) Papadino's is a humble, main street trattoria with homemade timber tables topped with floral decoupage cut from magazines. It bakes the kind of two-inch-thick, lead weight pizzas the Italians never made and Australians haven't made since the '70s. One feed will last you a week.

## Getting There & Away
**CityRail** ( ☎ 13 15 00; www.131500.com.au) trains run to Lithgow from Sydney's Central Station (one-way adult/child $18/9, three hours, hourly).

# SOUTHERN HIGHLANDS

The Southern Highlands was one of the first inland areas settled by Europeans, who promptly levelled the scruffy native foliage to make way for agriculture and English-style villages. Their arrival was early enough in Australia's history for the settlers to regard themselves as English landed gentry rather than Australian farmers, their affinity with the old world manifesting itself in a landscape of grassy slopes, brooding pines, distinct seasons and stone architecture.

Modern Australia has crept in the back door, but the Highlands towns coiling away from the Hume Hwy retain a gentrified air, accented by beautiful English gardens, antique shops and historic buildings.

## MITTAGONG & BOWRAL AREA
☎ 02 / pop 17,000
Mittagong and Bowral form the Southern Highlands' municipal epicentre, a status cemented by their steady bleed into one another. Mittagong is a broad, functional town with rural sensibilities; Bowral plays at being an English hamlet, with teahouses, a village green and lofty self-esteem. Both towns pride themselves on their chattering main streets,

and mature deciduous trees that erupt into autumnal russet reds.

If you're driving between Bowral and Mittagong, take the scenic route via the **Mt Gibraltar lookouts** for excellent valley views.

## Information
The **Southern Highlands visitors centre** ( ☎ 4871 2888; 1300 657 559; www.southern-highlands.com.au; 62-70 Main St, Mittagong; ⏰ 9am-5pm Mon-Fri, to 4pm Sat & Sun) is a capacious information centre with serious staff and free accommodation booking. Pick up a copy of *Craigie's Visitors Map of the Southern Highlands* ($8) which covers the area in detail.

## Sights
Legendary, to the threshold of sainthood, Sir Donald Bradman (aka 'The Don') started cracking cover drives and grafting centuries in Bowral. Fans pay homage at the **Bradman Museum of Cricket** ( ☎ 4862 1247; www.bradman.com.au; St Jude St, Bowral; adult/child/family $9/4/22; ⏰ 10am-5pm), which has an engrossing collection of Ashes and Don-centric memorabilia that even cricket-loathers admit is worthwhile.

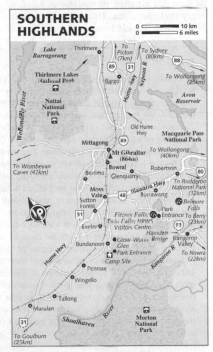

The museum is a couple of blocks east of Bowral's main street, next to the white-picketed Bradman Oval.

## Festivals

For two weeks over September and October, Bowral bursts into vivid hues during the **Bowral Tulip Time Festival** ( ☎ 1300 657 559; www.tuliptime .net.au). Rich soil and a cool climate ensure this floral extravaganza is always a success, attendees tiptoeing through Corbett Gardens, off Merrigang St. Jazz, folk dancing, cultural activities and plenty of fine regional food and wine enhance the mood.

## Sleeping

**Moss Vale Village Caravan Park** ( ☎ 4868 1099; www .mossvalevillagecaravanpark.com.au; Willow Dr, Moss Vale; unpowered/powered sites per 2 people $18/24, caravans/cabins from $47/77) At Moss Vale, 11km south of Bowral, this spacey caravan park has plenty of foliage and spots to park a tent. Spotless cabins offer the usual linoleum bedazzlements; facilities include barbecues, golf practice net and playground.

**Mittagong Hotel** ( ☎ 4872 2255; fax 4872 2242; 89 Old Hume Hwy, Mittagong; s/d from $40/60) Roomy, beery and megalithic (the biggest thing in Mittagong), this old boozer seems to be in a constant state of renovation. Pub meals, pool table and country music downstairs; fluttering NSW flag and tidy, good-value rooms (most with en suite) upstairs.

**Ranelagh House** ( ☎ 4885 1111; www.ranelagh-house .com.au; Illawarra Hwy, Robertson; r incl breakfast $55-150) This commanding English manor (1924) in wee Robertson manages to be simultaneously creepy and distinguished, with lavish rooms, mournfully wandering peacocks, wind in the pines and any number of windows from which unseen faces might peer… Devonshire teas and whodunnit weekends are a speciality.

**PortOCall Motor Inn** ( ☎ 4861 1779; fax 4861 1063; cnr Bundaroo & Bong Bong Sts, Bowral; r $69-115) Functional, central and immaculate, the PortOCall is festooned with the kind of abstract art that mums used to buy in 1985 when they wanted to be cool. Fear not – PortOCall is a quality mOtel with a capital O. Good disabled access.

Other recommendations:

**Bong Bong Motel** ( ☎ 4868 1033; fax 4869 2393; 238 Argyle St, Moss Vale; s/d from $75/95) How can you pass up a name like this? A clean, affordable, bong-water-coloured motel with an 'Everyone knows me!' manager.

**Best Western Grand Country Lodge Motel** ( ☎ 4871 3277, 1800 815 923; www.highlandsnsw .com.au; Old Hume Hwy, Mittagong; r $105-185; 🖳 ) A solid overnight option next to the Southern Highlands

---

### THE DON

Sir Donald Bradman was the greatest batsman cricket has ever seen. Born in Cootamundra (p280) in NSW's Central West in 1908, young Donald tuned his eye-hand coordination by spanking a golf ball against a corrugated metal water tank using a cricket stump as a bat. After many hours by the tank, the mature Don dazzled the world with his balletic footwork and devilishly good eye.

Bradman crashed world cricket's party, humbling England with his withering batting during the 1930 Test series. Shell-shocked English captain Douglas Jardine devised a cunning plan known as 'Bodyline', specifically to plug Bradman's run-scoring volcano. Bodyline involved crowding fielders around the legside of the wicket, then delivering fast, head-high 'bouncers' at the helmetless opposition. The Australians would be faced with a terrible choice: collect a cricket ball in the temple, or defend with the bat and spoon a catch to the vulture-like legside fielders.

Bodyline was viciously effective, several Australian batsmen receiving serious injuries during the 1932–33 Ashes Test series. After Australian captain Bill Woodford was struck on the chest, he uttered his famous words, 'There are two sides out there. One is trying to play cricket, the other is not.' Bradman's batting average fell to 56.57, a massive slide from his domestic average of 150. England won the Ashes but lost a legion of fans – Bodyline was eventually outlawed.

Bradman's vengeance was sweet and merciless: 19 Test centuries against England between 1928 and 1948. Affectionately known as 'Our Don Bradman' or simply 'The Don', he lifted the spirit of an entire nation after WWII. Captain of the 1948 Test team, still regarded as Australia's best-ever side, Sir Donald retired the same year with a Test batting average of 99.94! His average would have been 100-plus had he not been dismissed for a duck (0) in his last innings. It's a measure of the man's character that he didn't play another match to boost his average. Cricket is, after all, a team game.

visitors centre. The virginal water nymph fountain is a nice touch.

## Eating

**Ouddy Thai House** ( ☎ 4861 5554; 238 Bong Bong St, Bowral; mains $11-19; ☉ lunch Mon-Sat, dinner daily) A pocket of spicy Southeast Asian adventure amongst Bowral's tea-and-cake conservatism, Ouddy serves simmering soups, tasty curries, stir-fries and noodle dishes, with chilli customised to suit your level of tolerance. Try the whisky prawns.

**Mittagong Hotel** ( ☎ 4872 2255; 89 Old Hume Hwy, Mittagong; mains $15-25; ☉ lunch & dinner) If you're hungry in Mittagong, go no further than the local pub bistro. Plates piled high with chips, schnitzels, pasta and steak fly through the kitchen doors and satisfy hungry hordes of local farmers, truckers and passers-through like you.

## Getting There & Away

A short detour from the Hume Hwy deposits you in Mittagong, 1½ hours from Sydney. Bowral is 10 minutes' drive south of Mittagong. The Illawarra Hwy links the area with the coast, running through Moss Vale and Robertson. Long-distance Hume Hwy buses stop at the Southern Highlands visitors centre in Mittagong. Companies operating from Sydney are **Greyhound** ( ☎ 13 14 99; www.greyhound.com.au), with a once-daily service (adult/child $21/17, 2½ hours), and **Firefly** ( ☎ 1300 730 740; www.fireflyexpress.com .au) with a twice-daily service (adult and child $40, 2½ hours).

**Berrima Coaches** ( ☎ 4871 3211; www.berrimabuslines .com.au) has a service from Mittagong to Moss Vale via Bowral (one-way adult/child $4/2, 15 minutes, frequently weekdays, four Saturday and Sunday). **CountryLink** ( ☎ 13 22 32; www .countrylink.info) runs buses between Wollongong and Moss Vale (one-way adult/child $9/6, one hour 30 minutes, three daily), some running via Bundanoon. **CityRail** ( ☎ 13 15 00; www.131500 .com.au) trains run from Sydney's Central Station to Mittagong and Bowral (one-way adult/ child $14/7, two hours, roughly hourly).

## WOMBEYAN CAVES

The convoluted limestone **Wombeyan Caves** ( ☎ 02-4843 5976; www.npws.nsw.gov.au; Wombeyan Caves Rd; admission adult/child/family $13/8/30, with tour $16/10/39; ☉ 9am-5pm Mon-Fri, to 4pm Sat & Sun) are at the end of an equally convoluted mountain road 65km northwest of Mittagong. The surrounding bushland is part of a national park with walking tracks and plenty of wildlife, the caves themselves are in a shady valley with mown lawns, poplars and pines.

The **guided tour** is usually at 1pm and 2.30pm on weekdays, with an extra 10.30am tour on weekends. If you're resolutely independent, you can take a self-guided roam of the cave system (pre-empting the argument: stalactites descend, stalagmites ascend). Cool off afterwards in the swimming hole at **Limestone Canyon**.

You can pitch your tent nearby at the **Wombeyan Camping Reserve** ( ☎ 02-4843 5976; unpowered sites per 2 people $15, cabins $68-90), where there's also a kiosk and a well-equipped communal kitchen.

From either Canberra or Melbourne, the Goulburn–Taralga route is quickest and involves only 4km of narrow, winding road. From Sydney, the road winding west from Mittagong has a narrow, precipitous 45km stretch – very scenic but *really* slow (two hours from Mittagong). Watch out for oncoming cars, especially on weekends.

## BERRIMA

☎ 02 / pop 880

Founded in 1829, Berrima blossomed as a stopover en route to the wide brown lands west of the Blue Mountains. Unfortunately this route soon became infested with bushrangers and eventually the railway bypassed the town.

These days Berrima is heritage-classified, the town's plaid-clad country gents shuffling between historic buildings and tourist-trap stores, nodding salutations beneath towering pines. If you're after more than just lunch, there are some first-rate food and wine offerings here – make it an overnight indulgence.

The pick of Berrima's buildings is the 1838 neoclassical **Berrima Courthouse**, next to the still-functioning Berrima Gaol. Inside the courthouse is an excellent **Museum & Information Centre** ( ☎ 4877 1505; www.berrimacourthouse.org .au; cnr Wilshire & Argyle Sts; adult/child/family $6/4/15, ☉ 10am-4pm), which screens a 15-minute slide show about harsh early-19th-century justice. There's also information on prison history, early settlers, bushrangers, and a mock-up of the courthouse's first trial (complete with 30 wax mannequins and soundtrack).

Near the banks of the Wingecarribee River, the **Berrima District Museum** ( ☎ 4877 1130; cnr Market

Pl & Bryan St; adult/child $4/free; 10am-4pm Sat & Sun, school & public holidays) houses a local history collection, the highlight of which is a tree-trunk canoe hacked out by some of Berrima's 320 WWI German internees. Nearby the **Surveyor General Inn** claims to be Australia's oldest continuously operating hotel (aren't they all…).

Three kilometres north of Berrima, **Berkelouw's Book Barn & Café** ( 4877 1370; www.berkelouw .com.au; Old Hume Hwy; 9.30am-4.30pm Mon-Fri, 9.30am-5pm Sat & Sun), a branch of the famous Sydney bookshops, stocks enough secondhand and antiquated tomes to give the biggest of bookworms their fill. Absorb your selection (everything from pug dogs to politics) with a couch-bound coffee by the wood fire.

## Sleeping & Eating

**Surveyor General Inn** ( 4877 1226; www.highlandsnsw .com.au/surveyorgeneral; Old Hume Hwy; r without bathroom $60-80) There's a real sense of authenticity at this friendly local; you might feel like you've just stepped off the Cobb & Co.

The Inn's **bistro** (mains $16-23; lunch & dinner) is definitely 21st century, dishing up modern, inventive pub fare (great Thai fish cakes). There's also a fancy barbecue (the kind you can just about drive) on which your sirloin or kangaroo rump is grilled to perfection.

**White Horse Inn** ( 4877 1204; www.whitehorseinn .com.au; Market Pl; s $70-135, d $80-150) This gorgeous old sandstone pub has four tasteful en-suite B&B rooms (cushions, dressers, fluffy towels etc), but most people are here for the restaurant (mains $17-24; open breakfast, lunch and dinner). French and Asian overtones inform the cooking, served in private dining rooms, each with a magnificent table, open fireplace, fine china and restored antique furniture. Great coffee too.

## Getting There & Away

**Berrima Coaches** ( 4871 3211; www.berrimabuslines .com.au) buses run between Bowral and Berrima (one-way adult/child $8/4, 15 minutes, four daily).

## BUNDANOON & AROUND

02 / pop 1965

Bundanoon's main appeal is its proximity to the northern escarpments of **Morton National Park** – gorge yourself on lookouts or bicycle and walking tracks starting just 1km from the town. Once the Southern Highlands' undisputed guesthouse capital, though the trees now

outnumber the bipeds, the village is arguably the region's prettiest and most secluded.

## Sleeping & Eating

**Bundanoon YHA** ( 4883 6010; www.yha.com.au; 115 Railway Ave; unpowered site per 2 people $31, dm/d/f $28/64/96) Bundanoon's YHA occupies a fastidiously restored Edwardian guesthouse (officially called 'Lynbrook'), complete with deep, shady veranda, commodious country kitchen and gallons of gingham. The family rooms are family-sized and there's oodles of room outside for the kids to get into trouble.

**Treetops Country Guesthouse** ( 4883 6372; www .treetopsguesthouse.com.au; 101 Railway Ave; d incl breakfast & dinner $150-350) A dinner, bed and breakfast extravaganza, Treetops features stained-glass windows, four-poster beds, open fireplaces, a sunny games room and spiffy dining room. The snooker table is big enough to graze sheep on.

**Ye Olde Bicycle Shoppe** ( 4883 6043; 9 Church St; mains $10-15; breakfast & lunch) Next to the post office, this bike shop (sorry, shoppe) and café regulates the town's caffeine supply while renting out bicycles (half-/full-day $19/30). The banana bread is a heavyweight contender.

## Getting There & Away

**CountryLink** ( 13 22 32; www.countrylink.info) trains link Sydney's Central Station and Bundanoon (one-way adult/child $21/15, two hours, twice daily). Trains also arrive here from Wollongong (one-way adult/child $12/8, two hours, twice daily); the earlier service is via Moss Vale. **CityRail** ( 13 15 00; www.131500.com .au) trains run from Sydney's Central Station (one-way adult/child $16/8, two hours 30 minutes, six daily); you may need to change at Macarthur.

## NATIONAL PARKS

**Morton National Park** is a vast, unruly wilderness area in the Budawang Range, covering 162,386 hectares. Vertigo-inducing sandstone cliffs launch waterfalls over their edges, torrents of droplets dappling down onto forest canopies in the valleys below. It's a geographically chaotic area – before you go, record your proposed walk and have a chat with the friendly **NPWS visitors centre** ( 02-4887 7270; www.national parks.nsw.gov.au; Nowra Rd, Fitzroy Falls; 9am-5.30pm) near Fitzroy Falls themselves at the park entrance. The car park here costs $3 per vehicle (technically your national park entry fee).

Camping fees for the **camp site** (adult/child $5/3 per night) near the Bundanoon entrance can be paid here and there's also guides to walking in the park ($2 to $7). For longer bushwalks you'll need dedicated topographic maps.

The closest roads that access the park are at Bundanoon, at Fitzroy Falls and via the Tallowa Dam Rd from Kangaroo Valley. There's also the road running to Sassafras (surrounded by the park) from both Nowra or Braidwood.

Beyond spectacular, the wheelchair accessible **Fitzroy Falls** plunge a staggering 82m, the liberated waters smashing into a rabble of boulders below. The less well-known **Twin Falls** are 1km from here along the eastern track. The **Glow-Worm Glen** (at its most glowing-est after dark) is a half-hour walk from the end of William St in Bundanoon. In the park's south is the nipple-shaped **Pigeon House Mountain**; see p331 for walking details.

On the northeast edge of Morton National Park is the smaller **Budderoo National Park** offering yet more waterfalls, lookouts and walking tracks. On the west side of the park is the **Minnamurra Rainforest Centre** (p325). Access to both is from Robertson to the north or from Jamberoo near Kiama.

To get to Morton National Park take bus 813 from Moss Vale to Bundanoon (one-way adult/child $5/3, 20 minutes, four daily Monday to Friday). **Kennedy's Bus Service** ( ☎ 02-4421 7596, 0403 040 029; 7 Flinders Rd, Nowra) runs from Moss Vale to Fitzroy Falls (one-way adult/child $4/2, 30 minutes, 9.30am Monday to Friday), continuing to Nowra.

## KANGAROO VALLEY

☎ 02 / pop 350

Heading south from Fitzroy Falls, the world disappears over the edge of a steep escarpment, the road descending alarmingly to deposit you in the unbelievably picturesque Kangaroo Valley. Pegged in by a fortress of rainforest-steeped cliffs, the valley floor is carpeted by cow-dotted pasturelands, river gums and gurgling creeks. In perfect harmony with its surrounds, the slow country town of Kangaroo Valley itself, with its old pub, bakery and general store, feels lost somewhere between 1920 and 1980. Even the coaches belching through from the coast fail to ruin the atmosphere.

The formal entry to the valley is the unexpected **Hamden Bridge** (1898), a few kilometres

north of the town. It's a castellated sandstone-and-iron suspension structure, with a one-way lane, 17m above the riverbed. Next to the bridge is the **Pioneer Museum Park** ( ☎ 4465 1306; elaineaa@bigpond.net.au; Hampden Bridge, Moss Vale Rd; adult/child/family $4/3/10; ☒ 10am-4pm Fri-Mon Oct-Easter, 11am-3pm Fri-Mon Easter Sep). This walkabout museum provides a visual encounter with rural life in the late 19th century. A collection of historical buildings includes an 1860s homestead, blacksmiths forge and reconstructed dairy.

If the scenery is boring you to tears, get active with **canoeing**, **mountain biking** and **bushwalking** in and around the Shoalhaven and Kangaroo Rivers. **Kangaroo Valley Escapes** ( ☎ 0404 807 991; www.kangaroovalleyescapes.com.au; Moss Vale Rd; tours half-day $30-80, overnight $65-75) offers environmentally conscious guided tours, which you design yourself combining various rigorous activities. It also hires out canoes (half-/full-day $25/50) and mountain bikes ($30/50).

**Kangaroo Valley Safaris** ( ☎ 4465 1502; www.kangaroovalleycanoes.com.au; 2210 Moss Vale Rd; full day $35-60) rents out one- to three-person canoes and provides transport to/from specified points on the Shoalhaven River. It also runs overnight canoe camping trips (two-/three-day trips $75/105 per person).

## Sleeping & Eating

**Glenmack Park** ( ☎ 4465 1372; www.glenmack.com.au; 215 Moss Vale Rd; unpowered/powered sites per 2 people $16/20, cabins without/with bathroom $50/70) Sprawling Glenmack has 26 cabins, all with kitchenettes, TVs and aging lino, plus lush river-flat lawns for tents. Trees and ducks proliferate, enhancing the impression of camping out in the wild. You can light a campfire here too (a rarity!), but there's an undercover barbecue if things get too rough.

**Friendly Inn Hotel** ( ☎ 4465 1355; 159 Moss Vale Rd; mains $15-25; ☒ lunch & dinner) Kangaroo Valley's nocturnal life revolves around this classic country boozer, ever-so-subtly renovated to retain its local character. The original drinking nooks are intact and there's an exquisite dearth of plastic furniture (shame about the pokies in the corner). Styled-up pub nosh includes steaks of monstrous proportions and a slew of veggie, fish and chicken dishes.

**Old Store** ( ☎ 4465 1360; 2167 Moss Vale Rd; pies around $6; ☒ breakfast & lunch) Leading a clandestine double life as the valley post office, this roadside store sells what are allegedly the 'world's best pies'. Lavish with the filling in deliciously flaky butter-crust, its steak and red wine creation is indeed a world beater.

### Getting There & Away
**Kennedy's Bus Service** ( ☎ 4421 7596, 0403 040 029; 7 Flinders Rd, Nowra) runs from Moss Vale to Kangaroo Valley (one-way adult/child $6/3, 45 minutes, 9.30am Monday to Friday) continuing to Nowra.

# CENTRAL COAST

The sun-stroked Central Coast, corralled by the Pacific Hwy to the west and the Pacific Ocean to the east, is a distillation of all that's good about coastal Australia. Heading north from Gosford, a series of small towns is connected by scenic roads swerving through national parks, around saltwater lakes and alongside first-rate surf beaches.

Central Coasters live the definitive beach lifestyle – sun, sand and surf – amid beachy suburbs that thin to skeletal populations during winter. During summer, city-slickers converge in their 4WDs and at times Terrigal looks more like Tamarama. Don't worry – there's plenty of space to evade the crowds, and the local pelicans make for unpretentious company. Looking about as gainly as jumbo jets, these huge pin-eyed birds paddle around in search of food and glide silently overhead.

## GOSFORD & AROUND
At the base of a steep incline below the Pacific Hwy, Gosford (population 154,000) is the Central Coast's largest town. It's a pretty place, with suburbia kept at bay by waves of dense bush curling over the hills, but a downtrodden, redneck vibe conspires to keep things as unremarkable as possible. For banks and supermarkets it's fine, but for a meal or a bed you'll be better off in Terrigal (p138).

### Orientation & Information
Gosford's main strip is Mann St, an extension of the Pacific Hwy, which hosts the post office, banks, hospital and police station. Next to the train station, the **visitors centre** ( ☎ 02-4323 2353, 1300 132 975; www.cctourism.com.au; 200 Mann St; ⏰ 9.30am-4pm Mon-Fri, 10am-12.30pm Sat) is staffed by volunteers who seem to mostly enjoy their own company, but they do have overflowing brochure racks. The **NPWS Office** ( ☎ 02-4320 4200; www.nationalparks.nsw.gov.au; Suite 36, 207 Albany St North; ⏰ 8.30am-4.30pm Mon-Fri) provides permits for local national parks.

### Sights & Activities
Thirteen kilometres west of Gosford, you can get acquainted with cold-blooded locals at the **Australian Reptile Park** ( ☎ 02-4340 1022; www.reptilepark.com.au; Pacific Hwy, Somersby; adult/child/family $20/10/52; ⏰ 9am-5pm). A bush oasis, the park specialises in lizards, snakes and crocodiles of all magnitude, and less toothy beasts like koalas, platypuses and kangaroos. Conservation-impassioned staff conduct regular feeding sessions and talks throughout the day.

There are more cuties and furries at the **Australian Rainforest Sanctuary** ( ☎ 02-4362 1855; www.australianrainforest.com.au; Ourimbah Creek Rd, Ourimbah; adult/child/concession/family $12/6/10/30; ⏰ 10am-5pm Wed-Sun, also 6-9.30pm Wed-Sun Nov-Jan), a private rainforest reserve full of wallabies, wallaroos and 100 nattering bird species. The bushwalking isn't too strenuous, and there are grassy picnic and barbecue areas.

South of Brisbane Water National Park, there are silvery Broken Bay views from **Warrah Lookout**. Not far away, but screened from the Umina and Woy Woy housing estates by the steep Mt Ettalong road, is **Pearl Beach**, a National Trust–listed hamlet on the national park's eastern edge.

### BRISBANE WATER NATIONAL PARK
On the north side of the Hawkesbury River, 9km southwest of Gosford, **Brisbane Water National Park** (www.nationalparks.nsw.gov.au) extends eastwards from the Pacific Hwy to Brisbane Water itself. Despite its name, the park is mostly sandstone outcrops and forest with only a short Brisbane Water frontage. This park is famed for its explosions of spring wildflowers and Guringai stone engravings, the most impressive gallery of which is the **Bulgandry Aboriginal Engraving Site**, 3km south of the Pacific Hwy on Woy Woy Rd.

Rock climbing, bushwalking and abseiling courses are provided by **Central Coast Bushworks** ( ☎ 02-4363 2028; www.bushworks.info; 2hr abseiling per person $66, half-day bushwalking $75). There's generally a minimum requirement of 10 people – the larger the group, the lower the rate.

The main national park road access is at Girrakool; travel west from Gosford or exit the Sydney–Newcastle Fwy at the Calga in-

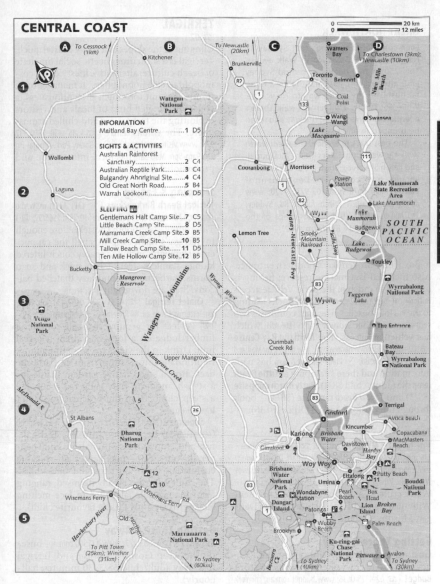

**CENTRAL COAST**

| INFORMATION | |
|---|---|
| Maitland Bay Centre.................1 | D5 |

| SIGHTS & ACTIVITIES | |
|---|---|
| Australian Raintorest Sanctuary.......................2 | C4 |
| Australian Reptile Park..........3 | C4 |
| Bulgandry Aboriginal Site......4 | C4 |
| Old Great North Road.............5 | B4 |
| Warrah Lookout.....................6 | D5 |

| SLEEPING | |
|---|---|
| Gentlemans Halt Camp Site...7 | C5 |
| Little Beach Camp Site.........8 | D5 |
| Marramarra Creek Camp Site.9 | B5 |
| Mill Creek Camp Site...........10 | B5 |
| Tallow Beach Camp Site......11 | D5 |
| Ten Mile Hollow Camp Site..12 | B5 |

**AROUND SYDNEY**

terchange. Wondabyne train station, on the Sydney–Newcastle line, is inside the park near several walking tracks (including part of the Great North Walk). Tell the guard if you want to get off at Wondabyne and you need to travel in the rear carriage. **Palm Beach & Hawkesbury River Cruises** (p114) run from Palm Beach to Patonga in the park. **Dangar Island Ferry Service** ( ☎ 02-9985

7566, 0415 274 020) operates ferries (adult/child $10/5, 15 minutes, 12 daily) from Brooklyn to Wobby Beach on a peninsula south of the park near some walking tracks.

**BOUDDI NATIONAL PARK**

Bouddi National Park, 19km southeast of Gosford, extends south from MacMasters Beach

**GREAT NORTH WALK**

Ever considered walking from Sydney to Newcastle? The Great North Walk awaits! This 250km trail begins in central Sydney and, after a short ferry ride, follows natural bushland the entire way to Newcastle. While not strictly a wilderness walk, there's adequate greenery along the way and it can be tramped in any season.

The best track reference, *The Great North Walk* by walk originators Garry McDougall and Leigh Shearer-Heriot, is out of print, but libraries stock copies. The **Department of Lands** (Map pp78–9; ☎ 02-9236 7720; www .lands.nsw.gov.au; 1 Prince Albert Rd, Sydney; ☺ 9am-5pm Mon-Fri) produces maps of the route in 'Discovery Kit' form ($12).

to Box Head, Broken Bay's northern entrance. Also included is a marine reserve; fishing is prohibited in much of the park. Vehicle access is limited but there are walking tracks leading to the various beaches. The park comprises two sections on either side of Putty Beach, which has vehicular access. The **Maitland Bay Centre** (☎ 02-4360 2833; www.nationalparks.nsw.gov.au; cnr Maitland Bay Dr & The Scenic Rd; ☺ 11am-3pm Sat & Sun) has park information and there's camping at **Little Beach camp site** (adult/child $8/4), **Putty Beach camp site** ($5/3) and **Tallow Beach camp site** ($8/4) – book through the Gosford NPWS Office (p136).

## Tours

The historic **MV Lady Kendall** (☎ 02-4323 1655; www .starshipcruises.com.au; Gosford Public Wharf, Dane Dr; adult/ child/concession $25/12/19; ☺ 10.15am Sat-Wed, leaves Woy Woy Public Wharf 10.40am) has 2½-hour Brisbane Water cruises. Ask about their less frequent Wine-tasting and Four Island cruises (Dangar, Milson, Scotland and Lion Islands).

## Getting There & Away

Gosford is easily accessible from the Sydney–Newcastle Fwy. Rent a car here from **Budget** (☎ 02-4325 0636; www.budget.com.au; cnr York & Melbourne Sts; ☺ 7am-7pm Mon-Fri, 7am-3pm Sat & Sun) or **Hertz** (☎ 02-4324 9859; www.hertz.com.au; 346 Mann St; ☺ 7.30am-5.30pm Mon-Fri, 8am-noon Sat & Sun) from $69 per day.

**CityRail** (☎ 13 15 00; www.131500.com.au) trains run from Sydney's Central Station to Gosford (adult/child $10/5, 1½ hours, at least hourly).

# TERRIGAL
☎ 02

Clinging to the slopes of a rocky coastal gulch, Terrigal is a sometimes hectic social omelette of beach culture, alternative lifestyle and cosmopolitan café hobnobbery. It manages to be trendy without too much pretentiousness, a constant mingled buzz of locals and visitors exploiting the tasty views and chilled atmosphere. The **visitors centre** (☎ 4385 4430, 1300 132 975; www.visitcentralcoast.com.au; Rotary Park, Terrigal Dr; ☺ 9am-5pm Mon-Sat) has local information and professional staff.

## Sleeping & Eating

**Terrigal Beach Backpackers** (☎ 4385 3330; www.yha .com.au; 12 Campbell Cres; 4-/8-bed dm $30/25, d/f $65/99; ☐ ) This roomy, slate-floored hostel is close enough to Terrigal's main strip to smell the cappuccino. Highlights include a spacey couch-littered lounge, stainless-steel kitchen, spick-and-span dorms, barbecue area and lazy thatched balcony. Staff are downright gracious.

**Chalet Terrigal** (☎ 4733 4924, 0407 434 969; www .chaletterrigal.com.au; 84 Riviera Ave; 3-bedroom lodge $95-180) Perfect for groups, this self-contained timber lodge on a lofty backstreet is a real find. Drink in the views (or something more traditionally intoxicating) from the barbecue deck atop a steep native garden. Inside it's a stylish, modern, fully gadgeted affair. It's a steep climb from the beach if you don't have a car.

**Supermex** (☎ 4384 6289; L1, cnr Church St & Campbell Cres; mains $17-29; ☺ dinner) Infusing Terrigal's fish-and-chip morass with red-hot chilli pepper flavours, Supermex serves up volcanic enchiladas, tacos, burritos and quesadillas. The chilli selection is fully itemised, ranging from manageable jalapeños to face-melting habañeros (Johnny Cash's favourite chilli).

## Getting There & Away

**Busways** (☎ 4368 2277; www.131500.com.au) buses run between Gosford Station and Terrigal (one-way adult/child $5/3, 30 minutes, half-hourly).

# THE ENTRANCE
☎ 02

Civilisation spreads decorously up the coast before turning abruptly into urban jungle at The Entrance, a dense cluster of cream brick, palm trees, plastic chairs and beer-bellied summer tourists with their inexhaustible kids. The

## WATERTAINMENT

The Central Coast's inland lakes and surf surplus generates plenty of aquatic activity.

**Central Coast Charters** ( ☎ 0427 665 544; www.centralcoastcharters.net; Terrigal & Ettalong; morning/afternoon charters per person $110/88) offers year-round morning fishing charters and afternoon charters between October and April. Ask about seasonal whale-watching cruises. **Hardys Bay Yacht Charters** ( ☎ 02-4360 1442; www.hbyc.com.au; Hardys Bay; 3hr twilight cruise per person $60, half-/full-day charter per boat $500/700) offers twilight cruises and yacht charters including a skipper. **Wandering The Lake Cruises** ( ☎ 1300 737 453; www.wanderingcruises.com.au; The Entrance; 2-3hr cruises adult/child/family from $23/10/61) runs cruises on the Wyong River and Tuggerah Lake, including lunch, wildlife spotting and morning tea, pelican feeding and twilight dinner cruises.

If you want to get more intimate with the water, **Ocean Planet** ( ☎ 02-4342 2222; www.oceanplanet .com.au; 25 Broken Bay Rd, Ettalong; tours adult/child from $95/50) has a range of sea- and river-kayaking day trips for all-comers. **Terry McDermott Surf Coaching** ( ☎ 02-4399 3388; www.surfcoaching.com.au; 2hr lesson incl equipment $45) provides expert surfing tutelage for novices and wannabes anywhere along the coast. **Central Coast Surf School** ( ☎ 0417 673 277; ccsurfschool@hotmail.com; Terrigal, Avoca & Umina beaches; 1hr lesson incl equipment $40) runs small-group surf lessons. For an even closer encounter, **Pro Dive** ( ☎ 02-4334 1559; www.prodivecentralcoast.com.au; 96 The Entrance Rd, The Entrance; 4-day course $375) provides learn-to-dive PADI courses and escorted dives for experienced submariners.

Entrance is the 'pelican capital of Australia', but everyone's really here for beautiful Tuggerah Lake and the grinding surf beach.

The volunteers at the **visitors centre** ( ☎ 4385 4430, 1300 132 975; www.visitcentralcoast.com.au; Marine Pde; ☒ 9am-5pm) swing between competent and confused, but have a wealth of information at their disposal. **The Entrance Bike Hire** ( ☎ 4333 3900; www.bikehiretours.com.au; bike hire per half-/full-day $15/35; ☒ 9am-5pm) is in the same building. It also runs four-hour local tours ($55 per person). On the beachfront nearby, the (voracious!) resident pelicans are fed daily at 3.30pm. Beside the bridge, **The Entrance Boatshed** ( ☎ 02-4332 2652; The Entrance Rd; ☒ 9am-6pm Sat & Sun, daily Dec-Feb) rents out aqua-bikes ($20 per hour), canoes ($15 per hour), rowboats ($20 per hour) and motorboats (from $30 per hour).

**Entrance Hotel** ( ☎ 4332 2001; www.entrancehotel .com.au; 87 The Entrance Rd; s/d incl breakfast $50/100) is a

genuine old-timer pub sitting defiantly unrenovated at the end of the patioed, tarted-up foreshore. Most rooms have bathrooms and views, but they're popular so book ahead.

The Hotel's **bistro** (mains $15-20; ☒ lunch & dinner) has a sizable courtyard and serves steaks, seafood and the odd curry (sometimes very odd).

If you're tent-bound, **Paradise Park** ( ☎ 4334 5555, 1300 658 865; www.paradisepark.com.au; cnr Pacific St & Tuggerah Pde; unpowered sites per 2 people $30, cabins $55-160) has timber cabins and villas with polished interiors and mod cons (some with spas). It's a tranquil spot facing Tuggerah Lake, with a fishing jetty and shoreline walking track just across the road.

**Red Bus Services** ( ☎ 4332 8655; www.131500.com .au) runs from Gosford Station to The Entrance (one-way adult/child $7/4, 45 minutes, roughly hourly).

# Hunter Valley

The vastness of the Hunter is readily recognised during a flight from Sydney, perhaps in a Dash 8. But the ample expanse is only really realised when you find yourself in the middle of the Wollemi or Yengo National Parks, or perhaps Barrington Tops. And the beauty is admired during a road trip on any given Sunday as you travel from Newcastle up to Scone. Forested mountains envelope rolling hills and sweeping valleys. And it's green, particularly if you have arrived after rain.

But poor weather is at the back of one's mind when holidaying in New South Wales' (NSW) second-largest city, Newcastle. Tanned bodies and surfie dudes populate the golden sands of Bar Beach, uninterested in the dozens of waiting coal loaders that adorn the horizon. Once home to the worst behaved convicts from the colony, the old steel city breathes a little easier these days by effortlessly embracing a barefoot surf culture, although telltale signs of the convict past are still scattered throughout the city and the Hunter in towns like Maitland, Morpeth, Wollombi and Stroud.

Money talks and farmed paddocks have slowly given way to the mining industry, which, in turn, now rivals the wineries. But today the farming is not just about grapes, with wineries sharing the focus and tempting foodies with selections of local produce such as olives, oranges, organic honey, macadamia nuts and even alpaca. And although the mining and energy industries still linger, you don't have to visit the Hunter vineyards on a busy weekend to realise the future here is in tourism.

## HIGHLIGHTS

- Cruise the **Lower Hunter Wineries** on the back of a trike (p151)
- Catch a wave at **Nobbys Beach** (p142) in Newcastle
- Survive The Steps, at night, in **Barrington Tops National Park** (p156)
- Back a winner at the **Scone Races** (p155)
- Greet ghouls at **Maitland Gaol** on a psychic tour (p147)
- Chill out on the grass at **Jazz in the Vines** (p151) in the Lower Hunter Wineries region
- Swim laps at **Merewether Ocean Baths** (p142) in Newcastle
- Learn viticulture speak at the **Hunter Valley Wine School** (p149)

Barrington Tops National Park

Scone

Lower Hunter Wineries

Maitland

Newcastle

# HUNTER VALLEY

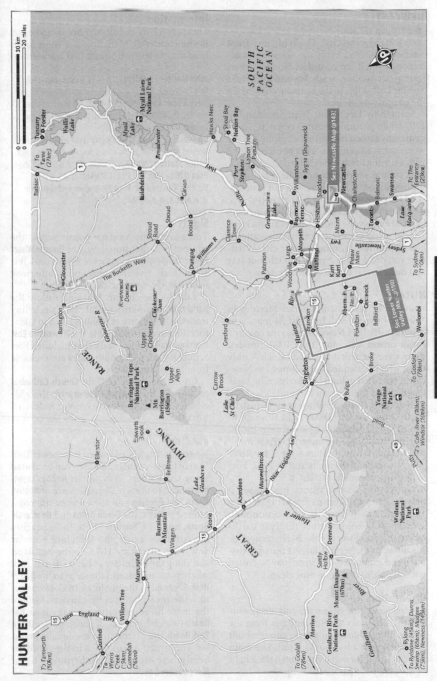

See Newcastle Map (p143)

See Lower Hunter Valley Map (p150)

**HUNTER VALLEY**

SOUTH PACIFIC OCEAN

# NEWCASTLE

☎ 02 / pop 483,300

'You gotta love this city', The Whitlams' front man croons. And everyone does. Most afternoons you'll see countless Novocastrians staring out over the beach, beyond the breaks and the coal ships, to the horizon, soaking up the coastal way of life.

Spotted by Lieutenant John Shortland in 1797 while pursuing escaped convicts, Newcastle was settled in 1801 as a colony for the worst behaved convicts. This past combined with a surfing lifestyle has helped shape a laid-back culture, making it one of the few cities in the developed world where you can grocery-shop barefoot and no one bats an eyelid.

Visit popular local beaches and bath in ocean baths or explore the endless dunes at Stockton. Dine at world-class restaurants both scattered and concentrated throughout the city. Whatever you do, don't just pass through, but stay and make sure it's for more than one day.

## History

Founded by Lieutenant Charles Menzies in 1801, he brought with him just 34 rebellious prisoners. By 1814 Newcastle was the colony's major prison with more than 1000 inmates. They were the worst of a bad bunch – only those who re-offended were shipped to Newcastle, banished to hard labour, burning lime, logging, and mining coal by hand.

Newcastle rivalled Sydney as an industrial centre from the late 1800s right through to World War II, when BHP played a significant role in producing war materials. As a result the steel city was the target of a Japanese submarine that fired shells at it in 1942. Fort Scratchley, of course, retaliated.

Newcastle's recent history has caused a massive shift away from misbehaving convicts and coal. The renewal has been rampant, spreading like wildfire since the 1989 earthquake and the closure of the BHP steelworks. It's home to the second-largest port in Australia and although the horizon may be dotted with coal ships, the air is now clean.

## Orientation

Central Newcastle sits on the end of a peninsula that separates the Hunter River from the sea and tapers down to a long convict-built spit heading east to Nobbys Head. The main street is Hunter St and it runs down the length of the peninsula parallel to King St.

## Information

There are ATMs and all your needs can be met in the Hunter St Mall, however most locals head to Charlestown Square (in Charlestown) for luxury items.

**John Hunter Hospital** ( ☎ 1921 3000, Lookout Rd, New Lambton)

**Juicy Beans Café** ( ☎ 4929 4988; 365 Hunter St; per 30 min $2; ☽ 6.30am-5pm Mon-Fri, to 3pm Sat) Has two terminals for internet access.

**Newcastle Region Library** ( ☎ 4974 5300; Laman St) Internet costs $3 for 30 minutes if you are checking email.

**Police Station** ( ☎ 4929 0999; cnr Church & Watt Sts)

**Post Office** ( ☎ 13 13 14; 1 Market St)

**Visitors Centre** ( ☎ 4974 2999; www.visitnewcastle.com.au; 361 Hunter St)

## Sights

There are many vantage points across the city, but your first stop should be **Queens Wharf Tower** (Queens Wharf; admission free; ☽ 8am-dusk). It is 40.3m high, has 180 steps and is otherwise referred to by locals as the 'Giant Penis'.

Take to the city on foot and follow the **Bathers Way**, a 5km coastal walk stretching from the lighthouse at Nobbys Head to Glenrock Reserve. Or negotiate the **Newcastle East Heritage Walk**, a 3km walk that includes Fort Scratchley. Maps for both walks are available from the visitors centre.

Climb the tower at **Christ Church Cathedral** or stop by the **Convict Lumberyard**, the oldest surviving example of a convict industrial workplace.

### BEACHES

Newcastle has six patrolled beaches within 5km of the city centre and each can be visited along the Bathers Way. From **Nobbys Lighthouse** head to the Art Deco elegance of **Nobbys Beach Surf Pavilion** and then follow the coast around to **Newcastle Ocean Baths** and **Newcastle Beach**, home of 'Surfest'. Both these beaches are fairly protected and therefore popular with young families. Hike up the headland and along the perimeter of King Edward Park where you can descend the steps to the **Bogey Hole**. Opened to the public in 1863, it was cut into the rock platform by convicts. One of the more favoured surfing breaks is at **Bar Beach** (which has loads of parking) but **Dixon Park Beach** and Merewether are equally popular. The largest ocean baths in the southern hemisphere are at the southernmost tip of **Merewether Beach**.

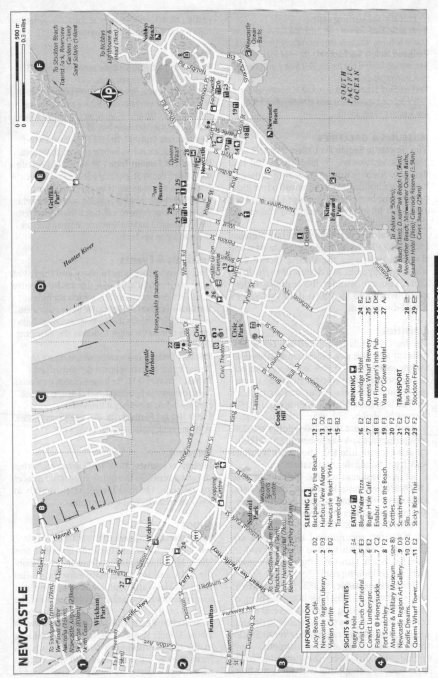

# NEWCASTLE

**HUNTER VALLEY**

Hone your surfing skills:

**Newcastle Surf School** ( ☎ 0405 500 469; lessons $30) Choose between Nobbys or the more private Cave's Beach.

**Redhead Mobile Surf School** ( ☎ 4944 9585; lessons $45, wetsuit & board hire for 2hr $25) A bit more personal with smaller groups.

**Surfest Surf School** ( ☎ 0410 840 155; www.surfest surfschool.com; lessons $25) Held at Nobbys Beach; buy four lessons and get one free.

### MUSEUMS & GALLERIES

The **Newcastle Region Art Gallery** ( ☎ 4974 5100; 1 Laman St; admission free; 🕑 10am-5pm Tue-Sun) is a dynamic space featuring travelling shows. It has school holiday workshops and a free kids' programme here on weekends at 11am, where your tiny tots (ages three to 15) can create their own masterpiece.

**Fort Scratchley Maritime & Military Museum** ( ☎ 4929 3066; Nobbys Rd; closed for refurbishment at time of research) overlooks the Pacific Ocean and was originally built as a deterrent to the Russians. You can wander the tunnels underneath, which are said to run all the way to King Edward Park.

## Activities

The lush grounds of the **Wetlands Centre Australia** ( ☎ 4951 6466; www.wetlands.org.au; Sandgate Rd, Sandgate; adult/child $5/3, 🕑 9am-5pm) were born out of a desperate bid to stop the highway storming through the guts of this former rubbish tip. The wetlands' humble beginnings in 1986 are now hidden by 45 hectares of rehabilitated wetlands and more than 250 wildlife species. Mosquitoes are aplenty so best keep walking/canoeing (canoe hire $8). The centre is a short walk from Sandgate train station.

Set in a bushland reserve, **Blackbutt Reserve** ( ☎ 4904 3344; www.newcastle.nsw.gov.au; Carnley Ave, Kotara; admission free; 🕑 9am-5pm) is a great venue for a picnic lunch, plus there are many walking tracks.

**Pacific Dreams** ( ☎ 4926 3355; 7 Darby St; day hire $50) hires out secondhand boards that are fibreglass – and hurt when they hit you in the white wash. However, the pain is a small sacrifice for looking cool.

**Fishers @ Honeysuckle** ( ☎ 4926 2722; Honeysuckle Dr; bike hire 1hr/2hr/day $15/20/35) hires bikes and buggies and is also a booking agent for several cruise companies in the area that specialise in drifting around the harbour, sauntering over to Stockton or floating as far afield as Morpeth.

Had enough? Feel like jumping from Strzelecki…? Paragliding with **Air Sports New-**

**castle** ( ☎ 0412 607 815; www.air-sports.com.au; tandem flight $165) is perhaps the answer.

## Tours

**Best Tours** ( ☎ 4950 4518; per person incl lunch $75) Tours the Lower Hunter vineyards.

**Hades Day Tours** ( ☎ 4981 0100; per person incl lunch $69) Goes to the vineyards also, but is a wee bit cheaper.

**Heliservices** ( ☎ 4962 5188; scenic flights from $69) Stuff the bus, take a chopper instead.

**Hunter River Cruises** ( ☎ 4958 7766; Queens Wharf; from $37) Sails around the harbour or inland to Morpeth.

**Newcastle's Famous Tram** ( ☎ 4977 2270; Newcastle train station, Hunter St; adult/child $12/6; 🕑 11am & 1pm) Take a 45-minute tour of the city's beaches and historic sites while receiving a running commentary and a little local gossip, delivered with typical Novacastrian zest. The best-spent 12 bucks in Newcastle. Vineyard tours are also available on weekends.

## Festivals & Events

This town knows how to party and the list of festivals is endless, so ask the visitors centre about its events calendar, which includes:

**Mattara – Festival of Newcastle** (www.mattarafesti val.org.au) This combines the Maritime Festival and Darby Street Fair to make the largest festival on offer throughout the year.

**Rainbow Festival** (www.rainbowvisions.org.au) An October festival celebrating Hunter gays and lesbians.

**Surfest** ( ☎ 4929 5833) The longest-running professional surfing competition in Australia, held at Newcastle Beach every March (and sometimes at Merewether).

**This Is Not Art Festival** ( ☎ 4927 0470) Young writers, artists and music-makers celebrate.

## Sleeping

**Terraces for Tourists** ( ☎ 4929 4575; www.terracesfortour ists.com.au) rents, as the name suggests, terraces for tourists. Or find longer term rentals at www.newcastle-real-estate.com.

### BUDGET

**Backpackers by the Beach** ( ☎ 1800 008 972, 4926 3472; www.backpackersbythebeach.com.au; 34-36 Hunter St; dm/d $25/55; 🖳 ) This one is just down the road from the YHA and is an alternative for those who despise YHAs (although Newcastle's one isn't nearly as institutionalised as some), or if the YHA is booked out.

**Newcastle Beach YHA** ( ☎ 4925 3544; www.yha .com.au; 30 Pacific St; dm/s/d $26/43/64; 🖳 ) Residing in the old 'Gentleman's Club' building, it's lucky they're a dying breed and the space is now better utilised by backpackers. There is a barbecue at the Brewery on Thursday night and a free dinner and plenty of craic at MJ Finnegan's Irish Pub (www.irishpub.com.au; 21-23 Darby St) Sunday to Tuesday nights.

## MIDRANGE

There are a string of motels along the Pacific Hwy at Belmont, which are great for exploring Lake Macquarie but not so much Newcastle proper.

**Travelodge** ( ☎ 1300 886 886, 4926 3777; www.travelodge.com.au; cnr King & Steel Sts; r from $100; **P** 🕱 ) Unexceptional rooms on offer here. No surprises or delights, but it's the cheapest room (with a bathroom) in town.

**Riverview Gardens** ( ☎ 4928 3048; www.riverviewgardens.com.au; 98 Fullerton St, Stockton; s/d incl breakfast $130/150) Spend lazy afternoons watching coal ships pass by the front door. It's a magical position giving some industrial insight into the harbour.

**Ashiana** ( ☎ 4929 4979; www.ashiana.com.au; 8 Helen St, Merewether; r incl breakfast $165; 🕱 ) Set back off the main road to the beach; soak up summer days in your swimmers and nights at the Beaches Hotel.

## TOP END

**Harbour View Manor** ( ☎ 4927 1448; www.harbourviewmanor.com; 110 Church St; r incl breakfast $175-300; 🕱 ) Fantastic views over the harbour at the top of town. The perfect stay in a quiet old street while still being amongst it. Closed on Sunday.

## Eating

There are three strips of eating places in Newcastle: **Beaumont St**, **Darby St** and the **Honeysuckle Boardwalk**. The first two are well established and will cater to every taste bud's whim. The third is a reasonably recent addition and features funky glass-fronted restaurants. Check out the website www.eatlocal.com.au for restaurant listings.

## BUDGET

**Scotties** ( ☎ 4926 3780; 36 Scott St; mains $9-15; 🕑 breakfast, lunch & dinner) A relaxed beach shack serving fish and chips and gourmet burgers with BYO.

**Estabar** ( ☎ 4927 1222; cnr Ocean St & Shortland Esp; light meals $10) Enjoy espresso and gelati practically on the beach. The Spanish-style hot chocolate is popular with those who cringe at the scent of coffee.

## MIDRANGE

**Sticky Rice Thai** ( ☎ 4927 0200; 19 Scott St; mains $11-19; 🕑 lunch & dinner) Beach-style Thai; this is not quite what you find in Koh Samui but it's close enough.

**Bogie Hole Café** ( ☎ 4929 1790; cnr Hunter & Pacific Sts; mains $18-24; 🕑 breakfast, lunch & dinner) Located at the top of Hunter St, it's just a hop, skip and jump to Newcastle Beach. The menu includes light summery meals like chicken and honeydew melon salad, to heavier options such as braised lamb shanks.

**Blue Water Pizza** ( ☎ 4929 5686; Queens Wharf; mains $18-24; 🕑 lunch & dinner) Just up from Scratchleys, this restaurant is a Newcastle institution.

## TOP END

**Scratchleys** ( ☎ 4929 1111; 200 Wharf Rd; mains $14-52; 🕑 lunch & dinner) It's fishy fresh and it's local, and if king prawns aren't big enough, they have jumbo prawns here. There are non-seafood options also.

**Silo** ( ☎ 4926 2828; Honeysuckle Dr; mains $27-38; 🕑 breakfast Sat & Sun, lunch & dinner daily) Laughter reflects from the red and white walls and ricochets off the glass chandeliers. Silo specialises in local produce and sports a tremendous selection of beers, cocktails, liqueurs and spirits. A DJ spins up a storm Friday and Saturday nights (from 9.30pm) and lazy Sunday afternoons.

**Jonah's on the Beach** ( ☎ 4929 5181; cnr Shortland Esp & Zaara St; mains $28-39; 🕑 breakfast, lunch & dinner) A concoction of contemporary Australian cuisine by the beach. Go for lobster and king prawn fettuccini for dinner or champagne-battered fish with lime aioli for lunch.

## Drinking & Entertainment

There has always been a lively music scene in the city. **Newcastle Music Week** ( ☎ 0425 236 156) and **Music and Moonlight Concert** ( ☎ 4914 5975) both celebrate this side of local culture. For a rundown on coming events check out www.tin.org.au/gigguide/livemusic or pick up a copy of *Drum Media*.

**Beaches Hotel** ( ☎ 4963 1574; www.thebeachhotel.com.au; cnr Frederick & Ridge Sts, Merewether) There is only one place to be on a Sunday afternoon and that is at this beachside pub.

**Queens Wharf Brewery** ( ☎ 4929 6333; www.qwb.com.au; 150 Wharf Rd) Newcastle has always been good at utilising its views, and this place and Beaches Hotel are the best two examples.

**Cambridge Hotel** ( ☎ 4962 2459; 789 Hunter St) Block out the spewy scent saturating the carpet; by midnight you won't even notice. Renowned for secret gigs where big acts will rock up to do an unadvertised show.

**Vass O'Gowrie Hotel** ( ☎ 4962 1248; 14 Railway St Wickham) Built in 1877, this is the oldest pub in Newcastle and has been the heart of the local music scene for the past 15 years. See local original acts here most nights.

**Greater Union Cinemas** ( ☎ 4926 2233; www .greaterunion.com.au; 183 King St) For a more subdued evening, head to the movies.

## Getting There & Away

### AIR
The airport is 40 minutes from Newcastle Station by bus. It runs irregularly, therefore most people make their way to town by taxi or hire car. **Aeropelican** ( ☎ 4928 9600), **Jetstar** ( ☎ 13 15 38), **QantasLink** ( ☎ 13 13 13) and **Virgin Blue** ( ☎ 13 67 89) all operate here.

### BUS
All local and long-distance buses leave from Newcastle Station. **Greyhound** ( ☎ 13 14 99) goes north as far as Byron Bay (adult/child $84/69), west to Tamworth (adult/child $66/54) and south to Sydney (adult/child $39/32).

Other options for travelling up the coast include **Premier Motor Service** ( ☎ 13 34 10) which travels through to Brisbane daily. Purchase a pass that allows you to jump on, jump off on the way (Backpacker Pass $109). Or take a trip up the coast with **Port Stephens Coaches** ( ☎ 4982 2940). It has multiple daily services that go as far north as Fingal Bay (adult/child $11/6). **Busways** ( ☎ 4983 1560) runs to Forster (adult/child $31/16) and Sydney daily.

For more westerly movements, **Rover Coaches** ( ☎ 4990 1699) has return services from Cessnock to Newcastle (adult/child $13/7) and **Sid Fogg's** ( ☎ 4928 1088) runs across to Dubbo, stopping at all major towns (adult/child $65/53).

### CAR
**Budget** ( ☎ 13 27 27) and **Thrifty** ( ☎ 4965 1535) usually have the best-value small cars. However, **Avis** ( ☎ 4965 1612), **Europcar** ( ☎ 4965 0162) and **Hertz** ( ☎ 13 30 39) also have cars at the airport. Otherwise, head to **Cheep Heep** ( ☎ 4961 3144; 141 Maitland Rd, Islington) and hire a cheap heap from as little as $33 a day.

### TRAIN
All **CountryLink** trains stop at Broadmeadow, just west of town, and run up and down the coast to

Coffs Harbour (adult/child $75/40). Change at Casino or Grafton for Byron Bay (adult/child $105/55). Trains also head to Tamworth (adult/child $30/25) and leave directly from Newcastle Station for Sydney (adult/child $30/15).

There are plenty of **CityRail** trains heading to Sydney and northwest to Maitland, Dungog and Scone, daily.

## Getting Around
All travel on the blue and white buses around the city centre is free.

**Newcastle Buses & Ferries** ( ☎ 13 15 00), offering a 23-hour service (adult/child $8/4 including bus and ferry), covers Newcastle and the eastern side of Lake Macquarie. Jump on the Stockton Ferry at Queens Wharf (adult/child one way $2/1).

If you have flown in, **Port Stephens Coaches** ( ☎ 4982 2940) runs to and from the airport almost hourly with reduced trips on the weekend ($6, 35 minutes). Otherwise call a **cab** ( ☎ 4979 3000).

## AROUND NEWCASTLE
Each grain of sand at **Stockton Beach** is constantly shifting, making it the largest moving dune mass in the southern hemisphere. It is the final resting place of the **Sygna**, a Norwegian bulk carrier that ran aground in 1974. And its sands are shipped over to Hawaii to cushion the fat alohas at Waikiki Beach. The main access to the dunes is via **Lavis Lane** off Nelson Bay Rd, but stop in at the **Metro** ( ☎ 4965 0401) on the roundabout to grab a vehicle permit (weekend pass $10).

Hoon across the dunes with **Sand Safaris** ( ☎ 4965 0215; www.sandsafaris.com.au; Lavis Lane, Williamtown) Two-hour trips cost $119/129 midweek/weekends. Or contact **Moonshadow 4WD Tours** ( ☎ 4984 4760; www.moonshadow4wd.com.au) for a more civilised approach (adult/child $20/15).

**Stockton Beach Tourist Park** ( ☎ 4928 1393; tourist park@stocktonbeach.com; Pitt St; sites $20-31, cabins $44-78, with bathroom $75-111; P ⟨image⟩ ) is very popular with the regional crowd and books out a year in advance for Christmas and Easter. You can hire linen ($12).

## MAITLAND
☎ 02 / pop 58,000
Molly Morgan stole some yarn and was therefore transported from England to the colony in Sydney. Married three times and transported twice, this vibrant character is part responsible for the birth and building of

Maitland. A cunning convict, she arrived with her 'ticket of leave' and a cedar-forested land grant on the banks of the Hunter River. The bullock track that dissected her property became High St, and the forested plains around her the township of Maitland.

## Orientation & Information
The main street, High St, is partly closed off and Heritage Mall is where most of your shopping needs will be met.

**Library** ( ☎ 4933 6952; 480 High St)

**Police Station** ( ☎ 4934 0200; 3 Caroline Place)

**Post Office** ( ☎ 13 13 18; 379-383 High St)

**Visitors centre** ( ☎ 4931 2833; www.maitlandhunter valley.com.au; cnr New England Hwy & High St) Look for the old steam train along the highway.

## Sights & Activities
The city's 19th-century wealth is reflected in the elaborate Georgian and Victorian buildings, so head to the visitors centre and grab information regarding heritage walks in town.

**Maitland Gaol** ( ☎ 4936 6482; John St; admission adult/child $10/7, tours adult/child $12/9) This is the second most haunted place in the country and the spooks rule the roost here. Ex-inmate tours give you insight into all the jailhouse goss and the psychic tours are even more informative.

**Walka Water Works Complex** ( ☎ 4932 0522; Sempill St; admission per car $3; powered/unpowered sites $15/11; ☯ 7am-dusk) Follow the signs from the roundabout at Maitland train station. Don't forget to pack lunch and the kids.

## Festivals & Events
**Steamfest** (www.steamfest.com.au) celebrates Maitland's steamy past and attracts 70,000 enthusiasts each April to ride trains throughout the Hunter.

## Sleeping
**LJ Hooker** ( ☎ 4933 5511) can hook you up with a rental property if you decide to linger longer.

**Belmore Hotel** ( ☎ 4933 6351; www.thebelmore.com .au; 476 High St; s/d $45/55 Mon-Thu, $65/75 Fri-Sun; P ☯ ). Respectable pub rooms and a friendly bar downstairs for a few cheeky ones.

**Molly Morgan Motor Inn** ( ☎ 4933 5422; New England Hwy; s/d $85/95, $10 more Sat; P ☯ ) One of the better motels in Maitland, all rooms are spacious and there is a good à la carte restaurant.

**Monte Pio Motor Inn** ( ☎ 4932 5288; New England Hwy, Rutherford; r $115; P ☯ ☯ ) West of town, it

is set in a historic building on acreage, with resort-standard facilities.

## Eating
**Maneeya** ( ☎ 4933 1717; 473 High St; mains $15-20; ☯ lunch Wed, dinner Thu & Fri) Centrally located on the main street, get a typical Thai feed here before heading out for the night.

**Café Blende Lorn** ( ☎ 4934 8224; 27 Belmore Rd, Lorn; mains $19-25; ☯ breakfast weekends, lunch Tue-Sun & dinner Wed-Sat) A quiet, comfortable little restaurant just over the river. There is a mixture of meals including pizza, pasta and meat-free steaks.

**Old George & Dragon Restaurant** ( ☎ 4933 7272; 48 Melbourne St, East Maitland; 2/3 courses per person from $57/70; ☯ dinner Wed-Sat) In a restored pub dating from the 1830s; owner and chef Ian Morphy's Anglo-French food attracts critical acclaim.

## Drinking & Entertainment
An epidemic spreads through town on Friday nights. It involves one-hit wonders, distasteful ballads and alcohol-dependent egos. Karaoke performances can be witnessed at both **Shenanigans** ( ☎ 4933 6566; 458 High St) and across the road at the **Belmore Hotel** ( ☎ 4933 6351; www .thebelmore.com.au; 476 High St).

**Clubhouse Hotel** ( ☎ 4933 5265; 41 Elgin St) serves dinner, but you should come back later as the crowds don't start pouring in until the wee small hours when the Belmore closes.

## Getting There & Away
**Rover Coaches** ( ☎ 4990 1699) has an hourly bus service to Cessnock on weekdays, with reduced services on Saturday. But **CountryLink** ( ☎ 13 22 32) travels slightly further afield, heading north to Scone (adult/child $20/10) and Tamworth (adult/child $45/25) daily, up the coast to Coffs Harbour (adult/child $72/36), and south to Sydney (adult/child $21/18).

**CityRail** has plenty of trains going into Newcastle and west to Scone, stopping at all major towns.

# MORPETH
☎ 02

Morpeth Cemetery looks over a sweeping green valley to the town, which hugs the Hunter River. In that cemetery are some of the oldest bones in NSW, as this was once the major port for passengers and products arriving in the Hunter. Sandstone buildings line the main street, where you can shop for

HUNTER VALLEY

expensive ladies' fashions, secondhand books and antiques.

**Morpeth Sourdough** ( ☎ 4934 4148; 148 Swan St; ⏲ 9am-5pm Wed-Sun) is housed in the original Arnott's Biscuits building; the grandson of the big-bickies business originator, Stephen Arnott, now handmakes bread.

For old-fashioned brews visit **Morpeth Ginger Beer Factory** ( ☎ 4933 1407; 5 Green St; ⏲ 10am-5pm Thu-Sun). There's also a range of gourmet foods upstairs.

Held in September, the **Morpeth Jazz Festival** (www.morpethjazz.com.au) features food, jazz and fine wine.

John Bradley scenes of Morpeth adorn the walls in the elegantly decorated **Bronte Guesthouse** ( ☎ 4934 6080; www.bronteguesthouse.com.au; 147 Swan St; r incl breakfast $140 Mon-Thu, $200 Fri-Sun).

**Kokepelli's** ( ☎ 4933 0337; 2/119 Swan St; mains $22-28; ⏲ breakfast & lunch daily, dinner Fri & Sat) does basic Aussie meals with a twist. Try kangaroo loin with blueberries and red wine.

**Blue Ribbon** ( ☎ 13 15 00) runs a bus from Maitland weekdays but, alas, they will leave you stranded on weekends. Not to worry; it is only six minutes in a cab and will cost about 10 bucks.

## AROUND MORPETH

The historic trail only begins in Morpeth, so cross the rickety bridge and continue north. One of the more pleasant drives in the valley, the road winds through broad green paddocks and hilly cattle country. **Largs** and **Woodville** are cute and quaint, but continue on to **Patterson** and stop for lunch at Yabbies Bistro at the **Paterson Tavern** ( ☎ 4938 5196; 25 Prince St; ⏲ lunch & dinner Wed-Sat).

## CESSNOCK

☎ 02 / pop 18,100

Clichéd it is, but Cessnock really is the gateway to the Hunter Valley vineyards. It has quickly built its identity on this, forgetting a coal mining past and focusing on more pressing viticultural issues. By basing yourself here you may be able to cut costs as there are slightly cheaper alternatives to sleeping in amongst the vines. However, there is no guarantee, as this town expertly rides the wave of the wine boom.

## Orientation & Information

Vincent St is the main street and runs perpendicular off Wollombi Rd. Several **ATMs** can be found along here.

**Grocery stores** (Cessnock Market Place, just off Wollombi Rd)

**Library** ( ☎ 4993 4399; 65-67 Vincent St) For internet access.

**Post Office** (Cessnock Market Place)

## Sleeping

Like grape country itself, Cessnock accommodation prices fluctuate on weekends, the definition of which can sometimes be vague. Also watch out for wounded bulls on long weekends and 'event' weekends. If you are looking to stay longer term, contact **Sylvester First National Real Estate** ( ☎ 4991 2577).

**Hunter Valley YHA** ( ☎ 4991 3278; www.yha.com.au; 100 Wine Country Dr; dm $29-32, s/d $64/77, with bathroom $79/97; 🖥 🐾 ) Wine tasting, pushbike riding, wine tasting, horse riding, wine tasting, flying lessons…best stick with the wine tasting.

**Wentworth Hotel** ( ☎ 4990 1364; 36 Vincent St; s/d incl breakfast $50/70 Mon-Thu, $75/95 Fri-Sun) For a good-value basic room you cannot go past The Werty. Particularly good news if you view accommodation costs in terms of cases of wine.

**Cessnock Motel** ( ☎ 4990 2699; 13 Allandale Rd; s/d $80/85 Sun-Thu, $90/95 Fri, $120/130 Sat; 🐾 ) The word swanky comes to mind. Think dark colours and minimalist furnishings.

**Potters Hotel & Brewery** ( ☎ 4991 7922; www.pottersbrewery.com.au; Wine Country Dr; r $99-149 Sun-Fri, $220 Sat, spa villa $200-300; 🐾 🐾 ) Stumble home from the brewery without getting lost. Shout yourself a spa package and you may never leave the grounds. Brewery tours ($6) leave at noon, 2pm and 4pm.

**Valley Vineyard Tourist Park** ( ☎ 4990 2573; Mt View Rd; sites $30; cabins midweek $65-85, weekends $85-110; 🐾 🐾 ) Set a little off the frantic Mt View Rd, this green park is a cheapish alternative if you possess a tent or caravan (linen hire $15).

## Eating

**Oak Brasserie** ( ☎ 4990 2366; 221 Vincent St; mains $12-24; ⏲ lunch & dinner) Inside the Royal Oak you'll be served huge and exquisitely presented meals like pork loin on sweet potato with pear salsa.

**Old Brickhouse Brasserie** ( ☎ 4991 7922; Wine Country Dr; mains $14-27; ⏲ lunch & dinner) Salads, pizzas, steaks and a whole section of the menu dedicated to 'Beer 'n' Food', ie brewer's lunch, beer 'n' fish basket, Hunter lager and lamb barbecue, and beer and steak pizza.

## Getting There & Away

**Keans** ( ☎ 6545 1945) has buses every day except Saturdays that run up the New England Hwy to Scone (adult/child $30/15) or down to Sydney.

## LOWER HUNTER WINERIES

People have been drinking wine for more than 5000 wonderful years. It is the oldest known agricultural product in the world. And Australia is the fourth biggest exporter in the world, sending 2.5 million bottles every day to 100 different countries. But don't worry, there is plenty left for Aussies. It's in our blood.

Wine came out with the First Fleet in 1788. It was one of our icons, Gregory Blaxland (of Lawson and Wentworth fame), who experimented with vines back in the 1820s. He had a little luck but it was not until James Busby put pen to paper and told the masses how to grow grapes that Australian viticulture truly began. Fiercely promoted by the government as a means of getting the convicts off harder spirits, there was hope the colony would become 'a healthy, sober, jolly, wine-drinking population'.

But nothing of a significant scale happened until 1828 when a free settler by the name of George Wyndham headed to the Hunter, land grant in hand. He cleared some land and planted the seed and Wyndham Estate was born. So too was Australian shiraz, semillion, chardonnay…

So here you are where it all started. With more than 140 wineries before you it can be a little overwhelming. The rigid few will grab a copy of the *Hunter Valley Wine Country Visitor Guide*. The rest will get to know the biggies and then go looking for the boutiques. 'Explore. Dream. Discover'.

## Information

**Hunter Valley Wine Country Tourism Centre** ( ☎ 02-4990 0900; www.winecountry.com.au; Wine Country Dr) Will book accommodation as well.

**Red Zebra Childcare Agency** ( ☎ 0419 411 636) The holy grail.

Grape picking starts in late January and continues through to late March. Contact the **Hunter Valley Vineyard Association** ( ☎ 02-4991 4533) for further info; otherwise it is a matter of contacting the vineyards individually in November and December.

## Sights & Activities

**Hunter Valley Gardens** ( ☎ 02-4998 4000; www.hvg.com.au; Broke Rd; adult/child $20/10) This is the most child-friendly destination in the vineyards. Young families can dine relatively cheaply here at several cafés and visit the Hunter Valley Chocolate Factory (where they have chilli chocolate samples for unsuspecting chocoholic traditionalists).

### GOLF

**Cypress Lakes Golf & Country Club** ( ☎ 02-4993 1800; www.cypresslakes.com.au; cnr McDonalds & Thompsons Rds, Pokolbin; green fees $84-98). Green fees include a motorised golf cart and disapproval of wannabe Happy Gilmores.

**Aqua Golf & Putt Putt** ( ☎ 02-4998 7896; Hunter Valley Gardens Village; putt putt adult/child $6/5, aqua golf

**HUNTER VALLEY**

---

### TOP FIVE ACTIVITIES

- Get up in the air for sunrise with **Balloon Aloft** ( ☎ 1800 028 568, 02-4938 1955; www.balloonaloft.com; 1443 Wine Country Dr; flights $295). Too much hot air? Take a joy flight with **Hunter Valley Aviation** ( ☎ 02-4991 6500; www.huntervalleyaviation.com; Main Rd, Cessnock Airport; 20min flight $60).

- Work up a canter at **Hunter Valley Horse Riding & Adventures** ( ☎ 07-4930 7111; 288 Talga Rd, Rothbury; per person $50). If you're not very horsey and prefer creatures of the night, go on a **4WD Night Wildlife Safari** (adult/child $30/15) instead.

- For a romantic clip-clop along the valley try **Pokolbin Horse Coaches** ( ☎ 02-4998 7305; McDonalds Rd; half-/full-day tours $45/69).

- Hire a tandem from **Hunter Valley Cycles** ( ☎ 02-4998 6633; Hunter Valley Gardens; per day $50) and let your better half do all the work while you drink the precious cargo.

- Become an instant wine connoisseur at **Hunter Valley Wine School** ( ☎ 02-4998 7777; Hermitage Rd, Hunter Resort; $25) and get some tips on the best buys in the valley. Or tie up your apron and take on the oven at the **Hunter Valley Cooking School** ($120).

# LOWER HUNTER VALLEY

0 ————— 5 km
0 ————— 3 miles

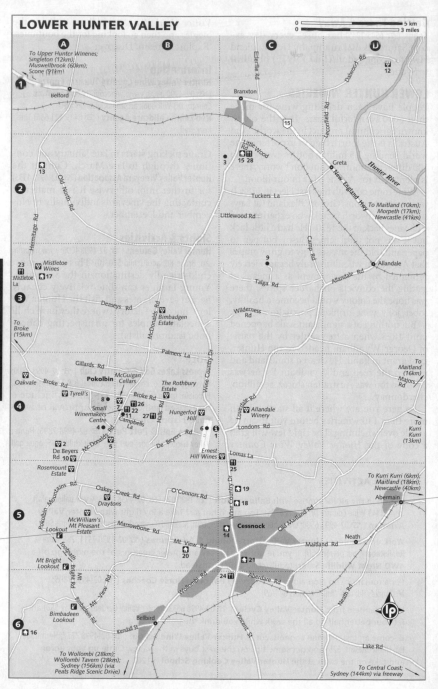

$7). Bad handicap? Let your frustrations out at Aqua Golf, where you don't have to go looking for the ball

## WINERIES

**Wyndham Estate** ( ☎ 02-4938 3444; 700 Dalwood Rd, Dalwood; ⏲ 10am-4.30pm) Where it all began back in 1828, this winery is the birthplace of Australian shiraz. The 'Shiraz Experience' tasting plate is essential to your full understanding of the drop. Tours through the winery leave at 11am.

**Lindemans Wines** ( ☎ 02-4998 7684; McDonalds Rd; ⏲ 10am-5pm) The naturally grand Lindemans with its amphitheatre of grapes is a cherished member of many families, even though Linde is kept in a cask on the bottom shelf of the fridge.

**Audrey Wilkinson Vineyard** ( ☎ 02-4998 7411; De Beyers Rd; ⏲ 9am-5pm) The single most beautiful vineyard in the valley is home to the first grapes planted in Pokolbin. Marvel at the expansive view while enjoying a drop of red, even if the wine was designed by a teetotaller.

## Tours

There are countless vineyard tours, so stop by the visitors centre for more info.
**Hunter Vineyard Tours** ( ☎ 02-4991 1659; www.hunter vineyardtours.com.au; day tours $50, with lunch $75)
**Tumbleweed Trike Tours** ( ☎ 02-4938 1245; 1st hr $150, thereafter $50; ⏲ weekends only) You won't be able to get the smile off your face, and that's before you have even started tasting.

## Festivals & Events

See www.winecountry.com.au/events for a full listing.
**Jazz in the Vines** (www.jazzinthevines.com.au) Food, wine and jazz all in the one place at the end of October.
**Lovedale Long Lunch** (www.lovedalelonglunch.com .au) A progressive lunch held at the end of May.
**Opera in the Vineyards** (www.wyndhamestate.com) Plenty of throat lubrication needed for this one.

## Sleeping

On the weekend you will find it hard to get a bed in the valley (especially for one night), so booking is essential. For budget or midrange accommodation it's best to base yourself at Cessnock (p148).

**Hunter Country Lodge** ( ☎ 02-4938 1744; Wine Country Dr; s/d incl breakfast $100/140 Mon-Thu, $145/200 Fri-Sun; ⏲ ⏲ ) Whitewashed walls, fresh air and a seat out on the veranda in the morning sun. Simplistic rooms next door to Shakey Tables restaurant.

**Billabong Moon** ( ☎ 02 6574 7290; www.hillabongmoon .com.au; 393 Hermitage Rd; cottages $200-220 midweek, $530-540 weekends for 2 nights; ⏲ ⏲ ) Self-contained cottages with original artworks, spa and four-poster bed. The bush setting is juxtaposed by a somewhat Roman feel.

**Hunter Valley Country Cabins** ( ☎ 02-4990 8989; www .huntervalleycabins.com.au; 1329 Mt View Rd; d incl breakfast $259 Sun-Thu, weekends for up to 4 adults $559; ⏲ ) Secluded wooden cabins with a seductive slow-combustion fire in winter. It offers vineyard tours and transfers to and from local restaurants.

**Hunter Valley Resort** ( ☎ 02-4998 7777; www.hunter valley.com.au; Hermitage Rd; $198-290 Sun-Fri, $230-325 Sat; ⏲ ⏲ ) The resort is beginning to show its age but is a handy place to stay if you want to get really familiar with the beverages at Blue Tongue Brewery.

## Eating

**Australian Regional Food Store & Café** ( ☎ 02-4998 6800; McDonalds Rd; mains $14-20; ⏲ breakfast & lunch)

After sampling the wines inside the Small Winemakers Centre, follow your nose to the regional produce section.

**Harrigan's** ( ☎ 02-4998 4000; Broke Rd; mains $16-35; breakfast, lunch & dinner) Featuring beers from Ireland and beyond, soak up the crate while tasting five at a time on weekends ($9 per person). Light meals include Guinness pie, but unfortunately most meals are uninspiring so go only for the beer when you're all wined out.

**Mill** ( ☎ 02-4998 7266; Mistletoe Lane; mains $31-33; breakfast, lunch & dinner) Glass-fronted with sweeping views of the valley, Mill has a tapas menu for early afternoon.

**Shakey Tables** ( ☎ 02-4938 1744; Wine Country Dr; mains $36; lunch Sun, dinner daily) Two A3 pages comprise the wine lists alone! Multi-award winning, funky and stylish, promoting atypical eating in the vineyards: pork belly and black truffle potato mash; roasted pigeon perhaps?

**Robert's Restaurant** ( ☎ 02-4998 7330; Halls Rd; mains $37-40; lunch & dinner) Try the tasty twice-roasted duckling with bok choy, pear and marmalade. But duck also if you are tall when entering the doorway of the restored 130-year-old settler's cottage.

No time for fine dining? Head to Pokolbin village for some slightly cheaper options or go gourmet with the excellent regional produce:

**Hunter Olive Centre** ( ☎ 02-4998 7524; Pokolbin Estate Vineyard, McDonalds Rd; 10am-5pm) The olives are roasted, they're marinated, and they are virgin. There are bush tucker sauces, vinaigrettes, tapenades, chutneys, condiments, conserves and wine jellies and jams (and it's all local).

**Hunter Valley Cheese Co.** ( ☎ 02-4998 7744; McGuigan Complex, McDonalds Rd; 9am-5.30pm) Cheese as well as gourmet produce such as organic pickled walnuts, and the alcoholic's favourite…whisky marmalade. Grab a pre-packaged Ploughman's Platter ($30) before heading to the Hunter Valley Gardens for respite. Cheese talk and tasting at 11am daily ($6).

### Getting There & Away

**Rover Coaches** ( ☎ 1800 801 012) runs a coach from Sydney daily (adult/child $40/30) with drop-offs in Cessnock and throughout the Lower Hunter Valley vineyards. It also has multiple daily services to Maitland (adult/child $9/4) and Newcastle (adult/child $12/6). Buses leave from in front of the visitors centre (p149).

## WOLLOMBI

☎ 02 / pop 355

The Wollombi Brook meanders through a narrow valley, passing the Wollombi Tavern at the foot of town. There's 175 years of European history preserved here, thanks to the demise of the **Great North Road** (see also p116): back in 1832 the government decided to open up the Hunter to free settlers and sent convicts restricted by leg-irons to build a road. Using retaining walls, stone abutments and pillars, the Great North Road was completed in 1836, opening an artery from Sydney to the north and placing Wollombi firmly on the map.

The old courthouse, now **Endeavour Museum** ( ☎ 4998 3375; Wollombi Rd; adult/child $2/1; 11am-2pm, to 3pm Mon & Fri, to 4pm Sat & Sun) houses a collection of local items dating back to the late 1800s.

Aborigines roamed these parts for 13,000 years prior to European settlement. This is remembered annually at **Wollombi Corroboree** (www.wollombi.org). Taking place in September, it is a celebration between local town folk and the original inhabitants of the area.

**Gray's Inn Guesthouse** and the **Water Hen Restaurant** ( ☎ 4998 3475; Maitland Rd; mains $25-32; breakfast & lunch Sat-Sun, dinner Wed-Sun) have a refined menu that reads like a taste bud's dream – pork medallions, veal cutlets, herb spatchcock, seafood paella and spiced vegetable stack.

An old wine bar was originally built at the current **Wollombi Tavern** ( ☎ 4998 3261; Great North Road; mains $16-20; lunch daily, dinner Fri & Sat) site. It burnt down in 1959 when the publican accidentally filled a kerosene fridge with petrol.

## WOLLEMI & YENGO NATIONAL PARKS

These two parks are inundated with Aboriginal paintings, with the 270-million-year-old outcrops being the perfect canvas for their art. Rock paintings often centre on Baiame, a prominent Dreamtime spirit in the area. The creator of all things, when he had finished his work he left this world from the top of Yengo Mountain, in Yengo National Park.

Furthermore, the infertile soils, dry climate and rugged terrain have kept the farmers away. So the parks have survived, forming the largest wilderness area in the state.

Sandstone ridges, gorges and escarpments mean the parks are popular for adventure sports such as rock climbing, canyoning, abseiling, and liloing. 'Tag-along' tours by 4WD are available through the **NPWS** 'Discovery' programme (see www.nationalparks.nsw

---

### CHANGING TIMES FOR THE GREAT NORTH ROAD

The first people to arrive in the Hunter Valley, via Great North Road, were war veterans then Irish, Scottish and English free settlers. Wollombi became a strategic hub of the region, but along with Wollombi's boom came the bushrangers. The Great North Road was their ultimate playground. Edward 'Jew Boy' Davis then 'Yellow Billy' ravaged the area between 1865 and 1866.

When the Wyndham Estate was established in 1828 it signified the beginning of something huge. Then coal was discovered near Cessnock so the mining industry began its migration from Newcastle to the Upper Hunter in 1887.

However, the Great North Road's importance declined as the wheat industry declined; the onset of the disease rust made farmers realise you can't grow wheat by the coast. The last straw was when *Sophia Jane* steamed in direct from Sydney to the port town of Morpeth, via the Hunter River. The Great North Road was left to fall into disrepair.

It is best preserved from Wiseman's Ferry north to Manning. However, you can still cycle or walk along its entire length (see www.nationalparks.nsw.gov.au). Look out for Australia's oldest bridge and convict graffiti.

---

.gov.au). Two of the more popular tracks are **Womerah Range Track** and **Finchley Track** in Yengo National Park near Wollombi.

There are glow-worm tunnels near Newness (near Lithgow), and **Dunns Swamp** (near Rylstone) is a canoeing capital and has **camping** (adult/child $3/2). Facilities can also be found at **Little Capertree** (near Newness Hotel), **Sheepskin Hut** and **Wheeny Creek**.

As well as being endowed with the very rare Wollemi Pine, the place unfortunately has some areas riddled with weeds, particularly **Colo River**, which is lined with willow trees. **Friends of Colo** ( ☎ 02-4588 5247) has annual rafting trips into the area focused on eradicating the willow. You can also contact Bulga **NPWS** ( ☎ 02-6574 5555) for further information.

### UPPER HUNTER WINERIES

If you have already toured the Lower Hunter vineyards…so what, the wine tastes different here. That is because it is hotter and the upper reaches of the valley don't receive coastal rains. They see just a trickle of customers midweek, so if you don't like crowds, get on your horse.

They specialise in cabernet sauvignon and shiraz; forget merlot but do dabble in the verdelho and chardonnay. **Cruikshank Collatoota Estate** ( ☎ 02-6547 8149; Wybong Rd, Wybong; ☻ 9am-5pm) is unique in that it is family run and absolutely everything takes place on the property, from grape pressing through to marketing. A favourite is the Velvet Cabernet.

**Yarraman Cellar Door** ( ☎ 02-6547 8118; Yarraman Rd, Wyhong; ☻ 10am-5pm) has a broad selection

of wines including some less familiar varietals (yes that's wine speak) such as chambourcin. There is a barbecue and an outdoor area, so collect your carnivorous snacks from Robert's Meats in Denman before heading out. Another favourite is the 2004 Gewurztraminer.

**Sandy Hollow Caravan Park & Country Cottages** ( ☎ 02-6547 4575; www.users.hunterlink.net.au/~mhbph; Golden Hwy; sites $16-22; d cottages $78-160, cabins $68-88; ☻ ) is the perfect low-cost base for the vineyards, and if you have a bike, even better, as numerous rides depart from the caravan park.

## DENMAN

☎ 02 / pop 1600

The sprouting wineries around its perimeter have done little to change the 182-year-old town. A historic main street is lined with numerous cafés serving Devonshire tea, clothing and craft stores, and gift shops that make you sneeze.

The main street is Ogilvie; there's an **ATM** halfway up the street and the **CTC** ( ☎ 6547 2799; 28 Ogilvie St) has tourist information and internet access.

There are plenty of B&Bs but the **Royal Hotel** ( ☎ 6547 2226; www.denmanroyal.com, Ogilvie St; s/d $25/35) is cheap and managed to survive the 1955 flood. Apparently the water came part way up the bar, and rumour has it the patrons, undeterred, kept drinking their beers. The hotel restaurant (mains $14 to $28) is open for lunch and dinner.

The little things are important at the **Denman Motor Inn** ( ☎ 6547 2462; denmanmotorinn@bigpond.com; 8 Crinoline St; standard s/d $80/90, deluxe r $95; ☻ ☻)… face washers, insect spray, hairdryer.

The very green **Denman Van Village** ( ☎ 6547 2590; www.denmanvillage.com.au; 10 Macauley St; unpowered/powered sites $15/20, cabins $40-85; ✗ ) is at the quiet end of an already quiet town.

**Sid Fogg's** ( ☎ 4928 1088) buses run between Dubbo and Newcastle (adult/child $65/53),

# SCONE

☎ 02 / pop 4560

It is the sport of kings, and although Kerry Packer was not quite royalty, Australia's recently departed richest man (his inheritance was worth five billion), did have property in Scone. This is thoroughbred country, nestled between the vines and the mines, and the culture in town is squarely focused on Mr Ed.

## Orientation & Information

The New England Hwy becomes Kelly St, the main shopping street. The **visitors centre** ( ☎ 6545 1526, www.upperhuntertourism.com.au; Susan St) is on the north side of town.

**Neighbourhood Resource Centre** ( ☎ 6545 2562; 214 Kelly St) Has internet access.

**NPWS** ( ☎ 6540 2300; 137 Kelly St)

**Post Office** (cnr Kelly & Liverpool Sts)

## Sights & Activities

The visitors centre has information about the heritage buildings in town. Kelly St is rife with historic façades but so too are Liverpool, Guernsey and Kingdon Sts.

**Upper Hunter Tours** ( ☎ 0417 439 776; www.upperhuntertours.com.au) can arrange visits to some of the area's horse studs. Tours generally go on demand and cost $95 per couple per stud.

Coal seams at **Burning Mountain** have been smouldering for 6000 years. They fooled the first Europeans who were certain it was an active volcano. A 3km return track leads up to the smoking vents. The turn-off from the New England Hwy to Burning Mountain is about 20km north of Scone.

## Festivals & Events

Held in the second week of May, the **Scone and Upper Hunter Horse Festival** (www.scone horsefestival.com) celebrates all things equine. The highlight for lonely lads and ladies is the B&S Ball.

## Sleeping & Eating

There are many accommodation options in town and an abundance of B&Bs, so drop into the visitors centre for a complete listing.

**Airlie House Motor Inn** ( ☎ 6545 1488; www.airlie house.com.au; 229 New England Hwy; r $82-99, ste from $140; ✗ ☑ ) Built in 1895 this old building was once the town doctor's residence. Stay in the hotel rooms or in a studio-type apartment

**Belltrees** ( ☎ 6540 1123, www.belltrees.com; Gundy Rd; cottages incl breakfast $218-380) First established in 1831 the wealthy estate once had 64 houses, including a store, post office, church and school. The cottages are suitably quaint and very agreeable.

**Scone Caravan Park** ( ☎ 6545 2024; 50 Kelly St; unpowered/powered sites $17/18, onsite van $37, cabins $50-60; ✗ ) This caravan park is a leafy, quieter alternative to the only other one in town. Linen hire is $10.

**Crowded House Café** ( ☎ 6545 2414; 95 Kelly St; meals $7-14; ☺ breakfast & lunch Mon-Sat) An attempt at cool has failed miserably thanks to a centrally hung horse portrait. Luckily they put together a great gourmet sandwich.

**Quince Restaurant** ( ☎ 6545 2286; 109 Susan St; mains $22-32; ☺ lunch Thu-Sun, dinner Thu-Sat) You can find this century-old wooden cottage next door to the visitors centre. The menu ranges from salads to lamb rump and there's some added pizzazz to what was once just a steak sandwich.

## Getting There & Around

**Greyhound** ( ☎ 13 14 99) buses has daily services to Sydney (adult/child $72/60), Newcastle (adult/child $50/41) and Tamworth (adult/child $44/36). And **Keans** ( ☎ 6545 1945) heads down to Sydney (adult/child $48/24) or out to Tamworth.

**CountryLink** has daily train services south to Sydney (adult/child $55/35) and north to Tamworth (adult/child $36/15). The railway station is located on Guernsey St behind the visitors centre, and you can also get **CityRail** trains east through the valley.

# GOULBURN RIVER NATIONAL PARK

Goulburn River National Park takes its name from the river, where you will spot wallabies and wallaroos dining on the grassy banks in amongst the river oaks. Keep an eye out for Aboriginal rock paintings on the Narrabeen sandstone outcrops, a favourite canvas used by Aborigines who travelled along here. And head to **Mount Dangar** for sweeping views over the Hunter Valley.

Go by 4WD along **Big River Trail** or canoe down the river (but you may get lodged on a rock if there hasn't been heavy rain). The park is 35km southwest of Merriwa, and access is from the road running south to Wollar and Bylong; all roads in the park are dry-weather roads only.

There are several (free) camping options; try **White Box Camp**, or **Spring Gully** and **Big River Camp** right on the river. Mudgee **NPWS** ( ☎ 6372 7199) has more information.

## THE BUCKETTS WAY

This old road is an engaging alternative to the Pacific Hwy as a route north of Newcastle, branching off the highway about 15km north of Raymond Terrace and rejoining it just south of Taree. The scenery is very English Cotswolds – well, just as charming if slightly less historic.

## Stroud

☎ 02 / pop 670

Rich in convict history, the town was established in 1826 by the Australian Agricultural Company. The town's newsagent and **visitors centre** ( ☎ 4994 5117; 54 Cowper St) has tourist information.

Several convict-built buildings are still standing, such as the old school **Quambi**, the **Anglican church** and the **courthouse**.

Stroud in Australia, the USA, England and Canada all participate in a **brick-throwing competition** held in unison in July.

The **Central Hotel** ( ☎ 4994 5197; The Bucketts Way; r $30-60) may be able to help you with some tourist information, but if they don't know they may also make it up. And **Stroud Monastery** ( ☎ 4969 0000; stroud@samaritans.org.au; r $28) has cheap rooms in a beautiful bushland setting. Or pay a little more for the clover-carpeted gardens at **Orchard Cottage** ( ☎ 0414 725 482; www.orchardcottage .bigpondhosting.com; 3 Broadway St; s/d $150/185).

**CountryLink** ( ☎ 13 22 32) buses go to Gloucester (adult/child $9/5) and connect through

to Newcastle. Otherwise head to Raymond Terrace (adult/child $9/5) to get to the North Coast.

## Gloucester

☎ 02 / pop 2500

A churchy town at the base of the goddess of all mountain ranges, Barrington Tops, Gloucester is a peaceful place where farmers still do business at the end of the bar in the local pub. With the last timber mill shutting recently, it's surprising that there appears to be a type of tourism resistance in certain sectors of town. Thankfully most recognise the beauty in their back yard and are comfortable sharing it with the rest of the world.

### INFORMATION

**Gloucester Online** ( ☎ 6558 1784; 34 King St) Has internet access.
**NPWS office** ( ☎ 6538 5300; 59 Church St)
**Post Office** ( ☎ 6558 1819; 9 Queen St)
**Visitors centre** ( ☎ 6558 1408; www.gloucester.org.au; 27 Denison St) Just off the main street.

### SIGHTS & ACTIVITIES

**Camp Cobark Trail Rides** ( ☎ 6558 5524; 2457 Scone Rd; 2hr ride per person $45) operates horse rides that take in stream crossings and unmatched panoramic views. But if you really want to liven things up a bit contact **Skydive Adventure Club** ( ☎ 1300 135 867; www.tandemskydiving.com.au; Gloucester Aerodrome, Jack's Rd; tandem jumps from $280). Jump at 14,000 feet, pull the cord at 3000 feet, and spend the next five minutes enjoying the view.

### SLEEPING & EATING

Stock up on groceries at the local IGA on the roundabout before heading bush. But if you aren't a bush hippy and camping gives you the creeps stay at **Gloucester Country Lodge Motel** ( ☎ 6558 1812; The Bucketts Way; s/d $74/88 Sun-Thu,

---

### RACE 6 MELVILLE HILL CHARDONNAY OVER 1600 METRES

A tribute to *The Jetsons*, the stadium centre is dedicated to betting. Excited voices echo out from its interior, 'C'arn Nordic Princess...'. Veins protrude from her neck and her nostrils flare but the old chum is pipped at the post by Mr Humerus. Tickets fly through the air before littering the ground. But on the hill the sun blazes and grass weaves between your toes...not even losing a couple of bucks can dampen the spirit. If you prize the odd punt or perhaps are a lover of horses, champagne or rather short men, then you are up for a fantastic day at the Scone Races.

Head out on Liverpool St, then right on Satur Rd and right at the TAFE. See www.racingnsw.com .au for upcoming events throughout the region.

$79/95 Fri & Sat). It's the better option on the outskirts of town. Or stay at **Gloucester Holiday Park** ( ☎ 6558 1720; Denison St; unpowered/powered sites $9/20; cabins $41 65; ⊗ ) if you are towing a van.

### GETTING THERE & AWAY
**Countrylink** ( ☎ 13 22 32) trains travel south to Broadmeadow (adult/child $20/10) and Sydney (adult/child $50/25) and north to Byron Bay (adult/child $90/45).

## BARRINGTON TOPS NATIONAL PARK
On top of the world – well, the Hunter – this is NSW's outdoor adventure capital: bushwalking, mountain biking, horse riding, canoeing, fishing and 4WDing. The **Barrington Trail** is particularly popular for 4WDing but it is closed during winter, which is AOK as it often snows and can get pretty chilly.

**Barrington Outdoor Adventure Centre** ( ☎ 02-6558 2093; www.boac.com.au; 126 Thunderbolts Way; 1-/2-day tours $125/335) specialises in mountain biking adventures with limited uphill legs. But if you would rather wrestle the rapids, **Canoe Barrington** ( ☎ 02-6558 4316; www.canoebarrington

.com.au; 744 Barrington East Rd; 2hr hire $40) hires canoes and kayaks.

Camping is possible throughout the park. The most popular grounds are at **Gloucester River** ($8) but there's free camping at **Devils Hole**, **Little Murray** and **Junction Pools**, although you need a 4WD to get there. The park can be accessed from Scone, Dungog and Gloucester. For more information contact Gloucester **NPWS** ( ☎ 6538 5300).

### Camping
**Barrington Wilderness Retreat** (The Steps; ☎ 02-6558 3048; www.australianoutdooradventures.com; 535 Manchester Rd, Barrington; sites $10, dm/s/d $28/32/70) The property fronts 600m of rapids, known in kayaking and canoeing circles as 'The Steps'. But a day spent rafting here is for sooks – this is the only place in the country where you can raft by moonlight.

**Riverwood Downs** ( ☎ 1800 809 772, 02-4994 7112; www.riverwooddowns.com.au; sites $10, dm $19, cabins $90-120) The ultimate retreat, it has come a long way in the past 10 years, so if you have been before, it's time to go again.

# North Coast

As the New South Wales coast tumbles north, the distance between rugged headlands widens and the urban interludes shrink. This is where the shoreline really unfurls, baring sandy horizons, kilometres of empty beach and banks of national park. To the west, green hummocks of farmland ripple at the base of mountains and ancient rainforest.

It's no wonder the stretch from Port Stephens to Tweed Heads is one of the most celebrated road trips in Oz, but for much of the journey the well-trodden tourist path is scarcely visible. Most folk make a beeline for Byron Bay, temptress of the north with her New Age glamour and halcyon tones. But the coast holds far more than a sea-change pursuit. Young families exhaust stimulus-needy rug rats with synthetic and natural fun in Coffs Harbour and Port Macquarie. Adolescent surfers (of all ages) cut their teeth in tiny surf settlements like Crescent Head and Angourie. Pernickety weekenders exploit gourmet cuisine, and cosy mountain cabins in hinterland towns like Dorrigo, Bellingen and Bangalow. Seasoned hippies create conformity-free utopias in Nimbin and beyond. Nature-lovers happily transgress in World Heritage national parks. And travellers and locals of any ilk make the most of that gorgeous shoreline.

Best of all, the resistance to development is strong in this enlightened neck of the woods. Locals here are fiercely protective of their exquisite home, and 'eco-friendly' is a tag worn with pride.

## HIGHLIGHTS

- Tune in, tone up and take time out in **Byron Bay** (p186)
- Chart a course around the magnificent **Myall Lakes National Park** (p160)
- Hide out with the surf and sun in blissful **Seal Rocks** (p161)
- Enjoy long, boozy afternoons and glistening harbour views in **Port Macquarie** (p163)
- Work the pins and gorge on views in **Dorrigo National Park** (p173)
- Channel Satchmo at the **Bellingen Jazz & Blues Festival** (p172)
- Catch the East Coast sunrise first from the summit of **Mt Warning** (p210)
- Shop at the Far North Coast Hinterland's bustling **weekend markets** (p191)

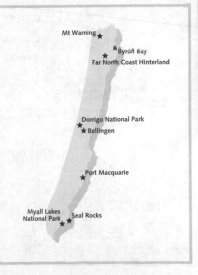

Mt Warning ★
★ Byron Bay
Far North Coast Hinterland

Dorrigo National Park ★
★ Bellingen

Port Macquarie ★

Myall Lakes National Park ★  ★ Seal Rocks

NORTH COAST

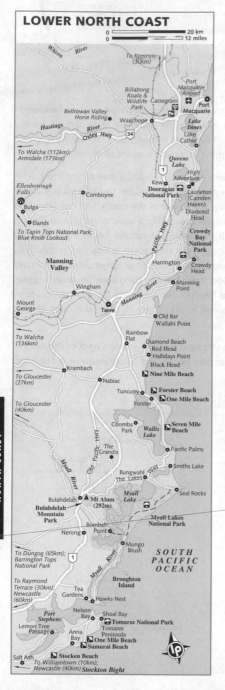

## LOWER NORTH COAST

Hovering just above Newcastle, the lower reaches of the North Coast are a meandering network of coastal towns with big sky, even bigger beaches and no attitude. It all starts with the beautifully haphazard waterways of Port Stephens, where whole neighbourhoods of urbanites relocate during school holidays. Beyond here, the quiet blue of Myall and Wallis Lakes hides tiny settlements in verdant pockets. The beach, peppered with undeveloped towns and impenetrable national park, zigzags its way north to cosmopolitan and pretty Port Macquarie.

## PORT STEPHENS

☎ 02 / pop 8040

The bay of Port Stephens incorporates a string of coastal towns and has a true family feel. Scalloping shorelines gives rise to shards of empty beach, and the scattered communities, who share a passion for the environment, do a good job of keeping things low-rise. This is an area where 'eco-accredited' certificates are sported like badges of honour. Locals and holidaying couples with youngsters in tow aren't the only fans – the bay is home to some 160 resident dolphins and the odd passing whale.

### Orientation & Information

**Nelson Bay** is the unofficial capital of Port Stephens, and home to the **visitors centre** ( ☎ 1800 808 900; www.portstephens.org.au; Victoria Pde). The area's most scenic beaches – Zenith, Wreck and Box Beach – back onto **Shoal Bay**, on the point, which is the next town along.

On the southern side of the Tomaree Peninsula is **Anna Bay**, another small town that has both surf and bay beaches. At the northern end of town, **One Mile Beach** is a gorgeous semi-circle of velvety sand and crystalline water, favoured by surfers, beachcombers and idle romantics…some of whom are nude by the time you reach **Samurai Beach**.

### Sights & Activities

Tiny Anna Bay is backed by the magnificent **Stockton Bight** – the longest moving sand dunes in the southern hemisphere, stretching 35km to Newcastle. These rolling moguls look strikingly similar to the Sahara Desert, and it's possible to lose yourself entirely in their shimmering midst.

The restored 1872 **Inner Lighthouse** at Nelson Head's Little Beach has displays on the area's history and suitably evocative views.

To get closer to those views mount a trusty steed for a beach ride with **Sahara Trails** ( ☎ 4981 9077; Port Stephens Dr; 2hr ride $90).

Local diving outfits include:

**Dive One Nelson Bay** ( ☎ 4984 2092; www.diveone .com.au) PADI courses $470.

**Pro Dive Nelson Bay** ( ☎ 4981 4331; D'Albora Marina) PADI courses $450.

## Tours

**Imagine Cruises** ( ☎ 4984 9000; www.imaginecruises .com.au; 123 Stockton St; 2hr cruise per adult/child $22/14) Eco-certified dolphin- and whale-watching tours.

**Moonshadow Cruises** ( ☎ 4984 9388; www.moon shadow.com.au; adult/child $60/20) Twilight dinner cruises.

**Sand Safaris** ( ☎ 4965 0215; www.sandsafaris.com .au; 173 Nelson Bay Rd, Williamtown; tours from $110) Eco-sensitive quad-bike fornys out on the dunes.

**Tamboi Queen Cruises** ( ☎ 4981 1959; 1½hr cruises per adult/child $17/9) Dolphin-watching cruises.

## Sleeping

**Winning Property** ( ☎ 4984 0100; www.kdwinning.com.au; 19 Stockton St) has prolific holiday rental listings.

**Melaleuca Surfside Backpackers** ( ☎ 4981 9422; www.melaleucabackpackers.com.au; 2 Koala Pl, One Mile Beach; camping per person $15, dm/d $25/85) It's all mates and smiles at this excellent backpacker retreat spread across a large green property. Camping is 'free range' on a grassy oval and cabins are made of glorious rust-red timber. It's wheelchair-friendly and the koalas dig it too.

**Leilani Haciendas** ( ☎ 4981 3304; leilani@hunterlink .net.au; Gowrie Ave, Nelson Bay; apt $110-180; 🐾 🔁 ) This cute block of units has more colour than a Wiggles convention. The one- and two-bedroom apartments, with sun-filled interiors and sliding doors onto the back patio, are ideal for families.

**O'Carrollyns Holiday Village** ( ☎ 4982 2801; www .ocarrollyns.com.au; 36 Eucalyptus Dr, One Mile Beach; d from $160; 🐾 🔁 ) A dishy eco-resort, O'Carrollyns scatters its eight cabins throughout a mini forest, complete with ponds, birdlife, grunting koalas and frogs. Digs have mezzanine bedrooms and five-star energy ratings (meaning minimal energy to heat and cool) and are wheelchair-friendly.

**Shoal Bay Resort & Spa** ( ☎ 1800 181 810, 4981 1555; www.shoalbayresort.com; Bearlhront, Shoal Bay; apt $180-240; 🐾 🔁 ) Praise be to the gods of pam-

pering, they surely had a hand in this classy number. A range of rooms treat fussy tushes and if you really want to impress the missus, opt for a Heritage Suite with ocean views and décor to die for.

Also recommended:

**Colonial Ridge Resort** ( ☎ 4982 0600; www.colonial ridge.com.au; 4 Fleet St, Salamanda Bay; r from $170; 🐾 🔁 ) Kitsch and comfy cabins.

**Halfax Holiday Park** ( ☎ 4981 1522; Beach Rd, Nelson Bay; powered sites from $32, cabins $90-160; 🐾 ) Excellent cabins and facilities.

## Eating

**RedNeds Gourmet Pie Bar** ( ☎ 4981 1355; Shop 3/17-19 Stockton St, Nelsons Bay; pies $5; 🍴 breakfast & lunch) The honey-chilli chicken, kangaroo teriyaki or two fat ladies seafood pies here will knock your socks off. There are more than 70 versions on the menu (and no ladies of any size are harmed in the making).

**E10 On The Marina** ( ☎ 4984 9700; Shop E10, D'Albora Marina; mains $16.25; 🍴 breakfast, lunch & dinner) This sunny, waterfront restaurant perfects casual dining with treats like Cajun-dusted calamari salad, mega burgers and fresh fish and chips. The sultry breeze off the water goes nicely with a crisp chardy.

**Catch** ( ☎ 4981 1555; Shoal Bay Resort & Spa; mains $28; 🍴 dinner) The ocean's elite find their way to dinner plates at this classy restaurant, and they arrive dressed for the occasion. Tempura nori of Atlantic salmon with blue swimmer crab and ginger mousse…you get the idea. Bring your manners and your appetite.

**Zest** ( ☎ 4984 2211, 16 Stockton St, Nelson Bay; 2/3 courses $55/65; 🍴 lunch Mon-Sat, dinner Wed-Sat) Port Stephens' finest restaurant dazzles even the harshest gastronomes with prosciutto-wrapped rabbit with tapenade filling or seared baby squid on strawberry and basil risotto. Dining is on an intimate deck with five-star service.

Also recommended:

**AquaBlue Bistro & Bar** ( ☎ 4984 9999; D'Albora Marina; mains $20; 🍴 breakfast, lunch & dinner) Cosmopolitan histro at the waterfront.

**bite me now** ( ☎ 0411 747 249; cnr Donald & Stockton Sts; meals $10; 🍴 breakfast & lunch) Healthy eats-on-the-run with attitude.

## Getting There & Around

Port Stephens is an area, not a town, so when driving follow the signs for Nelson Bay.

**Port Stephens Coaches** ( ☎ 4982 2940; www.ps coaches.com.au) runs daily from all towns of Port

Stephens to Sydney ($32) and services the coast to Newcastle.

**Port Stephens Ferry Service** ( ☎ 0412 682 117, 0419 417 689) departs Nelson Bay for Tea Gardens at 10am, noon and 3.30pm, returning at 10am, 2.30pm and 5pm (additional services over Christmas). The trip takes around an hour (return fare per adult/child $20/10).

**Shoal Bay Bike Hire** ( ☎ 4981 9444; Cnr Shoal Bay & Government Rds, Shoal Bay) rents bikes to explore the good network of paths.

## TEA GARDENS & HAWKS NEST
☎ 02

Tea Gardens is a small settlement with soft suburban alcoves and an abundance of stoic pelicans, which seem to revel in their capacity to sleep one-legged on a post. Across the bridge, Hawks Nest has impressive views out to Cabbage Tree Island and a smattering of modern accommodation.

The **visitors centre** ( ☎ 4997 0111; Myall Rd, Tea Gardens) is run by helpful volunteers. **CTC @ Tea Gardens** ( ☎ 4997 0749; Shop 4 Myall Plaza, Tea Gardens; per hr $10) has internet access.

### Activities
**Hawks Nest Dive Centre** ( ☎ 4997 0422; www.hawks nestdive.com.au) Snorkelling and diving.

**Naturally Amazing** ( ☎ 0409 993 470; half-day tours per person from $49) Small-group 4WD tours to Barrington Tops, Stockton Bight and more.

### Sleeping & Eating
**Tea Gardens Club Inn** ( ☎ 1800 635 790, 4997 0911; www .bestwestern.com.au/teagardens; Yalinbah St, Tea Gardens; r from $90; ✱ ) Behind the Bowls Club, this sturdy motel has good-sized rooms with creature comforts and spas. Some rooms have sliding doors right onto the bowling green – you can watch the greenkeepers battle with the birds in the morning.

**Ocean Side** ( ☎ 4997 0941; www.oceansidehawksnest .com.au; Cnr Booner & Bennet Sts, Hawks Nest; apt $140-180; ✱ ✎ ) Flashy and revamped, this place offers very comfortable apartments, some with spas, some with hot tubs (we'll let you spot the difference). All rooms have spiffy insides and the facilities are excellent.

**Aqua** ( ☎ 4997 0966; Cnr Booner & Tuloa Sts, Hawks Nest; mains $15-25; ☽ breakfast, lunch & dinner) This eatery touts itself as a cosmopolitan café, and boy does it bring home the bacon. Menu creations include artichoke and hokkien noodle stir-fry or pesto-stuffed, free-range chicken roulade.

**Pie Man** ( ☎ 4997 1733; Shop 3, 17-19 Stockton St; pies $4; ☽ breakfast, lunch & dinner Mon Fri) Taking the humble pie to a fine art, this bakery offers variations like spaghetti bolognaise, curry beef and spicy chicken. As for the sausage rolls…Lord help us.

Also recommended:

**Hawk's Nest Beach Caravan Park** ( ☎ 1800 072 244; www.hawksnestcaravan.com.au; Booner St, Hawks Nest; camp sites/cabins $31/77) Near a good surf beach.

**Mumm's** ( ☎ 4887 1162; 46 Marine Dr, Tea Gardens; mains $17; ☽ breakfast, lunch & dinner) Outstanding seafood.

## MYALL LAKES NATIONAL PARK & AROUND
☎ 02 / pop 1160

These stunning lakes form the largest natural freshwater system in NSW. Pooling in deep blue basins, they weave around clumps of forest and small settlements. The **Lakes Way** ribbons its way through the scenery and is a magnificent drive.

Canoes, sailboards and runabouts are available at **Bombah Point**. Here you'll also find **Bombah Point Eco Cottages** ( ☎ 02-4997 4401; www .bombahpoint.com; 969 Bombah Point Rd; d per 2 nights $440), which makes an environmentally friendly and romantic getaway.

Alternatively, **Eco Point Myall Shores Resort** ( ☎ 1300 769 566; www.myallshores.com.au; Myall Lakes National Park, Bombah Point; camp sites $26, cabins $95-260; ✱ ) has a huge range of cabins and villas.

There is a track from Bombah Point to Seal Rocks, but it's testing, even with a 4WD, and the park rangers are rather unsympathetic to over-ambitious drivers.

The **Bulahdelah visitors centre** ( ☎ 1800 802 692, 4997 4981; cnr Pacific Hwy & Crawford St) is just opposite the road to Myall Lake. Looming over the town is **Mt Alum**, the largest aboveground deposit of alum (a salt used in dyeing, medicine and manufacturing) in the world. The mining has ceased and the mountain is now the **Bulahdelah Mountain Park**, with some walking tracks to historic sites. The entrance is a couple of blocks back from the highway, on the same street as the police station.

The tallest tree in NSW, the 400-year-old **Grandis**, towers over dense rainforest not far from Bulahdelah and is an awesome sight. To reach it, take the signposted turn-off 12km from Bulahdelah.

The **National Parks & Wildlife Service** office (NPWS; ☎ 6591 0300; www.nationalparks.nsw.gov.au; The

Ruins Camping Ground, Booti Booti National Park, The Lakes Way, Pacific Palms) has information on the many local national parks, including **Booti Booti National Park** (admission per vehicle per day $7). The view from Cape Hawke here is a 360-degree panorama of the confluence of lakes, ocean, forest and teeny towns. On sunny days the horizon is lost and the water is so crystalline you'll want to sprout wings and jump in.

## SEAL ROCKS

This idyllic cove embodies the Australian ideal of utopia – few people, magical views, great surf and little to do but swim and sit. Surrounded by national parks and boasting the odd whale, it's the perfect spot for urban fugitives. The **historic lighthouse** is well worth the walk to witness the rocks that have claimed many ships over the past 150 years.

The **Seal Rocks Camping Reserve** ( ☎ 1800 112 234, 4997 6164; www.sealrockscampingreserve.com.au; camp sites/cabins from $25/70) has tidy cabins, a manicured-to-bowling-green-perfection lawn and a blissful location right on the beach.

Turn right at the general store for the intimate **Treachery Camp** ( ☎ 02-4997 6138; www.treacherycamp.com.au; 166 Thomas Rd; camp sites/cabins from $12/77), with lovely timber cabins and secluded camping.

## FORSTER-TUNCURRY

☎ 02 / pop 18,000

Forster and Tuncurry are twin towns separated by the sea entrance to **Wallis Lake**. This is a great spot for water babies to wade a while, with a string of spectacular beaches providing unhurried and unpretentious coastline. In winter you can slip into the ether here without fear of tourist tack or prices, but summer sees the lakes come alive with water sports, screaming kiddies and sunburnt adults.

### Orientation & Information

Forster (*fos*-ter), on the southern side of the entrance, is the big brother of the pair. The Lakes Way leads into town from the south, first becoming MacIntosh St then turning sharply left into Head St, which runs east to a large roundabout that marks the town centre.

The helpful **visitors centre** ( ☎ 6554 8799; Little St, Forster) is just beside the lake. There's internet access at **Leading Edge Computers** ( ☎ 6555 2065; Shop 3, cnr Head & Beach Sts; per hr $6).

## Sights & Activities

**Tobwabba Art** ( ☎ 6554 5755; www.tobwabba.com.au; 10 Breckenridge St, Forster; admission free; ☼ 10am-4.30pm Mon-Fri) is owned by the Worimi people of the Great Lakes region. The centre exhibits their paintings and artefacts.

For local history and a look at a classroom of yesteryear, visit the **Great Lakes Historical Museum** ( ☎ 6554 3012; Capel St, Tuncurry; adult/child $2/50c; ☼ 10am-2pm Wed, 1-4pm Sun).

Beaches are of the highest quality in this area, with **Nine Mile Beach** the pick of the surf spots, **Forster Beach** a good family option with its swimming **pools**, and **One Mile Beach** also popular.

Kids love a good adventure park, and Forster-Tuncurry has two: the **Big Buzz Fun Park** ( ☎ 6553 6000; The Lakes Way; adult/child $25/15; ☼ 10am-4pm Sat & Sun) is big on water slides, while **Ton O Fun** ( ☎ 6554 3090; Ton O Fun Rd, adult/child $33/21; ☼ 10am-4pm Sat & Sun) has quad bikes and water slides.

More activities include:

**Amaroo Cruises** ( ☎ 0419 333 445; www.amaroocruise .com.au; 2hr cruise $40) Shark and sea-turtle spotting.

**Boomerang Rainforest Tours** ( ☎ 6554 0757; tours per person $80-95) Excellent small-group 4WD tours.

**Dive Forster** ( ☎ 6554 7478; www.diveforster.com.au; Fisherman's Wharf; per adult/child $60/30) Cruises and dolphin swims.

## Sleeping & Eating

**Forster Dolphin Lodge YHA** ( ☎ 6555 8155; www.yha .com.au; 43 Head St, Forster; dm/d $25/65) Catering to backpackers (well, the handful who come), families and the lone traveller, this hostel has snug common areas and friendly staff. Some rooms have en suites.

**Barkley Inn** ( ☎ 6555 2552; www.barkleyinn.com; 38 Head St, Forster; s/d $85/90; ☷ ☻ ) A comfy option, the Barkley has neat and petite rooms with plenty of sunlight and furniture from the recent past. Most rooms have tree-lined windows and it's a stroll to town.

**Lakeside Escape Bed & Breakfast** ( ☎ 6557 6400; www.lakesideescape.com.au; 85 Green Point Dr; s/d incl breakfast $135/165) It's well worth getting out of town, with its motel mania, to spend a few nights in this pleasant B&B in the small Green Point fishing village. Rooms have spas and gorgeous lake views.

**Forster Beach Caravan Park** ( ☎ 1800 240 632, 6554 6269; www.escapenorth.com.au/forstercaravanpark.htm; Reserve Rd, Forster; camp sites/cabins from $22/55) This sprawling park manages to maintain spick-and-span order. It's backed by the mighty breakwall and has decent villas and cabins.

**Wharf Bar & Grill** ( ☎ 6555 7200; 1/32 Wharf St, Forster; mains $26; ☾ lunch & dinner) Grills like salt-and-pepper tempura whiting or prosciutto-wrapped chicken breast stuffed with macadamias keep this restaurant in fine form, as do the second-storey water views.

More eats:

**Casa del Mundo** ( ☎ 6554 5906; 12 Wharf St; mains $15-30; ☾ lunch & dinner) Nooky Spanish joint dishing up tapas and sangria.

**Forster Beach Kiosk** (Beach St; snacks $5; ☾ breakfast & lunch) Beachside burgers, rolls and sandwiches.

### Getting There & Away

**Busways** ( ☎ 1300 555 611) runs down to Bulahdelah ($30). **CountryLink** ( ☎ 13 22 32), **Greyhound** ( ☎ 13 14 99) and **Premier Motor Service** ( ☎ 13 34 10) all stop in Forster-Tuncurry.

## THE MANNING VALLEY

This valley extends west from the Manning River delta (between Old Bar and Harrington) through farmland to Taree and Wingham, then north through forests to the plateau containing Bulga and Comboyne. There are better coastal options to the north and south, but the rainforests and national parks are rewarding to investigate.

### Taree

☎ 02

Although it's the largest town in the Manning Valley, Taree offers little to the visitor and with the **Big Oyster**, its coveted landmark, retired to car-sales duties, the town should be used as little more than a reference point.

The **visitors centre** ( ☎ 1800 182 733, 6592 5444; 21 Manning River Dr) is on the north side of town.

Motels are out in force along the Old Pacific Hwy and you're sure to pick up a cheap deal during the week.

### Wingham

☎ 02 / pop 4670

This is the oldest town in the area and its English influence is reflected in a large, central green square that now features the **Log** (a 16m, 19-tonne log representing the town's timber-felling origins) and a replica **Vampire fighter jet** commemorating the 50th anniversary of the RAAF.

Down by the riverside lies **Wingham Brush**, a subtropical floodplain rainforest where

you can take to the boardwalk and see flying foxes.

If you need to hang the boots here, the **Wingham Motel** ( ☎ 6553 4295, fax 6553 4878; 13 Bent St; s/d $80/90; ☒ ☲ ) has decent little rooms right near the guts of town.

**Bent on Food** ( ☎ 6557 0727; www.bentonfood.com; 22 Bent St; mains $12; ☾ breakfast & lunch) is quite the hip café, serving meals like smoked pork loin stuffed with mango. You can also pick up cheeses, relishes and coffee to go.

## THE COASTAL WAY

This meandering route has sweet, sleepy towns and good surf beaches. The first section consists of **Black Head**, **Red Head** and **Diamond Beach**.

The next offering comes at **Old Bar**, which has a long surf beach. Just south is **Walabi Point**, where there's a lagoon for swimming. **Manning Point**, a hamlet serving the oyster farms along the river, is 12km up the coast.

Just across the river – but a hefty drive because there is no bridge shortcut – is **Harrington**, a lovely sneeze of a town with another lagoon and respectable surf beaches nearby. The **Harrington Hotel** ( ☎ 02-6656 1205; 28 Beach St; mains $15; ☾ lunch & dinner) is a beauty. The expansive bistro has glorious water views and upstairs there are wonderfully creaky old pub rooms ($45).

**Crowdy Head** is the prettiest of these towns, with sweeping views from the 1878 lighthouse out to sea and overlooking the Crowdy Head National Park.

You can take the unsealed but well maintained road to **Diamond Head** through the **rainforest** and, if you desire, pitch a tent at one of the camp sites ($6), but bring your own water.

Wedged between Dooragan National Park and the ocean is **Camden Haven**, which constitutes Laurieton, North Haven and Dunbogan villages. These quaint towns cluster around the wide sea entrance of **Queens Lake**.

Laurieton Lookout, inside **Dooragan National Park**, is 5km up a winding wooded road. The views from the top are jaw-dropping. Right in front is a bird's-eye view of Camden Haven, and a walking track descends down the mountain for 2km.

Your final march up the coastline will take you past the biggest town, **Lake Cathie** (cat-eye), on a lake with safe beaches ideal for youngsters. The road then enters the sprawling outer suburbs of Port Macquarie.

## PORT MACQUARIF
☎ 02 / pop 41,141

Port, as it's affectionately known, reclines over a spectacular headland at the entrance to the subtropical coast. Renowned for a handsome and undulating shoreline, it has a placid ambience that belies its population. Although this is the largest town between Newcastle and Brisbane, you'd never guess it – the urban tentacles here are well hidden behind the pretty harbour. The palm-lined centre has a touch of the cosmopolitan about it, enhanced significantly by a bevy of good restaurants and swank places to stay.

## Orientation
The city centre corners on the mouth of Hastings River. A string of magnificent beaches rolls south and a spread of suburbs follows.

## Information
**NPWS office** ( ☎ 6586 8300; 152 Horton St)
**Port Surf Hub** ( ☎ 6584 4744; 57 Clarence St; per hr $7; ☾ 9am-7pm) Internet access.
**Visitors centre** ( ☎ 1300 303 155; www.portmacquarie info.com.au; cnr Gordon & Gore Sts) Excellent info on the greater Port Macquarie area.

## Sights
### HISTORIC BUILDINGS & MUSEUMS
Convict labour has produced some striking architecture throughout the town. The 1824 **St Thomas' Church**, which sits on a hump of a hill, and the 1869 **old courthouse** ( ☎ 6584 1818; cnr Clarence & Hay Sts; adult/child $2/50c; ☾ 10am-3.30pm Mon-Fri) down in town are time warriors. The 1835 **Garrison shopping precinct** (cnr Clarence & Hay Sts) has been renovated – some say spoiled – and now houses 21st-century shops and cafés.

The 1836 **Port Macquarie Historical Society Museum** ( ☎ 6583 1108; 22 Clarence St; adult/child $5/4; ☾ 9.30am-4.30pm Mon-Sat) has a rich stock of 19th-century household items and excellent exhibits of local characters. There are also one-tonne Victorian-era frocks and frightening dentistry tools. Up on the point, the old pilot's cottage (1882) houses the **Maritime Museum** ( ☎ 6583 1866; 6 William St; adult/child $4/2; 10am-4pm Mon-Sat) with wreck relics, photographs of early navigators and a room devoted to Matthew Flinders' cat Trim.

The **Alma Doepel** ( ☎ 6581 8000; Lady Nelson Wharf; adult/child $3/1; ☾ 9am-4pm) is a resplendent three-masted trading vessel built in 1903, now

spending its retirement as Port Macquarie's centrepiece.

### OTHER SIGHTS
For those looking for answers beyond the horizon of the Pacific Ocean, sneak a peek through the telescope at the **observatory** ( ☎ 6583 1933; Rotary Park, William St; adult/child $5/4; ☾ 7.15-9.30pm Wed & Sun, 8.15-10pm during daylight savings).

**Timbertown** ( ☎ 6586 1940; www.timbertown.com.au; Oxley Hwy, Wauchope; entry by donation; 9.30am-3.30pm) is a heritage theme park suited to families, with old dust-swept streets, intimate shops and the old (working) steam train. Admission is free but you pay for rides.

### WINERIES
Several wineries are scattered around the Port Macquarie area. Its reputation as the region's pioneering vineyard has made **Cassegrain** ( ☎ 6582 8377; www.cassegrainwines.com.au; 764 Fernbank Creek Rd; ☾ 9am-5pm), 15km out of town, a favourite. **Ça Marche Restaurant** ( ☎ 6582 8320; mains $30; ☾ lunch & dinner) here has won awards and is worth the trip.

More wineries to visit include:
**Bago Vineyards** ( ☎ 6585 7099; www.bagovineyards .com.au; Bago Rd, Wauchope; ☾ 9am-5pm)
**Douglas Vale Historic Vineyard** ( ☎ 6584 3792; www.douglasvalevineyard.com.au; Oxley Hwy, Port Macquarie; ☾ 9am-1pm Wed-Sat)
**Inneslake Vineyards** ( ☎ 6581 1332; The Ruins Way, Port Macquarie; ☾ 10am-5pm)

### WILDLIFE & NATURE RESERVES
Port Macquarie shares its beautiful gum trees with one of Australia's icons, the koala. Unfortunately, people's housing needs have seen these little fellas' land rights diminish and, with that, their own homes. While searching for their lost oasis, many end up at the **Koala Hospital** ( ☎ 6584 1522; www.koalahospital.org.au; Roto House, Lord St; admission by donation; ☾ feeding time 8am & 3pm), which you can visit to cheer the little battlers up (no flash photography).

If hand-feeding fighting-fit koalas, kangaroos and the odd emu appeals, **Billabong Koala & Wildlife Park** ( ☎ 6585 1060; 61 Billabong Dr; adult/child $12/8; ☾ 9am-5pm) is a wonderful family experience. Patting times are 10.30am, 1.30pm and 3.30pm.

The **Kooloonbung Creek Nature Reserve** (cnr Gordon & Horton Sts; admission free) encompasses 50 hectares of bush and is great for bird-watching. There are trails, a lake, boardwalks and a cemetery.

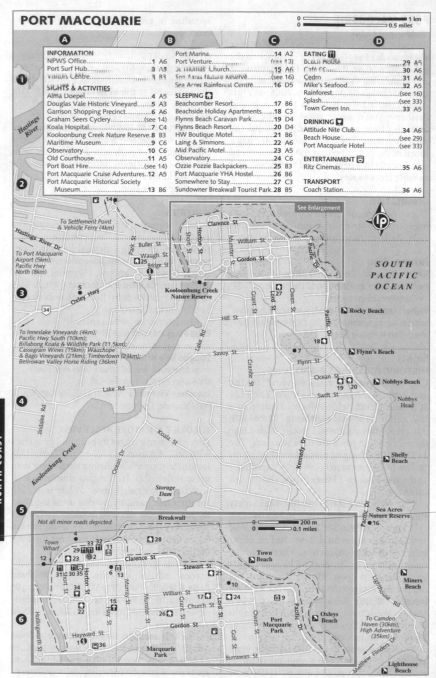

# PORT MACQUARIE

0 _____ 1 km
0 _____ 0.5 miles

**INFORMATION**
NPWS Office.................................1 A6
Port Surf Hub...............................2 A5
Visitors Centre.............................3 B3

**SIGHTS & ACTIVITIES**
Alma Doepel................................4 A5
Douglas Vale Historic Vineyard.......5 A3
Garrison Shopping Precinct............6 A6
Graham Seers Cyclery............(see 14)
Koala Hospital..............................7 C4
Kooloonbung Creek Nature Reserve.8 B3
Maritime Museum.........................9 C6
Observatory................................10 C6
Old Courthouse...........................11 A5
Port Boat Hire......................(see 14)
Port Macquarie Cruise Adventures.12 A5
Port Macquarie Historical Society
   Museum..................................13 B6

Port Marina.................................14 A2
Port Venture.........................(see 12)
St Thomas Church.......................15 A6
Sea Acres Nature Reserve........(see 16)
Sea Acres Rainforest Centre........16 D5

**SLEEPING**
Beachcomber Resort....................17 B6
Beachside Holiday Apartments......18 C3
Flynns Beach Caravan Park...........19 D4
Flynns Beach Resort.....................20 D4
HW Boutique Motel.....................21 B6
Laing & Simmons........................22 A6
Mid Pacific Motel........................23 A5
Observatory................................24 C6
Ozzie Pozzie Backpackers.............25 B3
Port Macquarie YHA Hostel.........26 B6
Somewhere to Stay......................27 C3
Sundowner Breakwall Tourist Park.28 B5

**EATING**
Beach House...............................29 A5
Café 66......................................30 A6
Cedro........................................31 A6
Mike's Seafood...........................32 A5
Rainforest............................(see 16)
Splash.................................(see 33)
Town Green Inn..........................33 A5

**DRINKING**
Attitude Nite Club.......................34 A6
Beach House........................(see 29)
Port Macquarie Hotel..............(see 33)

**ENTERTAINMENT**
Ritz Cinemas..............................35 A6

**TRANSPORT**
Coach Station.............................36 A6

See Enlargement

To Settlement Point
& Vehicle Ferry (4km)

Hastings River

Hastings River Dr

To Port Macquarie
Airport (5km);
Pacific Hwy
North (8km)

Park St
Buller St
Waugh St
Bridge St

Horton St
Short St
Clarence St
Munster St
William St
Gordon St

Pacific Dr

SOUTH
PACIFIC
OCEAN

Oxley Hwy

To Ineslake Vineyards (4km);
Pacific Hwy South (10km);
Billabong Koala & Wildlife Park (11.5km);
Cassegrain Wines (15km); Wauchope
& Bago Vineyards (21km); Timbertown (23km);
Bellrowan Valley Horse Riding (36km)

Kooloonbung Creek
Nature Reserve

Hill St

Savoy St

Grant St
Lord St
Owen St

Rocky Beach

Flynn's Beach

18

7

Flynn St

Ocean St
19 20

Nobbys Beach

Nobbys
Head

Lake Rd

Grante St

Swift St

Koala St

Ocean Dr

Kennedy Dr

Shelly
Beach

Kooloonbung Creek

Jindalee Rd

Storage
Dam

Sea Acres
Nature Reserve
16

Pacific Dr

**Enlargement:**

Not all minor roads depicted

Breakwall

0 _____ 200 m
0 _____ 0.1 miles

Town Wharf

28

33 32
29  11
23  @ 2
31 30 35
34
15
22

Short St
Horton St
Murray St
Munster St
Hay St

Clarence St

6
13

26

William St
Grant St
Church St
Gordon St

Stewart St

21

10

17  24

9

Lord St

Town
Beach

Miners
Beach

Port
Macquarie
Park

Oxleys
Beach

Golf St

Lighthouse Rd

To Camden
Haven (30km);
High Adventure
(35km)

Hollingworth St

Hayward St

1  36

Macquarie
Park

Burrawan St

Matthew Flinders Dr

Lighthouse
Beach

NORTH COAST

**Sea Acres Rainforest Centre** ( ☎ 6582 3355; Pacific Dr; adult/child $10/6; 🕥 9am-4.30pm) protects 72 hectares of coastal rainforest alive with birds, goannas, brush turkeys and, unfortunately, mosquitoes. There's a wheelchair-accessible boardwalk and excellent guided tours.

## Activities

A walking track curls around the headland and offers splendid views with your morning exercise. You can get offshore with **Port Boat Hire** ( ☎ 6583 8514; Port Marina), which rents vessels from $25 per hour for two people.

**High Adventure** ( ☎ 0429 844 961; www.highadventure.com.au; 10 Rosewood Crt, Laurieton; tandem flight from $110) delivers adrenaline and dramatic landscapes courtesy of hang-gliding.

Readers rave about **Bellrowan Valley Horse Riding** ( ☎ 6587 5227; www.bellrowanvalley.com.au; Crows Rd, Bellrowan Valley; 2hr per person $75), which organises guided horse-riding trails in the hinterland, about 30 minutes drive from Port Macquarie.

**Edge Experience** ( ☎ 0427 324 009; www.edgeexperience.com.au; full-day tours from $85) offers adventure combo-tours that mix mountain biking and abseiling, as well as vineyard and jazz tours.

More active pursuits:
**Graham Seers Cyclery** ( ☎ 6583 2333; Port Marina; half-/full-day hire $25/40) Bike hire.
**Port Macquarie Surf School** ( ☎ 6585 5453; www.portmacquariesurfschool.com.au; 2hr lessons per person from $40)
**Scuba Haven** ( ☎ 6559 5530; www.scubahaven.com.au; PADI courses $400)

## Tours

**Australian Wilderness Tours** ( ☎ 6587 7144; adult/child $99/59) Small-group 4WD wilderness tours.
**Port Macquarie Cruise Adventures** ( ☎ 6583 8483; 1300 555 890; www.cruiseadventures.com.au; Town Wharf; 3½hr per person from $35) Dolphin- and whale-watching tours.
**Port Venture** ( ☎ 1300 795 577, 6583 3058; Town Wharf; 2hr cruise per person $25) River cruises.

## Sleeping

For holiday apartment rentals, get in touch with **Laing & Simmons** ( ☎ 6583 7733; www.portrealestate.net; cnr William & Horton Sts).

### BUDGET

**Ozzie Pozzie Backpackers** ( ☎ 1800 620 020, 6583 8133; www.ozziepozzie.com; 36 Waugh St; dm $25, d without/with bathroom $55/65; P ) This small, charming and

colourful hostel is just the ticket to make you feel like one of the crew. Dorms with wide, steel-tubed bunks arrange themselves around a wee courtyard, with spotless bathrooms and kitchen and a cosy TV room.

**Port Macquarie YHA Hostel** ( ☎ 1800 880 008, 6583 5512; www.yha.com.au; 40 Church St; dm/d $23/55; P ) Homier than nanna's spare room, this sunflower-yellow weatherboard has neat four- to six-bed dorms, a sociable lounge and an open kitchen. It's family-friendly and the owners are unfailingly caring.

**Flynns Beach Caravan Park** ( ☎ 6583 5754; www.flynnsbeachcaravan.com.au; 22 Ocean St; camp sites/cabins from $30/90; P ) Get back to the bush in this well-treed pocket of a park. Dappled sunlight filters through the eucalypt canopy, settling on tidy cabins, grassy camp sites and good amenities.

More options:
**Somewhere to Stay** ( ☎ 6583 5850; wizbangent@hotmail.com.au; Cnr Lord & Burrawan Sts; r $90; P ) Cheerful and cheap.
**Sundowner Breakwall Tourist Park** ( ☎ 1800 636 452, 6583 2755; www.sundownerholidays.com; 1 Munster St; camp sites $25-47, cabins $75-290; P ) Fabulous facilities.

### MIDRANGE

Basic motels pepper Port's outskirts.
**Mid Pacific Motel** ( ☎ 1800 024 894, 6583 2166; midport@bigpond.com.au; cnr Clarence & Short Sts; r $110; P ) An oldie but a goodie, this medium-rise motel sits right on the grassy esplanade and has vibrant little rooms with kitchenettes and lovely views. The staff are super friendly.

**HW Boutique Motel** ( ☎ 6583 1200; www.hwport.com.au; 1 Stewart St; apt $125-165; P ) A handsome full-service hotel, HW has renovated a dowdy shell and turned its units into chic and spacious rooms with gorgeous views. Rooms have wi-fi and broadband and some have glossy spas.

**Beachcomber Resort** ( ☎ 6584 1881; www.beachcomberresort.com.au; 54 William St; r $135-175; P ) This low-rise condo-block has spiffy apartments with kitchenettes and bright, open living spaces. Some of the units have water views and the complex has a pool and barbecue courtyard AND two old-school video arcade games – ace!

**Beachside Holiday Apartments** ( ☎ 6583 9544; www.beachsideholidays.com; 48 Pacific Dr; apt $140-190; P ) Right across the road from Flynn's Beach, these apartments are spacious, have balconies and face either the ocean or the pool. There's also a lovely rooftop barbecue for sundowners and snags.

**Observatory** ( ☎ 1300 888 305; 6586 8000; www.observatory.net.au; 40 William St; apt from $166 210, ꔰ ꔰ ꔰ ) Oh so schmick, these as-new apartments are like showroom models. Soft colourings, suede couches and glass doors that open onto balconies with huge ocean vistas make them extremely comfortable. The same-sameness of them is a tad clinical, though.

### TOP END

**Flynns Beach Resort** ( ☎ 1800 833 338; www.flynns beachresort.com.au; cnr Pacific Dr & Ocean St; apt $180-275; ꔰ ꔰ ꔰ ) Holiday Inn meets boutique style in these two-bedroom apartments. Some have pool-and-tennis-court views, some have water views, all have sleek kitchens, cheerful décor and oodles of room. The complex is also extremely secure.

### Eating

**Mike's Seafood** ( ☎ 6583 7721 Shop 4/13 Hay St; mains $11; ꔰ lunch & dinner) We love the slogan – 'It's all good!' And it is. Mike's is a great little takeaway specialising in paper parcels of fishy goodness. Tuesday is 'buy one get another for a buck' night.

**Cedro** ( ☎ 6583 5529; 70 Clarence St; mains $10-15; ꔰ breakfast & lunch) Punters sun themselves on the patio here while the kitchen whips up Moroccan lamb or roast pumpkin, haloumi and pesto burgers. This spot begs for beautifully languid weekend brekkies.

**Beach House** ( ☎ 6584 5692; Horton St; mains $18; ꔰ breakfast, lunch & dinner) Take in the water views from the sea of seats outside and launch into a lunch of salmon and Caesar salad, Malaysian curry or an overflowing fisherman's basket. Stick around for beer and a burger, oysters and wine or a gourmet pizza for dinner.

**Town Green Inn** ( ☎ 6583 1011; cnr Clarence & Horton Sts; mains $15-20; ꔰ lunch & dinner) The bistro in the old Port Macquarie Hotel is a stylish and bright space serving scrummy fajitas, tuna steaks and korma prawn pizzas. Or you could even grill your own steak.

**Splash** ( ☎ 6584 4027; 3/2 Horton St; meals $25-30; ꔰ lunch & dinner) Is there such a thing as five-star Mod Oz? Yes there is! It tastes like seaweed and dashi crusted yellowfin tuna with spiced vegetables and snow-pea leaf salad, and it's served at this intimate and uncomplicated restaurant.

Also recommended:

**Cafe 66** ( ☎ 6583 2484; 66 Clarence St; mains $10-20; ꔰ breakfast & lunch) Massive Italian menu; family-friendly

**Rainforest** ( ☎ 6582 1444, 3ed Acres Rainforest Centre; mains $15; ꔰ breakfast & lunch) Beautiful leafy setting and fine cafe fare.

### Drinking & Entertainment

**Beach House** (see Eating), hogging an enviable position right on the grassy esplanade, is a beautiful pub perfect for a beer in the sun in the late afternoon. As the wee morning hours draw near folk head inside and mingle on the low-slung black leather couches.

**Port Macquarie Hotel** ( ☎ 6583 1011; cnr Horton & Clarence Sts) The old man of Port's pubs, this place simmers with afternoon drinkers and picks up for live bands on weekends and trivia on Sunday.

**Attitude Nite Club** ( ☎ 6583 5466; Galleria Bldg, William St; admission $5) Even a dress code doesn't prevent this club from ending up loud, beery and sticky in the early morning. Perfect for a younger crowd.

**Ritz Cinemas** ( ☎ 6583 8400; cnr Clarence & Horton Sts) It's all mainstream releases, but there are cheap tickets on Wednesday, Friday and Sunday.

### Getting There & Around

**QantasLink** ( ☎ 13 13 13) flies to Sydney.

**Greyhound** ( ☎ 13 14 99) and **Premier Motor Service** ( ☎ 13 22 32) both run to Sydney ($66) and Coffs Harbour ($44). **Keans** ( ☎ 6543 1322) runs three times a week to Tamworth. The coach station is on the corner of Horton and Gordon Sts.

The **Settlement Point ferry** ($3 per car, passengers free) operates 24 hours. A 10-minute trip on a flat punt gives you access to the north beach and Pilots Beach.

# MID-NORTH COAST

As the coast climbs further north, the pace of life becomes increasingly languid. Quiet towns in varying stages of sun-blissed slumber dodge in and out of national parks and station themselves above astonishing views. Inland, the woodsy towns of Dorrigo and Bellingen cultivate gourmet cuisine, thespian legacies and acclaimed festivals. In the background lie the humbling World Heritage rainforests of Dorrigo National Park. Turning all of this on its head is brash Coffs Harbour, with an abundance of cheap, raw-adventure activities.

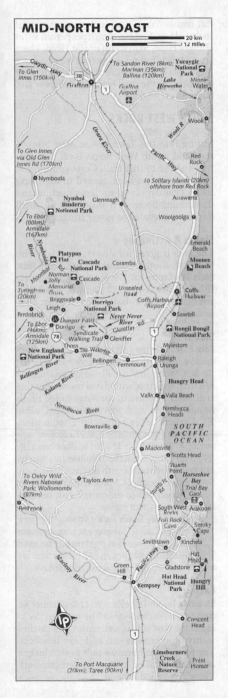

**MID-NORTH COAST**

## KEMPSEY

☎ 02 / pop 8460

Kempsey, a large rural town serving the farms of the Macleay Valley, is a gateway of sorts to the western rainforests and the eastern coastal towns. From Kempsey comes a couple of facts that will hold you in good stead at any pub trivia competition.

The town is the home of the **Akubra hat** – if you want to know more, there's a video at the excellent **visitors centre** ( ☎ 1800 642 480, 6563 1555; Pacific Hwy), which shares the space with the **sheepshearers museum** (adult/child $4/2), on the south side of town.

The late Slim Dusty was born here and, presumably, got his inspiration for songs like 'Duncan' from this unassuming town. Plans have been laid for the **Slim Dusty Heritage Centre** ( ☎ 6562 6533; www.slimdustycentre.com.au), although they haven't made it to vertical stage yet. You can give them a shove via a donation. If you still need more Slim-mania you can head to the **Pub With No Beer** ( ☎ 6564 2100; Taylors Arm Rd) about 60km northwest of Kempsey. Slim's aria to the pub became the biggest selling single in Australia in 1958. And it actually does serve beer.

All critters large and small are welcome at **Ned's Bed Horse-O-Tel** ( ☎ 6565 0085; www.nedsbed.com; 123 Kawana Lane; d/horse/dog $100/17/11; ⊠ ⊠ ), where self-contained units sit on a sizable plot of land. Our competition, *Lonely Pooch*, rates the place very highly.

Alternatively, **Moon River Motor Inn** ( ☎ 6562 8077; 157 Pacific Hwy; s/d from $55/70; ⊠ ⊠ ) is a wee shrub of a spot with 33 comfortable rooms.

**Fredo Pies** ( ☎ 6566 8226, 75 Macleay St, Frederickton; pies $3; ⊗ 7am-7pm) perfects the Oz institution by filling golden casings of pastry goodness with crocodile, kangaroo, beef and just about any other filling you can imagine.

**Greyhound** ( ☎ 13 14 99) and **Premier Motor Service** ( ☎ 13 34 10) run daily to Coffs Harbour ($45) and Sydney.

**CountryLink** ( ☎ 13 22 32) trains run to Grafton and Sydney.

## CRESCENT HEAD

☎ 02 / pop 1200

In surfing circles, this is where the Malibu surfboard gained prominence in Australia during the '60s. Now younger generations are living the surfing legacy this town cherishes. It's wonderful to watch the longboard riders surf the epic waves of **Little Nobby's Junction**

**NORTH COAST**

when the swell's up. Crescent Head itself is an intimate town that caters mainly for family getaways and the odd backpacker who has ventured off the beaten track.

For holiday rentals try **Point Break Realty** ( ☐ 1800 332 272, 6566 0306; www.pointbreakrealty .com.au).

**Mediterranean Motel** ( ☎ 6566 0303; www.cres centheadaccommodation.com.au; 35 Pacific St; s/d $110/130; ⊠ ⊠ ) is the best motel in town. It has a Mediterranean restaurant (mains $20; open breakfast, lunch and dinner), comfy and spotless rooms in the main building, and cute 'surf shacks' out the back (from $120) that sleep eight.

Right at the mouth of the river, **Crescent Head Holiday Park** ( ☎ 6566 0261; Pacific St; camp sites/cabins from $30/115) is a lovely spot to pitch a tent.

The turn-off to Crescent Head is near the visitors centre in Kempsey. **Busways** ( ☎ 1300 555 611) runs to and from Kempsey.

## HAT HEAD NATIONAL PARK

This coastal park of 6500 hectares runs north from near Hat Head to **Smoky Cape** (south of Arakoon), protecting scrubland, swamps and some excellent beaches backed by significant dune systems. Birdlife is prolific on the wetlands. Rising up from the generally flat landscape is Hungry Hill, near Hat Head, and sloping Hat Head itself, where there's a walking track.

Surrounded by the national park, the village of **Hat Head** is much smaller and quieter than Crescent Head. **Hat Head Holiday Park** ( ☎ 02-6567

7501; camp sites/cabins $16/60) is close to a beautiful sheltered bay. You can camp (per person $3) at Hungry Head, 5km south of Hat Head. There are pit toilets but no showers or water.

The park is accessible from the hamlet of Kinchela, on the road between Kempsey and South West Rocks.

## SOUTH WEST ROCKS
☎ 02 / pop 6000

Jutting into the Tasman Sea on a hooked headland, South West Rocks is off the highway and the tourist trail. Crass commercial development has been capped in the rising folds of eucalypts and endless shoreline, and the housing boom of mansions fit for small nations is relegated to newer fringes.

### Sights & Activities
The area is great for divers, especially **Fish Rock Cave**, south of Smoky Cape. **South West Rocks Dive Centre** ( ☎ 6566 6474; 5/98 Gregory St) and **Fish Rock Dive Centre** ( ☎ 6566 6614; www.fishrock .com.au; 134 Gregory St) both offer two dives for around $120.

### Sleeping
**Rock Pool Motor Inn** ( ☎ 1800 180 133; www.rockpool motorinn.com.au; 45 Mcintyre St; r/ste from $135/165; ⊠ ⊠ ) 'Motor inn' usually summons visions of a tired structure with dated rooms, but this is actually a pleasant, four-star hotel. Fresh rooms contain contemporary colours, cable TV, kitchenettes and plush little bathrooms.

**Heritage** ( ☎ 6566 6625; www.heritageguesthouse .com.au; 21-23 Livingstone St; d incl breakfast from $130; ⊠ ) This renovated 1880s house has lovely, old-fashioned rooms with discreet mod cons. Some also have spas. Choose from the simpler rooms downstairs or the more lavish versions upstairs with ocean views.

**Horseshoe Bay Beach Park** ( ☎ 6566 6370; www .horseshoebaypark.com.au; Livingstone St; camp sites/cabins $26/70) In a central position right on the sheltered Town Beach, the 82 sites and 12 cabins here are usually booked out over summer holidays.

### Eating
**Riverside Tavern** ( ☎ 6566 5700; 92 New Entrance Rd; mains $15-22; ⊗ lunch & dinner) The wooden decking at the bow of this waterfront pub catches plenty of afternoon sun and lazy lunchers. The food is scrubbed-up pub nosh: chicken and corn fajitas or lemon-scented calamari. There's also a kid's menu.

---

### LOCAL LAND RIGHTS

In 1996, Crescent Head became the first town on mainland Australia to experience the effects of the Mabo decision, which, in 1992, overrode the doctrine of *terra nullius* (which maintained that Australian land was owned by no-one) and recognised that rights to native title existed under Australian law. The government recognised that the Dunghutti people had native-title rights on 12.4 hectares of land. The land in question has been turned into a residential subdivision (the Dunghutti people were reasonably compensated), so while it may be hard to spot this historic piece of land on a drive through the town, it is strong in essence.

**Geppys** ( ☎ 6566 6169; cnr Livingstone & Memorial Sts; mains $20; ☯ dinner) This cosmopolitan restaurant sizzles up Mod Italian with a splash of Mod Oz...Mod Ozalion. Tuck into sashimi of yellowfin tuna with wasabi mayo or mud crab cooked in Singapore chilli. Live jazz and blues fills the room on Wednesday nights.

**Hermitage restaurant** ( ☎ 6566 6625; 21 23 Livingstone St; mains $25; ☯ breakfast & lunch daily, dinner Fri & Sat) Serves carnivorous concoctions such as a whopping 400g eye fillet with scallops and prawns.

More eateries:

**Seabreeze Hotel** ( ☎ 6566 6909; Livingstone St; mains $8-18; ☯ lunch & dinner) Great pub food and alfresco dining.

**South West Rocks Seafood** ( ☎ 6566 7703; Livingstone St; basket $6) Fish and chips.

## Getting There & Away
**Cavanaghs** ( ☎ 6562 7800) has two runs daily to and from Kempsey, leaving from the town bus stop at Horse Shoe Bay.

## TRIAL BAY & ARAKOON STATE RECREATION AREA
Imposing and profoundly historic, Trial Bay occupies the west headland of the town, and the **Trial Bay Gaol** ( ☎ 02-566 6168; adult/child $5/3; ☯ 9am-4.30pm) dominates the area. Pity (or perhaps envy) the wretched souls incarcerated here during the 19th century; they had to endure breathtaking views of the ocean, forests and freedom. Actually it's been mostly unoccupied, aside from a brief interlude in WWII when it housed Germans. Today it's a worthwhile museum.

The **Arakoon State Recreation Area** is behind the gaol and the camp sites are basic but picturesque. Great food and views are on offer at the **Kiosk** ( ☎ 02-6566 7100; Trial Bay; mains $15; ☯ breakfast & lunch). From South West Rocks it's a pleasant walk to Trial Bay along the beach: look out for the **love shack**, formerly a fisherman's abode, about halfway between the two.

## NAMBUCCA HEADS
☎ 02 / pop 8000
Spacious, sleepy and unspoilt, Nambucca Heads is strewn over a dramatically curling headland where estuaries from the Nambucca River interlace. It has beautiful buttery beaches and lucent water. Although the town seems to be in a constant state of refurbishment, nothing seems to change.

The Nambucca (which means 'many bends') Valley was occupied solely by the Gumbainggir people until European timber cutters arrived in the 1840s. There are still strong Aboriginal communities in Nambucca Heads and up the valley in Bowraville.

## Orientation & Information
The town is just off the Pacific Hwy. Riverside Drive runs alongside the estuary of the Nambucca River, then climbs a steep hill to Bowra St, the main shopping street. A right turn onto Ridge St at the top of the hill leads though the old part of town to the beaches.

The **visitors centre** ( ☎ 6568 6954; cnr Riverside Dr & Pacific Hwy) is very helpful and doubles as the main bus terminal.

## Sights & Activities
Of the numerous lookouts, **Captain Cook Lookout**, with its 180-degree views, best exploits the staggering views.

The only patrolled beach in town is **Main Beach**. Beilby's and Shelly Beaches are just to the south, closer to the river mouth – where the best surf is – and can be reached by going past the Captain Cook Lookout.

For boating enthusiasts, **Beachcomber Marine** ( ☎ 6568 6432; Riverside Dr) rents various vessels by the hour or day – call for rates.

The **V-Wall** is a clever snapshot of life: graffitied memoirs of newlyweds, newly-borns and travellers who've left their colourful mark. For art of a similar genre, the **Mosaic Wall** (Ridge St) in the town centre was made by a local artist from materials such as tiles and broken crockery.

Worth a visit is the **Headland Historical Museum** ( ☎ 6568 6380; Main Beach; adult/child $2/50c; ☯ 2-4pm Wed, Sat & Sun) with local history exhibits, including a collection of more than 1000 photos.

## Sleeping
Typical of this stretch of coast, you'll need to book ahead in summer.

**Beilby's Beach House** ( ☎ 6568 6466; www.beilbys .com.au; 1 Ocean St; r incl breakfast $70 110; ☒ ☐ ☒ ) The owners speak English, French and German, but even if you don't want to test your linguistic mettle it's worth staying for the comfortable rooms. It's near the beach and has a buffet-style, all-you-can-eat breakfast. Children welcome.

**Miramar Motel** ( ☎ 6568 7899; 1 Nelson St; s/d $80/85; ☒ ) Above a plunging valley, this motel has breezy, generous rooms with leafy outlooks. It's clean, quiet and comfy.

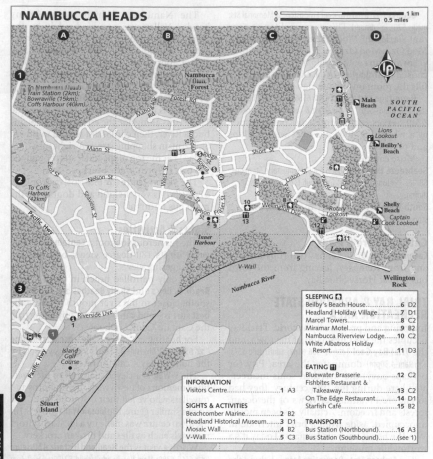

## NAMBUCCA HEADS

**SLEEPING**
Beilby's Beach House.................6 D2
Headland Holiday Village...........7 D1
Marcel Towers...........................8 C2
Miramar Motel...........................9 B2
Nambucca Riverview Lodge......10 C2
White Albatross Holiday
  Resort..................................11 D3

**EATING**
Bluewater Brasserie..................12 C2
Fishbites Restaurant &
  Takeaway.............................13 C2
On The Edge Restaurant...........14 D1
Starfish Café............................15 B2

**INFORMATION**
Visitors Centre...........................1 A3

**SIGHTS & ACTIVITIES**
Beachcomber Marine..................2 B2
Headland Historical Museum......3 D1
Mosaic Wall...............................4 B2
V-Wall.......................................5 C3

**TRANSPORT**
Bus Station (Northbound)..........16 A3
Bus Station (Southbound)..........(see 1)

---

**Nambucca Riverview Lodge** ( ☎ 6568 6386; www
.here.com.au/riverview; 4 Wellington Dve; s/d $90/115; ❄ )
What a humble moniker for Nambucca's oldest pub. Built in 1887, this double-decker hotel has eight unique rooms, all with balconies and views. Each is stuffed with charming furniture, plus a TV, DVD, VCR and lounge.

**Headland Holiday Village** ( ☎ 6568 6547; www
.headlandtouristpark.com.au; Liston St; camp sites/cabins
$19/85) Literally on the peak of the headland, this grassy knoll has an enviable position and infinite ocean vistas. It has clean and orderly facilities and decent cabins.

Also recommended:

**Marcel Towers** ( ☎ 6568 7041; www.marceltowers
.com.au; 12-14 Wellington Dr; apt $95-125; 🖳 ) Compact apartments.

**White Albatross Holiday Resort** ( ☎ 6568 6468;
www.white-albatross.com.au; Wellington Dr; camp sites/cabins from $35/80) Prime sites and cabins and great views.

## Eating

**Starfish Café** ( ☎ 6569 4422; 5 Mann St; mains $14-28;
☺ breakfast, lunch & dinner) Starfish's modern menu of seafood, steaks and fusion specials complements the gorgeous views from the back veranda. Live music occasionally tops the act.

**Fishbites Restaurant and Takeaway** ( ☎ 6569 4444;
1 Wellington Dr; mains $23; ☺ lunch Tue, Fri & Sun, dinner Tue-Sun) This ambient waterfront restaurant infuses local seafood with Asian flavours, like king prawn tails in coriander batter or oysters

with ginger, mirin and soy. Next door, the takeaway focuses on unfussy fish and chips.

**On the Edge Restaurant** ( ☎ 6569 4494; Headland Dr; mains $20; ☯ dinner Wed-Sat, brunch Sun) Behind a small, slate-coloured exterior lies one of Nambucca's finest spots to satiate your hunger. The menu is a powwow of full-bodied ingredients (try bacon-wrapped eye fillet with parsnip pudding) served to candlelit tables.

**Bluewater Brasserie** ( ☎ 6568 6394; V Wall Tavern; Wellington Dr; mains $18; ☯ lunch & dinner daily, breakfast Sat & Sun) A legion of outdoor tables on the wide balcony at this unfussy tavern makes for long, boozy lunches and balmy dinners. There's salads, steaks and seafood, it's family-friendly, and mums eat free every Monday.

## Getting There & Away
**Keans** ( ☎ 6543 1322) runs three times a week to Tamworth ($65).

**Premier Motor Service** ( ☎ 13 34 10) and **Greyhound** ( ☎ 13 14 99) charge around $70 to both Sydney and Byron Bay.

The train station is about 3km out of town. **CountryLink** ( ☎ 13 22 23) has trains to Coffs Harbour and Sydney.

## URUNGA
☎ 02 / pop 2000
Urunga is a comely family retreat, with safe river beaches, good fishing and an innocent atmosphere. Hungry Head, just down the coast, is popular with surfers.

The informative **Bellingen Shire visitors centre** ( ☎ 6655 5711; Pacific Hwy) is on the highway, just before you reach the river.

The **Ocean View Hotel** ( ☎ 6655 6221; 15 Morgo St; s/d incl breakfast $40/70) is the most prominent building in town. It offers simple accommodation and fine views and is good for a meal (mains $15; open breakfast, lunch and dinner).

**Urunga Heads Holiday Park** ( ☎ 6655 6355; Morgo St; camp sites/cabins $20/50; ☒ ) is next to the Urunga Lagoon in the centre of town.

## MYLESTOM
☎ 02 / pop 380
Mylestom is just north of Urunga and is another attractive, unassuming place. It has promising beaches on one side and a wide, influential river on the other.

Just south of the Raleigh Bridge, **Raleigh Winery** ( ☎ 6655 4388; www.raleighwines.com; 36 Queen St, Raleigh; ☯ 10am-5pm Wed Sun) produces good dry whites, rosés and liqueurs.

**North Beach Caravan Park** ( ☎ 6655 4250; Beach Pde; camp sites/cabins from $20/40), next to the waves, is a family affair with clean facilities.

## BELLINGEN
☎ 02 / pop 2500
Scattered around the banks of the Bellingen River, this charming hill town has an evergreen hue tempered by seasonal colours. Thick with gourmet cuisine and accommodation, Bellingen has a confident, laid-back personality, and artistic and alternative lifestyles are the norm.

The valley was part of the extensive territory of the Gumbainggir people until European timber cutters arrived in the 1840s. Until tourism boomed at Coffs Harbour in the 1960s, Bellingen was the most important town in this area.

## Information
**Bellingen Book Nook** ( ☎ 6655 9372; 25 Hyde St) Glorious for avid bookworms.
**Technicality** ( ☎ 6655 1121; 7d Church St; per hr $6) Internet access.
**www.bellingen.com** The excellent community website.

## Sights & Activities
To get a feel for the place, head to the magnificent **Hammond & Wheatley Emporium** (Hyde St), formerly an old department store. It's been very well restored and now houses a shop selling very stylish duds, as well as an art gallery and café.

The historic **Old Butter Factory** ( ☎ 6655 2150; 1 Doepel Lane; ☯ 9.30am-5pm) houses craft shops, a gallery, opal dealers, a masseur and a great café.

From December to March a huge colony of flying foxes descends on **Bellingen Island**. It's an impressive sight when thousands head off at dusk to feed (best seen from the bridge). There's also an interesting walk to **rope swings** into the river, near the YHA hostel.

**Bellingen Canoe Adventures** ( ☎ 6655 9955; 4 Tyson St, Fernmount; day tours per adult/child $77/39) operates wonderful guided canoe tours on the Bellingen River. You can also hire canoes (half-/full-day per person $33/55) or take one of its full moon tours (per adult/child fully clothed $20/15).

**Heartland Didgeridoos** ( ☎ 6655 9881; 2/25 Hyde St) sent the first 'didg' into space. The indigenous owners also know a thing or two about quality, with a growing international reputation. You can make your own didg here.

NORTH COAST

On the second Saturday of the month the **Natural Produce Market** holds court at the Bellingen Showground. On the third Saturday of the month the **Community Market** does the same at Bellingen Park.

## Festivals & Events

**Stamping Ground** (www.stampingground.com.au) A festival of international dance performances in January.

**Bellingen Jazz & Blues Festival** (www.bellingenjazz festival.com.au) Features a strong line-up of jazz names in late August.

**Global Carnival** (www.globalcarnival.com) A multicultural mix of music and performances in early October.

## Sleeping

**Bellingen YHA** ( ☎ 6655 1116; www.yha.com.au; 2 Short St; dm/d $24/60; 🖳 ) Bellingen's award-winning YHA attracts backpackers via the grapevine and then keeps them here with a tranquil, engaging atmosphere inside a renovated weatherboard house.

**Maddefords Cottages** ( ☎ 6655 9866; www.mad defordscottages.com.au; 224 North Bank Rd; d $135; 🐾 ) These polished mountain cabins have cosy interiors with country furnishings and big, sunny windows. Timber balconies overlook a private valley tumbling below, and your first night includes a sizable brekkie hamper.

**Rivendell Guest House** ( ☎ 6655 0060; www.riven dellguesthouse.com.au; 10-12 Hyde St; d incl breakfast $140;

🐾 ) Right in the thick of things, Rivendell has three large en suites and a twin with its own bathroom across the hall. All rooms have French door access to a shady veranda, and in winter the open fire is deliciously toasty.

More accommodation options:

**Casa Belle Country Guest House** ( ☎ 6655 0155; www .casabelle.com; 90 Gleniffer Rd; r incl breakfast $185; 🐾 ) Lavish Tuscan villa.

**Koompartoo Retreat** ( ☎ 6655 2326; www.koom partoo.com.au; cnr Rawson & Dudley Sts; d $145; 🐾 ) Delightful chalets.

## Eating & Drinking

**Boiling Billy Coffee House** ( ☎ 6655 1947; 7 Church St; mains $7-14; ☟ breakfast daily, lunch Mon-Sat) Gourmet sandwiches, Moroccan tagines and spicy Bombay curries are dished up amid terracotta hues and a beautifully blithe atmosphere. The divine smells drift all the way to the wicker seating out the front.

**Relish Bar & Grill** ( ☎ 6655 1003; 77 Hyde St; meals $8-15; ☟ lunch & dinner) Within the heritage-fronted Federation Hotel, this spot has the aesthetics of a chic, inner-city bar yet the atmosphere of a warm country hotel. The side veranda hosts live music and happy punters when the sun's out.

**Riverstone Cafe** ( ☎ 6655 9099; Shop 3, 105-109 Hyde St; mains $14-18; ☟ breakfast, lunch & dinner) Suck in the scent of fresh coffee while you pore over artsy

**A THESPIAN LEGACY** *Justine Vaisutis*

'He's nicked off,' said the waiter, of the chef. Under different circumstances I might have found this disconcerting, but I'd just packed an entire steak (medium-rare) into my belly and there was barely room for coffee. It was well past dining hour and the handful of other patrons appeared to be in similar states of cuisine-coma. Truth be told I had actually seen the chef scamper across the road throughout the evening, but small Australian towns are cauldrons of eccentricity, and I just let it slide. Turns out it was the eve of opening night, and the mad dashes were to final rehearsals at the tiny theatre across the road. Chef was one of the leads in the latest production from the **Dorrigo Drama Club** ( ☎ 6657 2243).

Dorrigo's population simmers beneath 1000, but the aptitude of its drama club proves that big things do come in small packages. This theatrical troupe has entertained audiences for almost a century and performs once or twice a year at the **Old Gazette Theatre** opposite **Misty's** (see opposite). Fortunately the key players have changed numerous times, so their rendition of *Hamlet* doesn't include an uncomfortable authenticity. The club's longtime patron, Ralda Nash, strutted the boards reciting the Bard in London for decades before overseeing things in Dorrigo. All the performers are local, competition is tight and the calibre of talent high. Hang around town for a few days and you'll discover that beneath Romeo, Horatio or Lady Macbeth lies a publican, chef or perhaps mechanic. It's a lucky dip with the emphasis on lucky – for the audience, that is. If you get the opportunity to see the Dorrigo thespians in action you will find yourself witnessing one of those rare treats of Australiana that make TV producers green with envy. You may want to book an early dinner, though.

tomes; this café-cum-bookshop-cum-music store titillates the taste buds and senses in a hip little package. The creative fare includes sake lamb with shitake mushrooms.

**No 2 Oak St** ( ☎ 6655 9000; 2 Oak St; mains $32; ☺ dinner Tue-Sat) The front window has donned culinary awards, but otherwise this renowned restaurant is utterly modest. Housed in a timber cottage, it specialises in Mod Oz with a French twist. Mains include slow-braised duck leg with caramel pears, button mushrooms and roast pumpkin.

More suggested eats:

**Lodge 241** ( ☎ 6655 2470; 117-121 Hyde St; mains $16; ☺ breakfast & lunch) Great organic and vegetarian food.

**Swiss Patisserie** ( ☎ 6655 0050; 7B Church St) Scrummy Swiss-Oz bakery hybrids.

## Getting There & Away
**Keans** ( ☎ 6543 1322) has twice-weekly services to/ from Coffs Harbour, Dorrigo and Armidale.

## AROUND BELLINGEN
There are some beautiful spots waiting to be discovered in the surrounding valleys. The most accessible is the tiny hamlet of **Gleniffer**, 10km to the north and clearly signposted from North Bellingen. There's a good swimming hole in the **Never Never River** behind the small Gleniffer School of Arts at the crossroads. Then you can drive around Loop Rd, which takes you to the foot of the New England tableland – a great drive that words don't do justice to.

If you want to sweat, tackle the **Syndicate Ridge Walking Trail**, a strenuous 15km walk from Gleniffer to the Dorrigo Plateau, following the route of a tramline once used by timber cutters. There's a very steep 1km climb on the way up. To get to the start, take the Gordonville Rd, turning into Adams Lane soon after crossing the Never Never River. The walking track commences at the first gate.

## DORRIGO
☎ 02 / pop 1000
The winding road from Bellingen to Dorrigo is less than 30km but reveals as dramatic a mountain pass as you'll find in NSW. In parts the northern side opens up to reveal thick-cut valleys cloaked in rainforest, with mist settling low. Dorrigo itself is a small and traditional T-junction of a country town, preserved beautifully by cool air and affable locals.

The **visitors centre** ( ☎ 6657 2486; 36 Hickory St; ☺ 10am-4pm) is run by volunteers who share a

passion for the area. The town's main attraction is **Dangar Falls** which cascade over a series of rocky shelves before plummeting into a pristine gorge. A lookout provides Kodak moments, and you can swim beneath the falls if you have a yen for glacial bathing.

## Sleeping & Eating
**Gracemere Grange** ( ☎ 6657 2630; www.dorrigo.com /gracemere; gracemere@dorrigo.com; 325 Dome Rd; s/tw without bathroom $35/70, d with bathroom $80) Oz hospitality doesn't get any warmer. Cosy bedrooms upstairs have slanted, attic-style roofs and the en-suite double has a skylight for views of the twinkling canopy. Rates include a continental breakfast and the owner is a gem.

**Dorrigo Hotel** ( ☎ 6657 2016; fax 6657 2059; cnr Cudgery & Hickory Sts; hotel/motel $55/65) The charm of this almighty pub's exterior is somewhat withered on the inside and the hotel rooms with shared bathrooms have a slightly smoky ambience. Nevertheless they have more character than the motel rooms, and no-one's arguing with the price. The bistro (mains $8-14; open lunch and dinner) whips up tasty pub nosh.

**Misty's** ( ☎ 6657 2855; www.dorrigo.com/mistys; 33 Hickory St; r incl breakfast $95) Misty's self-contained cottage dates from the 1920s and has a gorgeous antique kitchen and bedroom. The bathroom is thankfully renovated and breakfast comes in the form of a generous hamper.

The main event, however, is **Misty's restaurant** ( ☎ 6657 2855; mains $26; ☺ lunch Sun, dinner Wed-Sun) housed inside a lead-lighted weatherboard. Expect culinary delights such as grilled salmon with saffron and vanilla cream. The food, presentation and service are impeccable, and all achieved by a two-man team.

More sleeping and eating options:

**Dorrigo Mountain Resort** ( ☎ 6657 2564; www .dorrigomountainresort.com.au; Waterfall Way; camp sites/cabins $20/62) Bird's-eye views.

**Lookout Motor Inn** ( ☎ 6657 2511; Maynard Plains Rd; s/d $75/95; ☒ ) Standard motel rooms and sensational views.

## Getting There & Away
Twice a week **Keans** ( ☎ 6543 1322) heads to/from Bellingen, Coffs Harbour and Armidale.

## DORRIGO NATIONAL PARK
The most accessible of Australia's World Heritage rainforests is simply spectacular and a must if you're in this neck of the woods. The

---

**DETOUR: AN ANCIENT FOREST MEANDER**

Northwest of Dorrigo, the rippled landscape is quilted in farmland and a medley of gold and green. Just past Bostobrick, Moonbar Rd is a dirt track veering off to the north. It navigates old-growth forests and pockets of three national parks. About 8km in, a sign directs you to take a track to the left to the Norman Jolly Memorial Grove, where an 800m walking track meanders through 600-year-old tallow wood trees. Some 5km further north on Moonbar Rd will place you at Platypus Flat in the Nymbol Binderay National Park, with remote and basic camping.

Moonbar Rd continues to loop its way around the two-house settlements of Cascade and Briggsvale and through Cascade National Park. It then heads south again to skirt Junuy Juluum National Park and finishes at Dangar Falls.

Moonbar Rd is almost 45km long and traverses rugged and ancient forests. It's a bumpy ride in parts and best travelled in a 4WD in wet weather, but a 2WD will be fine otherwise.

---

turn-off to the park is just south of Dorrigo. The **Rainforest Centre** ( ☎ 02-6657 2309; Dome Rd; ⊙ 9am-5pm), at the park entrance, has information about the park's various ecosystems and can advise which walk to conquer given the weather and time of year. The track that best reveals the rainforest, featuring two waterfalls and trees up to 1000 years old, is the 6.6km Wonga Walk. It begins right next to the **Skywalk**, an elevated walkway in front of the rainforest centre that sits above the rainforest canopy and provides jaw-dropping views. It's well worth making the drive down to the **Never Never rest area** in the heart of the national park, from where you can walk to waterfalls or begin longer walks.

## COFFS HARBOUR
☎ 02 / pop 49,678

Leaning gum trees dominate the Coffs Harbour skyline, and this scenic city nestles delicately at their base. It's a hugely popular holiday destination for families, due to a string of fabulous beaches. The town makes a good stab at appealing to everyone and settles successfully on the 'middle Australian' market. Consequently its attractions swing heavily in favour of water-based fun, wild action sports, unabashed kitsch and encounters with soft and fuzzy wildlife. According to one website, the CSIRO has somehow scientifically declared Coffs Harbour's climate the best in Australia. No arguments here.

### Orientation

The town is split into three areas: the jetty (which isn't on the water), town centre and beaches. The Pacific Hwy turns into Grafton St and then Woolgoolga Rd on its run north through town.

### Information

**Jetty Village Internet Shop** ( ☎ 6651 9155; Jetty Village, Harbour Dr; per hr $6; ⊙ 10am-8pm Mon-Sat, to 4pm Sun) Internet access.
**Main post office** (Park Beach Plaza Shopping Centre)
**Planet Games** ( ☎ 6652 5188; Max Murray Mall, 20 Gordon St; per hr $6; ⊙ 10am-7pm) Internet access.
**Visitors centre** ( ☎ 1300 369 070, 6652 1522; www .coffscoast.com.au; Pacific Hwy) Exhaustive information.

### Sights

Clumps of indigenous scrub and rainforest mingle with foreign foliage at the **North Coast Botanic Gardens** ( ☎ 6648 4188; Hardacre St; entry by donation; ⊙ 9am-5pm), which hugs a curve of Coffs Creek. Paths crisscross beneath the canopy, kookaburras laugh from up high, and there's a vast grassy lawn begging for Frisbee action.

Coffs' main claim to fame is a ferocious, concrete **Big Banana** ( ☎ 6652 4355; www.bigbanana .com; Pacific Hwy; ⊙ 9am-4.30pm), hailed by many as a national icon. After purchasing the all-important souvenir banana key ring, you can go ice skating ($12, without bananas) or tobogganing ($5, not on a banana).

**Clog Barn** ( ☎ 6652 4633; www.clogbiz.com; 215 Pacific Hwy; per adult/child $5/4; ⊙ 7.30am-5pm) is a bizarre miniature Dutch village with windmills and a clog barn with a ridiculously large range of collectable spoons. It makes the Big Banana look sophisticated. Kids will like it, adults will be bamboozled.

At the **Pet Porpoise Pool** ( ☎ 6652 2164; Orlando St, beside Coffs Creek; adult/child $25/13; ⊙ 9am-4pm, shows 10am & 1pm) dolphins, penguins and sea lions all interact with the public during acrobatic shows. It's a hit with all ages.

**Coffs Harbour Zoo** ( ☎ 6656 1330; Pacific Hwy; adult/child/fam $16/8/40; ⊙ 9.30am-4pm) has koalas, pythons and echidnas on display. As far as zoos go, this one's pretty good.

**Muttonbird Island**, at the end of the northern breakwater, is occupied by some 12,000 pairs of muttonbirds from late August to early April, with cute offspring visible in summer.

### GALLERIES

**Coffs Harbour City Gallery** ( ☎ 6648 4861; cnr Coff & Duke Sts; ☑ 10am-4pm Wed-Sat) embraces the work of regional artists as well as contemporary international work. The curatorship is thoughtful and doesn't shy from social themes.

### BEACHES

Sweeping **Park Beach** attracts plenty of swell, along with punters and lifeguards, from October to April. **Jetty Beach** is just south and a safer option. **Diggers Beach**, to the north, is partially nudist and sensational (for the surf). **Moonee Beach** lies 14km further north and **Emerald Beach** is a further 6km.

## Activities

**Valery Horse Trails** ( ☎ 6653 4301; www.valerytrails.com .au; 758 Valery Rd, Valery; 2hr ride $45), has 60 'well disciplined horses' and plenty of acreage to explore the surrounding hills.

**Liquid Assets** ( ☎ 6658 0850; www.surfrafting.com; 38 Harbour Dr; half-/full-day per person from $40/125) keeps thrill junkies giddy with surf or white-water rafting, river kayaking and platypus spotting on the Nymboida River.

**Coffs City Skydivers** ( ☎ 6653 2067; www.coffscentral .dnet.tv/CoffsCitySkyDivers; Coffs Harbour Airport; tandem jump $320) obliges all urges to fling yourself from a plane.

A gravel track fringed by clumps of gum trees and utilised by dog-walkers and joggers skirts Coffs Creek and provides the perfect opportunity to do as the locals do.

More active options:

**East Coast Surf School** ( ☎ 6651 5515; www.eastcoast surfschool.com.au; Diggers Beach; 2hr lesson per person from $50) Adult and kids' surf camps.

**Jetty Dive Centre** ( ☎ 6651 1611; www.jettydive.com .au; 398 Harbour Dr) PADI courses from $215.

## Tours

**Mountain Trails** ( ☎ 6658 3333; tours per person from $65) Award-winning ecofriendly 4WD tours. A reader fave.

**Spirit of Coffs Harbour Cruises** ( ☎ 6650 0155; www .spiritofcoffs.com.au; International Marina; 2hr tours per person $49) Whale watching.

## Festivals & Events

**Gold Cup** ( ☎ 6652 1488) Early August – Coffs' premier horse race.

**Coffs Harbour Food & Wine Festival** Last weekend in October.

**Pittwater to Coffs Yacht Race** New Year – starts in Sydney and finishes here.

## Sleeping

**Pacific Property & Management** ( ☎ 1800 658 569; 6652 1466; www.coffsholidayrentals.com.au; 101 Park Beach Rd) has holiday rental listings.

### BUDGET

**Aussitel Backpackers Hostel** ( ☎ 1800 330 335, 6651 1871; www.aussitel.com; 312 Harbour Dr; dm/d $22/60; P ⬛ ⬛ ) In an oversized brick house, this hostel has a relaxed ambience, homely dorms and a shady courtyard. By night it brews a party atmosphere. Diving is offered (PADI courses from $245), as is kayaking, skydiving and rafting.

**Coffs Harbour YHA** ( ☎ 6652 6462; www.yha.com .au; 51 Collingwood St; dm/d from $24/70; P ⬛ ⬛ ) Readers rave about this snazzy hostel, and why wouldn't they? The staff are like family, dorms and en-suite doubles are spacious and modern, and the TV lounge and kitchen are immaculate. You can hire surfboards and bikes as well.

**Ocean Palms Motel** ( ☎ 6652 1264; www.oceanpalms motel.com.au; cnr Ocean Pde & Park Beach Rd; s/d $65/70; P ⬛ ) Behind a high brush fence and towering palms, this cheerful motel has quiet rooms with kitchenettes and glass sliding doors. The central lawn and pool are family-friendly.

Also available:

**Ocean Parade Motel** ( ☎ /fax 6652 6733; 41 Ocean Pde; s/d/tr $60/70/88; P ⬛ ) Nifty motel with friendly owners. Good wheelchair access.

**Park Beach Holiday Park** ( ☎ 1800 200 111, 6648 4888; www.parkbeachholidaypark.com.au; 1 Ocean Pde; camp sites $25, cabins $64-130; P ⬛ ) Prim and trim; fine cabins and sites.

### MIDRANGE

**Caribbean Motel** ( ☎ 6652 1500; caribbean@stayincoffs .com.au; 353 High St; d $90-200, f $130-220; P ⬛ ⬛ ) Close to the jetty and the marina, this motel complex has modern rooms, some with balconies or spas, plus great-value one-bedroom suites with kitchenettes. All have enough space to swing numerous bunches of bananas.

**Bangalow Waters** ( ☎ 6653 7999; www.bangalow waters.com.au; 95 James Small Dr, Korora; apt $130-160;

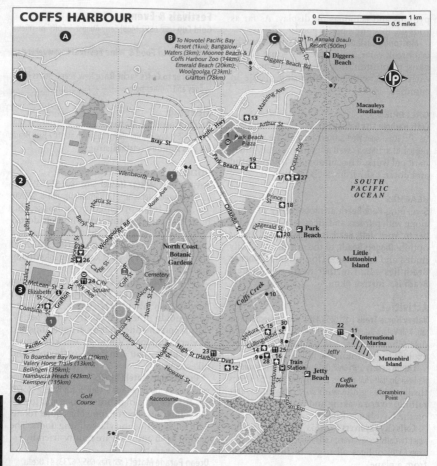

**COFFS HARBOUR**

P X 图 ) The 12 mock-Balinese *bures* at this private retreat overlook a lagoon and have atmospheric interiors, two bedrooms and full kitchens. Some also have spas. Week-long stays attract significant discounts.

**Observatory Holiday Apartments** ( ☎ 1300 302 776, 6650 0462; www.theobservatory.com.au; 30-36 Camperdown St; apt $140-170; P X ) Some have window spas with ocean views, some have balconies, and some have enough room for six people. All the apartments at this quiet, compact block are bright and airy with sunny décor.

**Aanuka Beach Resort** ( ☎ 6652 7555; www.aanuka .com.au; 11 Firman Dr; r $170, apt incl breakfast from $215; P X 图 ) Lodged in luscious leafage, this classy resort has excellent studios and apart-

ments, all with spas and dishy interiors. It sits right on a quiet neck of Diggers Beach and has a restaurant and tennis courts.

More midrange options:

**Boambee Bay Resort** ( ☎ 6653 2700; 8 Barber Cl; apt $150-180; P X 图 ) Spacious (but dated) apartments and a tropical setting. Good disabled unit.

**Quality Inn City Centre** ( ☎ 6652 6388; www.city centre.com.au; 22 Elizabeth St; s/d $125/135; P X 图 ) Reliable rooms with wi-fi access and good facilities.

**TOP END**

**Novotel Pacific Bay Resort** ( ☎ 1300 363 360, 6659 7000; cnr Pacific Hwy & Bay Dr; r $180-230; P X 图 ) The colossal Novotel sprawls its way around a nine-hole golf course, and its restaurant is so big it has palm trees on the inside. Rooms are suitably fabulous and facilities include a day spa and a kids club.

## Eating

### CITY CENTRE

Everything downtown shuts in the evening.

**That Fabulous Delicatessen & Café** ( ☎ 6652 5855; City Sq; mains $8; ☆ breakfast & lunch Mon-Sat) Yes, actually it is all fabulous at this European-style deli. Nibble on dolmades, dips and gourmet cheeses, or tuck into Turkish rolls stuffed with chilli-blasted chicken (ouch!).

**Starfish Café** ( ☎ 6651 5005; City Sq; mains $8-13; ☆ breakfast & lunch Mon-Fri) The coffee and people-watching are first class at this popular café. Fresh quiches, pastas and salads are changed daily, but they all take second billing to delectable burgers (try the pumpkin, basil, sun-dried tomato, char-grilled zucchini and hummus one).

### MARINA

**Fisherman's Co-op** ( ☎ 6652 2811; 69 Marina Dr; meals $7-10; ☆ breakfast, lunch & dinner) The place to head for grilled or battered catch of the day in a cardboard box. Ask what's freshest – New Zealand and southern seafood is sometimes served. You can also buy fish uncooked.

**Tide & Pilot** ( ☎ 6651 6888; Marina Dr; mains café $6-12, restaurant $20-30; ☆ breakfast, lunch & dinner) This cosmopolitan institution sizzles the who's who of the deep with finesse; herb and goat's cheese-crusted swordfish on roast garlic, for example. The casual 'lower deck' specialises in unfussy fish and chips.

### JETTY

**Crying Tiger** ( ☎ 6650 0195; 384s Harbour Dr; mains $10-20; ☆ dinner) Swimming in ambience and fragrant

smells, the Crying Tiger keeps inquisitive diners happy with red duck curry, or king prawns in lime leaf and coconut. You can turn the chilli gauge as high or low as you like.

**Vibes at the Jetty** ( ☎ 6651 1544; 382 Harbour Dr; mains $15-25; ☆ breakfast, lunch & dinner Tue-Sun) This trendy restaurant nails Mod Oz with salt-and-pepper squid with raspberry vinaigrette, or double-roasted duck with cumin and orange cognac glaze. The back courtyard is bliss on balmy evenings.

**Mangrove Jacks** ( ☎ 6652 5517; The Promenade Centre, Harbour Dr; mains $25; ☆ breakfast & lunch daily, dinner Tue-Sat) Overlooking a quiet bend of Coffs Creek, this restaurant serves sultry dinners like lamb shanks slow-cooked in shiraz, honey seeded mustard and sun dried tomatoes. Brekkie and lunch are far more casual.

## Drinking

**Plantation Hotel** ( ☎ 6652 3855; Pacific Hwy) Underneath the glossy façade of neon lights, mirrored walls and colourful wedge seating, the Plantation is still a pub at heart, so beer, live rock and the occasional 'Miss Indy' quest are still mainstays. It's a good spot to meet the young and local drinking constituency...or Miss Indy.

**Hoey Moey Pub** ( ☎ 6652 3833; Ocean Pde) The kind of place that may leave you deaf in one ear and with a layer of stick from the carpet on your shoes, the Hoey Moey isn't too proud to turn thongs away. Pool comps, live music and terrifying karaoke sessions are nightly norms.

More entertainment:

**Coffs Hotel** ( ☎ 6652 3817; cnr Pacific Hwy & West High St) Bands and DJs till late on weekends.

**Pier Hotel** ( ☎ 6652 2110; cnr Hood & High Sts) Classic 1930s local, complete with grizzly regulars.

NORTH COAST

## Getting There & Away

### AIR

**Virgin Blue** ( ☎ 13 67 89) and **Qantas** ( ☎ 13 13 13) fly to Sydney, Brisbane and Melbourne. **Brinda-bella Airlines** ( ☎ 1300 668 824) flies to Newcastle and Port Macquarie.

### BUS

Buses leave from the visitors centre.

**Greyhound** ( ☎ 13 14 99) and **Premier Motor Service** ( ☎ 13 34 10) stop in Coffs; fares include Port Macquarie ($45) and Byron Bay ($55).

**Keans** ( ☎ 6543 1322) has two services a week to Bellingen ($15), Dorrigo ($19) and Armidale ($25). **Busways** ( ☎ 6652 2744) has three buses daily to Bellingen ($8). **Ryans Buses** ( ☎ 6652 3201) runs to Grafton ($20) twice daily.

### TRAIN

**CountryLink** ( ☎ 13 22 32) trains head to Grafton, Sydney and Casino.

## Getting Around

All the major car rental companies are in town.

**Coffs Bike Hire** ( ☎ 6652 5102; cnr Orlando & Collingwood Sts; per day $25) rents mountain bikes.

For a cab, **Coffs District Taxi Network** ( ☎ 13 10 08) operates a 24-hour service.

# COFFS HARBOUR TO GRAFTON

## Woolgoolga

☎ 02 / pop 3800

A less developed coastal town just north of Coffs, Woolgoolga is renowned for its surf and sizable Sikh community. As you drive in, there's the impressive Sikh **Guru Nanak Temple**, the *gurdwara* (place of worship). Don't confuse it with the **Raj Mahal**, an Indian-influenced decrepit concrete extravagance with two giant elephant statues out the front and a tacky emporium inside. If you drive straight through town up to the point, you'll get a magnificent view of the **Solitary Marine Reserve**.

About 5km south of Woolgoolga and signposted off the Pacific Hwy, the small **Lake Russell Gallery** ( ☎ 6656 1092; www.lakerussellgallery.com.au; 12 Smiths Rd, Emerald Beach; ⏲ 10am-5pm) exhibits work by local artists and has coffee and cake to fuel the cultural concentration. The gallery sits on the verge of a lily-padded pond and boasts two private and very indulgent cottages (double rooms including breakfast $250) with air-con.

The **Woolgoolga Beach Caravan Park** ( ☎ 6654 1373; Beach St; camp sites/cabins from $35/60) right on the beach can't be beaten on position.

On the beachfront, **Bluebottles Brasserie** ( ☎ 6654 1962; cnr Wharf & Beach Sts; mains $23; breakfast & lunch daily, dinner Thu-Sat) serves fine seafood and vegetarian gems like spiced cous cous with roasted tomatoes and goat's cheese. On sultry summer afternoons you can catch live jazz here.

## Red Rock

☎ 02 / pop 290

Red Rock, a site that's sacred to the Gunawarri tribe, is a sleepy village with a beautiful inlet and gorgeous surroundings. Soak up the sun or catch a fish while camping at **Red Rock Caravan Park** ( ☎ 6649 2730; 1 Lawson St; camp sites/cabins from $13/65).

## Yuraygir National Park

Yuraygir (20,000 hectares) is the southernmost in a chain of coastal national parks and nature reserves that runs almost all the way north to Ballina. The beaches and bushwalking paths are gorgeous. The park is in three sections, from **Red Rock** to the Wooli River (turn off the highway just north of Red Rock); from the township of **Wooli** to the Sandon River (turn off the highway 12km south of Grafton); and from near **Brooms Head** to **Angourie Point** (accessible from those towns). There is no vehicle access between the sections; on foot you'd have to cross the challenging Wooli and Sandon Rivers.

Walkers can bush camp and there are basic camping areas (per person $5) at **Station Creek** in the southern section; at the **Boorkoom** and **Illaroo** rest areas in the central section; on the north bank of the Sandon River; and at **Red Cliff** at the Brooms Head end of the northern section. These are accessible by car; there is also a walk-in camp site in the northern section at Shelly Beach.

## Wooli

☎ 02 / pop 600

Wooli's beauty is its backdrop – Yuraygir National Park on land and the Solitary Islands Marine Park offshore. This means you are encircled by wildlife and crisp waters.

On the June long weekend the locals hold their big event, the **Goanna Pulling Championships**, which is devoid of reptilian participants but involves locals using their leather-strapped heads in a tug-of-war. You couldn't write this stuff.

The **Wooli Hotel Motel** ( ☎ 6649 7532; North St; s/d $66/76) has a gorgeous paved beer garden, good pub nosh (mains $10-18; open lunch and dinner) and standard motel rooms.

The **Solitary Islands Marine Park Resort** ( ☎ 1800 003 031, 6649 7519; North St; camp sites/cabins from $21/70) has a mouthful of a name and lovely cabins in a scrubby bush setting. Kayak rental is available for $15/25 per half-/full-day.

## Solitary Islands Marine Park

This group of five islands is the meeting point of warm tropical currents and cooler southern currents, making for a wonderful combination of corals, reef fish and seaweeds. Dubbed the 'rivers of life', this is the best area in which to dive or snorkel (look out for extremely rough conditions).

# FAR NORTH COAST

As the Pacific Hwy enters its final NSW run, loftier hills increase their ground cover, and each sign of civilisation is laced with New Age nuance. The string of national parks and fishing villages that stumble up the coast to Ballina are exquisitely beautiful. Coupled with the beaches and divine subtropical climate are rivers rich in depth and colour; the striking blue Clarence River is one of the most beautiful Down Under. By the time you reach Byron Bay, with its good looks and copious activities, the holiday hype gears up a notch. This region ticks to the tourist dollar, and backpackers, surfers, families, romantic couples, yuppie weekenders, rugby fanatics, yoga gurus, gastronomes and everyone else gets in on the act.

## GRAFTON

☎ 02 / pop 18,500

Nestled into a quiet bend of the Clarence River, Grafton is a charming grid of wide streets awash with hanging evergreens, grand pubs and splendid old houses. Heritage buildings line the avenues, and an aimless wander is a delight in itself. The town has 24 parks and, in late October, is carpeted in mauve flowers from the prolific Brazilian jacarandas.

## Orientation & Information

The Pacific Hwy bypasses the town and you enter over a lovely old double-decker (road and rail) bridge.

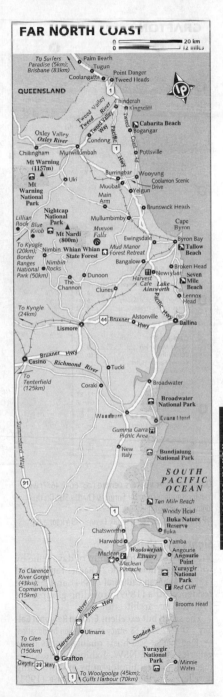

**FAR NORTH COAST**

NORTH COAST

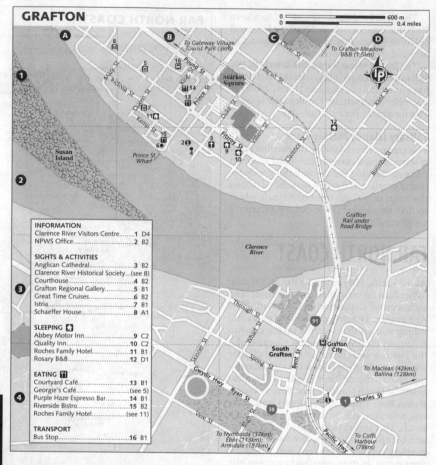

**GRAFTON**

0 ____ 600 m
0 ____ 0.4 miles

**Clarence River visitors centre** ( ☎ 6642 4677; www
.clarencetourism.com; cnr Spring & Charles Sts) On the
highway south of the town.
**NPWS office** ( ☎ 6641 1500; Level 3, 49 Victoria St)

## Sights & Activities

Victoria St is the focal point of days gone by
with the **courthouse** (1862), **Roches Family Hotel**
(1870), **Anglican Cathedral** (1884) and private
residence **Istria** (1899) providing glimpses of
19th-century architecture.

The small but excellent **Grafton Regional Gallery** ( ☎ 6642 3177; 58 Fitzroy St; admission by donation;
🕙 10am-4pm Tue-Sun) hosts quality works from
galleries around NSW. Exhibits include indigenous pieces, photography and stunning
jewellery. Further up, **Schaeffer House** (1903)

is where you'll find the **Clarence River Historical
Society** ( ☎ 6642 5212; 190 Fitzroy St; adult/child $3/1;
🕙 1-4pm Tue, Wed, Thu & Sun), which claims to
have the largest public showing of Wedgwood
in NSW.

**Susan Island**, in the middle of the river, is
home to the largest fruit bat colony in the
southern hemisphere. Their evening departure is a spectacular summer sight. Access
to the river is by boat or canoe; you can hire
a tinny from **Seelands Boat Hire** ( ☎ 6644 9381; 67
Old Punt Rd; per day $60), 6km north of Grafton, or
just sit on the banks and marvel.

Several outfits cruise the lower Clarence
River including **Great Time Cruises** ( ☎ 6642 3456;
Prince St Wharf; 2hr cruise incl lunch from $15), which
takes you around Susan Island.

## Festivals & Events

**Horse Racing Carnival** (www.racenet.com.au/grafton) Every July; one of the richest in Australia.

**International Philosophy, Science and Theology Festival** (www.pstf.com.au) Held in June, *the* event to discover what the golly 'it' is all about.

**Jacaranda Festival** (www.jacarandafestival.org.au) Late October to early November; Australia's longest-running floral festival.

## Sleeping

**Roches Family Hotel** ( ☎ 6644 2866; www.roches.com .au; 85 Victoria St; s/d $30/40) This historic hotel has been spruced up with a lick of new paint and a flourish of potted trees. The quaint and made-over rooms upstairs share a TV lounge and new bathrooms. Ask for a room with French doors to the glorious old balcony.

**Grafton Meadow B&B** ( ☎ 6643 2331; www.grafton meadow.com; 95 Crown St; s/d incl breakfast $70/85) At the end of a cul-de-sac, with horse paddocks to one side, this modern homestead has lovely rooms with balconies or courtyards, and classic jacarandas out the front.

**Abbey Motor Inn** ( ☎ 6642 6122; fax 6643 1615; 59 Fitzroy St; s/d $76/86; 🔀 ) So retro it's cool again, the Abbey Motor Inn is a slice of 1960s Australiana, right down to the chocolate vinyl swivel chairs and beseeching air-con (but not the free wi-fi access). Everything is in mint condition.

**Rosary B&B** ( ☎ 6642 2292; johnmelenhorst@bigpond .com; 41 Bacon St; s/d incl breakfast $75/90; 🔀 🍷 ) This beautifully cluttered Federation home has stood its ground since 1905. The rooms are comfortable and it's close to Grafton's main shopping area.

Also available:

**Gateway Village Tourist Park** ( ☎ 1800 012 019, 6642 4225; www.thegatewayvillage.com.au; 598 Sumer-land Way; camp sites/cabins from $27/95; 🍷 ) Massive holiday park with excellent facilities.

**Quality Inn** ( ☎ 6640 9100; www.qualityinngrafton .com.au; 51 Fitzroy St; r from $120; 🔀 ) Modern rooms and self-contained units.

## Eating

**Purple Haze Espresso Bar** ( ☎ 6642 8866; Shop 6, 4 King St; mains $7; 🕒 lunch & dinner Mon-Fri) Jimi Hendrix would stick out like a punk at a Tupperware convention here, but he wouldn't mind the no-fuss, great-value lavish wraps, cooked brekkies and strong coffee. If he was lucid (and alive) he might grab a table in the sun.

**Courtyard Café** ( ☎ 6642 6644; 120 Fitzroy St; mains $9-15; 🕒 breakfast & lunch) Tucked behind a beautiful sandstone building, this sheltered café whips up delights like seared lemon prawns with mint and ginger yoghurt or peppered beef fillet with asparagus and kumera salad.

**Georgie's Café** ( ☎ 6642 6996; 158 Fitzroy St; mains $20; 🕒 10am-4pm Tue-Sun, dinner Tue-Sat) Inside the Grafton Gallery, Georgie's serves a creative menu to tables in the central courtyard. Daylight meals of fresh, deli-style salads and sandwiches make way for finer treats at night.

For a generous counter meal settle into a booth at **Roches Family Hotel** (mains $10-15; 🕒 lunch & dinner) or the Crown Hotel's **Riverside Bistro** ( ☎ 6642 4000; 1 Prince St; mains $12-18; 🕒 breakfast & lunch daily, dinner Mon-Sat).

## Getting There & Around

**Busways** ( ☎ 6642 2954) has several daily services to Yamba. **Ryans Buses** ( ☎ 6652 3201) has four buses daily to Coffs Harbour. **Greyhound** ( ☎ 13 14 99) and **Premier Motor Service** ( ☎ 13 34 10) stop at the train station and travel to Byron Bay ($45) and Coffs Harbour ($35).

**CountryLink** ( ☎ 13 22 32) has trains to Sydney and Casino and buses to Coffs Harbour ($13).

There's an interesting route from Grafton to Armidale via Nymboida and Ebor, passing turn-offs to Dorrigo and the New England and Cathedral Rock National Parks. Heading west to Glen Innes, the Gwydir Hwy passes through the superb Washpool and Gibraltar Range National Parks.

**Grafton Radio Taxis** ( ☎ 6642 3622) operates a 24-hour service.

## CLARENCE RIVER VALLEY

The Clarence River rises in Queensland's McPherson Ranges and runs south through the mountains before thundering down a gorge in the Gibraltar Range west of Grafton. It then serenely meanders northeast to the sea at Yamba, watering a beautiful and fertile valley along the way.

The delta between Grafton and the coast is a patchwork of farmland in which the now immense and branching Clarence River forms about 100 islands, some very large. If you're driving, the profusion of small bridges and waterways makes it hard to keep track of whether you're on an island or the mainland.

This is the start of sugar-cane country and also the beginning of Queensland-style domestic architecture: wooden houses with high-pitched roofs perched on stilts to allow air circulation in the hot summer. The burning of the cane fields (May to December) adds a smoky tang to the air.

## INLAND FROM GRAFTON

The Clarence River can be navigated as far upstream as the village of **Copmanhurst**, about 35km northwest of Grafton. Further up, the Clarence River descends rapidly from the Gibraltar Range through the rugged **Clarence River Gorge**, a popular but potentially dangerous site for white-water canoeing.

Private property flanks the gorge. Land on the south side is owned by the Winters family, who allow day visitors and have cabin accommodation at **Winters' Shack** ( ☎ 02-6647 2173; s/d/f $25/50/70). Access is via Copmanhurst. It's best to ring first to get permission and to arrange for the gates to be unlocked.

On the north side, **Wave Hill Station** ( ☎ 02-6647 2145; www.wavehillfarmstay.com.au; per person $25) has accommodation in the beautifully rustic Dingo Dam Cottage, and regular horse-riding trips to the gorge (per person per hour from $25).

## MACLEAN

☎ 02 / pop 3250

Some might say, given the tartan power poles, Maclean takes its Scottish heritage a little too seriously. That said, the town does sweep alongside a lazy sprawl of the delta in vaguely Celtic fashion, and with your Glenmorangie goggles (firmly) fastened, you might mistake the Clarence River for a Highlands loch. The **Lower Clarence visitors centre** ( ☎ 6645 4121; Pacific Hwy) is on the southern entry to town.

To take in the beautiful surrounds, head up the hill to **Maclean Lookout**. The **Maclean Historical Society** ( ☎ 6645 3416; www.macleanhistory .org.au; cnr Wharf & Grafton Sts; adult/child $3/1; ⏰ 1-4pm Wed & Fri, 10am-4pm Sat) tells you all about the town's Scottish roots.

The small but innovative **Witzig Gallery** ( ☎ 6645 2804; 80 River St; admission free; ⏰ 10am-4pm) specialises in contemporary works from Papua New Guinea and Australian surf art.

The 1867 **Historic Gables B&B** ( ☎ 6645 2452; gables@northnet.com.au; 2b Howard St; d $95) is a charming Federation house with six bedrooms, an open fireplace and a wide veranda for epic sunsets over the Clarence.

Alternatively, **Motel Maclean** ( ☎ 6645 2473; www.motelmaclean.com; 65 Cameron St, Old Pacific Hwy; s/d $60/70; ▨ ) has decent rooms.

## YAMBA

☎ 02 / pop 6500

'Yamba, it's yours' greets you in cheerful font as you enter this gem of a town. If only; beaches on three fronts, kilometres of grassy esplanade, stunning views and a warm and charming population would make a perfect kingdom. Fishing rods are a fifth appendage of the town folk.

### Activities

**Yamba Kayak** ( ☎ 6646 1137; www.yambakayak.com.au; pick-up at Gorman's Restaurant at Yamba Bay; half-day $55) operates on demand. To use the motorised version, **Yamba Boat Hire** ( ☎ 6645 8525; Boat Harbour Marina; full day for 8 people $120) has simple, square boats. There's a **community market** at the Yamba Oval on the fourth weekend of each month.

### Sleeping

**Pacific Hotel** ( ☎ 6646 2466; 18 Pilot St; dm $45, r without/ with bathroom $60/100) Gorgeously situated overlooking the ocean, this fabulous pub corners the budget and midrange markets with bright, four-bed bunk rooms and handsome hotel rooms with million-dollar views.

**Pegasus Motel** ( ☎ 6646 2314; pegasusmotel@yambansw .com.au; cnr Yamba & Angourie Rds; r/apt $80/95; ▨ ▣ ) Applause all round for this excellent motel, which defies boring stereotypes. Standard rooms are fancied up with smart and fresh linen and décor, and 'courtyard suites' are one-bedroom apartments with kitchenettes and private courtyards. All rooms are a steal.

**On The Rocks** ( ☎ 6646 1760; www.ontherocks.com.au; 6 Ocean St; r/apt per 2-nights from $370/400; ▨ ) Bondi, eat yer heart out! These genteel studios hover right over the ocean and come with plenty of glass to exploit the views. The milky-white interiors are chic and polished and scream (quietly) 'romantic getaway'.

More options:

**Calypso Holiday Park** ( ☎ 6646 8847; www.calypso yamba.com.au; Harbour St; camp sites/cabins from $23/70; ▨ ▣ )

**Eco Point Angourie Resort** ( ☎ 6646 8600; 166 Angourie Rd; apt $140-299; ▨ ▣ ) Appealing, eco-certified complex with sleek apartments.

### Eating

**Caperberry Cafe** ( ☎ 6646 2322; 17 Yamba Rd; mains $5-11; ⏰ breakfast & lunch) Offering sophisticated food in humble surrounds, with heart-kicking coffee and more Turkish toasties than the mother country. Overflowing frittatas, bakes, salads and a mean lamb burger are also on offer.

**Restaurant Castalia** ( ☎ 6646 1155; 15 Clarence St; mains $20-30; ❤ breakfast Sat, lunch Fri & Sat, dinner Mon-Sat) Relaxed yet stylish, Castalia has built a name for itself with fancy bush tucker like kangaroo striploin with bush spices and beetroot relish. The inventive menu is worthy of several visits.

More eating options:

**Clarence River Fish Co-op** ( ☎ 6646 2099; Yamba Rd; meals $10; ❤ breakfast & lunch) Takeaway fish and chips for less than $10.

**Pacific Hotel** ( ☎ 6646 2466; 18 Pilot St; mains $15-25; ❤ lunch & dinner) Outstanding views and delicious pub grub.

## Getting There & Away

A passenger-only ferry (adult/child $5/3, four times daily) runs to Iluka, on the north bank of the Clarence River.

**Busways** ( ☎ 6642 2954) and **Countrylink** ( ☎ 13 22 32) buses go to Grafton ($11), Lennox Head ($14) and Byron Bay ($15).

## ANGOURIE

☎ 02 / pop 626

Five kilometres south of Yamba, this tiny surf haven climbs a pretty headland and beckons seasoned surfers (who wear helmets and leap off rocks) with epic breaks. Less hardened surfers can cool off in the **Blue Pool**, a quarry next to the beach filled with fresh water from a spring.

**Frangipani** (The Crescent; mains $24; ❤ breakfast, lunch & dinner Tue-Sun) is an edgy and atmospheric restaurant with fine food along the lines of salmon steak with caper butter terrine or chicken saltimbocco with prosciutto.

## ILUKA

☎ 02 / pop 1860

Iluka is a carbon copy of Yamba but less developed due to its distance from the Pacific Hwy. Anglers love this area, as do nature enthusi-

asts. The town acts as a gateway to the World Heritage–listed **Iluka Nature Reserve**.

## BUNDJALUNG NATIONAL PARK

This 4000 hectares of coastal land has 30km of unspoilt beaches for surfing and swimming. The entrance is 60km north of Grafton or 55km south of Ballina and there are four main areas.

The **Gumma Garra** picnic area has creeks, islands, rainforests and a midden that can be seen by the river. You can get there via Evans Head on the Bundjalung road. The second is **Black Rocks & Booroora** picnic area and camping, which is tucked in behind the sand dunes of the 10-mile beach. You can sit in the shade of the tuckeroo tree. The third area is the **Woody Head Camping Area** ( ☎ 6646 6134; camping per person $8, cabins $55-77), which has rock pools, lovely picnic tables, camp sites and self-contained cabins. It's 6km north of Iluka. The fourth area is **Shark Bay**, where you can bushwalk and swim. There's a photogenic lookout here with views of the coastline all the way around to Cape Byron.

## EVANS HEAD

☎ 02 / pop 2610

Evans Head is a great way to escape the hectic tourist lifestyle present in its northern counterparts. Locals endearingly call it 'the jewel in the crown'. It has an intense prawn and fishing industry.

The **Silver Sands Caravan Park** ( ☎ 6682 4212; Park St; camp sites/cabins from $18/60) is orderly and populated by permanent residents. Cabins are militarily clean (and organised). For a pub room, try the **Hotel Illawong** ( ☎ 6682 4222; Evans Head; s/d $35/55) and for a motel room try **Pacific Motor Inn** ( ☎ 6682 4318; 38 Woodburn St; r $68-75).

**Cafe Spirit** ( ☎ 6682 4055; 18 Oak St; mains $10-15; ❤ breakfast & lunch) is a funky little eatery, with

---

**DETOUR: ITALY ON A SHOESTRING**

About 40km north of Iluka on the Pacific Hwy, the **New Italy Museum** ( ☎ 02-6682 2622; admission by donation; ❤ 10am-3pm) follows the Marquis de Ray's ambitious plan to colonise New Guinea (known as New Ireland) with 340 unwitting Italians. Many died on the journey and, because de Ray failed to discuss his plan with the original inhabitants of the island, more of the group died from headhunters, starvation and disease once they reached 'paradise'. After making their way to Sydney in 1888, the surviving members relocated to New Italy. Sadly none remain in the area, but the museum is a tribute to the migrants' strength and resilience. As for de Ray – unsurprisingly he was consigned to a lunatic asylum in France. Adjoining the museum is a coffee shop and licensed Italian restaurant.

tables inside and out, serving toasted sambos and good cooked breakfasts.

Evans Head is 10km east of the highway; turn off at Woodburn.

## BROADWATER NATIONAL PARK

Extending from north of Evans Head to Broadwater, this small coastal park (3750 hectares) protects a 7km stretch of beach backed by coastal heath. You can drive through the park on the roads between Evans Head and Broadwater. Camping is not allowed in the park.

## BALLINA

☎ 02 / pop 34,700

With Byron above and the idyllic fishing villages south of the Richmond River below, Ballina is planted somewhere between a commercial centre and a wannabe tourist lure. This is actually the town's saving grace as it has maintained a coastal ambience without tarting itself for the holiday bucks. For travellers it's a pleasant spot for a day or two to explore the waterways and the kilometres of esplanade. Urban sprawl is rearing its head in ready-made suburb developments on the outskirts, but you won't encounter the effects in town.

## Orientation & Information

The Pacific Hwy approaches from the west and turns into River St, the main drag.

**Ice Creamery Internet Café** ( ☎ 6687 5783; 178 River St; ⏰ 8.30am-9pm; per hr $6) Internet access.

**Visitors centre** ( ☎ 6686 3484; cnr Las Balsas Plaza & River St)

## Sights

Behind the visitors centre, the **Naval & Maritime Museum** ( ☎ 6681 1002; Regatta Ave; admission by donation; ⏰ 9am-4pm) has a remarkable collection of model ships, ranging from bottle-sized 17th-century trading vessels to replica aircraft carriers up to 2m in length. There's also the remains of a balsawood raft that drifted across the Pacific from Ecuador as part of the Las Balsas expedition in 1973.

White and sandy, **Shelly Beach** is patrolled, and glassy **Shaws Bay Lagoon** is popular with families.

Just north of Ballina, the **Thursday Plantation** ( ☎ 1800 029 000; Pacific Hwy; admission free; ⏰ 9am-5pm)

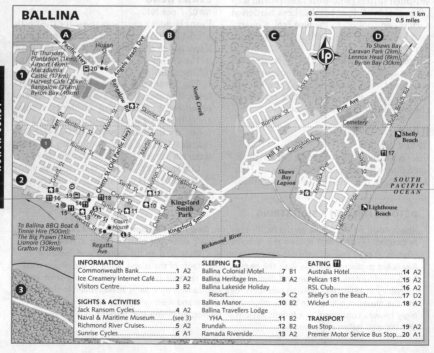

## BALLINA

0 _____ 1 km
0 _____ 0.5 miles

| INFORMATION | | |
|---|---|---|
| Commonwealth Bank | 1 | A2 |
| Ice Creamery Internet Café | 2 | A2 |
| Visitors Centre | 3 | B2 |

| SIGHTS & ACTIVITIES | | |
|---|---|---|
| Jack Ransom Cycles | 4 | A2 |
| Naval & Maritime Museum | (see 3) | |
| Richmond River Cruises | 5 | A2 |
| Sunrise Cycles | 6 | A1 |

| SLEEPING 🛏 | | |
|---|---|---|
| Ballina Colonial Motel | 7 | B1 |
| Ballina Heritage Inn | 8 | A2 |
| Ballina Lakeside Holiday Resort | 9 | C2 |
| Ballina Manor | 10 | B2 |
| Ballina Travellers Lodge YHA | 11 | B2 |
| Brundah | 12 | B2 |
| Ramada Riverside | 13 | A2 |

| EATING 🍴 | | |
|---|---|---|
| Australia Hotel | 14 | A2 |
| Pelican 181 | 15 | A2 |
| RSL Club | 16 | A2 |
| Shelly's on the Beach | 17 | D2 |
| Wicked | 18 | A2 |

| TRANSPORT | | |
|---|---|---|
| Bus Stop | 19 | A2 |
| Premier Motor Service Bus Stop | 20 | A1 |

has a teatree maze and specialises in high-quality therapeutic products. It is well worth a visit.

The **Big Prawn** (Pacific Hwy) is beached unceremoniously next to a transit centre at the town's southern entry. It's quite fabulous in its absurdity and exacts equal measures of fear and laughter. It could also be a pinup for a campaign about the dangers of nuclear power.

## Activities

Ballina is renowned for its great walking and bike tracks, so hiring a bike can be rewarding. **Sunrise Cycles** ( ☎ 6686 6322; Hogan St; per day $20) and **Jack Ransom Cycles** ( ☎ 6686 3485; 16 Cherry St; per day $17) both offer bike hire.

**Ballina BBQ Boat & Tinnie Hire** ( ☎ 0403 810 277; cnr Brunswick St & Winton Lane; per 30min/half-day $55/80) has tinnies for fishing and catamarans for the more adventurous.

**Richmond River Cruises** ( ☎ 6687 5688; www.ballina web.com/rrcruises; Regatta Ave; 2hr tour per adult/child $24/10; ⏰ 10am & 2pm Wed, 2pm Sun) has morning and afternoon tea cruises along the Richmond River on a double-decker vessel. It's also wheelchair-friendly.

## Tours

**Ballina Kayak Tours** ( ☎ 6685 3722; www.ballina kayaks.com; per person $55) Three-hour kayak adventures with the chance to spot bottlenose dolphins.
**Ballina Ocean Tours** ( ☎ 6680 7906; www.ballina oceantours.com; per person $75) Small-group whale-watching tours.
**Baysail** ( ☎ 1300 857 443, 6626 6889; www.baysail.net .au; per person $85) Whale-watching tours.
**Explorer Experience** ( ☎ 6681 4111; www.explorer experience.com.au; half-/full-day tours per person $85/160) Small-group hinterland tours in a 4WD coach.

## Sleeping

**Ballina Travellers Lodge YHA** ( ☎ 6686 6737; 36-38 Tamar St; www.yha.com.au; dm $22, d $55-65; 🅿 🗗 ) In a quiet residential street, this lodge has a super-tidy setup with airy motel rooms and an excellent hostel wing. All rooms are modern and spotless, and there are bikes and bodyboards available for hire.

**Ballina Lakeside Holiday Resort** ( ☎ 1800 888 268; 6686 8755; www.ballinalakeside.com.au; Fenwick Dr; camp sites/cabins from $27/70; 🗗 ) None-too-subtly disguised as a suburb, this park has roads, sparkling cabins and amenities, and a great location right on the lake. It *doesn't* have too much privacy and is teeming during holidays.

**Ballina Heritage Inn** ( ☎ 6686 0505; www.ballina heritageinn.com.au; 229 River St; s/d $100/120; 🗗 ) In the centre of town, this tidy inn has neat, bright and very comfortable rooms that are a significant leap in quality from the nearby confluence of motels. Ballina's best midrange option.

**Brundah** ( ☎ 6686 8166; www.babs.com.au/brun dah; 37 Norton St; s/d incl breakfast $135/185; 🗗 ) This comely white B&B has three gorgeous en-suite bedrooms with plush beds and handsome chests, chairs and furnishings. Brekkie is a fully cooked affair, and there's a pretty garden in which to contemplate your navel.

**Ballina Manor** ( ☎ 6681 5888; www.ballinamanor .com.au; 25 Norton St; r from $190; 🗗 ) Ballina's best is a heritage-listed building filled to the hilt with restored 1920s furnishings, carpets and drapes. It used to be a school for fine young ladies and the structure itself has been beautifully maintained. Though antique in design, the three types of rooms are indulgent and extremely comfortable.

Also available:
**Ballina Colonial Motel** ( ☎ 6685 7691; www.colonial motel.net; cnr Bangalow Rd & Skinner St; s/d $70/85; 🅿 🗗 ) Cheerful, charming and cheap.
**Ramada Riverside** ( ☎ 1800 006 362, 6681 9200; www.ramadariverside.com.au; Fawcett St; r/apt from $130/210; 🗗 🗗 ) Swish apartments with that as-new scent.

## Eating

**Shelly's on the Beach** ( ☎ 6686 9844; Shelly Beach Rd; mains $15; ⏰ breakfast & lunch) This casual little café dishes up sensational food and superb views. The bacon-and-egg-and-paper brigade fills the tables early on weekend mornings, but it's worth losing a sleep-in for. Lunch is salads, sambos and the usual café fare.

**Pelican 181** ( ☎ 6686 9181; 12-24 Fawcett St; mains $10-20; ⏰ breakfast & lunch) This sprawling upscale fish-and-chippery serves excellent seafood au natural. Make sure you check out the overflowing prawn baguettes beneath the counter before settling on any decision. Dining is largely alfresco with right-on-the-water views.

**Wicked** ( ☎ 6686 2564; 37 Cherry St; mains $24-30; ⏰ dinner Wed-Sun) Pulling all sorts of flavours out of the hat, Wicked focuses firmly on seafood and delivers it with international flair. Mozambique peri-peri seafood, Boston clam chowder and Thai fish cakes all get a go on the extensive menu.

You can also tuck into pub grub for around $15 at the architecturally fearsome **RSL Club**

( ☎ 6686 2544; cnr Grant & River St; ⊙ lunch & dinner) or the **Australia Hotel** ( ☎ 6686 2015; cnr Cherry & River Sts; ⊙ lunch & dinner).

## Getting There & Away

**Regional Express** (Rex; ☎ 13 17 13), **Virgin Blue** ( ☎ 13 67 89) and **Jetstar** ( ☎ 13 15 30) all fly to/from Sydney.

**Greyhound** ( ☎ 13 14 99) stops at the Big Prawn and **Premier Motor Service** ( ☎ 13 34 10) stops at Ampol Pied Pier. Both head to Brisbane ($40), Coffs Harbour ($45) and Sydney ($97).

**Blanch's Bus Service** ( ☎ 6686 2144) operates a service to Lennox Head, Mullumbimby, Byron Bay and Bangalow. All stop on Tamar St.

**CountryLink** ( ☎ 13 22 32) buses head to Evans Head, Lennox Head and Lismore (all $6). They also head to Casino ($7) for train connections.

If you're heading to Byron Bay, take the coast road through Lennox Head. It's much prettier than the highway and much shorter as well.

## AROUND BALLINA

Inland from Ballina, the closely settled country of the north coast hinterland begins, with winding, hilly roads running past tropical fruit farms, tiny villages and the occasional towering rainforest tree that has somehow escaped the wholesale clearing of the forest.

Macadamia-nut nuts may enjoy the café and gift store at the **Macadamia Castle** ( ☎ 6687 8432; Pacific Hwy; admission free; ⊙ 8.30am-5pm), 17km north of Ballina.

**Harvest Café** ( ☎ 6687 2644; 18 Old Pacific Hwy, Newrybar; mains $10-22; ⊙ breakfast & lunch Tue-Sun), 20km north of Ballina, is a must for gastronomes. In 2004 it won a national award for the 'Best Breakfast Restaurant in Australia'. Them's spectacular eggs. For lunch you can tuck into Thai barramundi fish cakes with salsa or plum sweet-chilli pan-seared prawns.

## LENNOX HEAD

☎ 02 / pop 4000

Flanked by picturesque coastline on either side, Lennox Head is a low-key, laid-back haunt of locals and surfers. Among the latter it's a must-stop destination due to a peeling right-hander off the point, and wetsuits sometimes outnumber the shorts-and-shirt brigade. **Lake Ainsworth** is a freshwater lake that is conducive to pleasant swimming and windsurfing. Swimming there can be some-

what beneficial to the skin as the dark colour is a result of teatree oil. If the wind's up, wind- or kite-surfing is the ticket, and **Wind & Water Action Sports** ( ☎ 6686 9555; www.windnwater .net; sailboard longboard per hr from $20; 1hr windsurfing lesson $70; 3hr kite surfing lesson $180) has a good line of equipment.

If you plan to stay awhile, it is worth getting in contact with the **Professionals** ( ☎ 6687 7579; www.professionals.com.au/lennoxhead; 66 Ballina St) for holiday apartments.

The YHA-affiliated **Lennox Head Beach House** ( ☎ 6687 7636; www.yha.com.au; 3 Ross St; dm/d $28/70) has immaculate rooms and a great vibe. For $5 you can use the surfboards, sailboards and bikes.

Clean and affordable **Lake Ainsworth Caravan Park** ( ☎ 6687 7249; www.bscp.com.au/lakeains; Pacific Pde; unpowered/powered camp sites $25/30 cabins without/with bathroom from $78/95) is set on a compact stretch of flat, green grass right across the road from the beach.

At the other end of the scale, **Lennox Point Holiday Apartments** ( ☎ 6687 5900; www.lennoxholiday apartments.com; Pacific Pde; apt $220; ✖ ⊛ ) are slick, stylish and new. Plus they're opposite the beach and close to the Lennox Point Hotel.

The **Red Rock Café** ( ☎ 6687 4744; 3/60 Ballina St; mains $10; ⊙ breakfast & lunch; ⬛ ) is nondescript from the outside but whips up a mean burger with homemade relish, as well as Vietnamese beef salads. For more good café food and chunky cakes try **Café de Mer** ( ☎ 6687 7132; Ballina St; mains $7-12; ⊙ breakfast & lunch).

**Ruby's by the Sea** ( ☎ 6687 5769; 17-19 Pacific Pde; bistro mains $18, restaurant mains $25; ⊙ lunch & dinner daily) has two wings within the Lennox Point Hotel. The bistro cooks up plenty of fresh seafood including barbecued tiger prawn Caesar salad, and the finer balcony restaurant upstairs serves char-grilled cuttlefish with saffron and aioli or Peking duck crepes.

**Premier Motor Service** ( ☎ 13 34 10) stops here on request; pick-up is from the CountryLink coach stop. **Blanch's Bus Service** ( ☎ 6686 2144) has services to Ballina, Byron Bay and Mullumbimby on a Freedom pass ($12 per day).

## BYRON BAY

☎ 02 / pop 9000

The high green moguls of the Northern Rivers hinterland meet the coast in spectacular fashion at the region's most celebrated haunt. Byron's beauty precedes it and then deftly exceeds expectations. But it's the town's escapism that has become the honey to roving bees. Deflated swarms of them bumble in to get drunk on the trademark New Age, laid-back, organic fusion lifestyle. They stay for a weekend, a week or for good (often in that order) to tune in, tune out, tone up and tan up. During the off season the mix is an ambling milieu, but come summer and school holidays it positively seethes.

## Information

**Accommodation booking office** ( ☎ 6680 8666; www.byronbayaccom.net) Run by the visitors centre.
**Backpackers World** ( ☎ 6685 8858; www.backpackers world.com.au; Shop 6, 75 Jonson St) Info and tours for budget travellers.
**Byron Books** ( ☎ 6680 9717; 3/1 Marvell St) Byron's best bookshop.
**Byron Bus & Backpacker Centre** ( ☎ 6685 5517; 84 Jonson St) For the lowdown on transport, accommodation and activities.
**Global Gossip** ( ☎ 6680 9140; 84 Jonson St; per hr $6) Internet access.
**Star Internet** ( ☎ 6680 8199; Ste 1, 9 Fletcher St; ⏱ 9am-9pm; per hr $5) Internet access.
**Visitors centre** ( ☎ 6680 9271; 80 Jonson St) A wealth of information.

## Sights

### CAPE BYRON

George Gordon (Lord) Byron may have incessantly raved about walking in beauty like the night, but his grandfather did a little travel of his own, sailing around the world in the 1760s – Captain Cook named this headland after him. The views from the summit are spectacular, particularly if you've just burnt breakfast off on the climbing track from Clarke's Beach. Ribboning around the headland, it dips and (mostly) soars its way to the lighthouse. The surrounding ocean also jumps to the tune of dolphins and migrating humpback whales in June and July. Towering over all is the 1901 **lighthouse** ( ☎ 6685 6585; Lighthouse Rd; ⏱ 8am-sunset), Australia's most easterly and most powerful lighthouse. The walking track descends around the northeast side of the Cape, delving into **Cape Byron State Conservation Park**, where you'll stumble across bush turkeys and wallabies. En route, photo-hungry walkers can work the lens at **Captain Cook Lookout**. The track winds up at Lighthouse Rd and is a 4km round trip. You can also drive right up to the lighthouse and pay $6 for the privilege of parking (or nothing at all if you park 300m below).

## BEACHES

**Main Beach**, right in front of the thick of town, is the most popular spot for swimming and beautiful-people-watching. At its eastern end is **Clarks Beach**, good for small, peeling waves when the swell's right. For the famous breaks, keep walking to the **Pass**, which leads onto the **Watego's** and **Little Watego's Beaches**. Dolphin sightings are common at these spots. To the west of Main Beach, clothing is optional at quieter **Belongil Beach**.

South of **Cape Byron** are the hallowed sands of **Tallow Beach**, which stretch 7km down to a rockier section around **Broken Head** (named appropriately). Your next decent line of sand is **Seven Mile Beach**, running down to Lennox Head.

## Activities

**Kidz Klub** ( ☎ 0429 770 147; www.kidzklub.com.au) offers excellent adventure tours, workshops, yabbying, bushwalking and school holiday programmes for kids aged four and up, plus baby-sitting for all little tackers. Rates are variable.

Once upon a time you wanted to run away and join the circus. Then you figured it was easier to just run away. But as luck would have it, you can still show mum and dad that you were serious by taking trapeze classes or circus skills workshops with **Circus Arts** ( ☎ 6685 6566; www.circusarts.com.au; 17 Centennial Circuit), located in Byron's Arts and Industry Estate, 2km west of town.

### ALTERNATIVE THERAPIES

Byron is alternative therapy heartland. The *Body & Soul* guide, available from the visitors centre, is a handy guide to the host of therapies on offer.
**Ambaji** ( ☎ 6685 6620; www.ambaji.com.au; 6 Marvell St; prices from $65; ⏱ 10am-4pm Mon-Sat, 11am-3pm Sun) Craniosacral balancing, aqua balance healing and more.
**Byron Ayurveda Centre** ( ☎ 6632 2244; www.ayur vedahouse.com.au; Shop 6 Middleton St; prices from $45; ⏱ 9am-6pm Mon-Sat) Indian medicinal therapies.
**Buddha Gardens** ( ☎ 6680 7844; www.buddha gardens.com; 21 Gordon St, Arts Factory Village; prices from $80; ⏱ 10am-6pm) Balinese-style day spa.
**Relax Haven** ( ☎ 6685 8304; Belongil Beachouse, Childe St; prices from $60; ⏱ 10am-8pm) Float tanks.
**Shambala** ( ☎ 6680 7791; www.shambala.net.au; 4 Carlyle St, prices from $35; ⏱ 9am-7pm) Massage, reflexology, acupuncture and more.

# BYRON BAY

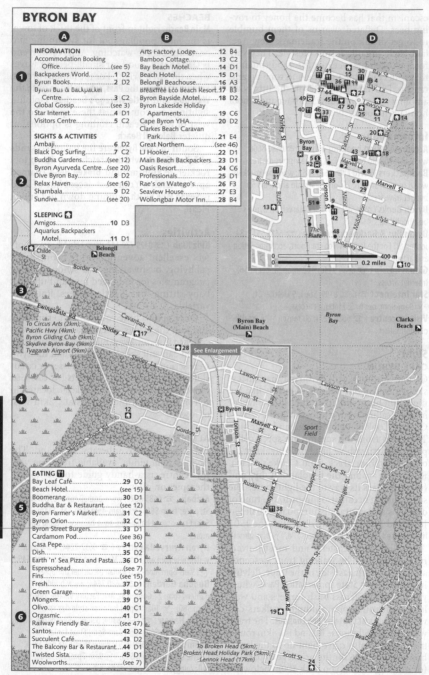

**A**

**INFORMATION**
Accommodation Booking
Office.....................................(see 5)
Backpackers World............**1** D2
Byron Books......................**2** D2
Byron Bus & Backpacker
Centre.............................**3** C2
Global Gossip................(see 3)
Star Internet.....................**4** D1
Visitors Centre.................**5** C2

**SIGHTS & ACTIVITIES**
Ambaji..............................**6** D2
Black Dog Surfing............**7** C2
Buddha Gardens..........(see 12)
Byron Ayurveda Centre..(see 20)
Dive Byron Bay................**8** D2
Relax Haven..................(see 16)
Shambala..........................**9** D2
Sundive.........................(see 20)

**SLEEPING**
Amigos.............................**10** D3
Aquarius Backpackers
Motel.............................**11** D1

**B**

Arts Factory Lodge............**12** B4
Bamboo Cottage.............**13** C2
Bay Beach Motel..............**14** D1
Beach Hotel......................**15** D1
Belongil Beachouse.........**16** A3
Breakfree Eco Beach Resort..**17** B3
Byron Bayside Motel.........**18** D2
Byron Lakeside Holiday
Apartments..................**19** C6
Cape Byron YHA..............**20** D2
Clarkes Beach Caravan
Park.............................**21** E4
Great Northern..............(see 46)
LJ Hooker.........................**22** D1
Main Beach Backpackers...**23** D1
Oasis Resort.....................**24** C6
Professionals....................**25** D1
Rae's on Watego's...........**26** F3
Seaview House.................**27** E3
Wollongbar Motor Inn......**28** B4

**EATING**
Bay Leaf Café.....................**29** D2
Beach Hotel....................(see 15)
Boomerang.......................**30** D1
Buddha Bar & Restaurant...(see 12)
Byron Farmer's Market.....**31** C2
Byron Orion.....................**32** C1
Byron Street Burgers........**33** D1
Cardamom Pod..............(see 36)
Casa Pepe........................**34** D2
Dish..................................**35** D2
Earth 'n' Sea Pizza and Pasta..**36** D1
Espressohead..................(see 7)
Fins..................................(see 15)
Fresh................................**37** D1
Green Garage....................**38** C5
Mongers...........................**39** D1
Olivo.................................**40** C1
Orgasmic..........................**41** D1
Railway Friendly Bar........(see 47)
Santos..............................**42** D2
Succulent Café..................**43** D2
The Balcony Bar & Restaurant..**44** D1
Twisted Sista....................**45** D1
Woolworths.....................(see 7)

**C**

Byron Bay
(Main) Beach

Byron Bay

**D**

Byron
Bay

Clarks
Beach

See Enlargement

0          400 m
0          0.2 miles

NORTH COAST

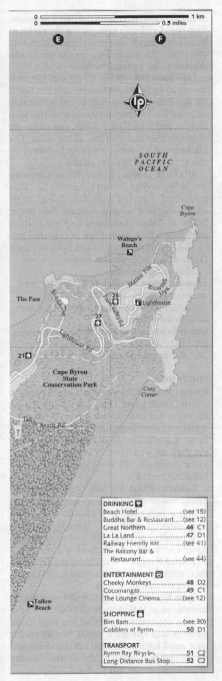

## DIVING & SNORKELLING

A number of dive outfits in Bryon Bay take advantage of the town's close proximity to the **Julian Rocks Marine Reserve**. About 3km offshore, this reserve has been rated one of Australia's top 10 dive sites, with more than 600 species of fish plus whales, dolphins and turtles.

Outfits with good reputations:

**Dive Byron Bay** ( ☎ 1800 243 483, 6685 8333; www .byronbaydivecentre.com.au; 9 Marvell St; PADI courses from $350, snorkelling $50)

**Sundive** ( ☎ 1800 008 755; www.sundive.com.au; Middleton St; PADI courses from $350; snorkelling $45)

## FLYING

**Byron Airwaves** ( ☎ 6629 0354; www.byronair.cjb .net) Tandem hang-gliding ($110) and courses (from $1050).

**Byron Bay Gliding** ( ☎ 6684 7572; www.byronbay gliding.com; Tyagarah Airport) Glider joy flights over the coast and hinterland from $90 for 20 minutes.

**Byron Gliding Club** ( ☎ 6684 7627; www.byrongliding .com; Tyagarah Airport) Glider joy rides from $80 plus lessons.

**Skydive Byron Bay** ( ☎ 6684 1323; www.skydivebyron bay.com; Tyagarah Airport) Tandem dives ($275) and Australia's highest dive at 14,000 feet ($390).

## KAYAKING

A couple of companies offer great half-day kayaking tours for $60 per person, in and around Cape Byron Marine Park. Exhibitionist dolphins are the main attraction, and the tours provide commentary and much-needed Tim Tams and coffee.

**Cape Byron Kayaks** ( ☎ 6685 4161)

**Dolphin Kayaking** ( ☎ 6685 8044; www.dolphinkayak ing.com.au)

## SURFING

**Blackdog Surfing** ( ☎ 6680 9828; www.blackdogsurf ing.com; Shop 8, The Plaza, Jonson St; 3hr lesson $60; 3-day $135) Small group lessons and a special course for women.

**Mojosurf Adventures** ( ☎ 1800 113 044; www .mojosurf.com.au; half-day lessons per person $65) Highly recommended. There's also five-day surf trips (per person $635) which include accommodation and meals.

**Samudra** ( ☎ 6685 5600; www.samudra.com.au) All-inclusive surf-and-yoga from $630 per two days per person. A reader fave.

**Surfaris** ( ☎ 1800 634 951; www.surfaris.com; Sydney-Byron Bay return trip $549) More five-day surf trips including camping and meals.

## Tours

The following offer small-group tours into the North Coast hinterland:

**Byron Bay Eco Tours** ( ☎ 6685 4030; www.byron-bay .com/ecotours; per person $85) Small-group 4WD tours with excellent commentary.

**Jim's Alternative Tours** ( ☎ 6685 7720; www.jims alternativetours.com; per person $35) Entertaining tours (with soundtrack!) to Nimbin.

**Mountain Bike Tours** ( ☎ 1800 122 504, 0429 122 504; www.mountainbiketours.com.au; per person $100) Environmentally friendly bike tours.

## Festivals & Events

**East Coast International Blues & Roots Music Festival** ( ☎ 6685 8310; www.bluesfest.com.au) Held over Easter, this international jam attracts high-calibre performers such as Michael Franti and Beth Orton. Local heavyweights also get in on the act. Book early.

**Splendour in the Grass** (www.splendourinthegrass .com) Held in July, this indie music festival gives punters a good run for their money, with funk, electronica, folk, rock, hip-hop and a host of other genres. Book early.

**Byron Bay Writers Festival** ( ☎ 6685 5115; www .byronbaywritersfestival.com.au) In July/August, this three-day event features workshops, writer forums and kids events. Top-shelf Australian writers attend.

## Sleeping

It's essential to book accommodation during school holidays and summer. Useful contacts for holiday house rentals:

**Byron Bay Accommodation** (www.byron-bay.com /accommodation)

**LJ Hooker** ( ☎ 6685 7300; www.ljhooker.com; 4/31 Lawson St)

**Professionals** ( ☎ 6685 6552; www.byronbaypro.com .au; cnr Lawson & Fletcher Sts)

### BUDGET

**Main Beach Backpackers** ( ☎ 1800 150 233, 6685 8695; fax 6685 8609; cnr Lawson & Fletcher Sts; dm $25, d $55-60; ☐ ) Size does matter. This small, personable hostel makes guests feel like more than a number with friendly staff, a sunny lounge, and dorms and doubles reminiscent of comfy bedrooms.

**Belongil Beachouse** ( ☎ 6685 7868; www.belongil beachouse.com; 25 Childe St; dm/d from $25/65; ☐ ) Tucked into a green pocket, this beachy warren has excellent self-contained cabins, clinically modern studio units and comfortable dorms. Pick of the bunch are the cosy, self-contained doubles.

**Great Northern** ( ☎ 6685 6454; Jonson St; s/d $55/65) Though spartan, the rooms here enjoy an overspill of character from the pub downstairs. You could end up a groupie for the night, as headlining bands also crash here. Either way you won't get much sleep on the weekends. All rooms have shared bathrooms.

**Cape Byron YHA** ( ☎ 1800 652 627; 6685 8788; www .yha.com.au; cnr Byron & Middleton Sts; dm/d from $26/70; ☐ ☒ ) This purpose-built hostel is one tidy ship and has five-bed, uncramped dorms with lockers and fans. The doubles and twins are also spacious and one has an en suite. The kitchen and TV room are snug, but there's a sunny courtyard to compensate.

**Arts Factory Lodge** ( ☎ 6685 7709; www.artsfactory .com.au; Skinners Shoot Rd; dm/d from $30/85; ☐ ) This celebrated complex embodies Byron at its alternative best. Guests nurture their inner hippy at didgeridoo, yoga and meditation workshops, then bunk down in colourful six- to 12-bed dorms. Couples can opt for 'cubes' (aptly titled) or pricier en suites.

Also recommended:

**Aquarius Backpackers Motel** ( ☎ 6685 7663; www .aquarius-backpackers.com.au; 16 Lawson St; dm/d $30/75; ☐ ☒ ) An urban castle with a myriad of dorms, doubles and motel rooms.

**Clarkes Beach Caravan Park** ( ☎ 6685 6496; clarkes@ bshp.com.au; off Lighthouse Rd; camp sites/cabins from $25/120) Tightly packed cabins and sites in a bush setting.

### MIDRANGE

**Amigos** ( ☎ 6680 8622; www.amigosbb.com; 32 Kingsley St; s/d from $80/100) Soaked in south-of-the-border flavours, this cute B&B has three bedrooms with crisp white linen and multicoloured Bolivian spreads. There's also a gorgeous cottage out the back with hammocks swinging nearby in the garden. An all-you-can-eat continental breakfast costs $5.

**Bamboo Cottage** ( ☎ 6685 5509; www.byron-bay .com/bamboocottage; 76 Butler St; s/d from $90/118) Featuring a lion's share of charm and global wall hangings, Bamboo Cottage treats guests to a handful of enigmatic rooms heavy on Asian overtones. Out the back is a semi-self-contained bungalow resembling the Taj's boudoir, complete with an elevated futon tucked behind romantic curtains.

**Byron Bayside Motel** ( ☎ 6685 6004; www.byronbay sidemotel.com.au; 14 Middleton St; s/d $110/115) So the interior aesthetics won't bowl you over (floral patterns and raw-brick walls), but all rooms have small kitchenettes and full laundries, and for the central location it's a steal. The cleaning detail could win an international competition.

## MARKETS OF THE HINTERLAND

### Weekly Markets

- **Bangalow Farmer's Market** (Byron St; 8-11am Sat)
- **Byron Farmer's Market** (Butler St; 8-11am Thu & Sat)
- **Lismore Farmer's Market** (Lismore Showground; 8am-noon Sat)
- **Rainbow Region Organic Markets** (Lismore Showground; 8-11am Tue)

### 1st Weekend of the Month

- **Brunswick Heads** (Memorial Park; Sat)
- **Lismore Car Boot Market** (Lismore Shopping Centre; Sun)

### 2nd Weekend of the Month

- **Alstonville Market** (Alstonville Showground; Sun)
- **Channon Craft Market** (Coronation Park; Sun)
- **Lennox Head Lakeside Market** (Lake Ainsworth Foreshore; Sun)

### 3rd Weekend of the Month

- **Aquarius Fair Markets** (Nimbin Community Centre; Sun)
- **Ballina Markets** (Circus Ground; Sun)
- **Lismore Car Boot Market** (Lismore Shopping Centre; Sun)
- **Mullumbimby Museum Market** (Stuart St; Sat)
- **Uki Produce & Craft Market** (Uki Village Buttery; Sat)

### 4th Weekend of the Month

- **Bangalow Village Market** (Bangalow Showground; Sun)
- **Evans Head Riverside Market** (Recreation Reserve; Sat)

### 5th Weekend of the Month

- **Aquarius Fair Markets** (Nimbin Community Centre; Sun)
- **Lennox Head Lakeside Market** (Lake Ainsworth Foreshore; Sun)

**Bay Beach Motel** ( 6685 6090; www.baybeach motel.com.au; 32 Lawson St; r $165-185; ) Finally someone has realised that 'motel' and 'dowdy' needn't be joined at the proverbial hip. The standard motor inn rooms here have been transformed into sharp and sassy bedrooms with suede furniture, Asian-influenced bedspreads and contemporary bathrooms.

**Oasis Resort** ( 1800 336 129, 6685 7390; www .byronbayoasisresort.com.au; 24 Scott St; ste from $195; ) This compact resort is engulfed by palms and has sizable one- and two-bedroom apartments with big balconies, or smart

'Tree Top Houses' (from $305). All accommodation is spotless and kitted out in cheery décor.

More midrangers:

**Breakfree Eco Beach Resort** ( 6639 5700; www .ecobeachbyron.com.au; 35-37 Shirley Street; r from $165; ) Fresh and funky.

**Byron Lakeside Holiday Apartments** ( 6680 9244; www.byronlakeside.com; 5 Old Bangalow Rd; r per 3-night stay from $450; ) Suburb-style holiday village with superb apartments.

**Wollongbar Motor Inn** ( 6685 8200; 19-21 Shirley St; r $95-140; ) A fine motel with spotless rooms. Good disabled rooms too.

NORTH COAST

## TOP END

**Beach Hotel** ( ☎ 6685 6402; www.beachhotel.com.au; Bay St; r incl breakfast from $250; 🅿 🈯 ) This classy beachfront joint has 'Garden View Rooms' doused in forest greens and polished wood, with marble bathrooms, Thai silk cushions and gourmet cookies (it's the little touches…). Top of the food chain are the Ocean View Loft Rooms and the East Coast Suite.

More Top Enders:

**Rae's on Watego's** ( ☎ 6685 5366; www.raes.com.au; 8 Marine Pde, Watego's Beach; ste $570-730; 🅿 🈯 ) Superlative boutique hotel.

**Seaview House** ( ☎ 6685 6486; www.seaviewbyron .com; 146 Lighthouse Rd; d $250; 🅿 ) Cushy B&B with Byron's best views.

## Eating
### CAFÉS

Most of Byron's cafés close at 5pm.

**Twisted Sista** ( ☎ 6680 9100; Shop 1/4 Lawson St; mains $8-15; 🕙 breakfast & lunch) Gluttonous goodies such as oversized quiches, frittatas and salads tumble over each other in a mass of fresh and fabulous ingredients at this warm café. The sweets are too big for solo efforts.

**Succulent Cafe** ( ☎ 6680 7121; Marvell Lane; mains $8-16; 🕙 breakfast & lunch) And succulent the steak sandwiches, grilled mahi mahi salads and chilli prawn linguini are! This narrow café packs plenty of flavour and ingredients into a fresh menu. Mosaic-tiled tables and great coffee.

**Bay Leaf Cafe** ( ☎ 6685 8900; Marvell St; mains $10-18; 🕙 breakfast & lunch) This bohemian café has a small but excellent menu that makes a task out of choosing. Soups, pastas and Turkish bread sambos change daily, but expect the likes of chorizo and aioli linguini. Seats are perched at elevated, open windows.

**Byron Orion** ( ☎ 6685 6828; 5/2 Jonson St; mains $14-20; 🕙 breakfast, lunch & dinner) Orion's open-door policy stops passers-by in their tracks. It could be the delicious red vinyl walls and supper cocktails, but we're pretty sure it's the hot and spicy scents courtesy of Gujarati beef, rogan josh and vindaloo. Breakfast is decidedly Australian free-range eggs.

**Casa Pepe** ( ☎ 6685 7121; Shop 4, 14 Middleton St; lunch mains $8-15, dinner mains $18-26; 🕙 lunch daily, dinner Sat & Sun) Hidden in a nondescript block of shops, this vegetarian restaurant is worthy of all dietary persuasions. Happy patrons sit in the sheltered courtyard and tuck into pizzas, pies, soups and tofu burgers for lunch and smart pastas and pizzas for dinner.

Also recommended:

**Espressohead** ( ☎ 6680 9783; Shop 13/108, Woolworths Plaza, Jonson St; mains $10; 🕙 breakfast & lunch) Fabulous coffee.

**Mongers** ( ☎ 6600 0000, 1 Day Lane, meals $9-13, 🕙 lunch & dinner) Nifty café with delicious seafood and hand-cut chips.

### RESTAURANTS

**Balcony Bar & Restaurant** ( ☎ 6680 9666; cnr Lawson & Johnson Sts; mains $20-30; 🕙 breakfast, lunch & dinner) Take up a voyeuristic seat overlooking the street action below, or embed yourself in an obese cushion. The Balcony dishes up Ottoman overtones and fabulous fare like a curry-rubbed BLAT (bacon, lettuce, avocado and tomato ciabatta) for breakfast, fresh fish with crushed Jerusalem artichokes and citrus butter for lunch, and midnight tapas to soak up the cocktails. The soundtrack is suitably somnific and the atmosphere cosy and chic. This place could teach any inner-city venue a thing or two about style.

**Fresh** ( ☎ 6685 7810; 7 Jonson St; mains $20-27; 🕙 breakfast, lunch & dinner) Serving up Mediterranean salads, spicy nasi goreng and Sumatran lamb, Fresh is an adaptable eatery and a favourite stomping ground for locals. Diners sip coffee outside in the morning sun and chatter over candlelight at night.

**Dish** ( ☎ 6685 7320; cnr Jonson & Marvell Sts; mains $27-35; 🕙 dinner) Ivy-clad walls and floor-to-ceiling glass create an atrium atmosphere at this dishy restaurant. The equally sophisticated cuisine includes Bangalow pork scotch fillet with roasted pistachio, chorizo and apple purée. The wine list is worthy of applause.

**Fins** ( ☎ 6685 5029; The Beach Hotel; mains $35; 🕙 dinner) Tucked behind the boisterous Beach Hotel pub, this elegant sibling serves fish tagines, Mauritian seafood sambals and tiger abalone. The marine mains are touted as the best on the coast, and celeb chefs pop in to prepare degustation nights.

More fine dining:

**Boomerang** ( ☎ 6685 5264; Shop 5, 2 Fletcher St; mains $40-60; 🕙 lunch Sunday, dinner daily) An inspired menu and wine list.

**Olivo** ( ☎ 6685 7950; 34 Jonson St; mains $20-30; 🕙 dinner) Chic and snug with global flavours from Europe.

The **Beach Hotel** (left) and the **Railway Friendly Bar** (opposite) serve great pub meals for $10 to $20 and you can also tuck into organic dinners for $15 to $20 before no-nonsense beers at the **Buddha Bar & Restaurant** (right)

### QUICK EATS
**Orgasmic** ( ☎ 6680 7778; 11 Bay Lane; mains $5-10; ✤ lunch & dinner) Proving unequivocally that it's not the size of the wave but the motion of the spatula, even the 'half pockets' at this cosy hole-in-the-wall eatery satisfy voracious patrons. Alternative climaxes include kofta, schnitzels and sublime Middle Eastern dips.

**Cardamom Pod** (Shop 8, Pier Arcade, 7 Lawson St; meals $7-14; ✤ lunch & dinner) Fusing flavours from the subcontinent with an Aussie twist, this teeny gem serves excellent salads, curries and samosas at a handful of tables. The whole menu is vegetarian and you can vacuum your tofu and pumpkin salad here or get it to go.

More quick fixes:

**Byron Street Burgers** ( ☎ 6685 5234; Shop 8 Byron St; mains $8-11; ✤ lunch & dinner) Organic veggie and meat burgers.

**Earth 'n' Sea Pizza & Pasta** ( ☎ 6685 6029; 11 Lawson St; mains $15-25; ✤ lunch & dinner) Mind-blowing pizzas.

### SELF-CATERING
Options for the DIY chef:

**Byron Farmers Market** ( ☎ 6685 9792; Butler St; ✤ 8-11am Thu & Sat) Great for picking up delicious local produce.

**Green Garage** ( ☎ 6680 8577; 68 Tennyson St; ✤ 7am-7pm) Organic goodies.

**Santos** ( ☎ 6685 7071; 105 Jonson St) Organic grocer.

**Woolworths** ( ☎ 6685 7292; Jonson St; ✤ 8am-9pm)

## Drinking
**Beach Hotel** ( ☎ 6685 6402; cnr Bay & Jonson Sts) When this mother ship of pubs is full, it seems the whole of Byron and beyond has stopped in for a drink. Buzzing folk settle at alfresco tables with smacking beach views, or in the stadium-sized interior. Big, festive and fun.

**Railway Friendly Bar** ( ☎ 6685 7662; 80 Jonson St) This indoor-outdoor pub has a cosy interior and a front beer garden conducive to boozy afternoons. You're likely to spark up new friendships over an upturned keg, and there's live music most nights.

**Great Northern** ( ☎ 6685 6454; Byron St) You won't need your fancy duds at this brash and boisterous pub. It's loud and beery most nights and even louder when hosting headline acts. Touring bands pop in most weekends and local musos fill the midweek gaps.

**Buddha Bar & Restaurant** ( ☎ 6685 5033; Skinners Shoot Rd) Once fed, the young and funky mingle on leather lounges beneath wickedly low lighting in Byron's sultriest drinking hole. The global soundtrack traipses from hip-hop to Latino, with jazz and electronic pitstops along the way. DJs and acoustic sets also get a go.

More drinking venues:

**Balcony Bar & Restaurant** (opposite) Smooth and chic.

**La La Land** ( ☎ 6680 7070; 6 Lawson St) Soft couches, sinful lighting, slinky young things.

## Entertainment
**Cheeky Monkeys** ( ☎ 6685 5886; 115 Jonson St) A backpackers' bonanza – cheap food, cheap drinks and cheesy tunes. Expect (dodgy) tabletop dancing, instant friends, long nights and easy, sleazy fun.

**Cocomangas** ( ☎ 6685 8493; 32 Jonson St) Sure, it's a little lacking in sophistication and style, but so are most of the patrons jumping to their heart's content on the dance floor. It's the stomping ground of twenty-somethings thrashing to indie rock, old school, techno and fusion.

**Lounge Cinema** ( ☎ 6680 9055; Skinners Shoot Rd; admission $10) The Arts Factory's cinema screens Hollywood fodder as well as art-house flicks and classic reruns.

## Shopping
**Bim bam** ( ☎ 6680 8813; Shop 3, 2 Fletcher St) This small gallery sells quality indigenous art and craft, some affordable for most wallets and some for the serious collector.

**Cobblers at Byron** ( ☎ 6685 6190; Shop 5, Feros Arcade) Hopeless shoe and leather addicts will struggle to keep their mitts off the fabulous boots, sandals, shoes, bags and wallets at this cobbler's.

## Getting There & Away
### AIR
The closest airport is at Ballina (see p186), but you're likely to get a cheaper flight into Coolangatta airport on the Gold Coast.

### BUS
Long-distance buses stop on Jonson St. **Greyhound** ( ☎ 13 14 99) and **Premier Motor Service** ( ☎ 13 34 10) have daily services to Brisbane ($40), Coffs Harbour ($55) and Sydney ($105).

**Kirklands** ( ☎ 6626 1499) has buses to Lismore and Coolangatta airports. **CountryLink** ( ☎ 13 22 32) has buses to Casino for train connections.

NORTH COAST

**Blanch's Bus Service** ( ☎ 6686 2144; www.tropicalnsw
.com.au/blanchs) runs daily to Ballina, Lennox
Head and Mullumbimby for less than $10.
Shuttle services:
**Airlink Byron Bay Airbus** ( ☎ 6684 3232; www.air
linkhyronbay com au) Coolangatta Airport ($35), Lismore
Airport ($40) and Ballina Airport ($15).
**Byron Bay Transport Services** ( ☎ 6685 5008;
www.byronbaytaxis.com) Ballina Airport (from $15) and
Coolangatta ($36).

## Getting Around
**Byron Bay Bicycles** ( ☎ 6685 6067; Woolworths Plaza,
Jonson St) Hires mountain bikes for $28 per day.
**Byron Bay Taxis** ( ☎ 6685 5008) On call 24 hours.

# BRUNSWICK HEADS
☎ 02 / pop 1860
Fresh oysters and mud crabs call the Brunswick River home, as do retirees and families
who love the good beaches and fishing.

**Chalet Motel** ( ☎ 6685 1257; www.brunswickvalley
.com.au/chaletmotel; 68 Tweed St; r from $85; ❄ ☒ ☲ ) is
the pick of the motels in town, with a towering
garden and cute and colourful rooms.

Alternatively, **Brunswick Sails Motor Inn**
( ☎ 6685 1353; 26-28 Tweed St; r $65-115; ❄ ☲ ) flags
you down with a garish blue exterior and
generically comfy rooms.

The **Terrace Reserve Caravan Park** ( ☎ 1300 762
072, 6685 1233; terrace@bshp.com.au; unpowered/powered
sites from $21/24, cabins $85-170), on the banks of
Simpson Creek, has plenty of sites and snazzy
cabins.

The splendid **Hotel Brunswick** ( ☎ 6685 1236;
www.hotelbrunswick.com.au; Mullumbimby St; s/d $40/70)
has decent pub rooms, an ecofriendly bent
and a magnificent beer garden that unfurls
beneath flourishing poincianas. The Bruns
serves great nosh (mains $15-20; open lunch
and dinner), there's live music on the weekends, and every Wednesday night you can
watch a movie.

**Yami** ( ☎ 6685 0186; 1 Park St; mains $8-14; ❄ breakfast
& lunch daily, dinner Fri-Sun) is yummy. It's a decadent little spot with couches inside, tables in
the sun and a tangy Middle Eastern menu.

**Kirklands** ( ☎ 6626 1499) has buses to Byron
Bay, Lennox Head and Lismore. **CountryLink**
( ☎ 13 22 32) has buses to Byron Bay and Tweed
Heads.

# THE TWEED COAST
As the coastline bleeds into Queensland's
(Qld) southern border, the development be-

gins to assert itself more distinctly. Concrete
and mortar stake their claim on the beach with
all the subtlety of a used-car salesman. But the
territory remains less tarnished than the glitz
of the Gold Coast, and surf culture still simmers within the cream brick ghettos.

# TWEED HEADS
☎ 07 / pop 55,860
Tweed Heads is in the grip of an urban-testos-
terone epidemic. High-rise apartment blocks
are shooting up quicker than you can say
Viagra, and bamboozled retirees and tourists
potter past gaping construction sites where
the milk bar used to be. But the beaches remain the area's best feature. The state border
is an invisible line, and Coolangatta (Qld) and
Tweed Heads (NSW) bleed into one.

## Orientation & Information
Coming from the south, after the bypass road
branches off, the old Pacific Hwy crosses the
river at Boyds Bay Bridge and becomes Wharf
St, the long main street. You then meet Boundary St, which will veer to the right to take you
up to **Point Danger** for sweeping views.

The **visitors centre** ( ☎ 1800 674 414; www.tweed
coolangatta.com.au; Centro Tweed Mall, Wharf St; ❄ 9am-
5pm Mon-Sat) is a small but helpful booth in the
middle of the shopping mall.

## Sights & Activities
There are sweeping views back down the
Tweed Coast and up to the glittering high-
rises of the Gold Coast from the **Mt Toonbara-
bah Lookout** (Mt Razorback). But beaches are
what you come up here for – **Kirra Point** is a
big favourite with surfers. Further round, **Kirra
Beach** is patrolled year-round.

The small **Minjungbal Aboriginal Cultural Centre**
( ☎ 5524 2109; cnr Kirkwood & Duffy Sts; adult/child $15/8;
❄ 9am-4pm Mon-Fri) provides an interesting insight into the traditional owners of the land,
the Minjungbal people. Exhibits demonstrate
their traditional lifestyle, the influence of Pacific Islander (Kanak) refugees, and the landscape prior to European arrival.

The **Tweed Maritime Museum** ( ☎ 5536 8625;
Kennedy Dr; adult/child $4/50c; ❄ 11am-4pm Tue, Thu &
Fri, 1-4pm Sun) has an interesting array of things,
with Boyd's fishing shed well worth a look.

**Tweed River Catch-a-Crab** ( ☎ 5599 9972; www
.catchacrab.com.au; Dry Dock Wharf; tours incl lunch & fishing
per adult/child $90/54) operates very fun crab-catch-
ing-and-eating tours. For fishing charters try

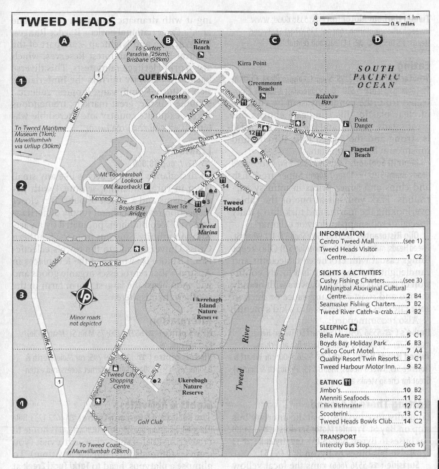

**TWEED HEADS**

**Seamaster Fishing Charters** ( ☎ 0415 593 901) or **Cushy Fishing Charters** ( ☎ 0418 631 076), both based at Tweed Marina on River Tce. Rates vary depending on duration of charter.

## Sleeping

Some of the best accommodation is on the NSW side of the invisible state line.

**Calico Court Motel** ( ☎ 5524 3333; 29-33 Minjungbal Dr, Tweed Heads; r from $75; 🅿 🖵 ) This single-storey brick block offers decent motel rooms with light interiors, cable TV and a free bus to the local bowls club. The owners are also happy to accommodate families with cots and extra beds.

**Bella Mare** ( ☎ 5599 2755; www.bellamare.com.au; 5 Hill St, Coolangatta; apt per night/week from $110/765; 🅿 🖵 )

This fancy apartment block is bathed in terracotta and Mediterranean hues. It houses cool and crisp apartments and villas with contemporary interiors and glistening mod cons.

**Quality Resort Twin Resorts** ( ☎ 5536 2277; www.twintowns.com.au; cnr Wharf & Griffith Sts, Tweed Heads; r from $205; 🅿 🖵 🖵 ) Some folk don't mind sharing a building with a small nation as long as there's a view. Which is why this alpha male of the high-rises, with its chic apartments, made-over hotel rooms and fabulous vistas, is popular.

Also recommended:

**Boyds Bay Holiday Park** ( ☎ 5524 3306; www.tchp.com.au/boydsbay; 3 Dry Dock Rd, Tweed Heads; camp sites from $24, cabins without/with bathroom from $95/110; 🖵 ) Neat and tightly packed.

### INFORMATION
| | |
|---|---|
| Centro Tweed Mall | (see 1) |
| Tweed Heads Visitor Centre | 1 C2 |

### SIGHTS & ACTIVITIES
| | |
|---|---|
| Cushy Fishing Charters | (see 3) |
| Minjungbal Aboriginal Cultural Centre | 2 B4 |
| Seamaster Fishing Charters | 3 B2 |
| Tweed River Catch-a-crab | 4 B2 |

### SLEEPING 🛏
| | |
|---|---|
| Bella Mare | 5 C1 |
| Boyds Bay Holiday Park | 6 B3 |
| Calico Court Motel | 7 A4 |
| Quality Resort Twin Resorts | 8 C1 |
| Tweed Harbour Motor Inn | 9 B2 |

### EATING 🍴
| | |
|---|---|
| Jimbo's | 10 B2 |
| Menniti Seafoods | 11 B2 |
| Cilio Ristorante | 12 C2 |
| Scooterini | 13 C1 |
| Tweed Heads Bowls Club | 14 C2 |

### TRANSPORT
| | |
|---|---|
| Intercity Bus Stop | (see 1) |

**Tweed Harbour Motor Inn** ( ☎ 5536 6066; www
.tweedharbourmotorinn.com.au; 135 Wharf St, Tweed
Heads; r $105; ⊠ ⚛ ) Cheap and central.

## Eating
**Scooterini** ( ☎ 5599 2298; Shop 1, Calypso Plaza, Griffiths
St, Coolangatta; mains $10-20; ✷ breakfast & lunch) Pro-
tected from the condo invasion by curtains
of clear plastic, this snug café churns out
great salads, paninis and burgers. The coffee
is strong and the grilled tofu, tomato and
mushroom breakfast is fab.

**Menniti Seafoods** ( ☎ 5599 2343; 2 River Tce, Tweed
Heads; mains $10; ✷ 10am-7.30pm) Super-fresh fish
and chips and super prices in unfussy surrounds. Park yourself at one of the tables
overlooking the marina and tuck into a daily
special of red snapper, dory or calamari.

**Olio Ristorante** ( ☎ 5536 9500; Shop 3 & 4, 1 Wharf St,
Tweed Heads; mains $18-27; ✷ dinner Tue-Sat) Olio keeps
things casual with crocheted tablecloths and
candlelight. But the menu is a lovely confu-
sion of flavours: seafood skewers with brandy
mango and roast capsicum sauce or duck in
sour cherry sauce. There's also a kid's menu.

Also recommended:
**Jimbo's** ( ☎ 5536 2090; 118 Wharf St; Tweed Heads;
mains $22; ✷ lunch & dinner) Classy fish and chips.
**Tweed Heads Bowls Club** ( ☎ 5536 3800; cnr Wharf &
Florence Sts, Tweed Heads; mains $15; ✷ lunch & dinner)
Great for cheap steaks and parmas.

## Getting There & Around
Long-distance buses stop at the intercity bus
stop on Bay St. **Premier Motor Services** ( ☎ 13 34 10)
has buses to Byron Bay ($24). **CountryLink** ( ☎ 13
22 32) also has buses to Byron Bay ($15).

**Surfside** ( ☎ 5536 7666) runs the local yellow
buses up to the Gold Coast and south to
Brunswick Heads.

# FAR NORTH COAST HINTERLAND

The undulating landscape of the Far North
Coast Hinterland is a gorgeous tapestry of
ecosystems. Native flora mingles with the
johnny-come-latelies of foreign soil. Orchards
roll into farmland, and dry eucalypt forests
converge in small clumps. Twenty-two million years ago an eruption of lava from Mt
Warning created the northern half of the
hinterland, flattening the valley and enclos-

ing it with dramatic mountain ranges. The
area's three national parks – Border Ranges,
Mt Warning and Nightcap – are part of the
Central Eastern Rainforest Reserves, which
are World Heritage rainforests. This diverse
backdrop perfectly mirrors the hinterland's
rich culture. Kombi vans, hippies, galleries,
sublime cuisine, great markets, tremendous
B&Bs, exquisite country and incredible waterfalls all call the area home.

# LISMORE
☎ 02 / pop 38,000
At first glance Lismore seems like any small
town in rural Australia, seasoned with pa-
rochialisms and a surfeit of pubs. But closer
inspection reveals a liberal supply of heritage
and Art Deco buildings populated by an artistic community. Students from the Southern
Cross University add to the town's eclectic-
ism. Lismore is also one of the few places in
Australia that reprocesses organic goods and
will soon boast the largest worm farm in the
southern hemisphere.

## Information
**NPWS office** ( ☎ 6627 0200; 75 Main St, Alstonville)
East of Lismore.
**Visitors centre** ( ☎ 1300 369 795; cnr Molesworth &
Ballina Sts; ✷ 9.30am-4pm) Internet access and exten-
sive information.

## Sights & Activities
The **Koala Care & Research Centre** ( ☎ 6622 1233; Rifle
Range Rd; admission free; ✷ 9.30-10.30am Sat) is home to
recovering koalas and well worth a visit (you
can view animals from outside any time). To
glimpse a platypus, head to **Tucki Tucki Creek** at
the southern end of Kadina St in Goonellabah.
Dawn or dusk yield the best opportunities to
spot these enigmatic monotremes.

There are more opportunities to spot fuzzy,
grey bums-in-the-gums at **Tucki Tucki Nature
Reserve** ( ☎ 6627 0200; Wyrallah Rd). About 16km
south of town, this reserve protects koala
habitat and enables rangers to study the animals as part of a programme to conserve them
in NSW.

For an insight into European settlement
and indigenous tribes visit the **Richmond River
Historical Society** ( ☎ 6621 9993; 165 Molesworth St;
admission $2; ✷ 10am-4pm Mon-Fri).

The diminutive Lismore **Regional Art Gallery**
( ☎ 6622 2209; 131 Molesworth St; admission by donation;
✷ 10am-4pm Tue-Fri, 10.30am-2.30pm Sat) has just

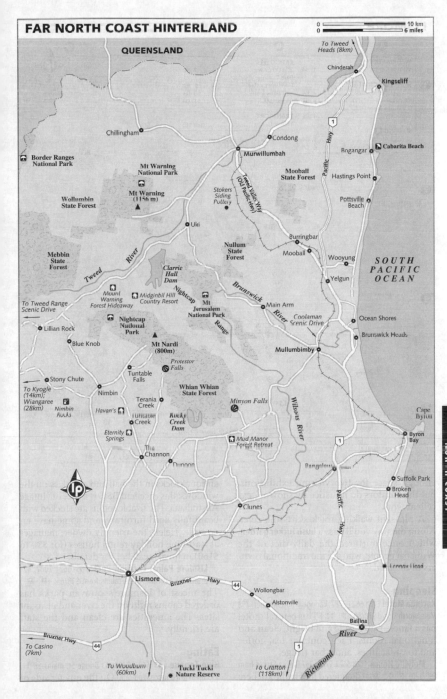

# FAR NORTH COAST HINTERLAND

0 ——— 10 km
0 ——— 6 miles

**QUEENSLAND**

To Tweed
Heads (8km)

Chinderah

Kingscliff

Chillingham

Condong

Murwillumbah

Rogangar

Cabarita Beach

Border Ranges
National Park

Mt Warning
National Park

Mooball
State Forest

Hastings Point

Mt Warning
(1156 m)

Stokers
Siding
Pottery

Pottsville
Beach

Wollumbin
State Forest

Tweed Valley Way
(Old Pacific Hwy)

Uki

Nullum
State
Forest

Burringbar

Mebbin
State
Forest

Tweed    River

Clarrie
Hall
Dam

Mooball

Wooyung

Yelgun

*SOUTH
PACIFIC
OCEAN*

To Tweed Range
Scenic Drive

Mount
Warning
Forest Hideaway

Midginbil Hill
Country Resort

Nightcap

Mt
Jerusalem
National Park

Brunswick    River

Main Arm

Coolaman
Scenic Drive

Ocean Shores

Lillian Rock

Nightcap
National
Park

Range

Brunswick Heads

Blue Knob

Mt Nardi
(800m)

Protestor
Falls

Mullumbimby

Stony Chute

Tuntable
Falls

To Kyogle
(14km);
Wiangaree
(28km)

Nimbin

Nimbin
Rocks

Havan's

Terania
Creek

Whian Whian
State Forest

Minyon Falls

Wilsons   River

Cape
Byron

Tuntable
Creek

Rocky
Creek
Dam

Byron
Bay

Eternity
Springs

The
Channon

Mud Manor
Forest Retreat

Dunoon

Bangalow

**NORTH COAST**

Suffolk Park

Broken
Head

Clunes

Pacific    Hwy

Lismore

Bruxner   Hwy   44

Wollongbar

Alstonville

Lennox Head

Ballina

Bruxner Hwy   44

To Casino
(7km)

To Woodburn
(60km)

Tucki Tucki
Nature Reserve

To Grafton
(118km)

*River*

Richmond

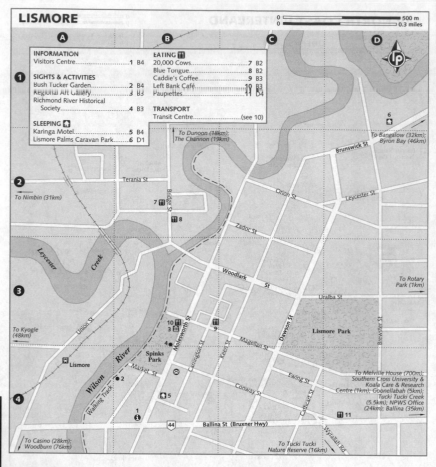

**LISMORE**

| INFORMATION | |
|---|---|
| Visitors Centre | 1 B4 |

| SIGHTS & ACTIVITIES | |
|---|---|
| Bush Tucker Garden | 2 B4 |
| Regional Art Gallery | 3 B3 |
| Richmond River Historical Society | 4 B3 |

| SLEEPING | |
|---|---|
| Karinga Motel | 5 B4 |
| Lismore Palms Caravan Park | 6 D1 |

| EATING | |
|---|---|
| 20,000 Cows | 7 B2 |
| Blue Tongue | 8 B2 |
| Caddie's Coffee | 9 B3 |
| Left Bank Café | 10 B3 |
| Paupiettes | 11 B4 |

| TRANSPORT | |
|---|---|
| Transit Centre | (see 10) |

enough space for two visiting exhibitions, but the curators do it justice by showing excellent works.

A pleasant walking track skirts the river. Along the way you'll pass a **bush tucker garden**, which once nurtured the daily diet of the Widjabal people, who are the traditional owners of the land.

## Sleeping

**Karinga Motel** ( ☎ 6621 2787; karinga@motorinn.net; 258 Molesworth St; s/d $70/80; P X ) This central motel has a fancied-up façade and bright, clean and functional rooms. Each contains tea, coffee and toast facilities, and a bar fridge.

**Melville House** ( ☎ 6621 5778; 267 Ballina St; s/d from $90/120; P X R ) Chequered tiles in the kitchen,

antique clocks in the hall and cut glass on the windows: this excellent B&B is a slice of vintage Australiana. The sizable rooms are stocked with beautifully aged furniture, and some have an en suite. Helen, the friendly owner, manages at least nine holiday rental houses (for $90 to $160) in town – call her for details.

**Lismore Palms Caravan Park** ( ☎ 6621 7067; 42-48 Brunswick St; camp sites/cabins from $18/65; P R ) The nicest of Lismore's caravan parks has ordered cabins right on the river and pleasant sites. The amenities are clean and the staff are friendly.

## Eating

**Blue Tongue** ( ☎ 6622 0750; 43 Bridge St; mains $8-11; ☽ breakfast & lunch Wed-Sun) On the quieter side of the river in a wonderfully worn building, Blue Tongue whips up solid café fare. The BLATs, toasted Turkish sandwiches and fine coffee taste better when consumed in the sunny courtyard with its anarchic foliage.

**Left Bank Café** ( ☎ 6622 2338; 133 Molesworth St; mains $10 18; ☑ breakfast & lunch Mon-Sat, dinner Fri & Sat) Attached to the gallery, this bright, open café serves artistic works of its own. In the umbrella-shaded courtyard or the glassy interior you can dine on rabbit sugo with parpadelle, or zucchini, mint and feta frittata.

**20,000 Cows** ( ☎ 6622 2517; 58 Bridge St; mains $15; ☑ dinner Wed-Sat) This vegetarian restaurant delivers international flavours with one-for-all and all-for-one social messages. Far right conservatives need not enter, and everyone else can enjoy the Yemeni pastries, Lithuanian kugelis, Egyptian dips, Thai soups, Indian curries and warm vibes.

Also recommended:

**Caddie's Coffee** ( ☎ 6621 7709; 20 Carrington St; meals $8-13; ☑ breakfast & lunch Mon-Fri, to 2pm Sat) Bohemian café with gluten-free goodies.

**Paupiettes** ( ☎ 6621 6136; 56 Ballina St; mains $15-25; ☑ dinner Tue-Sat) Superb Mod Oz menu and local produce.

### Getting There & Around

**Regional Express** (Rex; ☎ 13 17 13) flies to Sydney.

**Greyhound** ( ☎ 13 14 99) has daily buses to Byron Bay ($45). **Kirklands** ( ☎ 6622 1499) also runs to Byron Bay ($14). **CountryLink** ( ☎ 13 22 32) buses head to Byron Bay and Murwillumbah. All leave from the transit centre.

There are also 24-hour **taxis** ( ☎ 13 10 08).

## THE CHANNON

The Channon is an intimate village between Nimbin and Lismore. If you can, time your visit for the second Sunday of the month for 'the mother of all markets', according to local pundits.

**Eternity Springs B&B** ( ☎ 02-6688 6385; www.eternitysprings.com; 483 Tuntable Creek Rd; camping per person $12, s incl breakfast $50-100, d incl breakfast $80-160) A true eco-haven, this idyllic plot has cosy 'cubbies' with private verandas and share bathrooms, en-suite doubles filled with impressive art, and the very stylish, self-contained, one-bedroom 'Lotus Room'. The real beauty of Eternity Springs, however, is the spring water, solar power, permaculture, flushing compost toilets and organic breakfasts. At the back of the property is a splendid open walled timber studio with views of the

surrounding valleys. Yoga workshops don't get any lovelier.

**Havan's** ( ☎ 02-6688 6108; www.rainbowregion.com/havan; Lot 1, Lawler Rd; s/d $75/120) is a pretty eco-tourist retreat set in the heart of a rainforest.

## NIGHTCAP NATIONAL PARK

Encompassing over 8000 hectares, this stunning national park contains diverse subtropical rainforests and wildlife. The bent-winged bat, red-legged pademelon (a relative of the wallaby) and endangered Fleay's barred frog all call the area home. With the highest annual rainfall in NSW, Nightcap has spectacular waterfalls, gorgeous green gullies and sheer cliff walls. The exposed rock pinnacles of the **Sphinx** can be seen from Lismore.

There are several access points and walks to suit all fitness levels. The short trek from the road to **Protestor Falls** (1.4km) ambles beneath thick palms and rainforest and around moss-carpeted rocks. There are also picnic spots and dramatic lookout points, including **Mt Nardi** (800m). The NPWS office at the visitors centre in Murwillumbah (p211) can supply detailed maps and advice on many walks.

## NIMBIN

☎ 02 / pop 400

Landing in Nimbin is like entering a social experiment. It's as if the residents have transmogrified into a dreadlocked, tie-dyed society, milling in a jetlag of marijuana and the 1970s. This is overkill, of course, and Nimbin's residents are far more eclectic, but the town's experimental curiosity is the showcase of its tiny main street. Nimbin is not for everyone, and plenty of day-trippers wander the streets dazed and a little frightened (and not from the cookies). But once the tourist buses have hit the road the stereotypes melt and Nimbin's warm and diverse culture becomes more conspicuous.

### Orientation & Information

Nimbin is very small and you'll find all points of interest on Cullen St, which runs through the centre.

**Nimbin Connexion** ( ☎ 6689 1764; www.nimbinconnexion.com; Cullen St; ☑ 9am-4pm) is at the northern end of town and has a wealth of knowledge, bike hire ($20 per day) and internet access ($6 per hour).

Any wwoofers out there? You're in luck. Nimbin is home to dozens of organic farms and many host **Willing Workers on Organic Farms** (www.wwoof.org.au). Nimbin Connexion can help you get your hands dirty.

## Festivals & Events

**Nimbin Mardi Grass** is held over the first weekend in May and delivers happy high fun courtesy of the hemp olympix, hemp-themed street parades, hemp-based discussions and more scoobs than a uni dosshouse.

## Sights & Activities

The wacky and wonderful **Nimbin Museum** ( ☎ 6689 1123; 62 Cullen St; admission free; ☼ 9am-5pm) pays homage to crashed kombis in psychedelic garb and the pursuit of 'loving the child within yourself' and sticking it to 'the man'. Though minute, the museum instils the ethos of those who moved here in the 1970s. Actually, the ethos is still pretty thick today.

The **Nimbin Artists Gallery** ( ☎ 6689 1444; 49 Cullen St; ☼ 10am-4pm) packs an eclectic collection of pottery, prints, weaving, glass work and much more into a modest space.

The **Hemp Embassy** (Cullen St; ☼ 9am-5pm) features none-too-subtle displays that dispel myths about hemp and marijuana, and might be banned under (more) despotic regimes. Once you've been converted you can buy paraphernalia to get high. Smokers are welcome at the coffee shop next door.

**Djanbung Gardens** ( ☎ 6689 1755; www.earthwise .org.au; 74 Cecil St; admission free; 10am-3.30pm Tue-Sat) is a permaculture education centre, café and bookshop spreading good environmental practice.

The **Rainbow Power Company** ( ☎ 6689 1430; www .rpc.com.au; No 1 Alternative Way; admission free; ☼ 9am-5pm Mon-Fri) designs and produces 'appropriate home-energy systems' that use nature's forces – the sun, wind and water – to generate electricity. The systems are exported to all corners of the globe.

At the old butter factory, the **Bush Theatre** ( ☎ 6689 1111) shows films several nights a week.

Nimbin hosts a colourful market on the third and fifth Sundays of the month.

## Tours

See p190 for more tour options from Byron Bay.
**Nimbin Tours & Shuttle Bus** ( ☎ 6680 9189; www.nim bintours.com; $5; ☼ tours 2pm Mon-Fri) One-hour tours of the Rainbow Power Company and Djanbung Gardens.

**Grasshoppers Eco Explorer** ( ☎ 0500 881 881; www .grasshoppers.com.au; tours per person incl lunch $35) Day tours from Byron Bay. A reader fave.

## Sleeping

**Nimbin Backpackers at Granny's Farm** ( ☎ 6689 1333; Cullen St; dm/d $20/54, 🖬 ) The hostel closest to town offers warm and colourful doubles and dorms, with enough room to swing a tofu cow. Most nights some sort of friendly drink fest takes place in the open-air lounge room. It's popular with bus tours.

**YHA Nimbin Rox Hostel** ( ☎ 6689 0022; www.yha .com.au; 74 Thornburn St; dm/d $24/56; 🖳 🖳 ) Tumbling down a landscaped native garden, this excellent hostel has clean and contemporary accommodation and great national park views. Dorms have four or eight beds, and one is suitable for wheelchairs. There are also safari tents.

**Grey Gum Lodge** ( ☎ 6689 1713; www.nimbinaustralia .com/greygumlodge; 2 High St; s/d from $40/55; 🐾 ) The rooms at this beautifully worn and creaky house fit better than your favourite jacket, and the high, comfy beds are the snuggy silver lining. Each room has a TV and en suite, and the back veranda provides outstanding conversations and sunsets.

More options:

**Nimbin Tourist Caravan Park** ( ☎ 6689 1402; 29 Sibley St; camp sites from $19)
**Rainbow Retreat Backpackers** ( ☎ 6689 1262; 75 Thorburn St; camp sites/dm/d $10/15/40) Rudimentary and serene retreat.

## Eating & Drinking

**Retro** ( ☎ 6689 0590; 76 Cullen St; mains $8; ☼ breakfast & lunch) A tidy café in a private corner pocket, Retro does great roast veggie wraps, frittatas, bakes, sambos and gluttonous sweets. It also serves stiff coffee.

**Rainbow Café** ( ☎ 6689 1997; 70 Cullen St; mains $6-13; ☼ breakfast & lunch) Pack a healthy appetite for this Nimbin institution – you'll need room for the generous burgers, wraps, nachos and salads. Creative combos include tofu and peanut sauce or Mediterranean sweet potato salad. The sunny courtyard is a time vacuum.

**Nimbin Hotel** ( ☎ 6689 1246; Cullen St; mains $15; ☼ lunch & dinner) Nimbin's local boozer cooks up hearty pub nosh à la steak or chicken parma. Wash it all down with a schooner on the back porch while appreciating the stunning views. On weekends it gets rolling with live music.

(Continued on page 209)

The Breadknife, Warrumbungle National Park (p252)

Early morning balloon trip, Hunter Valley (p140)

Barrington Tops National Park (p156)

Sunrise over Mt Warning National Park (p210)

RICHARD I'ANSON

Busker at a market in Byron Bay
(p186)

PETER PTSCHELINZEW

Mother and child at Byron Bay (p186)

BECCA POSTERI

St Georges Basin (p330), Jervis Bay

MARK ANDREW KIRBY

Ebor Falls (p221), near Armidale

MARK PARKES

Fishing boats moored at Coffs Harbour (p174)

RICHARD I'ANSON

Starfish, Merimbula (p339)

Little penguins, Montague Island (p335)

Seahorse Inn (p341), overlooking Twofold Bay, near Eden

Parkes Radio Telescope (p243)

Japanese Garden, Cowra (p245)

Giraffes in the Western Plains Zoo (p241), Dubbo

CHRISTOPHER GROENHOUT

Aerial view of Parliament House (p349), Canberra

ROB BLAKERS

National Carillon (p349), Lake Burley
Griffin, Canberra

New Parliament House (p349), looking back towards the old one, Canberra

RICHARD NEBESKY

Floriade flower festival (p356), Canberra

ROSS BARNETT

Australian War Memorial (p351), Canberra

OLIVER STREWE

Aboriginal Tent Embassy (p351), Canberra

PATRICK HORTON

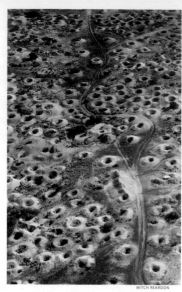

Opal-mining area, White Cliffs (p264)

Outback art, Silverton (p271)

Sculpture Symposium (p269), Broken Hill

*(Continued from page 200)*

**Nimbin Trattoria and Pizzeria** ( ☎ 6689 1427; 70 Cullen St; mains $10-20; ☾ lunch Thu-Sun, dinner daily) Outstanding pizzas worthy of gorging on and delicious pastas are churned out in ample supply at this toasty trattoria. Leave room for dessert.

## Getting There & Away
The **Nimbin Tours & Shuttle Bus** (see p200) operates between Byron Bay and Nimbin (per person $12).

You can also hitch a ride with **Wallers Bus Company** ( ☎ 6687 8550) to/from Lismore (per person $10).

## AROUND NIMBIN
**Nimbin Rocks**, an Aboriginal sacred site, lies about 6km south of town, well signposted off Stony Chute (Kyogle) Rd. **Hanging Rock Creek** has falls and a good swimming hole; take the road through Stony Chute for 14km, turn right at the Barkers Vale sign, then left onto Williams Rd; the falls are nearby on the right.

See Nightcap National Park (p199) for information on Mt Nardi.

## BANGALOW
☎ 02 / pop 1230
Beautiful Bangalow could make a painting weep with envy. Against a hilly backdrop, the ascending main street is a strip of old buildings populated by galleries, boutiques and fine eateries. There's a good **farmer's market** (open 8-11am Saturday) selling local organic produce. Just 14km out of Byron Bay, Bangalow makes for a lovely day trip, or even lovelier overnighter.

## Sleeping
**Riverview Guesthouse** ( ☎ 6687 1317; www.riverviewguesthouse.com.au; 99 Byron St; r $75-195) A stately Victorian house circumnavigated by a wide veranda and lush gardens, Riverview is a B&B pinup. Filled to tasteful sufficiency with antiques and classic cream colourings, it offers fine rooms and gourmet brekkies.

**Village View Bed & Breakfast** ( ☎ 6687 2619; terisu@hotkey.net.au; 11 Barby Cres; s/d incl breakfast $120/130) This contemporary B&B dwells in the heights of Bangalow's residential pocket. It sleeps guests in a private cottage out the back, with spa, balcony and gobsmacking views of the surrounding green hills. The delectable breakfast will keep you going well after lunch.

## Eating
**Ate** ( ☎ 6687 1010; 33 Byron St; mains $16; ☾ breakfast, lunch & dinner) Creating more than just meals, this crafty café prepares food with passion. The result is inventions like crab spaghetti with capers, chives and tomatoes or osso bucco with Middle Eastern spices.

Upstairs from Ate is **Satiate** (degustation $50; ☾ dinner Tue-Sat) which does designer degustation and chic cocktails in exotic surrounds.

**Utopia** ( ☎ 6687 2088; 13 Byron St; mains $16-24; ☾ breakfast, lunch & dinner) Contemporary jazz throbs softly in the background, lulling diners into sopor while they wait for gluten-free sausages with red pepper and mustard relish or Victorian mussels steamed with saffron. Yes – it is gastronomic utopia.

**Urban Café** ( ☎ 6687 2678; 33 Byron St; mains $12-16; ☾ breakfast & lunch daily, dinner Thu-Sat) Casual and creative, this café specialises in fresh salads, sambos and burgers with deli ingredients, and fine coffee. There's live jazz, blues or country on the weekends.

## MULLUMBIMBY
☎ 02 / pop 3200
Referred to as Mullum by most, this serene town is a coast-hinterland hybrid, drawing aesthetics and character from both. Wide streets with swaying palms are occupied by unhurried locals, and everything shuts on the weekends except the pubs and cafés, leaving little choice but to eat, drink and be merry. Mullumbimby is also a community centre for the valley, and consequently a good spot to stock up if you're going walkabout.

## Orientation
Burringbar St is the main shopping street and runs off Dalley St, the main road through town.

## Sights & Activities
**Crystal Castle** ( ☎ 6684 3111; Monet Dr; admission free; ☾ 10am-5pm) has tranquil, labyrinthine gardens, Australia's biggest stone-carved Blessing Buddha (15 tonne worth of enlightenment) and an impressive collection of crystals.

The **Brunswick Valley Historical Society Museum** ( ☎ 6684 1149; Stuart St; admission free; ☾ 11am-3pm Fri, 9am-noon third Saturday of every month) is housed in the old post office, itself worth a photo, and offers a comprehensive insight into days gone by.

NORTH COAST

## Sleeping & Eating

**Mullumbimby Motel** ( ☎ 6684 2387; www.mullumbimby motel.com.au; 121 Dalley St; s/d/tw $75/80/85;  ) Under a bank of foliage, this is a reliable budget option with generic but sizable motel rooms including cable TV and the odd ghastly and extremely comfortable easy chair.

**Middle Pub** ( ☎ 6684 3229; fax 6684 3121; 46 Burringbar St; r without/with bathroom $35/90;  ) Mullumbimby's social hub has clean and frugal rooms with fans and shared bathrooms, or quite fabulous hotel rooms with country-kitsch king-size beds. Beware the din from the weekend warriors downstairs.

**Poinciana Café** ( ☎ 6684 4036; 55 Station St; mains $8-16;  breakfast & lunch) Casually constructed around two stunning poinciana trees, this atmospheric eatery has a chic menu boasting a kicking swordfish, tomato and aioli burger. At the time of research the brand-new owners were still finding their dinner feet with promises of similarly delectable options.

**Milk And Honey** ( ☎ 6684 1422; 59A Station St; mains $15-20;  dinner Wed-Sat) The thin-crust, wood-fired pizzas toasted at this edgy little pizzeria draw diners from surrounding towns. The changing menu always features a good range of carnivorous and vegetarian delights.

Also recommended:

**Café Ripe** ( ☎ 6684 2915; 72 Burringbar St; mains $9-14;  breakfast & lunch) Genovese fish stews, Indonesian rendangs and hearty pot roasts.

**Maca's Camping Ground** ( ☎ 6684 5211; Main Arm Rd; camp sites $10-15) Basic facilities on a macadamia nut plantation.

## Getting There & Away

**Blanch's Bus Service** ( ☎ 6686 2144) runs daily to Byron Bay ($5.60). **CountryLink** ( ☎ 13 22 32) has buses to Lismore ($8.80) and Byron Bay.

## WHIAN WHIAN STATE CONSERVATION AREA

Timber is still produced in this forest and is regarded as a prime example of how forestry resources can be best utilised and managed. The forest adjoins the southeast side of Nightcap National Park and is home to threatened species including the spotted quoll.

The spectacular **Minyon Falls** are found here, plunging 100m into a rainforest gorge and surrounded by a flora reserve with several walking tracks. Take a dip under the falls for an unforgettable experience.

The historic **Nightcap Track** (16km long) passes through both the state forest and Nightcap National Park; it was the original track used by postal workers and others in the late 19th and early 20th centuries. **Rummery Park** isn't far off the road down from the falls; it's a well-provided picnic spot with barbecues and cold showers. **Peate's Mountain Lookout**, just on from Rummery Park, has a great view from Jerusalem Mountain in the north, to Byron Bay in the east.

The **Mud Manor Forest Retreat** ( ☎ 02-6688 2205; www.mudmanor.com; r from $120;  ) is a perfect haven for those looking to escape the crowds. Built from mud bricks, this retreat has a permaculture garden and rooms with hand-crafted luxuries, spas and large decks.

## UKI
☎ 02 / pop 210

Uki (uke-i) is a cute town overshadowed by the dominating peak of **Mt Warning**. It has a pretty warren of steep streets and a warm and alternative atmosphere.

The **Uki Café** ( ☎ 6679 5351; 1 Rowlands Creek Rd; mains $7-12;  breakfast & lunch daily, dinner Fri & Sat) has good food, a sweeping veranda and a toasty pot belly stove inside for winter afternoons. Across the highway, **Babareki Beads** ( ☎ 6679 5677; Room 4, The Buttery;  10am-3pm Wed-Mon) sells colourful and unique handmade jewellery and **Precious Earth** ( ☎ 6679 5885; The Buttery;  10am-4pm) runs come-one-come-all pottery workshops on Saturday mornings.

**Midginbil Hill Country Resort** ( ☎ 6679 7158; www .midginbilhill.com.au; Town Green; s/d incl breakfast $95/135;  ) is a working cattle farm right at the base of Nightcap National Park. It offers accommodation during school holidays and horse riding (per person $50) as well as canoeing on the Clarrie Hall dam (per person $30).

Alternatively, **Mount Warning Forest Hideaway** ( ☎ 6679 7277; www.foresthideaway.com.au; 460 Byrrill Creek Rd; d/ste from $80/130;  ) has comfortable, self-contained studios and suites in an isolated patch of rainforest about 12km southwest of Uki.

A few kilometres east, **Stokers Siding Pottery** ( ☎ 6677 9208; www.stokerspottery.com.au; 224 Stokers Siding Rd;  9.30am-5pm) is well worth the short side trip to see the beautiful pottery, glass work and wood work shaped by local hands.

## MT WARNING NATIONAL PARK

Relatively small in size (2380 hectares), this is the most dramatic feature of the hinterland, with Mt Warning (1156m) towering over the valley. The peak is the first part of mainland Australia to be touched by sunlight each day. This has resulted in 60,000 people each year making the steep 4.4km, five-hour round-trip trek to the summit from **Breakfast Creek** (don't forget a torch). Mt Warning is known to the Bundjalung people as Wollumbin, meaning 'cloud catcher', 'fighting chief of the mountain' and 'weather maker'. Although everyone does it, you should be aware that under Bundjalung law only specifically chosen people are allowed to climb the mountain, and consequently they ask you not to go out of respect. The unnerving European name was given to the peak in 1770 by Captain Cook to warn seamen of the offshore reefs.

You can't camp at Mt Warning, but the **Mt Warning Caravan Park & Tourist Retreat** ( ☎ 02-6679 5120; www.mtwarningholidaypark.com; Mt Warning Rd; camp sites/cabins from $18/55) on the Mt Warning approach road is a viable option, with good kitchen facilities, budget and en-suite cabins and a well-stocked kiosk.

**Wallers Bus Company** ( ☎ 6687 8550) runs from Lismore ($20) to the turn-off for Mt Warning every morning and runs past in the afternoon. Call for changing times.

## MURWILLUMBAH
☎ 02 / pop 7700

Sitting pretty on the plateau of the Tweed Valley, Murwillumbah is surrounded by the NSW–Qld Border Ranges. Peppered with plenty of heritage façade and charm, the town's streets tumble on top of one another,

with stunning views of Mt Warning peeking around every corner.

### Information
The **visitors centre** ( ☎ 6672 1340; www.tweedcoolangatta.com.au; cnr Alma St & Tweed Valley Way) has national park passes, information on accommodation and a great rainforest display.

### Sights
The exceptional **Tweed River Art Gallery** ( ☎ 6670 2790; www.tweed.nsw.gov.au/artgallery; cnr Mistral Rd & Tweed Valley Way; free admission; ☒ 10am-5pm, Wed-Sun) is an architectural delight and home to some of Australia's finest art works. Temporary exhibits complement the permanent fixtures and the spectrum includes portraits, indigenous work, photography, sculpture and woodwork.

**Murwillumbah Museum** ( ☎ 6672 1865; 2 Queensland Rd; adult/child $2/1.50; ☒ 10am-4pm Wed Fri) This small museum, housed in a beautiful old building, features a solid account of local history and an interesting radio room.

Just north of town, **Tropical Fruit World** ( ☎ 6677 7222; www.tropicalfruitworld.com.au; Duranbah Rd; adult/child $32/25; ☒ 10am-5pm) allegedly has the world's largest collection of tropical fruit. This doesn't justify the melon of an entry fee because there's really only so much (PG) fun you can have with fruit.

### Sleeping
**Mount Warning-Murwillumbah YHA** ( ☎ 6672 3763; www.yha.com.au; 1 Tumbulgum Rd; dm/d from $25/54) Free

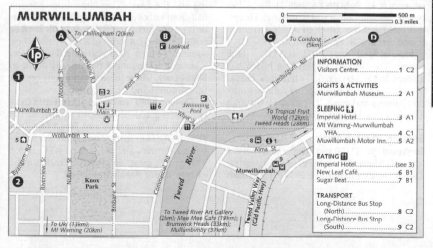

MURWILLUMBAH

| | 0 | 500 m |
| --- | --- | --- |
| | 0 | 0.3 miles |

To Chillingham (20km)

To Condong (5km)

Lookout

Queensland Rd

Mooball St

Bent St

Main St

Murwillumbah St

Swimming Pool

Wharf St

Wollumbin St

Byangum Rd

Riverview St

Nullum St

Brisbane St

Commercial Rd

Knox Park

Tweed River

To Uki (13km); Mt Warning (20km)

To Tweed River Art Gallery (2km); Moo Moo Cafe (19km); Brunswick Heads (33km); Mullumbimby (37km)

To Tropical Fruit World (12km); Tweed Heads (28km)

Alma St

Murwillumbah

Tumbulgum Rd

Tweed Valley Way (Cld Pacific Hwy)

**INFORMATION**
Visitors Centre.....................1  C2

**SIGHTS & ACTIVITIES**
Murwillumbah Museum.........2  A1

**SLEEPING** 🛏
Imperial Hotel.......................3  A1
Mt Warning-Murwillumbah
YHA.................................4  C1
Muwillumbah Motor Inn.......5  A2

**EATING** 🍴
Imperial Hotel...................(see 3)
New Leaf Café.....................6  B1
Sugar Beat..........................7  B1

**TRANSPORT**
Long-Distance Bus Stop
(North).............................8  C2
Long-Distance Bus Stop
(South).............................9  C2

NORTH COAST

ice cream is generally enough to win any back-packer's loyalty but this hostel does it for kicks, not business. Bohemian cheer swims in the colourful waterfront house with eight-bed dorms. There's canoe and bike hire, and four-night stays attract free tours.

**Imperial Hotel** ( ☎ 6672 2777; fax 6672 8188; 115 Main St; s/d with shared bathroom $30/45, d with bathroom $55) These grand old pub rooms look like they haven't been altered since the opening ceremony – shabby chic without even trying. Snug interiors are aged like a good quaffing wine, with antique robes and floral bedspreads.

**Murwillumbah Motor Inn** ( ☎ 1800 687 224, 1800 023 105; www.murwillumbahmotorinn.com.au; 17 Byangum Rd; s/d $84/96; ⌧ ⬜ ⬛ ) It's a little on the frumpy side but all rooms in this motel have cable TV and microwaves. There's also a pleasant courtyard out the back with a communal barbecue.

### Eating
**New Leaf Café** ( ☎ 6672 2667; Shop 10, Murwillumbah Plaza; meals $5-10; ⏲ breakfast & lunch) The food here is creative and vegetarian, with plenty of Middle Eastern flavours and salads on offer. Dine inside, alfresco, or take away.

**Sugar Beat** ( ☎ 6672 2330; Shop 2/6-8 Commercial Rd; mains $10; ⏲ breakfast & lunch) Park yourself by the sunny window or settle into a corner of the long bench seating. Then tuck into tofu and veggie gado gado, sesame chicken with Japanese dressing or an equally elaborate salad or burger. Or just blow the diet and have cake.

**Moo Moo Café** ( ☎ 6677 1230; Tweed Valley Way, Mooball; mains $8-11; ⏲ breakfast & lunch) Halfway between Murwillumbah and Brunswick Heads, this café takes cow kitsch to udder extremes. It also serves a decent sandwich.

**Imperial Hotel** ( ☎ 6672 2777; mains $15; ⏲ lunch & dinner) The Imperial's sprawling bistro has a short but snazzy menu – tempura barramundi, freshly wrapped spring rolls or gourmet bangers and mash. It's pub grub through a sophisticated looking glass.

### Getting There & Away
**Greyhound** ( ☎ 13 14 99) and **Premier Motor Service** ( ☎ 13 34 10) have daily services to Coolangatta/ Tweed Heads and Byron Bay ($15). **Kirklands**

( ☎ 6626 1499) charges around the same for daily buses to Byron Bay and Brunswick Heads. **CountryLink** ( ☎ 13 22 32) buses run to Byron Bay, Tweed Heads and Brisbane.

## BORDER RANGES NATIONAL PARK
The Border Ranges National Park, a World Heritage area (31,500 hectares), covers the NSW side of the McPherson Range, which runs along the NSW–Qld border and some of its outlying spurs. The park has large tracts of superb rainforest, and it has been estimated that a quarter of all bird species in Australia can be seen here.

The eastern section – which includes the escarpments of the massive Mt Warning caldera – is the most easily accessible, via the Tweed Range Scenic Drive. You can access the smaller central section from the Lions Rd, which turns off the Kyogle–Woodenbong road 22km north of Kyogle. The large and rugged western section is almost inaccessible except to well-equipped bushwalkers.

The **Tweed Range Scenic Drive** – gravel but usable in all weather – loops through the park from Lillian Rock (midway between Uki and Kyogle) to Wiangaree (north of Kyogle on the Woodenbong road). The signposting on access roads isn't good (when in doubt take roads signposted to the national park), but it's well worth the effort of finding it. The road is unsuitable for caravans and large vehicles.

The road runs through mountain forest most of the way, with steep hills and breathtaking lookouts over the Tweed Valley to Mt Warning and the coast. The adrenaline-charging half-hour walk out to the crag called the **Pinnacle** is not for vertigo sufferers! **Antarctic Beech** is, not surprisingly, a forest of Antarctic beeches, some more than 2000 years old. From here, a walking track (about 5km) leads down to **Brindle Creek**, where there is stunningly beautiful rainforest and a picnic area.

There is **NPWS camping** at **Sheepstation Creek** (per person $3), about 15km north of the turn-off at Wiangaree, and **Forest Tops** (per person $3), 6km further on. There are toilets but no showers and it's best to BYO water. There's free camping at Byrill Creek, on the eastern side of **Mebbin State Forest**.

# New England

If Tamworth is the heart of New England, then Armidale is the brains. Tamworth holds the boot-scooting label and is home to the Country Music Festival, where all people (that way inclined or not) party all week long. When you have swung those tassels till they have almost fallen off, boot scoot over to more conservative Armidale. A cosmopolitan energy focuses on the town centre and there is a string of national parks to the east, with unforgettably deep gorges and waterfalls.

But dotted around these two regional centres is a mottling of small country towns, which are usually located on a river or straddling a couple of highways. Focused on a broad main street they typically feature wide awnings reaching for oversized gutters and a couple of two-storey iron-laced hotels.

Whether you are travelling the Fossickers Way or not, get out the shovel and dig a little deeper as each town carries its own signature gem. Whether it be horse riding or an emerging arts scene, the towns in between are the essence of the New England Tableland.

## HIGHLIGHTS

- Discover the largely undiscovered **Kwiambal National Park** (p229)
- Fly high in **Manilla** (p227), away from it all
- Line dance at the Tamworth **Country Music Festival** (p215)
- Cruise in a chopper over the gorges of the **Waterfall Way** (p221)
- Crack the whip at **Leconfield Jackaroo & Jillaroo School** (p215)
- Listen to bird chitchat in **Washpool National Park** at Granite Lookout (p224)
- Fossick for minerals along the **Fossickers Way** (p226)
- Drink and laugh at Inverell's **Graman Pub** (p229)

★ Kwiambal National Park

★ Washpool National Park

Inverell ★

★ Fossickers Way

★ Manilla     ★ Waterfall Way

★ Tamworth

NEW ENGLAND

# NEW ENGLAND

# TAMWORTH

☎ 02 / pop 37, 120

Jackie Cole, Keith Urban, Slim Dusty... 'Pub with no Beer'. That's enough to get anyone's attention (that is if you're still reading). Fair enough, country music may not be your cup of tea, but this fantastically friendly city has a vibrant nightlife, and emerging foodie scene, as well as the rather large golden guitar. So dust off your boots and oil up the chaps, we are going to the country music capital of Australia...yeehaa!

## Information

To get into the string of things, drop into to the guitar-shaped **visitors centre** ( ☎ 6767 5300; www.visittamworth.com.au; cnr Peel & Murray Sts) and check out the **Walk a Country Mile museum** (adult/child $6/2). Then scoot on down to Peel St (the main street, where you'll find ATMs) to get your bearings before you get the show on the road.

**Hospital** ( ☎ 6767 7700; Dean St) When the boot scooting gets too much.

**Library** ( ☎ 6767 5457; 466 Peel St) For free internet access.

**Post Office** ( ☎ 6755 5988; 406 Peel St)

## Sights

### COUNTRY MUSIC

Tassel phobes should skip the **Australian Country Music Foundation** ( ☎ 6766 9696; 93 Brisbane St; adult/child $6/4; ☒ 10am-4pm Mon-Fri, to 1pm Sat); it's not much of a display really. Ditch the curator and it should take as little as five minutes to see in its entirety, though it all depends on your level of interest of course.

The **Big Golden Guitar Tourist Centre** ( ☎ 6765 2688; New England Hwy; ☒ 9am-5pm) has a café and souvenir shop where you can stock up on 'golden guitar' jewellery, stationery, clothing and snow domes. And when you have finished stocking up check out the Wax Museum (adult/child $8/4). It must be alright being a country music star, just look at the smiles plastered across their chops.

By appointment only, **Lindsay Butler Studios** ( ☎ 6762 1104; ☒ 10am-5pm) will open its doors to visitors.

### OTHER ATTRACTIONS

And you thought this town was just guitars and mullets. **Oxley Marsupial Park** (Endeavour Dr; ☒ 8am-5pm) has overly friendly cockatoos and other native animals at this council-run park

at the end of Endeavour Dr, the northern continuation of Brisbane St.

Grab a bottle of wine, the one you love (anyone will do), and follow Jacaranda-lined White St to the very top where you'll reach **Oxley Scenic Lookout** (Scenic Rd). This is the best seat in the house as the sun goes down over Tamworth and the surrounding Liverpool Ranges.

Containing three million bucks worth of bikes, **Motorcycle Museum** ( ☎ 6766 7000; New England Hwy; adult/child $7/5; ☒ 9am-5pm) memorabilia has been collected by none other than the owner of the Quality Powerhouse Hotel next door. Three cheers for capitalism. There's not much floor space left, not even for the humble Norton 500.

The **Calala Cottage** ( ☎ 6765 7492; 142 Denison St; adult/child $4/2; ☒ 2-4pm Tue-Fri, from 10am Sat & Sun) is where you may get a hand-held tour but gee it's informative. The slab hut, coach house and blacksmiths were all built just before the manor in 1875. Coffee freaks will love the old wrought-iron coffee-grinder.

The course at **Leconfield Jackaroo & Jillaroo School** ( ☎ 6769 4328; 'Bimboola' at Kootingal; 5-day course $490), covering mustering, milking, shearing, shoeing, and lamb slaughtering, will transform you into a budding horseman/woman in no time.

## Festivals & Events

Held at the end of January, New England's biggest annual party, the **Country Music Festival** lasts 10 days. There are over 800 acts, of which 75% are free. Or if you missed the big one in summer, get along to **Hats off to Country Music** during the June Queen's-birthday long weekend.

## Sleeping

Most of the accommodation in town is booked out months in advance for the Country Music Festival in January, so get in early and contact the visitors centre for an information pack.

### BUDGET

**YHA Tamworth** ( ☎ 6761 2600; 169 Marius St; dm/d $23/48; ☒ ) A clinical little white building slotted snugly into the city. Closed 12.30pm to 4pm.

**Tudor Hotel** ( ☎ 6766 9564; 327 Peel St; s/d $35/45) The pick of the pubs in terms of accommodation. The French Riviera feel is enhanced after many alcoholic beverages and the lift,

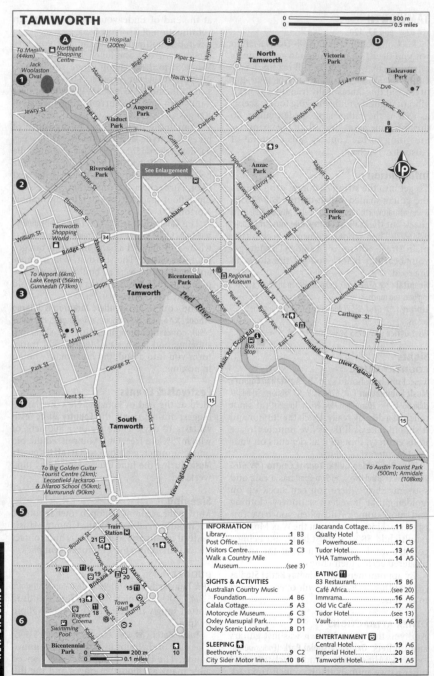

# TAMWORTH

**INFORMATION**

| | |
|---|---|
| Library | 1 B3 |
| Post Office | 2 B6 |
| Visitors Centre | 3 C3 |
| Walk a Country Mile Museum | (see 3) |

**SIGHTS & ACTIVITIES**

| | |
|---|---|
| Australian Country Music Foundation | 4 B6 |
| Calala Cottage | 5 A3 |
| Motorcycle Museum | 6 C3 |
| Oxley Marsupial Park | 7 D1 |
| Oxley Scenic Lookout | 8 D1 |

**SLEEPING**

| | |
|---|---|
| Beethoven's | 9 C2 |
| City Sider Motor Inn | 10 B6 |

| | |
|---|---|
| Jacaranda Cottage | 11 B5 |
| Quality Hotel Powerhouse | 12 C3 |
| Tudor Hotel | 13 A6 |
| YHA Tamworth | 14 A5 |

**EATING**

| | |
|---|---|
| 83 Restaurant | 15 B6 |
| Café Africa | (see 20) |
| Immrama | 16 A6 |
| Old Vic Café | 17 A6 |
| Tudor Hotel | (see 13) |
| Vault | 18 A6 |

**ENTERTAINMENT**

| | |
|---|---|
| Central Hotel | 19 A6 |
| Imperial Hotel | 20 B6 |
| Tamworth Hotel | 21 A5 |

at that stage in the night, is a lot safer than the stairs.

**Austin Tourist Park** ( ☎ 1800-826 967, 6766 2380; www.austintouristpark.com.au; 581 Armidale Rd; unpowered/powered sites $21/25, cabins $52-87; P ✕ ✈ ) Warning – sleep-walkers should stay away from this park. There is a river and it is quite a steep drop-off.

**MIDRANGE**

The New England Hwy is midrange heaven and during off-peak times there are plenty of bargains.

**City Sider Motor Inn** ( ☎ 6766 4777; 237 Marius St; d/ste $89/120; P ✕ ✈ ) Squat rooms in a 'Mediterranean kinda' inspired–complex. Lookout for this one if you are coming in from Armidale; it's gaudy and yellow.

**Jacaranda Cottage** ( ☎ 6766 4281; 105 Carthage St; r incl breakfast $90-135; P ) Built in the 1930s this B&B is in a very peaceful street (forgetting the fire station next door of course). There are two rooms in the house but the more private option is the self-contained loft out back.

**Beethoven's** ( ☎ 6766 2735; 66 Napier St; r $120 Mon-Thu, $140 Fri-Sun; P ) A lovingly restored building with four rooms including bathrooms and a magnificent open fire in the guest lounge. Conveniently located across the road from the bowling club.

**TOP END**

**Quality Hotel Powerhouse** ( ☎ 6766 7000; www.qualityhotelpowerhouse.com.au; New England Hwy; r $170-210; P ✕ ✈ ) Prices at the old powerhouse do drop depending on the time of year/week you stay. For example, you may score a cheap room on a Friday night in nonpeak periods.

## Eating

There is a meal in Tamworth to suit every tastebud. You can have Chinese, Indian, Thai, Mexican, Italian and even African. And if you are more about quantity than quality, head to **83 Restaurant** ( ☎ 6766 2383; 199 Marius St; ✕ lunch & dinner) for all-you-can-eat.

**Immrama** ( ☎ 6761 3504; 306 Peel St; mains $5-10; ✕ breakfast & lunch) Finally a place where people can go to rejuvenate and relax, receive reiki ($30), or get a clairvoyant reading ($45). Meditation and natural-healing sessions happen on Monday night.

**Old Vic Café** ( ☎ 6766 3435; 261 Peel St; mains $10-18; ✕ breakfast & lunch, closed Sun) An earthy coun-

try feel in terms of cheesecloth and Betty Crocker rather than tassels and bow legs. Get anything from a sandwich to a rump steak.

**Tudor Hotel** ( ☎ 6766 2930; 377 Peel St; mains $9-24; ✕ lunch & dinner) Elegantly decorated with romantic '80s music oozing from the restaurant. Garlic prawns and avocado taste good whether you are downstairs or up as it is the same menu on both levels.

**Vault** ( ☎ 6766 6975; 429 Peel St; mains $9-26; ✕ breakfast & lunch daily, dinner Tue-Sat) Residing in an old heritage bank, it cooks up basic meals with a gourmet twist.

**Café Africa** ( ☎ 6766 9995; cnr Brisbane & Marius Sts; mains $13-35; ✕ lunch & dinner, closed Mon) Herbivores stay away, you will be confused by the Kalahari Bushman Skewers, and distraught by the Game of the Day. But carnivores are you ready for the Massai Challenge? Eat two Massai 1kg rumps and get the third one free.

## Entertainment

**Imperial Hotel** ( ☎ 6766 2613; www.imperialhotel.com.au; cnr Brisbane & Marius Sts) This is where the young folk tend to hang out. It goes off Thursday nights but you can catch local live acts most weekends in Studio 181.

**Central Hotel** ( ☎ 6766 2160; cnr Brisbane & Peel Sts) It has an older crowd and bands or a DJ on weekends. A bit more of a laid-back affair. You will make friends here whether you like it or not.

**Tamworth Hotel** ( ☎ 6766 2923; 147 Marius St) This place says country club and so do the slightly conservative crowd that drink here. There is a brassiere but no loud bands, just the faint sizzle of steaks and subtle hint of pretension wafting throughout the hotel.

## Getting There & Away

**QantasLink** ( ☎ 13 13 13) has four to five daily flights to and from Sydney.

If you decide to bus it, **Greyhound** ( ☎ 13 14 99) has daily services along the New England Hwy to Armidale (adult/child $40/35) and through to Sydney (adult/child $90/75). And **Keans** ( ☎ 6545 1945) runs to Armidale, Coffs Harbour and Port Macquarie, and south to Scone.

**CountryLink** ( ☎ 13 22 32) trains go to Scone and Sydney daily. Buses travel to Manilla (adult/child $7/4) and Inverell (adult/child $46/26) daily.

NEW ENGLAND

## Getting Around

**Tamworth Coaches** ( ☎ 6762 3999) operates extensively throughout town; stops are visible and obvious. **Tamworth Taxis** ( ☎ 6766 1111) can be waved down around town. And there are plenty of hire-car companies to choose from including **Avis** ( ☎ 6765 2000), **Budget** ( ☎ 6765 5910), **Hertz** ( ☎ 6762 5545), **Tamworth Hire Cars** ( ☎ 6766 1909) and **Thrifty** ( ☎ 6765 3699).

## OXLEY WILD RIVERS NATIONAL PARK

There will always be one old duck eager to tell you how they saw a brush-tailed rock wallaby. But the truth is sightings are rare, even in World Heritage–listed Oxley, the main refuge for the endangered species. However, large colonies of them do hang out at **Dangar Gorge**. So keep your eye out because if you don't see one someone back up at the car park will have.

But for the most part this park is known for its rivers, gorges and waterfalls. **Wollomombi Falls**, 40km east of Armidale, is the highest in Australia with a drop of 220m. The spectacular **Apsley Falls** are 18km east of Walcha at the southern end of the park.

Lots of water makes for lots of water sports and canoeing and kayaking are popular in the park. Mountain-biking and horse riding are allowed on the fire trails as long as they are not within designated 'wilderness' areas. You can 4WD on **Race Course Trail** on the border of Oxley Wild Rivers and **Werrikimbe National Park**. The National Parks & Wildlife Service (NPWS) run the '**Discovery**' programme here during school holidays (www.nationalparks.nsw.gov.au).

The park can be accessed via Walcha, Dorrigo and Armidale along the Waterfall Way. **Youdales Hut** is a little primitive but is also a popular camping destination accessed by 4WD only via Walcha and Kangaroo Flats Rd. Call **Walcha NPWS** ( ☎ 6777 4700) for bookings.

## URALLA

☎ 02 / pop 2300

The name Uralla is said to be Aboriginal for 'ceremonial meeting place'. But the town is probably more well know as the home of legendary bushranger Captain Thunderbolt (see the boxed text, below). Although born in Windsor and married in Stroud, Thunderbolt was killed just south of town.

Foodworks in the main street, Bridge St, has an **ATM**. The **post office** is on Hill St and the **CTC** has internet access in the old Courthouse on the corner of Hill and Maitland Sts. Visit Paul at the **visitors centre** ( ☎ 6778 4496; www.uralla.com; 104 Bridge St) who will happily point you in the right direction for fossicking around town.

An old flour mill, the **McCrossin's Mill Museum** ( ☎ 6778 3022; cnr Bridge & Salibury Sts; adult/child $4/2; 🕒 12pm-5pm Mon-Fri, from 10am Sat & Sun) is where you can view Captain Thunderbolt's muzzle loader and revolver and learn about the evolution of the cricket bat.

## Sleeping & Eating

**Coachwood and Cedar Hotel/Motel** ( ☎ 6778 4110; www.toppuburalla.com.au; Bridge St; s/d motel $55/70, s/d hotel $35/70) Stay the night in a cheaper pub room or in the mini motel out the back. With enormous, bold bathrooms and funky coloured paintwork, these rooms are the trendier option in town if not all of New England!

**Uralla Caravan Park** ( ☎ 6778 4763; www.urallacaravanpark.com.au; 17 Queen St; sites unpowered/powered $15/18, cabins $60) Forget about the on-site vans as they are tiny and you forgot to pack linen anyway. The cabins are a better option but Fido must stay outside. Linen is available for hire ($5).

**Stoker's Restaurant** ( ☎ 6778 3777; 37 Bridge St; mains $19-24; 🕒 dinner Mon-Sat) Built in the 1820s they serve up an odd selection of mains (apparently) reflecting the position of the town

---

### THUNDERBOLT

Born to an Irish convict in 1835, dead by 36. A typical timeline for your average Aussie bushranger. Supported by the poorer locals, their legends still ignite a 'them-and-us' sense only capable in a population grown from a convict state. This one inspired the public imagination even further by escaping the inescapable Cockatoo Island Gaol in Sydney Harbour, not once but twice. Swimming to shore in Balmain, he survived the next six years by intercepting and robbing the wealthy aristocrats as they travelled past his bush hideouts throughout the Hunter and New England. Stop at his many lookouts, inspect his hideout north of Tenterfield (5km south of Uralla), the scene of his shooting, and mourn his passing over a beer at the Bottom Pub (see Top Pub, opposite) before checking out his grave on the edge of Uralla Cemetery (John St).

NEW ENGLAND

and a need to appeal to all tastes. So keep this in mind when noticing a menu of Italian and Indian dishes and Guinness pie.

**Top Pub** ( ☎ 6778 4110; Bridge St; mains $17-30; ☺ lunch & dinner) Known as the Top Pub because it is at the top of the main street, this drinking hole is popular with students from Armidale. The 'Funk Lush Room' outside is a great place to chow down on anything from Thai curry, pizza and steak, to kangaroo fillet.

### Getting There & Away
**Keans** ( ☎ 6545 1945) buses travel to Coffs Harbour and down the coast to Port Macquarie. They head south to Tamworth and Scone. And **Greyhound** ( ☎ 13 14 99) travels back up the New England Hwy, as far as Tenterfield (adult/child $60/50) and south to Tamworth (adult/child $40/32) and Sydney (adult/child $100/85). An **Edwards** ( ☎ 6772 3116) bus does five trips a day to Armidale on weekdays only.

## AROUND URALLA
An unusual hexagonal-shaped woolshed, a vine-covered chapel and 199 elm trees turn this unique destination, **Gostyck**, into a little piece of England. Go there in the thick of autumn when it is covered in an array of orange tones, and on the first Sunday of the month for a peak inside. Gostyck is just 10 minutes' drive east of Uralla; admission is free, and as it's on public land you can visit it at any time

## ARMIDALE
☎ 02 / pop 25,000
It is a university town but even the hundreds of virile students don't seem to soften the pensive mood here. SAD (seasonal affective disorder) or not, the town's history and culture shine through. You can mope in museums, mill around the market or be joyless in a joy-flight over the local gorge country and waterfalls.

Go there in autumn and hear the fallen leaves crinkle under foot when the cooler breeze paints the town orange hues. With its historic streetscapes, excellent eating options, and World Heritage–listed national parks, there will always be something to do to lift the mood.

### Information
The New England Hwy turns into manic Marsh St. Thankfully Beardy St is the main street and is closed off to traffic.

**AMAC Digital Products** ( ☎ 6771 1287; 209 Beardy St) For internet access.
**Armidale Outdoors** ( ☎ 6772 7744; 152 Rusden St) For all your camping accessories. Stocks a handful of maps.
**Library** (Faulkner St; ☺ 10am-6pm Mon-Fri, 10am-1pm Sat) Has free internet.
**National Parks & Wildlife Service** (NPWS; ☎ 6738 9100; 145 Miller St)
**Visitors centre** ( ☎ 1800 627 736, 6772 4655; www .armidaletourism.com.au; 83 Marsh St) Located behind the Mobil service station.

### Sights
#### UNIVERSITY OF NEW ENGLAND
The key to finding your way around the university is to locate **Booloominbah** ( ☎ 6773 3909; University campus, Queen Elizabeth Dr). Not an easy feat in itself, unless you head up Queen Elizabeth St and turn right on Elm Ave, following the elms to the very end. From there you can do a self-drive tour of the university grounds or park and walk (visitors' parking for two hours only; it's better get a parking permit).

A **walking tour** brochure can be picked up from the **visitors centre** in town, and gives a brief description of some of the key university buildings, such as the **Museum of Antiquities** (admission free; ☺ 9am-5pm Mon-Fri) where you can learn about Australia's history from back when *Homo erectus* first arrived, 40,000 years ago.

#### MUSEUMS
With staff who are both knowledgeable and upbeat, **New England Regional Art Museum** ( ☎ 6772 5255; Kentucky St; admission free; ☺ 10am-5pm Tue-Fri, 9am-4pm Sat & Sun) is the *crème de la crème* gallery of the region. Stop for a coffee at NERAM Café on the way out.

We have all come to equate Aboriginal art with dot paintings. Come to the **Aboriginal Cultural Centre & Keeping Place** ( ☎ 6771 3606; 128 Kentucky St; art exhibit $2; ☺ 10am-5pm Tue-Fri, 9am-4pm Sat & Sun) to broaden the mind and let the kids make their own priceless piece with the help of the resident artist.

### Activities
There is a free, yes you heard right free, **Heritage Tour** of Armidale that departs from the visitors centre at 10am daily. They also have details of heritage walks around town.

Better still, get on a bike from **Armidale Bicycle Centre** ( ☎ 6772 3718; 244 Beardy St; per hr $5.50); you'll cover more ground that way.

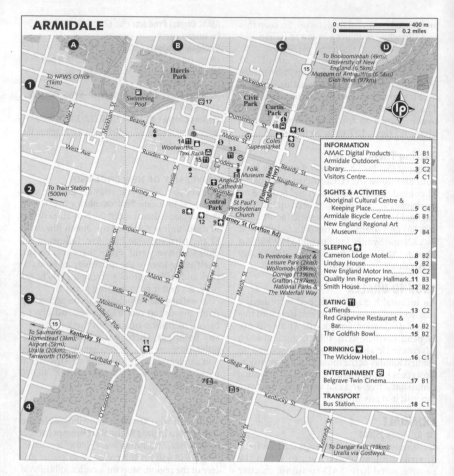

## ARMIDALE

Catch a close view of the gorgeous gorges with **Fleet Helicopters** ( ☎ 6772 2348; www.fleethelicopters.com.au; Armidale Airport). A 30-minute flight over Dangar and Gara costs $180 per person, but catch a glimpse of all six in one hour for $330.

## Festivals & Events

Armidale is at its picturesque best in March for the **Autumn Festival**, which includes a street parade and plenty of live music. The National Sheep Dog Trials are held at the **Wool Expo** and on the last Sunday of each month there is a **market** on Beardy St.

## Sleeping

Watch out as premiums may rise and hotels will book-out quickly during graduation.

### BUDGET

**Smith House** ( ☎ 6772 0652; www.smithhouse.com.au; 100 Barney St; incl breakfast s/d $40/50; P ) Smith has provided everything you will need including heating, TV, fridge, microwave and even internet connection.

**Cameron Lodge Motor Inn** ( ☎ 6772 2351; cnr Dangar & Barney Sts; s/d $65/72; P ✕ ) Value for money conveniently located just one block from Beardy St. Although the faux-fur bedspreads really do ooze Miami Vice, or is it more '80s porn?

**New England Motor Inn** ( ☎ 6771 1011; www.newenglandmotorinn.com.au; 100 Dumaresq St; s/d $85/95; P ✕ ) This very pink motel is across the road from the Wicklow and has comfortable rooms that are very popular so you may need to book ahead.

**Pembroke Tourist & Leisure Park** ( ☎ 6772 6470; 39 Waterfall Way; unpowered/powered sites $19/24; dm $24; cabins from $56; **P** **⚓** ) Very friendly, very leafy.

**MIDRANGE**
**Quality Inn Regency Hallmark** ( ☎ 6772 9800; 208 Dangar St; r $105-130, spa ste $175; **P** **R** **⚓** ) A touch pricey and a little luxurious, this is one of several options in town. A confused French restaurant features overpriced French cuisine and Asian dishes, so head into town for a better feed.

**TOP END**
**Lindsay House** ( ☎ 6771 4554; www.lindsayhouse.com .au; 128 Faulkner St; incl breakfast deluxe/exec d $165/220; **P** ) Antique-filled rooms house lavish four-poster beds. The front rooms overlook the immaculate gardens and Central Park, and are the perfect place to sit and just chill from the chill on a cold winter's day.

## Eating
**Goldfish Bowl** ( ☎ 6771 3271; Dangar St; mains $6-9; ❤ breakfast & lunch) Are Aussies really ready for proper espresso, and although everyone wants to be Italian, do we really need to hover over our coffee? So will you please sit down and watch the *baristas* make the best coffee in town.

**Caffiends** ( ☎ 6772 0277; Beardy St Mall; mains $9-15; ❤ breakfast & lunch) Basic through to gourmet sandwiches, salads, pizzas, laksa, nachos and even steak! A real mixed bag to suit every tastebud but not every wallet, bring cash only.

**Red Grapevine Restaurant & Bar** ( ☎ 6772 2822; 1st fl, 113 Jessie St; mains $19-26; ❤ dinner Tue-Sat) It arrives hot, it's hearty, rich and filling. Chorizo, tomato and cannellini bean, it is the way soup was always meant to be. This restaurant is not trying to be anything other than a fantastic Italian dining experience. BYO bottled wine only.

## Drinking & Entertainment
A curfew is strictly enforced in Armidale, so pick your establishment prior to 12.30am and settle in.

**Wicklow Hotel** ( ☎ 6772 2421; cnr Marsh & Dumaresq Sts) There is a selection of 20 local and imported beers on tap, so dump the young folk in the Kids Club where they can watch Sponge Bob Squarepants while the adults do all the socialising.

**Belgrave Twin Cinema** ( ☎ 6771 3388; www.bel gravecinema.com.au; 137 Dumaresq St) It shows mainstream and occasional art-house films.

## Getting There & Away
The airport is 5km southeast of town. **Qantas-Link** ( ☎ 13 13 13) has four flights a day to Sydney during the week and three on weekends.

**Greyhound** ( ☎ 13 14 99) runs twice daily north past Glen Innes (adult/child $44/36) and south to Tamworth (adult/child $40/32). One daily service departs Armidale for Sydney (adult/child $100/82). **Keans** ( ☎ 6545 1945) runs east to Coffs Harbour (adult/child $37/20) or as far south as Scone (adult/child $37/21).

**CountryLink** ( ☎ 13 22 32) goes daily to Tamworth (adult/child $20/10), Broadmeadow-Newcastle (adult/child $75/35) and Sydney (adult/child $95/50).

## Getting Around
**Edwards** ( ☎ 6772 3116) run a local bus service about town. They ferry students to and from the university as well as heading down to Uralla. Or hire a car from **Avis** ( ☎ 6772 6216), **Budget** ( ☎ 6772 5872) or **Hertz** ( ☎ 6772 0620), who all have vehicles at the airport. **Realistic** ( ☎ 6772 8078) or **Thrifty** ( ☎ 6772 4551) are in town. For taxi services call **Armidale Radio Taxis** ( ☎ 6771 1455).

# AROUND ARMIDALE
## Saumarez Homestead
A magnificent National Trust–owned house 3km from Armidale Airport, this **homestead** ( ☎ 02-6772 3616; Saumarez Rd; tours adult/child $8/6; ❤ 10am-4pm Mon-Fri, to 5pm Sat & Sun) represents two eras in Australian history. The bottom floor was constructed in 1888 and the second added in 1906. Closed from mid-June until 1st September.

## The Waterfall Way
The best thing about the national parks in this area is that they can each be visited in turn (waterfalls included) on a trip from Coffs Harbour or Grafton to Armidale. They are part of what is appropriately known as the **Waterfall Way** and are conveniently close to Armidale.

Forget the water, more surprising are the vast open cavities in the ground. Trees cling to the edge and the voids are so unexpected you would think whole herds of cattle could simply fall in. **Ebor Falls** is unique in that the water runs down three separate steps formed by ancient lava flows. Whereas the highly vertical **Wollomombi, Apsley** and **Dangar** all flow over volcanic rock sporting spectacularly hexagonal columns reaching up to the head of the falls.

## NEW ENGLAND NATIONAL PARK

This national park is home to cool temperate rainforest and the very rare Antarctic beech. It is just one of only four core refuge areas in the world for the 80-million-year-old tree.

There are multiple walks to choose from, or if you are feeling a little less than energetic drive to the top to **Point Lookout**. It is so high up here your echo won't even come back and you are bound to have a Leonardo DiCaprio 'I'm the king of the world' moment.

The park is 85km east of Armidale on the Waterfall Way near the township of Ebor. Caravans cannot be towed into the park but there is a serene little camping ground by a stream just before the park. **Thungutti Rest Area** has three cabins that can be hired out through Dorrigo **NPWS** ( ☎ 6657 2309)

Within the national park lies **Yaraandoo** ( ☎ 6775 8401; janniene@email.com; r $55-135, Wollomombi), which generally targets larger groups but does have a lodge, cottage and cabins available, and a huge range of activities on offer from fly-fishing to skirmish and everything in between.

## GUY FAWKES RIVER NATIONAL PARK

This is one of the more controversial parks in the state, where old-growth forest was continually removed until a group of protestors chained themselves to the actual trees. The logging of old growth (in what is now national park) has ceased but take care dodging logging trucks (yes, the pests are still hanging about).

You won't realise how high you have climbed until you stop at the **Misty Creek Lookout**. Just a short walk over a small incline and the extent (or height) of your bumpy trip will be revealed as you peer down into **Guy Fawkes River Gorge** and to the river 630m below. The park has the usual diverse collection of walks but also a 30km-long overnight wilderness walk, **Guy Fawkes River Walk**.

**Chaelundi Falls** (site per adult/child $3/2), may not actually be falling (depending on recent rain) but the short walk is worth it for the endless views through the valley and there are more

good chances of spotting the world's only egg-laying amphibious mammal as it definitely does look like platypus country here. The camping grounds are at least an hour's drive off the Gwydir Hwy. But if you only want to stop for a bit of a walk, the **Mt Hyland Track** is just 18km into the park.

Access (not always easy) is from Hernani, 15km northeast of Ebor, and its 30km to the **Chaelundi Rest Area**, with camp sites and water. The Dorrigo **NPWS** ( ☎ 6657 2309) office has all necessary information.

## CATHEDRAL ROCK NATIONAL PARK

This park engulfs the **Snowy Range**, the highest point in the New England Tablelands, and therefore can get quite chilly. Gone is the lush greenness seen at Guy Fawkes National Park. This is granite country with huge boulders that precariously balance (like sumo wrestlers attempting the Kama Sutra).

The camping grounds at **Native Dog Creek** (adults/child $3/2) are smallish, fairly private and accessible by car and caravan. Turn off the Waterfall Way and head towards the Guyra. But if you prefer listening to the crickets at night, rather than the cars careering past, stay at **Barokee Picnic and Camping Area** (8km off Waterfall Way). There are several walking tracks and the **Cathedral Rock Circuit** leaves from the rest area and leads you to the top of Cathedral Rock itself.

The park is near Ebor, off the Ebor–Guyra Rd. It is 60km west of Dorrigo off the Waterfall Way and 74km east of Armidale. Contact the Dorrigo **NPWS** ( ☎ 6657 2309) office for more details.

## GLEN INNES

☎ 02 / pop 6250

Glen Innes is as Scottish as a plastic-backed tartan picnic rug. But that is the gimmick and the locals are sticking with it. Frustrated by the lack of pagan activity back in the Stone and Bronze Ages, the town went about erecting their own standing stones.

The town itself is beautiful in its own right, the fairy lights strung up through the main street enhance the mystical air which is only emphasised more by the presence of the rare blue sapphire. The prettiness of the area coupled with heaps of heritage-listed buildings makes for a nice destination to visit. So leave your kilts and haggis at home and come in search of the rare blue sapphire instead.

## Orientation & Information

The town is at the intersection of the New England Hwy and Gwydir Hwy with historic Grey St running parallel to the former. The **visitors centre** ( ☎ 6730 2400; www.gleninnestourism.com; 152 Church St) is on the New England Hwy. There's an ATM at the Commonwealth Bank on the main street.

**Computer Future** ( ☎ 6732 5100; 266 Grey St) $5 per hour internet access or head down Grey St for free access at the library.

**NPWS** ( ☎ 6732 5133; 68 Church St)

**Stocks Service Station** ( ☎ 6732 1948; 271 Grey St) Sells fishing gear, bait and camping equipment.

## Sights & Activities

Overlooking the town from the Centennial Parklands are the **Australian Standing Stones**, a national monument to the Celtic people who helped pioneer Australia. But stifle giggles by continuing up the hill for a bird's-eye view of town at **Walters Lookout**.

The town has a generous portion of iron-laced pubs built in the late 1800s. But find your way to the old railway station at the **Railway Refreshment Rooms** ( ☎ 6732 1070; Lambert St, mains $10-18; ⊙ lunch & dinner) where the trains may have stopped running, but the beer never has.

Do not underestimate the capacity to interest at **Land of the Beardies History House** ( ☎ 6732 1035; cnr Fergerson St & West Ave; adult/child $6/1; ⊙ 10am-noon Mon-Fri & 1-4pm daily). It is quite surprising how much has been jammed into the old hospital, although the highlight for some will be the free morning/afternoon tea (10am and 3pm).

Combining two of the area's interests is **Pub Crawls on Horseback** ( ☎ 6732 1599; www.pubcrawlsonhorseback.com.au; Bullock Mountain Homestead; horse riding per hr from $30, weekend ride $375). You will come to a fork in the road at which point you should take a right (a left if you're a fan of 'Free Willy'). Depending on your skill level you will be riding Martini, Budweiser or maybe Baileys. The meals are forgettable so don't go expecting gourmet, but do expect a fantastic time on horseback.

## Festivals & Events

**Minerama** ( ☎ 6730 2400; www.minerama.gleninnes.biz) or possibly Hawkerama is held on the second weekend of March and attracts hundreds of mineral enthusiasts to the area. The **Celtic Festival** (www.theaustraliancelticfestival.com) is held at the end of April each year when you can watch grown men in medieval dress poke each other with big sticks in the jousting competition. But the **Beardies Festival** (www.beardiesfestival .com) is where you will see the beard-growing competition, a popular event open to both men and women.

## Sleeping

Prices go up and digs book out quickly during the Celtic Festival, but generally you won't find any very dear upmarket choices in town.

**Red Lion Tavern** ( ☎ 6733 3271; New England Hwy, Glencoe; s/d $65/75; mains $10-27) The old pub burnt down in 1968 and they say the locals frantically saved what they could. No furniture of course, just the liquor. The new pub is built from recycled bits of a court house and church. The meals are tasty, rooms are cosy, and the publican's wife is just lovely. Food is served all day.

**New England Motor Lodge** ( ☎ 1800-619 159, 6732 2922; nemlgleninnes@bigpond.com; 160 Church St; s/d from $69/79, spa ste $151; 🐾 🏋 ) Fantastic rooms (and restaurant) but what distinguishes this place is the very '80s rock waterfall by the pool. It accommodates discrete spa-frolicking and is in desperate need of a facelift.

**Silent Grove Farmstay** ( ☎ 6733 2117; www.silentgrovefarmstay-bandb.com.au; Silent Grove, Ben Lamond; r incl breakfast $85) Dorothy's your typical hard-working all-Aussie no-nonsense lady. Staying here is just like stopping over at Grans. The kids will love the baby animals, walks on the farm and fishing for yabbies.

**Craiglebuln Tourist Park** ( ☎ 6732 1283; www .gleninnes.com/craigieburn; New England Hwy; unpowered/powered sites $16/20, cabins $48, with bathroom $60-67) The pick of the caravan parks, with on-site fossicking for sapphires with Take a Wee-Brek ( ☎ 0417-272 440). Just don't underestimate the hobbitesque shower heads.

## Eating

Head down the main street to IGA for groceries if you are not venturing out tonight.

**Crofters Cottage** ( ☎ 6732 5668; Centennial Parklands; mains $3-14; ⊙ lunch Tue-Sun) At the top of the hill, this place offers light meals such as quiche and salad, as well as vegemite sandwiches for the really broke ($2.50). There is a guy in a kilt but the most Scottish thing about the place would be the IRN-BRU in the fridge.

**Tasting Room** ( ☎ 6732 6500; 296 Grey St; mains $7-15; ⊙ breakfast & lunch Tue-Sat) What this café is lacking in pretension it makes up for with a delicious array of gourmet sandwiches and light meals, including appealing vegetarian options such as eggplant fettuccine and sweet potato soup.

**Crystal Room Restaurant** ( ☎ 6732 4292; Glen Innes & District Services Club, cnr Lang & Grey Sts; mains $15-21; ☼ lunch & dinner) Have we really regressed to an age when our (seared) meat is served on a heated rock which the chef expects you to cook yourself at your table? Wilma and Fred would be flabbergasted.

**Ramona's** ( ☎ 6732 2922; 160 Church St; mains $24-29; ☼ dinner). Fabulous cuisine focused on organic and local produce. Try chicken breast, pork loin, boneless lamb steak or kangaroo fillet. Yes sure, the carpet screams 'picnic', but it may in some freaky subconscious way help the appeal of the place.

### Getting There & Away

**Greyhound** ( ☎ 13 14 99) runs down the New England Hwy to Armidale (adult/child $45/36) and Tamworth (adult/child $55/45). And there is a bus that leaves daily for Sydney (adult/child $105/85) picking up at the Caltex on Church St. **Black & White** ( ☎ 6732 3687; www .blackandwhitebus.com) runs to Inverell twice a day. And **CountryLink** ( ☎ 13 22 32) has buses down to Armidale (adult/child $18/8) out to Grafton (adult/child $18/15) and the coast, and up to Tenterfield (adult/child $10/8).

## GIBRALTAR RANGE & WASHPOOL NATIONAL PARKS

There is an unmanned **NPWS visitors centre** at the turnoff to **Mulligans Hut**. Better stop to sign the visitors book and 'take the piss' (in true Aussie style) in the comments column, like all those before you.

The best place in all of New England would have to be **Granite Lookout**. If you are lucky enough it won't be completely fogged-in and you will find yourself alone listening to the birds' chitchat echoing up the valley. If you have to choose between the two, visit **Washpool**, although the rockier **Gibraltar Range** has more accessible roads and is known for its bushwalks and mountain-bike tracks.

**CountryLink** ( ☎ 13 22 32) buses between Glen Innes and Grafton stop at the Gibraltar Range visitors centre and at the entrance to Washpool. The **NPWS** Grafton ( ☎ 6641 1500); Glen Innes ( ☎ 6732 5133) offices have more information on camping and walks.

## TENTERFIELD

☎ 02 / pop 3300

Forget Sir Henry Parkes and his vision of 'one people, one destiny', that began Australia's road to federation, the real star of Tenterfield is Peter Allen of 'When my baby smiles at me I go to Rio de Janeiro' fame. Wherever he went it is always remembered in Tenterfield that his roots are firmly here.

But you can also have fun hankering around historic buildings, get into the gourmet cuisine, and immerse yourself in the wilderness at Boonoo Boonoo and Bald Rock National Parks.

### Information

The New England Hwy turns into Rouse St and is dissected by High and Manners Sts. See Biddy at the **visitors centre** ( ☎ 6736 1082; www.tenterfield.com; 157 Rouse St) for help finding the only ATM in town.

**Library** ( ☎ 6736 1454; Manners St)
**Post Office** ( ☎ 6736 1295; cnr Rouse & Manners Sts)

### Sights & Activities

Built in 1888 from riches acquired through tin mining, **Stannum House** ( ☎ 6736 3780; 114-116 Rouse St) was intended to be the House of Parliament back when Tenterfield was hoped to be the capital of NSW.

The squat little shop, **Tenterfield Saddler**, immortalised in Peter Allen's song about his father, was Peter's grandfather's business.

The famous Henry Parkes speech that shaped the nation took place at **School of Arts** ( ☎ 6736 3592; cnr Manners & Rouse Sts; adult/child $5/2; ☼ 10am-4pm). It now houses a library and a small museum with exhibits relating to the politician's career.

Refrain from mentioning you're a geologist or endure a specimen-by-specimen tour of the entire exhibit at **Emmaville Mining Museum** ( ☎ 6734 7025; 86 Moore St; ☼ 10am-4pm Fri-Tue). Interesting for those into rocks, those who aren't can entertain themselves at the historical and 'handsome' **Emmaville Hotel**.

The king of 4WD parks is **Rover Park** ( ☎ 6737 6862; www.roverpark.com; Rover Park Rd; sites $30, on-site vans $55, bunkhouse $60); it's best you don't drive a hatchback in if you have some pride. There are over 300km of 4WD tracks to traverse and, if you don't have your own vehicle, hire one for the day for $45 plus fuel. You can go horse riding, mountain-biking, fossicking or fishing. The park is 35km east of Tenterfield on Casino Rd.

NEW ENGLAND

There is plenty of work fruit picking on farms near town from October through to May. Pick stone fruit, cherries, tomatoes and grapes. Phone Barbara at **Tenterfield Lodge & Caravan Park** ( ☎ 6736 1477) for further information.

## Festivals & Events

If you are going to one event in Tenterfield this year, make sure it's the **Oracles of the Bush**. Where state-wide competitors prepare by preening their prose and perfecting there pronunciations. **Gemfest** ( ☎ 6734 7210) is Emmaville's day to shimmer and shine. Held at the start of September, it's the one day of the year where you can go onto local properties fossicking.

## Sleeping

**Peter Allen Motor Inn** ( ☎ 6736 2499; 177 Rouse St; s/d $70/86; 🐾 ) No relation to the Boy from Oz himself except perhaps for the flamboyantly coloured bathroom tiles.

**Wangrah Wilderness Lodge** ( ☎ 6737 3665; www .wangrah.com.au; Bluff River Rd; on-site vans $60, cottages $132-150) Don't be put off by the 'Private Property' sign, as you follow 12.6km of dusty meandering road and river. At the end of the road is a haven for those who want to relax and unwind. But there is also tennis, bushwalking, 4WD adventures, mountain-biking, fishing and kayaking.

**Tenterfield Lodge and Caravan Park** ( ☎ 6736 1477; tenterfieldlodge@ozemail.com.au; 2 Manners St; unpowered/ powered sites $15/19, dm $25, on-site vans s/d $35/40, cabins $45-65; 🖳 ) A great place to base yourself while fruit picking in the area ($110 a week) but even better if you have canines. There is a dog-friendly cabin where Buster can bunk in with the rest of the family.

## Eating

You really need to have basic bases in some parts of regional NSW, then build from that, easing in the gourmet slowly, no sudden moves. Foodworks is on Rouse St.

**Destination Field Good** ( ☎ 6736 5777; 399-401 Rouse St; mains $3-13; 🕙 10am-5pm, closed Tue) The sweet gardens and decking out back are perfect for basking in spring sunshine. The mostly organic menu contains gluten- and wheat-free choices and generous servings of cake.

**Kurrajong Downs Vineyard** ( ☎ 6/36 4590; Casino Rd; mains $14-27; 🕙 lunch Thu-Mon, dinner Fri & Sat by appointment) Overlooking the vineyard and rolling yellow hills you can enjoy basic meals with a gourmet edge. The rib fillet on the bone is grown 2km down the road…and boy do those cows look happy.

**Saddler Cafe & Wine Bar** ( ☎ 6736 4400; cnr Rouse & Manners Sts; mains $22-24; 🕙 breakfast & lunch Mon-Sat, dinner Thu-Sat) Specialising in local produce and local wines, the oven-roasted duck with red cabbage potatoes and wine sauce is a delish choice. Who would have thought cabbage could taste so damn good!

## Getting There & Away

Buses leave town from the Community Centre on Manners St. **Greyhound** ( ☎ 13 14 99) runs a service down the New England Hwy stopping at Tamworth (adult/child $63/52) and Sydney (adult/child $105/86). **Kirklands** ( ☎ 6626 1499) runs from Tenterfield across to Lismore (adult/child $30/15).

**CountryLink** ( ☎ 13 22 32) has bus services travelling south along the New England Hwy to Glen Innes (adult/child $16/8) and to Armidale (adult/child $35/18), where you can change for Sydney (adult/child $62/52).

## BOONOO BOONOO NATIONAL PARK

Just 20km from Tenterfield, **Boonoo Boonoo** (bun-na-b'*noo*) is home to the endangered brush-tailed rock wallaby and the glossy black cockatoo. A day pass for one vehicle costs $7 and it's an extra $5/3 per adult/child to camp the night. Just to the south of the **Boonoo Boonoo Falls Lookout** turnoff are the **Black Swamp Falls** but don't attempt this road without a 4WD and map. The puddles change in magnitude depending on the season but the consistency of the signage does not.

## BALD ROCK NATIONAL PARK

You still can't pronounce Boonoo Boonoo so carry on a further 10km to Bald Rock National Park. Several walks begin in the car park at the camping ground (adult/child $5/3). There is Carrolls Creek Walk (18km), Border Walk (14km), and **Bald Rock Climb** (3km) which is of course the reason you are here. There is the summit direct steep-grade option for the lunatics out there and the Bungoonaa Walk for the less obsessive among us – though you'll still need to be interested enough to walk for three hours to view the southern hemisphere's largest granite monolith. Stop off to check out **Thunderbolts Hideout** on the way back to Tenterfield. Park entry is $7 per vehicle.

# THE FOSSICKERS WAY

Starting at Nundle this road takes you through the New England slopes as far north as Warialda, then east over the northwest slopes to Glenn Innes. It passes through the Tertiary basalts of the central volcanic province. Hurled from volcanoes they bear various valuable minerals and contain crystals of corundum otherwise known as sapphire. Forget about fuel prices, you could actually make money on this trip.

## NUNDLE

☎ 02 / pop 240

Lush grape vines shade the veranda in spring and summer but the leafless vines in winter give way to snow-capped mountain views. Oh... you are actually sitting on the back veranda of the Peel Inn. And unfortunately the mountains only have snow three or four days a year. But you can be guaranteed that the Peel River will still be flowing and trout still biting.

The **visitors centre** ( ☎ 6769 3158; 96 Jenkins St) is part of Café Nundle, where you can get information about the **Go For Gold Festival** in Easter; where all the locals dress up as Chinamen (and women) to celebrate the early mining heritage.

**Hanging Rock**, 10km to the east, offers superb views and picnic opportunities; you can camp for free by the **Sheba Dams**, which were built during the gold rushes. But if you are planning to retire, forget the camping and grab a pan from Café Nundle, as there is gold waiting to be uncovered at **Swamp Creek Reserve**.

### Sleeping & Eating

Accommodation gets booked out over Christmas and the Easter long weekend and during the Tamworth Country Music Festival at the end of January.

**Peel Inn** ( ☎ 6769 3377; www.peelinn.com.au; r $35-70, s/d incl breakfast $50/65) When was the last time you walked into a pub through saloon doors? Get good value unintentionally retro pub rooms (think Austin Powers), and a restaurant serving steak and seafood meals ($10 to $26).

**Jenkins St Guest House** ( ☎ 6769 3239; 85 Jenkins St; r $130-170) Share honey-glazed lamb shanks with your honey. Or prawn chilli linguine with the love of your life. Lunch is served daily and dinner from Thursday to Sunday. Meals range from $20 to $26.

**Fossickers Tourist Park** ( ☎ 6769 3355; www.fossickersatnundle.com.au; Jenkins St; unpowered/powered sites $15/20, on-site vans $45, cabins $55-80; 🖳 ) Adjacent to the Peel River and opposite the visitors centre. Ask for the cabin with river views.

There is a school bus that heads to Tamworth on school days at 7.15am, however, all roads around here lead somewhere, so it's probably best if you come by car.

## MANILLA

☎ 02 / pop 2110

The town is just a tipple of its former glory but the three remaining pubs still stand gregariously proud on the main street. Manilla boasts some of the best conditions in the world for paragliding and the talk of this place becoming a hub for the extreme sport is not all just hot air. Extreme sports aside Manilla is also fisherman fantasy world with the Namoi River and Lake Keepit quite close by.

### Orientation & Information

There is a SPAR for groceries and ATM located on the main street. The post office is opposite the Post Office Hotel of course.

---

**FOSSICKING THE FOSSICKERS WAY**

'Left ta right, side ta side, then turn it ova, just like Mum's flippin a cake', Ross explains, his beady eyes awash with hope as they search through the wash of pebble looking for just a hint of blue. This is the home of the **blue sapphire** and only one of a few places on earth where they are found. Learn to fossick with an expert like Ross or hire gear from town and head to **Boolabinda**, **Kookabookra** or **Dwyers** Fossicking Reserves. Or partake in group fossicking come March when hundreds converge on Glen Innes for **Minerama**. And remember, size doesn't matter, apparently it's all to do with the quality of the crystal. But if sapphires don't light your fire, what about agate, emerald, topaz, garnet, or gold, all waiting to be unearthed along The Fossickers Way. **Take a Wee-Brek** ( ☎ 0417-272 440; www.fossickingtours.gleninnes.com; Grey St; per bucket $10-15; ⏱ 9am-5pm in summer, ⏱ 9.30am-3pm in winter).

NEW ENGLAND

---

### VIEW FROM ABOVE

Receiving sporting medals from the prime minister alongside Steve Waugh and Kieran Perkins was a less-celebrated man who has certainly gone the distance. Meet Godfrey Wenness, the man who bought his own mountain and proceeded to fly the very first hill-launched Open-Distance Hang Gliding World Record from it. Not content with the solo record, his girlfriend Suzi joined him up in the clouds for a tandem flight of 223km that netted the world record and saw them land near the Queensland border.

Manilla has become world-famous in the flying community for long-distance flights and Godfrey's mountain is known in flying circles as God's takeoff point.

---

They are big on fish here so grab your bait, licence and some greasy take-away from **North Manilla Store** ( ☎ 6785 1900) just north of the bridge before heading to **Lake Keepit** ( ☎ 6769 7605) or north to Warrabah National Park for the big bites.

The man wanted to fly so he bought a mountain. **Godfrey's Manilla Paragliding** ( ☎ 6785 6545; www.flymanilla.com; tandem flights $120) will take you to the top of Mt Borah so you can paraglide back down again. Complete a nine-day course ($1320 including accommodation), just turn left on Charles St north of the river.

Bulging brown tree-freckled hills, it's hard to imagine **Warrabah National Park** ever being green. You will pass oodles of ostriches on your 35km trip northeast of Manilla. The beautiful brook along the side of the road is the Namoi River and you can bushwalk, canoe, fish (murray cod and catfish), swim or camp on its banks (adult/child $3/2).

### Sleeping & Eating

**Manilla River Gums Caravan Park** ( ☎ 6785 1166; therivergums@bigpond.com; 86 Strafford St; unpowered/powered sites $15/18 on-site vans $20-45, cabins $55; 🖳 ) Just $10 a night for a bed in the 'crash pad'. You can hire canoes for $5, and ask Joe where he can get you a great deal on pushbikes.

**Chinese Restaurant** ( ☎ 6785 1566; 25 Court St; mains $9-17; 🕙 lunch & dinner Tue-Sun) If you are counting calories you might as well starve, as one of the only other options is the local Chinese restaurant. Found where all small-town Chinese restaurants reside, inside of the local RSL Club.

### Getting There & Away
**CountryLink** ( ☎ 13 22 32) coaches depart Manilla for Inverell (adult/child $35/18) daily. Get to Manilla from Tamworth (adult/child $7/4) or Sydney (adult/child $81/41).

## BARRABA
☎ 02 / pop 2140
Settled in the 1830s, Barraba was put on the map during the gold-fever days of the late 1800s. But the old wide streets and elegant awnings cannot hide an artsy underbelly centred on music. You may need to do a little digging to find it, but that's OK because the shovel's in the back next to the pick and pan – this place is great for fossicking.

Everything you need is on Queen St. The **library** ( 🕙 Tue-Fri) has internet access if you happen to be in town when it's actually open. The **visitors centre** ( ☎ 6782 1255; www.barraba.org; 116 Queen St) is also on the main street and has a leaflet detailing a **Heritage Walk** that trundles past the oldest buildings throughout town.

The **Festival of Barraba** is held on the first weekend in November and is a celebration of 'music, trees and gardens'.

But if it's rocks that you are into and you're feeling a bit fossicky, head to the visitors centre and pick up a pamphlet and purchase a gold pan. Travel 3km out of town and turn right onto Woodsreef Rd, 14km more and you will come to Ironbark Goldfield and **Woodsreef Reserve**.

Andy at **Andy's Backpackers** ( ☎ 6782 1916; www.andysbackpackers.com.au; 98 Queen St; dm $20, meals by donation) has 'spasmodic' work available in return for free board. He can organise bushwalking, horse riding and fossicking tours.

Otherwise stay at **Barraba Caravan Park** ( ☎ 6782 1818; www.baraba.org; Bridge St; sites unpowered/powered $16/18, cabins $30-55).

**CountryLink** ( ☎ 13 22 32) departs Barraba from Barraba Food & Fuel for Tamworth (adult/child $16/8) daily.

## BINGARA
☎ 02 / pop 1300
This is a small town straddling the Gwydir River. There is not much here if you are not horsey, but it is a nice place to stop over on your way to Tamworth or Copeton Dam.

The post office and IGA are on the main street, but the only ATM will force you into the pub. The **visitors centre** ( ☎ 6724 0066; www.bingara.nsw.gov.au; Roxy Theatre, 74 Maitland St) is situated in the **Roxy** which is a Greek-influenced, refurbished Art Deco cinema. It is still utilised today for films, concerts and theatrical pursuits in general.

There are 3000 acres to ride on but most people want to swim with the horses at **Gwydir River Trail Rides** ( ☎ 6724 1562, qwydirrides@northnet.cm.au; 17 Keera St; 2½hr trail ride $55, canoe hire $30). For fair-dinkum Aussieness complete the five-day Jackeroo/Jillaroo Adventure. You will come back able to ride a horse, crack a whip and brand cattle among other things. All meals and accommodation included ($350). Or you can giddy up with horse riding lessons for $20 an hour.

The **Fossickers Way Motel** ( ☎ 6724 1373; www .bingaramotel.com.au; Finch St; r $60; 🐾 ) has a tidy appearance and a very quiet setting on the edge of parkland, just across the road from the Gwydir River.

Cheap accommodation can be found at the **Sportsman's Hotel** ( ☎ 6724 1139; 31 Maitland St) and if you have finished horse riding and feel famished, get anything from sandwiches and melts to steak and burgers (mains $10 to $16).

**CountryLink** ( ☎ 13 22 32) coaches depart Bingara for Inverell (adult/child $18/9), Tamworth (adult/child $26/13) and Sydney (adult/child $100/50). All bookings can be made at the local newsagents.

## INVERELL
☎ 02 / pop 11,000

What this place lacks in character it does not make up for in any other way. It is, however, a regional centre refreshingly not driven by the tourist dollar. The three reasons to go are all located outside of town. The very surprising Kwiambal National Park, the very empty Copeton Dam (just 23% capacity at the time of writing) and the very beery and cheery Graman Pub (see opposite).

## Information
Pick up a map of the area's fossicking sites at the **visitors centre** ( ☎ 6728 8161; www.inverell-online .com.au; Campbell St) as there are plenty of gems that can be visited by car.
**Post office** ( ☎ 6722 5241; 97 Otho St)

## Sights & Activities
The **Inverell Pioneer Village** ( ☎ 6722 1717; Tingha Rd; adult/child $8/4; 🕙 10am-5pm Tue-Sun) is a place where you step back in time and discover the people who helped shape Oz.

An ideal outing for car enthusiasts is the **Transport Museum** ( ☎ 6721 2270; Taylor Ave, Bannock-

burn Rd; adult/child $6.60/4.40; 🕙 10am-4pm), which features some rare and exotic mobiles that can only be viewed here in Inverell.

One of the more popular fossicking reserves around town is **Billabong Blue Sapphire Fossicking Park** ( ☎ 6728 8161; Woodstock Rd; adult/child $20/10; 🕙 10am-4pm Wed-Sun) . However, prospecting individuals may want to check out **7 Oaks** ( ☎ 6725 1582; Rickey's Lane) as well. **Fishing & Camping World** ( ☎ 6722 3620; 112 Byron St) can sort out your fossicking and fishing needs.

## Festivals & Events
There is dancing in the streets at the **Sapphire City Festival** when locals put on a parade in October. But if you are feeling fishy the **Great Inland Fishing Festival** is held at Copeton Dam

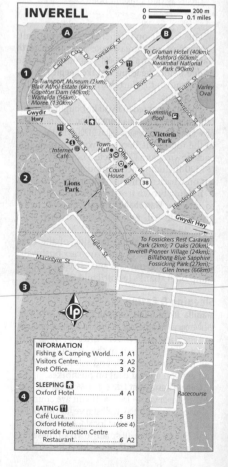

in December. It is a catch-and-release comp where you score points depending on what you have hooked.

## Sleeping

Warning... expect price hikes during festival and peak times.

**Oxford Hotel** ( ☎ 6722 1101; 61 Otho St; s/d $25/35) Very cosy bargain rooms mean you will soon forget about the one-inch gap above the doorway.

**Blair Athol Estate** ( ☎ 6722 4288; www.babs.com .au/blairathol; Warialda Rd; s/d incl breakfast from $100/120) Built on an extinct volcano, the stunning grounds are peppered with a bizarre to almost disturbing mix of flora from Himalayan cedars to boabs. The initial owners are buried in the front yard.

**Fossickers Rest Caravan Park** ( ☎ 6722 2261; www fossickersrest.com.au; Lake Inverell Dr; unpowered/powered sites $14/18, cabins $45-55) Located in a beautiful shady setting 3km east of Inverell.

## Eating

**Café Luca** ( ☎ 0267-210 160; 103 Byron St; ☽ breakfast & lunch) Located within a hardware store, the café offers a range of original melts as well as the Steamer, flavour-infused milk.

**Oxford Hotel** ( ☎ 6722 1101; 61 Otho St; mains $5-16; ☽ lunch & dinner, closed Sun) Frighteningly, it's the pick in town in terms of value, thanks to large servings of steak and seafood.

**Riverside Function Centre Restaurant** ( ☎ 6721 1244; Campbell St; mains $22-28; ☽ breakfast & lunch daily, dinner Mon-Sat) In a town lacking choice, this restaurant is the most upmarket option. The key here is flavour and they actually use herbs, homemade sauces and dressings, distinguishing it from all other eating options in town.

## Getting There & Away

**Black & White** ( ☎ 6732 3687) departs Inverell for Glen Innes weekdays only. **CountryLink** ( ☎ 13 22 32) departs Sydney for Inverell daily (change over at Tamworth). And runs south to Tamworth (adult/child $28/35), connecting through to Scone (adult/child $40/35) and Sydney (adult/child $62/52).

If you would prefer to fly **Big Sky Express** ( ☎ 1800 008 759) depart daily from Sydney to Inverell, via Gunnedah.

## AROUND INVERELL

**Copeton Dam** ( ☎ 6723 0260; Gumflat Rd; per car $8, boat hire per hr $20, bike hire $14) There are a number of activities from water skiing and sailing to golf, although the kangaroos don't appear to take their game too seriously. Be careful of these fellows on the road, they're big buggers and remember to stop at Gum Flat Worm and Yabbie Supplies for all your live bait needs.

**Green Valley Farm** ( ☎ 6723 3370; Tingha; admission $5; ☽ 9.30am-5pm Sat & Sun & school holidays) Head south of Inverell to the small township of Tingha and Green Valley Farm. There is 18 hole mini golf ($2), water slides ($6), a museum, a zoo and topiary grotesqueries, such as an 'eight-legged kitten' and 'Siamese pigs'.

**Graman Pub** ( ☎ 6725 6482; Yetman Rd, Graman; ☽ lunch & dinner) Craig is the publican and what you see is what you get, which is always lots of laughs. You will meet brilliant characters and have a wonderful time, this may just be one of the best pubs you will visit in NSW.

## KWIAMBAL NATIONAL PARK

Pronounced Kigh-am-bal (the 'w' is silent), the park is located on the junction of the Macintyre and Severn Rivers. Largely undiscovered (admission free), it is an important conservation area for the tumbledown gum and Caley's ironbark.

When you pull up in the car park of the **Macintyre Falls Lookout** at **Lemon Tree Flat Camping Area**, you immediately notice the hypnotic humming in the trees and the rush of water. Find time to complete a (1km-long) walk as there are several to choose from that either take you over the rocks, down to the plunge pool or along the beach.

The park is also known for the **Ashford Limestone Caves**. You can feel the cold seep into your bones as you approach the entrance. This place is creepy (particularly if you forget to bring a torch) and is home to the very rare Large Bent-wing and Eastern Horseshoe bats.

Head 90km north of Inverell toward Ashford and follow the signs. The road may be hard to negotiate after rain so contact the **NPWS** (Glen Innes office; ☎ 6732 5133) or **Inverell visitors centre** ( ☎ 6728 8161) before you go to check its condition.

# Central West

It was gold that began the Central West, and it's the history of gold that you feel every time you enter one of the region's fascinating Victorian-era towns. They're steeped in bushranger and gold rush history: streets lined with stately buildings, parks with well-tended English gardens, folk museums filled with memorabilia, and roads named after admired drovers. Stretching 400km inland from the Blue Mountains and gradually shifting from fields to vast plains, the Central West is unique in New South Wales (NSW) for its many close and fair-sized towns.

It started with Edward Hargraves, a clever man with an intense dislike for work. Returning empty-handed from the Californian goldfields, he was inspired by a government reward for discovering payable gold, so he headed west in 1851 and found gold in Lewis Ponds Creek. He named the field Ophir after the biblical city of gold. Within a week gold fever gripped the region; for the rest of the century tens of thousands of fossickers came to the Central West in the hope the streams and hillsides would yield enough of the promised metal to change their lives forever.

Then the agriculturalists moved in. These days, the Central West is 21st-century agribusiness. It is the university city of Bathurst, the public-service enclave of Orange, the thrusting new small businesses of Mudgee, tourist towns like Wellington and Parkes, and extraordinary places like Dubbo with its Western Plains Zoo. The Central West is solid, respectable and, above all, a re-affirming successful rural hub.

---

### HIGHLIGHTS

- Watch giraffes mate at Dubbo's **Western Plains Zoo** (p241)

- Scoff down fresh-baked cherry pie in **Young** (p247), the cherry capital of Australia

- Stroll in the serene Japanese Gardens in **Cowra** (p245)

- Talk to **Pieter Ven Gent** at his vineyard in Mudgee (p235), where you sit in old choir stalls, and the muscat is liquid gold

- Dream of being a moon-walker at the **Parkes Radio Telescope** (p243)

- Explore the subterranean wonderland of lakes, chambers and stalactites at **Wellington Caves** (p240)

- Swish silent as the breeze in a hot air balloon in **Canowindra** (p247)

- Stretch your neck to see the teeth of Tyrannosaurus Rex at the **Australian Fossil & Mineral Museum** (opposite) in Bathurst

Dubbo ★
Wellington ★        ★ Mudgee
Parkes ★        Orange
Canowindra ★        ★ ★ Bathurst
        ★ Cowra
        ★ Young

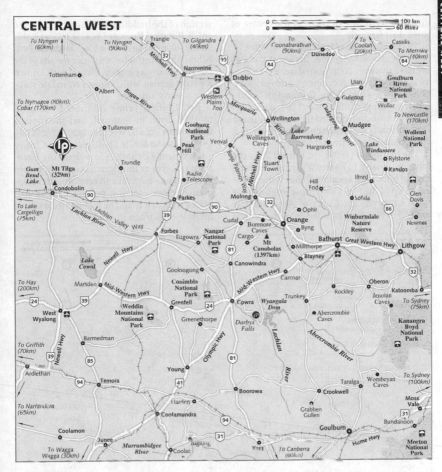

CENTRAL WEST

## BATHURST

☎ 02 / pop 37,100

There are dinosaurs in Bathurst, but even though it's Australia's oldest inland settlement, it's no dinosaur of a town. It boasts European trees, a cool climate and stacks of places of architectural and historical interest. But best of all, Bathurst is the bastion of Australian motor sport, hosting numerous events.

### Orientation & Information

The city is laid out on a grand scale with a large grid of wide streets. William St between Durham and Keppel Sts is the main shopping area.

The **visitors centre** ( ☎ 6332 1444; Kendall Ave; www.bathurst.nsw.gov.au; ☼ 9am-5pm) is particularly helpful. Internet is free at the **Bathurst Library** ( ☎ 6332 2130; 70-78 Keppel St), part of the Bathurst Regional Art Gallery.

### Sights & Activities

See Tyrannosaurus Rex, Australia's only complete skeleton, at the **Australian Fossil & Mineral Museum** ( ☎ 6331 5511; 224 Howick St; adult/child $8/4; ☼ 10am-4pm Mon-Sat, 10am-2pm Sun). You'll also see the internationally renowned Somerville Collection, the personal collection of geologist Warren Somerville, with more than 6000 fossils from every period of the earth's history, some specimens being the only examples in the world. And the collection of crystal is stunning, plus there's the country's finest collection of fossils in amber, and opalised dinosaur teeth. It's all there in the centre of town. Just fantastic.

The **Bathurst Regional Art Gallery** ( ☎ 6331 6066; 70-78 Keppel St; admission free; ☑ 10am-5pm Tue-Sat, 11am-2pm Sun) has a dynamic collection of work featuring local artists as well as exciting touring exhibitions. The work of Grace Cossington-Smith, whose paintings of the Sydney Harbour Bridge under construction defined the event for many Australians, is well represented but restricted; you must ask at the front desk.

The **courthouse** (1880), on Russell St, is the most impressive of Bathurst's many interesting old buildings. Local myth has it there was a mix-up of the plans with those intended for India's magnificent Court of Appeals! The **court** ( ☑ 9.30am-1pm & 2-4pm Mon-Fri) is the central

section of the building. In the east wing is the small **Historical Museum** ( ☎ 6332 4755; adult/child $2/1; ☑ 10am-4pm Tue, Wed, Sat & Sun). **Machattie Park**, behind the courthouse, was once the site of the jail and is now a pleasant formal park known for its begonias, which flower from late summer to early autumn.

Ben Chifley, prime minister from 1945 to 1949, lived in Bathurst, and the modest **Chifley Home** ( ☎ 6332 1444; 10 Busby St; adult/child $6/4; ☑ 11am-3pm Sat-Mon) is on display. The Chifley government's initiatives in welcoming European refugees as immigrants were important to Australia's cultural and economic development. Before entering politics Chifley had been a train driver and he maintained a simple lifestyle even when in office.

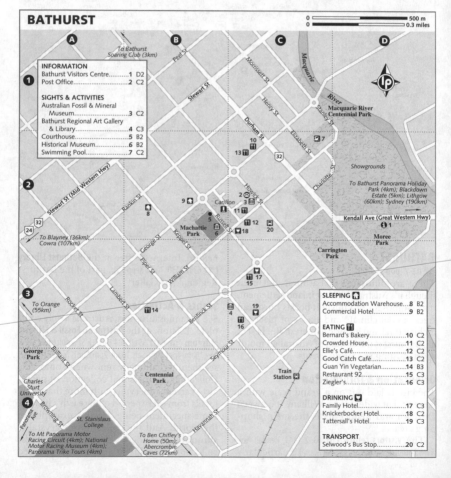

## BATHURST

0 ——————— 500 m
0 ——————— 0.3 miles

**INFORMATION**
Bathurst Visitors Centre...........1 D2
Post Office................................2 C2

**SIGHTS & ACTIVITIES**
Australian Fossil & Mineral
  Museum.................................3 C2
Bathurst Regional Art Gallery
  & Library...............................4 C3
Courthouse................................5 B2
Historical Museum.....................6 B2
Swimming Pool..........................7 C2

**SLEEPING** 🛏
Accommodation Warehouse...8 B2
Commercial Hotel..................9 B2

**EATING** 🍴
Bernard's Bakery....................10 C2
Crowded House......................11 C2
Ellie's Café............................12 C2
Good Catch Café....................13 C2
Guan Yin Vegetarian..............14 B3
Restaurant 92........................15 C3
Ziegler's................................16 C3

**DRINKING** 🍷
Family Hotel..........................17 C3
Knickerbocker Hotel...............18 C2
Tattersall's Hotel....................19 C3

**TRANSPORT**
Selwood's Bus Stop................20 C2

Rev-heads will enjoy the **National Motor Racing Museum** ( ☎ 6332 1872; Pit Straight; adult/child/family $7/5/16; ☒ 9am-4.30pm).

## Activities

Bathurst has a stack of adventurous activities available, from caving to vintage joy flights, harness racing to motorcycle cruising.

The 6.2km **Mt Panorama Motor Racing Circuit** is the venue for one of Australia's most popular car races: the Bathurst Motorsport Spectacular in October, when the visitors centre runs a private-homestay scheme for the extra crowds. You can drive around the circuit, but it's a two-way public road with a 60km limit (boring!).

If that doesn't do it, take a three-wheeler joyride around the circuit, or in the Mt Panorama area, with **Panorama Trike Tours** ( ☎ 6331 9629, 0422 182 020; Pit Straight; spins from $10), or glide across the area with **Bathurst Soaring Club** ( ☎ 4757 1824, 6337 1180; www.bathurstsoaring.org.au; 167 Freemantle Rd; ☒ 9am-9.30pm Mon-Sat). Prices are given on request.

## Sleeping

**Commercial Hotel** ( ☎ 6331 2712; 135 George St; www .geocities.com/commercialhotelbathurst; dm/s/d $20/29/49) This quaint old pub has a cosy bar downstairs and small but inviting rooms upstairs, opening onto a veranda. There's darts, pool comps and trivia nights, the shared kitchen is well stocked, the pub grub is first-rate and there are good weekly deals available.

**Bathurst Panorama Holiday Park** ( ☎ 6331 8286; www.bathurstholidaypark.com.au; Great Western Hwy; camp site per adult $26, cabins from $60; ☒ )This is the main caravan park, but during race periods other camping areas are opened.

**Accommodation Warehouse** ( ☎ 6332 2801; www .accomwarehouse.com.au; 121a Keppel St; s/d $60/80; ☒ ) This soaring brick building with its arched windows and Juliet balconies has lovely self-contained apartments, or stylish rooms with shared kitchen.

**Blackdown Estate** ( ☎ 6331 7121; www.blackdown estate.com.au; 90 Eleven Mile Dr; d queen/ste $150/170; ☒ ), This dreamy retreat off the road to Sofala has majestic rooms, claw-footed bathtubs and views across the historic outbuildings and lakes to the low ranges. The courtyards, formal gardens and romantic corners are a treasure.

## Eating

**Bernard's Bakery** ( ☎ 6331 2042; 81 George St; gourmet sandwiches $7; ☒ 6.30am-6pm Mon-Fri, 7am-4pm Sat &

Sun) This is a local favourite with its crusty rolls and bacon-and-egg sandwiches, or grab yourself a pie for $4.

**Guan Yin Vegetarian** ( ☎ 6332 5388; 166A William St; mains $10-14; ☒ lunch Mon-Fri, dinner Wed-Fri) This cosy restaurant serves 'I can't believe it's not meat' dishes where vegetarian Mongolian beef is the order of the day.

**Restaurant 92** ( ☎ 6332 1757; 92 Bentinck St; mains $8-15; ☒ 10am-3pm Mon-Sat & 6-11pm Tue-Sat) An upmarket deli-cum-wine bar with a soothing atmosphere and a focus on local produce.

**Good Catch Café** ( ☎ 6331 1333; 85 George St; mains $9-16; ☒ 11am-8.30pm Tue-Sun) This cheerful café sells a range of seafood and salads. Eat in or take away an attractive boxed meal.

**Ellie's Café** ( ☎ 6332 1707; 108 William St; mains $11-15; ☒ 7.30am-6pm Mon-Wed, till late Thu-Sat, 8.30am-5pm Sun) Ellie's great range of hot meals, such as fish with tomato and olive tapenade, or the crepes and sandwiches, will set you up for more touring. It's comfortable inside, and the courtyard and veranda are just as popular.

**Ziegler's** ( ☎ 6332 1565; 52 Keppel St; mains $16-24; ☒ 9am-10pm Tue-Sat, 9am-3pm Sun-Mon) The leafy courtyard at Ziegler's is the perfect place for coffee, which you can see being roasted. It also has tasty main dishes like crispy-skinned salmon on caponata with aioli.

**Crowded House** ( ☎ 6334 2300; www.crowdedhouse cafe.com.au, 1 Ribbon Gang Lane off William St; mains $16-30; ☒ 10am-3pm & 6-11pm Tue-Sat) From a restored 1850s church with soaring ceilings, the restaurant spills out onto a medieval courtyard dotted with olive trees and lavender bushes. The food is just as elegant and interesting as the surroundings.

## Drinking

Bathurst is a student town and they know how to party.

**Knickerbocker Hotel** ( ☎ 6332 4500; 110 William St; ☒ to 11pm Mon-Thu, till late Fri-Sun) It has big screens for Fox Sports, a jukebox, cover bands, a mixed crowd of all ages and a smart beer garden.

**Family Hotel** ( ☎ 6331 1353; cnr Russell & Bentinck Sts) This hotel is exactly that, with a pleasant beer garden and an Italian-style bistro. There is free jazz on Thursday nights and local bands get the place rocking on Friday and Saturday.

**Tattersall's Hotel** ( ☎ 6331 5544; Keppel St) This little, low-slung, atmospheric pub is popular with the uni crowd for its cheap drinks.

**PRIDE & PRODUCE**

Orange, Dubbo, Young, Mudgee, Cowra, Bathurst…the names trip off the tongue. Driving through the countryside in spring, your senses are overwhelmed by Young's cherry blossoms, young vines in Mudgee and lambs almost everywhere, the buzz of the native bees and the smell of newly cut forage. You know this area had a winter, that it was frosty and that it is over. New season, new hope.

These 'regions' are flexing their political muscle to ensure they have the same access to modern infrastructure as their city cousins. Now every small holder trades electronically, centres are being sympathetically renovated and new uses found for old buildings. If many of them are service- or tourist-oriented, it's because they're leading the way by providing opportunity and employment.

In early summer, stone fruits ripen, lambs fatten and vines bud. Each year sees new products, encouraged by both local and city chefs and gastronomes. Once asparagus was green and came in tins. Now it is white and purple and delivered daily to Sydney Markets in Flemington. Once there was leg of mutton, now there is lamb and baby goat. Once Mudgee and Orange wineries were an aberration, now they are appellation controlled. And there is cheese of every variety, virgin olive oil and verjuice.

The towns compete to provide the best services to visitors and take pride in their locality: there's tours of local wineries and honey producers; places to try the local produce; fish to be caught and smoked; museums and galleries; and restaurants and cafés inviting you to experience everything the past and the present has to offer.

The Central West is not in the heart of Australia, but it exudes an aura of being its heart.

## Getting There & Away

**Australian Rail Maps** (www.railmaps.com.au) website has details of the services in the region; click on the relevant route. **Selwood's Coaches** ( ☎ 6362 7963) links Bathurst with Orange ($9, 45 minutes) and Sydney ($30, four hours) three times daily.

The quick **CountryLink** ( ☎ 13 22 32; www.country link.info) XPT trains stop here on the daily Sydney ($34, 3½ hours) and Dubbo ($31, 1½ hours) service.

**Broken Hill Outback Explorer** stops here each Monday ($88 to Broken Hill).

## Getting Around

**Taxis** ( ☎ 6331 1511, 13 22 32) run 24 hours a day. **Bathurst Coaches** runs a local bus service, which stops outside Bathurst Panorama Holiday Park every day except Sunday. Grab a timetable from the visitors centre.

## AROUND BATHURST

About 70km south of Bathurst along awesome winding roads are the famous **Abercrombie Caves** ( ☎ 02-6368 8603; www.jenolancaves .org.au; self-guided/guided tours $13/16; ☼ 9am-5pm). The Grand Arch is one of the world's largest natural tunnels and even the side passages are huge. In the Hall of Terpsichore you can still dance on the dance floor installed by miners 120 years ago. Beneath all the limestone is a river with a few particularly beautiful pools. There's swimming and **accommodation** ( ☎ 026368 8603; camp site per person/family $7.50/18, cabin std/deluxe $50/90) near the cave, with good facilities nearby.

**Sofala**, Australia's oldest surviving gold town and a quaint little place, has some unusually well-preserved timber buildings. The films *The Cars that Ate Paris* and *Sirens* were shot here.

Northwest of Sofala, pretty **Hill End** was the scene of an 1870s gold rush, then it became an artists' colony where Donald Friend lived and worked for years. Inside the old hospital is the **NPWS office** ( ☎ 02-6337 8206; Hospital Lane; ☼ 9.30am-12.30pm & 1.30-4.30pm) where you book for the two **NPWS camping grounds** (adult/child $5/3) and a fascinating **museum** (admission $2.50).

Hang out with the few residents at their local, the dusty but still regal **Royal Hotel** ( ☎ 02-6337 8261; Beyers Ave; s/d $40/65), the only pub remaining of an original 52 in the district. The rooms are pleasant, amenities are shared, and downstairs is the **bistro** (mains $16-24; ☼ breakfast, lunch & dinner).

Further northeast towards Mudgee, the small town of **Rylstone** features pretty sandstone buildings and access to **Wollemi National Park**.

## MUDGEE
☎ 02 / pop 8500

Mudgee, an Aboriginal word for 'nest in the hills', is the centre for the new regional gourmet food and wine industries. So it's a popular weekend getaway, combining attractive natural surroundings with gastronomic exploration. Local farms now specialise in sheep and goat's cheeses, olives, hazelnuts and, of course, the renowned Mudgee honey.

### Orientation & Information

Mudgee is about 120km north of Bathurst and Lithgow, on the banks of the Cudgegong River. Most wineries are north of the river. The main shopping street is Church St.

The **visitors centre** ( ☎ 1800 816 304, 6372 1020; www.visitmudgeeregion.com.au; 84 Market St; ☼ 9am-5pm Mon-Fri, to 3.30pm Sat, 9.30am-2pm Sun) is near the post office. If you're going wine tasting, grab a copy of the Mudgee–Gulgong visitors guide.

### Sights & Activities
#### WINERIES

The vineyards are clustered in two groups north and southeast of town. This makes them ideal

for cycling between as long as you don't get the wobbles. The vintage is later than in the Hunter Valley because of Mudgee's higher altitude.

**Poet's Corner** ( ☎ 6372 2208; Craigmoor Rd; ☼ 10am-4.30pm) has produced a vintage annually since 1858, making it one of Australia's oldest. The atmospheric cellar holds musical evenings – ask at the visitors centre.

Get some old-fashioned winery atmosphere at **Pieter Van Gent** ( ☎ 6373 3807; Black Springs Rd; ☼ 9am-5pm Mon-Sat, 10.30am-4pm Sun), where tastings can be taken in old choir stalls, and the muscat is nectar of the gods.

**Simon Gilbert Wines** ( ☎ 6373 1245; www.simongilbert wines.com.au; Castlereagh Hwy; ☼ 9am-5pm) offers stunning views along the Cudgegong River Valley, along with its wine tasting. The winemakers platter ($15) includes local produce to add to your taste treat.

See Festivals & Events (p236) for more winery-related events.

#### OTHER ATTRACTIONS

If you really want to embrace the foodie experience, **Heart of Mudgee** ( ☎ 6372 3224; www.mudgee hampers.com.au; cnr Court & Short Sts; ☼ 9am-4pm Thu-Tue)

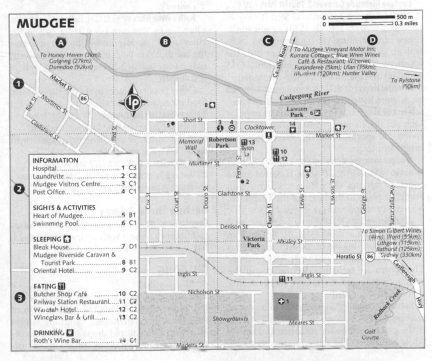

**MUDGEE**

0 —————— 500 m
0 —————— 0.3 miles

To Honey Haven (3km);
Gulgong (27km);
Dunedoo (92km)

To Mudgee Vineyard Motor Inn;
Kurrara Cottages; Blue Wren Wines
Café & Restaurant; Wineries;
Furundere (5km); Ulan (35km);
Mudgee (120km); Hunter Valley

To Rylstone
(90km)

Cudgegong River

Lawson Park

Short St

Clocktower

Market St

Memorial Wall

Robertson Park

Byron La

Mortimer St

Perry St

Gladstone St

Denison St

Victoria Park

Mealey St

To Simon Gilbert Wines
(4km); Ilford (55km);
Lithgow (115km);
Bathurst (125km);
Sydney (330km)

Horatio St

Inglis St

Nicholson St

Showground

Meares St

Golf Course

Madeira St

| INFORMATION | |
|---|---|
| Hospital | 1 C3 |
| Laundrette | 2 C2 |
| Mudgee Visitors Centre | 3 C1 |
| Post Office | 4 C1 |

| SIGHTS & ACTIVITIES | |
|---|---|
| Heart of Mudgee | 5 B1 |
| Swimming Pool | 6 C1 |

| SLEEPING | |
|---|---|
| Bleak House | 7 D1 |
| Mudgee Riverside Caravan & Tourist Park | 8 B1 |
| Oriental Hotel | 9 C2 |

| EATING | |
|---|---|
| Butcher Shop Café | 10 C2 |
| Railway Station Restaurant | 11 C3 |
| Waratah Hotel | 12 C2 |
| Wineglass Bar & Grill | 13 C2 |

| DRINKING | |
|---|---|
| Roth's Wine Bar | 14 C1 |

is a good place to start. It showcases products produced by people living in Mudgee – the best the region has to offer – with a tasting table that runs down the middle of the shop.

If that wasn't enough, **Honey Haven** ( ☎ 6372 4478; cnr Gulgong & Hargraves Rds; ☷ 9am-5pm) has endless varieties to trial (the wonderfully named 'Beeagra' included!). Kids can watch the bees hard at work in their hive.

## Festivals & Events

In September, there's a fabulous **wine festival** (www.mudgeewines.com.au) to celebrate the region's new-release wines, complete with wine show, tastings, food and concerts.

**Huntington Estate** ( ☎ 6373 3825; www.huntington estate.com.au; Cassilis Rd; ☷ 9am-5pm Mon-Fri, 10am-5pm Sat, to 3pm Sun) hosts the immensely popular **Huntington Music Festival** in early December, featuring the Australian Chamber Orchestra.

## Sleeping

If you come to Mudgee on a weekend or during the wine festival, you should book, and the rates are a bit higher. Ask at the visitors centre for a list of the many B&Bs in the valley.

**Mudgee Riverside Caravan & Tourist Park** ( ☎ 6372 2531; www.mudgeeriverside.com.au; 22 Short St; camp site per adult $20, cabin/villa d $60/72; ☒ ) It's right in the centre of everything yet it's green and leafy, with an aviary and as many birds outside the wire netting. There's mountain bike rental ($15 half-day) and the cabins are self-contained.

**Oriental Hotel** ( ☎ 6372 1074; www.orientalhotel.com .au; cnr Lewis & Mortimer Sts; B&B s/d $35/45) Help yourself to breakfast in a lovely breakfast room, or look out on the hills from the veranda. The rooms are spacious and the shared facilities bright and clean.

**Mudgee Vineyard Motor Inn** ( ☎ 6372 1022; 252 Henry Lawson Dr; s/d/f $75/85/120; ☒ ☐ ☒ ) Located only a couple of minutes' drive from town, this is an attractive place in the heart of the vineyards, with pretty rooms and great views.

**Bleak House** ( ☎ 6372 4888; www.geocities.com/bleak housemudgee; 7 Lawson St; B&B d $165; ☒ ☒ ) Built in 1860, it is anything but bleak with its gracious verandas, soaring ceilings and pretty gardens. The rooms are tastefully decorated and the scrumptious breakfast will have you powering through the vineyards.

**Kurrara Cottages** ( ☎ 6373 3734; www.kurrara.com.au; Henry Lawson Dr; 1-/2-bedroom B&B $160/295; ☒ ) This is the place to come for romance and fluffy, white bathrobes. The self-contained cottages

are for couples only, some with spa baths, all set amid rolling hills and small lakes.

## Eating & Drinking

This is such a foodie town that you'll be around for a while trying out the many restaurants.

**Butcher Shop Café** ( ☎ 6372 7373; 49 Church St; mains $7-15; ☷ breakfast & lunch daily, dinner Fri & Sat) A hip eatery in an old butchery, with stained glass and interesting artwork. Cameron, the chef, makes the best scrambled eggs with smoked salmon to start your day. Dinner is well-presented Mod Oz, including pastas and salads.

**Waratah Hotel** ( ☎ 6372 1842; cnr Market & Church Sts; mains $11-18; ☷ lunch & dinner) Locals like this place with its long timber tables and chatty atmosphere. It's good value, with grand Greek, Caesar or green salads served with the freshly prepared mains.

**Blue Wren Wines Café & Restaurant** ( ☎ 6372 6205; Cassilis Rd; mains $24-29; ☷ lunch, dinner Wed-Sat) An exceptional restaurant in an interesting space, Blue Wren is the place to indulge in dishes like Moroccan spiced lamb tagine. There is also a generous BYO policy – considering it *is* a winery.

**Roth's Wine Bar** ( ☎ 6372 1222; 30 Market St; ☷ noon-6.30pm Mon-Fri, 10am-noon Sat) After a day in the vineyards a late-afternoon tipple is probably the last thing on your mind, but Roth's is the oldest wine bar in NSW and the atmosphere is still there.

Other popular places to try the superb local food include the following:
**Railway Station Restaurant** ( ☎ 6372 0177; Inglis St; mains $22-28; ☷ breakfast Sat & Sun, lunch daily, dinner Wed-Sun) Shawn cooks dishes such as Jamaican jerk chicken with apricot and fig pilaf.
**Wineglass Bar & Grill** ( ☎ 6372 3417; Cobb & Co Ct, cnr Market & Perry Sts; mains $28-32) Where you can try dishes such as poached snapper with polenta.

## Getting There & Away

**CountryLink** ( ☎ 13 22 32; www.countrylink.info) buses to Lithgow connect with Sydney trains ($23, five hours 20 minutes, twice daily).

## GULGONG

☎ 02 / pop 2500
This little time-warp town was known as 'the hub of the world' during the roaring days of gold fever. It's narrow, old rambling streets lined with authentic old shops and miners' cottages was created almost overnight in the rush

that began in 1870. After 1880 the rush tapered off, but it left behind a well-established town that is today classified by the National Trust. Gulgong later called itself 'the town on the $10 note', but since plastic $10 notes, it isn't.

## Orientation & Information

Gulgong's main street is Herbert St, which leads south to Mudgee. Winding across town is Mayne St, a delightful old thoroughfare that becomes Wellington Rd down the hill. The **visitors centre** ( ☎ 6374 1202; www.mudgee-gulgong .org; 109 Herbert St; ☒ 8am-1pm & 1.30-5pm Mon-Fri, 9.30am-2pm Sat & Sun) has guides to some terrific walks around the area.

## Sights & Activities

The **Gulgong Pioneer Museum** ( ☎ 6374 1513; 73 Herbert St; admission $5; ☒ 9am-5pm) is one of the most eclectic country-town museums in the state. The huge collection of the important and the trivial borders on chaos, but it's all fascinating. Photographs of early Gulgong from the Holterman Collection are displayed, and there are also pin-up photos of the stars who drove the diggers wild at the local opera. Music aficionados can get their fix a few doors down in the sight-and-sound section and might even get to play a record on the gramophone run by car batteries.

Author Henry Lawson spent part of his childhood in the area after his parents followed the rush to the goldfields. The **Henry Lawson Centre** ( ☎ 6374 2049; 147 Mayne St; adult/child $4/2.50; ☒ 10am-3.30pm Wed-Sat, to 1pm Sun-Tue) looks at Lawson's early memories of Gulgong; this town was where he learned to dislike the squalor and brutalising hard work and poverty of the goldfields – a bitterness that never quite faded. There is a good selection of his works for sale.

Originally built from bark, the **opera house** ( ☎ 6374 1162; 99-101 Mayne St) is one of the oldest surviving theatres in Australia and still holds several performances a year. It was immortalised in Henry Lawson's poem, 'The Last View', and played host to such stars as Dame Nellie Melba.

Around the corner, Herbert St has some exciting galleries, like the **Cudgegong Gallery** ( ☎ 6374 1630; www.cudgegonggallery.com.au; 102 Herbert St; ☒ 10am-5.30pm) which features internationally recognised Australian artists.

**Gulgong Golf Club** ( ☎ 6374 1571) welcomes players to its nine-hole treed and grassy course between Tallawang Rd and Fisher Street. There are golf clubs for hire, and payment is by donation.

## Festivals & Events

The long weekend in June is the time for the big **Henry Lawson Festival** ( ☎ 6373 4623). There is music, dramatisation of Lawson stories at the opera house, and literary awards, some of them sponsored by Norwegian organisations – Lawson's father was a Norwegian immigrant.

Gulgong also hosts the popular **Gulgong Folk Festival** ( ☎ 6373 4623) over the New Year period with concerts, bush dances, jam sessions, street parades and more. In March, the **Gulgong Show** ( ☎ 6374 1225) has rodeos, wood chopping, animals and crafts.

## Sleeping & Eating

**Henry Lawson Van Park** ( ☎ 6374 1294; www.henrylaw soncaravanpark.com.au; 111 Mayne St; camp site per adult $19, cabin std/deluxe $36/63) Across from the Goldfields Motor Inn on the road to Wellington, this park spreads prettily among the trees. It also has an animal farm with friendly llamas and a great aviary.

**Goldfields Motor Inn** ( ☎ 6374 1111; cbailey@hwy .com.au; 112 Mayne St; std s/d $58/74, self-contained s/d $62/80; ☒ ☒ ) This place has the usual spacious clean rooms, but the views are fabulous, your hosts friendly, kitchens in the self-contained units are modern and the pool/barbecue area includes a sauna. It's a few minutes' walk up the hill to the centre of town. Ask about the family discounts.

**Stables Guesthouse** ( ☎ 6374 1668; www.thestables guesthouse.com.au; 149 Mayne St; B&B stable s/d $85/130, heritage s/d $100/160; ☒ ☒ ) A gentleman's residence in 1885, Stables is authentically renovated, with lovely gardens, gourmet breakfast and spacious dining rooms, all in the centre of town.

**Regional Ceramic Gallery** ( ☎ 6374 1202; 109 Herbert St; snacks $7; ☒ 8am-4.30pm Mon-Fri, 9.30am-2pm Sat & Sun) This is a fascinating spot, with interesting works to look at while you sip excellent coffee and enjoy light snacks, focaccias and cakes.

**Meg's Kitchen** ( ☎ 6374 1166; 97 Mayne St; mains $8-21; ☒ lunch & dinner) This delightful little den, tucked behind the Prince of Wales Hotel, has delicious food cooked by Meg herself. The creamy garlic prawns really excite the mouth, or there are takeaway homemade pizzas ($7 to $10).

**Larsen's Brasserie** ( ☎ 6374 2822; 137 Mayne St; mains $14-25; ☽ 11am-2pm & 6-10pm Fri & Sat) Relax in the nice courtyard while enjoying some excellent homemade fare featuring the local produc and a fine selection of local wines.

## Getting There & Away

**CountryLink** ( ☎ 13 22 32; www.countrylink.info) runs two buses to Mudgee ($5.50, 25 minutes, twice daily) from Gulgong.

## ORANGE

☎ 02 / pop 39,000

No, it doesn't grow oranges. It's in a fertile agricultural area, but the town was actually named in 1846 after Prince William of Orange. With four distinct seasons (due to an altitude of 950m), the city's parks and gardens are a kaleidoscope of colours throughout the year; cold winters bring occasional snowfalls.

### Orientation & Information

Suburban Orange sprawls over quite a large area, but the city centre, with its grid-pattern streets, is compact and easy to get around.

Summer St is the main street and the town centre begins just west of the train line.

The **visitors centre** ( ☎ 6393 8226; www.orange.nsw .gov.au; Byng St; ☽ 9am-5pm) has a range of handy brochures, including a walking tour of the city and winery tours around the district.

Internet access is available in many places. Try **DNA Coffee** ( ☎ 6363 1400; Orange City Centre, Anson St; per hr $5; ☽ 7.30am-6pm Mon-Wed, to 11pm Thu-Sat, 8.30am-5pm Sun).

The autumn apple-picking season lasts for about six weeks. **Octec Employment Service** ( ☎ 6362 8169; www.octec.org.au; 247 Anson St) can help you find work in the area. Some orchards have accommodation.

### Sights & Activities

The excellent **Orange Regional Gallery** ( ☎ 6393 8136; Civic Sq; admission free; ☽ 10am-5pm Tue-Sat, 1-4pm Sun) has an ambitious, varied programme of exhibitions as well as works by modern Australian masters.

The **Botanic Gardens** ( ☎ 6361 5186; Kearneys Dr; admission free; ☽ 7.30am-dusk) is on Clover Hill (with good views between the trees), 2km north of the city. The gardens were established in 1981

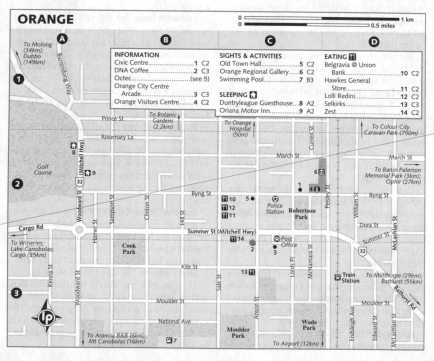

ORANGE

| INFORMATION | | SIGHTS & ACTIVITIES | | EATING 🍴 | |
|---|---|---|---|---|---|
| Civic Centre | 1 C2 | Old Town Hall | 5 C2 | Belgravia @ Union | |
| DNA Coffee | 2 C3 | Orange Regional Gallery | 6 C2 | Bank | 10 C2 |
| Octec | (see 5) | Swimming Pool | 7 B3 | Hawkes General | |
| Orange City Centre | | | | Store | 11 C2 |
| Arcade | 3 C2 | SLEEPING 🛏 | | Lolli Redini | 12 C2 |
| Orange Visitors Centre | 4 C2 | Duntryleague Guesthouse | 8 A2 | Selkirks | 13 C3 |
| | | Oriana Motor Inn | 9 A2 | Zest | 14 C2 |

to preserve the native woodlands of the area and to grow other plants suited to this cool climate. This is an interesting project, as most botanic gardens in the state were established long ago and are rigidly formal, echoing the gardens 'back home' in Britain.

Poet Banjo Paterson (who wrote the lyrics to 'Waltzing Matilda') was born on Narrambla Station near Orange in 1864. The site of the station is now **Banjo Paterson Memorial Park**, about 3km northeast of Orange on the Ophir road, with picnic facilities under the giant oak trees.

Orange has a reputation for distinctive cool-climate wines, with many award-winning vineyards around the town. Get your *Cellar Doors of Orange* booklet from the visitors centre. It gives you a summary of each vineyard then you can follow its maps in every direction.

Australia's first real gold rush took place at **Ophir**, 27km north of Orange along mostly unsealed roads. After the diggers left, deep mining was begun and continues today at Doctors Hill. A few fossickers still come here, and small finds by visitors aren't uncommon.

## Festivals & Events

**Orange Food Week** (www.orangefoodweek.com .au) is the city's annual celebration of all things epicurean and gustatory. Held during autumn, events range from cooking classes to **Opera in the Vineyard**. Then come back in October for **Orange Wine Week** (www.winesoforange .com.au) to celebrate wine with concerts, tastings, markets and vineyard tours.

**Orange National Field Days** (www.anfd.com .au/index.cfm), the largest in the state, are held in the middle of October. Here you can check out the latest farm machinery and watch events such as sheepdog trials.

The **visitors centre** ( ☎ freecall 1800 069 422) has info on where to stay, and free shuttlebus timetables during these festivals.

## Sleeping

**Colour City Caravan Park** ( ☎ 6362 7279; kpratt@orange .nsw.gov.au; cnr Margaret St & Leeds Pde; camp site $19, cabin s/d $44/52; ⚡ ) Just at the northeast corner of the city centre, this squeaky-clean place is in a large grassed park with a great barbecue area. There's plenty of space for camping, and ask about the longer-term rates.

**Oriana Motor Inn** ( ☎ 6362 3066; www.orianamotorinn .com.au; 178 Woodward St; s/d $64/82; ⚡ 🖵 ) A pleas-

ant set of units, it's set back in a spacious garden and just a stroll down from the centre of town.

**Duntryleague Guesthouse** ( ☎ 6362 3822; www .duntryleague.com.au; Woodward St; s/d $110/135; ⚡ ) A grand mansion built in 1876, now run B&B-style with grand rooms, four-poster beds and the Orange golf course right there in the grounds.

**Arancia Bed & Breakfast** ( ☎ 6365 3305; www.arancia .com.au; Wrights Lane; s/d $145/185; ⚡ ) The rooms are luxurious, the views are stunning and the breakfast delicious. It is set amid rolling hills, a delightful five-minute drive that takes you close to the wineries and golf courses.

## Eating

**Zest** ( ☎ 6360 4860; Orange Arcade, Summer St; snacks $4-11; ⚡ 8am-6pm Mon-Fri, 10am-3pm Sat & Sun) All glass and shine, the food shines too, with fresh salads and sandwiches to go with fresh-squeezed juices.

**Hawkes General Store** ( ☎ 6362 5851; 46 Sale St; mains $6-14; ⚡ 9.30am-5.30pm Mon-Fri, 10am-1.30pm Sat) This is a popular meeting place for those who like to shop for knick-knacks while they wait for the coffee – there's an excellent selection plus light meals and a pretty outdoor area to laze in.

**Belgravia @ Union Bank** ( ☎ 6360 0495; cnr Sale & Byng Sts; mains $18; ⚡ 10am-8pm Sun-Thu, till late Fri & Sat) This exciting new cellar door and wine bar in the centre of town has a range of tapas and other tasty snacks, great décor, excellent service and great weekly events such as music in the courtyard on Friday and old movies in the kitchen each Wednesday.

**Lolli Redini** ( ☎ 6361 7748; 48 Sale St; mains $22-33; ⚡ dinner Tue-Sat) It could be Italian, but Mod Oz prevails in this atmospheric timber-and-soft-light romantic spot, with slow-cooked wagyu beef cheeks, roasted beetroot and parsnip purée very hard to pass. Beware, the desserts are equally imaginative and tempting. Fortunately it also opens for lunch in summer.

**Selkirks** ( ☎ 6361 1179; 179 Anson St; 2/3-courses $66/77; ⚡ dinner Tue-Sat) In a lovely old sandstone house, this is one of NSW's premier restaurants. The menu follows the seasons, and Michael Manners, your chef who is passionate about the region's food, presents a balanced mix of fine dishes, recommending a particular local wine with each. Don't miss the dessert platter – absolute bliss.

## Getting There & Away

**Regional Express Airlines** (Rex; ☎ 13 17 13) flies to Sydney daily. The airport is 13km southeast of Orange.

**Selwood's** ( ☎ 6362 7963; www.selwoods.com.au) buses leave for Sydney ($39, four hours 15 minutes) and Bathurst ($9, 45 minutes) from the train station three times daily. **CountryLink** ( ☎ 13 22 32; www.countrylink.info) trains go to Sydney ($41, five hours) and Dubbo ($20, one hour 45 minutes) daily.

## WELLINGTON

☎ 02 / pop 5200

This thriving town at the junction of the Bell and Macquarie Rivers was the first settlement established west of Bathurst. With its steep green hills overlooking the town, and the wide Bell River running through, it's a very pleasant spot. But more than that, it has the amazing limestone caves with the world's largest stalagmite, a phosphate mine complex, significant fossil sites, a Japanese garden, and the parks and water sports at Lake Burrendong, a lake so big it contains 3½ times the volume of water in Sydney Harbour.

## Orientation & Information

The town meanders along the east bank of the Bell River, which joins the Macquarie River just north of the town centre. Nanima Cres curves past Bell River; Cameron Park runs down to the river from Nanima Cres, and across the river is the pleasant Pioneer Park.

In Cameron Park is the very helpful **visitors centre** ( ☎ 6845 1733; www.wellington.nsw.gov.au; ☉ 9am-5pm) which has a brochure with attractions, activities and festivals.

## Sights & Activities

The **Wellington Caves & Phosphate Mine** ( ☎ 6845 1733; adult/child 1 cave $14/9, 2 caves or cave & mine $24/17; ☉ tours daily; ☒ ☒ ) were discovered in 1830 by a colonist, George Ranken, who accidentally fell into one of the caves. These exquisite and unusual formations, plus subterranean waters, marsupial fossils and 'living fossils', are an absolute highlight. Cathedral Cave is famous for its majestic 32m-wide and 15m-high stalagmite! The phosphate mine is wheelchair-friendly.

Across the road from the caves is **Japanese Garden** (admission free; ☉ 9am-4pm), a gift from Wellington's Japanese sister city, Osawano.

You'll be entranced by the **Burrendong Botanic Garden & Arboretum** ( ☎ 6846 7454; www.burrendongarboretum.org; admission per car $4; ☉ 7.30am-sunset), an area overlooking Lake Burrendong that's been transformed into a wonderland of native vegetation – 50,000 plants and the largest range in Australia. The colour and variety is spectacular, especially the Western Australian collection, and so is fern gully, an oasis of rainforest plants that have flourished across Australia for millions of years.

## Festivals & Events

The horse-racing carnival in March culminates in the running of the town's answer to the Golden Slipper (Australia's premier event for two-year-olds), the **Wellington Boot** ( ☎ 0427 732 710). At the same time there is the annual **Wellington Vintage Fair** ( ☎ 6845 1736), the largest swap meet in NSW – certainly the place to come if you are into antique motors. For a special December, come to **Carols in the Cathedral Cave** ( ☎ freecall 1800 621 614).

## Sleeping & Eating

**Wellington Caves Holiday Complex** ( ☎ 6845 2970; www.wellington.nsw.gov.au/tourism; Caves Rd; camp site per adult $21, cabin/unit $52/68; ☒ ) It's a buzz to camp out at the caves, with camp sites and cabins hidden between the trees around a golf course. The attractive cabins range from basic to self-contained brick units.

**Hermitage Hill Resort** ( ☎ 6845 4469; www.hermitagehill.com.au; 135 Maxwell St; guesthouse/cottage d $89/165; ☒ ☒ ) A stunning complex of heritage buildings and classic gardens, the main house features wide verandas with views over the town and nearby Mt Arthur. There's fun shared areas with wide-screen TV, spa baths in some rooms, and an excellent restaurant; Red Rosellas (mains $20 to $30; open for lunch and dinner) is the place for romance, or a dining delight any time, with its classic décor and interesting dishes on the menu, such as chicken breast in bacon on a rosemary skewer.

**Cactus Café & Gallery** ( ☎ 6845 4647; 33-5 Warne St; dishes $5-11; ☉ 10am-4pm Wed-Sun). It's nothing like being in school, drinking coffee in the former Sacred Hearts Infants School built in 1929–30 in the Spanish Mission style. The gallery features local artists and there are Mexican handcrafts for sale, as well as home-cooked meals using seasonal produce.

**Lion of Waterloo Tavern** ( ☎ 6845 3636; cnr Gipps & Montefiores Sts; mains $12-20; ☉ lunch & dinner) Located in a really old hotel – you need to duck to get in the door – that takes you back in time while you enjoy fab food like Waterloo chicken, washed down with local wines or well-priced beers.

## Getting There & Away

**CountryLink** ( ☎ 13 22 32; www.countrylink.info) Dubbo XPT service stops daily at Wellington on its way to and from Sydney ($62, 6½ hours).

## DUBBO

☎ 02 / pop 40,000

Home to the grand Western Plains Zoo, Dubbo is also a rural centre and transport crossroads on the northern fringe of the Central West region. One of the larger towns in the state, busy but clean and attractive, it's here you'll find plenty of attractions and great shops before you head north or west into the outback.

## Orientation & Information

Dubbo's grid-pattern city centre lies just east of the Macquarie River, with parkland bordering both banks of the river.

The Mitchell and Newell Hwys cross at a roundabout just west of the river. The Newell Hwy becomes Whylandra St then Erskine St as it bends east around the top end of the city centre; the Mitchell Hwy becomes Cobra St and skirts the city centre to the south. The main shopping street is Macquarie St, which runs between the two.

The **visitors centre** ( ☎ 1800 674 443, 6801 4450; www.dubbotourism.com.au; cnr Macquarie & Erskine Sts; ☻ 9am-5pm) is in a park at the northern end of town.

The **library** (Talbragar St) provides free internet access and there's a **laundrette** (Brisbane St) near the corner of Bultje St.

## Sights & Activities

With more than 1500 animals, the **Western Plains Zoo** ( ☎ 6882 5888; www.zootopia.com.au; Obley Rd; 2-day pass adult/child/family $32/18/84; ☻ 9am-5pm, last entry 4pm) is Dubbo's star attraction. You can park your bike or car beside different paddocks or pools and feel a connection. Stand so close to the giraffes that you can sense their stillness and majesty. To witness their mating ritual is to watch a ballet in slow motion,

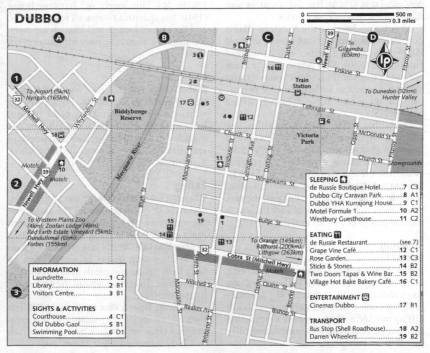

DUBBO

| 0 | 500 m |
| 0 | 0.3 miles |

**INFORMATION**
Laundrette......................1 C2
Library...........................2 B1
Visitors Centre................3 B1

**SIGHTS & ACTIVITIES**
Courthouse.....................4 C1
Old Dubbo Gaol...............5 B1
Swimming Pool................6 D1

**SLEEPING** 
de Russie Boutique Hotel............7 C3
Dubbo City Caravan Park............8 A1
Dubbo YHA Kurrajong House........9 C1
Motel Formule 1......................10 A2
Westbury Guesthouse...............11 C2

**EATING** 
de Russie Restaurant.................(see 7)
Grape Vine Café.......................12 C1
Rose Garden............................13 C3
Sticks & Stones.......................14 B2
Two Doors Tapas & Wine Bar.....15 B2
Village Hot Bake Bakery Café.....16 C1

**ENTERTAINMENT** 
Cinemas Dubbo........................17 B1

**TRANSPORT**
Bus Stop (Shell Roadhouse)........18 A2
Darren Wheelers.......................19 B2

To Airport (5km);
Nyngan (165km)

Biddybunge Reserve

To Western Plains Zoo (4km); Zoofari Lodge (4km); Red Earth Estate Vineyard (5km); Dundullimal (6km); Forbes (155km)

Train Station

To Dunedoo (92km); Hunter Valley

To Gilgandra (65km)

Victoria Park

Showgrounds

To Orange (145km); Bathurst (200km); Lithgow (263km)

Motels

Motels

quiet and solemn. Then there's the rare black rhinos, flown in from Zimbabwe as part of an international project to save these magnificent beasts from extinction. You can almost cuddle the fat little puddings. The exciting Asian Wetlands exhibit brings you up close to crazy, acrobatic otters and other wildlife found in a Nepalese village. The Bengal tigers alone are worth the admission price. You can walk the 6km, hire a bike ($13) or join the crawling line of cars. Guided morning zoo walks start at 6.45am ($3) every Saturday and Sunday.

Be met by a warder and taken off to **Old Dubbo Gaol** ( ☎ 6801 4460; 90 Macquarie St; adult/child $12/5; ✆ 9am-4.30pm). Fortunately it's now a museum. 'Animatronic' characters tell their stories – you hear from a condemned man due to meet with the gallows. It's rather creepy but imparts an authentic feel for life in the 1800s.

Dubbo has some lovely old country-town buildings such as the **courthouse** (Brisbane St), an impressive neoclassical edifice. The visitors centre has maps for both a heritage walk and a heritage drive.

**Cinemas Dubbo** ( ☎ 6881 8600; 49 Macquarie St; adult/child/family $12.50/10.50/38) has five theatres and shows all the first-release movies.

About 2km beyond the Western Plains Zoo, **Dundullimal** ( ☎ 6884 9984; Obley Rd; adult/child $6/3; ✆ 10am-5pm), is a timber-slab homestead built in the 1840s. Slab houses, made from rough-cut tree trunks laid vertically around the frame, were the earliest form of permanent European housing in the newly settled areas of NSW.

Dubbo has a full range of activities, like cinemas, tenpin bowling, golf, cycleways and boomerang-throwing lessons. The visitors centre has the details, if you can tear yourself away from the vineyards, such as **Red Earth Estate Vineyard** ( ☎ 6885 6676; www.redearthestate.com.au; 18 Camp Rd; ✆ 10am-5pm Thu-Tue), just past the zoo, where you can taste for free or kick back with a grand platter of cheeses and fruits ($18).

## Sleeping

### BUDGET

**Dubbo YHA Kurrajong House** ( ☎ 6882 0922; dubboyha@iinet.net.au; cnr Brisbane St & Newell Hwy; camp site per adult $8, dm/s/d/f $23/30/46/55; 🖵 ) A homey little fan-cooled place with open verandas. It fills up quickly, as the hosts have a reputation for being friendly and accommodating. Bike hire ($8) is available.

**Motel Formule 1** ( ☎ 6882 9311; cnr Mitchell & Newell Hwys; d/q $49/69; P 🐾 🐾 ) Cheap and cheerful, it's a great option with firm, comfortable beds, even though the rooms are a tad squashy.

**Dubbo City Caravan Park** ( ☎ 6882 4820; www.dubbo caravanpark.com.au; Whylandra St; camp site per adult $24, cabin std/deluxe $46/92; 🐾 🐾 ) Right on the riverbank and an easy walk across the bridge into town, this is a busy spot set around an attractive pool. The barbecue area, kids' playground and camp kitchen are all excellent, and the cabins nestle privately between the trees.

### MIDRANGE

There's so many motels along Cobra and Whylandra Sts that the night is bright with their neon signs.

**de Russie Boutique Hotel** ( ☎ 6882 7888; www.de russiehotels.com.au; 95 Cobra St; s/d $88/95; P 🐾 🖵 🐾 ) This very new B&B is just delightful, with architectural features that make you forget you're even in a motel. The continental breakfast is good and there's wireless internet available.

**Westbury Guesthouse** ( ☎ 6884 9445; westbury dubbo@bigpond.com; cnr Brisbane & Wingewarra Sts; s/d $90/110; 🐾 ) This lovely old heritage home (1910) has spacious rooms, all with ensuites, and the shared lounge and kitchen are comfortable. Ask about the rates for longer-term stays.

### TOP END

**Zoofari Lodge** ( ☎ 6881 1488; www.zoofari.com.au; Western Plains Zoo; s/d $318/530; 🐾 ) For an African safari experience, spend the night in total luxury just steps from the savannah. Charges include two days in the park with bicycles and exclusive tours, fine dining, discounts and a night under canvas.

## Eating

**Village Hot Bake Bakery Café** ( ☎ 6884 5454; 113 Darling St; snacks $4-10; ✆ 6am-6pm Mon-Fri) The awards on the wall prove it has Australia's best pies, but don't mention the best big breakfast ($10).

**Grape Vine Café** ( ☎ 6884 7354; 144 Brisbane St; mains $11-15) Enjoy soup, pastas, focaccias, cakes, all tasty fresh snacks and meals in a coffee house atmosphere. Take your cup out the back to the lovely courtyard.

**Two Doors Tapas & Wine Bar** ( ☎ 6884 4338; 215b Macquarie St; mains $14-16; ✆ dinner) Enjoy a great range of tapas, or just kick back with a drink in a leafy courtyard below street level.

**Rose Garden** ( ☎ 6882 8322, 208 Brisbane St; mains $14-17; ⓨ lunch & dinner) A local institution in Dubbo, this is a cosy spot with good Thai cuisine, richly coloured décor and very friendly staff.

**Sticks & Stones** ( ☎ 6885 4852; 215 Macquarie St; mains $14-19; ⓨ dinner) The wood-fired pizzas are gourmet and the pastas are pretty good too in this happy, atmospheric restaurant. If you're hungry, you'll love the country-style servings.

**de Russie Restaurant** ( ☎ 6882 7888; 93 Cobra St; mains $23-25; ⓨ dinner Mon-Sat) For a special meal, this pretty restaurant is perfect. Chef Wade Holding has a light touch, preparing beautifully balanced meals like braised duck with black grapes.

## Getting There & Around
**QantasLink** ( ☎ 13 13 13) and **Regional Express Airlines** (Rex; ☎ 13 17 13) have regular flights to Dubbo.

**CountryLink** ( ☎ 13 22 32; www.countrylink.info) runs the XPT train, and one coach service, to/from Sydney ($60 to $78, 6½ hours) daily.

**Darren Wheelers** ( ☎ 6882 9899; 25 Bultje St; ⓨ closed Sun) rents mountain bikes for $15 per day.

## PARKES
☎ 02 / pop 10,500
A visit to the Parkes gold diggings by NSW premier Sir Henry Parkes in 1871 prompted the locals to change the name of their village from Currajong and name the main street after Parkes' wife, Clarinda. It's said that Sir Henry later influenced the decision to route the railway through the town.

Today, Parkes is happy to be known as the home of the radio telescope, made famous by the film *The Dish*. The town is still the sleepy charming place that was portrayed there. There's a festival in July called the Astrofest, held at the Dish; contact **CSIRO telescope** ( ☎ 6861 1700) for information.

## Orientation & Information
From the south, the Newell Hwy takes a twisting route through the centre of Parkes, becoming Grenfell St, Welcome St and finally joining Clarinda St, the main shopping street, to begin its run north to Dubbo. This is a three-way intersection, with Dalton St, the road running west to Condobolin, also joining Clarinda St here. South of this intersection, Clarinda St curves eastwards and becomes the main route to Orange.

The **visitors centre** ( ☎ 6863 8860; www.visitparkes .com.au; cnr Newell Hwy & Thomas St; ⓨ 9am-5pm Mon-Fri,

10am-4pm Sat & Sun) is in Kelly Reserve. Parkes Shire **library** ( ☎ 6861 2309, Dogan St; ⓨ 10am-7pm Mon-Fri, to noon Sat) has internet access.

## Sights & Activities
### MUSEUMS
Along the Newell Hwy on the Dubbo side of town the **Sir Henry Parkes Museum** ( ☎ 6862 3509; adult $5; ⓨ 10am-3.30pm Mon-Sat) is more like someone's house than a traditional exhibition space, but it has some Parkes memorabilia and more than 5000 pieces of antique machinery. A reconstruction of Moat House Cottage in Coventry, where Parkes was born in 1815, contains a gallery and an audiovisual story of Federation.

### PARKES RADIO TELESCOPE
The Radio Telescope, built by the CSIRO in 1961, is 6km east of the Newell Hwy, about 20km north of Parkes. As one of the world's most powerful telescopes it has helped Australian radio astronomers become leaders in their field, and brought pictures of the *Apollo 11* moon landing to an audience of 600 million people. The telescope has also played a vital role in detecting thousands of new galaxies at the edge of the known universe. More than half the known pulsars (rapidly spinning 'cores' of dead stars) have been discovered at Parkes.

Although the telescope is off-limits, you can get close enough for a good look, and the renovated **visitors centre** ( ☎ 6861 1777; www .csiro.au/parkesdish; admission free; ⓨ 8.30am-4.15pm) has hands-on displays and screens that show you what the astronomers see. **3-D films** (adult/child $6.50/5.00) such as *Journey to Mars* screen throughout the day. The **Dish Café** ( ☎ 6862 1566; Parkes Radio Telescope, Telescope Rd; meals $6-12; ⓨ 8.30am-4.15pm), in the shade of the telescope, makes great coffee, does breakfasts like Meteor Muesli and Dish Big Breakfast, and known for the excellent lunches, is like Space Station Steak Sandwich, served with rocket fuel if you want.

## Festivals & Events
The **Parkes 2PK Country Music Spectacular** (www .country.com.au) with concerts and street entertainment, and **Antique Motorbike Rally** ( ☎ 6862 2547) for vintage and classic motorcycles built before 1964, both bring the crowds for the Labour Day long weekend in early October. But perhaps the most unusual event is the

annual **Parkes Elvis Revival Festival** ( ☎ 6863 8860; www.visitparkes.com.au/elvis.htm), held in conjunction with Elvis' birthday on the second weekend in January. There's Elvis lookalike, soundalike, and even movealike competitions.

## Sleeping & Eating

**Currajong Tourist Cara Park** ( ☎ 6862 3400; Newell Hwy; camp site per adult $20, cabin/cottage $45/75; ✕ ⍾ ) Just a few metres north of the visitors centre is this small, quiet and pretty place, with a spacious aviary to keep you entranced.

**Spanish Lantern Motor Inn** ( ☎ 6862 3388; www .spanishlantern.com.au; Newell Hwy; s/d $64/74; ✕ ⍁ ⍾ ) This is great value, and your friendly hosts, John and Pam, know lots about the area.

**Bushmans Motor Inn** ( ☎ 6862 2199; Currajong Rd; r $99-110; ✕ ⍾ ) The motel is settled into a lovely garden around a central court and overlooks a lush paddock at the back.

**Bella's Caffe Espresso** ( ☎ 6862 4212; 245 Clarinda St; mains $8-18; ⍾ 8am-6pm Mon-Fri, to 2pm Sat & Sun) This small but shiny new coffee stop has excellent stir-fries, soups and snacks. The staff are as bubbly as the espresso machine.

**Marty's Restaurant** ( ☎ 6863 4333; Newell Hwy; mains $17-25; ⍾ 7-9am & 6-9pm Mon-Sat) Located in the Country Comfort hotel, this is a peaceful spot for a home-cooked meal like corned silverside with potato bake. The drinks menu features local wines – try the Limestone Creek Vineyard range.

## Getting There & Away

**Regional Express Airlines** (Rex; ☎ 13 17 13) has daily flights to Sydney (excluding Sunday).

**CountryLink** ( ☎ 13 22 32) buses connect to trains departing Orange and Lithgow for Sydney ($57, 6½ hours, twice daily). The *Indian Pacific* between Sydney and Perth stops here, and the *Broken Hill Outback Explorer* also stops on Monday, en route to Sydney.

# FORBES

☎ 02 / pop 9975

Perched on the banks of the Lachlan River, Forbes is one of NSW's prettiest towns, retaining much of its 19th-century flavour thanks to its beautifully restored buildings. It is also famous for its connections to Ben Hall, a landowner who became Australia's first official bushranger, and who was betrayed and shot near Forbes. Visit the town's cemetery where people still leave notes on his grave.

The first Europeans to set foot on the future town site were members of explorer John Oxley's party in 1817. Oxley was so unimpressed with the clay soil, poor timber and swamps that he concluded, 'It is impossible to imagine a worse country.' Pity he wasn't here in the 1860s to see the gold rush, when more than 8000kg of gold was found!

## Orientation & Information

Forbes has two main roads: Dowling St (Newell Hwy) and, parallel, Rankin St. The cheerful **visitors centre** ( ☎ 6852 4155) in the old train station at the northern end of town also exhibits works by local artists. The **NPWS office** ( ☎ 6851 4429; 83 Lachlan St; ⍾ 8.30am-4.30pm Mon-Fri) has information about national parks in the region.

Internet access is available at **Western Internet Services** ( ☎ 6851 1624; Lachlan St; per hr $5; ⍾ Mon-Sat).

## Sights & Activities

Forbes' wide streets are lined with grand 19th-century gold-funded buildings including the **Town Hall** (1891) and **courthouse** (1880). At the tower atop the **Albion Hotel** on Lachlan St a watch was kept for Cobb & Co coaches.

The Albion also contains the interesting **Bushrangers Hall of Fame** ( ☎ 6851 1881; 135 Lachlan St; adult/child $5/3; ⍾ 10am-6pm), which has guided tours of old underground tunnels used to transfer gold from banks into waiting coaches. On the corner of Court and Lachlan Sts is the **post office** (1879–81) which has an unusual three-storey clock tower.

Osborne Hall on Cross St was the dance hall of the Osborne Hotel and now houses the **Forbes Museum** ( ☎ 6852 1694; adult/child $2/1; ⍾ 3-5pm Oct-May, 2-4pm Jun-Sep) of local history, with Ben Hall relics.

Just off the Newell Hwy about 4km south of Forbes, **Gum Swamp** is an enchanting wetland area that is home to many species of birds. There's a hide to watch them from. While sunset and sunrise are the best viewing times, it is an idyllic spot at any hour.

## Sleeping & Eating

**Forbes Apex Riverside Tourist Park** ( ☎ 6852 2694; www.touristpark.com.au; 88 Reymond St; camp site per adult $24, cabin std/luxury $50/90; ✕ ⍾ ) Running down to the Lachlan River, southwest of town, this fishing haven has lovely grassy areas, plenty of shade trees and modern amenities.

**Vandenberg Hotel** ( ☎ 6852 2015; info@vanden berghotel.com.au; / Court St; s/d/f $30/40/50) This impressive pub has grand old rooms along a wide corridor. Rooms have a fridge and TV, and most open onto a balcony overlooking Victoria Park.

**Ben Hall Motor Inn** ( ☎ 6851 2345; 5-7 Cross St; r $70; ☒ ) It's a budget motel only in price. The rooms are spacious and it's all quite charming.

**Mezzanine Style** ( ☎ 6851 4056; 23 Rankin St; mains $5-11; ☒ 9am-5.30pm) Indeed a mezzanine, from where you look over a funky furniture and book shop. Choose a luscious meal like sweet chilli chicken burger from the blackboard menu.

**Forbes Inn Restaurant** ( ☎ 6851 6888; 43 Rankin St; mains $18-26; ☒ lunch daily, dinner Tue-Sat) Upstairs in the Forbes Inn is this elegant, award-winning, fine dining restaurant with old favourites like grilled lamb cutlets using local produce.

## Getting There & Away

**CountryLink** ( ☎ 13 2232) buses connect to trains to Sydney ($57, eight hours, twice daily).

## COWRA

☎ 02 / pop 13,147

Ever since August 1944, when 1000 Japanese prisoners broke out of a POW camp here (231 of them died, along with four Australians), Cowra has aligned itself with Japan and with the cause of furthering world peace. The break-out is immortalised in the film *Die Like the Carp!*

## Orientation & Information

Cowra straggles up the side of a steep hill above Lachlan River, its main street, Kendal St, abuzz with alluring shops.

The **visitors centre** ( ☎ 6342 4333; www.cowratour ism.com.au; Olympic Park, Mid Western Hwy; ☒ 9am-5pm) has a great introduction to the break-out, with a strange but fascinating hologram film on the subject. The **Japanese War Cemetery** (Doncaster Dve) is 5km north of town, off Binni Creek Rd. A nearby **memorial** marks the site of the break-out, and you can still see the camp foundations.

## Sights & Activities

Built as a token of Cowra's connection with Japanese POWs (but with no overt mention of the war or the break-out), the **Japanese Garden** ( ☎ 6341 2233; Binni Creek Rd; adult/child $8.50/5; ☒ 8.30am-5pm) and the attached cultural centre on Bellevue Hill are well worth visiting. The large garden, serene and beautifully maintained, was a gift from the Japanese government. The cultural centre is a peaceful place, with displays that include a collection of *ukiyo-e* paintings depicting everyday events in pre-industrial Japan. A **sakura** (cherry blossom festival) is held around the second weekend in October.

Nearby is the **Bellevue Hill Flora & Fauna Reserve**, a complete contrast to the formality of its neighbour.

The darkest place for star-gazing in all of Australia is **Darby Falls Observatory** ( ☎ 6345 1900; Mt McDonald Rd; adult/child $10/7; ☒ 7-10pm, 8.30-11pm during daylight saving). From town, take Darbys Falls Rd for 22km and turn onto Mt McDonald Rd, then follow the signs. Turn off your headlights as soon as you see the red fairy lights leading up to the observatory.

Kids will enjoy the **War, Rail & Rural Fun Museum** ( ☎ 6342 2801; www.caravancitycowra.com.au; Mid

---

**DOWN THE LACHLAN**

'I had written him a letter which I had, for want of better
Knowledge, sent to where I met him down the Lachlan, years ago'

*Banjo Patterson*

The scenic Lachlan Valley Way runs by the Lachlan River from Forbes to **Condobolin**, the main service centre and home town of Australian singer Shannon Noll. There are several camping sites and fishing spots along the winding road.

The 40-hectare **Gum Bend Lake**, 3km west of Condobolin, is the area's water playground; however, it is sometimes closed in summer due to low water levels. About 8km north of 'Condo' is **Mt Tilga**, officially the geographical centre of NSW.

North of Condobolin, the farmland begins to blur into the outback, with several routes heading north to the Barrier Hwy (if you have a decent map). And for the rest of Banjo Paterson's poem, go to http://oldpoetry.com and search for 'Clancy of the Overflow'.

Western Hwy; adult/child $9/7; ⊙9am-5pm) with its working steam engines, hands-on railway and farming displays, and the POW camp. They'll also enjoy a visit to **Smokehouse Deli** ( ☎ 6341 1489; Mid Western Hwy; ⊙ 9.30am-6pm Wed-Mon) where you can feed and catch trout and watch your catch being smoked, ready to eat or take away with you. It's in a massive container shed, where you can also sample the local produce and buy up big as it's all fresh direct to you.

Each August, Lachlan Valley Railway celebrates the rail travel of yesteryear with **Vintage Train Rides** ( ☎ 6342 5101; Cowra railway station).

### WINERIES

There are some excellent wineries in the area for wine tasting and trying the local produce; the visitors centre has a guide to cellar doors, and **Ideal Tours** ( ☎ 6341 3350; www .australianacorner.com; 1 Kendal St) runs bus tours of the area. Right in town is the **Mill** ( ☎ 6341 4141; www.windowrie.com.au; 6 Vaux St; ⊙ 10am-6pm), Cowra's oldest building, where its millstone first turned in 1861. Now it's a well-regarded winery – try the region's famous chardonnay.

## Sleeping & Eating

**Cowra Van Park** ( ☎ 6340 2110; Lachlan St; camp site $22, cabin std/deluxe $60/70) Shady and green, and overlooking the lovely Lachlan, this is really handy to everything.

**Imperial Hotel** ( ☎ 6341 2588; 16 Kendal St; s/d $40/50, d with bathroom $80) This is one of several old pubs in Cowra that offer comfortable rooms. But inside the Imperial the rooms are crisply modern and motel-like.

**Breakout Motel** ( ☎ 6342 6111; www.breakoutmotel .com.au; 181 Kendal St; s/d $88/98; ▨ ▣) This very modern and quite delightful place, right in the centre of things, uses slate, blue and beige amid its covered walkways to set a peaceful atmosphere.

**Vineyard Motel** ( ☎ 6342 3641; vineyard@dodo.com .au; Chardonnay Rd; s/d $90/100 d incl spa $110; ▨ ▣) Located just 4km out of town, this place overlooks the lush Lachlan Valley. Surrounded by fields of grapevines, it's secluded and peaceful, with wide vine-covered verandas for a romantic feel.

**Naked Lady** ( ☎ 6341 1455; mains $9-17; ⊙ breakfast & lunch) Gourmet delights, like lamb kofta skewers with baba ganoush, are served at this cheerful eatery, where you are surrounded by waterfalls and statues.

**Neila** ( ☎ 6341 2188; 5 Kendal St; mains $29; ⊙ dinner Thu-Sat) This small gem on Cowra's main drag fuses regional goodies with Mod Oz creativity. It's decidedly laid-back, but the food certainly isn't – try the caramelised pork hock with green papaya and cashew-nut salad.

### Getting There & Away

**CountryLink** ( ☎ 13 22 32) has a twice-daily service to Sydney ($58, 5½ hours).

## AROUND COWRA

About 40km west of Cowra, **Grenfell** is a quiet country town with a curvy Main St and some beautiful old buildings. Henry Lawson was born here in 1867 and a memorial marking his birthplace is off the highway at the eastern edge of town. The annual **Henry Lawson Arts Festival** (www.henrylawsonfestival.asn.au) is held around the writer's birthday on 17 June. For something completely different, Grenfell hosts the **National Guinea Pig Races** (www.lisp.com.au /grenfell) during Easter and in June.

Nineteen kilometres southwest of Grenfell, **Weddin National Park** (8361 hectares) is a rugged place with lots of wildlife, Aboriginal sites and some good walking tracks. **Holy Camp** in the northwest and **Seatons Camp** in the northeast are camping areas; both have road access and you can walk between them. The NPWS office in Forbes (p244) has more information.

## YOUNG

☎ 02 / pop 11,957

Colourful hills of cherry orchards – pink, red, green – tell you you're coming into Young, Australia's 'cherry capital' on the edge of the western slopes of the Great Dividing Range. Nicole Jasprizza, who arrived during the gold rush, first planted cherries here in 1860. His orchard was an immediate success and expanded rapidly. Today there are about 130 orchards producing a large proportion of Australia's crop. Prunes are also an important local industry, but 'prune capital' doesn't have quite the same ring.

The notorious White Australia policy of Australia's early years had its origins near Young – goldfield riots at Lambing Flat in 1861 led to the government restriction on Chinese immigration.

## Orientation & Information

Entering town from the south, the Olympic Hwy becomes Short St, then enters Main St, turns east into Boorowa, the main shopping strip, north into Zouch, where the best restaurants are, and continues across the railway line north up to Cowra. The **visitors centre** ( ☎ 6382 3394; 2 Short St; ☼ 9am-5pm Mon-Fri, 9.30am-4pm Sat & Sun) is near the creek as you enter town.

The cherry harvest is in November and December. In January other stone fruits are harvested and in February the prune harvest begins. The **Ready Workforce office** ( ☎ 6382 1403; 187 Boorowa St; ☼ 9am-5pm Mon-Fri) can help you find fruit-picking work.

## Sights & Activities
### WINERIES
This area produced wine grapes from the 1880s until the 1930s, when the more profitable cherry orchards took over. In the 1970s the Barwang vineyard was established, and there are now about 15 small vineyards in the area producing award-winning cool-climate wines. The visitors centre has a booklet. Two that are excellent are **Lindsay's Woodonga Hill** ( ☎ 6389 2972; 1101 Cowra Rd; ☼ 9am-5pm) northeast of Young, and **Chalkers Crossing** ( ☎ 6382 6900; www.chalkerscrossing.com.au; 387 Henry Lawson Way; ☼ 10am-4pm) is north.

### OTHER ATTRACTIONS
The **Lambing Flat Folk Museum** ( ☎ 6302 2248; Campbell St; adult/child $4/1; ☼ 10am-4pm) displays artefacts from the goldfields including the remarkable 'Roll Up' banner carried by European miners in protest against the Chinese in 1861. The Sydney Chinese community raised money to build the **Chinese Tribute Garden** (Pitstone Rd; admission free; ☼ daily), a tranquil spot featuring a pagoda and dam, to remember the contribution the Chinese miners made, including an ingenious troughlike structure to transport the water up to 3km away.

Pick your own fruit – the visitors centre staff has a list of orchards. If you fancy some horse riding, try the **Lirambenda Riding Club** ( ☎ 6383 4237; Old Forbes Rd; ☼ by appt). **JD's Jam Factory** ( ☎ 6382 4060; Grenfell Rd; admission free; ☼ 8am-6pm) is a small jam factory that started life as a roadside stall and now supplies companies like SPC and Yoplait. Sample or buy some of the produce, just don't leave Young without trying their glorious cherry pie.

A spectacular garden that you can wander through for a small fee is **Jacaranda Hill** ( ☎ 6382 4657; Noonan Rd).

## Festivals & Events
Young's two main **festivals** ( ☎ 6382 3394; www.visityoung.com.au) are the **Cherry Festival**, held on the first weekend in December, with markets, heritage train rides, street art and a cherry-pip spit competition, and the **Lambing Flat Festival**, held mid-April, with a legendary bush dance, historic re-enactments, street dances and much more fun. If you want to see the trees in blossom, come in early October.

## Sleeping & Eating
**Young Tourist Park** ( ☎ 6382 2190; Zouch St; camp site per adult $20, cabin std/deluxe $60/77; ☒ ) A new camp kitchen and drive-through sites with bathrooms for caravans make this a comfortable option. It's run by a young couple who welcome pets, and it's just a short stroll over the railway line into town.

**Empire Hotel** ( ☎ 6382 1665; www.empirehotelyoung.com; cnr Lovell & Main Sts; s/d/f $30/50/60). Another grand old pub, which has plenty of pleasant

---

### DETOUR: LET'S GO BALLOONING

Canowindra is the Ballooning capital of Australia, because of its gentle winds and attractive countryside. Several outfits offer flights including **Aussie Balloontrek** ( ☎ 6364 0211; www.aussiebal loontrek.com.au; Nanami Ln, Canowindra; 30min/1hr flights from $160/280). And there's a barbecue breakfast and champagne along with the view.

On Anzac Day weekend, **Marti's Balloon Fiesta** ( ☎ 6344 2422; www.martisfiesta.com.au) sees up to 50 hot air balloons competing.

Canowindra's main thoroughfare, Gaskill St, follows the crooked route of the old bullock track and every building is heritage listed. The **Age of Fishes Museum** ( ☎ 6344 1008; cnr Gaskill & Ferguson Sts; admission $7.70; ☼ 10am-4pm) displays the fish fossil collection which made Canowindra world famous in 1956 for the 360 million year old fossil find. Ask about going on a fossil dig.

From Cowra, follow the signs to **Canowindra**, to the north of the Lachlan River. Continue north to Orange, through fields of yellow canola and budding vineyards.

rooms, each with TVs and kettles, and shiny, clean shared facilities.

**Goldrush Motel** ( ☎ 6382 3444; goldrush@bigpond.net.au; 6 Campbell St; s/d/f $65/85/110; 🅿 🆒 ) A friendly place with cheery rooms, free Austar, a great barbecue and playground, and a self-contained cottage (2-/8-person $100/250).

**Marina Homestead B&B & Alpaca Farm** ( ☎ 6382 6770; Moppity Rd; B&B d $120) No wonder the alpacas are content. There's a beautiful rambling garden around this historic homestead, all rooms have private bathrooms, the sitting room has a wood fire, and breakfast features local produce. It's just 5km southeast of town.

**Country Providore** ( ☎ 6382 7255; 143 Boorowa St; mains $8-16; 🕙 8.30am-6pm Mon-Fri, to 2pm Sat) This is a busy licensed place with attractive giftware on display. Take your meal outside if you prefer, and there's a takeaway menu.

**Zouch** ( ☎ 6382 2775; 26 Zouch St; mains $19-29; 🕙 lunch daily, dinner Thu-Sat) The old Masonic Hall houses this charming restaurant that serves lashings of exotic country cooking using local fruit, veg, meat and oil, and features an extensive range of local wines.

**Café de Jour** ( ☎ 6382 1413; cnr Lovell & Zouch Sts; mains $21-27; 🕙 lunch & dinner Tue-Sat) This is a lovely restaurant with great atmosphere, where Stephen and Kelly present meals with a finesse well acknowledged by food critics. The chicken breast pocketed with prawn and crab farce is like a work of art.

## Getting There & Away

Buses stop at the old train station on Lovell St. **Fraser's Coaches** ( ☎ 13 22 32; www.fraserscoaches.com.au) runs a daily service between Cootamundra and Dubbo, which connects with the XPT train to Melbourne ($72).

# Northwest

A big sky umbrellas the mega cash crops below. Kilometres of cotton and a sprinkling of canola, cow peas, field peas and other fruits of the soil dominate today's northwestern New South Wales landscape. About 17 million years ago the Warrumbungle volcano erupted, the remnants of which characterise the Coonabarabran horizon.

When the Australian plate drifted north away from Antarctica, the earth became warm and the ice caps melted. If you were heading to Lightning Ridge back then you'd pack your togs, as it was covered by an inland sea (with perfect chemistry for opal formation). Mountains formed, the artesian basin boiled, and rivers flowed – the Namoi, the Macquarie, the Castlereagh, the Barwon – each depositing the rich alluvial soils over vast flood plains that now bare the colossal cotton crops of the northwest.

A labour of love, the soils are worked and the crops raised, only too often to be destroyed by drought or flattened by flood. As the weather dictates the lives of those who work the land, it also inadvertently shapes a culture of hardened and hard-working farmers, who are down-to-earth with a certain admiration and respect for mother nature. The northwest is populated by locals who openly appreciate the wilderness in their backyards, with the Warrumbungle's a perfect example of a community utilising and loving their landscape. Linger a little longer at Lightning Ridge and you'll also recognise this respect in the eyes of the opal miners.

## HIGHLIGHTS

- Noodle for opals and meet the locals at **Grawin and Glengarry Opal Fields** (p256) near Lightning Ridge
- Get an eyeful of geologic monstrosities such as the Breadknife in the **Warrumbungle National Park** (p252)
- Star gaze at the **Skywatch Observatory** (p251) in Coonabarabran
- Contemplate the universe at **Australia Telescope Compact Array** (p253) just out of Narrabri
- Relax in **spa baths** (p255) in Moree and let your troubles float away
- See the sunset from **Siding Spring Observatory** (p251), west of Coonabarabran
- Camp in style on **Mt Kaputar** (p254) with a bottle of wine and corkscrew, that's all you'll need

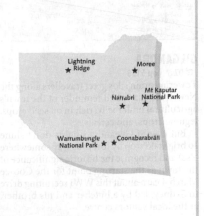

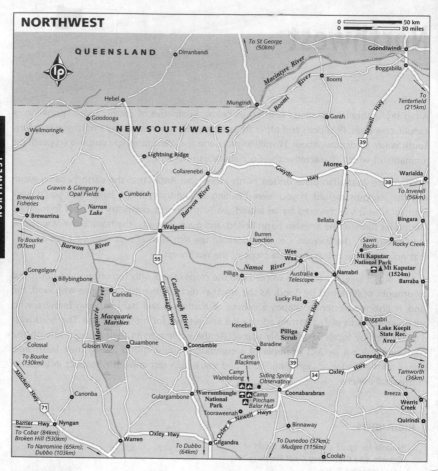

# NORTHWEST

## GILGANDRA

☎ 02 / pop 5156

Towering grain silos greet travellers along the Newell Hwy, a proud reminder of the town's agricultural underbelly, rich in oil seed crops, legume crops, and cereals.

But even if Gilgandra's lights don't shine so bright do stop by (on your way somewhere else) and recognise the historic significance of the town as the starting point for the Coo-ee March. Learn about this WWI recruiting drive to Sydney, led by a butcher and his brother, at the local visitors centre.

## Orientation & Information

Wedged between the Oxley and Newell Hwys, Gilgandra is snug up against the Castlereagh River. The Newell Hwy turns into Castlereagh St and then Miller St.

**Post office** (cnr Warren Rd & Wamboin St)

**Visitors centre** ( ☎ 6847 2045; www.gilgandra.nsw .gov.au; Newell Hwy; ⏰ 9am-5pm)

## Sights

Are you interested in farming equipment, machines such as the Howard Rotary hoe, first invented in Gilgandra in 1920? If so, you'll probably leave the **Rural Museum** ( ☎ 6847 0806; Newell Hwy; adult/child $5/3; ⏰ 10am-4pm Sat & Sun) without the feeling that you've been the museum's only visitor all day. Otherwise head to the **Gilgandra Observatory** ( ☎ 6847 2646; Willie St; adult/child $9/6; ⏰ 7-10pm Mon-Sat, from 8.30pm during summer) and look for the rings of Saturn, or perhaps spot some Martians leaving the Rural Museum.

## Sleeping & Eating

Many motels line the Newell Hwy, all with similar deals that target travellers stopping over on their way somewhere else. There's an IGA supermarket at the northern end of the main street.

**Cooee Motel** ( ☎ 6847 2981, 1800 266 333; www.cooee motel.com; Hargraves Lane, off Newell Hwy; s/d/f $68/74/90; 🖫 ) A clean neat motel set back off the highway. It's a pity the block-out blinds don't block out the highway noise as well.

**Anna's Place** ( ☎ 6847 2790; mikenlibby@bigpond.com; 13 Morris St; s/d incl breakfast $85/110; 🖫 🖭 ) This is a pleasantly peaceful, pet friendly B&B in what was previously the town hospital.

**Gilgandra Rotary Caravan Park** ( ☎ 6847 2423; Newell Hwy; unpowered/powered sites $16/18, cabins $40-60; 🖫 🖭 ) The trees are thick with rosellas in this pretty park, but it is a little exposed and you can *still* hear the highway. **Rest-A-While Cabin & Van Park** ( ☎ 6847 2254; 108 Miller St; unpowered/powered sites $15/17, cabins $55; 🖫 ) is a little quieter, but not nearly as friendly.

**Ellam's Bistro** ( ☎ 6847 2004; Royal Hotel, 73 Miller St; mains $8-17; lunch & dinner) Whether you choose roast of the day, bangers and mash, or the more extravagant 'deluxe steak sandwich', this classic pub grub has changed little since the 1980s...not even the price.

**Next Grind** ( ☎ 6847 2707; Newell Hwy; mains $10-17; 🕑 9am-5pm Tue-Fri, to 4pm Sat & Sun) Serenely set in the grounds of a nursery it serves the freshest, lightest scones in the southern hemisphere. It is the perfect rest stop for travellers and has plenty of room for cars towing caravans.

## Getting There & Away

**CountryLink** ( ☎ 13 22 32) buses run north to Lightning Ridge and south to Dubbo once daily. A **Greyhound** ( ☎ 13 14 99) coach ferries passengers between Brisbane and Gilgandra daily (adult/child $140/110).

## COONABARABRAN

☎ 02 / pop 3012

Coo-na-bar-ra-brn. Fun to say, it was actually derived from an Aboriginal word meaning 'an inquisitive person'. When you notice all the white dome structures that dot the countryside around town the definition becomes fitting. They are private observatories people use to peer into outer space.

But the most fantastic thing is when you first drive toward town and see the outrageously knobbly nodular shapes of the Warrumbungles, the focal point of town.

## Orientation & Information

The extremely helpful ladies at the **visitors centre** ( ☎ 6842 1441; www.coonabarabran.com; John St; 🕑 9am-5pm) can provide you with details on the area and the Warrumbungles. You will find all you need along the main street, including the **post office** and an **ATM**.

**CTC** ( ☎ 6842 2929; 71 John St; per hr $6; 🕑 9am-5pm Mon-Fri) For internet access.

**NPWS** ( ☎ 6842 1311; 30 Timor St; 🕑 8.30am-4.30pm Mon-Fri)

**Top Shop** ( ☎ 6842 2066; 9 Camp St; 🕑 9am-5pm) This store specialises in all things fishing.

## Sights & Activities

**Skywatch Observatory** ( ☎ 6842 3303; Timor Rd; adult/child $15/9; 🕑 viewing 7-10pm) Just west of the town centre it has a planetarium and astronomy exhibition and night-time star gazing. Or head to **Siding Spring Observatory** ( ☎ 6842 6211; www .sidingspringexploratory.com.au; National Park Rd; guided tours adult/child $11/9; 🕑 9.30am-4pm Mon-Fri, 10am-2pm Sat & Sun) 27km west of town, for some of the world's major, and Australia's largest, telescopes.

## Sleeping

**Imperial Hotel** ( ☎ 6842 1023; imphotel@tpg.com.au; 70 John St; s/d $25/35; 🖫 ) A heater, electric blanket, sink, TV...what more could one want? This place is perfect for the low maintenance traveller.

**Coachman's Rest Motor Lodge** ( ☎ 6842 2111; coachmans_rest@bigpond.com.au; Newell Hwy; s/d $77/88; 🖫 🖭 ) A good place to base yourself when in Coona. The gardens are stately but the brick interior is a bit ick. There is a restaurant with some tasty choices (mains $20 to $25).

**John Oxley Caravan Park** ( ☎ 6842 1635; Newell Hwy; camp sites $14-19, cabins $39-49) Very friendly, so nice the owners will hire you linen ($8). Large basic cabins on the south side of town.

## Eating

**Bi Lo** ( ☎ 6842 1911; 64 Dalgarno St) is good for groceries.

**Woop Woop Café** ( ☎ 6842 4755; 38a John St; mains $10-15; 🕑 breakfast & lunch) This rustic little restaurant is pretty hard to find, so ask if you're lost. Family run with friendly service they recommend you try the Farmhand Platter. Open till 5.30pm weekdays and 5-ish on weekends.

**Wattagan Estate Winery** ( ☎ 6842 2456; Oxley Hwy; ☷ 10am-5pm Fri-Mon) While Erne the Emu instinctively ducks, dives, and weaves outside, step indoors to view a range of emu oil products (rendered from farmed emus yoo, they're basically boiled up for the oil). Luckily the port tastes sooo good. Oh and the chardonnay. Did you sample the sparkling…?

### Getting There & Away

**CountryLink** ( ☎ 13 22 32) buses connect with trains at Lithgow and run to Coonabarabran every day except Saturday (adult/child $70/45). **Greyhound** ( ☎ 13 14 99) coaches have a service connecting Brisbane to Coonabarabran (adult/child $120/100).

## WARRUMBUNGLE NATIONAL PARK

Snap, crackle, pop went the Warrumbungle volcano as it erupted 17 million years ago. The honey lava slowly oozed from numerous vents, often solidifying before hitting the ground, building massive lava domes. Many years under the weather and the softer sandstones eroded away to reveal monstrosities such as the **Breadknife**.

This is the most striking, geologically significant, and accessible national park in the Northwest. Culturally embraced by the locals with a calendar of events catering for everyone, from **Wildflower Week** to the **Warrumbungle Marathon**. There is a NPWS 'Discovery' programme during school holidays where you can learn about Aboriginal culture, identify flora and fauna, go on guided bushwalks, or get your rocks off learning about the local geology.

The best time to visit is in the shoulder seasons, spring and autumn. Summer can be very hot and Jack Frost will visit your camp in winter.

### Information

The **Warrumbungle National Park visitors centre** ( ☎ 6825 4364; ☷ 9am-4pm), 37km west of Coonabarabran, has loads of information on the park's flora, fauna and facilities. A shop sells ice and camping supplies and grab your $7 (daily) entry permit before pursuing the peaks.

For more information on the park, *Warrumbungle National Park* by Peter Fox is an excellent guide published by the NPWS. It has detailed walking information. Lonely Planet's *Walking in Australia* details the Grand High Tops walk.

### Sleeping

Tooraweenah is a hidden little hamlet at the foot of the Warrumbungles. Weenah by name, weeny by nature, everything here is tiny. Even the butchers shop (opposite the pub) is cutesy! Park yourself at **Tooraweenah Tourist Park** ( ☎ 6848 1133; unpowered/powered sites $15/18; cabins $40-55; ☷ ) or perhaps **Mountain View Hotel/Motel** ( ☎ 6848 1017; s/d $40/60).

But there's a more civilised accommodation option closer to the park at **Kookaburra Cabin** ( ☎ 6842 2663; www.warrumbunglesglasshouse .com; Tibuc Rd; r $85) a quaint little cottage that is ideal for some peace and quiet. It's adjacent to the **Glass House Gallery** ( ☷ Wed-Mon 10am-5pm).

**Tibuc Cabins** ( ☎ 6842 1740; www.coonabarabran .com/tibuc; Timor Rd; r $90-110) Think mountainous wilderness, mudbrick cottage, a toasty log fire and tender moments with the one you love (or perhaps the one you lust). Bring your own linen, or hire on-site. The turn-off to the farm is 17km from Coonabarabran.

### Camping

A third alternative is to camp inside the park at a couple of camping grounds that can be booked through the NPWS visitors centre. The main and largest is **Camp Blackman** (unpowered sites adult/child $5/3, powered sites adult/child $8/4), but **Camp Wambelong** (sites adult/child $5/3) is a tad more peaceful. Maybe leave the car behind and head for the walk-in camps such as **Camp Pincham** and **Balor Hut** (adult/child $3/2). Or camp in the back country for free and pitch your tent wherever you like (within reason of course).

### Getting There & Away

The park entrance is 33km west of Coonabarabran, but you can also get here on smaller roads from Gulargambone or Coonamble, both on the Castlereagh Hwy to the west of the park.

## GUNNEDAH

☎ 02 / pop 9500

Gunnedah's adopted daughter Dorothy Mackellar penned her most famous poem 'My Country' around these parts. She was inspired by the Gunnedah landscape in the heart of the Liverpool Plains. And today the country is still sunburnt and in desperate need of flooding rains. You get the feeling not much ever changes here, even the koalas look settled.

## Information

The **visitors centre** ( ☎ 6740 2230; www.infogunnedah .com.au; Anzac Park off South St; ☻ 9am-5pm Mon-Fri, 10am-3pm Sat & Sun) is just south of the railway lines from the town centre – look for a statue of Dorothy on her horse.

**Library** ( ☎ 6740 2190; 291-293 Conadilly St) For free internet access.

**Post office** ( ☎ 6740 2040; cnr Elgin & Conadilly Sts)

## Sights

Cute and cuddly, they cling to the trees outside the visitors centre and have been known to wander down the road to the shops, probably for eucalyptus drops. Take a stroll along the **Bindeah Walking Track** and up to **Porcupine Lookout**, as you are sure to spot some more koalas there.

**Water Tower Museum** ( ☎ 6742 1184; adult/child $3/1; ☻ 2-5pm Sat) Just uphill from the visitors centre it contains the usual array of old local items plus a Dorothea Mackellar display.

**Gunnedah Rural Museum** ( ☎ 6742 4690; Oxley Hwy; adult/child $5/2; ☻ 9am-3pm) You could check out all things rural here, although you would be better off satisfying your farming jollies all at once at **Ag-quip** ( ☎ 6740 2230; www.agquip.farmonline .com.au) It attracts 100,000 other like-minded individuals in August each year.

**Waterways Wildlife Park** ( ☎ 6742 1826; Oxley Hwy, 7km west of Gunnedah; adult/child $5/3; ☻ 10am-4pm) One wonderful selfless woman has been rescuing little critters since the beginning of time. Sure the park has seen better days, but it's nice to support her work and it's a great day out for the kids.

## Sleeping & Eating

**Alyn Motel** ( ☎ 6742 5028; alynmotel@bigpond.com; 351 Conadilly St; s/d $81/91; ☒ ☒ ) Modern simple rooms keep the bod warm at night thanks to electric blankets. It's worth paying a little bit extra to stay in a deluxe room.

**Roseneath Manor** ( ☎ 6742 1906; 91 Maitland St; s/d incl breakfast $85/95) Built in 1878 this Victorian manor is found in the quietest and oldest street in Gunnedah. It's enveloped in a Federation picket fence and guarded by two very placid Dobermans.

**Gunnedah Tourist Caravan Park** ( ☎ 6742 1372; 51 Henry St; powered sites $22, cabins $59-75; ☒ ☒ ) If you are towing a caravan it's best you stop here as it is the only place in town.

**Two Rivers Brasserie** ( ☎ 6742 0400; 313 Conadilly St; mains $14-26; ☻ lunch & dinner) Located inside the

Gunnedah Services & Bowling Club this is the local favourite, which is understandable when you can get lunch for $8.

**Red Embers Restaurant** ( ☎ 6742 6766; 359 Conadilly St; mains $24-29; ☻ dinner Tue-Sat) An elegant mix of old and new, this is the ultimate dining experience in a tired old town. Malay fish curry is delivered complete with coconut for texture and fruit chutney to take the edge off.

## Getting There & Around

**Harvey World Travel** ( ☎ 6742 2211; 149 Conadilly St) will take care of most travel bookings. **Big Sky Express** ( ☎ 1800 008 759) flies to Sydney daily (except Saturday) or get a daily **CountryLink** train (adult/child $90/50). **Lowder & Sons Bus & Coach Service** ( ☎ 6792 1665, 0427 944 421) has a school bus run to Narrabri (but it runs on school days only).

## NARRABRI

☎ 02 / pop 7250

The younger sibling to Moree, Narrabri also boasts a snail-paced main street. It turns into a highway that bisects the cotton crops to link the two towns. Cotton dandruff litters the roadside verges and green space-invaders harvest crops along the Newell Hwy. Head northeast for respite in Mt Kaputar National Park.

## Information

The **visitors centre** ( ☎ 6799 6760; www.visitnarrabri .com.au; Newell Hwy; ☻ 9am-5pm Mon-Fri, to 2pm Sat & Sun) is located on the main street, Maitland St, which runs parallel to Narrabri Creek. Here you will find multiple ATMs to withdraw those hard-earned dollars.

**Joblink** ( ☎ 6792 5188; 5/100 Maitland St) For cotton jobs, also check out www.jobsearch.gov.au/harvesttrail or ring 1800 062 332

**Library** ( ☎ 6799 6790; Doyle St) For free internet.

**Post office** (cnr Doyle & Maitland St) For all your postal needs.

## Sights & Activities

The **Australian Cotton Centre** ( ☎ 6792 6443; Newell Hwy; adult/child $8/6; ☻ 8.30am-4.30pm) An exhibition dedicated to the region's big cash crop. It will take you from the cotton seed to the T-shirt.

**Australia Telescope Compact Array** ( ☎ 6790 4070; Yarrie Lake Rd; admission free; ☻ 11am-4pm) OK so they're not as big as the telescope at Parkes (featured in the Aussie film *The Dish*), but hey, there are six here, so who's complaining? This is the first point of call for UFOs entering the atmosphere and you don't have to be nerdy to enjoy the displays, but it does help.

## Sleeping & Eating

There are bakeries and pubs on Maitland St and visit **Woolworths** (opposite the visitors centre) for all your grocery needs.

**Narrabri Backpackers Bed & Breakfast** ( ☎ 6792 6473; dshweiki67@hotmail.com; 30 Mooloobar St; dm/tr incl breakfast $20/40; ☐ ) It is housed in an old pub in what was once the happening side of town. You will find friendly hosts, clean rooms, and good value accommodation.

**Aalbany Motel** ( ☎ 6792 4211, 1800 024 211; 38 Cooma Rd; s/d $72/81; ✖ ☳ ) One of many that line the Newell Hwy all offering the same services at the same standard, which is pretty standard.

**Highway Tourist Village & Caravan Park** ( ☎ 6792 1438; www.caravanparknarrabri.com.au; 86-92 Cooma Rd; sites $26-36, cabins $51-85; ✖ ) Set a little off the highway, the cabins aren't the cheapest in town but they are clean and in the prettiest park. The camping area looks out over the river.

**Outback Shack Bar & Grill** ( ☎ 6792 1202; Narrabri RSL Club, 7 Maitland St; mains $15-32; ☯ lunch & dinner) It's not 'Dan Kelly's herb bread' that makes this a unique place to dine, or the 'outback yabbies' caught up the road and served with lettuce and sweet chilli sauce. It actually rains inside.

## Getting There & Around

**QantasLink** ( ☎ 13 13 13) flies from Narrabri to Sydney via Moree twice daily. And **CountryLink** ( ☎ 13 22 32) has a daily service that runs between Narrabri and Sydney (adult/child $100/55). **Lowder & Sons Bus & Coach Service** ( ☎ 6792 1665, 0427 944 420) has buses that run to and from Gunnedah on school days as well as a town loop service (Rte 457C).

## MT KAPUTAR NATIONAL PARK

Looking like the Raj fortresses of India, resistant rocky outcrops cling to the mountain tops of a 21-million-year-old volcano. The older sister to the Warrumbungles, the thing that most distinguishes this park from the rest is that it is so accessible by car. There's even short walks to lookouts such as the **Governor** that are accessible by wheelchair.

Feel the temperature drop and watch the vegetation change as you drive to the summit where a handful of steps leads to an expansive view. Learn more about the mountain ecology with the **NPWS 'Discovery' programme** run during school holidays. Ring the local office or check

out www.nationalparks.nsw.gov.au for information on upcoming walks and talks.

Just 27km from Narrabri, head out along Tibhereena St and then Old Gunnedah Rd to the westernmost spur of the Nandewar Range. This park is popular for bushwalking, rock climbing, mountain-biking (Barraba Track) and wild flowers.

**Dawson's Spring** and **Bark Hut** are both established **camp sites** (sites per adult/child $3/2) with good facilities including warmish showers and septic loos. There are also three **cabins** (per night $55; min 2-night stay) at Dawson's Spring that can be booked at the local **NPWS office** ( ☎ 6792 7300; 100 Maitland St). Get in early as these are popular with the locals.

A slightly more civilised alternative is **Dulcinea Holiday Cabins** ( ☎ 6793 5246; dulcineacabins@hotmail.com; Mt Kaputar Rd; r $70; ✖ ) located just outside the park.

**Sawn Rocks**, at the northern end of the park, is a spectacular 40m cliff formed of octagonal columns of basalt which took shape from very slow-cooling lava. The site is signposted off the Bingara Rd about 40km northeast of Narrabri. There's a 900m walking track that starts at the car park (suitable for wheelchairs).

## MOREE

☎ 02 / pop 10,000

Colonnaded walkways shrouded in grapevine greenery do add some charm to the hectic main street. Fit for royalty, maybe not. A major cotton producing area, Moree has also tapped into the warm artesian waters without consciously tapping into the tourist dollar.

## Information

Frome St encapsulates the best thing about small towns. In the block just south of Heber St you will find the **post office**, art gallery, Westpac Bank, and the Postman Hotel (opposite the post office of course).

**Library** ( ☎ 6757 3360; cnr Albert & Balo Sts) Free internet.

**Visitors centre** ( ☎ 6757 3350; cnr Newell & Gwydir Hwys; ☯ 9am-5.30pm Mon-Fri, to 1pm Sat & Sun)

Cotton related work is available throughout the year for skilled workers who are not afraid of a little blood, sweat and tears. However, anyone can partake in cotton chipping over long hot days through November to January. Contact Julie at **Joblink** ( ☎ 6752 8488) for further info on **Project Harvest** or check out www .jobsearch.gov.au/harvesttrail.

## Sights & Activities

**Hot Springs Health Resort** ( ☎ 6752 2122; cnr Newell Hwy & Innes Ave; adult/child $4/3; ☯ 8am-8pm) Located behind the gaudy blue 'Health Resort', this place lends a certain 1920s atmosphere of swimming caps, deck chairs, and strongman competitions. But there are not many here, just a few locals frolicking in the hotter of the artesian pools (42°C).

**Moree Plains Gallery** ( ☎ 6757 3320; cnr Frome & Heber Sts; admission by donation; ☯ 9am-5pm Mon-Fri, 10am-2pm Sat) The Kamilaroi exhibit upstairs is a diverse display of local Aboriginal art. Kids' art classes are held on weekday afternoons conducted by **Red Art Shed** ( ☎ 6752 7216; lessons $20; ☯ Tue-Thu).

## Tours

Go nuts on the **Pecan and Nut Tour** or a **Cotton Gin Farm Tour** ( ☎ 6752 3841; adult/child $25/13). The tours are seasonal and pretty much leave on demand, so ring ahead and book your place. If you still haven't cottoned on to the local industry, perhaps go on a day tour out to Lightning Ridge instead (adult/child $55/28).

## Sleeping

Strange as it seems, motel rooms can book out quite quickly midweek.

**Moree Hotel** ( ☎ 6752 1644; 7 Alice St; s/d $33/50; ☒ ) Great rooms with balconies and TVs more than compensate for the garish green carpet and the primitive bathrooms. Special rates for long-termers; this is the place to stay while working on the cotton farms.

**Sundowner Moree Motel** ( ☎ 6752 2466, 1800 637 678; moree@sundownermotorinns.com.au; 2 Webb Ave; standard/deluxe r $67/95; ☒ ☒ ) The roar of 1500 semitrailers a day is juxtaposed with the tranquillity of lily-filled Broadwater Creek. Thankfully the Sundowner embraces the latter with deluxe rooms overlooking the greenery and bubbling brook.

**Mehi River Van Park** ( ☎ 6752 7188; www.big4 .com.au; 28 Oak St; sites $15-20, cabins $55-67; ☒ ☒ ) Neat cabins with or without linen; 24-hour highway noise with or without sleep; dreaming of sheep roaring down the highway and semitrailers jumping fences? There are no highway-free options in this town.

## Eating

**Moree on a Plate** ( ☎ 6757 3350) Is held in May each year. But even with all this foodie expertise about town you will still need to speak up if you don't like salt and pepper, otherwise your sandwich is automatically doused in it.

**Café 2400** ( ☎ 6752 6700; 123 Balo St; mains $5-12; ☯ breakfast & lunch) There's the happy hum of the espresso machine, light meals or gourmet sandwiches with homemade relishes and dressings and free-range poultry. Long live happy chooks.

**Explorers Restaurant & Bar** ( ☎ 6752 3377; Newell Hwy; mains $20-30; ☯ dinner Mon-Sat) It's fine dining in Moree's most elegant restaurant located inside the Burke & Wills Motor Inn.

## Getting There & Away

**Qantas** ( ☎ 13 13 13) flies to/from Sydney twice daily (once on Saturdays). You could also catch a daily train (adult/child $105/55). Otherwise travel to Dubbo on a **Greyhound** ( ☎ 13 14 99) coach Friday to Monday (adult/child $70/55); and catch a coach from there to Sydney. **Crisps** ( ☎ 07-4661 8333) runs a bus to Brisbane.

## LIGHTNING RIDGE

☎ 02 / pop 2200

This town was named after an unfortunate event in 1963 when a flock of sheep, their drover, and his faithful dog were struck down by lightning. Their singed woolly carcasses were still wafting with smoke when the town took its name from said event.

They come here from far and wide to try their luck hunting down the elusive black opal. They build castles, astronomer's monuments, tin shacks, and even houses made out of bottles. Gamesome and grandiose dreams hang overhead as they search for the precious stone, itself simply a piece of solidified silica that refracts light to give off a stunning array of colour. So the streets are trodden by eccentric artisans, true-blue bushies, and the general unconventional collective. And that is all just ridgy didge in the Ridge.

## Orientation & Information

The road in from the highway becomes Morilla St, where an **ATM, post office** ( ☎ 6829 0320; 46 Morilla St) and **medical centre** ( ☎ 6829 1977; 1/48 Morilla St) all reside. The **visitors centre** ( ☎ 6829 1670; www.lightningridge.net.au; Morilla St; ☯ 9am-5pm) is on your right as you enter town.

## Sights & Activities

Head to the visitors centre for maps showing the **Car Door Tours**. The yellow tour is the pick if you have to choose one. Follow the signs to

---

**DETOUR: OPAL FIELDS PUB AND PIT TOUR**

Start the tour at the **Walk-In Mine** and once you have learnt to watch for potch, head south of town to the **Grawin and Glengarry Opal Fields**. In the lush grounds of the golf course you will find the **Club in the Scrub**. Have a beer here and then you're on your way, before the white dust has a chance to settle. Follow the winding road, it is as rough as the miners' hands that innervate its underbelly. The dumps on your left reveal oodles of noodlers. Stop and spend some time searching through the waste rock. Then have a quick drink at the **Sheepyard** before heading to the **Glengarry Hilton**. You should have finished the Pub and Pit Tour in a different state. If not, drive north on the Castlereagh Hwy and find the historic **Hebel Hotel**, just over the Queensland border.

---

Homebrew Valley then Junk Pile Museum, to get better access to the open cut and a unique view on how the other half live.

**John Murray Art Gallery** ( ☎ 6829 1130; www.johnmurrayart.com.au; Opal St; ⏰ 9am-5pm Mon-Fri, to 1pm Sat & Sun) He's left his mark at the Lightning Ridge turn-off, on the flying panel van, and all over the Hebel Hotel (just over the border).

**Walk-In Mine** ( ☎ 6829 0473; adult/child $8/3; ⏰ 9am-5pm) Visit the mine to get a feel for the type of environment encountered by the average opal miner. Great for those without time but make sure you take yourself out to the Grawin and Glengarry Opal Fields for the real thing.

**Bottle House** ( ☎ 6829 0618; Opal St; adult/child $5/1; ⏰ 9am-5pm) Heres an idea, let's collect 40 years worth of junk, put it in a house made of over 5000 bottles and charge an entry fee to come see it. Do go if you're extra keen on salt and pepper shaker collections or if you have spent a couple of days in town and are yet to meet one of the locals.

**Hot Artesian Bore Baths** (Pandora St; admission free; ⏰ 24hr) If you need to relax (but not cool off!), try the 52°C pool at the northern edge of town. Four words – warm artesian water, free.

## Tours

**Black Opal Tours** ( ☎ 6829 0368; adult/child $25/10; ⏰ tours at 8.30am, 9.30am & 1.30pm) and **Outback Opal Tours** ( ☎ 6829 4110; www.outbackopaltours.com.au; adult/child $25/10; ⏰ tours at 8.15am, 9.00am, 1.15pm & 2pm) offer virtually the same product just a different size bus.

## Festivals & Events

Prove your worth and join in the shenanigans on Easter Saturday at the **Great Goat Race**. Catch a feral beast, give it some lessons on racing etiquette, let it go with 50 other goats, and bet money on which one will win. The **Opal & Gem Festival** is held at the end of July.

## Sleeping

**Bluey Motel** ( ☎ 6829 0380; 32 Morilla St; s/d $45/55; 🐕 ) A successful attempt at a budget motel that offers everything you need: a corkscrew and face washer. Simplicities that keep smiles on faces.

**Fossickers Cottages** ( ☎ 6829 0066; www.fossickerscottages.com; 2 Morilla St; 1-/2-bedroom cottage $120/130; 🐕 ) Fully self-contained and handy to town as well as being Fido friendly.

**Lightning Ridge Hotel/Motel and Caravan Park** ( ☎ 6829 0304; www.ridgehotelmotel.com.au; Onyx St; sites $13/15, s/d powered sites $16/18, cabins $60-80; 🐕 🏊 ) All your accommodation needs in the one place plus Nobbie's Bistro a short walk away.

## Eating

Of the people mining The Ridge, 80% were born outside of Australia. With such a multicultural population it's astounding to think the most exotic cuisine in town can be found at Wong's Chinese. Perhaps most locals are too focused on finding opal.

**Star Dust Café** ( ☎ 6829 2725; 4 Opal St; mains $8-16; ⏰ breakfast, lunch & dinner, closed Sun) One steak and salad sandwich, $7; A Dolly Parton CD for your listening pleasure, $26; a meal delivered with, 'Here you go darl'…priceless.

**Ridgez Restaurant** ( ☎ 6829 0408; 1 Agate St; mains $18-25; ⏰ lunch daily, dinner Tue-Sat) There is a wide selection of cocktails which reflect the success of your day. Tropical Margarita for those who discovered opal, Harvey Wallbanger for those who didn't. Located inside the bowling club.

## Getting There & Away

All bookings can be made at the **Opal Cave** ( ☎ 6829 0333; www.opalcave.com; 51 Morilla St; ⏰ 8.30am-5.30pm) with the buses stopping two doors up in front of Ridge Real Estate. **CountryLink** ( ☎ 13 22 32) runs daily trains between Sydney and Lightning Ridge connecting to a coach at Dubbo (adult/child $90/55).

# Back o' Bourke

Vast sunburnt plains, crimson sunsets and empty horizons – far west NSW is every bit as spacious as you could imagine, rough and rugged, and oh so dry. Yet this dry country is one of the most interesting areas in the state, and much more diverse than it first appears. It produces much of New South Wales' wealth, particularly from the mines of Broken Hill, and it is home to some of the state's most interesting national parks; a wondrous combination of stunning natural environments and vastly significant Aboriginal heritage.

A startlingly empty land, the outback is sparsely populated both with plants and animals and with people. You need to be rather special to live out here. So the people you meet are special – larger than life, yet calm and caring. You won't hear a car horn in these towns.

From November to February the heat is intense – by 10am the Celsius landmark of 40°C is passed. That leaves another 10 hours of daylight for the current record, 51.7°C, to be broken. There's plenty to see and do, and you can get into the towns and most national parks in a 2WD. But seek local advice if you want to venture onto unsealed roads, even in a 4WD. They're corrugated dust, some with a high central hump, and a few drops of rain polishes them slick to swish you out of control.

Although the country is flat to the horizon with small clumps of saltbush all over, there are plenty of birds, mobs of emus, cattle, feral goats and kangaroos along the roadside to watch – and to watch out for!

**BACK O' BOURKE**

---

## HIGHLIGHTS

- Feel deeply moved as the sun sets on the **Broken Hill Sculpture Symposium** (p269)
- Squeeze down a mine shaft, digging your feet nervously into the rough-hewn steps, at **Daydream Mine** (p268) at Broken Hill
- Slip softly through the water of the **Menindee Lakes** (p272) looking for a good fishing spot
- Get up and out there on a camel trek at historic **Silverton** (p271)
- Wake to see birds of every colour bathing in the Bogan River at **Nyngan** (p262)
- Sleep underground, with your purchase of opals under your pillow, at **White Cliffs** (p265)
- Photograph baby pelicans from an **1895-replica paddle-wheeler** on the magnificent Darling River at Bourke (p259)
- See for yourself the extraordinary plains, dunes and archaeological records at **Mungo National Park** (p273)

Bourke ★
White Cliffs ★
Nyngan ★
Silverton ★ ★ Broken Hill
★ Menindee Lakes
Mungo National Park ★

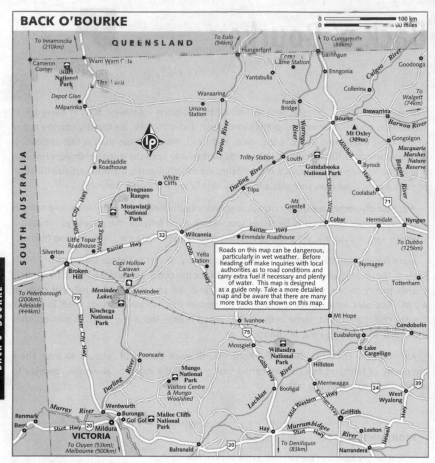

## BACK O'BOURKE

Roads on this map can be dangerous, particularly in wet weather. Before heading off make inquiries with local authorities as to road conditions and carry extra fuel if necessary and plenty of water. This map is designed as a guide only. Take a more detailed map and be aware that there are many more tracks than shown on this map.

## BOURKE

☎ 02 / pop 3924

Immortalised for Australians in the expression 'back of Bourke', that is anything remote, this easy-going town on the Darling River sits right on the edge of the outback. Beyond Bourke, green pastoral lands stop abruptly, settlements are few and the country is flat, brown and alluring. Bourke itself is gorgeous, historic and quaint, sprawled along its beautiful river with its river gums and water birds. Besides, the space is exhilarating, and the very remoteness attractive.

## History

The Ngemba people lived in a large area centred on the Brewarrina Fisheries – a series of stone traps on the Darling River – including Bourke and Louth.

The first Europeans to see this area were in Charles Sturt's party of 1828. Sturt was unenthusiastic about the country but by 1860 there were enough grazier settlers for a paddle-wheeler to risk the difficult journey up to Bourke. By the 1880s, many of the Darling River's 200 paddle-steamers were calling at Bourke; it was possible for wool leaving here to be in London in just six weeks.

Bourke is still a major wool-producing area, but droughts and low prices have forced farmers to look to products such as cotton and rock melons. There's even a vineyard.

Bourke has hosted Australian legends. Poet and writer Henry Lawson lived at the Carriers

Arms Hotel in 1892 while painting the Great Western Hotel. Fred Hollows, the ophthalmic surgeon and hero for his philanthropic work in developing countries, chose to be buried here in the 'land without fences'.

## Orientation & Information

The Mitchell Hwy winds through town then heads out across the old bridge to North Bourke (just a pub) 6km away. The shopping centre is on Oxley St between Sturt St and Richard St.

The **visitors centre** ( ☎ 6872 1222, 6872 2280; www.visitbourke.com; tourinfo@ozemail.com.au; Anson St; ☺ 9am-5pm, closed Sun in summer) has an excellent leaflet called *Bourke Mud Map Tours*, detailing a town walk and drives to places in the district.

Limited seasonal work is available: picking grapes (December to January), rock melons (November or December), citrus fruits (May to October) and cotton chipping (weeding; November or December). Nearly all these activities take place in summer and it can be *hot!* For work opportunities contact **Bourke Joblink** ( ☎ 6870 1041; www.joblinkplus.com.au; 26 Oxley St).

## Sights & Activities

The **Back O' Bourke Exhibition Centre** ( ☎ 6872 1321; www.backobourke.com.au; Kidman Way; stage 1 adult/child $3.50/2.50) follows the legends of the back country from both indigenous and settler perspectives by using oral histories and innovative displays. It is fascinating and the final form of the three-stage exhibition (adult/child $15/7.50) promises a unique experience.

There are many reminders of the time when the big paddle-wheelers were Bourke's lifeline. The impressive three-tiered **wharf** at the northern end of Sturt St is a faithful reconstruction of the original built in 1897 and, on the river, the **PV Jandra** ( ☎ 6872 1321; Kidman's Camp Tourist Park; adult/child $14/10; ☺ cruises 9am & 3pm Mon-Sat, 2.30pm Sun) is a replica of an 1895 paddle-wheeler. The one-hour cruise on the *Jandra* lets you experience the legendary Darling, hear about the local history and see the great range of river birds, like the blue-eyed corellas and pelicans, and their babies.

Many old buildings in town are reminders of Bourke's important past. The **courthouse** (1900), on the corner of Oxley and Richard

BACK O' BOURKE

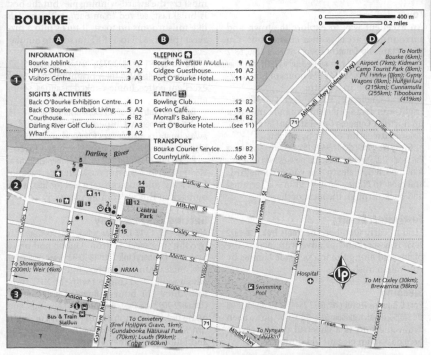

**BOURKE**

| | 0      400 m |
|---|---|
| | 0      0.2 miles |

**INFORMATION**
Bourke Joblink.................1 A2
NPWS Office....................2 A2
Visitors Centre.................3 A3

**SIGHTS & ACTIVITIES**
Back O'Bourke Exhibition Centre...4 D1
Back O'Bourke Outback Living.....5 A2
Courthouse......................6 B2
Darling River Golf Club..........7 A3
Wharf...........................8 A2

**SLEEPING**
Bourke Riverside Motel............9 A2
Gidgee Guesthouse...............10 A2
Port O'Bourke Hotel.............11 A2

**EATING**
Bowling Club....................12 B2
Gecko Café......................13 A2
Morrall's Bakery................14 B2
Port O'Bourke Hotel.........(see 11)

**TRANSPORT**
Bourke Courier Service........15 B2
CountryLink..................(see 3)

To North Bourke (6km); Airport (7km); Kidman's Camp Tourist Park (8km); PV Jandra (8km); Gypsy Wagons (8km); Hungerford (215km); Cunnamulla (255km); Tibooburra (419km)

Darling River

To Showgrounds (200m); Weir (4km)

To Cemetery (Fred Hollows Grave, 1km); Gundabooka National Park (70km); Louth (99km); Tilpa (160km)

To Mt Oxley (30km); Brewarrina (98km)

To Nyngan (203km)

Bus & Train Station

Sts, is topped by a crowned spire, signifying that it can hear maritime cases!

**Bourke's Historic Cemetery** (Kidman Way) predates the town with many epitaphs saying simply 'perished in the bush'. Here too is the deeply emotive headstone to Professor Fred Hollows, the eye surgeon who was determined to help restore the sight of people going needlessly blind. It was carved by a team of international sculptors when he was buried here in 1993.

**Darling River Golf Club** (☎ 6872 2210; Kidman Way) is a great spot to enjoy some green grass amid the native trees. Just turn up and have a hit, but you need your own clubs. There's a basketball and squash court here, and ask about the tennis courts on Mitchell St.

**Back O' Bourke Outback Living** (☎ 6872 4242; Sturt St; �9 10am-5pm Mon-Fri, to 2pm Sat) is a gem for local art and crafts and historical displays. There's a Crossley engine out the back, next to the wharf.

Cotton is picked in March and April. From about May to August you can see the cotton gin in action by phoning **Clyde Agriculture** (☎ 6872 2528).

## Tours

An excellent way to explore the town and surrounding areas is in a coaster bus. Go with **Mateship Country Tours** (☎ 6872 2280, 6872 1222; tourinfo@ozemail.com.au; adult/child $25/11; �9 tours 2pm Mon-Fri, 9.30am Sat) for 3½ hours of fun, leaving from the tourist centre.

For a challenge, the Gidgee Guesthouse (right) can arrange a farmstay and camel trek up north at **Comeroo Camel Station** (☎ 6874 7735; come@lisp.com.au) for one to five nights.

**Gypsy Wagons** (☎ 0429 927 185; Kidman's Camp Tourist Park; adult $10; �9 tours 11am) harnesses two cuddly-looking Clydesdales to take you past vineyards and bush to Nancy Bird-Walton Air Terminal and back through the local orchards.

## Festivals & Events

Held in early October, the **Poets Trek** (☎ 6872 2055) is a weekend of adventure across the plains and along the tracks made famous by Australian bush poets.

## Sleeping

**Port O'Bourke Hotel** (☎ 6872 2544; 32 Mitchell St; B&B s/d $40/55, d with bathroom $75; ☒ ) The pub's been renovated and is a cheerful place, serving breakfast in an elegant old dining room.

**Gidgee Guesthouse** (☎ 6870 1017; gidgee@auzzie .net; 17 Oxley St; dm/s/d $28/40/58; ☐ ) The old London Bank building is now a great guesthouse with changing art exhibitions, music gear for use, and pleasant rooms around a peaceful sculpture garden. Your hosts will give you all the goss, arrange tours and get you up on a camel.

**Bourke Riverside Motel** (☎ 6872 2539; www.bourke riversidemotel.com; 3 Mitchell St; standard s/d $75/95, heritage d $125; ☒ ☐ ☒ ) In an enchanting riverside garden, and reflecting all the magic that is Bourke itself, this friendly place includes the historic Telegraph Hotel, and many unique rooms, with antique furniture, even four-poster beds.

**Kidman's Camp Tourist Park** (☎ 6872 1612; Kidman Way; camp site $23, cabin standard/with bathroom $69/88; ☒ ☒ ) This quiet camping ground, just north of town, looks out on the plains along the Darling's banks. The deluxe cabins with timber decks look grand amid the trees.

## Eating

**Morrall's Bakery** (☎ 6872 2086; 37 Mitchell St; mains $7.50-10; �9 breakfast & lunch daily, dinner Thu-Sun) You must try the award-winning pies but the best is breakfast, served from 6am, with specials like mushrooms on toast. It turns into a pizzeria (pizzas $15 to $18) Thursday to Sunday evening.

**Gecko Café** (☎ 6872 2701; 29 Oxley St; meals $8.50-10.50; �9 9am-4pm Mon-Fri) A bright place serving excellent coffee, home-cooked lasagnes, soups and curries.

**Bowling Club** (☎ 6872 2190; Richard St; mains $12-18; �9 lunch & dinner) A Chinese restaurant hidden away upstairs also serves Oz food and delights like Mongolian lamb, using local produce.

**Port O'Bourke Hotel** (☎ 6872 2544; Mitchell St; mains $15; �9 lunch Tue-Sun, dinner Mon-Sat) It's a great spot for a roast and you can get a feel for life in the outback in this welcoming place.

## Getting There & Away

**Air Link** (☎ 13 17 13; www.airlinkairlines.com.au) has five flights a week to/from Dubbo and on to Sydney. **CountryLink** (☎ 13 22 32; www.countrylink .info) buses run to Dubbo (four hours, four days a week) and connect with the XPT train to Sydney (11 hours). **Bourke Courier Service** (☎ 6872 2092; cnr Oxley & Richard Sts) sells bus and plane tickets (opening hours depend on flight times). Tickets from Bourke to Dubbo are $63 and Dubbo to Sydney $60.

---

**DETOUR: PICNIC AT GUNDABOOKA NATIONAL PARK**

Pack a basket of goodies and set off to **Gundabooka National Park**, about 70km southwest of Bourke off the Kidman Way (watch for the turn-offs), where there are wonderful views between the wild flowers and mulga, gorges and rusty cliffs. The rock pools often have water in them and Mt Gundabooka is of great cultural significance to the Ngemba and Paakintji Aboriginal people, whose rock-art painting can still be seen. Outback talk is that there may be some volcanic activity in Mt Gundabooka, and 60km away at Mt Oxley. Check it out on www.outbackonline.net/MysteriousOxley.htm before you go, and if you're game to stay overnight, visit the **National Parks & Wildlife Service** (NPWS; ☎ 6872 2744; 51 Oxley St; ☷ 8.30am-4.30pm Mon-Fri) and ask about accommodation. There's camping at Dry Tank, beds in a shearers' quarters, or the Belah Governess's Cottage. Ask, too, for the Gundabooka key (needed to open gates to see rock art).

---

A **road condition report** ( ☎ 6872 2055, 0419 722 055) is posted at service stations. All unsealed roads are closed when wet.

## DARLING RIVER

Although it passes through some of the driest country in the state, the Darling River usually has some water and its banks are lined with massive river red gums. With the Murray, the Darling forms one of the world's longest exotic rivers – one that for much of its length flows through country from which it receives no water.

An unsealed road runs along the Darling's south bank downstream from Bourke to Wilcannia with a few places to check out on the way.

Tiny **Louth** (population 34), about 100km from Bourke, hosts up to 4000 people during the annual race meeting on the second Saturday in August. During the week before the races the local Shindy's Inn comes alive each night with events such as a damper bake-off. **Old Louth Post Office** ( ☎ 6874 7362; dr.white@bigpond.com; s/d $45/90) has been lovingly restored and now operates as a B&B.

**Trilby Station** ( ☎ 6874 7420; www.trilbystation.com.au; camp site d/f $20/25; bunkhouse s/d $30/60, standard/large cottage d $85/95; ☷ ☷ ), 20km west of Louth, offers an insight into outback life, including feeding animals, watching cattle mustering or sheep shearing, and listening to the School of the Air. Yabbying is fun, or go fishing and canoeing. The self-contained cottages are roomy, the bunkhouse cosy or you can camp by the river near the barbecue and gazebo.

Further downstream is the **Tilpa Hotel** ( ☎ 6837 3928; Tilpa; s/d/f $30/40/60), all scrunched and dusty, its name painted across the low-slung corrugated iron roof that holds up its veranda posts. There are meals (mains $17 to

$20; open lunch and dinner) like Bushman's Steak to fortify you, fuel and of course beer. The basic accommodation is in a separate building.

From Tilpa, the Darling flows down to **Wilcannia**, then through a system of lakes at **Menindee** (p272), surrounded by **Kinchega National Park** (p272), past **Pooncarie**, a pretty hamlet and a jumping-off point for **Mungo National Park** (p273), until it meets the Murray at **Wentworth** (p293). These places are accessible by sealed roads from Broken Hill.

## CORNER COUNTRY

Out here, it's a different world. The outback is both harsh and peaceful, stretching forever to the endless sky. This far western corner of NSW is a semidesert of red plains, heat, dust and flies; to quote Henry Lawson (1893): 'There are no mountains out west, only ridges on the floor of hell'. But it's also pastoral lands, with huge properties running beef and sheep. Corner Country produces over a million kilograms of fine merino wool each year.

If you've come west from Bourke, the 413km to Tibooburra via Wanaaring has been an adventurous drive, on a challenging unsealed road. If you've come north on the Silver City Hwy which is mostly sealed but still monstrous after rain, you've passed through **Milparinka**, where members of Charles Sturt's expedition were forced to camp for six months in 1845. Milparinka courthouse is a fine sandstone building, which houses a local history centre and has maps for a heritage walking track. About 14km northwest at **Depot Glen** is the grave of James Poole, Sturt's second-in-command, who died of scurvy.

Whatever the adventures on the way, it's worth being here to experience for yourself the space, physical features and wildlife.

Watch out for kangaroos and emus, goannas and other lizards on the road, and wedge-tailed eagles above. Along the Queensland border is the dingo-proof fence, patrolled daily by boundary riders.

## Tibooburra
☎ 08 / pop 150

Tiny Tibooburra, the hottest town in NSW, has two fine sandstone pubs and a small outdoor cinema. The town used to be called the Granites after the 400-million-year-old granite outcrops nearby, which are good to visit on a sunset walk. This is the closest town to Sturt National Park and there's a large **National Parks & Wildlife Service office** (NPWS; ☎ 8091 3308; ☼ 8.30am-4.30pm Mon-Fri) in the main street. Next door is the well-presented **Courthouse Museum**. **Keeping Place** ( ☎ 8091 3435) features indigenous artefacts as well as art for sale from the Wadigali, Wengkumara and Malyangapa tribes.

Internet access is available at the **Telecentre** ( ☎ 8091 3388; tibooburra2880@hotmail.com; Sturt St; per ½/1hr $4/6).

There's camping in the national park north of town at **Dead Horse Gully** (camp site $7); despite the immediate beauty it is rather exposed and dusty. In town, the **Granites Motel & Caravan Park** ( ☎ 8091 3305; Brown St; camp site $18, cabin standard/deluxe $50/60, motel s/d $56/70; ☼ ☎ ) has a communal kitchen, cheery rooms, pleasant cabins and a few small trees struggling to provide shade.

The **Family Hotel** ( ☎ 8091 3314; motel unit s/d $60/70; ☼ ) and **Tibooburra Hotel** ( ☎ 8091 3310) both have basic hotel rooms with shared facilities (single/double $30/50). Both bars have character; the Tibooburra has a collection of more than 60 well-worn hats on the walls.

**TJ's Roadhouse** ( ☎ 8091 3477; meals $12-18.50; ☼ 7am-9pm, to 6pm Sun) has bank, post office and laundry facilities, tourist and road information, and good country cooking. **Corner Country Store** ( ☎ 8091 3333; ☼ 7am-6pm), looking modern and cool, serves all-day breakfast, snacks and coffee, and has a barbecue area. It also sells fuel, groceries and camping equipment.

### GETTING THERE & AWAY
There is fuel halfway between Milparinka and Broken Hill at the **Packsaddle Roadhouse** ( ☎ 8091 2539), which features meals, accommodation and wool industry memorabilia. If you're travelling west from Bourke, there's fuel at Wanaaring and White Cliffs (p264). Phone for **road info** ( ☎ 08 8082 6660, 13 27 01, 08 8091 5155).

## Sturt National Park
Taking in vast stony plains, the towering red sand hills of the great Strzelecki Desert and the unusual flat-topped mesas around the Olive Downs, this park covers 340,000 hectares of classic outback terrain. Thanks to the protection of the dingo-proof fence, there are large populations of western grey and red kangaroos.

Sturt NP has 300km of drivable tracks, camping areas and walks. The NPWS at Tibooburra has brochures for each. A favourite destination for visitors is **Cameron Corner**. A post marks the spot where Queensland, South Australia and NSW meet. The Corner is reached by a well-signposted dirt road (allow two hours). In the Queensland corner, vine-covered **Cameron Corner Store** ( ☎ 08 8091 3872) has fuel, meals, accommodation and good advice on road conditions.

## BARRIER HIGHWAY
The Barrier Hwy, part of the direct route between Sydney and Perth and an alternative route to Adelaide, is an excellent sealed road heading from Nyngan 594km to Broken Hill.

## Nyngan
☎ 02 / pop 2500

Nyngan is a leafy country town on the banks of the Bogan River at the junction of the Barrier and Mitchell Hwys. Nyngan is also close to the centre of NSW; a cairn marks the exact spot 72km south.

The great flood of 1990, when the Bogan River overwhelmed the town and the entire population was evacuated by helicopter, still looms large in local memory. You can see photos of the flood at the **Railway Station Museum** (adult/child $2/50c; ☼ 10am-4pm). There is good bird-watching in Nyngan with 107 varieties that love the many little islands in the Bogan. Ideal spots are the **Rotary Park** near the Peter Sinclair Bridge and **Riverside**. Nyngan makes an excellent jumping-off point for visiting the Macquarie Marshes Nature Reserve (Map p250). The **visitors centre** ( ☎ 6832 1705, 13 20 77; 12 Old Warren Rd) is at the Nyngan Caravan Park, east of town over the railway line. West of town, over the bridge, there are free sheltered camping spots off Temples Lane.

**Canonba Hotel/Motel** ( ☎ 6832 1559; 129 Pangee St; s/d $35/55; ☼ ) has motel-style rooms behind the pub, and your usual pub counter meals inside.

**Country Manor Motor Inn** ( ☎ 6832 1447, 1800 819 913; www.countrymanor.com.au; 145 Pangee St; s/d $69/80; ☒ ☒ ) is an attractive new place near the pub. Owner Colin Duel will tell you about the local attractions.

**Beancounters House** ( ☎ 6832 2270; www.beancoun tershouse.com.au; 103 Pangee St; d incl breakfast $99-130; ☐ ) is mostly on top of the Westpac bank with a modern kitchen off the verdant courtyard garden. Settle in for a comfortable stay in minimalist bedrooms, smart shared bathrooms and veranda access to watch the world go by.

**Nyngan Riverside Caravan Park** ( ☎ 6832 1729; enquiries@nynganriversidc.com.au; Barrier Hwy; camp site $20, cabin standard/deluxe $50/70), west of town, is set on a sandy river beach on the Bogan, a great spot for water-skiing, swimming, canoeing and fishing. Day entry into the park is adult/child $5/3. Your hosts provide a free taxi into town in the evenings.

The **Windmill Tavern** ( ☎ 6832 1244; 11 Pangee St; mains $7.50-16; ☽ lunch & dinner) is a basic but spacious bar and bistro, serving meals like rissoles and veg.

**CountryLink** ( ☎ 13 22 32) bus/XPT service between Sydney ($78; nine hours) and Broken Hill ($64; 6½ hours) stops here daily, and another bus runs to Bourke ($27; two hours) four times weekly.

## Cobar
☎ 02 / pop 5020

Cobar is a bustling mining town with a productive copper mine. Rich copper ore was discovered in 1871. Both the Great Cobar and

Cornish, Scottish & Australian (CSA) mines closed in the 1920s. The CSA mine reopened in the 1960s; it is 1km deep. The Endeavor mine, 47km west of Cobar, is currently exploiting a rich plug of zinc, lead and silver.

### INFORMATION
The **visitors centre** ( ☎ 6836 2448; cobarmus@bigpond .com; Barrier Hwy, Cobar; ☽ 8.30am-5pm), at the eastern end of town, is in the Great Cobar Heritage Centre. Pick up a Mud Map and Heritage Walk. There's also a **NPWS office** ( ☎ 6836 2692; 16 Barton St).

### SIGHTS & ACTIVITIES
In the Mines Office (1910) of the Great Cobar Heritage Centre is the **Cobar Museum** (adult/child/ family $7/5/15; ☽ 8.30am-5pm) and many of the displays reflect this association. The hospital train carriage is interesting and there are also sophisticated displays on the environment, local Aboriginal life and the early Europeans. Don't miss it.

Next to the museum is the **Stele Monument**, dedicated to the town and its mining past. You'll find a surprising number of interesting buildings in Cobar including the enormous **Great Western Hotel** (1898), which has perhaps the longest iron-lace veranda in the world. The town also has some legendary characters; stories can be found at the visitors centre.

Take a sealed road to **Fort Bourke Lookout** and view Cobar and its surroundings There is a viewing platform – look down on the old open-cut gold mine and watch the trucks

BACK O' BOURKE

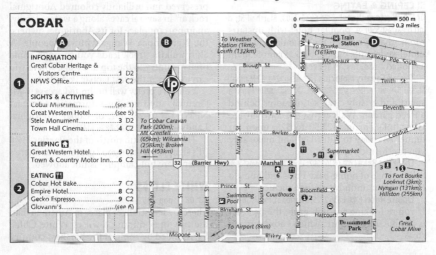

COBAR

**LET'S TALK ABOUT THE ROADS**

Who would have thought, but the roads out here are a favourite topic. The dust that makes a road Is so fine that you could use it to lubricate your engine. A sprinkle of rain turns it to glass. Slippery glass. Those dips in sealed roads aren't for fun. They make canals to carry rain away as it doesn't soak into the glassy soil. Those ribbans of mud you see ahead are deep waterways waiting to whoosh you out onto the plains.

The mere hint of rain and everyone has a tale, of being land-locked for days, of digging all night to get out of a ditch, you know the sort of thing.

Then there are the animals. They look like clumps of mulga until they rush at you. No reason, they just rush out. This happens most at dusk and dawn. You're hungry, they're hungry. Great combination. One guy thought he'd died when everything went black and he saw dimly that he was covered in blood. Kangaroo blood, as it turned out, from it bounding through the windscreen.

You'll even meet the odd person who's tried to pass a road train and lived to tell about it.

Get up to Corner Country and road conversations are electrified with anxiety, challenge, simmering with details of walkie-talkie contact, two-way HF radio contact, CB radios, GPS readings, tracks, traps, fuel stocks, water stocks, flares, spare tyres and the sad situation of mobile phones that don't have network coverage anywhere you might need it. Everyone's read the advice at www.flyingdoctor .net/travelinfo.htm, and got brochures and travel advice by calling ☎ 1800 633 060.

The roads are the adventure out here, the land they slice through merely their backdrop.

heading down the deep decline through to the new mine

The **Weather Station** ( ☎ 6836 2149; Louth Rd; tour free; ☽ 8.45am) offers a 45-minute guided tour which includes the spectacular launching of its weather balloon at 9.15am (10.15am during daylight saving).

If you're in town on the weekend, check out the **Town Hall Cinema** ( ☎ 6836 38195; www .cinemacafé.com.au; Barton St; adult/child $12/6; ☽ Fri-Sun) which screens current films in the afternoon and evening.

**SLEEPING & EATING**

**Great Western Hotel** ( ☎ 6836 2503; Marshall St; d incl breakfast $50) A popular hotel with upstairs rooms that open onto the veranda, and basic motel-style units out the back. From 5.30am a cooked breakfast is served.

**Town & Country Motor Inn** ( ☎ 6836 1244; 52 Marshall St; s/d $79/90, deluxe s/d $98/108; ☒ ☐ ☒ ) Has a smart and crisply clean set of rooms behind a treed garden. Walk across the courtyard to Giovanni's (mains $22.50 to $28; open for dinner Monday to Saturday) and make sure you try the rack of lamb.

**Cobar Hot Bake** ( ☎ 6836 2007; 13 Barton St; meals $2-8) Sells a range of home-baked pies and buns to take to Drummond Park for a picnic.

**Empire Hotel** ( ☎ 6836 2725; 6 Barton St; meals $8-17) If you're looking for pub grub, the best bet is the bustling Empire, which cooks a mean steak.

**Gecko Espresso** ( ☎ 6836 4888; 35 Marshall St; meals $6.30-9.50; ☽ 8am-6pm Thu & Fri, to 4pm Mon, Wed & Sat) A cheery and bright coffee bar with good cakes and excellent salads and wraps.

**GETTING THERE & AWAY**

**CountryLink** ( ☎ 13 22 32) bus/XPT service between Sydney ($82; 10½ hours) and Broken Hill ($51; five hours) stops here daily.

## Mt Grenfell Historic Site

Taking in part of the Mt Grenfell Station, the Mt Grenfell historic site protects well-preserved and brilliantly coloured Aboriginal rock art in several caves along a watered gully, an important place for its Aboriginal owners, the Ngiyampaa Wangaaypuwan people. A 5km walking track leads you through some pretty country to the top of a ridge where you can look over the vast Cobar Pediplain.

You have pretty well unlimited access to Mt Grenfell, any time; for information, contact NPWS ( ☎ 02-6836 2692) or Cobar Aboriginal Lands Council ( ☎ 02-6836 1144).

The site is 32km north of the Barrier Hwy (it's signposted) on a good gravel road. There's water there but camping is not allowed.

## WHITE CLIFFS

☎ 08 / pop 225

There are few stranger places in Australia than the tiny opal-mining town of White Cliffs. Surrounded by some of the harshest country the outback has to offer, many residents have gone underground to escape the heat.

The town centre (a pub, a post office and a general store) is on flat land south of the main digging area. At the digging area, there are thousands of holes in the ground and miners' camps surrounded by car graveyards. The two bare hills, Turley's Hill (with the radiotelephone mast on top) and Smith's Hill (south of the centre), command the plains like diminutive city-states.

Although the town is still a key opal producer, tourism brings in almost as much money these days. You can fossick for opals around the old diggings, but watch the kids around those deep, unfenced holes. There are a number of opal showrooms with hand-crafted jewellery, souvenirs, rough opal and Aboriginal art for sale, or just talk to the artists. The **visitors centre** ( ☎ 8091 6611; ☺ 8am-8pm) at the White Cliffs Store has information, maps and a Heritage Trail guide map. It also sells takeaway food and fuel.

Many of the underground homes offer inspections to tourists. **Parkers' Dug-Out Home Tours** ( ☎ 8091 6635; adult/child $5/free; ☺ 10am-4pm) includes a tour of a unique home and a display area of fossils, an opalised log and memorabilia.

In the town's centre is the **solar power station** ( ☺ tours 2pm) where emus often graze out the front. Local businesses each spent up to $60,000 a year on diesel-generator electricity before the Australian National University updated their original solar-power project in 1993 and got them on the grid.

## Sleeping & Eating

White Cliffs is busy during holiday periods, so it's best to book ahead. In the underground buildings, the walls need to stay dry to be stable, so bathrooms are near the exits and shared. You'll be glad the walls are stable when you're there.

**White Cliffs Underground Motel** ( ☎ 8091 6677; www.undergroundmotel.com.au; s/d $79/99; 3-course set-menu dinner $35; ☐ ☒ ) Custom-built with a tunnelling machine, its corridors are wide and lead to the lovely dining room with windows looking out onto the pool. Or take the back stairs up to a viewing platform that looks out over the town. It's all delightfully comfortable and when the lights are off the silence is total. Claustrophobics need not despair; there are two aboveground rooms available.

**PJ's Underground** ( ☎ 8091 6626; www.babs.com.au/pj; Turley's Hill; s/d with breakfast & mine tour $100/130; self-help dinner $35) Was once a mine and the owners have converted it into a cool sanctuary. Self-caterers can pay $5 to use the barbecue and there's one room with an en suite ($160).

**White Cliffs Opal Pioneer Reserve** ( ☎ 8091 6649; camp site $9.50) Simmering peacefully under the sun, there's powered sites on flat dusty earth between saltbush clumps, a barbecue area and laundry.

## Getting There & Away

The road north from Wilcannia is sealed, straight and fast. All other roads into White Cliffs are unsealed. **Road info** ( ☎ 8087 0660, 8091 5155) is posted outside the general store.

---

### TOP FIVE DRINKING SPOTS

There's a good spot for a drink wherever you go out here, but these represent the range you'll find, all with a connection to the history of outback Australia.

**Mungo Lodge** ( ☎ 03-5029 7297; Mildura Rd, Mungo National Park) Sit around an open fire and chat to your Irish hosts about the latest archaeological finds in this extraordinary park (p273).

**Mario's Palace Hotel** ( ☎ 08-8088 1699; cnr Argent & Sulphide Sts, Broken Hill) Lounge across the very long bar under a glorious ceiling of murals, wide screen sports at one end, bristle-haired lads at the other, and wonder just where in the world are you (p270).

**Tilpa Hotel** ( ☎ 02-6837 3928; Darling St, Tilpa) Perched on the bank of the Darling River with a shady beer garden, this is a classic bush pub. Have a yarn with the shearers or donate some money to the Flying Doctor Service for your chance to scribble on the walls (p261).

**Family Hotel** ( ☎ 08-8091 3314; Briscoe St, Tibooburra) Built in 1883, the Family is covered in original works of the artists Clifton Pugh, Russell Drysdale and Rick Amor, who, fascinated by the desert, came here to paint it (p262).

**Silverton Hotel** ( ☎ 08-8088 5313; Laynard St, Silverton) Make like Mad Max and take a drink at the pub that has been used as a film location at least 140 times (p272).

## MUTAWINTJI NATIONAL PARK

The exceptional Mutawintji National Park lies in the Byngnano Ranges, the eroded and sculptured remains of a 400 million-year-old seabed. The area teems with wildlife around its stunning gorges, dark rock pools and mulga plains that stretch to the horizon.

The reliable water supply was vital to the Malyankapa and Pandjikali people who lived in the area for over 8000 years. There are important **rock engravings**, stencils and paintings as well as the scattered remains of the day-to-day life of the people. Some rock art has been damaged by vandals but can still be seen on **Mutawintji Heritage Tours** ( ☎ 08-8088 7000; adult/child/family $20/10/40; ⊙ tours 11am Wed & Sat) between April and November.

There are many graded, marked walks for all levels of fitness, through crumbling sandstone hills and craggy cliffs to rock pools and tranquil valleys where rock paintings can be seen in the unrestricted areas.

There's a **camping ground** (adult/child $5/3) at Homestead Creek, with toilets, showers and gas barbecues. Fuel and food are not available in the park; collect firewood from the signposted areas near the park entrance.

### Getting There & Away

Most people head out to Mutawintji from Broken Hill, up the Silver City Hwy to the turn-off then 68km to the park entrance along a good unsealed road – impassable after a little rain. The road down from White Cliffs is also good, albeit challenging, or take the Wakibag Rd off the Barrier Hwy. **Road closure info** ( ☎ 08-8082 6660, 13 27 01, 08-8091 5155).

## BROKEN HILL

☎ 08 / pop 20,440

The Silver City, as Broken Hill is known, is a fascinating destination for its comfortable, oasislike existence in an extremely unwelcoming environment. Some of the state's best national parks are in the area, plus interesting near-ghost towns. Elements of 'traditional' Australian culture that are disappearing in other cities can still be found in Broken Hill, showing the sensibilities that come with access to a huge, unpopulated landscape. This has also inspired a major arts centre with

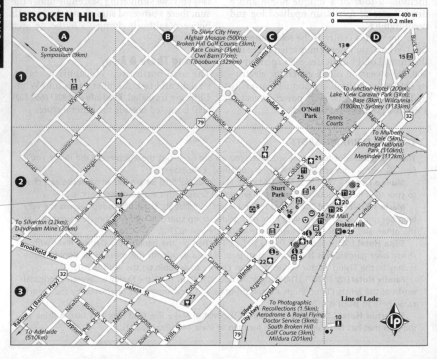

poets, writers, artists and sculptors offering a surprisingly different and delightful view of the great outback.

## History

Charles Sturt stood on this hill of incredible wealth in 1842 and looked out across the plains, searching for an inland sea. Unfortunately it had dried up 20 million years earlier. It was another 41 years before the world's biggest hill of silver was noticed by a boundary rider, Charles Rasp, laying the foundations that took Australia from an agricultural country to an industrial nation.

An early syndicate of seven men formed to start mining, but one couldn't raise the £230. The group elected to play poker, including him if he won. He lost, which made it the richest game of poker ever played.

The Broken Hill Proprietary Company (now international giant BHP Billiton) was formed in 1885. Other mining claims were staked, but BHP was always the 'big mine' and dominated the scene. Rasp went on to amass a personal fortune and BHP, which later diversified into steel production, became Australia's largest company.

Early conditions in the mine were appalling. Hundreds of miners died and many more suffered from lead poisoning and lung disease. This gave rise to the other great force in Broken Hill, the unions. Many miners were immigrants, but all were united in their efforts to improve mining conditions.

The first 35 years of Broken Hill saw a militancy rarely matched in Australian industrial relations. After many unsuccessful campaigns the turning point was the Big Strike of 1919–20, which lasted for over 18 months. The miners won a great victory, achieving a 35-hour week

and the end of dry drilling, responsible for the dust that afflicted so many miners. The concept of one big union, which had helped to win the strike, was formalised in 1923 with the formation of the Barrier Industrial Council.

Today the world's richest silver, lead and zinc deposit is still worked, though not by BHP, which ceased work in 1940, but by Zinifex, the only remaining operator. The ore body is diminishing and modern technology has greatly reduced the number of jobs. But while mining has declined, art has thrived.

## Orientation & Information

The city is laid out in a grid with the streets named after metals and their compounds. Argent St is the main street.

The **visitors centre** ( ☎ 8088 9700; www.visit brokenhill.com.au; cnr Blende & Bromide Sts; ⏰ 8.30am-5pm) has the excellent free booklet *Broken Hill, the Accessible Outback*, which is full of helpful regional information, and there is a handy guide to the art around town.

The visitors centre is also where buses arrive (book through the town's travel agents) and there's a car-rental desk on the premises.

The **NPWS office** ( ☎ 8080 3200; 183 Argent St; ⏰ 8.30am-4.30pm Mon-Fri) can help with local national park inquiries and bookings.

The **Royal Automobile Association of South Australia** (RAASA; ☎ 8088 4999; 261 Argent St; ⏰ 8.30am-5pm Mon-Fri, to 11.30am Sat) provides reciprocal service to other auto-club members.

Internet access is available at **Fully Loaded Computer Supplies** ( ☎ 8088 4255; www.fullyloaded.net .au; 195 Argent St; per 15/30/60min $3/4/6; ⏰ 10am-5pm) and **Tourist Centre Café** ( ☎ 8088 9700; cnr Blende & Bromide Sts; per 10min $1; ⏰ 8.30am-5pm). **Hungry Jack's** (cnr Argent & Iodide Sts) has a free 24-hour wifi hot spot.

## Sights & Activities

### MINES

There's an excellent underground tour at **Delprat's Mine** ( ☎ 8088 1604; adult/child over 5 yr $40/30; ☽ tours 10.30am Mon-Fri, 2pm Sat) where you don miners gear and descend 130m in a cage for a two-hour tour of stopes and working equipment. Delprat's is signposted across the railway tracks.

The first mines were walk-in, pick-and-shovel horrors. For an amazing experience, tour the historic **Daydream Mine** ( ☎ 8088 5682; adult/child $15/8; ☽ 10am-3.30pm), where you squeeze down the steps with your helmet-light quivering on your head. Daydream was established in 1882 and the guide has tales of baby-faced miners, which will have you giggling nervously. Sturdy footwear is essential for the one-hour tour. It's a scenic drive off the Silverton road, and the café serves the best Devonshire teas ($6.50) while you wait for the next group to venture into the mine.

### LINE OF LODE

The huge silver skimp dump, which makes up Broken Hill's stark backdrop, also features the moving **Miners Memorial** ( ☎ 8087 1318; Federation Hill; admission $4; ☽ 9am-6pm, later in summer). The memorial commemorates the deaths of over 800 men who have died in the mines since 1883. The list of the dead includes Dario Palumbo, an architecture student from the University of South Australia, who died suddenly during his work on the memorial, and whose story truly captures the emotions. The Broken Earth Café & Restaurant (p271) is attached.

### ROYAL FLYING DOCTOR SERVICE

Flynn of the Inland's dream was a flying doctor service. Go to the airport to see the reality. The **Royal Flying Doctor Service** ( ☎ 8080 1714; www .flyingdoctors.org; airport; adult/child $5.50/2.20; ☽ 9am-

5pm Mon-Fri, 11am-4pm Sat & Sun) exhibition includes the fascinating **Mantle of Safety Museum** with lots of quirky stories and things to see. The tour includes a DVD about the service, and you inspect the headquarters, aircraft and the radio room that handles calls from remote towns and stations. Tours run during the week, or visit the museum at any time.

### SCHOOL OF THE AIR

For a back-to-school experience, sit in on **School of the Air** (Lane St; admission $4.40; ☽ broadcasts 8.30am Mon-Fri), which broadcasts to kids in isolated homesteads. You must book through the visitors centre the day before. During school holidays a tape will be played for you.

### GALLERIES

With its dramatic scenery and empty spaces Broken Hill is an inspiring place, so it's not strange to find that the city houses a vibrant community of artists, from painters to performers. There are many galleries, including the **Pro Hart Gallery** ( ☎ 8088 2992; 108 Wyman St; adult $4; ☽ 9am-5pm Mon-Sat). Pro Hart who died early in 2006 was a former miner. He is Broken Hill's best-known artist and his charming gallery displays many of his works from his private collection (like *The Holy Tower* and *Dragon Fly*), a superb collection of Australian art (such as Whiteley's *Nude*, Lindsay's *Selena* and Tucker's *Australian Girl in Paris*) and several works by international artists such as Picasso and Dali.

**Broken Hill Regional Art Gallery** ( ☎ 8088 6897; 404-408 Argent St; entry by donation; ☽ 10am-5pm) was established in 1904 to meet the needs of a 'city in isolation', making it the oldest regional gallery in NSW and with 1500 works in its permanent collection, possibly the largest. One room of the gallery is devoted to the artists of Broken Hill. Special exhibitions have included Brushmen of the Bush.

---

### PHONES, TIMES & FOOTBALL

When the NSW government refused to give Broken Hill the services it needed, saying the town was just a pinprick on the map, the Barrier Industrial Council replied that Sydney was also a pinprick from where it was, and Broken Hill would henceforth be part of South Australia. Since the town was responsible for much of NSW's wealth there was an outcry, the federal government stepped in, and Broken Hill was told it was to remain part of NSW. In protest, the town adopted SA time, phone area code, and football, playing Australian Rules from then on.

Tourists beware, time in Broken Hill is Central Standard Time (CST), 30 minutes later than the surrounding area on Eastern Standard Time (EST); you're in the 08 phone code region; and don't talk about soccer in the pub.

**Thankakali Gallery** ( ☎ 8087 6111; cnr Buck & Beryl Sts; ☺ 9am-4pm Mon Fri) is the Aboriginal cultural centre, located in an old brewery. There is an extensive gallery downstairs as well as a range of hand-painted arts, crafts and didgeridoos by local artists, including Badger Bates' paintings – all for sale.

While on Argent St make sure you have a look at the murals in Mario's Palace Hotel (p270).

### SCULPTURE SYMPOSIUM
A striking range of work on a hilltop northwest of town was created in 1993 by 12 international sculptors. They were responding to the limitless landscape, using some 52 tonnes of Wilcannia sandstone, borrowing the local miners' old tungsten carbide chisels to dent the tough rock, and camping in tents near their work. Their pieces took shape with names like *Under the Jaguar Sun* and *Moon Goddess*. The colours of the stone change constantly with the light. Bring water in summer, and consider visiting at dawn or sunset, to add another dimension to the romance of this wonderful place. The sculptures are signposted off to the right along Nine Mile Rd. Get the keys for the gates from the visitors centre and drive up to the top car park, where there's also wheelchair access to the sculptures. Or it's a 20-minute climb to the sculpture site from the lower car park.

### HISTORIC BUILDINGS
Broken Hill has a rich and varied architectural heritage. It is well worth buying a copy of the *Heritage Trails* booklet from the visitors centre ($2.20). The many listed sights include the old miners cottages and the slag heap. Locals say there is millions of dollars' worth of silver left in the slag heap but it can't be touched because of the heritage listing!

**Trades Hall** (cnr Sulphide & Blende Sts; ☺ 10am-3pm Mon-Tue & Thu-Fri, 1-4pm Sat), built between 1898 and 1904, houses the Barrier Industrial Council. It features a pressed-iron ceiling over its elaborately detailed interior, restored in 1988.

**Afghan Mosque** (cnr William & Buck Sts; admission $2.50; ☺ 2-4pm Sun) is a simple corrugated-iron building c 1891. Afghan cameleers helped open up the outback and the mosque was built on the site of a camel camp.

The **former synagogue** (Wolfram St) dates from 1900, but it closed in 1962 and the religious scrolls were sent to Melbourne.

### GOLF & TENNIS
**Broken Hill Golf Course** ( ☎ 8087 9099; Racecourse Rd; 9/18 holes $16/25, club hire from $12; ☺ 7.30am-5.30pm), a spectacular course around green rolling hills sprinkled with kangaroos and emus, provides a perfect break.. Then check out the fun at **South Broken Hill Golf Course** ( ☎ 8087 4639; Jameison St; 18 holes $4), which has gravel fairways and sand-scrape greens. It's open the same hours and will lend you some clubs.

**Tennis** (O'Neill Park, Beryl St; day/night $5/7) is available, played on synthetic grass, if you have your own rackets and balls. Get the key from the visitors centre ($20 deposit).

### OTHER ATTRACTIONS
The wonderful **Photographic Recollections** ( ☎ 8087 9322; old Central Power Station, Eyre St; adult/child $5/2; ☺ 10am-4.30pm Mon-Fri, 1-4.30pm Sat & Sun) exhibition is a pictorial history of Broken Hill.

There is more local history at the **Railway, Mineral & Train Museum** ( ☎ 8088 4660; cnr Blende & Bromide Sts; adult/child $2.50/$2; ☺ 10am-3pm). The museum is in the Silverton Tramway Company's old station. The tramway was a private railway running between Cockburn (SA) and Broken Hill via Silverton until 1970.

**GeoCentre** ( ☎ 808/ 6538; cnr Bromide & Crystal Sts; adult/child $4/2.50; ☺ 10am-4.45pm Mon-Fri, 1-4.45pm Sat & Sun) is an interactive geology museum bringing you beautiful and rare minerals and crystals. There are lots of touch-and-feel exhibits that display the story of Broken Hill's geological history and how minerals are processed. It's also home to a 42kg silver nugget and the *Silver Tree*, a large and intricate silver sculpture created in 1878 by German silversmith Harry Steiner.

**Silver City Mint & Art Centre** ( ☎ 8088 6100, 60 Chloride St; admission $5; ☑ 10am-4pm) is home to the *Big Picture*, the largest continuous canvas in Australia, an amazing 100m-by-12m diorama of the Broken Hill outback.

**Owl Barn** ( ☎ 8088 5301; Silver City Hwy, Stephens Creek; admission by donation; ☑ 10am-4pm, closed Thu) has hundreds of owls, local crafts and memorabilia on display in a quirky old pub with its roof burnt off.

## Tours

Two-hour guided walks (for a donation) of Broken Hill commence from the tourist centre at 10am Monday, Wednesday and Friday. Plenty of companies offer tours of the town and nearby attractions, some going further out to White Cliffs, Mutawintji National Park and other outback destinations. The visitors centre has information and takes bookings.

For a real buzz, hitch a ride with the **Bush Mail Run** ( ☎ 0411 102 339; adult $88; ☑ 7am Wed & Sat), an outback mail delivery service that covers over 550km, stopping at isolated homesteads for the occasional cuppa. Several outfits have longer 4WD tours of the area, for example **Broken Hill's Outback Tours** ( ☎ 1800 670 120; www .outbacktours.net) has deluxe tours for up to nine days, and **Tri State Safaris** ( ☎ 8088 2389; www.tristate .com.au), a tourism award winner, runs half- to 20-day tours and goes to places like Corner Country, Birdsville and the Simpson Desert.

## Festivals & Events

Held annually on the Saturday two weeks before Easter is **St Patrick's Race Day**. Thousands of people flock to the dirt-track racecourse on the outskirts of the city. Celebrations begin in town on the preceding Wednesday, and the actual event is followed by a recovery party at the Silverton pub on the Sunday. But there's stacks more to do, so look at the calendar of events at www.visitbrokenhill .com.au/events.asp.

## Sleeping

### BUDGET

**Tourist Lodge YHA** ( ☎ 8088 2086; 100 Argent St; s/tw/d $30/44/50; ☒ ☐ ☒ ) This popular and central YHA has a laid-back atmosphere and is set around a charming courtyard with a small pool. Its gallery sells opals and arranges tours, its kitchen provides meals, and since there's no stairs it's also popular with seniors. Bike rental is $15 a day

**Laledonian B&B** ( ☎ 8087 1945; www.caledonianbnb .com.au; 140 Chloride St; s/d $55/69; ☒ ☒ ) This cosy B&B is in a beautifully refurbished pub (1898). Your charming hosts cook up a storm and will swap your hearty breakfast for a gourmet affair (extra $5) served at an antique dining table and surrounded by the colourful art work by local artist Allan Duffy.

**Mario's Palace Hotel** ( ☎ 8088 1699; cnr Argent & Sulphide Sts; s/d/tr/q $55/75/85/95; ☒ ☒ ) Star of the hit Australian movie *The Adventures of Priscilla, Queen of the Desert*, this is an impressive old pub (1888) with large TV screens, great veranda and a coating of murals, like the owner Mario Celetto's tribute to Botticelli's *Birth of Venus* on the ceiling and walls of lavish Australiana landscapes. Stay in the Priscilla Room for $110, or there are $22 rooms with shared facilities. It's all a bit of fun.

**Mulberry Vale** ( ☎ 8088 1597; Menindee Rd; cabin d $77; ☒ ☒ ) About 5km out of Broken Hill is this small oasis. The accommodation is comfortable; however, it's the peaceful environment that is the drawcard and it costs less the longer you stay.

**Quandong Cottage** ( ☎ 8087 1653; Lduffy@westnet .com.au; 78 Williams St; 4/6 people $100/130; ☒ ) This gorgeous stone cottage (others are available), with its seriously thick walls for total peace, is set in a large native garden with a playground. There's a minimum two-night stay, but ask about the discount for longer stays and guess what – pets are welcome.

**Lake View Caravan Park** ( ☎ /fax 8088 2250; 1 Mann St; camp site $19, cabin $58, 2-room cottage with/without spa $110/90; ☒ ☒ ) Looking down on Imperial Lake, you're high enough for cooling breezes and it's pleasantly green with grass and trees around a grand swimming pool.

### MIDRANGE

**Astra** ( ☎ 8087 5428; www.theastra.com.au; 393 Argent St; d/deluxe/ste $175/195/250; ☒ ☒ ☐ ) Sweep up the broad staircase to wide corridors and elegant rooms that open onto a magnificent veranda. Each room features stained glass, a spa and a homely feel. Ask about a single rate.

**Imperial** ( ☎ 8087 7444; imperial@pcpro.net.au; 88 Oxide St; d $180; ☒ ☒ ☒ ) These rooms retain the feel of the grand old hotel the Imperial once was. There is a full-size billiard table in the guest lounge. Use the guest kitchen if you wish to cook, and a help-yourself breakfast is provided.

## Eating

Broken Hill's many clubs welcome diners if you like a background clang of pokies.

### BUDGET

**Charlotte's at the Grand** ( ☎ 8087 2230; 317 Argent St; meals $6-13; ☺ breakfast & lunch) A cosy place for lunch, with lots of tasty vegetarian and gluten-free options, sandwiches and smoothies.

**Southern Cross Hotel** ( ☎ 8088 4122; 357 Cobalt St; meals $11-22; ☺ lunch & dinner) Has a good menu with standouts being the fresh fish, although the chicken with camembert and mango is very good. The dining room is pleasant and the staff friendly.

### MIDRANGE

**Argent St Café & Restaurant** ( ☎ 8087 2637; 343 Argent St; mains $15-25; ☺ 8.30am-4.30pm & 6pm-midnight Tue-Sat) Bright and shiny new, with Badger Bates' protégés' artworks on display, this place features an artists studio throughout summer. There's good old Aussie tucker (like lamb shanks Italian style!), and a great range of dairy-, lactose-, gluten- or meat-free meals. Great all-day breakfast, BYO and dine-and-wine. And coffee to walk a mile for.

**Alfresco's Café** ( ☎ 8087 5599; cnr Argent & Oxide Sts; mains $17-24; ☺ breakfast, lunch & dinner) Always busy, serving plates of pancakes, roasts, salads and pasta dishes, but it's best known for its gourmet pizzas.

### TOP END

**Broken Earth Café & Restaurant** ( ☎ 8087 1318; Line of Lode visitors centre; mains $26-34; ☺ 8.30am-10pm) With its stunning views over Broken Hill, airy modern design and something-for-everyone menu, this is certainly the place to come. There's all-day coffee and cakes, fab Sunday breakfast, and the light lunch menu includes an excellent grilled kangaroo on sweet potato rosti.

## Drinking & Entertainment

Broken Hill stays up late and people feel safe here, so you'll find pubs doing a roaring trade until almost dawn on Thursday, Friday and Saturday.

**Rising Sun Hotel** ( ☎ 8087 4856; 2 Beryl St) Has free games of pool and gets very lively on Friday night.

**Southern Cross Hotel** ( ☎ 8088 4122; 357 Cobalt St) Here you'll find a mellow atmosphere with '70s- and '80s-style music and an extensive cocktail list.

**Musicians Club** (267 Crystal St) A jolly place with a heaving mix of young and old. Country-music bands play on the weekends while the drinks flow. Two-up (gambling on the fall of two coins) is played on Friday and Saturday night from 10pm to 2am – Broken Hill claims to have retained the atmosphere of a real two-up school and the locals are happy to give you lessons.

## Getting There & Away

**Regional Express Airlines** (Rex; ☎ 13 17 13) flies between Broken Hill and Adelaide (daily), and to and from Sydney via Dubbo (daily except Saturday).

**CountryLink** ( ☎ 13 22 32) runs the Broken Hill Outback Explorer to Sydney ($106; 13½ hours). Dubbo XPT connects with a bus to Broken Hill daily ($78; 16½ hours). The **CountryLink booking office** ( ☎ 8087 1400; ☺ 8am-5pm Mon-Fri) is at the train station.

The **Indian Pacific** ( ☎ 13 21 47; www.trainways .com.au) goes through Broken Hill on Tuesday and Friday (departing 6.30pm CST) bound for Sydney ($200; 16 hours), and on Thursday and Sunday (8.20am CST) heading for Adelaide ($87; seven hours) and on to Perth ($425; 49 hours).

## Getting Around

Some of the clubs have a free bus to drive you home after your night out. It leaves hourly between 6pm and midnight.

**Murton's Citybus** ( ☎ 8087 3311) operates four routes around Broken Hill. Pick up a timetable at the visitors centre. Its new **Dial'n'Ride** ( ☎ 0429 179 552) operates Friday and Saturday nights till 12.30am.

**Hertz Car & 4WD Hire** ( ☎ 8087 2719) has an office at the visitors centre. There are several other car-rental companies or you can call for a **taxi** ( ☎ 8087 2222).

## SILVERTON

☎ 08 / pop 50

It's absolutely obligatory to visit Silverton, an old silver-mining town, where you walk inside a Drysdale painting and discover the charm of the outback. Silverton's fortunes peaked in 1885, when it had a population of 3000 and public buildings designed to last for centuries like the old gaol (now the museum). But in 1889 the mines closed and the people (and some houses) moved to the new boom town at Broken Hill.

Today it's a ghost town with a new lease of life due to the spirits at the pub (beer too) and a small community of artists. Several, including leather and leadlight workers, painters, and coin carvers, have studios here. The **visitors centre** ( ☎ 8088 7566; ☉ 8.30am-5pm) is in the original ice-cream shop, where you can find locally made gifts and a walking-tour map describing the old buildings.

Silverton was used as the setting for films such as *Mad Max II* and *A Town Like Alice*. The **Silverton Hotel** ( ☎ 8088 5313; ☉ 9am-9pm) displays photos taken on the film sets; ask at the bar about the infamous 'Silverton test'.

The friendly **café** ( ☎ 8088 6601; mains $16; ☉ 8am-4pm Tue-Sun) has a menu with staples such as stockman's balls and damper. Not game? Then try the roast.

**Barrier Range Camel Safaris** ( ☎ 8088 5316; www .silvertoncamels.com; ½-/1hr tours $15/25, 2hr sunset trek $50) runs a variety of **camel tours** from Silverton, on friendly and quiet camels. The day/night safari ($170) gives you an unforgettable taste of the outback.

Lush, green and treed **Penrose Park** ( ☎ 8088 5307; camp site s/f $7/15, bunkhouse/self-contained cottage $40/65) was established as a picnic and camping ground for miners' families. The buildings sleep six to eight. The road beyond Silverton leads to the **Mundi Mundi Lookout** where you look over the vast expanse of the Mundi Mundi Plain.

## MENINDEE
☎ 08 / pop 980
This small town on the Darling River, an outback township since 1860, provides access to the Menindee Lakes, with Australia's best inland fishing, and Kinchega National Park.

The **visitors centre** ( ☎ 8091 4274; Menindee St; ☉ 10am-4pm) has stacks of useful information and touristy gifts and artefacts for sale.

**Ah Chung's Bakehouse Gallery** ( ☎ 8091 4322; ☉ 2-5pm, closed Wed & Sun), a cute old building (1880) off Haberfield St, has original ovens and bread-making tools and an interesting range of paintings and artefacts.

**Menindee Lakes** are a series of nine natural, ephemeral lakes adjacent to the Darling River (camping is free), but they have been dammed to ensure year-round water. Water was trans-

ported from here to Broken Hill by rail until 1960. The last water train to leave Menindee was derailed by floodwaters that broke the drought! Geoff Looney runs **boat tours** ( ☎ 8091 4437; per hr for 2 people $50) throughout the lake system, for fishing or bird-watching. Get his *Menindee Wetlands Fishing & Birdwatching Guide* from the visitors centre.

There are caravan parks and cabins out by the lakes. **Copi Hollow Caravan Park** ( ☎ 8091 4880; Menindee-Broken Hill Rd; camp site/cabin $18.50/40) is set around a lovely tree-lined swimming hole at the far end of the lakes and is very popular for its fishing, skiing and bushwalking.

Explorers Burke and Wills stayed at the historic **Maidens Hotel** ( ☎ 8091 4208; Yartla St; s/d/f $35/55/70) where little old rooms, with crisp white linen on the new beds, open onto a courtyard. Or cross the road to **Burke & Wills Motel** ( ☎ 8091 4313; Yartla St; s/d/tr $60/70/80; ✖ ) for a little outback luxury.

**Menindee Café** ( ☎ 8091 4644; Menindee St; mains $9.80-16; ☉ 8am-9pm) feeds you very well, offering sandwiches, pies and pastas with enthusiasm.

The **Indian Pacific** ( ☎ 13 21 47; www.trainways.com .au) will stop at Menindee (if arranged) on its twice-weekly run between Broken Hill ($21; 1½ hours) and Sydney ($119; 14 hours). The visitors centre sells tickets. **CountryLink** ( ☎ 13 22 32) Broken Hill Outback Explorer to Sydney (13½ hours) stops here once weekly.

**Central Darling** (www.centraldarling.nsw.gov.au) bus service runs between Menindee and Broken Hill ($10; daily Monday to Friday).

If you are driving, call **roads info** ( ☎ 08 8087 0660, 08 8091 5155).

## KINCHEGA NATIONAL PARK
Kinchega National Park is 20km out of Menindee and includes the Darling River and several of the lakes in the Menindee system. These glittering lakes are a haven for water birds living among the backwaters and drowned forests. The visitors centre is at the site of the old Kinchega homestead, about 16km from the park entrance. Kinchega shearing shed has been beautifully restored; the shearers quarters have **bunk accommodation** ( ☎ 8080 3200; adult/child $16.50/8.25) but you must book, and there are plenty of **camp sites** (adult/child $3/2) among the red gums along the Darling's banks. Pay the $7 per day vehicle fee at the self-registration box near the woolshed.

# MUNGO NATIONAL PARK

This remote, beautiful and most important place, full of great significance for the human species, covers 27,850 hectares of the Willandra Lakes World Heritage area. The echoes of over 400 centuries of continuous human habitation are almost tangible here, in Mungo National Park.

The story of both Australia and its oldest inhabitants is told in the dunes of Mungo. At least 60,000 years ago, Aborigines settled on the banks of the fertile lakes, living on the plentiful fish, mussels, birds and animals. Some of the animals were megafauna, much larger than their modern relatives (see a life-size replica at the visitors centre). After 45,000 years the climate changed, the lakes dried up and the Aborigines adapted to life in a harsh semidesert, with only periodic floods filling the lakes. The constant westerly wind drifted sand from the lakebed up onto the dunes, gradually burying old camp sites.

Europeans arrived with their sheep in the early 19th century, then Chinese miners came looking for work when the Victorian goldfields lost their appeal. These men named a fabulous 25km semicircle (lunette) of huge shimmering white sand dunes the **Walls of China**. Walk between these high sand sculptures that nature created with her westerly wind to feel how homesick the wall must have made the men.

Along with the remains of incredibly ancient animals and people, the dunes hold tracks of the Cobb & Co coaches, which cut across the lake last century. In 2006 the wind, which continually exposes ancient remains, revealed a walking track that's 23,000 years old yet the footprints look like they were made yesterday. Archaeologists have established the size, weight and fitness of the people who include a one-legged 1.98m-tall athlete who hopped along this track unaided.

## Information

There's a visitors centre in the park by the old Mungo woolshed. A road leads across the dry lake bed to the Walls of China, and you can drive a complete 70km loop of the dunes when it's dry. There's a self-guided drive brochure at the visitors centre, which also runs lots of interesting **guided walks** (adult/child/family $5.50/3.20/13.20) during all states' school holidays. The whole area is a playground for

photographers, bird-watchers, artists and 4WD enthusiasts.

## Tours

Award-winning **Harry Nanya Tours** ( ☎ 1800 630 864, 03-5027 2076; www.harrynanyatours.com.au) has daily tours to Lake Mungo from Mildura and Wentworth, employing Aboriginal guides like charismatic Graeme Clark, who has lots of local knowledge of culture and history, Dreamtime stories, plants, animals and archaeology.

## Sleeping & Eating

Places fill up during the school holidays. Book through the **NPWS** ( ☎ 03-5021 8900) at Buronga. There's no water supply out here, so these places use an interesting poly-tarp system to catch rain water.

**Mungo Lodge** ( ☎ 03-5029 7297; mungoldg@ruralnet .net.au; cabin s/d $88/118) On the Mildura road, about 4km from the visitors centre, this is the place to be, with a great bar and restaurant (you must book ahead, and ask for the salt-bush lamb!). The little cabins with verandas are comfortable and quiet, and there's self-contained cottages for an extra $10 a night. In low season (summer) ask for the special rates. The restaurant (mains $18 to $24; open for breakfast, lunch and dinner) serves delicious, home-cooked meals with veggies straight from the garden to you. The Aussie Clean system it uses to regenerate all sewerage keeps the garden blooming.

The **Main Camp** (camp site adult/child $3/2) is between the lodge and the visitors centre. It's a pleasant spot with plenty of flat ground, but can be extremely cold at night. **Belah Camp** (camp site adult/child $3/2) is on the eastern side of the dunes.

To pay your camp fees and park entrance fee (per day $7) put money in an envelope at the visitors centre.

## Getting There & Away

The closest towns to Mungo are Mildura (110km) and Balranald (150km) but the corrugated, unsealed roads become instantly impassable after rain. Call **roads info** ( ☎ 08-8087 0660, 8091 5155) to make sure they're open. These towns are also the closest places selling fuel. If you take the sealed road towards Pooncarie you are left with only 65km of unsealed road from the Mungo turn-off.

# The Riverina

This green, endlessly rolling country with some of the state's best farming and grazing areas is called the Riverina because the mighty Murray and Murrumbidgee Rivers are its lifeblood. Irrigation schemes along these important waterways have allowed crops such as rice, lettuce and grapes to flourish in several centres, while the small towns of the Riverina are welcoming oases, especially for visitors who are serious about food and wine.

Before the Europeans arrived, the rivers of the region provided an idyllic home for the Aborigines, and the area around Deniliquin was probably the most densely populated part of the continent. But John Oxley, the first European to visit the area, wasn't impressed by the arid plains carved by the waterways as they changed course over the millennia, saying, 'There is a uniformity in the barren desolation of this country which wearies one more than I am able to express'.

A century later the Murrumbidgee Irrigation Area (MIA) had turned those dry flatlands into fertile farmland and graziers had established sheep stations on the plains. These days you'll find thriving townships, looking their best in the balmy climate. There's a grand sense of history everywhere. And as well as the farms and stations, there's small industries preparing all sorts of gourmet delights to send to the cities.

It's a popular region for holidays, especially for water sports on the rivers. And away from the rivers, it's all low key, where people seem to find time to chat to you – all part of the Riverina's attraction.

## HIGHLIGHTS

- Feast on glorious Italian fare in **Griffith** (p286)
- Test the chocolate and liquorice at the Liquorice Factory in **Junee** (p280)
- Embrace the sights and smells of the **livestock sales market** (p277) in Wagga Wagga
- Spin down the **orange-red sand dunes** (p293) near Wentworth
- Watch the kangaroos from the beautifully restored homestead at **Willandra National Park** (p287)
- Glow in the colourful reflections at the **National Glass Art Collection** (p277) in Wagga Wagga
- Catch yabbies before setting up the barbecue in **Corowa** (p289)
- Laze the days away on a magnificent sandy river-beach at **Deniliquin** (p291)

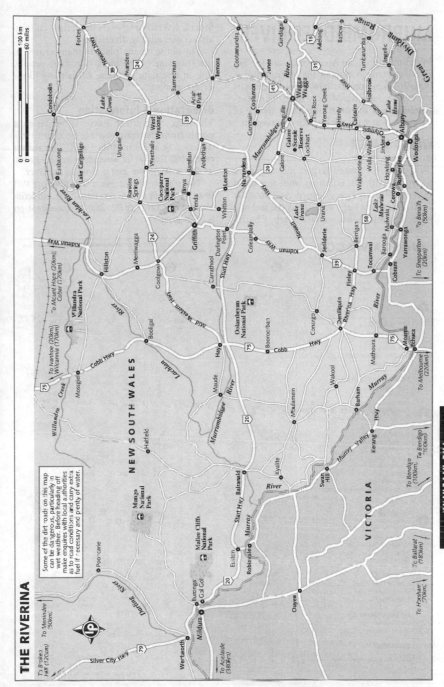

THE RIVERINA

NEW SOUTH WALES

VICTORIA

Some of the dirt roads on this map can be dangerous, particularly in wet weather. Before heading off make enquiries with local authorities as to road conditions and carry extra fuel if necessary and plenty of water.

THE RIVERINA

# MURRUMBIDGEE RIVER

Murrumbidgee is an Aboriginal word for 'big river', and true to its name the Murrumbidgee flows 1578km from the Snowy Mountains to its confluence with the Murray River. The Murrumbidgee is the most important source of irrigation water for the lush Riverina region.

## WAGGA WAGGA

☎ 02 / pop 58,000

'Wagga' is the state's largest inland city, a pretty city with fine buildings, wide tree-lined streets and lovely riverside gardens. Though it sprawls across a large area, it has the feel of a relaxed country town, with the nearby Charles

Sturt University and some interesting cultural attractions adding diversity.

The name means 'place of many crows' in the language of the local Wiradjuri people, but an alternate meaning is 'dancing like a drunken man'.

### Orientation & Information

The long main street, Baylis St, which runs north from the train station, becomes Fitzmaurice St at its northern end. The **visitors centre** ( ☎ 1300 100 122; www.tourismwaggawagga.com .au; Tarcutta St; ☼ 9am-5pm) is close to the river.

There's internet access at **Civic Video** ( ☎ 6921 8866; 21 Forsyth St; per hr $5; ☼ 10am-10pm) and **Scribbles Internet Café** ( ☎ 6921 8860; 22 Fitzmaurice St; per hr $4; see p278).

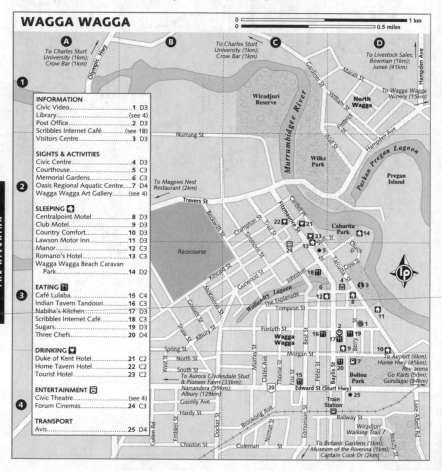

WAGGA WAGGA

| INFORMATION | |
|---|---|
| Civic Video | 1 D3 |
| Library | (see 4) |
| Post Office | 2 D3 |
| Scribbles Internet Café | (see 18) |
| Visitors Centre | 3 D3 |

| SIGHTS & ACTIVITIES | |
|---|---|
| Civic Centre | 4 D3 |
| Courthouse | 5 C3 |
| Memorial Gardens | 6 C3 |
| Oasis Regional Aquatic Centre | 7 D4 |
| Wagga Wagga Art Gallery | (see 4) |

| SLEEPING 🏠 | |
|---|---|
| Centralpoint Motel | 8 D3 |
| Club Motel | 9 D3 |
| Country Comfort | 10 D3 |
| Lawson Motor Inn | 11 D3 |
| Manor | 12 C3 |
| Romano's Hotel | 13 C3 |
| Wagga Wagga Beach Caravan Park | 14 D2 |

| EATING 🍴 | |
|---|---|
| Café Lulaba | 15 C4 |
| Indian Tavern Tandoori | 16 C3 |
| Nabiha's Kitchen | 17 D3 |
| Scribbles Internet Café | 18 D3 |
| Sugars | 19 D3 |
| Three Chefs | 20 D4 |

| DRINKING 🍷 | |
|---|---|
| Duke of Kent Hotel | 21 C2 |
| Home Tavern Hotel | 22 C2 |
| Tourist Hotel | 23 C2 |

| ENTERTAINMENT 🎭 | |
|---|---|
| Civic Theatre | (see 4) |
| Forum Cinemas | 24 C3 |

| TRANSPORT | |
|---|---|
| Avis | 25 D4 |

## Sights & Activities

The Civic Centre houses the **Wagga Wagga Art Gallery** ( ☎ 6926 9660; admission free; ☼ 10am-5pm Tue-Sat, noon-4pm Sun), home to the wonderful **National Art Glass Collection**. The Glass Collection provides an overview of the history and development of the studio glass movement in Australia from the 1970s. The gallery space is a superb configuration of water, light and glass, and the permanent exhibition is one of diverse colour and beauty.

To check out the town, make use of Wagga's bikeways, flat paths that completely circle the city. The **Oasis Regional Aquatic Centre** ( ☎ 6937 3737; www.wagga.nsw.gov.au/oasis/; Morgan St; adult/child $5/3.50; ☼ 6.30am-8pm Mon-Fri, 8.30am-6pm Sat & Sun) has several pools and includes a wave ball with mats to ride the wave, an excellent gym and a fun free playground out the front.

The **Botanic Gardens** (Macleay St; ☼ sunrise-sunset) has a small **zoo**, geese and peacocks that roam free, and a free-flight aviary containing some colourful native birds. The entrance is just before the archway telling you you're entering Lord Baden Powell Drive, which itself leads to a good lookout and the scenic **Captain Cook Drive**.

Wagga is a major centre for **livestock sales** (Boman industrial area) and you can see the farmers (and animals) in action every week. Cattle are sold on Monday in an amphitheatre-style ring, while sheep are sold outdoors by the thousands on Thursday. The smells and sounds are exhilarating.

The **Museum of the Riverina** ( ☎ 6925 2934; Baden Powell Dr; admission free; ☼ 10am-5pm Tue-Sat, noon-4pm Sun) operates from both the Civic Centre and the Botanic Gardens; the latter site focuses on Wagga's people, places and events. The section on the Wiradjuri people is particularly good, but best is the Sporting Hall of Fame. Countless sports stars grew up in the area, from AFL luminary Wayne Carey to test cricketer Mark Taylor.

The **Wiradjuri Walking Track** is a 30km circuit based from the visitors centre (get your map there) that includes some good lookouts and places of Aboriginal significance. There's another 10km loop past the **Wollundry Lagoon**. From the **beach** near Cabarita Park you can swim and fish, and ponder the famous 'Five O'Clock Wave' (ask a local for an explanation).

The **Wagga Wagga Winery** ( ☎ 6922 1221; Gundagai Rd; ☼ 11am-10pm Wed-Sun) has delicious barbecue meals (from $17). Charles Sturt University has an award winning **winery** ( ☎ 6933 2435; ☼ 11am-5pm Mon-Fri, to 4pm Sat & Sun), reached through the Agriculture Research Unit, about 3km north of Wagga, off Olympic Way.

**Rev-arena Go Karts** ( ☎ 6921 9544; www.revarena.com.au; 28 Nagle St; per 15 laps $19; ☼ 10am-10pm Mon-Sat, to 6pm Sun) offers a lot of action and fun, helmets, kiosk, and many packages.

## Festivals & Events

The **Wagga Wagga Jazz Festival** (www.waggajazz.org.au), held each September, hosts international and national musicians who play in a variety of locations. The festival is well regarded, and prices for single sessions are reasonable.

**Wagga Gold Cup Festival** (www.visitwagga.com.au) in May is the biggest and best race meeting in the Riverina, held over two days, with bands, fashions and prize money to attract the best horses.

## Sleeping

### BUDGET

**Wagga Wagga Beach Caravan Park** ( ☎ 6931 0603; www.wwbcp.com.au; 2 Johnston St; camp site per adult $19, cabin std/deluxe $55/75; 🞩 ) At the bend of the river where the water spreads wide, the banks make a swimming beach, there's stacks of cabins, and you can see the grand old buildings of the town centre.

**Romano's Hotel** ( ☎ 6921 2013; cnr Fitzmaurice & Sturt Sts; s/d $30/50) This is an airy old pub with quaint rooms, grand beds and bleak bathrooms – ask for a room on the quieter 2nd floor.

**Club Motel** ( ☎ 6921 6966; theclub1@tpg.com.au; 73 Morgan St; s/d $65/85; 🞩 **P** ) This is perfect if you want to walk to everything. The rooms are spacious enough and very clean.

### MIDRANGE

There are many motels in town, especially along Tarcutta St.

**Manor** ( ☎ 6921 5962; 38 Morrow St; B&B s/d $70/98, with bathroom $95/110, suite $170; 🞩 **P** ) A charming well-restored guesthouse, the Manor is furnished with antiques like four-poster beds and leather-lined desks. Take your breakfast onto the balcony to look over the Memorial Gardens. Equally elegant is the Manor Restaurant (mains $20-32; open for dinner Monday to Saturday) where the favourite dish is chicken with garlic and prawns.

**Centralpoint Motel** ( ☎ 6921 7272; 164 6 Tarcutta St; s/d $85/108; 🞩 **P** ) This motel uses 'allergy-conscious' cleaning products and all rooms, including studio and one-bedroom, are self-contained. Ask about weekly and family rates.

**Country Comfort** ( ☎ 6921 6444; www.country comforthotels.com; cnr Morgan & Tarcutta Sts; d from $120; ❄ P ⛱ ) This sprawling place is huge, with facilities for families and long-stay guests. It's set in pretty gardens and offers many self-contained units.

**Lawson Motor Inn** ( ☎ 6921 2200; www.thelawson .com.au; 117 Tarcutta St; std/garden/river d $125/145/165; ❄ P ⛱ ) Right on the Murrumbidgee, the Lawson is elegant. From it, you can walk straight onto the riverbank walking tracks.

## Eating

**Nabiha's Kitchen** ( ☎ 6921 7813; Neslo Arcade, Baylis St; mains $4-9; ❄ lunch & dinner Mon-Sat) A small Lebanese takeaway (with tables) where everything is cooked in front of you. The menu includes Indian and vegetarian options, home-grown vegetables and free-range eggs.

**Sugars** ( ☎ 6921 7710; 54 Forsyth St; mains $6-11; ❄ 7.30am-5pm Mon-Fri, 8.30am-4pm Sat & Sun) For a delicious breakfast, this sunny spot is perfect. There are wraps and light meals throughout the day.

**Scribbles Internet Café** ( ☎ 6921 8860; 22 Fitzmaurice St; mains $8-15; ❄ breakfast & lunch daily, dinner Thu-Sat) Shabby but fun; it has paper tablecloths for doodling and a pile of favourite board games for you (or your children).

**Café Lulaba** ( ☎ 6931 8903; 10 Best St; mains $11-13; ❄ 9am-5.30pm Tue-Fri, to 4pm Sat) It's known for its dhal curry, but how could you go past the quiche? It's a cheery spot with a large zebra watching over you.

**Indian Tavern Tandoori** ( ☎ 6921 3121; 81 Peter St; dishes $11-19; ❄ dinner) Locals who love a vindaloo support this multi-award-winning eatery which also serves a range of dishes from the tandoori oven.

**Magpies Nest Restaurant** ( ☎ 6933 1523; cnr Old Narrandera & Pine Gully Rds; dishes $15-27; ❄ lunch & dinner Wed-Sun) This is housed in restored stone stables, with sweeping views of the town. The focus is on local produce; vegetables come straight from the garden!

**Three Chefs** ( ☎ 6921 5897; 70 Morgan St; mains $28-35; ❄ breakfast daily, lunch Mon-Fri, dinner Mon-Sat) A white-tablecloth fine-dining place which has kept a warm and comfortable atmosphere. The sweet suckling pork with caramelised shallot tart is a taste treat.

## Drinking

This is a university town of sorts, and the pubs can get really packed.

**Tourist Hotel** ( ☎ 6921 2264; 91 Fitzmaurice St) The Tourist is a glass-fronted old place which has regular live music and a relaxed atmosphere. You will find plenty of locals here, despite its name.

**Home Tavern Hotel** ( ☎ 6921 3117; 142 Fitzmaurice St) This low, basic old pub is more of a pool hall. But it's a popular spot, and there are nightly pool competitions where backpackers are always ready to throw out a challenge.

**Crow Bar** ( ☎ 6933 2040; Charles Sturt University) It has cheap drinks and a line-up of local bands; visitors are welcome – get a student to sign you in. You'll be mixing with a spunky 18- to 28-year-old group from all over the world.

**Duke of Kent Hotel** ( ☎ 6921 3231; Fitzmaurice St) Pretty in pink and blue tiles, the Duke is popular; rowdy but fun.

## Entertainment

Wagga Wagga often has a number of arts events going on at any one time; they just aren't highly publicised.

**Civic Theatre** ( ☎ 6926 9680; ❄ 10am-5.30pm Mon-Fri, to 12.30pm Sat) The Civic has a booking office, not only for its own productions but for much of the locally created entertainment, from youth theatre to performances by the Riverina Conservatorium.

**Forum Cinemas** ( ☎ 6921 6863; 77 Trail St) Six huge screens show both the latest blockbusters and arthouse flicks.

## Getting There & Away

**QantasLink** ( ☎ 13 13 13; www.qantaslink.com.au) flies daily to Sydney and **Regional Express** (Rex; ☎ 13 17 13; www.regionalexpress.com.au) flies several times daily to Melbourne and Sydney.

**CountryLink** ( ☎ 13 22 42; www.countrylink.com.au) buses leave from **Wagga train station** ( ☎ 13 22 32, 6939 5488), where you can make bookings. The Melbourne/Sydney XPT service stops at Wagga twice daily. The service costs $68 to both Sydney and Melbourne. **Greyhound** ( ☎ 13 14 99; www.greyhound.com.au) buses runs daily from Sydney ($61; eight hours) to Melbourne ($63; 6½ hours) and another to Adelaide ($131; 16 hours).

**Avis** ( ☎ 6921 9977) car rentals is near the train station at the corner of Edward and Fitzharding Sts.

## AROUND WAGGA WAGGA

### The Rock & Around

On the Olympic Way about 25km southwest of Wagga, The Rock is a small town near a large craggy hill rising out of the flat plain. The town was called Hanging Rock until the boulder balanced on top of the hill fell off late in the 19th century.

Surrounding the hill is the **Rock Nature Reserve**; there's a 3km walking track to the summit, from which you can see Mount Kosciuszko and the Victorian Alps on a clear day. Near the top, the going is steep and you have to be careful of falling rocks.

### Galore Scenic Reserve

Henry Osborne (owner of the first station in the region) walked from Wollongong to Adelaide in 1840 and on the way he climbed this sudden hill (it rises 215m from an almost flat plain), exclaiming at the top, 'There's land, and galore'. Now a scenic reserve, Galore Hill is worth a visit for its bush, the plantings near the base of the hill, and the 360-degree views from the platform at the top. You can't camp here.

Galore Hill is 14km south of the Sturt Hwy – turn off about 60km west of Wagga Wagga. It's also accessible from **Lockhart**, a little town known for its beautiful late-19th-century verandas – both sides of the main street, are lined with them

### Culcairn

☎ 02 / pop 1400

The train from Sydney finished at Culcairn back in 1880, so people stayed there overnight then caught the bus to Melbourne. The town's main feature, the **Culcairn Hotel** (1891), still shows how significant it was. It's a majestic

hotel, the largest between the two cities until the 1930s, with a beer garden that deserves a more lavish name – it has a fountain!

The old stationmaster's residence and half the main street are classified by the National Trust.

**Morgan's Lookout** is a low hill with a cluster of huge boulders on top. Allegedly this was Mad Dog's lookout where he watched for approaching victims and police (see below). You can climb up for great views, and there are gas barbecues. The lookout is about 18km southwest of Culcairn on the sealed road to Walla Walla. While you're out that way, stop to see the old wagon in a glass case on the side of the road in Walla Walla. It tells of the German immigrants' journey from South Australia to settle in the area.

### Henty

☎ 02 / pop 1700

Henty is 'Home of the Header' because, in 1913, local farmer Headlie Taylor invented the header harvester, which revolutionised grain harvesting around the world. There's a display commemorating the invention in **Henty Memorial Park**.

The **Henty Machinery Field Days** (www.hmfd.com) are held in the third week in September. About 50,000 people turn up to check out the best in leading-edge farm equipment in Australia.

## JUNEE

☎ 02 / pop 5890

Once known as the 'Rail Centre of the South', Junee is a small, friendly country town with an extraordinary number of impressive buildings. Get some tourist information and a map from the **shire offices** ( ☎ 6924 8100; Belmore St) opposite the police station.

---

**MORGAN COUNTRY**

The area known as Morgan Country is a rough circle of pretty country containing some interesting little towns, including Henty, Culcairn and Jindera.

This was once the stamping-ground of Dan 'Mad Dog' Morgan, allegedly the most brutal and callous bushranger in Australia's history. Unlike Ned Kelly, Morgan was a bushranger no-one respected. He began his career in Victoria in the 1850s but was captured and spent six years on a prison hulk in Port Phillip Bay. On receiving parole he escaped and moved into NSW, where for two years he terrorised this small area. Declared an outlaw, he fled to Victoria (where he was still wanted) in 1865, resolving to 'take the flashness out of the Victorian people and police'. With a £1000 bounty on his head he didn't get very far. At Peechelba station, just south of the Murray River, he was shot dead. His head was cut off and it's said that his scrotum became a tobacco pouch.

## Sights & Activities

### MONTE CRISTO

Built in 1884, the mansion of **Monte Cristo** ( ☎ 6924 1637; www.montecristo.com.au; Monte Cristo Rd; adult/child/family $10/5/2.50; ☯ 10am-4pm) was the home of Christopher Crawley, a shrewd landowner who predicted or, rather, manipulated the railway's arrival (via his land) in Junee and the subsequent boom in land prices.

Monte Cristo homestead has been faithfully decorated in high Victorian style, and it's full of superb antiques that have been collected by the owners during their 30-year restoration of the property. It had nearly been destroyed by weather, and vandals who weren't deterred by the house's reputation for supernatural goings-on.

The admission price includes an informative guided tour. You can get to Monte Cristo from John Potts Dr.

### RAILWAY ROUNDHOUSE

The only surviving, working roundhouse in Australia, the **Junee Roundhouse** ( ☎ 6924 2909; Harold St; adult/child/family $6/4/16; ☯ 9.30am-4.30pm, closed Mon & Fri) was built in 1947. Back then, its 30m turntable was the largest in the southern hemisphere. Railway enthusiasts should visit the **Roundhouse Museum** in the same complex. As well as the large display about the history of rail in Australia, and an impressively large model-train set, there's also an interesting general transport display.

### OLD BUILDINGS

If you like pubs, you'll lament the closing of many of Junee's watering holes. Some magnificent old pubs with massive verandas dripping with iron lace now stand empty.

The 1915 **Commercial Hotel** (cnr Lorne & Waratah Sts) still has a busy bar crowded with after-work drinkers. The **Loftus** ( ☎ 6924 1511; 6 Humphreys St) was the town's grandest hotel, with a frontage running for an entire block. It was sold in late 1999 for only $32,000!

Across the tracks, the **Junee Hotel** ( ☎ 6924 1124; Seignior St) was built by Christopher Crawley in 1876. The pub hasn't had a lot done to it over the years, but that means the original fittings are still intact.

The station's **Railway Refreshment Room** (Lorne St; sandwiches from $4) is a glorious place with huge mirrors and soaring arched ceilings. Apart from admiring your surroundings you can get drinks and a range of sandwiches, cakes and snacks.

### LIQUORICE FACTORY

Everyone loves watching **Green Grove Organics** ( ☎ 6924 3574; www.greengroveorganics.com; 8-18 Lord St; adult/child $4/2.50; ☯ 10am-4pm) make liquorice and chocolate in the old Junee Flour Mill (1935). In fact it won the Best Tourist Attraction 2006. There's a great gift shop with local arts and crafts, snacks and lunches ($9.50), and tours run every hour from 10.30am to 2.30pm.

## Sleeping & Eating

**Junee Caravan Park** ( ☎ 6924 1316; Broadway St; camp site per adult $22, cabin std/deluxe $65/85) This pretty caravan park by the lake won the inland tourism award 2006 for its attractive, spacious amenities such as pool, barbecue and playground.

**Loftus B&B** ( ☎ 6924 1511; 6 Humphreys St; B&B s/d $60/90, d with bathroom $105) A 100-year-old pub located in the centre of town, complete with sweeping staircases and an endless balcony. Downstairs is Betty & Muriel's ( ☎ 6924 2555; mains $20 to $31; open 10am to 10pm Tuesday to Saturday) where you dine with Hollywood stars. Try, if you dare, a Pamela Anderson (two half chicken breasts stuffed with smoked salmon and brie).

## Getting There & Away

**Junee Buses** ( ☎ 6924 2244), on Main St near the railway level crossing, runs weekday services to Wagga Wagga.

**CountryLink** ( ☎ 13 22 42) XPT trains stop at Junee on the main Sydney ($64; six hours) and Melbourne ($68; 5½ hours) run twice daily.

## COOTAMUNDRA

☎ 02 / pop 7600

Cootamundra, founded around 1860, is a prosperous service centre for surrounding farmlands and an important railway junction. Best known for being the birthplace of cricket great Don Bradman, the town's neat grid of streets contains many fine examples of Federation-style houses and a few earlier Victorian gems. Cootamundra is in the foothills of the Great Dividing Range.

## Orientation & Information

Parker St is the main shopping street, and its intersection with Wallendoon St, where you'll find the impressive post office, town hall and several banks, is the centre of town. At the train station on Hovell St the **visitors centre** ( ☎ 6942 4212, 1800 350 203; www.cootamundra.com; ☯ 9.30am-5pm) can tell you about the host of festivals throughout the year, or look at the calendar on the website. There's also a self-drive map of the highlights, and snacks available (from $3).

## Sights & Activities

Stand in the old weatherboard hospital, now a **museum** ( ☎ 6940 2100; 89 Adams St; adult/child $3/free; ☺ 9am-5pm), where Sir Donald Bradman, Australia's greatest cricketer, was born in 1908. The Bradmans moved to Bowral when the Don was still very young, and it's there he learned his craft (see p132).

Cootamundra's climate means that European trees flourish (the elms along Cooper St are over 100 years old) and there are several formal parks. **Albert Park** (Hovell St) is near the train station and **Jubilee Park**, on the other side of the city centre, features the **Captains' Walk**, a series of busts of Australia's cricket captains.

Cootamundra is also known for the **Cootamundra wattle** (*Acacia baileyana*); its profuse yellow flowers bloom in July and August each year. Although native to this area, Cootamundra wattle has been planted throughout the cooler areas of southern Australia. The **Wattle Time Festival** (www.cootamundra.biz) is held in August.

## Sleeping & Eating

**Cootamundra Caravan Park** ( ☎ 6942 1080; 55 Mackay St; camp site per adult $20, cabin without/with bathroom $44/60) Situated in pretty Jubilee Park, this sits beside Muttama Creek. It's calm here, prob ably because of all the space between sites and the mix of European and native trees.

**Albion Hotel** ( ☎ 6942 1177; StephanSellars@bigpond .com; cnr Parker & Wallendoon Sts; dm/s/d/f $20/35/55/80) This is the oldest pub, yet it has spacious rooms with private bathrooms and TVs.

**White Ibis B&B** ( ☎ 6942 1850; www.whiteibis.com .au; 21 Wallendoon St; s/d $50/80) This B&B has been restored to a boutique hotel, pretty with its Juliet balconies, and it's just a block from the station. Ask about longer-term rates.

**Harrison Deep** ( ☎ 6942 7799; 115 Parker St; mains $20-25; ☺ lunch Wed-Fri, dinner Thu-Sat) There are many cafés, especially along Parker St, but top restaurants such as this one are too good to miss. Harrison Deep is known for its specialist lamb dishes using local texel lamb. Start with the cutlets with Asian mint on kumara rosti.

**Delv's Cafe** ( ☎ 6942 3400; 248 Parker St; mains $15-29; ☺ 8.30am-5pm Mon-Thu, to midnight Fri-Sun) This friendly place is buzzing, especially on open-mic nights, and in summer when there's live music in the courtyard. The fave meal is Coota by the Bay, a New York–style steak topped with scallops and garlic prawns.

## Getting There & Away

There's a **CountryLink Travel Centre** ( ☎ 6940 2921) at the train station. Fast trains (XPTs) running between Sydney ($72; five hours) and Melbourne ($90; 6½ hours) stop here twice daily. Buses to Mildura ($98; 8½ hours) connect with the XPT service.

---

**SPITFIRES OVER AUSTRALIA**

Aviation enthusiasts shouldn't miss **Temora**, a prosperous town and home to the **Temora Aviation Museum** ( ☎ 6977 1088; www.aviationmuseum.com.au; 1 Menzies St; ☺ 10am-4pm).

During WWII, Temora was home to the No 10 Elementary Flying Training School (10 EFTS) with more than 10,000 personnel at the school training more than 2400 pilots. Since then it has hosted more sport-aviation activities including gliding, parachuting and ultra-light aircraft operations.

Sydney businessman David Lowy completed an aviation museum here in 2002 with Australia's oldest flying Tiger Moth, a Canberra bomber, Vampire jet fighter and many more. Aircraft are housed in a 1980-sq-metre hangar, and the museum holds Flying Weekends about every month. When a second Spitfire was bought in 2006, the September air show became the talk of town, because for the first time there would be two Spitfires flying in formation over Australian soil.

Just to tempt you, watch the 2005 air display on www.recreationalflying.net and click on Temora airshow Oct 05 review.

If you're not so wild about planes, keep your feet on the ground at the enormous **Rural Museum** ( ☎ 6977 1291; Junee Rd; ☺ 2-4.30pm) which includes Sir Donald Bradman's first home, a hardwood slab hut, working machinery, pioneer buildings and Jimmy Sharman's boxing troupe memorabilia.

Contact Temora's **visitors centre** ( ☎ 6977 1511; www.temora.nsw.gov.au; 294 Hoskins St) for further information.

THE RIVERINA

# NARRANDERA

☎ 02 / pop 6600

On the banks of Lake Talbot and the Murrumbidgee River, Narrandera is known for its beautiful green avenues and parks. With good services and accommodation, it makes a pleasant stopover for a day or two.

## Orientation & Information

The Newell Hwy runs through town as Cadell St; the Sturt Hwy passes just south of the town. East St is the commercial centre. The helpful **visitors centre** ( ☎ 1800 672 392; Narrandera St; ☉ 9am-5pm) is in Cadell St. Here you'll find 'the largest playable guitar in the southern hemisphere' – although you need two people to play, and you wouldn't get much of a tune out of it.

## Sights & Activities

In the best tradition of small-town museums, the **Parkside Cottage Museum** ( ☎ 6959 1372; Twynam St; adult/child $2/0.50; ☉ 2-5pm Mon & Tue, 11am-5pm Wed & Sun) has an extremely eclectic collection, from '1000 years of monarchy' to skis from Scott's Antarctic expedition.

**Lake Talbot Complex** ( ☎ 6959 1211; Lake Dr; adult/child $2.50/1.50; ☉ 6-8am, 10am-1pm, 4-6pm Mon-Fri, 10am-7pm Sat & Sun) is a beautiful but faded watersports reserve, partly a long artificial lake and partly a swimming centre with an exhilarating 100m water slide.

Bush (including a koala regeneration area) surrounds the lake and a number of trails make up the **Bundidgerry Walking Track**. The visitors centre has a map and brochure.

The **John Lake Centre** ( ☎ 6959 9021; Buckingbong Rd; adult/child $5.50/2.75; ☉ 8.30am-4pm), at the Narrandera Fisheries, breeds endangered fish species of the Murray Darling river system. There are guided tours throughout the day (look out for a huge Murray cod named Agro).

## Festivals & Events

In early February, **water-skiing championships** take place on Lake Talbot. March sees the **John O'Brien Bush Festival** which celebrates the bush poetry of Father Hartigan ('We'll all be rooned said Hanrahan, in accent most forlorn'). Check these, and other events at www.narrandera.nsw.gov.au/events.html.

## Sleeping

**Lake Talbot Tourist Park** ( ☎ 6959 1302; www.laketalbot.com; Gordon St; camp site per adult $22, cabin std/deluxe $35/65) This place spreads itself around a picturesque grassy setting on a hill overlooking Lake Talbot, right next to the swimming complex. Dense redgum forest stretches to the horizon. Ask about the weekly rates.

**Murrumbidgee Hotel** ( ☎ 6959 2011; cnr East & Audley Sts; s/d $25/35) This nice old place has big, clean rooms and friendly service, excellent shared bathrooms and living room, and one gorgeous veranda.

**Narrandera Gateway Motor Inn** ( ☉ 6959 1877; ourmotel@ozemail.com.au; 152 East St; s/d/f $65/70/75; ⓟ ⌧ ▭ ⌨ ) It's very quiet and comfortable staying in these spacious, colourful rooms right in the centre of town. The pool is large, with a barbecue area, and there are mountain bikes for hire

**Historic Star Lodge** ( ☎ 6959 1768; www.historicstarlodge.com.au; 64 Whitton St; s/d $66/88, d with bathroom $110) This impressive old hotel (c 1916), complete with verandas and iron lace, is now a beautiful, if old-fashioned, B&B. Your host and chef, Pat St George, will look after you very well. There's a two-bedroom flat available ($120).

## Eating

**Narrandera Bakery** ( ☎ 6959 3677; cnr East & Bolton Sts; dishes $4-7; ☉ 7.30am-5.45pm Mon-Fri, to 2.30pm Sat) This serves sandwiches and fresh baked pies, in bright and cheery surroundings.

**Classique Café Restaurant** ( ☎ 6959 1411; 124 East St; mains $6-10; ☉ 9am-5.30pm Mon-Fri, to 4.30pm Sat) A cosy place with seriously good coffee and an interesting range of gourmet sandwiches and salads.

**Bellissimo Pizza & Pasta** ( ☎ 6959 3010; 131 East St; dishes $8-20; ☉ 7.30am-10pm) This is a friendly family restaurant that the locals unashamedly recommend for the cheap but tasty Italian dishes.

**Charlies on East** ( ☎ 6959 2042; 77 East St; dishes $16-21; ☉ lunch daily, dinner Mon-Sat) Inside or out, it's a lovely place to eat the excellent food like Beef Wellington with mushroom farce. It's olive green with pressed tin ceiling, and play equipment out by the deck. And there's a pub menu ($7 to $17 with an $8.50 roast on Sunday) if you'd rather.

## Getting There & Away

**Regional Air Express** (Rex; ☎ 13 17 13; www.rex.com.au) flies into Narrandera, including flights to/from Sydney three times daily. **Greyhound** ( ☎ 13 14 99) buses go daily to Sydney (10 hours) and Adelaide (12 hours), stopping at the Mobil roadhouse on the Sturt Hwy. **CountryLink** ( ☎ 13

22 32) XPT train/bus service stops twice daily between Sydney ($90; 7½ hours) and Griffith ($14; one hour), and goes daily to Melbourne ($90; seven hours).

## LEETON

☎ 02 / pop 12030

As the headquarters of the Murrumbidgee Irrigation Scheme (MIA), Leeton is at the centre of one of Australia's largest regions for growing fruit, vegetables and rice.

Leeton was founded as a MIA town in 1913; there was no settlement here before the water came. The first of the Walter Burley Griffin–designed towns, it remains close to the architect's original vision, and is developing into a thriving commercial centre.

## Orientation & Information

Most streets are named after trees or local products; the main street is Pine Ave, named after the Murray pine, a native species.

The **visitors centre** ( ☎ 6953 6481; www.leetontourism .com.au; 10 Yanco Ave; ☒ 9am-5pm Mon-Fri, 9.30am-12.30pm Sat & Sun) has several maps including forest drives and heritage walks. It's in a beautiful house, formerly the MIA manager's home, and has a charming statue, in memory of women workers at Letona processing factory, in its gardens.

There's internet access at the **Shire Library** (cnr Myrtle & Willow Sts; per hr $6; ☒ 9am-5pm Mon-Fri, 9am-12.30pm Sat) and the **Soldiers Club** ( ☎ 6953 3444; Acacia Ave; per hr $4; ☒ 11am-11pm).

## Sights & Activities

Rice-growing began near Leeton in 1924, and today the Riverina exports 80% of its million-tonne-plus crop each year. Learn all about it at the **SunRice Centre** ( ☎ 6953 0596; www.sunrice.com .au; Calrose St; admission free; ☒ 9am-5pm Mon-Fri), which has presentations at 9.30am and 2.45pm.

**Lillypilly Estate** ( ☎ 6953 4069; www.lillypilly.com; Lillypilly Rd; ☒ 10am-5.30pm Mon-Sat) and **Toorak Wines** ( ☎ 6953 2333; www.toorakwines.com.au; Toorak Rd; ☒ 9am-5.30pm Mon-Sat) are two local wineries open for tastings and sales.

Leeton has several Art Deco gems, including the majestic 1930s **Roxy Theatre** (Pine Ave), which still operates in all its neon glory on Friday and Saturday nights. The visitors centre has a map outlining other buildings of note.

## Sleeping & Eating

**An Oasis Caravan Park** ( ☎ 6953 3882; fax 6953 6256; 90 Corbie Hill Rd; camp site per adult $17, cabin std/deluxe

$47/56; ☒ ) This accommodation option spreads prettily in the bush; it's a relaxing spot with plenty of shade.

**Leeton Hotel** ( ☎ 6953 2027; fax 6953 3765; 71 Pine Ave; dm/s/d $13/25/35) This offers clean basic rooms above an airy pub with a water feature on the outside deck. It's right in the centre of town.

**Historic Hydro Motor Inn** ( ☎ 6953 1555; hydro@dragnet.com.au; Chelmsford Pl; s/d $65/99) This is a huge, delightfully faded old home with a National Trust listing. There's a range of rooms, including spa suites (from $95) and a three-bedroom apartment ($160). If you're not staying, there are daily tours so you can look around.

**Mick's Bakehouse** ( ☎ 6953 2212; 56 Pine Ave; mains $4-10; ☒ 6am-5.30pm Mon-Fri, 7am-2pm Sat & Sun) It has excellent pies, pastas, coffee and cakes, in a grand room with a jukebox and lounge chairs.

**Pages on Pine** ( ☎ 6953 7300; 119 Pine Ave; mains $19-24; ☒ lunch & dinner Wed-Sun) It serves a range of tapas, such as grilled oysters with pancetta, that are perfect before a night at the movies across the road, or stay for delights like lamb shanks on mash. There's American pancakes on Sunday.

## Getting There & Away

**CountryLink** ( ☎ 13 22 32) buses between Griffith ($9; one hour) and Wagga Wagga ($14; two hours), and **Greyhound** ( ☎ 13 14 99) buses between Sydney ($155; 10 hours) and Adelaide ($165; 14 hours) both stop daily at the visitors centre.

## GRIFFITH

☎ 02 / pop 24,910

Griffith is small but sophisticated; its cultural mix of Europeans, Indians and South Pacific Islanders gives it a cosmopolitan atmosphere. Quite clearly the wine-and-food capital of the Riverina, Griffith's vineyards, cafés and restaurants offer a variety and quality that's recognised nationally.

## Information

The **visitors centre** ( ☎ 6962 4145; www.griffith.com.au; cnr Banna Ave & Jondaryan Aves; ☒ 9am-5pm) has a life-size WWII Fairey Firefly plane outside. The **NPWS office** ( ☎ 6966 8100; www.npws.nsw.gov.au; 200 Yambil St; ☒ 8.30am-4.30pm Mon-Fri) has information on Cocoparra, Willandra and newly-created Oolambeyan National Parks. Access the internet at the **library** (cnr Banna Ave & Kooyoo St; per hr $6).

# GRIFFITH

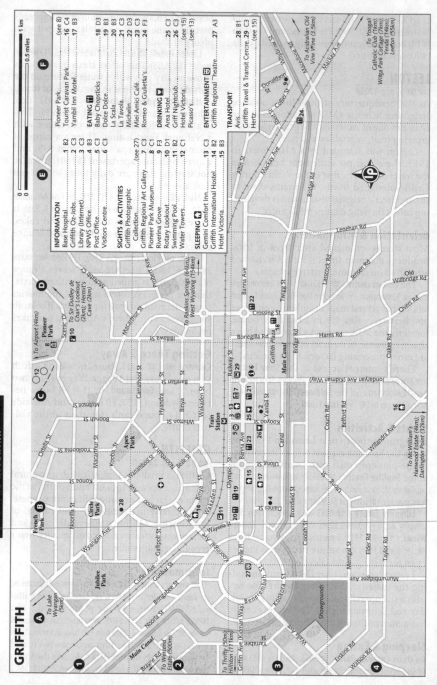

| INFORMATION | |
|---|---|
| Base Hospital | 1 B2 |
| Griffith Oz-Jobs | 2 C3 |
| Library (Internet) | 3 C3 |
| NPWS Office | 4 B3 |
| Post Office | 5 C3 |
| Visitors Centre | 6 C3 |

| SIGHTS & ACTIVITIES | |
|---|---|
| Griffith Photographic | |
| Collection | (see 27) |
| Griffith Regional Art Gallery | 7 C3 |
| Pioneer Park Museum | 8 C1 |
| Riverina Grove | 9 F3 |
| Rotary Lookout | 10 D1 |
| Swimming Pool | 11 B2 |
| Water Towers | 12 C1 |

| SLEEPING | |
|---|---|
| Gemini Comfort Inn | 13 C3 |
| Griffith International Hostel | 14 B2 |
| Hotel Victoria | 15 B3 |

| EATING | |
|---|---|
| Baby Chopsticks | 18 D3 |
| Dolce Dolce | 19 B3 |
| La Scala | 20 B3 |
| La Tavola | 21 C3 |
| Michelin | 22 D3 |
| Miei Amici Cafe | 23 C3 |
| Romeo & Giulietta's | 24 F3 |

| DRINKING | |
|---|---|
| Area Hotel | 25 C3 |
| Griff Nightclub | 26 C3 |
| Hotel Victoria | (see 15) |
| Picasso's | (see 13) |

| ENTERTAINMENT | |
|---|---|
| Griffith Regional Theatre | 27 A3 |

| TRANSPORT | |
|---|---|
| Avis | 28 B1 |
| Griffith Travel & Transit Centre | 29 C3 |
| Hertz | (see 15) |

Pioneer Park........(see 8)
Tourist Caravan Park........16 C4
Yambil Inn Motel........17 B3

With the lowest unemployment rate in Australia, it's hard *not* to get a job in Griffith. Grape harvesting usually begins in February and lasts six to eight weeks. A multitude of other crops such as oranges, melons and onions are harvested during the year. The **Griffith Oz-Jobs** ( ☎ 6964 3232; Karin.Penninga@chandlermacleod .com; 108b Yambil St) can help you find casual and seasonal work: **harvest hotline** ( ☎ 1300 720 126).

Very few of the vineyards and orchards have accommodation, or even space to camp, so you'll probably have to stay in Griffith, which means that you'll need your own transport.

## Sights & Activities

High on a hill north of the town centre, **Pioneer Park Museum** ( ☎ 6962 4196; cnr Remembrance & Scenic Drs; adult/child $8/4; �}9am-4.30pm) is a re-creation of an early Riverina village, with an old hospital, a music room and other fascinating displays in original old buildings. The new **Italian museum** even includes a very early knitting machine brought here by migrants.

Not far from Pioneer Park is the **Rotary Lookout**, with great views of the town and the surrounding farmland. Also up here on Scenic Hill are three **walking tracks**: Trates Loop (2km), Barinji Loop (5km) and Narinari Loop (6.5km). About 1.5km east of Pioneer Park is **Sir Dudley de Chair's Lookout**. Just below is the **hermit's cave**, home of an Italian recluse for many years (see p286).

With the high quality of produce in the area, a stop at **Riverina Grove** ( ☎ 6962 7988; www .riverinagrove.com.au; 4 Whybrow St; �}8am-5pm Mon-Fri, 9am-noon Sat) becomes a real indulgence. This mecca of gourmet food allows you to sample everything from marinated fetta to rich nougat, and you won't leave empty handed.

Though small, the Art Deco **Griffith Regional Art Gallery** ( ☎ 6962 5991; 167-185 Banna Ave; adult/child $2/1; �}10.30am-4.30pm Tue-Sat) has a lovely sense of space. Exhibitions change monthly and there's also a permanent collection of contemporary Australian jewellery.

The **Griffith Regional Theatre** ( ☎ 6961 8388; theatre@griffith.nsw.gov.au; Neville Pl; adult/child $2.50/free; �}9am-5pm Mon-Fri) has a massive, community-produced soft-sculpture curtain depicting the region and its activities. You can see it at 11am, 2pm and 4pm provided there's no concert under way. The theatre is also home to the interesting **Griffith Photographic Collection**, dating back to the foundation of the city, and the community's **Mosaic Lifecycle** project.

**Griffith Regional Aquatic Leisure Centre** ( ☎ 6964 7071; 5 Wayeela St; adult/child/family $5/4/12; �}6am-7.30pm Mon-Fri, 8am-5.30pm Sat, 10am-5pm Sun) has a great spread of indoor pools looking out onto grassy play areas, gymnasium and crèche.

### WINERIES

The Griffith area has a large number of wineries, featuring beautiful surroundings and award-winning wines. **McWilliam's Hanwood Estate** ( ☎ 6963 0001; Jack McWilliam Rd, Hanwood; �}tastings 9am-5pm Mon-Sat) is the oldest (1913). Also among the best for quality and range are **Westend Estate** ( ☎ 6964 1506; Brayne Rd; �}8am-5pm Mon-Fri, 10am-4pm Sat & Sun), started in 1945, and **Australian Old Vine Wine** ( ☎ 6963 5239; Rosetto Rd, Beelbangera; �}10am-4pm), a boutique winery with wine to suit everyone's taste.

Check out www.griffith.nsw.gov.au and then click on the visitors centre's attractions section to download a wineries map and get opening times.

## Festivals & Events

Held on Easter Saturday, **La Festa** (www.lafesta.org .au) is a big occasion celebrating the multicultural community with music and food from around the world, displays of award-winning wines, and food stalls covering the streets. Then mid-October, everybody is in town for the **Festival of Gardens** (www.griffith.nsw.gov.au), when the magic of springtime is celebrated, unique gardens opened and amazing citrus sculptures produced.

## Sleeping

If you are doing seasonal work in Griffith, there are two options for cheap longer-term accommodation, but they fill up quickly.

**Pioneer Park** ( ☎ 6962 4196; Remembrance Dr; d nightly/weekly $15/85) In former shearers' quarters built of corrugated iron, the dorms are small and basic (this is a historic building) but there's a large communal kitchen and lounge. Unfortunately it's a steep walk from town and there's no public transport.

**Griffith International Hostel** ( ☎ 6964 4236; 112 Binya St; d nightly/weekly $20/110; ☐ ) On a pleasant street near the town centre, this Griffith hostel is rough around the edges, with large dorms. Available long-term for international travellers, Australians are welcome to an overnight bed ($12).

**Tourist Caravan Park** ( ☎ 6964 2144; 919 Willandra Ave; caravan/site with bathroom $19/24, cabin $49-66; ☐ )

This is the most convenient caravan park; its small, all crisp and organised, and has a pool and grassy play or sitting areas.

**Yambil Inn Motel** ( ☎ 6964 1233; 155 Yambil St; s/d $86/93; ⚑ P ⚒ ) This small place has a pretty tropical-garden feel with a good pool to relax by on hot days. Walk a block to the city centre.

**Hotel Victoria** ( ☎ 6962 1299; 384 Banna Ave; B&B s/d $85/95; P ⚒ ▣ ) The Victoria features bright corridors, cheerful rooms, good bathrooms and friendly staff. If you like it quiet, ask for a room away from the pub noise.

**Gemini Comfort Inn** ( ☎ 6962 3833; www.geminigriffith.com.au; 201-27 Banna Ave; budget $70, std s/d $85/95, s/d incl spa $108/117; P ⚒ ) A comfortable place in the perfect location, right in the centre of town, with a popular cocktail bar and super-friendly staff.

## Eating

The quality of the food in Griffith, in particular the Italian cuisine, is outstanding; it's hard not to spend the whole day eating!

**Baby Chopsticks** ( ☎ 6964 5412; Griffith Plaza, Yambil St; dishes $5-9; ☽ 11am-8pm Tue-Fri, to 4pm Sat-Mon) This serves grand amounts of filling fried rice, Mongolian beef, sweet chilli chicken – eat in or take away.

**Dolce Dolce** ( ☎ 6962 1888; 449 Banna Ave; mains $5-10; ☽ 9am-5pm Wed-Sun) Come here for fine Italian torte and pastries, a morning coffee and an excellent selection of lunch dishes.

**Miei Amici Cafe** ( ☎ 6962 5999; 350 Banna St; dishes $6-12; ☽ 7am-5pm Mon-Fri, to 2pm Sat) This tiny place is where everyone meets over the great breakfasts. Try the bacon-and-pancake stack, and get acquainted at 'My Friends' Café'.

**Romeo & Giulietta's** ( ☎ 6962 7728; 40 Mackay Ave; mains $9-19; ☽ dinner Thu-Sun) Try here for traditional wood-oven pizzas, grilled fish and pasta.

**La Tavola** ( ☎ 6962 7777; 188 Banna Ave; mains $10-19; ☽ lunch & dinner) A bright and cheery restaurant with an excellent range of Italian dishes such as saltimbocca. The owner is Italian, loves food, and will be very pleased to help you with your selection.

---

### INLAND ITALIANA

Griffith used to make headlines for its alleged links to the Mafia, the murder of an anti-drugs crusader and police corruption. But today the emphasis is on tasty produce, and the large Italian community is working hard to free itself of a quarter of a century of infamy.

Italians have been in Griffith since the early days of the Murrumbidgee Irrigation Scheme; three pioneering Italians, Enrico Lucca, Luigi Gulielmini and Francesco Bicego left the mines in Broken Hill (p267) and took up farming in 1913. Many more miners and construction workers joined them when war broke out. Originally from the Veneti region around Verona, they lived in shacks, working hard to repay the cost of their fare from Italy.

Valentino Ceccata was one of these irrigation pioneers. He slowly started a modest building business and got occasional contract work through the MIA Commission. When the Italian consulate in Sydney heard about this, it directed new immigrants to Valentino's home. Within a few months he had over 40 people camped on his property. Valentino rotated his six staff every week to give everyone a chance at earning some pay. Eventually the stream of arrivals became too much, and Valentino had to travel to Sydney to inform the consul.

It was a difficult time: during the Depression, prices collapsed and fruit was left to rot. One Italian farmer who lived in a tent couldn't sell his Griffith grapes, so he decided to make some wine. Eighty years later his grandson, Darren de Bortoli, is the managing director of a company that makes half a million cases of wine a year.

Others were not so lucky. Valerio Recitti arrived in Australia in 1916, and in the 1920s sought refuge in a cave near Griffith. Valerio kept entirely to himself, creating a private utopia of massive stone galleries, cliffside gardens and floral-painted walls. After falling and injuring himself he was discovered and interned at Hay during WWII on suspicion of being a spy.

While Australian-born farmers and inexperienced soldier settlers went broke and left for the cities, this was not an option for the Italians whose support networks were confined to the area. So they pooled their resources and bought farms at the bedrock prices. In 1929 Italians held 67 small lots; these days they own almost all the irrigated farms. Many came to Griffith from Calabria, in southern Italy, after WWII. In the last 30 years, 'tribal' distinctions between the Veneto and Calabrese communities have become less distinct.

THE RIVERINA

**La Scala** ( ☎ 6962 4322; 455b Banna Ave; dishes $21-7; ☺ dinner Tue-Sat) Hidden down atope and behind an old pink door is La Scala, a cellar with a great reputation and a happy laid-back feel. The menu includes old favourites like scallopine al funghi. But it's hard to go past the steak, and there's an extensive list of local wines.

**Michelin** ( ☎ 6964 9006; 72 Banna Ave; dishes $27-9; ☺ lunch Tue-Sun, dinner Tue-Sat, brunch Sun) The elegant dining room is just the start. Chef Antony More prepares stunning Mod Oz meals like spiced lamb rump with eggplant caviar, Persian fetta pepperoncini and olive crusted kipfler potatoes. The reputation is well deserved.

## Drinking

**Yoogali Catholic Club** ( ☎ 6962 2519; Leeton Rd) The biggest night out in Griffith is Dusk til Dawn, held one Saturday night each month, although the club is open till late every night.

**Hotel Victoria** ( ☎ 6962 1299; 384 Banna Ave) If you miss out on Dusk til Dawn, console yourself at this popular watering hole open till late with live music Fridays and Saturdays.

**Picasso's** ( ☎ 6962 9662; 201-227 Banna Ave) At the Gemini Comfort Inn (opposite), Picasso's has an extensive cocktail list and a relaxed atmosphere in delightful surroundings.

**Griff nightclub** ( ☎ 6962 4325; cnr Kooyoo & Yambil Sts) The ugly modern Griff Hotel can be a fun place, especially on Saturday night. It often has local bands and is open late.

**Area Hotel** ( ☎ 6962 1322; 202 Banna St) is the in place this week. Revamped but still gloriously ugly in that grey-and-pink carpet, brown wall, backdoor bar stool sort of way, it features local bands and has regular jukebox parties.

## Getting There & Away

**Regional Express** (Rex; ☎ 13 17 13; www.rex.com.au) flies between Griffith and Sydney.

All buses, except CountryLink (which stops at the train station), stop at the **Griffith Travel & Transit Centre** ( ☎ 6962 7199; 121 Banna Ave) in the Shell petrol station opposite the plane memorial. You can book Greyhound, V/Line and CountryLink tickets here, with connections to regional coach lines. All services run daily to Adelaide ($108; 14 hours), Melbourne ($98; nine hours), Sydney ($98; 10 hours) and Mildura ($80; six hours).

## Getting Around

Griffith has a **taxi service** ( ☎ 6964 1444) and **airport express bus service** ( ☎ 0418 696 280). Bookings are essential.

Car-rental companies are at the airport and also at the following places.

**Avis** ( ☎ 6962 6266; 7 Wyangan Ave)
**Hertz** ( ☎ 6964 1233; Yambil St) At the Yambil Inn Motel.
**Thrifty** ( ☎ 6962 9122; 2 Griffin Ave) At Westpoint Motors.

## LAKE CARGELLIGO

☎ 02 / pop 1300

On the flat western plains north of Griffith, Lake Cargelligo, 'the Lake', is an unexpected oasis. The **visitors centre** ( ☎ 6898 1501; 1 Foster St; ☺ 10am-4pm) can give you information about the hotels and motels around the lake, plus where to see local and indigenous art. The 8km-wide lake is home to numerous species of birds including pelicans, swans and black cockatoos, and is popular for **water sports**.

**Lake View Caravan Park** ( ☎ 6898 1077; Naradhan & Womboyn Sts; camp site $11-15, cabin $44; ⊠ ) is right by the lake and has a large barbecue area.

## WILLANDRA NATIONAL PARK

Like Mungo National Park (p273), Willandra is part of a huge sheep station on a system of dry lakes. The lakes here, especially **Hall's Lake**, tend to become temporary wetlands more often than Mungo's ancient basins, and **birdlife** is abundant. During spring there are magnificent displays of **wild flowers**, and **emus** and **kangaroos** can be found on the open plains throughout the year.

The historical interest of Willandra centres on the wool industry and station life, although there were certainly Aboriginal civilisations in the area, probably of the same antiquity as those at Lake Mungo. In 1869 some enterprising Melbourne grocers formed the sheep station **Big Willandra** – the national park (about 19,400 hectares), formed in 1972, is less than 10% of Big Willandra.

The **Willandra Homestead** ( ☎ 6967 8159), built in 1918, is gloriously traditional, low-slung and U-shaped, with a wide veranda all the way around that's great for shade and trike races. Established rose gardens and shade trees surround it. The homestead was the centre of station life and the distance of accommodation from the homestead indicated the status of the workers; furthest away is the tin-lined shearers' quarters (take time to explore the graffiti in each room) – much less comfortable in the heat than the thatched ram shed, where the kings of the station (the rams who made all the money) lived.

THE RIVERINA

There are walking tracks in the park, none of them very long, and there's the **Merton Motor Trail**, which takes you on a loop around the eastern half of the park.

## Sleeping

**Willandra Homestead** (r/f/whole homestead $60/80/350) has been faithfully restored, with bathrooms, sitting rooms and a spacious kitchen. The old station's **men's quarters** (r $25) has two double bunks per room and an outside loo. The most popular option is the **cottage** (q $50, per extra person $10), which sleeps eight. Book through **Griffith NPWS office** ( ☎ 6966 8100; fax 6962 5480).

There are several **camp sites** (site per adult/child $3/2) along Willandra Creek, with pit toilets, fireplaces and showers. Bring your own drinking water.

## Getting There & Away

Main access to the park, around 40km west of Hillston, is via the Hillston–Mossgiel road. Entrance costs $7 per day per vehicle. It takes very little rain to close the roads: **Road Info** ( ☎ 6965 1306; www.carrathool.nsw.gov.au/).

## HAY

☎ 02 / pop 3550
This might be flat, one-tree plains country but Hay is colourful, busy, and its position at the junction of the Sturt and Cobb Hwys makes it an important transit point. It's also very much the centre of this rural area. Just watch the main street fill with utes (utility trucks) on Saturday morning as station hands from far and wide come to play in Hay's sporting teams.

The **visitors centre** ( ☎ 6993 4045; www.visithay .com.au; 407 Moppett St; ☾ 9am-5pm Mon-Fri, to noon Sat & Sun) also has an **Amenities Centre** (free; ☾ 6am-6pm) with showers, toilets and picnic area.

There is internet access at **Share a Little Software** ( ☎ 6993 1104; 387 Moore St; per hr $5; ☾ 9am-5.30pm Mon-Fri, to 1pm Sat) and **Hay Newsagency** ( ☎ 6993 1081; 142 Lachlan St; per hr $6; ☾ 9am-6pm).

## Sights & Activities

Shearers enjoy legendary status in this part of Australia, and the innovative **Shear Outback** ( ☎ 6993 4000; cnr Sturt & Cobb Hwys; adult/child $15/8; ☾ 9am-5pm) is devoted to these colourful characters. If you've ever felt the draw of a bushman's life, the interactive displays at Shear Outback will give you all the incentive you need.

Hay housed three internment camps during WWII, and the **Hay POW & Internment Camp Interpretive Centre** ( ☎ 6993 2112; Murray St; adult $2; ☾ 9am-5pm), at the 1882 railway station, gives an insight into that time, telling the stories of the 'Dunera boys', and Japanese and Italian internees.

There are several impressive old buildings in town, including **Bishop's Lodge** ( ☎ 6993 1727; Roset St; adult $4; ☾ 2-4.30pm Mon-Sat Apr-Dec, 10am-12.30pm Jan-Mar), a mansion built entirely of corrugated iron as a residence for the Anglican bishop in 1888. It's set amid acclaimed heritage rose gardens that surround the magnificent verandas.

From an insane asylum to a maternity hospital, the **Old Hay Gaol** (Church St; adult/child $2/1; ☾ 9am-5pm) has had many uses but is now a museum with a fascinating collection of memorabilia from around the district. One cell is set up as it was when the gaol was a detention centre for wayward girls, its last incarnation before it closed in 1973.

## Festivals & Events

Every month features exhibitions in Hay, but the **Booligal Sheep Races** (www.visithay.com.au) over the September long weekend really attracts the crowds.

## Sleeping & Eating

**Hay Plains Holiday Park** ( ☎ 6993 1875; camp site per adult $19, cabin std/deluxe $45/55; ☒ ☒ ) This small park very close to everything has quaint little cabins and a pleasant swimming pool and barbecue area.

**Riverina Hotel** ( ☎ 6993 1137; Lachlan St; s/d/f $30/40/45) This offers basic rooms that have been recently renovated, and large shared bathrooms. The rooms are well away from the bright modern bar area, which sports a magnificent timber bar.

**Bidgee Motor Inn** ( ☎ 6993 2260; Lachlan St; s/d $65/75; P ☒ ) Right in the centre, yet pleasantly open and quiet, the Bidgee has spacious rooms set around a playground, barbecue and saltwater pool.

**Bank B&B** ( ☎ 6993 1730; www.users.tpg.com.au /users/tssk; 86 Lachlan St; s/d $80/120; ☒ ) On the main street, this is a charming place in a building with heaps of character, although the facilities are modern. The lounge area opens onto the balcony of this historic mansion, built in 1891. It feels rather special out there, watching the people passing below.

**Haveachat** ( ☎ 6993 2031; 125 Lachlan St; meals $3-9; ☺ 9am-5pm Mon-Fri, to 1pm Sat) A large blue café, the meeting place for many locals, with grand steak sandwiches and big breakfasts.

**Cumquats** ( ☎ 6993 4399; 161 Lachlan St; meals $7-15; ☺ 9am-5pm Mon-Fri, 9am-2pm Sat & Sun) It's charming here, with interesting dishes such as the warm Thai chicken salad and decent coffee among buckets of fresh flowers.

**Jolly Jumbuck** ( ☎ 6993 4718; 148 Lachlan St; mains $10-25; ☺ lunch & dinner) Located at the Riverina Hotel, it has $10 lunch specials but lash out and order the fantastic lamb cutlets from its extensive range of country style meals. There's a large selection of wines.

## Getting There & Away

Long-distance buses stop at the Mobil petrol station, Sturt Hwy South Hay. **Greyhound** ( ☎ 13 14 99) buses stop here on the daily run between Adelaide (11 hours) and Sydney (13½ hours).

**CountryLink** ( ☎ 13 22 42) XPT train/bus services stop here daily from Sydney ($110; 11½ hours), continuing to Mildura ($51; four hours) or Melbourne ($119; 11 hours).

# MURRAY RIVER

Albury, the largest town on the Murray River, is covered on p316.

## COROWA

☎ 02 / pop 10,970

This historic river town is known as the 'Birthplace of Federation'. When Victoria was proclaimed a colony in 1850 it caused so many customs hassles across the Murray River that people in the area pushed for federation of the colonies. In 1893 a conference was held in Corowa that began the process of Federation, achieved in 1901. There had been previous conferences, but Corowa's was the first to capture the attention of the public.

Another lasting product from Corowa is the Tom Roberts painting *Shearing the Rams*, which was researched in the woolshed of Brocklesby station.

## Orientation & Information

The main street, where you'll find most of the pubs and shops, is Sanger St. It leads down to the Foord Bridge across the Murray River to Wahgunyah. Federation Ave is a leafy street cutting through town to the Mulwala road. The **visitors centre** ( ☎ 6033 3221, 1800 814 054; www .corowa.nsw.gov.au; 88 Sangar St; ☺ 10am-5pm Mon-Sat, to 1pm Sun) hires bikes (per day $15).

## Sights & Activities

The **Federation Museum** ( ☎ 6033 1568; Queen St; adult/child $2/0.50; ☺ 2-5pm Sat & Sun), opposite the neat Ellerslie Gardens, has displays on the history of Federation. There are also sketches by Tommy McCrae, a member of the Bangerang people who lived in the area at the time of first contact with Europeans. The sketches are among the few records of an indigenous people's reaction to European arrival.

The **Star Hotel** (Sanger St) has old cellars which are filled with memorabilia from the town; ask at the pub for access.

You can catch your own yabbies and cook them at the **Murray Bank Yabby Farm** ( ☎ 6033 2922; www.yabbyfarm.com; 76 Federation Ave; family $25; ☺ by appt Nov-Apr). Note that yabbies sleep during winter.

Corowa is home to the **Australian Soaring Centre** ( ☎ 6033 5036; www.australian-soaring-corowa .com; Redlands Rd). Come out to Corowa airport between October and March when the thermals are good. Joy flights run from $100, or try some skydiving (priceless).

## Festivals & Events

Australia Day Weekend is **Corowa National Federation Festival** (www.corowa.nsw.gov.au) with art exhibitions, horse racing, rowing and motor sports. Corowa is a prime place to base yourself in June, for Victoria's grand wine festivities and the nearby **Rutherglen Winery Walkabout** (www.rutherglenvic.com).

## Sleeping & Eating

**Bindaree Motel & Caravan Park** ( ☎ 6033 2500; www .bindaree.net; 454 Honour Ave; camp site per adult $20, cabin std/deluxe $55/65, self-contained motel unit d $80; 🅿 🛠 🖵 ). Pleasantly spread along the river, with a boat ramp and beach, or a pool and spa if you'd rather - plenty of relaxing can be done here.

**Royal Hotel** ( ☎ 6033 1395; 95 Sanger St; s/d $30/60) It's newly renovated and looking gorgeous, which adds to the value of these pleasant rooms that open onto the amazing veranda.

**Murray Bank Holiday Units & Yabby Farm** ( ☎ 6033 2922; www.yabbyfarm.com; 76 Federation Ave; d/f $65/100) A delightful place, with self-contained units spread around the lake. Your hosts' craftwork, like hand-felted scarves, is also for sale. Ask about long term and single rates.

**Brunch 'n' Lunch** ( ☎ 6033 2068; 100 Sanger St; mains $6-13; ◷ 8am-5pm) A spacious, friendly place that offers a good range of burgers, sandwiches and blackboard lunch specials such as smoked chicken risotto.

**D'Amico's** ( ☎ 6033 0666; 235 Sanger St; mains $15-28; ◷ dinner Thu-Tue) This is just the spot for delicious, award-winning Italian meals to go with an extensive wine list.

## Getting There & Around

**CountryLink** ( ☎ 13 22 42) buses run two services between Albury and Corowa: via Rutherglen ($7; 1½ hours; daily Monday to Friday), and via Howlong ($7; one hour; twice daily Monday to Friday). CountryLink's daily XPT service from Sydney ($102; nine hours) stops here then continues to Echuca ($34; three hours).

**Taxis** ( ☎ 6033 1634) are available 24 hours.

## TOCUMWAL

☎ 03 / pop 1530

With its mild winters, long summers and lovely river beaches Tocumwal is an attractive holiday town well worth a stop. The **visitors centre** ( ☎ 1800 677 271; www.toconthemurray.com.au; Deniliquin St; ◷ 10am-5pm Mon-Fri, to 2pm Sat & Sun) has a range of brochures and maps for the whole district, plus an interesting historic walk past buildings dating back to 1881.

A huge statue of a **Murray cod** stands in the centre of town; in the bar of Tattersalls Hotel across the road you'll see some stuffed Murray cod almost as big. There are **riverboat cruises** ( ☎ 5871 2184, 0427 531 407; Thompsons Beach, Cobram; adult/child incl afternoon tea $18/12; ◷ 1.30pm) on the *Matilda*; book at the visitors centre.

**Tocumwal Swim Centre** (Deniliquin Rd; adult/child $4/1.50; ◷ 3.30-7pm) has a small pool in attractive grassy grounds.

Tocumwal is a haven for golfers during winter (summers are scorchers!) with its 36-hole championship course at **Tocumwal Golf Club** ( ☎ 5874 9172, 1800 631 197; www.tocumwalgolf.com.au; Barooga Rd; ◷ from 7am). Fees per 9/18 holes are $15/30 plus club hire $10/18.

Taking you back in time, **Chrysties Museum** ( ☎ 5874 3358; Thornburns Rd, via Barooga Rd; adult/child $5/free; ◷ 10am-4pm) has impeccable working vintage cars, log trucks, tractors, caravans and more.

## Sleeping & Eating

**Boomerang Way Tourist Park** ( ☎ 5874 2313; www .boomerangwaytouristpark.com.au; 65 Murray St; camp site

per adult $24, cabin std/deluxe $72/72; ❄ 🐾 🖥 ) This is a most attractive place, only minutes from both the town and the river. The facilities are sparkling new and include an electric barbecue.

**Thomas Lodge Motel** ( ☎ 5874 2344; 115 Deniliquin St; r $59; ❄ ) Cool under sail cloth, the Thomas is not only close to everything, but has gorgeous rooms, attractive gardens, chocolates on the bed and a very friendly owner.

**Coachmans Cottages** ( ☎ 5874 2699; 16 Barooga Rd; d cottage/spa cottage $97/106; ❄ 🐾 ) This is luxurious, with pretty self-contained cottages tucked away in delightful gardens, all with their own private views. The kidney-shaped pool is a retreat of sparkling blue, but you might find it hard to tear yourself away from your own spa bath.

**Pavilion** ( ☎ 5874 2196; 21 Deniliquin Rd; mains $6-17; ◷ 6am-4.30pm Mon-Fri, to 3.30pm Sat & Sun) Perfect for an early breakfast, or a meal out on the balcony overlooking the foreshore. Front up to the cheery service bar to see the day's specials.

**Woodfired Kreations** ( ☎ 5874 2010; 48 Henessy St; mains $10-29; ◷ lunch Thu-Sun, dinner Wed-Sun) In the popular Farmers Arms hotel, Chef Brian Whiteman offers an exotic and extensive menu, such as pork rack with spicy plum sauce, to be enjoyed in a casual room, a small dining room, or in the beer garden.

## Getting There & Away

**CountryLink** ( ☎ 13 22 42) buses pass through Tocumwal three times weekly on the Echuca–Albury service ($15 to Albury and $25 to Echuca).

**V-Line** ( ☎ 13 61 96; www.viclink.com.au) services between Tocumwal and Melbourne ($75; 4½ hours) run twice daily (once Saturday and Sunday).

## DENILIQUIN

☎ 03 / pop 8220

Deniliquin is a busy town, big enough to offer most services but small enough to retain an easy-going rural feel.

## History

The flood plains and their networks of creeks and billabongs provided plenty of food for the early tribes of the Deniliquin area, one of the most densely populated parts of Australia. When the enterprising Ben Boyd found the river in 1842 he established a station and a pub called Deniliquin, after a local Aboriginal wrestler who was respected for his size and strength. Boyd's shaky empire fell apart soon after, but the town kept growing, and by 1849 it was officially recognised. It prospered because it was at the end of major droving routes leading down from Queensland. Later, it became a wool and sheep centre.

## Orientation & Information

Deniliquin is on a bend in the Edward River. Although the town covers a wide area, its centre, the blocks around Napier and Cressy Sts, is compact.

The **visitors centre** ( ☎ 1800 650 712; www.deniliquin.nsw.gov.au; George St; ☻ 9am-4pm) is part of the Peppin Heritage Centre.

## Sights & Activities

The **Island Sanctuary**, on the riverbank in town, has a pleasant walking track set among the river redgums. The sanctuary is home to plenty of wildlife including kangaroos, possums and birds.

The attractive **Peppin Heritage Centre** ( ☎ 1800 650 712, 5898 3120; George St; adult/child $2/free; ☻ 9am-4pm) is devoted to the wool industry with interesting historical displays.

The Graeco Roman–style **courthouse** (Poictiers St) is an extremely imposing building constructed in 1883.

For swimming, head to **McLean Beach** one of the finest riverside beaches in Australia with golden sand, picnic facilities and a walking track. There is also a spread of pools – Olympic

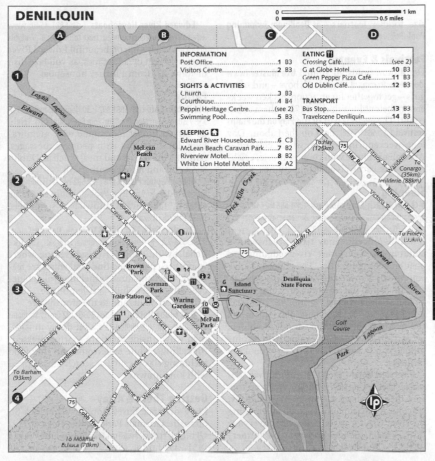

DENILIQUIN

**INFORMATION**
Post Office......................................1 B3
Visitors Centre...............................2 B3

**SIGHTS & ACTIVITIES**
Church............................................3 B3
Courthouse.....................................4 B4
Peppin Heritage Centre...........(see 2)
Swimming Pool...............................5 B3

**SLEEPING**
Edward River Houseboats..............6 C3
McLean Beach Caravan Park...........7 B2
Riverview Motel..............................8 B2
White Lion Hotel Motel...................9 A2

**EATING**
Crossing Café............................(see 2)
G at Globe Hotel...........................10 B3
Green Pepper Pizza Café................11 B3
Old Dublin Café............................12 B3

**TRANSPORT**
Bus Stop.......................................13 B3
Travelscene Deniliquin..................14 B3

---

**DETOUR: TRACKING DOWN NED**

Jerilderie, up there on the Kidman Way, is Ned Kelly country. The Kelly Gang held up Jerilderie for three days in 1879, earning themselves an Australia-wide reputation for brazenness. The NSW government declared him an outlaw and the colony was no longer a safe haven. Yet the speech Ned made to his captives in the Royal Mail Hotel (still operating as a pub; 22 Jerilderie St) and the letter he wrote complaining at his treatment at the hands of the authorities aroused the suspicion that young Ned might be a latent political activist.

The streets of Jerilderie reflect young Ned's days. Pop into the old post office, now called **Willows** ( ☎ 5886 1666; Powell St; ☿ 10am-4pm), to have a cuppa, check out the museum of the gang's memorabilia and collect your maps for the National Ned Kelly Trail and Horgan's Walk.

Down the street is the **blacksmith's shop** ( ☎ 5886 1513; Powell St; ☿ by appt) where the gang had their horses shod and charged it to the NSW government. Cheeky. Stay the night in the atmospheric **Do Book Inn** ( ☎ 5886 1513; horseshoebendjerilderie@bigpond.com; 17 Powell St; d/q $75/125), a fascinating B&B cottage made mostly of recycled materials. It overlooks a billabong and has wonderful sculptures in the garden.

---

size, toddler, learners – at **Deniliquin Swimming Pool** (Poictiers St).

## Festivals & Events

Deniliquin holds an annual **Ute Muster** (www .deniutemuster.com.au), when bush boys – and some girls – get together for an action-packed weekend in their utility vehicles, 6172 of them at last count! The event is part of the **Play on the Plains Festival** ( ☎ 5881 3388), held on the Labour Day long weekend in October, which celebrates Australian culture with country music, celebrity guests, carnivals and competitions.

## Sleeping

**McLean Beach Caravan Park** ( ☎ 5881 2448; www .mcleanbeachcaravanpark.com.au; Butler St; camp site per adult $20, cabin std/deluxe $65/95; ☒ ) This is next to a magnificent sandy river beach with a children's safe enclosure, river redgums and boat launching facilities. The children's play equipment is spectacular, the cabins are self-contained and the amenities are shiny new.

**White Lion Hotel Motel** ( ☎ 5881 2699; 53 Russell St; s/d/tr/f $40/50/60/100; ☒ ) These pleasant motel rooms are set around the edge of the block, away from the pub. Great value, with a communal family room, but there's no cooking facilities.

**Riverview Motel** ( ☎ 5881 2311; www.riverviewmotel .com.au; 1 Butler St; s/d $65/75; ☒ ▢ ) Wake up to a view through a haze of gums from your lovely, spacious room with private porch overlooking the river. Can't tear yourself away? Riverview Bistro (mains $15 to $20; open for dinner) serves the best steak with chips and veg.

**Edward River Houseboats** ( ☎ 5881 4540; www .edwardriverhouseboats.com.au; next to bridge; 3-/7-nights from $580/890) It's fun on beautiful Edward River passing 36km of landscapes, as you laze, fish or water-ski from a luxury houseboat.

## Eating

**Old Dublin Café** ( ☎ 5881 3921; 30 Napier St; mains $5-9; ☿ 7.30am-5pm Mon-Fri, 8am-2pm Sat & Sun) Go Irish, go carved timber mezzanine with memorabilia, local artwork with people's messages, fantastic breakfasts and meals such as Dublin roast roll and rissoles with mash.

**Green Pepper Pizza Café** ( ☎ 5881 4177; Hardinge St; mains $10-12; ☿ 9am-10pm Mon-Sat) Eat in this large café, or take away, sandwiches, schnitzels, pasta and pizzas.

**Crossing Café** ( ☎ 5881 7827; Peppin Heritage Centre; mains $18-22; ☿ 9am-3pm daily, dinner Fri & Sat). It's like a chalet with an idyllic riverside setting, where wood-fired pizzas and fine local wines are featured. Weekend dinners include grilled blue-eye with sweet-chilli-and-lemonade sauce, while local bands add to the atmosphere.

**G at Globe Hotel** ( ☎ 5881 2030; 202 Cressy St; mains $16-30; ☿ lunch & dinner) It's a bit dingy outside, then wow! Inside there are soaring pressed-tin ceilings, white tablecloths and fine food including classics such as scotch fillet topped with king prawns.

## Getting There & Away

Long-distance buses stop on Whitelock St, opposite Gorman Park. **CountryLink** ( ☎ 13 22 42) buses run between Deniliquin and Wagga ($51; 3½ hours; four days a week) or Albury ($29; 3½ hours; the other three days), both linking with the XPT train to Sydney ($110; 10 hours). **V/Line** ( ☎ 13 61 96) coaches run daily between Deniliquin and Melbourne ($37; four hours), stopping at Echuca ($4; one hour). **Travelscene Deniliquin** ( ☎ 588 7744; tonta@mpx.com.au; 358 Cressy St) is the ticket agent.

## WENTWORTH

☎ 03 / pop 7240

This charming historic river port nestles at the junction of the Murray and Darling Rivers, shaded by stately river redgums. There are plenty of lookouts, self-guided walking tracks, a heritage drive trail and brilliant bike-riding and bird-watching opportunities. The **visitors centre** ( ☎ 5027 3624; www.wentworth.nsw.gov.au; 66 Darling St; ⏰ 9am-5pm Mon-Fri, 10am-2pm Sat & Sun) is on the main road.

Local history is displayed at the **Old Wentworth Gaol** ( ☎ 5027 3327; Beverley St; adult $6; ⏰ 10am-5pm), the first colonial Australian–design gaol. Across the road in the **Rotary Folk Museum** (adult $2; ⏰ 10am-4pm, closed Sat) there is a large collection of photos of the paddle-steamers that once made this a major port, and replicas of the mega fauna that once roamed the area.

The **Perry Dunes** are stunning orange-red sand dunes that date back 40,000 years. They're just 6km north of town, off the road to Broken Hill. Go bananas, running up the 200 hectares of rolling sand, but keep your eyes peeled as you roll back down as fossils of mega fauna have been found.

**Harry Nanya Tours** ( ☎ 1800 630 864; www.harrynanyatours.com.au; 33 Darling St) runs day and sunset tours (adult/child $130/85 including meals) with Aboriginal guides into Mungo National Park (p273).

## Sleeping & Eating

**Wombat Lodge Backpackers** ( ☎ 0439 808 217; 162 Darling St; dm $15) This is the spot for some home comforts and lots of information. The small timber home mostly features lounges, a kitchen and sitting areas while most of the bedrooms are out back in the garden.

**Sportsmans Inn Motel** ( ☎ 5027 3584; 120 Adams St; s/d $55/65; ⛄ ) It's a favourite with travellers, who pass through Wentworth regularly for the no fuss value you get at this typical red-brick 1960s motel built around a central courtyard. The rooms are spacious, the owners delightful and it's a pleasant walk to the centre.

**Wentworth Grande Resort** ( ☎ 5027 2225; wentworthresort@bigpond.com; 61-79 Darling St; std/with spa from $110/135; ⛄ 🛏 ) Situated on the banks of the Murray at its junction with the Darling, this resort offers glorious river views from many of its modern rooms. Others overlook the pool or tropical garden. It has golf, tennis, a gym, and houseboats to hire.

**Crown Hotel** ( ☎ 5027 3061; 52 Darling St; mains $10-18; ⏰ lunch & dinner Mon-Sat) A friendly family pub. Start with the pea-and-ham soup. It's perfect, and you'll hear no complaints about the home-cooked schnitzels or roasts either. On Thursday nights, there's a $5 dinner and pool comp.

Staying on a houseboat is popular. The boats accommodate from six to eight people. Expect to pay from $950 for three nights on a six-berth boat. The visitors centre has a complete listing of boat operators

## Getting There & Around

Most long-distance buses run through Mildura. **Coomeallan Bus Lines** ( ☎ 5027 4704) runs to Mildura ($5, three times daily), from the Post Office corner. If you'll be driving on unmade roads, call **Road Condition Info** ( ☎ 5027 5090).

THE RIVERINA

# Southeast

Kosciuszko National Park dominates this inland area of New South Wales (NSW) and with it comes a mixture of winding mountain roads, spectacular scenery and, perhaps unexpectedly in Australia, snow. Small towns that hardly rate a mention in summer become hives of activity in winter, when day-trippers and holidaymakers pass through on their way to live it up in Thredbo and Perisher Blue.

When the white powder isn't falling (or being made artificially), the dense bushland, native wildlife, cascading waters and limestone caves attract just as many outdoor and adventure types as it does the kind of folk who just want to get away from it all. And there's plenty of room for both!

For most visitors it's necessary to access the park via the flat expanse of the arid Monaro Tableland to the northeast or the sloping autumnal orchard and timber country to the west. Whichever way you approach, the contrasting natural environments are worthy touring country and provide – much like the Hume Highway on the western border – an ideal opportunity for side-trips to smaller remote towns, where smiles are served up as readily as cold beer.

## HIGHLIGHTS

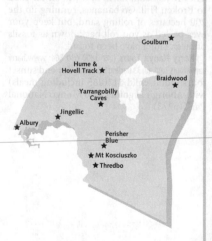

- Admire the pointed peak views from **Mt Kosciuszko** (p298), Australia's resplendent rooftop
- Dodge stalactites at **Yarrangobilly Caves** (p302) before slipping into the nearby thermal pool
- Spend a night in the rustic charm of a brewery worker's cottage in **Goulburn** (p312)
- Float peacefully with the current around the Murray River 'loop' at **Albury** (p316)
- Carve up the snow-coated slopes at **Thredbo** (p298) or **Perisher Blue** (p301)
- Take a reviving dip in the natural rock swimming holes near **Braidwood** (p303)
- Swing off a rope into the fast-flowing Murray River at **Jingellic** (p318)
- Follow (at least some of) the footsteps of early European trailblazers on the **Hume & Hovell Track** (p309)

SOUTHEAST

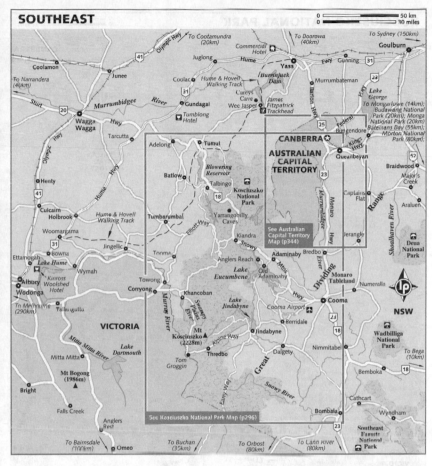

SOUTHEAST

# KOSCIUSZKO NATIONAL PARK

NSW's largest and most spectacular national park covers 690,000 hectares and provides year-round activity, from skiing and snowboarding in winter to bushwalking and camping in summer. What's more it's home to Australia's highest mountain, **Mt Kosciuszko** (koz-zy-*os*-ko), where a drive to within 8km of the summit (2228m) can make you feel on top of the world.

## Orientation & Information

Mt Kosciuszko and the main ski resorts are in the south-central area of the park. From Jindabyne, Kosciuszko Rd leads to the resorts of Smiggin Holes (30km), Perisher Valley (33km) and Charlotte Pass (40km), with a turn-off before Perisher Valley to Guthega and Mt Blue Cow. From Jindabyne, the Alpine Way leads to Thredbo (33km) and to Khancoban (103km).

The main visitors centre for the park, run by the National Parks and Wildlife Service (NPWS), is at Jindabyne (p307). There's an **education centre** ( ☎ 02-6450 5666) at Sawpit Creek (15km from Jindabyne), which runs programmes during school holidays (but is otherwise closed), and visitors centres at Yarrangobilly Caves (p302) and Tumut (p309) in the north of the park.

Entry to the national park costs $27 a day per car in summer and $16 at other times. If

# KOSCIUSZKO NATIONAL PARK

0 [_____] 20 km
0 [_____] 12 miles

To Hume
Hwy (27km)
Adelong
Falls &
Gold Battery
Tumut
To Gundagai (38km)
Adelong
Boonderoo
Wines
Thomas Boyd
Trackhead

To Mutrumbateman
(35km); Yass (94km);
Goulburn (92km)
CANBERRA
Queanbeyan

Bogong
Peaks
Wilderness
Area
Goobarragandra River

Blowering
Reservoir
Hume &
Hovell's
Lookout
Batlow

AUSTRALIAN
CAPITAL
TERRITORY
(ACT)

To Braidwood (90km);
Araluen (120km);
Batemans Bay (137km)

Paddy's River
Dam & Waterfalls
Laurel Hill
Talbingo

Tumut 3 Power
Station (Currently
Closed)
Yarrangobilly

To Rosewood
(4km)
Bago
State
Forest
Talbingo
Reservoir
Thermal
Pool
Yarrangobilly
Caves

Glenburnie
Vineyard
Tumbarumba
Henry Angel
Flat Trackhead

Currango

Pilot Reef
Mountain
Kosciuszko
National
Park

Tantangara
Reservoir

Tumut 2
Power Station
(Currently
Closed)
Kiandra
Mt Selwyn
Eucumbene
River

To Albury
(120km)
Tooma
Cabramurra
Providence
Portal
Adaminaby
Bredbo

Monaro
Tableland

Tooma River
Anglers
Beach
Old
Adaminaby

Tintaldra
Lake
Eucumbene
Braemar
Bay
Frying Pan
Creek

Chakola

Towong
This road is closed
during winter
Eucumbene
Buckenderra
Bunyan

Corryong
Jagungal
Wilderness
Area
Great Dividing Range

Khancoban
Murray 1
Power Station
Kosciuszko
National
Park
Cooma

To Tallangatta
(60km)
Khancoban
Pondage
Kosciuszko
Mountain
Retreat
Sawpit
Creek

Scammell's
Lookout
Olsen's
Lookout
Mt
Blue
Cow
Guthega Smiggin
Holes
Sawpit
Creek
Lake
Jindabyne
Berridale

Geehi
Camp Site
Mt Twynam
Perisher
Blue
Perisher Valley
Bullocks Flat
Skitube
Kosciuszko Rd
Jindabyne
Nimmitabel

Blue Lake
Club Lake
Lake Albina
To Bega
(50km)

VICTORIA
Mt Kosciuszko
(2228m)
Charlotte
Pass
Ngarigo
Thredbo
Valley
Distillery
Snowy River

Tom Groggin
Camp Site
Thredbo
Dead
Horse Gap
Thredbo
Diggings
Camp Site
Pilot
Lookout

Beloka
Dalgety
Maffra

Leatherbarrel
Creek Camp
Site
NSW

Snowy
Mountains

Pilot
Wilderness
Area
Byadbo
Wilderness
Area

The Pilot
(1830m)

Bombala

To Buchan
(50km)
To Orbost
(70km)

you intend to stay a while, buy the $190 annual parks permit, which gives you unlimited access to every national park in NSW.

## Bushwalking

Contact the NPWS visitors centres in Jindabyne (see p307) or Khancoban (p311) for information on the many walks in the park.

From Charlotte Pass you can walk to the Mt Kosciuszko summit (18km return), or take the easier walk to the summit from Thredbo (13km return). Other walking tracks from Charlotte Pass include the 21km glacial lakes walk.

Bush camping (without car access) is permitted in most of the national park, but not in ecologically fragile areas (such as near the glacial lakes or other water catchment areas). Some car-based camp sites have riverside picnic areas, fireplaces and pit toilets.

Cattlemen's huts, scattered throughout the park, are available for emergency shelter and shouldn't be used for accommodation – but they do make great bushwalking destinations. The only formal camping area is the **Kosciuszko Mountain Retreat** ( ☎ 02 6456 2224; www .kositreat.com.au; powered/unpowered sites from $32/$23, cabins from $66), a tranquil place amid the gums at Sawpit Creek along the road to Perisher Valley. These guys know about bushwalks.

## Sleeping

There's no longer a problem finding accommodation in summer, especially at the year-round resort of Thredbo (p298). In all cases the prices will be considerably lower, some less than half the peak-season prices.

In winter, a two-bedroom apartment in Thredbo costs from about $3000 for a week during peak ski season (roughly mid-July to early September) and a double room in a lodge costs around $1000, including some meals.

Travel agents in most regions book accommodation and ski packages.

**Perisher Blue Snow Holidays** ( ☎ 1300 655 811)
**Snowy Mountains Holiday Centre** ( ☎ 1800 641 064)
**Snowy Mountains Reservation Centre** ( ☎ 1800 020 622)
**Thredbo Accommodation Service** ( ☎ 1800 801 982)
**Thredbo Resort Centre** ( ☎ 1300 020 589)

## SKIING & SKI RESORTS

Skiing or snowboarding in Australia is oft derided for its short season and unpredictable snowfalls. But don't be put off. Thredbo has recently forked out a fortune to automate its

snowmaking machines (ensuring 25% of ride-able terrain is covered), and Perisher Blue has upgraded its facilities to enable more reliable connections between major chairlifts. If the outcome is not exactly 100% guaranteed snow, it's a pretty good start.

When there is snow on the ground there's plenty of fun to be had, with long meandering runs to keep beginner and intermediate skiers happy and enough short sharp black runs for the more experienced. The scenery is also worth getting excited about, making Nordic (cross-country or *langlauf*) skiing popular too. Some of the best trails run along old cattle-herders' huts.

Off the slopes there are excellent restaurants, lively nightlife and enough to keep you occupied if you've had enough snowploughing (or face-planting). There's also a plethora of facilities and activities catering for families. Thredbo and Perisher Blue have designated kids' ski programmes, lessons, crèches and daycare.

On the downside, the resorts tend to be particularly crowded on weekends and the short seasons mean operators have to get their returns quickly, so costs are high.

## Information

For snow and road reports contact the visitors centres at **Thredbo** ( ☎ 1900 934 320) and **Perisher Blue** ( ☎ 1900 926 664) or try www.ski.com.au. Also tune in to 97.7 Snow FM locally. Snow chains must be carried during winter even if there's no snow – heavy penalties apply (try $300) if you're caught without them.

## Costs
### THREDBO

During the peak season an adult two-/five-day lift ticket costs $178/388. Children's tickets cost $96/221. A combined two-hour adult lesson and lift pass costs $178/388 (for beginners) or $238/488 (for experienced skiers). A child's combined lesson and lift pass costs $128/254 (for beginners) or $159/322 (for more experienced skiers). Private lessons are also available. Friday Flat is a purpose-built beginners' area with its own slow-speed quad chairlift ($43).

Boots, skis and stocks can be hired for adults/children $58/31 per day and snowboards and boots for adults/children for $74/42.

### PERISHER BLUE

During the peak season at Perisher Blue an adult one-/five-day lift ticket costs $91/393

SOUTHEAST

or $112/479 including return Skitube tickets. Children's tickets cost $50/228 or $61/271. Noon start, quad chair and night ski passes are also available. A combined two-hour lesson and lift pass costs $98/440 (or $119/526 including Skitube pass) for beginners and $122/497 (or $143/583 with Skitube pass) for experienced skiers. Private lessons are also available.

Boots, skis and stocks can be hired for adults/children $65/44 per day and Snowboards and boots for adults/children for $73/56.

At both resorts, equipment will cost less for longer periods; less, too, if you hire it away from the mountain, but if you have a problem with the fit you may be stuck. There are hire places in towns close to the resorts and many garages hire out ski equipment and chains.

## Thredbo

☎ 02 / pop 3000

At 1370m, **Thredbo** ( ☎ 1300 020 589; www.thredbo .com.au) has the longest runs and some of the best skiing to be had in this big ol' sunburnt country. The village itself is eye-candy compared with other Australian ski villages, with blue, green and grey tones ensuring chalets and lodges blend with the surrounding snow gums and alpine flora. It sleeps approximately 4300 people and most of the infrastructure has been built on one side of the valley so that visitors holed up in their lodges on the other can kickback and watch the ski action. And of course Thredbo is an all-season resort, so if you can't afford it in winter, summer has got a lot to offer too.

### INFORMATION

The Thredbo **visitors centre** ( ☎ 6459 4294; Friday Dr) is good for bookings, but quality information is best obtained from the Jindabyne (p307) and Cooma (p305) visitors centres.

There is internet at **Hot Shots** ( ☎ 6457 6422; level 1, Upper Concourse, Alpine Hotel; per hr $25) and an internet kiosk at **Snowflakes Bakery** ( ☎ 6457 7157; Village Square; per 10 min $2).

### SEASONAL WORK

Thredbo employs about 200 year-round full-time staff and close to 750 in winter. For job vacancies and info, check out the recruitment page at www.thredbo.com.au. The length of the season lends itself well to overseas travellers with a working holiday visa, who are limited to working for three months. It's also worth checking the noticeboard at the supermarket in the village centre for jobs and accommodation.

### SIGHTS & ACTIVITIES

#### Winter

Thredbo's **skiing** terrain is roughly 16% beginner, 67% intermediate and 17% advanced and no matter what category you fit into you should try to have a crack at a long run. The Supertrail (3.7km) begins at Australia's highest lifted point then drops 670m through some pretty awesome scenery. From up here you can also take the 5km easy Village trail to Friday Flats, or black-run junkies can crank it up a notch on the 5.9km hair-raiser from Karels T-Bar right down to Friday Flats. These back valley slopes are best in the morning; head to the front valley in the afternoon for more freestyle action.

The **Thredbo Leisure Centre** ( ☎ 6459 4100/51; Friday Dr) organises all sorts of activities, summer and winter, including hiking, mountain biking, canoeing, white-water rafting, abseiling and horse riding. **Thredbo Snow Sports Outdoor Adventures** ( ☎ 6459 4044; www.thredbo.com.au) has a diverse range of high-energy activities including snowshoeing, snow climbing, telemark and back-country alpine touring. It also hosts a cool five-star **snow camping expedition** (per person $275) where you snowshoe to a secret camp site, feast on gourmet cuisine and test your snow survival skills overnight.

Get out of the lodge with a self-guided walk – there is a map available from the information centre.

#### Spring, Summer & Autumn

Thredbo is generally cool in summer with average temperatures of between 14 and 21°C. But locals have seen both the mercury soar to 30°C and snow on the ground, so be prepared.

First and foremost it's an excellent area for **bushwalking**, with 10 or so tracks snaking out into the national park from the village centre. The Kosciuszko Express chairlift to the top of Mt Crackenback runs through summer (adult/child return $26/13) and it's the easiest way to explore Australia's rooftop. From here it's a pleasant 2km walk or cross-country ski to a good view of **Mt Kosciuszko** (which, from here, looks more like a small hill) or 6km to the top of the mountain itself.

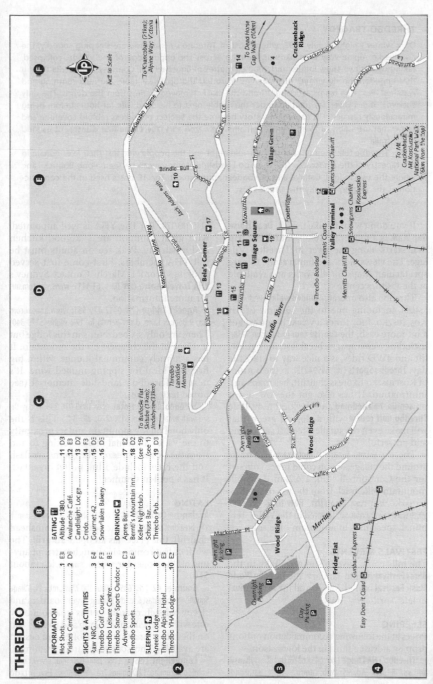

**THREDBO**

Kosciuszko Alpine Way

To Khancoban (71km);
Alpine Way (70km)

Not to Scale

To Dead Horse
Gap Walk (10km)

Crackenback
Ridge

Crackenback Dr

Ramshead Dr

Brindle Bull

Jack Adams Dr

Buckwong Pl

Diggings Tce

Thyne Reid Dr

Village Green

Bela's Corner

Mowamba Pl

Village Square

Kosciuszko Alpine Way

Bango Dr

Buckle La

Diggings Tce

Mowamba Pl

Friday Dr

Footbridge

Valley Terminal

To Mt
Crackenback;
Mt Kosciuszko
National Park Walk
(6km from the top)

Ramshead Chairlift

Kosciuszko
Express

Tennis Courts

Thredbo Bobsled

Snowgums Chairlift

Thredbo
Landslide
Memorial

To Bullocks Flat
Skitube (7km);
Jindabyne (33km)

Bobuck La

Thredbo River

Merritts Chairlift

River View Summit Way

Wood Ridge

Mountain Dr

Overnight
Parking

Highway Tce

Valley Cl

Wood Ridge

Mackenzie Pl

Chimney Way

Overnight
Parking

Merritts Creek

Wood Ridge

Gunbarrel Express

Overnight
Parking

Friday Flat

Day
Parking

Easy Does It Quad

SOUTHEAST

**THREDBO TRAGEDY**

On a winter's night in July 1997, when most of Thredbo's residents were sleeping soundly, the Kosciuszko Alpine Way embankment, running across the upper edge of the village, collapsed, taking with it two snow lodges and 2000 cu metres of liquefied soil. Courtesy of a media throng that engulfed the ski village, Australians sat around the breakfast table the next morning and watched as rescue teams, working around the clock, removed victims from the debris. The only survivor, Stuart Diver, lay trapped under the rubble next to his dead wife for hours before being miraculously rescued. His courageous story became the subject of endless tabloid coverage and somewhat inevitably, a TV movie. He remains the name and face of the first disaster of its kind in Australia.

For Thredbo folk, memories of that terrible night and the people who lost their lives remain in the tapestry of the landscape. The Thredbo Landslide Memorial can be seen along Bobuck Lane where the two lodges, Carinya and Bimbadeen, once stood. The 18 posts used in the construction of the platform signify the 18 lives lost.

If you don't want to take the lift, **Dead Horse Gap Walk** is a moderate 10km, four-hour trip that starts along the river in Thredbo Village. The views, flora and fauna at the top are spectacular. Maps for all walks are available at the visitors centre.

Thredbo also operates **guided walks** (adult/child $34/20), including one to the summit of Mt Kosciuszko, four times a week. If you've got a bit more cash, the **sunrise tour** (per person $138), including a champagne breakfast, tour guide, lift and 4WD rides, is a nice way to start the day. **Thredbo Sports** ( ☎ 6459 4119), at the bottom of Kosciuszko Express chairlift, has maps and information. It has also got the low-down on **tennis**, **bobsledding** and the local nine-hole **Thredbo golf course** with a sloping green that will make even the smallest tee-off seem long and powerful.

There are two lengthy **mountain-bike tracks** around the village, or you could brace yourself for the Cannonball Run, a 4.2km downhill mountain-bike track from the top of the Kosciuszko Express chairlift. **Raw NRG** ( ☎ 6457 6990; www.rawnrg.com.au), located in the Valley Terminal, specialises in mountain-bike rides.

**FESTIVALS & EVENTS**
The hills come alive in summer. Take in the **Blues Festival** in mid-January, the **Thredbo World Music Festival** in mid-March and the **Jazz Festival** in late April/early May.

**SLEEPING**
Prices at the following accommodation options drop by at least a third in the low season.
**Thredbo YHA Lodge** ( ☎ 6457 6376; thredbo@yhansw .org.au; 8 Jack Adams Path; dm/d/r with bathroom $145/163/179; 🖳 ) The YHA is well appointed, with great common areas, a good kitchen and a balcony. Peak season adults must be full YHA members. First-come-first-served bookings from 1 March. Contact Sydney's **YHA Travel Centre** ( ☎ 02-9261 1111; www.yha.com.au) for more information.

**Aneeki Lodge** ( ☎ 0417 479 581; www.aneeki.com .au; 9 Bobuck Lane, d per person for two nights $170-340) There are only six bedrooms in this lodge but it is one of the cheapest on the mountain. It has a homely communal lounge with a big fireplace ideal for sipping mulled wine. It's next to Thredbo's landslide memorial (see boxed text, above).

**Thredbo Alpine Hotel** ( ☎ 1800 026 333; Friday Dr; s/d with breakfast from $190/270; 🖳 🎯 ) This is the only hotel on the mountain and its proximity to the Valley Terminal makes getting to and from the slopes a breeze. The rooms are flash and the rates include a full buffet breakfast. It has a pool in summer.

**EATING**
**Avalanche Café** ( ☎ 6457 6131; Shop 7, Valley Terminal; ☯ breakfast & lunch) At the bottom of Ramshead chairlift, this place has an open-air grill. The whiff of fried onions is enough to tempt anyone off the slopes for a steak sandwich (about $10).

**Gourmet 42** ( ☎ 6457 7500; 100 Mowamba Pl, Village Square; ☯ breakfast & lunch) Hung-over boarders and sleepy bar staff rock up to this small but busy café with excellent coffee. Soup and pasta is also on the menu for about $10. Coffee and dessert are available Thursday to Saturday evening.

**Candlelight Lodge** ( ☎ 1800 020 900; www.candle lightlodge.com.au; 32 Diggings Tce, ☯ dinner) For a true

Alpine experience – the fondue – try this lodge's Swiss Gruyere and Emmental with white wine and schnapps ($30 for two people) or eye fillet fondue ($64). It also has accommodation (see the website).

**Altitude 1380** ( ☎ 6457 6190; Shop 5, Upper Concourse, Alpine Hotel; ☺ breakfast & lunch) Grab a BYO bottle from the boozer two doors down and kick back here for great food at prices that don't bite. Dinner is available Wednesday to Saturday night. Cash only.

**Credo** ( ☎ 5457 6844; 2 Diggings Tce; ☺ dinner) For a Mediterranean feast in a groovy establishment, this gets a good rap. It's a five-minute walk from the village centre.

## DRINKING
**Aprés Bar** ( ☎ 6457 6222; Diggings Tce) Cosy couches and crimson leather poufs are crammed together in this cosy over-25s atmosphere. The tunes are spot on and vino by the glass is affordable. It's downstairs at the Denman Hotel.

**Schuss Bar** ( ☎ 6459 4200; Upper Concourse, Alpine Hotel) Live bands give this place a bit of energy as do the young folk fresh from the slopes. Beers are on tap and schnapps costs $6. Monday is comedy night ($10 entry from 8.30pm).

Other recommendations:
**Bernti's Mountain Inn** ( ☎ 6457 6332; 4 Mowamba Pl) Not shy of putting on the TV for some live sporting action.
**Thredbo Pub & Keller Night Club** ( ☎ 6459 4200; Friday Dr; ☺ from 4pm Thu-Sat) Has a huge balcony overlooking Thredbo River to the slopes. Skip the food.

## Perisher Blue
☎ 02 / elevation 1680m
Perisher Valley, Smiggin Holes, Mt Blue Cow and Guthega make up the massive resort of **Perisher Blue** ( ☎ 6459 4495, 1300 655 811; www.perisherblue.com.au). The terrain is roughly 22% beginners, 60% intermediate and 18% advanced with most of the action in Perisher Valley. Guthega (1640m) and Mt Blue Cow (1640m) are mainly day resorts so they're smaller and less crowded. From Guthega, cross-country skiers head to the Main Range or Rolling Ground. Mt Blue Cow is accessible via the **Skitube** ( ☎ 1300 655 822; adult/child same-day return $38/21). Because of Perisher Blue's sporadic layout, it doesn't have the village ambience of Thredbo, but it's widely held (though still debated) that the skiing is superior. Boarders should head for the half-pipe park where there are rails, boxes, kickers etc

and good skiers shouldn't leave without giving the knees a workout on Toppers Dream, the freestyle mogul course groomed for Winter Olympics training.

## SEASONAL WORK
Perisher Blue jobs are seasonal and vary depending on snow conditions and business demands. For job vacancies and information check out the employment page at www.perisherblue.com.au. For the majority of positions, applicants need a working visa; however, Perisher Blue can apply for sponsored work visas on behalf of instructors, snow groomers and ski patrollers with two to three seasons under their belt. Staff housing isn't guaranteed but local real estate agencies should be able to help.

## SLEEPING
Most accommodation is in Perisher Valley and Smiggin Holes. The following rates include either breakfast and lunch or breakfast and dinner.

**Sundeck Hotel** ( ☎ 6457 5222; sundeck@acr.net.au; Kosciuszko Rd; d/tw from $165) One of the oldest lodges in Perisher, Sundeck has a comfy bar and great views from the guest lounge over the Quad 8 Express.

**Perisher Valley Hotel** ( ☎ 6459 4455; pvh@perisher.com.au; Perisher Valley; d/tw from $231) This hotel is in a prime locale, two minutes from the Skitube terminal at the bottom of the Quad 8 Express. Rooms are spacious and have views. You can make use of the indoor spa that overlooks the on-snow action.

**Heidi's Chalet** ( ☎ 1800 252 668; www.heidis.com.au; Munyang Rd, Smiggin Holes; two night packages tw/tr/dm from $260/236/236) This is one of the cheaper options in Smiggin Holes and it's just a short snowplough to the ski lifts. Closed in summer.

Other recommendations:
**Aurora Ski Club** ( ☎ 0412 363 206; auroraperisher@yahoo.com.au; Perisher Valley; dm from $95) A budget hotel – it pays to book early.
**Chalet Sonnenhof** ( ☎ 6457 5256; www.sonnenhof.com.au; Perisher Valley; tw/dm from $145/130) Has a restaurant, lounge bar, open fire and large spa.

## EATING & DRINKING
The Perisher Centre (Perisher Valley) and Skitube terminals at Blue Cow and Perisher Valley have plenty of fast food.

**Snow Gums Restaurant** ( ☎ 6459 4443; Perisher Valley; ☺ lunch & dinner) In the Perisher Valley Hotel, this is a fine dining option in a cosy room with a fireplace and an atmospheric bar. The à la carte menu has something for everyone but the gnocchi ($18) is especially good.

**Ruffles Restaurant** ( ☎ 6457 5291; Perisher Valley; ⏲ lunch & dinner) Does a gourmet take on lunch time favourites such as steak sandwiches, fish and chips and Caesar salads (around $18). It has a piano bar for cocktails – just turn a blind eye to the dated décor.

**Smiggin's Chargrill** ( ☎ 6457 5375; Smiggin Holes; ⏲ lunch & dinner) Has good pizzas ($17) and a bistro menu the kids will love. It's reasonably priced with a late-night bar and live band on Wednesday nights.

**Jax Bar & Grill** ( ☎ 6459 4437; Perisher Centre; ⏲ lunch & dinner) Check out the ski bunnies from this big glassed-in bar at the bottom of Mitchell T-bar. There are a couple of pool tables, beers are on tap and you can cook your own steak (around $20).

## Charlotte Pass
☎ 02 / elevation 1780m

There are just over 600 beds in the village, which doesn't represent many skiers on the slopes. At the base of Mt Kosciuszko, this is one of the highest, oldest and most isolated resorts in Australia and in winter you have to 'snowcat' (use oversnow transport) the last 8km from Perisher Valley ($30 each way, book ahead). Five lifts service rather short, but uncrowded, runs and this is good ski-touring country. In summer, it's the start of a number of walks including to the summit of Mt Kosciuszko (18km return), the Main Range (25km return) and the Blue Lake Lookout (10km return).

**Kosciuszko Chalet** ( ☎ 1800 026 369; www.charlotte pass.com.au; Fri & Sat r with 2 meals & lift pass per person $693) is a grand old place dating from the 1930s. **Alitji Alpine Lodge** ( ☎ 6457 5223; enquiry@alitji.com.au; r with 3 meals from $85) is a cheaper option. **Stillwell Lodge** ( ☎ 6457 5073; www.stillwell-lodge.com.au; d from $135) is good for students.

## Bullocks Flat & Around
☎ 02

Bullocks Flat, on the Alpine Way between Jindabyne and Thredbo, is the site of the Skitube terminal, one of Perisher Blue's most underrated drawcards. Simply park the car, buy a ticket, board the train and within 15 minutes you're on the slopes. The **Skitube train** ( ☎ 1300 655 822; adult/child same-day return $38/21) runs

from here mostly underground to Perisher Valley and Mt Blue Cow. In summer it runs to a reduced timetable but operates daily during school holidays. Parking and national park entry fees are included in the ticket price. Combine a mountain pass with the Skitube pass to save money (see p297).

The **Novotel Lake Crackenback Resort** ( ☎ 1800 020 524; www.novotellakecrackenback.com.au; 1650 Alpine Way; d summer/winter from $180/200) is a village resort close to the Skitube terminal. **Crackenback Cottage** ( ☎ 6456 2198; www.crackenback.com.au; adult/child summer $75/$35, adult/child winter $150/75; ⚑ ), on the road towards Jindabyne, has a sensational guesthouse, gorgeous restaurant and a maze to keep the kids entertained.

Across the road the **Thredbo Valley Distillery** ( ☎ 6457 1447; www.wildbrumby.com; Alpine Way; ⏲ 11am-5pm) makes Wildbrumby schnapps. Sit down for a bowl of schnapps and a shot of soup!

## Cabramurra
☎ 02 / pop 160

Australia's highest town, Cabramurra (1488m), has great views when the weather allows and is worth diverting 4km from the main route. The general store has snacks, a clean toilet and petrol but no gas. **Tumut 2 Power Station** was once the main reason for visiting Cabramurra but it is currently closed.

## Yarrangobilly Caves

Perhaps the most underrated caves in Australia, the **Yarrangobilly Caves** ( ☎ 6454 9597; car entry $3, tour adult/child $13/9 at 11am, 1pm & 3pm or self-guided $7; ⏲ 9am-4pm) were formed in a belt of limestone around 440 million years ago. There's also a thermal pool, which retains a constant 27°C: if it's snowing, even better. There's a **NPWS visitors centre** ( ☎ 6454 9597) but not much in the way of food or petrol so come prepared.

## Getting There & Around
**Greyhound Ski Express** ( ☎ 13 14 99) buses run from Sydney and Canberra to Thredbo via Jindabyne and Bullocks Flat daily, June to October.

**Transborder** ( ☎ 6421 0033) runs a service from Canberra ($64) to Thredbo and back daily, which also stops at Jindabyne ($45) and Bullocks Flat ($60). All year round.

**Wayward Bus** ( ☎ 1300 653 310) runs a summer-only service to Melbourne ($120) four times weekly.

In winter you can normally drive as far as Perisher Valley, but snow chains must be carried and fitted where directed. The simplest and safest way to get to Perisher Valley and Smiggin Holes during the winter is to take the Skitube train (p301). See the Alpine Way (below) for western routes into the national park.

## THE ALPINE WAY

From Khancoban, this spectacular route runs through dense forest, around the southern end of Kosciuszko National Park to Thredbo and on to Jindabyne. All vehicles have to carry chains, which can be hired at **Khancoban Lakeside Caravan Resort** ( ☎ 6076 9488; www.klcr.com.au; Alpine Way) and dropped off at **Margaritta Hire** ( ☎ 6456 1959; 8 Kosciuszko Rd, Jindabyne) or vice versa. The fine for not carrying chains is steep (about $300). Motorbikes are not permitted along the Alpine Way from June to October.

In winter, check conditions at Khancoban or Jindabyne. There's no fuel available between Khancoban and Thredbo (71km). If you're driving between Khancoban and Jindabyne, you can get a free transit pass, but if you stop en route you must have a day pass ($27).

**Murray 1 Power Station** ( ☎ 6076 5115; admission free; ⊙ 9am-4pm Mon-Fri, from 10am Sat & Sun), south of Khancoban, has an informative visitors centre explaining the Snowy Mountains hydro-electric scheme and a pleasant café on the pondage.

Further south is **Scammels Lookout** then **Geehi**, a beautiful grassy camping area with lots of kangaroos, on the Swampy Plains River. At **Tom Groggin** the road skirts the upper Murray River – a clear, cool stretch that's good for a swim on a hot day. There's a good camping and picnic site here and a smaller site at **Leatherbarrel Creek**, about 7km further on. After Tom Groggin the road climbs 800m to the **Pilot Lookout** (1300m), with views across a wilderness area to The Pilot (1830m), the source of the Murray River. There's another climb to **Dead Horse Gap** (1580m), named after some brumbies that froze here, then a descent to Thredbo (1400m), the Skitube terminal at Bullocks Flat, and Jindabyne. **Thredbo Diggings** and **Ngarigo** are two more picnic and camping areas on the banks of the Thredbo River near Bullock's Flat.

# MONARO TABLELAND

The legacy of the Snowy Mountains hydro-electric scheme yields unexpected scenery in this elevated expanse of land northeast of Kosciuszko National Park. The rugged grey countryside, known for its unforgiving soil, is also home to massive fishing lakes formed when the Snowy scheme flooded part of the tablelands more than 50 years ago. The Snowy scheme provides electricity to Canberra, NSW and Victoria and is hailed as one of Australia's greatest engineering feats. Its historical importance was enhanced by workers from 30 countries immigrating to work on a project that was a source of immense national pride attitudes to new immigrants changed and Australia's multiculturalism began. From an environmental point of view, however, it has been viewed as a national catastrophe, contributing to fishery depletion and the salination crisis.

Cooma and Jindabyne are the major town centres and while they're pretty laidback in summer, they pick up the pace in the winter when the state's snow bunnies stop through on their way to Thredbo and Perisher Blue. In the smaller towns you'll be surprised to find decent coffee, cute pubs and locals who can point you in the direction of a good feed.

### Getting There & Away

**Regional Express** (Rex; ☎ 13 17 13) flies from Cooma to Sydney and back daily.

Cooma is the main transport hub in winter, with crowds coming to the ski-fields from Melbourne, Canberra and Sydney.

If driving from Canberra, the Monaro Hwy runs down to Cooma (1½ hours). The quickest route from Sydney is to take the Hume Hwy to Goulburn, then the Federal Hwy to Canberra. From Cooma, the Monaro Hwy heads south to Bombala and the Victorian border.

The Barry Way is a largely unsealed, narrow and winding mountain road running from near Jindabyne to Buchan in Victoria. It's a spectacular route through national parks, but it can be difficult when wet. Fuel isn't available anywhere along this road.

# BRAIDWOOD

☎ 02 / pop 1100

Braidwood has long been on the radar of visiting Canberrans because of its well-preserved historic buildings. But more recently it's the

SOUTHEAST

food scene that makes passers-by pull up to the kerb. On any given weekend the small town buzzes with the sound of chatting latte drinkers and foodie folk fond of perching streetside under big umbrellas for the best food just outside the capital. When you've had your fill, Braidwood is also a great base for bushwalking in the national parks.

## Information

**Braidwood visitors centre** ( ☎ 4842 1144; www.braidwood-tourism.com; 92 Wallace St; ⏲ 10am-4pm) has a walking-tour map of the town (free), books and topographical maps of scenic drives and bushwalks in the nearby national parks.

## Sights & Activities

A stroll along **Wallace St**, with its restored Victorian buildings and wrought-iron lacework, is rather pleasant. Pop into the Italianate **Studio Altenburg** ( ☎ 4842 2384; 104 Wallace St; ⏲ 1-5pm) in the impressive old bank (1888); it displays work by local artists and craftspeople. **Carriages by Cupid** ( ☎ 0417 456 093) is the town's horse-drawn taxi alternative and local history tour guide. Flag it down for a ride ($10 per person for an hour).

Just out of town there are two pristine bush **swimming holes**. One of them 'starred' in the classic Australian movie *The Year My Voice Broke*. The visitors centre can give directions.

## Festivals & Events

On the first or second Saturday in February, the **Braidwood Cup** is one of those great country race meetings (see the boxed text, p314). The **Braidwood Show** is held in mid-March.

## Sleeping

**Royal Mail Hotel** ( ☎ 4842 2488; 147 Wallace St; r $30) Spic-and-span pub rooms with shared bathrooms. Downstairs, The Coach House bistro has $7 lunchtime 'hunger-busters' and a beer garden.

**Country Style B&B** ( ☎ 4842 2577; Wallace Street; r $75) Behind Eureka Pizza on the main street, this cute 1870s B&B is self-contained and sleeps 12 people. It has a cosy lounge for colder months and a front veranda ideal for sipping cool ale in summer.

**Mona B&B** ( ☎ 4842 1288; Kings Hwy; r from $300) This is one for high-rollers or honeymooners with no expense spared. The owner's immaculate taste makes for a lavish weekender on a country estate with all the trimmings.

## Eating

**Café Altenburg** ( ☎ 4842 2077; 104 Wallace St; mains $8-13; ⏲ 10am-5pm) This pleasant and relaxing café in the courtyard of Studio Altenburg (left) has homemade soups, pies, pastries, savoury tarts, cakes, tempting pastas and salads, all at reasonable prices.

**Braidwood Natural Foods & Dojo Bread** (91 Wallace St; ⏲ 9am-3pm Tue & Thu, 11am-6pm Fri, 9am-1pm Sat) Two scrumptious organic shops in one of Braidwood's oldest buildings, behind Eureka Pizza.

**Serrated Tussock Café** ( ☎ 4842 2346; 118 Wallace St; mains $9; ⏲ breakfast & lunch) This place is gorgeous; it's a bookshop-cum-café with a rear courtyard, couches, cake and spot-on coffee.

Other recommendations:

**Eureka Pizza** ( ☎ 4842 1019; 91 Wallace St; mains $13-26; ⏲ dinner) Tasty wood-fired pizzas and cheaper traditional Italian-style fare. Tuck in on the veranda.

**Somewhere Special on Wallace** ( ☎ 4842 1999; 123 Wallace St; entrees $18, mains $24; ⏲ dinner) Braidwood's newest upmarket restaurant.

## Getting There & Away

**Murrays** ( ☎ 13 22 51) has a bus that stops outside the post office on Wallace St daily on its run between Canberra ($20) and Batemans Bay ($17).

**Rixons** ( ☎ 4474 4243) has a bus that stops Monday, Wednesday and Friday in each direction between Woden and Narooma at the Ampol service station, where you can buy tickets and get info on other bus lines.

Braidwood is on the Kings Hwy between Canberra (89km) and Batemans Bay (59km). An alternative route to the south coast at Moruya runs through Araluen and some beautiful country on the northern edge of Deua National Park. The road is sealed as far as Araluen, but after that it's not suitable for caravans.

If you're heading to Cooma, consider taking the scenic, partly sealed road via Numeralla. Floods can sometimes cut the road, so if it has been raining, change your plans.

## AROUND BRAIDWOOD

The **Budawang** and **Morton National Parks** and the new **Mongo National Park** are accessible from Braidwood. Monga has a beautiful **2WD scenic loop** accessing walking tracks, picnic areas and Penance Grove, where an interpretative boardwalk winds through ancient cool temperate rainforest, a legacy of the Gondwanan Age.

**Major's Creek**, an old gold-mining town 16km south of Braidwood, has a number of historic buildings and a good country pub with comfortable rooms – the **Elrington Hotel** ( ☎ 02-4846 1145; 1 George St, s/d $30/40).

### SEASONAL WORK

From November to February, there is peach-picking work in the peaceful little town of Araluen, 26km south of Braidwood on the road to Moruya. **Araluen Valley Hotel** ( ☎ 02-4846 4073; Main Rd; s $45) has all the info and great pub rooms.

## Adaminaby

☎ 02 / pop 400 / elev 1017m

Adaminaby, on the Snowy Mountain Hwy, is so small-town it could be accused of going backwards. Fortunately, it remains the biggest place between Cooma and Tumut and the closest town to **Mt Selwyn ski-fields**, so it still pulls a crowd. Fishing in nearby **Lake Eucumbene** is also a big attraction and one that accounts for the giant rainbow trout greeting visitors in the town park.

**Snowy Mountains Holiday Centre** ( ☎ 1800 641 064; www.smhc.com.au; 9 Denison St) on the main street has plenty of info and books tickets for the **Adaminaby Bus Service** ( ☎ 1800 641 064) to Mt Selwyn, which leaves from the giant trout daily at 9am (return adult/child $30/25). It also offers a charter transport service for bushwalkers in summer. You can hire ski gear from several shops in town.

**Tanderra Lodge** ( ☎ 6454 2470; www.tanderra.com; 21 Denison St; d/tr/q/f $100/110/120/150) has basic rooms and plenty of '70s fishing and ski-ing ambience here. Adjacent, **Snow Goose Hotel/Motel** ( ☎ 6454 2202; cnr Denison & Baker Sts; motel s/d with breakfast $85/130) has pub and motel rooms and counter meals. It's one of the few places open in the evening (until 9pm) year-round.

The **Cooma visitors centre** ( ☎ 1800 636 525) can point you towards **farmstays** in the region.

## COOMA

☎ 02 / pop 8000

Proximity to the snowfields keeps this little town punching above its own weight during winter but it slows down considerably during summer. On the main street there are petrol stations aplenty, pubs for a different kind of refuelling and all the cafés and fast food necessary for a road trip.

## Orientation & Information

Sharp St, the main street, becomes the Snowy Mountains Hwy to the west and the Monaro Hwy to the east.

The **Cooma visitors centre** ( ☎ 1800 636 525; www .visitcooma.com.au; 119 Sharp St; ⊗ 9am-5pm Mon-Sat) is next to Centennial Park. It makes accommodation bookings and may know of special deals being offered. It has internet access ($6 per hour) as does the **library** (Vale St; per hr $6). Nearby, **Public Internet Access** (67 Sharp St; per hr $15) has coin-operated internet access.

## Sights & Activities

Off the Monaro Hwy, 2km north of the town centre, the **Snowy Mountains Scheme Information Centre** ( ☎ 1800 623 776; www.snowyhydro.com.au; admission free; ⊗ 8am-5pm Mon-Fri, to 1pm Sat & Sun) has the best info on this feat of engineering. The **Cooma Monaro Railway** ( ☎ 6452 7791; ⊗ 11am, 1pm & 2pm Sat & Sun, public holidays & summer school holidays; ⊗ 1pm & 2pm Sun during winter) runs 45-minute train rides ($12) aboard restored 1923 CPH rail motors. There's also a signposted **rail history walk**.

Out of town, 3km west, **Mt Gladstone lookout** has picnic tables.

## Festivals & Events

The **Cooma Street Fair** and **Snowy Ride** are held in early November and **Cooma Race Day** is on the first Saturday in December (see the boxed text, p314). Punters can catch the train to and from the racetrack. Cooma is a major centre for **cattle sales** and a big sale is worth seeing. The saleyards are just southeast of town on the Monaro Hwy.

## Sleeping & Eating

**Royal Hotel** ( ☎ 6452 2132; 59 Sharp St; s/d $30/50) The oldest licensed hotel in Cooma is a beautiful old sandstone place with decent pub rooms, shared bathrooms and a great veranda.

**Bunkhouse Motel** ( ☎ 6452 2983; www.bunkhouse motel.com.au; 28 Soho St; s/d winter $45/60, dm/s/d summer $25/35/60) This is the best value for money in Cooma – a neat, friendly place with a slightly cramped and rustic feel. Some rooms have cooking facilities.

**Lott** ( ☎ 6452 1414; 178-180 Sharp St; ⊗ breakfast & lunch) A great place, as cosy as mumma's kitchen. The colourful cushions, produce piled high on the counter and the smell of fresh brewed coffee wafting around the room will make you feel right at home.

SOUTHEAST

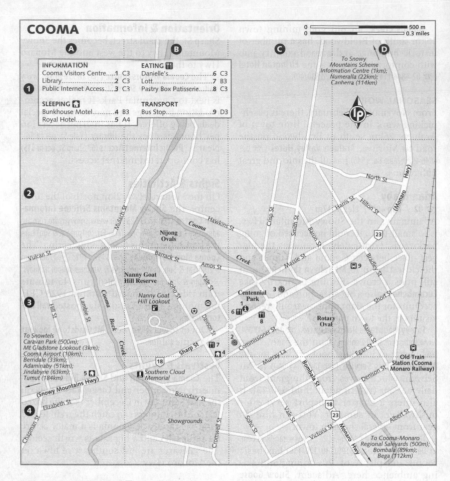

## COOMA

0 — 500 m
0 — 0.3 miles

INFORMATION
Cooma Visitors Centre.....1 C3
Library.........................2 C3
Public Internet Access....3 C3

SLEEPING
Bunkhouse Motel..........4 B3
Royal Hotel..................5 A4

EATING
Danielle's....................6 C3
Lott...........................7 B3
Pastry Box Patisserie......8 C3

TRANSPORT
Bus Stop......................9 D3

To Snowy
Mountains Scheme
Information Centre (1km);
Numeralla (22km);
Canberra (114km)

**Pastry Box Patisserie** ( ☎ 6452 5159; 100 Sharp St; ☺ breakfast & lunch) Opens at about 6am (knock and the pastry chef will let you in) with a selection of French patisseries, chunky beef pies, wraps, flans and sandwiches.

**Danielle's** ( ☎ 6452 4488; 121 Sharp St; mains $16-25; ☺ lunch & dinner Tue-Sun, breakfast Sat & Sun) Next door to the visitors centre, Danielle's is probably Cooma's best restaurant. It's licensed, and has a menu of Italian-influenced dishes and a second-storey view over the main street.

### CAMPING
**Snowtels Caravan Park** ( ☎ 6452 1828; info@snowtels .com.au; 286 Sharp St; powered/unpowered sites $22/18; cabins from $45) On the highway, 1.5km west of town,

this is a big, well-equipped place with rates that don't seem to fluctuate.

## Getting There & Away
The airport is about 10km southwest of Cooma on the Snowy Mountains Hwy. **Rex** ( ☎ 13 17 13) flies from Cooma to Sydney and back daily.

**Greyhound Ski Express** ( ☎ 13 14 99) buses run from Sydney and Canberra to Thredbo, Bullocks Flat Skitube and Jindabyne daily.

**SkiBus** ( ☎ 6456 2957) buses run daily from Thredbo and Perisher via the Skitube, Jindabyne and Cooma (on request) to Canberra.

The **Snowy Mountains Express Shuttle** ( ☎ 1800 679 754) meets every Rex flight and runs between the airport and Jindabyne, Alpine Way, Perisher Blue and Thredbo.

**Transborder** ( ☎ 6241 0033) buses run daily from Thredbo via the Skitube ($21), Jindabyne ($25) and Cooma ($35) to Canberra ($64).

Victoria's **V/Line** ( ☎ 13 61 96) has an interesting twice-weekly run from Melbourne to Canberra via Cooma ($63). The nine-hour trip from Melbourne takes you by train to Bairnsdale, then by bus.

Heading to Batemans Bay, you can travel via Numeralla to Braidwood on a partly sealed road skirting Deua National Park. If you're heading to Bega, be warned there's no petrol until Bemboka.

There are two car-hire companies available in Cooma. **Europcar** ( ☎ 13 13 90) is located at the airport, but if you're not coming by plane a taxi to the airport costs $50 or $60. **Thrifty** ( ☎ 13 12 86) is central but has more restrictions for travelling above the snowline.

## NIMMITABEL
☎ 02 / pop 300

Pretty Nimmitabel, on the Monaro Hwy 35km south of Cooma, is a good spot for a coffee fix but you'll have to look elsewhere for petrol.

The **Royal Arms** ( ☎ 6454 6422; www.royalarms.com.au; Snowy Mountain Hwy; d from $100), a restored hotel, is the main source of tourist info. **CJ Harvey's Coffee Bar** ( ☎ 6454 6464; 43 Bombala St; ⏰ breakfast & lunch) is an unexpected surprise in such a small place. It is ultra modern with 'out-there' sculptures and good coffee.

The **CountryLink** ( ☎ 13 22 32) bus between Canberra and Eden passes through daily in both

directions. It stops outside the elephant statue (shipped over from Bali by the local baker).

## JINDABYNE
☎ 02 / pop 4420

Jindabyne has a split personality. As the closest town to Kosciuszko National Park's major ski resorts, it sleeps more than 20,000 visitors in winter. But in summer the crowds go elsewhere and the town reverts to its relatively peaceful small-town self where fishing is the mainstay activity.

### Orientation & Information

As with many other towns on the Monaro Tableland, today's Jindabyne is a modern incarnation of an original settlement that is now submerged in Lake Jindabyne.

The impressive **Snowy Region visitors centre** ( ☎ 6450 5600; fax 6456 1249; www.nationalparks.nsw.gov.au; Kosciuszko Rd; ⏰ 8am-5pm), on the main road, is operated by the NPWS. There are display areas, a cinema and a good café.

Nearby is **Nugget's Crossing** (Kosciuszko Rd), the town's main shopping centre, with three banks, cafés and shops. The post office is located behind the centre.

### Summer Activities

**Jindabyne Adventure Booking** ( ☎ 1800 815 588; 2 Thredbo Tce) offers a variety of tours and packages including mountain biking, white-water rafting, kite boarding, wake boarding, abseiling and guided walks up to the top of Mt Kosciuszko.

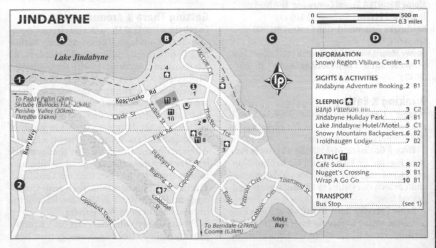

SOUTHEAST

**Paddy Pallin** ( ☎ 1800 623 459; www.paddypallin .com.au; cnr Kosciuszko & Thredbo Rds) is a kitted-out adventure centre 2.5km out of Jindabyne, just past the Thredbo Rd turnoff. It has tents, skiing and walking equipment for hire, and national park bushwalks.

## Sleeping

The influx of snow bunnies in winter sends prices through the roof, but it's still generally cheaper than at the resorts. Plan well ahead.

**Snowy Mountains Backpackers** ( ☎ 1800 333 468; www.snowybackpackers.com.au; 7-8 Gippsland St; Jun-Oct Sun-Thu dm $30-42, d $90-120, Fri & Sat dm $35-44, d $90-130) A well-oiled machine with clean rooms, internet (20 minutes for $3) and service with a smile. The way a backpackers should be.

**Lake Jindabyne Hotel/Motel** ( ☎ 1800 646 818; Kosciuszko Rd; d five night with breakfast Sun-Thu $600-675, d two nights with breakfast Fri & Sat $380-495; 🛋 ) A big place by the lake in the centre of town, with a heated pool, spa and sauna. Expect rate decrease in summer.

Other recommendations:

**Banjo Paterson Inn** ( ☎ 1800 046 275; www.banjo patersoninn.com.au; 1 Kosciuszko Rd; d $70-250)

**Jindabyne Holiday Park** ( ☎ 6456 2249; www.jindabyne holidaypark.com.au; Kosciuszko Rd; powered/unpowered sites from $35/$22, add $10 on weekends)

**Troldhaugen Lodge** ( ☎ 6456 2718; 13 Cobbodah St; s/d with breakfast from $50/70)

There are many places offering cheap accommodation in flats, apartments and lodges, but they can fill up quickly. Agents in Jindabyne:

**Alpine Resorts & Travel Centre** ( ☎ 1800 802 315)

**Jindy Real Estate** ( ☎ 1800 020 657)

**Kosciuszko Accommodation Centre** ( ☎ 1800 026 354)

**Snowy Mountains Holiday Centre** ( ☎ 1800 641 064)

**Snowy Mountains Reservations Centre** ( ☎ 1800 020 622)

## Drinking & Eating

Nugget's Crossing on Kosciuszko Rd is a well-stocked shopping centre with a supermarket and numerous places to eat.

**Wrap A Go Go** ( ☎ 6457 1887; Shop 1 Lakeview Plaza, Snowy River Ave; 🕙 lunch & dinner) Up behind Nugget's Crossing, this place does a damn good chilli prawn quesadilla ($17) and similar well-priced fare.

**Banjo Paterson Inn** ( ☎ 1800 046 275; www.banjo patersoninn.com.au; 1 Kosciuszko Rd) This is a flash establishment where locals flock for a piss-up in the main bar or a quiet glass of wine next door at Clancy's bar. It has lake views, accommodation and a restaurant.

**Café Susu** ( ☎ 6456 1503; 8 Gippsland St; mains $12; 🕙 breakfast, lunch & dinner) This is handy to Snowy Mountains Backpackers with reasonably priced curries, stir-fries and pasta. Friday night is sushi night!

## Getting There & Away

**Alpine Express** ( ☎ 6456 7340) has a three-hour bus from Canberra to Jindabyne, which continues on to Thredbo. This bus connects with the Sydney–Canberra bus. The bus stop is outside the visitors centre.

**Greyhound Ski Express** ( ☎ 13 14 99) buses run from Sydney and Canberra to Thredbo, Bullocks Flat Skitube and Jindabyne daily.

**Jindabyne Coaches** ( ☎ 6457 2117) runs buses to Bullocks Flat in winter, and may go as far as Thredbo depending on demand.

**Transborder** ( ☎ 6241 0033) is the main service between Canberra and Jindabyne ($45).

# WEST OF THE SNOWIES

The western slopes of the Snowy Mountains are steeper than on the east, and the area is more intensively farmed, although there's still plenty of bush. The farms and small towns in the area blaze with colour in the autumn when poplars and fruit trees prepare to shed their leaves. It's good touring country with some great little towns.

## Getting There & Around

**CountryLink** ( ☎ 13 22 32) runs a bus from Cootamundra to Gundagai, Tumut, Adelong, Batlow and Tumbarumba daily except Saturdays. At Cootamundra it connects with the Sydney to Melbourne XPT (express) train.

If driving or riding a motorcycle, there are several approaches from the Hume Hwy. The main route, the Snowy Mountains Hwy (18), leaves the Hume about 30km south of Gundagai and takes you to Tumut, Kiandra, Adaminaby and Cooma. Or try the **Snowy Valleys Way** (www.snowyvalleysway.com.au), an alternate tourist route to the Hwy through Gundagai, Tumut and Tumbarumba, then onto Corryong and Beechworth in Victoria, joining the highway again near Wangaratta.

From Albury you can travel on Victoria's Murray Valley Hwy to Corryong, then head across the river to Khancoban for the Alpine Way. From Holbrook on the Hume Hwy, a sealed road runs through to Jingellic and along the river to Corryong. Another sealed road runs from the Hume to Tumbarumba where you can join the winding Elliott Way to get to Mt Selwyn and the Snowy Mountains Hwy at Kiandra.

# TUMUT & AROUND
☎ 02 / pop 6000

Is Tumut a small big town or a big small town? It's hard to say. But it is certainly set in a picturesque valley where, if you've got a car, you can quite happily base yourself for a day or two. It's the closest centre to the northern end of Kosciuszko National Park and home to many pine plantations, orchards and rolling countryside. The **Festival of the Falling Leaf** kicks off on the last weekend in April.

## Information
The **Tumut visitors centre** and **NPWS office** ( ☎ 6947 7025; www.tumut.nsw.gov.au; 5 Adelong Rd; ☉ 9am-5pm) are in the refurbished Old Butter Factory north of the town centre. The **library** ( ☎ 6947 1969; 169 Wynyard St; ☉ 10am-6pm Mon-Fri, 9am-noon Sat) has internet access ($7 per hour).

## Sights & Activities
Tumut is a popular spot for powered hang-gliding and half-hour microlight 'trike' flights; contact **Air Escape** ( ☎ 6947 1159; 8 Twomeys La). **Selwyn Snow & Water** ( ☎ 6947 6225), near the swimming pool on Fitzroy St, hires bikes as well as ski and water-sports gear.

For a tipple, **Boonderoo Wines** ( ☎ 6947 2279; Boonderoo Rd) is a family-run boutique vineyard on the road to Blowering Reservoir. It is open most weekends.

There's a 3km paved **river walk** along the shady bank of the Tumut River (also good for bikes) or stretch your legs strolling to the scenic lookout from the main street (Wynyard St).

**Mountain biking** in Tumut State Forest is becoming popular with more than 7km of constructed single track covering three connected loops. Mundowie Loop (3.3km) and Womboyne Trail (2.3km) are intermediate rides while the steep and rocky GC Mile (1.6km) is for advanced riders. Maps and info are available from the NPWS office. To get to the trailhead car park, head to the western end of Herbert St, and turn off just before the golf course.

The Thomas Boyd Trackhead, part of the **Hume & Hovell Walking Track** (see boxed text, below), is 25km southeast of Tumut on the beautiful Goobarragandra River. It has camping facilities ($5) and is perfect for kayaking, fishing, liloing and wildlife watching.

**Blowering Reservoir**, nearly 20km long, has numerous picnic and camping areas, and the lake is popular for water sports. You can drive or walk up to the top of the 112m-high dam for a good view; gates close at 4pm.

At the southern end of the reservoir is the small town of **Talbingo**, the birthplace of famous author Miles Franklin (*My Brilliant Career*). The surrounding high country is ideal for walks and picnics. West of Tumut, the gorgeous little town of **Adelong**, with its old-fashioned main street, is worth visiting. Stop at **Adelong Falls & Gold Battery** (Tumblong Rd) for a picnic.

## Sleeping & Eating
There are plenty of hotels and just as many holiday parks and camping areas around Tumut. Wynyard St is the place to got for takeaway shops and pub food.

---

### HUME & HOVELL WALKING TRACK

You're bound to see many references to this 440km walking track between Yass and Albury. It follows the historic route taken by explorers Hamilton Hume and William Hovell in their 1824 expedition to Port Phillip Bay (present-day Melbourne).

The six-man outfit took only four months to complete the return journey to Port Phillip, passing to the west of the Snowy Mountains and through the relatively flat plains of Victoria.

The Yass–Albury walk takes about 24 days, winding through numerous state forests along the shores of Lake Burrinjuck and Blowering Reservoir, and close to Wee Jasper, Tumut, Tumbarumba, Lankeys Creek and Woomargama. It's divided into 12 stages with six major trackheads, and there are various side trips and day walks off the main track.

The route is well signposted and there are 16 camp sites along the way. A good resource is *The Hume & Hovell Walking Track Guidebook* (1993), by H Hill.

**Oriental Hotel** ( ☎ 6947 1174; cnr Fitzroy & Wynyard Sts; s $25) Known as The Ourie, this is a good-looking old pub with standard rooms leading onto the big balcony. The owners are friendly too.

**Royal Hotel** ( ☎ 6947 1179; 88 Wynyard St; s/d from $42/55) If you can forgive the pink décor in the main bar, this has good motel-style units and hotel rooms.

**Old Butter Factory Café** ( ☎ 6947 4150; 5 Adelong Rd) Next to the visitors centre, this is a community based café that does good coffee and a classic Aussie hamburger complete with bacon and egg, beetroot and pineapple ($7).

**Coach House Gourmet Eatery** (Russell St; mains $8-10; ☺ breakfast & lunch) Is the pick of the cafés, with excellent coffee, gourmet sandwiches and a couple of tasty hot dishes that change daily.

**Brandy's** ( ☎ 124 Wynyard St; mains $20-25; ☺ dinner) The building is not very special, but this is Tumut's best restaurant, serving mostly steaks and seafood.

## Getting There & Away

**CountryLink** ( ☎ 13 22 32) buses, which run to Cootamundra, Adelong, Gundagai, Batlow and Tumbarumba, stop daily (except Saturday) outside the National Australia Bank on the corner of Russell and Wynyard Sts. **Harvey World Travel** ( ☎ 6947 3055), in the Hub centre on Wynyard St, sells tickets.

There's a mostly unsealed road from Tumut north to Wee Jasper (69km), from where you can get to Yass, and another running east through the Brindabella Range to Canberra (125km).

## BATLOW

☎ 02 / pop 1500

Batlow, on one side of a bowl-shaped valley, is an apple-orchard town. Tourist information for the area can be found at **Springfield Orchard** ( ☎ 6949 1021), just north of town and at **Tumut visitors centre** ( ☎ 6947 7025; www.tumut.nsw.gov.au; 5 Adelong Rd, Tumut; ☺ 9am-5pm).

The trees blossom in October (when there's an Apple Blossom Festival) and the apple harvest starts around mid-March, but there are also stone fruits and cherries, so picking work is usually available from December to May. The best way to find work is to contact **Riverina Community College** ( ☎ 6947 3886; Wynyard Centre, Wynyard St, Tumut; ☺ 9am-5pm Mon-Fri).

Fruit can be savoured at a number of roadside stalls. If you've never seen the inside of an apple-packing factory, **Joyson** ( ☎ 6949 1835; 1 Cottams Rd; tour $3; ☺ Mon-Fri), 6km south of town, is the place for a short, guided tour. Otherwise stop at **Batlow Hotel** ( ☎ 6949 1001; 12 Pioneer St; s/d $25/35) for a beer. It has good honest pub rooms and toast- and coffee-making facilities.

## TUMBARUMBA

☎ 02 / pop 3940

There's a classic Australian bush poem by John O'Brien called *Tumba Bloody Rumba* about a bloke who goes 'shootin' kanga-bloody-roos' here. Once you've read the poem, it's hard to refer to this pretty little town by any other name. Set in a valley, Tumba was first settled by graziers, who wintered their cattle here when the snows came to the high plains. Today, forestry and cold-climate fruit orchards are the major industries but tourism and wine have also made their mark.

The **visitors centre** ( ☎ 6948 3333; 10 Bridge St; ☺ 10am-5pm) is at the southern end of The Parade, the main street. It has details of the area's walks and a small pioneer museum. There's internet access at the **library** ( ☎ 6948 2725; ☺ 1-5pm Tue, 2-5pm Wed-Fri, 10am-noon Sat; per hr $4) in the Bicentennial Gardens on Prince St, and at **Bridson Internet Cafe** ( ☎ 6948 3322; 16 Bridge St; per hr $4).

---

**SOUTHEAST**

### DETOUR: THE ELLIOTT WAY

Ignoring the superstar Alpine Way for a minute, one of the best drives in the Snowy Mountains region is the back road from Tumbarumba to Adaminaby. Take Tooma Rd south out of Tumba for about 18km until you reach a T-junction. Turn left onto the Elliott Way, which will take you through rolling farmland, with Pilot Reef Mountain on your right. You'll know you're in the Kosciuszko National Park when the landscape changes from grassy paddocks to soaring eucalypt forest. The road cuts around and follows the Tumut River, which it crosses at the site of the Tumut 2 power station. From there you climb up and out of the forest. Take a left and you're onto the eerily vacant highlands, a unique and rugged landscape. The road joins the Snowy Mountains Hwy at Kiandra, and from here it's another 40km to Adaminaby.

Anyone looking for **fruit picking work** should check out the noticeboard at Tumbarumba Creek Caravan Park (see below).

**Tumbarumba Rodeo** is held on New Year's Day and **Tumbafest**, a weekend of food, wine and entertainment, is celebrated in early February.

### Sights & Activities

The **Pioneer Women's Hut** ( ☎ 6948 2635; Wagga Rd; 10am-4pm Sat & Sun, from 11am Wed) might sound dire but in fact, it's lauded as one of the most interesting small museums in the country. **Glenburnie Vineyard** ( ☎ 6948 2570; Black Range Rd; ✆ 10am-6pm) is 4km north of town. The cellar is in a renovated shearing shed. On a cold day (Tumba boasts a few), **Old Mason's Cinema** ( ☎ 6948 2950; Winton St; $10), with its modern façade and big comfy seats, brings new and old films to the bush. Out of town, just before the turnoff to Elliott Way, **Paddy's River Flats** is a picture-perfect spot for a picnic and a paddle.

### Sleeping & Eating

**Café Red B&B** ( ☎ 6948 3228; 34 The Parade; s/d $75/90) This place is great value, with cosy timber motel-style rooms and a lavish cooked breakfast included. The café is definitely the hippest in the region, serving imaginative food and great coffee.

**Tumbarumba Motel** ( ☎ 6948 2494; tumbarumbamotelelms@bigpond.com; cnr Albury Close & Mate St; s/d $88/92) Modern and spacious, this friendly motel is ideal for families. It has a good restaurant (entrees $10, mains $25) with a pretty view of town.

**Glenburnie Cottage** ( ☎ 6948 2570; Black Range Rd; s $85, d $95-120) Set amid the vineyard this cute weatherboard house is perfect for a family or group. It has two queen-sized rooms and is equipped with all the essentials.

**Old Mason Cinema Café** ( ☎ 6948 3300; Winton St; snacks $12, mains $24; ✆ lunch & dinner Wed-Sun) Whether or not you're catching a film, this groovy café with an enticing menu and a long list of wines by the glass is the ticket.

#### CAMPING

**Tumbarumba Creek Caravan Park** ( ☎ 6948 3330; www.tumbarumbacreek.com.au; Lauder St; camp sites $12, bunkhouse $14, d cabins from $40) This tidy little park among the trees is backpacker central with a handy noticeboard for fruit-picking jobs and a community atmosphere. The public pool is across the road.

### Getting There & Away

**CountryLink** ( ☎ 13 22 32) buses stop in town. Bookings can be made at the newsagency on The Parade. From Tumbarumba, roads run west to the Hume Hwy, north to Tumut, east to the Snowy Mountains Hwy, and south to Khancoban, the Alpine Way and Corryong (in Victoria). The ski slopes at Mt Selwyn are about an hour away on the Elliott Way. You'll need chains to drive there in winter.

## KHANCOBAN

☎ 02 / pop 310

Originally constructed by the Snowy Mountains Authority to house 7000 construction workers, Khancoban is now a sleepy hollow with good facilities (ie a public pool) considering the decreasing population.

There's a **NPWS office** ( ☎ 6076 9373; ✆ 8.30am-noon & 1-4pm) where you can buy park entry permit and get information.

Khancoban Pondage and the Swampy Plains River that runs through it provide top-notch swimming spots. In summer, head to 'the beach' – Khancoban's very own sandy **swimming spot**. It's near the pondage boat ramp.

**Live Adrenalin** ( ☎ 1300 791 793; www.adrenalin.com.au) organises adventure activities around Khancoban. A one-day white-water rafting trip costs $220 and a two-day camping trip costs $440. **Rapid Descents** ( ☎ 1800 637 486; www.rapiddescents.com.au) has caving, abseiling and rafting trips at similar prices.

**Lakeside Caravan Resort** ( ☎ 6076 9488; www.klcr.com.au; powered/unpowered sites $15/20, vans $28, cabins $44), by the Khancoban Dam, is a well-equipped place with ski equipment, snow chains and boats for hire. On the hill, **Queens Cottage B&B** ( ☎ 6076 9033; Pendergast St; s/d with bathroom $95/110) has modern and tasteful hillside cabins with clean bathrooms and views across the beautiful valley.

**Alpine Inn Hotel/Motel** ( ☎ 6076 9471; trout@alpineinn.com.au; Alpine Way; s/d from $55/65; 🍺 ) has good basic accommodation and counter meals and the adjoining **Pickled Parrot Restaurant** ( ☎ 6076 9471; Alpine Way; ✆ breakfast, lunch & dinner) has retro décor and bistro food.

The **General Store** ( ☎ 6076 9559; Mitchell Ave) has good-value takeaway food including a monstrous chicken schnitzel ($5).

### Getting There & Away

There are no regular bus services to Khancoban. If you're heading towards Albury, you can grab a ride in the mail truck, which leaves the post office at 12.30pm weekdays.

# THE HUME HIGHWAY

Like all big swathes of four-lane bitumen, the Hume Hwy, running nearly 900km from Sydney to Melbourne, is somewhat lacking in aesthetic. Sure visitors will spot some of Australia's most beloved animals – kangaroos, wombats and koala – but they're likely to be roadkill. Despite this, the highway is easily navigable, and an effortless way to traverse the country by car. It also provides an opportunity to visit small towns where a true picture of Australia, outside the big cities, can be seen.

Much of the highway is speed limited to 110km/h. Due to increasing death tolls on Australian roads, this speed limit is rigorously implemented with speed cameras and roadside police cars. Drivers will do well to take heed for safety reasons but also for the back pocket. Speeding fines are hefty.

## GOULBURN & AROUND
☎ 02 / pop 27,200

Goulburn lays claim to the title of Australia's first inland city and it has the history and architecture to prove it. While the old town centre is relatively peaceful and worth a stroll, the city's food scene has picked up a notch and alfresco dining and lattes are becoming the norm.

Backpackers looking for canning work should know that this is not the Goulburn of Goulburn Valley canned fruit fame.

### Orientation & Information

The main shopping street in Goulburn is Auburn St.

The **Goulburn visitors centre** (☎ 4823 4492/1800 353 646; www.igoulburn.com; 201 Sloane St; ☺ 9am-5pm), opposite Belmore Park, has regional information, free internet access and local produce.

### Sights

First stop should be the **Old Goulburn Brewery** (☎ 4821 6071; 23 Bungonia Rd; adult/child/concession $6/3/4; ☺ tours 11am & 3pm) where you can see the workings of a brewery but, more importantly, sip on a beer. Accommodation is also available (see right).

The heritage bicycle-tour map takes riders (or drivers on a wet day) to a stack of places

including the **Goulburn War Memorial lookout**, and past the ominous **Goulburn Correctional Centre**, which holds some of the most notorious criminals in NSW (including serial backpacker murderer Ivan Milat).

The three-storey-high **Big Merino** (Cowper St; admission free; ☺ 8am-8pm) should be put out to pasture. It is soon to be relocated next to the Hume Hwy where all things 'big' belong.

About 40km southeast of Goulburn and abutting Morton National Park, **Bungonia State Conservation Area** (☎ 4844 4277; Lookdown Rd) has a dramatic forested gorge and some deep caves ideal for abseiling. Contact **Abseiling Adventures Goulburn** (☎ 0409 438 503; www.abseilingadventures .com.au; 11 Mannifera Place). (If Goulburn's five-year drought breaks, canoeing also gets a thumbs-up). **Wombeyan Caves** (☎ 4843 5976; www .jenolancaves.org.au) are part of the Jenolan Caves limestone system but are cheaper than tours of the main caves, with smaller group tours. Follow the Tourist Drive 13 signs via Taralga.

### Festivals & Events

The **Australian Blues Music Festival** (www.australian bluesfestival.com.au) kicks off in the second week of February, the **Irish Music Festival** is in the second week of June and **Taralga Annual Australia Day Rodeo** (www.argylecountry.com.au/taralgarodeo) is on the last weekend of January.

### Sleeping

**Tattersall's Hotel** (☎ 4821 3088; 76 Auburn St; dm $20) This is as close as you'll get to a backpackers. The rooms upstairs are basic – there are four bunks to a room, but most likely you'll have a room to yourself.

**Goulburn Brewery** (☎ 4821 6071; 23 Bungonia Rd; per person $44) This is the real deal with lumpy mattresses and ageing furniture in a terrace of old brick houses once used to accommodate brewery workers. It has seven guest rooms with a mix-match of beds.

**Mike's Manor** (☎ 4822 8414/0417 462 664; www .mikesmanor.com; 197 Braidwood Rd; s/d/f $70/80/120) Owned by a Formula 3 racing driver, this is *the* place to get the lowdown on the local motorsport (Wakefield Park is the nearby racing circuit). It's well kept with clean, tidy motel-style rooms and a sociable lounge, suited to backpackers, couples and families alike.

**Mandelson's** (☎ 4821 0707; www.mandelsons.com.au; 160 Sloane St; s/d with breakfast from $120/130) A charming and luxurious B&B in a restored heritage building.

## Eating & Drinking

**Greengrocer Café** ( ☎ 4821 0033; 37 Clifford St; ☯ break-fast & lunch) This innovative café with an eclectic mix of stools, couches and comfy chairs has good coffee, local produce and a tasty chalked-up menu. Breakfast starts at 6am and dinner is available Thursday and Friday evening.

**Paragon Café** ( ☎ 4821 3566; 174 Auburn St; mains from $9; ☯ breakfast, lunch & dinner) When every other café on Auburn St is closed, the Paragon's lights still shine. It is licensed and has reasonable pasta dishes ($11).

**Sasso Pizza & Bar** ( ☎ 4822 8564; 173 Bourke St; mains $18; ☯ lunch Sat & Sun, dinner Wed-Sun) This is Goulburn's best-kept secret. It's a funky little place with an edgy cosmopolitan ambience. Traditional Italian pizzas and organic wood-fired bread are just the start.

**Goulburn Club** ( ☎ 4821 2043; 19 Market St) If you're over 25 and enjoy live music and boutique beer, this place is staffed by volunteers, has art on the walls and is a well-known local hangout. Thursdays is blues night.

## Getting There & Away

**Greyhound** ( ☎ 13 14 99) buses between Goulburn and Adelaide (from $138), via Canberra ($15) and Melbourne (from $81), stop at the service station at the southern entrance to the city. **Murrays** ( ☎ 13 22 51) also run buses three times a week to Canberra ($21) and Wollongong ($28), and **Fearnes** ( ☎ 1800 029 918) has daily services to Wagga Wagga ($41) and Sydney ($53, stopping outside the courthouse).

Trains to Sydney ($30) and Melbourne ($104) stop here daily. The **CountryLink Travel Centre** ( ☎ 02-4827 1485; ☯ 9am-4.45pm Mon-Fri) is at the train station. It also serves as the booking office for buses to Canberra and to Sydney.

## YASS

☎ 02 / pop 12,940

Yass is a pretty place. It's quiet (thanks to the highway bypass) but atmospheric with a wide main street (Comur St), shops and pubs of the wide-veranda variety, and heritage buildings. You'll see alfresco dining on the footpaths at lunchtime and big sun umbrellas promoting good coffee.

## Orientation & Information

The Yass Valley Way (the old highway) becomes Comur St, then Laidlaw St as it passes through town. **Yass visitors centre** ( ☎ 6226 2557;

tourism@yass.nsw.gov.au, Comur St; ☯ 9am 4.30pm Mon-Fri, to 4pm Sat & Sun) is in Coronation Park on the Sydney side of town.

**Yass Library** (Banjo Paterson Park, Meehan St; 9.30am-5.30pm Mon-Wed & Fri, 9.30am-7pm Thu, 10am-1pm Sat) has free internet access and Yass visitors centre is planning to have access also.

## Sights

Next to the visitors centre, the **Hamilton Hume Museum** ( ☎ 6226 2700; adult/child $2/1; ☯ 10am-4pm Tue, Wed, Sat & Sun summer) has a model reconstruction of the town in the 1890s. Hume's house (1835), **Cooma Cottage** ( ☎ 6226 1470; adult/child $4/2; 10am-4pm Wed-Mon), is on the Yass Valley Way on the Sydney side of town. **Riverbank Park** is a great place for a picnic or a quiet sit by the river. Check out the **Aboriginal murals** on the toilet blocks and underneath the bridge.

## Festivals & Events

**Yass Valley Festival** (www.yassvalley.nsw.gov.au) is held at Riverbank Park on the third weekend in November each year; **Yass Picnic Race Day** is held on the first Saturday in March (see the boxed text, p314); and the **Yass Rodeo and Ute show** is held in mid-November. Details for all events can be found at the visitors centre.

## Sleeping & Eating

There is a broad range of accommodation available in and around Yass, from fine old B&Bs and guesthouses to hotels, motels and caravan parks. **Yass visitors centre** can provide a complete list of accommodation and prices.

**Globe B&B** ( ☎ 6226 3680; www.globe.com.au; 70 Rossi St; s/d/f $90/120/150) A lovely old National Trust-classified guesthouse in a restored Victorian hotel in the middle of town. The owner has immaculate taste.

**Kerrowgair** ( ☎ 6226 4932; www.kerrowgair.com.au; 24 Grampian St; d with breakfast from $130) Another National Trust-listed building set in ample gardens on a hill overlooking the town.

**Galutzi** ( ☎ 6226 5261; Meehan St; sandwiches $5-8; ☯ 9am-5pm Mon-Fri, to 3pm Sat) Probably Yass' hippest café – there's a plethora of gourmet sandwich ingredients to choose from and the coffee is excellent.

**Café Dolcetto** ( ☎ 6226 1277; Comur St; sandwiches $4-7, mains $15; ☯ breakfast & lunch Mon-Sat) A cosy café with outdoor tables for summer and a log fire in winter. The food is fresh without being too fancy.

SOUTHEAST

---

**PICNIC RACES**

Care for a bet on the nags? Here's a tip: get along to a picnic race day. Held annually in a large number of country towns, these community race meets are the lifeblood of the rural social calendar and a bloody good bash for everyone else. They are traditionally held on a Friday and are the only day of the year when farmers and graziers feel at liberty to swap their work attire for a pair of polished RM Williams boots and a chambray shirt. Today, town and city folk are cottoning on to the fun and some picnic race days are held on a Saturday.

Expect to see a fraternity of frocked-up women gathered around gourmet picnic hampers, Akubra-donned men downing cold beer at the outdoor bar and a bustling betting ring. Some tracks are better than others (Yass' Marchmont track has a back straight hidden from public view, prompting endless rumours of jockey-swapping), but all of them kick up enough dust to raise a whoop or whimper from the barracking-mad punters in the (often) not-so-grand stands. Pluck that little dress out of the backpack and try your luck with Fashions on the Field.

Race days that coincide with Melbourne's November Spring Carnival are particularly good fun. See the racing diary at www.racingnsw.com.au or contact visitors centres.

---

## Getting There & Away

**V/Line** ( ☎ 13 61 96) buses heading to Melbourne stop at the visitors centre; heading to Sydney they stop at the NRMA garage across the road. **Firefly** ( ☎ 1800 631 164) and **Greyhound** ( ☎ 13 14 99) daily services to Sydney (from $42) and Melbourne (from $73) stop at the Caltex petrol station at the southern entrance into town. **Transborder** ( ☎ 6241 0033) and **Fearnes** ( ☎ 1800 029 918) have daily services between Yass and Canberra ($16). They leave from Rossi St. **CountryLink Trains** ( ☎ 13 22 32) between Sydney and Melbourne stop daily at Yass Junction, 2km north of town. Some bus services can be booked at the NRMA garage.

## WEE JASPER

☎ 02 / pop 80

About 55km southwest of Yass following Tourist Drive No 7, Wee Jasper (www .weejasper.org) is a small village in a beautiful valley near the southern end of Burrinjuck Dam. It's a favourite getaway for the Canberra weekender set, but during the week you may have the valley to yourself (and the 80 or so locals).

You can join the **Hume & Hovell Walking Track** here, and visit the limestone **Careys Cave** ( ☎ 6227 9622; www.weejaspercaves.com; adult/child $11/7), open Friday to Monday in the afternoon and Wednesday on school holidays, but call first to confirm. There is a store and a pub, and fuel is available.

The **Stables** ( ☎ 6227 9619; Yass-Wee Jasper Rd; cabins $50) has good-sized cabins, some with open fireplace and kitchens. Ask at the **General Store**

( ☎ 6227 9640) for more accommodation options or contact the **ranger** ( ☎ 6227 9626) for camping details.

The road from Yass has an 8km unsealed section but it's usually pretty good. Continuing southwest to Tumut, the road deteriorates for the climb out of the valley and is not recommended for campervans or hire cars. Another unsealed road cuts across to Canberra. Both these roads are OK when dry.

## MURRUMBATEMAN

☎ 02 / pop 500

On the Barton Hwy southeast toward Canberra, Murrumbateman is a small town that has recently been hit with the gastronomy stick. Locals say the name hails from colonial days when punters would ask Bateman, a local publican, for 'more rum' but today they're likely to be asking for more wine. The area has a number of cool-climate wineries open for sales and tastings – and with good wine comes great food. The **Murrumbateman Moving Feast**, at the end of September, celebrates the region's top-notch wine and cuisine.

**Schonegg Country Guesthouse and Café** ( ☎ 6227 0344; www.schonegg.com.au; 381 Hillview Dr; s/d $140/160; breakfast, lunch & dinner) is the pick of this wine region with six sleek contemporary bedrooms. Up the road, **Helm Winery** ( ☎ 6227 5953; www .helmwines.com.au; Butts Rd; 10am-5pm Thu-Mon) is the granddaddy of the region's wineries and has a cute weatherboard tasting room. **Clonakilla Winery** ( ☎ 6227 5877; Crisps Lane; 10am-5pm) specialises in Shiraz Viognier with access via the Murrumbateman Rd turnoff in the centre of town.

# GUNDAGAI

☎ 02 / pop 2500

Gundagai, on the Murrumbidgee River 398km from Sydney, is very small-town in a relaxed easy-going kind of way. It is one of the more interesting small towns along (or bypassed by) the Hume Hwy.

The **visitors centre** ( ☎ 6944 0250; www.gundagai.nsw .gov.au; 249 Sheridan St; ☑ 8am-5pm Mon-Fri, from 9am Sat & Sun) is on the grand main street and has plenty of info on B&Bs and farmstays in the area.

## Sights

The **Prince Alfred Bridge** (closed to traffic, but you can walk it) is the star of Gundagai's sights. It crosses the flood plain of the Murrumbidgee River and provides a perfect spot for breathing in the country air.

At the visitors centre, take a peek at **Rusconi's Marble Masterpiece**, a cathedral model, and grab a walking map of the local **heritage**.

In town, **Green Dog Gallery** ( ☎ 6944 1479; Sheridan St; ☑ 10.30am-5.30pm Thu-Sat) and **Lannigan Abbey Art Gallery** ( ☎ 6944 2852; www.laniganabbey.com.au; 72 First Ave; ☑ 9am-5pm) are worth a bo peep. Lannigan is also a B&B (double rooms are $175).

The **Mt Parnassus lookout** has picnic facilities and good views over the town; take the steep walk (or drive) up Hanley St.

About 8km east of town, the **Dog on the Tuckerbox** is Gundagai's most famous monument. A sculpture of a dog from a 19th-century bush ballad, it's well-known along the Hume Highway, but most people will be disappointed to find the only thing worth stopping for is petrol.

## Festivals & Events

Held in mid-November, the **Snake Gully Cup** is Gundagai's famed annual race day (see the boxed text, opposite). It coincides with the **Dog on the Tuckerbox** festival. The **Festival of the Turning Wave** (www.turningwave.org.au) is a four-day Irish festival in mid-September.

## Sleeping & Eating

**Star Hotel** ( ☎ 6944 1030; Mount St; s/d $25/45) This typical country town pub is slightly cheaper than the Criterion, and a continental breakfast is included in the rate. It's in the heart of town on the main street.

**Criterion Hotel** ( ☎ 6944 1048; 172 Sheridan St; s/d with breakfast $35/55) The closest visitors will get to backpacker-style accommodation. It has reasonable pub rooms, a lively public bar and a rear beer garden.

**Poet's Recall** ( ☎ 6944 1777; poets.recall@bigpond.com; cnr West & Punch Sts; s/d $75/95; ☑ ) Touches like slate bathrooms and comfy furniture make this the best motel in town. Locals also rate the restaurant, which has an Irish chef.

**Old Bridge Inn** ( ☎ 6944 4250; 1 Tumut St) On the south of town, the Inn is a lovely old building with B&B accommodation. Ring ahead for availability and room prices. The excellent restaurant has menu favourites such as filet mignon ($25), salt and pepper calamari ($7) and chicken schnitzel ($13).

**Gundagai Tourist Park** ( ☎ 6944 1620; Junee Rd; camp sites unpowered/powered $19/22, cabins $44) Near the swimming pool, this place has well-presented vans and cabins.

Other recommendations:

**Coach Lamp Café** ( ☎ 6944 4295; Sheridan St; ☑ breakfast & lunch) Near the Arts & Craft Emporium, it's a tad twee but has surprisingly good coffee.

**Niagara Café** ( ☎ 6944 1109; 124 Sheridan St; ☑ breakfast, lunch & dinner) Steak meals cost $14 and it's licensed.

---

### ALTERNATIVE STOPS

The Hume Highway is notoriously long and boring, but for an enjoyable snapshot of country Australia, traditional old pubs can give travellers an insight into local life. The **Commercial Hotel** (Map p295; ☎ 6227 6008; Leake St), just south of the Yass turnoff at Bowning, has B&B rooms ($70) that open onto the rickety old veranda, cook-your-own barbies out the back and, of course, a classic old bar complete with a 'beer and bullshit' corner. South past the Gundagai turnoff, 100km away, you'll recognise the **Tumblong Hotel** (Map p295; ☎ 6944 9202; Hume Hwy) by the Toohey's beer truck that sits atop the corrugated iron roof. Pop in here for a cold beer in a public bar cluttered with Australiana or stretch your legs by the open fire in the lounge. Near Albury, the **Kinross Woolshed Hotel** (Map p295; ☎ 6043 1155; 47 Old Sydney Rd, Thurgoona; ☑ 10am-late) was once a working woolshed and it still retains the original round timber supports and corrugated iron walls. But for the pool table and icy cold beer you'd think you were about to give the shears a whirl.

SOUTHEAST

## Getting There & Away

The tourist office sells bus tickets for the services that depart from outside. **Greyhound** ( ☎ 13 14 99) buses go to Melbourne and Sydney (from $42) via Canberra (from $67), and **V/Line** ( ☎ 13 61 96) buses also stop here between Melbourne and Canberra. **CountryLink** ( ☎ 13 22 32) runs buses north to Cootamundra ($9) and south to Tumut ($7) and Tumbarumba ($21). **Fearnes** ( ☎ 1800 029 918) has buses from Wagga to Sydney ($53) via Gundagai ($25).

## ALBURY

☎ 02 / pop 42,000

Albury is a major regional centre on the Murray River, just below the big Hume Weir. Outsiders often refer to it as Albury-Wodonga because its Victorian neighbour is just across the river, but a certain amount of cross-border snobbery will have New South Wales locals putting you straight: 'the former is all that's required'.

After years of lobbying, the locals have finally lost their battle for a bypass and the city is about to be bisected by a fully fledged Hume Highway (as opposed to a main road). For travellers, this means Albury is the most convenient stopover between Melbourne and Sydney with all the necessary amenities (including good coffee).

It's also a good base for trips to the Riverina, Snowy Mountains and Victorian wineries and high country, but that's not to say it's the hole in the doughnut – the river, among

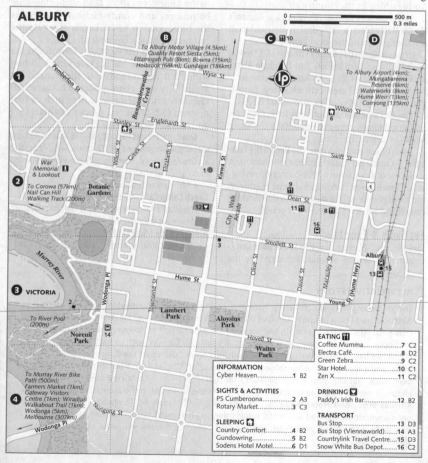

**ALBURY**

0 — 500 m
0 — 0.3 miles

| INFORMATION | |
| --- | --- |
| Cyber Heaven.................1 B2 | |

| SIGHTS & ACTIVITIES | |
| --- | --- |
| PS Cumberoona.................2 A3 | |
| Rotary Market.................3 C3 | |

| SLEEPING ⌂ | |
| --- | --- |
| Country Comfort.............4 B2 | |
| Gundowring.................5 B2 | |
| Sodens Hotel Motel.........6 D1 | |

| EATING ⊞ | |
| --- | --- |
| Coffee Mumma....................7 C2 | |
| Electra Café....................8 D2 | |
| Green Zebra....................9 C2 | |
| Star Hotel....................10 C1 | |
| Zen X....................11 C2 | |

| DRINKING ⊡ | |
| --- | --- |
| Paddy's Irish Bar.................12 B2 | |

| TRANSPORT | |
| --- | --- |
| Bus Stop....................13 D3 | |
| Bus Stop (Viennaworld).......14 A3 | |
| Countrylink Travel Centre....15 D3 | |
| Snow White Bus Depot........16 C2 | |

To Albury Motor Village (4.5km); Quality Resort Siesta (5km); Ettamogah Pub (8km); Bowna (15km); Holbrook (68km); Gundagai (186km)

Guinea St

To Albury Airport (4km); Mungabareena Reserve (6km); Waterworks (8km); Hume Weir (13km); Corryong (135km)

Pemberton St

Bungambrawatha Creek

Wyse St

Wilson St

Stanley St

Englehardt St

Swift St

Wilcox St

Creek St

Elizabeth St

Kiewa St

War Memorial & Lookout

To Corowa (57km); Nail Can Hill Walking Track (200m)

Botanic Gardens

Dean St

City Walk Arcade

Smollett St

Murray River

Olive St

David St

Macauley St

Young St

Albury

St (Hume Hwy)

VICTORIA

Wodonga Pl

Hume St

To River Pool (200m)

Townsend St

Lambert Park

Aloysius Park

Hovell St

Noreuil Park

Waites Park

To Murray River Bike Path (500m); Farmers Market (1km); Gateway Visitors Centre (1km); Wiradjuri Walkabout Trail (1km); Wodonga (5km); Melbourne (307km)

Nungong St

Wodonga Pl

other attractions, provides a handy diversion on a long car trip.

## Orientation & Information

The long Lincoln Causeway over the Murray River's flood plain links Albury with Wodonga. Central Albury is a reasonably compact grid, but the city sprawls northwards into the residential suburb of Lavington. Dean St is the main shopping strip.

The **Gateway visitors centre** ( ☎ 1300 796 222; www.destinationalbury/wodonga.com.au; ◷ 9am-5pm) is part of a large 'island' complex on the Lincoln Causeway on the Victorian side of the river.

**Cyber Heaven** ( ☎ 6023 4320; 505 Kiewa St; per hr $9; ◷ 10am-6pm Mon-Fri, 10am-2pm Sat) has internet access.

## Sights & Activities

The paddle steamer **PS Cumberoona** ( ☎ 6021 1113; adult/child $16/8), moored on the river behind Noreuil Park, has one-hour weekend trips between October and April.

For a cleansing river swim, turn right into Noreuil Park just before the Lincoln Causeway where there's a swimming **pool** in the river or try the **loop**, a magical 20-minute float (on your back) around a big bend that ends close to where you began. Start below the Lincoln Causeway's Union Bridge or anywhere near there. Finish just before you reach the Cumberoona paddle steamer or its concrete mooring ramp.

Just out of Albury, towards the airport, turn right to **Mungabareena Reserve** or continue 1km to the **Waterworks** for two more picturesque swimming options.

Near the visitors centre, a paved **bike & walking track** starts at Union Bridge and follows the winding river to Wodonga. For more river action, go **canoeing**. Popular day- and half-day trips begin at Mungabareena Reserve and end at Noreuil Park. The visitors centre has information on hiring canoes.

If the wineries and food producers of Victoria aren't on your itinerary, the **Farmers Market**, held every second Saturday near the visitors centre, is an excellent means of scoping the local food scene. On Sunday mornings, the **Rotary Market**, in the tax office car park on Smollett St, is also worth browsing.

The **Botanic Gardens** (4 hectares), at the northern end of Wodonga Place, are old, formal and beautiful; somewhere the kids can run wild while mums and dads sink a tinnie. The **Nail Can Hill Walking Track** rambles over the

steep, bush-covered ridges on the western side of town or head up Dean St to the **war memorial** (with a good view) and pick up the trail there. The visitors centre has a map.

The **Wiradjuri Walkabout trail** is an easy interpretive trail around Gateway Island starting from the visitors centre.

## Festivals & Events

The **Albury-Wodonga Food & Wine Festival** (www .hmfb.org) is on in late September/early October, the Aboriginal **Ngan Girra (Bogong Moth) Festival** is held at the Mungabareena Reserve in late November and the **Albury Gold Cup** ( ☎ 6025 1333) is a big social event at the end of March (see the boxed text, p314).

## Sleeping

**Albury Motor Village YHA** ( ☎ 6040 2999; www.yha.com .au; 372 Wagga Rd; powered sites $20, dm/d $22/50, d cabins $62; P ⊠ ) About 4.5km north of the centre, this is a tidy park with a range of cabins, vans and backpacker beds in clean dorms.

**Sodens Hotel Motel** ( ☎ 6021 2400; cnr David & Wilson Sts; r $45-60) Two blocks from the main street, this is an old-style pub with a grandiose veranda. It has 50 rooms within stumbling distance of the beer garden.

**Quality Resort Siesta** ( ☎ 6025 4555; www.siesta .com.au; 416 Wagga Rd; r from $70-270; P ⊠ ) Possibly the most garish-cum-luxurious option. This is a vaguely Mexican-themed 4½-star resort with a bewildering array of options – spa, sauna, steam room, solarium, gym, a couple of decent restaurants and the Cantina Bar.

**Country Comfort** ( ☎ 6021 5366; www.countrycomfort .com.au; cnr Dean & Elizabeth Sts; $99-200; P ⊠ ) Travelling salespeople head straight for this tall semicircular landmark at the western end of Dean St. There's a decent cocktail bar here and live music on weekends.

**Gundowring** ( ☎ 6041 4437; thudson@albury.net.au; 621 Stanley St; s/d with breakfast $110/130; P ) The best B&B near the centre. It's in a gorgeous Federation house a short walk from the botanical gardens.

## Eating

The Albury eating scene has really picked up recently – Dean St is a long strip of takeaways, cafés, restaurants and plenty of nightlife.

**Electra Café** ( ☎ 6021 7200; 3/441 Dean St; ◷ breakfast, lunch & dinner Wed-Sun) This place has excellent coffee and a sunny footpath eating area. The poached eggs and grilled country mushrooms

**SOUTHEAST**

is a breakfast worth pulling off the highway for ($13).

**Green Zebra** ( ☎ 6023 1100; 484 Dean St; 🕑 8am-6.30pm Mon-Fri; 8am-4pm Sat) The homemade pasta is always a winner. This modern café with a gourmet approach to food makes fresh fettuccini and tasty tagliatelle on site.

**Coffee Mumma** ( ☎ 6041 2600; 5/501 Olive St; 🕑 7.30am-4.30pm Mon-Fri, 8am-2pm Sat) This relatively new café does the best coffee in town and has a handy footpath takeaway service area for travellers who don't want to stop for long.

**Star Hotel** ( ☎ 6021 2745; 502 Guinea St) This local favourite has a huge beer garden out the back and a front bar with pool tables where the gregarious owners will keep you entertained. It's a little off the main drag but worth the walk down Olive St.

Other recommendations:

**Paddy's Irish Bar** ( ☎ 6021 3599; 491 Kiewa St) Your typical Irish theme-bar.

**Zen X** ( ☎ 6023 6455; 467 Dean St; mains from $15; 🕑 lunch & dinner) Does excellent sushi and *teppanyaki*.

## Getting There & Away

The airport is 10 minutes out of town on Borella Rd. **Rex** ( ☎ 13 17 13) flies to Sydney and Melbourne. **Brindabella** ( ☎ 1300 668 824) flies to Canberra.

Long-distance buses running on the Hume Hwy between Sydney and Melbourne stop at the train station. Most also stop at Viennaworld (a petrol station/diner) across from Noreuil Park. You can book buses at the **CountryLink Travel Centre** ( ☎ 6041 9555; 🕑 8.30am-5pm Mon-Fri, 9.30am-4.30pm Sat & Sun) at the train station.

**Greyhound** ( ☎ 13 14 99) has coaches to Melbourne (from $43, four hours), Wagga Wagga (from $33, two hours) and Sydney (from $65, nine hours). **CountryLink** ( ☎ 13 22 32) runs to Echuca ($85) in Victoria via several towns in the southern Riverina three times a week. CountryLink buses leave from the train sta-

tion bus stop. **V/Line** ( ☎ 13 61 96) coaches run to Mildura.

**XPTs** (express trains) running between Sydney ($98) and Melbourne ($64) stop here. If you're travelling between the two capital cities ($125), it's much cheaper to stop over in Albury on a through ticket than to buy two separate tickets (it's sometimes even cheaper to fly). **V/Line** runs a cheaper, daily train to Melbourne (from $50).

## Getting Around

If you need a lift to some of the outlying areas, **Snow White Bus Depot** ( ☎ 6021 4368; 474 David St) is the pick-up point for mail, freight and passenger buses that run just about everywhere (eventually).

## AROUND ALBURY

About 8km north, the lopsided **Ettamogah Pub** ( ☎ 6026 2366; www.ettamogah.com; Burma Rd, Tabletop), off the Hume Hwy towards Sydney, is a real-life re-creation of a famous Aussie cartoon pub by Albury-born Ken Maynard.

Follow Borella Rd past the airport northeast to the **Hume Weir** for water sports and swimming.

About 15km further north at **Bowna** there's a turn-off to **Wymah** (22km on) where you can cross by vehicle ferry to the Murray Valley Hwy on the other side of the river. Alternatively wind your way around the unsealed river road to **Jingellic**, a picturesque little place on the Murray River. It has a great pub and a basic but bloody good camping spot. Give the rope swing a go.

Further up the highway **Holbrook Farm Hosts** ( ☎ 0407 303 138; $110 per person) is a collective of local property owners who offer bed and breakfast on a farm. Be welcomed into local homesteads as part of the family, enjoy gourmet cuisine and help round up the cattle (or at least watch the professionals do it). You'll recognise Holbrook by the huge submarine in the main street. Ahoy!

# South Coast

If it's off-road rugged beauty you're after, the compass should be pointed squarely in this direction. The spectacular south coast, stretching 400km by road to the Victorian border, retains its remarkable undiscovered air. By detouring, often only slightly, off the main roads into national parks, it's possible to find secluded beaches, remote mountaintops and rugged bushland where isolation reigns supreme. Have a sense of adventure in tow!

In between these spots of solitude, small towns and historic villages hug the coastline and the hinterland. In some cases urban sprawl is an eyesore, but in most, there's a surprising mix of coastal hamlet hip and cosmopolitan cool. A decent coffee can be found in small, blink-and-you'll-miss-it towns, wineries have spread their green leaves over the countryside and sea-changing city chefs have transported their culinary expertise here.

If the latte set is exactly what you're trying to escape, there are ways and means. Cheap, fresh oysters and seafood are as common as vegemite sandwiches, and campervanners and campers can purchase them roadside to eat in nature's very own dining room – on the picnic tables and barbecue areas that dot the beaches, headlands and lookouts. Some of the best camping spots are at basic bush camps run by the National Parks and Wildlife Service (NPWS).

Despite these places being busy during school holidays and at Christmas time, especially around Batemans Bay and Kiama, at other times you're likely to have the wildlife and the beach all to yourself. And when you're not eating or sleeping it's all about getting off your behind. Eco tourism is definitely in and there's a myriad of swimming, surfing, whale-watching and diving opportunities, particularly in the crystal waters around Merimbula and Jervis Bay. And, of course, the staggeringly beautiful national parks are out there, waiting to be explored.

## HIGHLIGHTS

- Take a boat tour to see the wildlife near Narooma on **Montague Island** (p335)
- Walk or drive across the new Sea Cliff Bridge at **Wollongong** (p323)
- Dive or snorkel in the coastal waters of **Merimbula** (p339)
- Flash-camp in a luxury bush tent at **Jervis Bay** (p329)
- Munch fresh oysters at **Pambula** (p341)
- Potter around in a houseboat from **Batemans Bay** (p333)
- Whale-watch at Twofold Bay in **Eden** (p341) during October and November
- Climb to the top of Pigeon House Mountain near **Ulladulla** (p331)

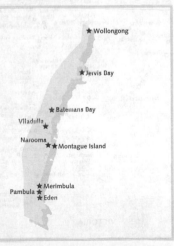

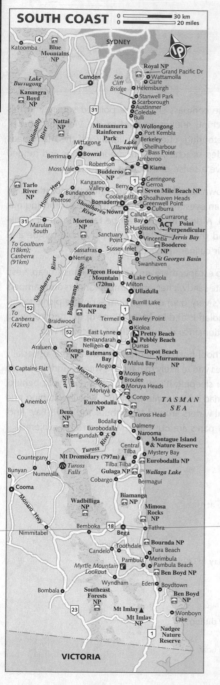

**SOUTH COAST**

VICTORIA

## Getting There & Around

### BUS

Nowra-based **Premier Motor Service** (☎ 13 34 10) has a jump-on jump-off service from Sydney to Eden ($66) and on to Melbourne($79). Two buses a day go as far as Eden.

**Sapphire Coast Express** (☎ 1800 812 135) runs from Batemans Bay through to Melbourne on Tuesday and Friday only; and **Murrays** (☎ 13 22 51) has daily services between Batemans Bay and Narooma ($23), Batemans Bay and Canberra ($24), and Canberra and Narooma ($37).

### CAR & MOTORCYCLE

There is no doubt, the south coast is best explored with your own transport. Princes Hwy starts at Sydney's George St and continues all the way to Adelaide via Melbourne. It's known as the coastal route, but in fact the highway runs a little way inland. Hence, along the length of this route there are turn-offs and scenic routes to interesting places, both on the coast and in the Great Dividing Range, where there's an almost unbroken chain of superb national parks and state forests. It's a longer, slower route between Sydney and Melbourne than the Hume Hwy, but it's infinitely more interesting.

# WOLLONGONG & AROUND

☎ 02 / pop 257,000

Wollongong, 80km south of Sydney, has the best of both worlds. The population (it's the state's third-largest city) is big enough to support a host of restaurants and bars, arts, culture and entertainment while its position, sitting pretty on the Illawarra coast, means residents still enjoy the laidback beachside lifestyle that cities such as Sydney can't compete with.

In recent years, the city's reputation as being home of the biggest steel industry in Australia has thankfully lost its sheen. Instead the stunning natural beauty of the area is attracting attention. There are 17 patrolled beaches, all unique, and a spectacular sandstone escarpment that runs from Royal National Park south past Wollongong and Port Kembla. The combination makes for a host of outdoor activities: excellent surf, safe beaches, bushwalks and sky-high activities to name a few. The opening of the impressive Grand Pacific Drive (see the boxed text, p323) is also attracting deserved attention.

## Orientation & Information

Crown St is the main street. Between Kembla and Keira Sts is a two-block pedestrian mall. Keira St is part of the Princes Hwy. Through-traffic bypasses the city on the Southern Fwy.

The **Wollongong visitors centre** ( ☎ 4227 5545/1800 240 737; www.tourismwollongong.com; 93 Crown St) can book accommodation. There's a **NPWS office** ( ☎ 4225 1455; 4/55 Kembla St; ☼ 8.30am-4.30pm Mon-Fri) and you can jump online at **Network Café** ( ☎ 4228 8686; upstairs, 157 Crown St; per hr $4; ☼ 10am-6pm Mon-Wed, to 9pm Thu, to 4pm Sun).

## Sights & Activities

Wollongong's fishing fleet is based at the southern end of the harbour, **Belmore Basin**. There's a fishing cooperative here (with a fish market and a couple of cafés) and an 1872 lighthouse on the point. Nearby, on the headland, is the newer **Breakwater Lighthouse**.

A bird's eye view of the coastline is perhaps the best. **Sydney Hang Gliding Centre** ( ☎ 4294 4294; www.hanggliding.com.au; ☼ 8am-8pm) has tandem flights ($165) from breathtaking Bald Hill at Stanwell Park. If the adrenalin still hasn't kicked in, skydive from 14,000ft and land in the sand. **Skydive the Beach** ( ☎ 4225 8444; www.sky divethebeach.com; Stuart Park) has awesome tandem jumps from $275. For something different **Sydney Microlight Centre** ( ☎ 4294 1031; www.sydmicro .com; ☼ 8am-5pm) has open cockpit microlight flights from $150.

**Just Cruisin'** ( ☎ 4294 2598; www.justcruisintours.com .au) has solo and sidecar Harley tours from $30, a fantastic option if you want to tour the new Grand Pacific Drive (p323).

The **Cockatoo Run** ( ☎ 1300 653 801; www.3801 limited.com.au; adult/child/family $40/30/110; ☼ Wed & Sun) is a heritage train that travels inland across the Southern Highlands. Along the Hwy, **Nan Tien Buddhist Temple** ( ☎ 4272 0600; www.nantien .org.au; Berkeley Rd, Berkeley; ☼ 9am-5pm Tue-Sun) has relaxation of a different kind with weekend retreats, vegetarian cooking classes, meditation and t'ai chi.

### FOR CHILDREN

Quizzical kids can indulge their senses at the **Science Centre & Planetarium** ( ☎ 4283 6665;

www.sciencecentre.uow.edu.au; Squires Way, Fairy Meadow; adult/child $10/7; ☼ 10am-4pm daily) or meet and greet a Tassie Tiger at **Symbio Wildlife Gardens** ( ☎ 4294 1244; 7-11 Lawrence Hargrave Dr, Stanwell Tops; adult/child $18/9; ☼ 9.30am-5pm). **Futureworld** ( ☎ 4426 9147; www.futureworld.org.au; Mill St, Coniston; ☼ 10am-4pm) has a fantastic interactive eco-technology exhibition.

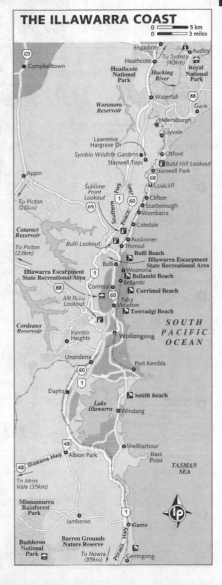

THE ILLAWARRA COAST

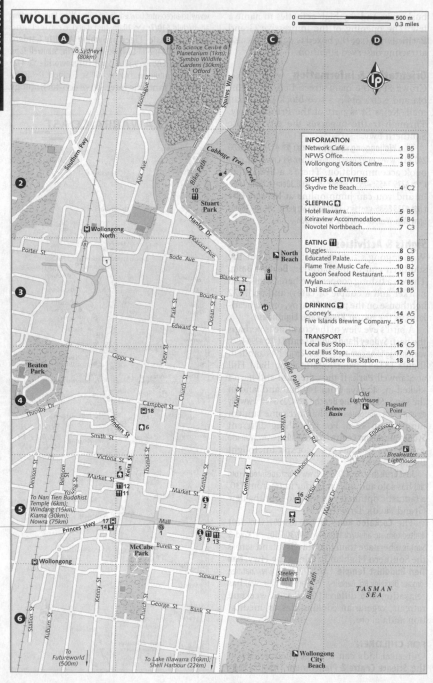

# WOLLONGONG

0 ────── 500 m
0 ────── 0.3 miles

**To Sydney (80km)**

**To Science Centre & Planetarium (1km); Symbio Wildlife Gardens (30km); Otford**

Cabbage Tree Creek

Squires Way

Southern Fwy

Ajax Ave

Montague St

Bike Path

Hanley Dr

Pleasant Ave

Porter St

Bode Ave

Blanket St

Bourke St

Park St

Ocean St

Edward St

Gipps St

View St

Church St

Marr St

Beaton Park

Throsby Dr

Campbell St

Flinders St

Smith St

Victoria St

Keira St

Thomas St

Kembla St

Corrimal St

Denison St

Belgrave St

Young St

Market St

Market St

To Nan Tien Buddhist Temple (6km); Windang (15km); Kiama (30km); Nowra (75km)

Princes Hwy

Mall

McCabe Park

Burelli St

Crown St

Stewart St

Steelers Stadium

Kenny St

Church St

Station St

Auburn St

George St

Bank St

To Futureworld (500m)

To Lake Illawarra (16km); Shell Harbour (22km)

Wilson St

Cliff Rd

Harbour St

Hector St

Marine Dr

Endeavour Dr

Bike Path

North Beach

Belmore Basin

Old Lighthouse

Flagstaff Point

Breakwater Lighthouse

**TASMAN SEA**

Wollongong City Beach

Wollongong North

Wollongong

Stuart Park

**INFORMATION**
Network Café.........................1 B5
NPWS Office.........................2 B5
Wollongong Visitors Centre...3 B5

**SIGHTS & ACTIVITIES**
Skydive the Beach..................4 C2

**SLEEPING** 🏠
Hotel Illawarra......................5 B5
Keiraview Accommodation......6 B4
Novotel Northbeach...............7 C3

**EATING** 🍴
Diggies.................................8 C3
Educated Palate.....................9 B5
Flame Tree Music Cafe..........10 B2
Lagoon Seafood Restaurant...11 B5
Mylan.................................12 B5
Thai Basil Café......................13 B5

**DRINKING** 🍸
Cooney's..............................14 A5
Five Islands Brewing Company...15 C5

**TRANSPORT**
Local Bus Stop......................16 C5
Local Bus Stop......................17 A5
Long Distance Bus Station.........18 B4

## SURFING

**North Beach** and **Wollongong City Beach** have beach breaks suitable for all visitors and are walking distance from the city centre. Look for the Acids Reef break on North Beach for more of a challenge. Up the coast, the options are varied and less crowded with fun beach breaks at **Coledale** and **Bulli** beaches and reef breaks at Sharkies (also at Coledale) and Headlands. While **Sharkies** is something of a misnomer in light of the minimal risk of meeting a finned friend here, surfers have occasionally come face to face with the odd humpback whale close to shore. Check out www.wannasurf.com for a full run-down on local waves and www.swellnet.com for a five-day forecast. **Taupu Surf School** ( ☎ 4268 0088; ☽ Mon-Sat) runs courses at Thirroul and North Wollongong starting at $125 for three lessons. Further south, Seven Mile Beach has surf camps (p328).

## SOUTH OF THE CITY

Southwest of Wollongong, the **Illawarra Escarpment** is a state recreation area. There is no vehicle access but the spot is good for bushwalking. The park is a number of separate sections from Bulli Pass to Bong Bong; it isn't very large but the country is spectacular. Contact the Wollongong NPWS office (p321) for information on bush camping.

Just south of Wollongong, **Lake Illawarra** is popular for water sports including windsurfing. Further south is **Shellharbour**, a popular holiday resort, now overrun with tacky housing.

## Sleeping

There is plenty of accommodation available in and around Wollongong from beachside camping resorts and B&Bs to self-contained apartments. The visitors centre can make reservations. Also try www.tourismshellharbour.com.au.

**Hotel Illawarra** ( ☎ 4229 5411; cnr Market & Keira Sts; s/d $50/70) The pub rooms and downstairs bar have recently been revamped and this funky place is experiencing a rebirth of cool. Best suited to the middy-drinking mindset.

**Keiraview Accommodation** ( ☎ 4229 9700; www.keiraviewaccommodation.com.au; 75-9 Keira St; dm/tw/d/f $29/40/100/110; ℗ 🖵 ) Slightly military in its rules, this complex contains the YHA hostel, which caters to students and backpackers in tidy four-bed dorms. The double and family rooms are pricier because they have verandas and kitchenettes.

**Novotel Northbeach** ( ☎ 4226 3555; www.novotel.com.au; 2-14 Cliff Rd; r incl breakfast $220-348; ℗ 🐾 🏊 ) Wollongong's flashiest joint is all class. The spacious and comfortable rooms have views of the ocean on one side or the escarpment on the other, as well as balconies to soak up the sunshine.

## CAMPING

**Coledale Beach Camping Reserve** ( ☎ 4267 4302; Beach Rd, Coledale; two-person unpowered/powered $20/25) Wake up and smell the surf, this is one of the best basic camping spots on the coast.

**Corrimal Beach Tourist Park** ( ☎ 4285 5688; corrimaltp@wollongong.nsw.gov.au; Lake Pde, Corrimal; cabins $66 161)

## Eating

**Thai Basil Café** ( ☎ 4228 8940; 5/166 Keira St; entrees $6, mains $11; ☽ lunch & dinner) Recommended as one of the highlights of the Asian precinct on

---

### DETOUR: GRAND PACIFIC DRIVE

Is the big smoke doing your head in? If so, ditch the traffic just out of Sydney for a cliff-hugging coastal drive to Wollongong. At Loftus, take a left off the Princess Hwy into Farnell Ave towards the **Royal National Park** (the world's second oldest) where you can visit tranquil **Wattamolla** and **Garie beaches**, picnic at **Bundeena** or stretch the legs on one of the many walking tracks.

Continue on to Otford and **Bald Hill** for eye-catching coastal views, then follow Lawrence Hargrave Dr to the spectacular new **Sea Cliff Bridge**, a ribbon of road that swings out from the cliff over the water. It has a pedestrian footpath perfect for dolphin and whale watching.

Further on, the small seaside towns dotted along the coast from Coalcliff to Bulli have superb beaches for swimming, surfing and soaking up the atmosphere. Pop into the pub at Scarborough, surely one of the best in Australia with beer, barbecues and brilliant views or, for something a little more sobering, a gelato at the Fireworks Café on the beach road at Austinmer.

Coledale, Bulli and Corrimal have camping sites slap bang on the beach (above) or you can continue on to Wollongong for the night. From here you can rejoin the Princes Hwy.

Keira St, between Smith and Crown, you'll find it among Thai, Vietnamese, Chinese and Japanese restaurants jam-packed with curry-lovers and noodle-tragics. This area is definitely the cheapest eats in town. Try the creamy green curry.

**Mylan** ( ☎ 4228 1588; 198 Keira St; mains $10-20; ☺ lunch & dinner Mon-Sat) This is another great choice in the same precinct, especially for its excellent Vietnamese seafood.

**Diggies** ( ☎ 4226 2688; 1 Cliff Rd, North Beach; ☺ breakfast & lunch) Right on the beach, this is the perfect spot for excellent coffee and a 'sunrise breakfast' of banana bread, low-fat yoghurt and fresh fruit ($10).

**Educated Palate** ( ☎ 4225 0100; 87 Crown St; ☺ breakfast & lunch) This culinary kitchen also has a coffee bar out the back with *baristas* on hand to make lattes par excellence. The bacon-and-egg Turkish bread breakfast is a bargain ($7).

**Lagoon Seafood Restaurant** ( ☎ 4226 1677; Sturt Park; entrees $16, mains $28; ☺ breakfast, lunch & dinner) In a tranquil setting, this is one of four top-quality seafood restaurants in Wollongong. It has delectable dishes worthy of fine dining and it's a stone's throw (with a good arm) from the water.

Further recommendations include these ones:

**Flame Tree Music Café** ( ☎ 4225 7409; 89 Crown St; mains $9; ☺ breakfast & lunch) A hippy-cum-bohemian-cum-affable café.

**R&R Catering** ( ☎ 4294 1410; 1/114 Parkes St, Helensburgh; ☺ breakfast & lunch Wed-Mon) This is a cute café in a sunny spot near Royal National Park.

## Drinking

**Five Islands Brewing Company** ( ☎ 4220 2854; WIN Entertainment Centre, cnr Crown & Harbour Sts) This feels more like a bar than a brewery but there are nine fine draught beers. The Pig Dog Pilsner is named after the owner (an ex-St George rugby player) who has an anecdote for each beer. It has plenty of outdoor seating and a good menu but the focus should remain on drinking.

**North Wollongong Hotel** ( ☎ 4229 4177; Princes Hwy) This has the biggest beer garden known to man, and the interior is as cool as some of the students who hang out here. It heaves on weekends.

**Cooney's** ( ☎ 4229 1911; 234 Keira St) This dark and nooky bar has dim lighting, booth seating, five pool tables and constant tunes. There's a

beer garden out the back and Saturday night is jazz night.

## Getting There & Away

All long-distance buses leave from the **bus station** ( ☎ 4226 1022; cnr Keira & Campbell Sts). **Premier Motor Service** ( ☎ 13 34 10) operates daily buses to and from Sydney ($15) and south to Eden ($66). **Murray's** ( ☎ 13 22 51) travel to Canberra ($31). **CountryLink** runs buses to Moss Vale from outside the train station and **CityRail** runs frequently to Sydney's Central station ($9) and south to Kiama ($6), Gerringong ($7) and Bomaderry/Nowra ($9).

**Wollongong Illawarra Regional Airport** has QantasLink ( ☎ 13 17 13) flights to Sydney and Melbourne.

## Getting Around

Two local bus companies, **Pioneer Motor Services** ( ☎ 13 34 10) and **Dions** ( ☎ 4228 9855), service the local area. The main stops are on Marine Dr, and the corner of Crown and Keira Sts. You can reach most beaches by rail and trains are fairly frequent. Bringing a bike on the train from Sydney is a great way to get around; a **cycle path** runs from the city centre north to Bulli and south to Port Kembla.

# KIAMA TO ULLADULLA

Shoalhaven is a large municipality stretching from north of Nowra almost as far south as Batemans Bay. It takes in some great beaches, state forests and, in the ranges to the west, the big Morton National Park (p134).

This area is a popular family-holiday destination, but it isn't yet as crowded as parts of the north coast and much of the tourism is confined to weekenders from Sydney.

There are regional visitors centres in Kiama, Nowra and Ulladulla, and you'll also find information at www.shoalhaven.nsw.gov.au.

## KIAMA & AROUND

☎ 02 / pop 22,000

Kiama is a pretty town at the epicentre of some good beaches and quaint villages – both rural and seaside. The **Kiama Area visitors centre** ( ☎ 4232 3322/1300 654 262; www.southcoast.com.au/kiama; ☺ 9am-5pm) is on Blowhole Point, so-called because of a **blowhole** that can spurt water up to 60m. A self-guided **heritage-tour** booklet is available from the visitors centre (free).

# Kmart Fuel Offer – Save: 4c/litre

## Expires: 11 December 2008

This receipt entitles you to receive a discount of

4c per litre off the pump price of all fuels

including LPG at Coles Express service stations.

Valid to one transaction only. Limit of 1 receipt per

fuel purchase up to 150 litres per vehicle per customer.

Fuel offer not valid for Fleet Card, Shell Card,

Motorpass etc. Business purchases or in conjunction

with any other fuel offers unless otherwise specified.

No other discounts apply. This section of receipt must

be surrendered on redemption.

1690123328981210404

The **Terrace** (Collins St) is a neat strip of restored houses that date back to 1886 and are now mostly occupied by browsing shops and restaurants.

There's a good **lookout** from the top of Saddleback Mountain, just behind the town, and a wave at **Surf** and **Bombo beaches**, and at **Werri Beach**, 10km south in Gerringong.

**Minnamurra Rainforest Centre** and an **NPWS visitors centre** ( ☎ 4236 0469) are in beautiful **Budderoo National Park** ( ☎ 4236 0469; car/motorcycle $10/4), about 14km inland from Kiama. On the way to Minnamurra you'll pass through the old village of **Jamberoo**, which has a nice pub. South along the coast, **Gerringong** and **Gerroa** have their fair share of picture-postcard scenery and restaurants to write home about.

## Sleeping

**Gerringong Real Estate** ( ☎ 4234 1177; www.gerringongrealestate.com.au; 135 Fern St) Has a holiday brochure for accommodation in Gerringong and Gerroa.

**Kiama Backpackers** ( ☎ 4233 1881; 31 Bong Bong St; dm/d $20/49; 🖳 ) Just up from the Grand Hotel, this decidedly drab building has clean male and female rooms and internet access ($5 per hr).

**Grand Hotel** ( ☎ 4232 1037; 49 Manning St; r per person $30) This is another option for backpackers. It's on the corner of Bong Bong St and has basic rooms. Bands crank up the volume on Saturday nights

**Kiama Harbour Cabins** ( ☎ 1800 823 824; Blowhole Point; 1-bedroom cabins from $190) These are fairly new and in the best position in town. The front verandas have barbecues so you can cook fish fresh from the co-op over yonder and enjoy dinner with a view.

### CAMPING

**Surf Beach Holiday Park** ( ☎ 4232 1791; Bourrool St; 2-person camp sites from $24, cabins from $42) This caravan park is a haven for anyone wanting to catch a wave. It also has cabins, some with water views and a spa (from $135 for two people).

## Eating

Stroll along Terralong St (the main street) and nearby Collins St for more restaurants.

**Ritzy Gritz** ( ☎ 4232 1853; 40 Collins St; mains $24; 🕒 lunch Fri-Sun, dinner daily) A few interesting variations on the Mexican theme can be sampled here and the margaritas are pretty good too.

**Seahaven Café** ( ☎ 4234 3796; 19 Riverleigh Ave, Gerroa; 🕒 breakfast & lunch Wed-Mon, dinner Fri & Sat) Pull

up a pew and take in the view; this is one of the south coast's best café-cum-restaurants. The gourmet food, tasteful maritime décor and seaside setting are all worth the detour. Try the eye fillet with sweet potato and coriander salad.

**Cargo's Wharf** ( ☎ 4233 2771; 2 Kiama Wharf; 🕒 lunch & dinner) This old cargo shed, built in 1868, is now home to a fine seafood restaurant right on the water. Ask for a table upstairs for added seaside ambience.

**Gerringong Gourmet Deli/Café** ( ☎ 4234 1035; 133 Fern St, Gerringong; 🕒 breakfast & lunch) A café that roasts its own coffee beans and serves up local produce in a down-to-earth style has mastered the art of success. It has tables and chairs on the footpath.

## Getting There & Away

**Premier Motor Service** ( ☎ 13 34 10) stops in Kiama (but only if there's a booking) outside the Leagues Club on Terralong St. **Kiama Coachlines** ( ☎ 4232 3466) runs to Gerringong and Minnamurra (via Jamberoo).

Frequent **CityRail** ( ☎ 13 15 00) trains run north to Wollongong ($6) and Sydney ($13) and south to Gerringong ($3) and Bomaderry/Nowra ($5).

If you're driving take the beach detour via Gerringong and Gerroa and rejoin the highway just north of Nowra.

## BERRY

☎ 02 / pop 2670

Inland and about 20km north of Nowra is the pretty little town of Berry, a worthy place for a stopover despite not being on the coast. It has a plethora of great eating venues and two pubs fit for shouting a round or two. **Queen St**, Berry's short main street, is worth a stroll for its National Trust–classified buildings, museum and antique shops.

**Pottering Around** ( ☎ 4464 2177; 97-99 Queen St), opposite the Great Southern Hotel, has some tourist information; otherwise try www.berry.net.au.

**Mild to Wild** ( ☎ 4464 2211; www.m2w.com.au; 84 Queen St) organises adventure tours such as half-day self-guided mountain bike rides ($40) and kayaking trips ($20).

## Sights & Activities
### WINERIES

There are several **wineries** in the area and the **Hotel Berry** ( ☎ 4464 1011; 120 Queen St; 🕒 11am Sat) runs a short, sweet and cheap wine tour ($15). Choose four wineries from the seven in the area. Two close to town are the **Silos** ( ☎ 4448 6082; B640 Princes Hwy, Jaspers Brush; ☺ 10am-5pm Mon-Sun), where the original cow barn now houses the cellar door, and **Bundewallah Estate** ( ☎ 4464 3600; 204A Bundewallah Rd; ☺ 10am-5pm Wed-Sun). Some wineries have a restaurant and accommodation. The **Shoalhaven Jazz & Blues Festival** is held mid-October at **Cambewarra Estate Winery** ( ☎ 4446 0170; www.shoalhavenjazz.com.au; Illaroo Rd, Cambewarra; from $35) northwest of Nowra. Also see activities listed on p328.

## Sleeping

There is accommodation aplenty in Berry but beware prices rise on the weekends. Holiday apartments can be booked through **Elders Real Estate** ( ☎ 4464 1600; 121 Queen St).

**our pick** **Hotel Berry** ( ☎ 4464 1011; 120 Queen St; s/d $35/70) This country pub is a rarity – it caters to weekending city slickers without totally losing its status as a local watering hole. The rooms are standard pub bedrooms with shared bathroom facilities, but are large and well presented. It has seven beers on tap!

**Great Southern Hotel** ( ☎ 4464 1009; s/d/tr $44/80/105) This is a boozer worth having a beer in if only to feast your eyes on the hub-cap collection, bullet-sprayed road signs and miscellaneous Aussie paraphernalia. The motel-style rooms have character albeit they're a tad overpriced.

**Village Boutique Motel** ( ☎ 4464 3570; www.berry motel.com.au; 72-76 Queen St; d $125; ☒ ☒ ) This good-looking place has stylish rooms (some with a spa) and a Roman bath–style swimming pool. Locals rave about the adjoining restaurant known as The Pavillion at Twenty Three at Berry (see below).

## Eating

**Cuttlefish Pizza Bar** ( ☎ 4464 3065; 98 Queen St; ☺ dinner Thu-Mon, lunch Sun) This modern Italian restaurant, with al fresco dining, has a good position overlooking Queen St. It also does take-away pizzas ($9 to $20), lasagne ($13) and, the best bit, rosemary roast potatoes ($9).

**Delicious – Food By Lisa** ( ☎ 4464 3650; 62 Albert St; ☺ breakfast & lunch) Off the main drag, this place uses local produce to whip-up homemade tarts, gourmet salads, pies and a tasty spinach and feta pastry ($9).

**Twenty Three at Berry** ( ☎ 4464 2323; 85 Queen St; ☺ dinner Wed-Sun) This upmarket place, part of the Village Boutique Hotel, is a hit with the locals. It has a log fire in winter and a courtyard in summer. The kangaroo fillet with garlic mash ($27) is a skip favourite.

## Getting There & Away

**Premier Motor Service** ( ☎ 13 34 10) buses between Kiama and Nowra ($30) stop here on request. Scenic routes to **Kangaroo Valley** and **Mittagong** leave the Princes Hwy south of Berry on Kangaroo Valley Rd and north via Woodhill and Wattamolla.

## NOWRA

☎ 02 / pop 25,000

Nowra is the largest town in the Shoalhaven area and therefore the central business district and transport hub. It's not, as many people expect, on the coast (the nearest beach is at Shoalhaven Heads, about 17km east) so it's not top of the pops in terms of beach holidays. It is, however, a handy base for excursions to beaches and villages around the region.

## Information

The **Shoalhaven visitors centre** ( ☎ 1300 662 808; www .shoalhavenholidays.com.au; Princes Hwy) is just south of the bridge near the naval helicopter. It has internet access for $5 per half hour. There's also an **NPWS office** ( ☎ 4423 2170; 55 Graham St).

## Sights & Activities

The 6.5-hectare **Nowra Wildlife Park** ( ☎ 4421 3949; wwww.nowrawildlifepark.com.au; Rock Hill Rd, North Nowra; adult/child $14/8; ☺ 9am-5pm), on the north bank of the Shoalhaven River, is a native-animal hangout the kids will enjoy.

Both **Nowra Museum** ( ☎ 4421 2021; cnr Kinghorne & Plunkett Sts; admission $1; ☺ 1-4pm Sat & Sun) and **Meroogal** ( ☎ 4421 8150; cnr West & Worrigee Sts; adult/child $8/4; ☺ 1-5pm Sat & 10am-5pm Sun, 10am-5pm Thu-Sun Jan) have the lowdown on local history.

Love planes? Visit **Fleet Air Arm Museum** ( ☎ 4421 1920; www.museum-of-flight.org.au; 489A Albatross Rd; adults/children $13/5; ☺ 10am-4pm), 10km south of Nowra. Prefer to jump out of one? Nearby **Nowra Skydive** ( ☎ 0419 446 904; www.skydivenowra .com.au; Braidwood Rd), has tandem jumps from 10,000ft for $380.

The visitors centre produces a handy compilation of walks in the area. To see the river, **Shoalhaven River Cruises** ( ☎ 0429 981 007; www.shoal havenrivercruise; $20) has tours that leave from the wharf just east of the bridge near the visitors centre.

## Sleeping

**Empire Hotel** ( ☎ 4421 2433; cnr Kinghorne & North Sts; s/d $25/50) These basic pub rooms overlook the beer garden of Carluci's Italian restaurant. The bedrooms have sinks and shared bathrooms.

**Hub** ( ☎ 4422 8006; www.nowrabackpackers.com; Scenic Dr; dm $30, d $60) A self-contained house, aimed at backpackers, in a good location by the river. There's an enclosed patio for bikes.

**Riverhaven Motel** ( ☎ 4422 8006; www.nowraback packers.com; Scenic Dr; s/d $65/75) Next to the Hub, this 22-room hotel is well run with the usual motel facilities.

**Whitehouse** ( ☎ 4421 2084; www.whitehouseguest house.com; 30 Junction St; d/tr $100/115) A friendly family operates this homely guesthouse with views of the Cambewarra mountains.

## CAMPING

**Nowra Wildlife Park** ( ☎ 4421 3949; camp sites per adult/ child $7/5) This animal park has camp sites in riverside bushland. Electricity is $2 a night.

**Shoalhaven Caravan Village** ( ☎ 4423 0770; 17 Terara Rd; camp sites per adult $16) This is a ship-shape place that backs onto the river.

## Eating

**River Deli** ( ☎ 4423 1344; Kinghorne St; ☒ breakfast & lunch Mon-Sat) Take a sunny seat outdoors for a latte, great snack food and fresh sandwiches. The Moroccan chicken wrap ($10) will fill that bottomless pit.

**Carluci's** ( ☎ 4421 4711; cnr Kinghorne & North Sts; ☒ lunch Tue-Fri, dinner Wed-Sat) A local hangout that is known as Nowra's best Italian restaurant.

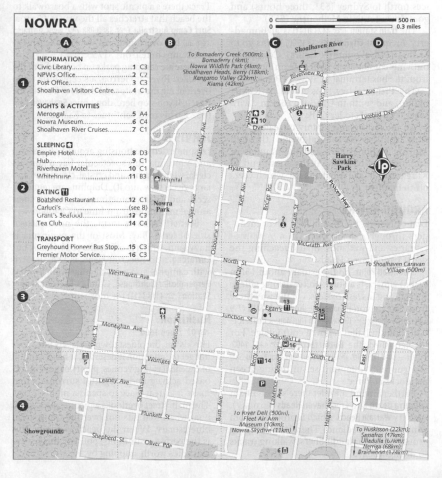

**NOWRA**

0        500 m
0        0.3 miles

The prices are reasonable: Wednesdays you can get steaks for $8 and pasta for $6.

**Boatshed Restaurant** ( ☎ 4421 2419; 10 Wharf Rd; mains $28-30; ☷ lunch Sat & Sun, dinner Tue-Sun) This is the place to go for an upmarket meal with a view – it overlooks the river just next to the bridge. The seafood is the freshest around.

Further recommendations:

**Grant's Seafood** ( ☎ 4421 2742; 9 Egan's Lane; mains $15; ☷ lunch daily, dinner Thu-Sun) Good-value fish and chips and juicy ribs.

**Tea Club** ( ☎ 4422 0900; 46 Berry St; mains $12; ☷ lunch & dinner Tue-Sat) Nowra's Bohemian set hangs out at this comfortable little café.

## Getting There & Away

**Premier Motor Service** ( ☎ 13 34 10) runs bus services north to Sydney ($31, three hours) and goes down south to Melbourne ($55).

The **train station** ( ☎ 4423 0141) is at Bomaderry. Frequent **CityRail** ( ☎ 13 15 00) trains go to Sydney ($16; about three hours). Coaches to outlying coastal areas depart from here and from the bus terminal in Stewart Place.

The Princes Hwy runs north to Kiama (42km) and south to Ulladulla (67km), with several turn-offs to Jervis Bay.

An interesting and mainly unsealed road runs from Nowra to Braidwood, through Morton National Park and the hamlets of Sassafras and Nerriga. At the south end of Kinghorne St take Albatross Rd, which veers off to the right.

## AROUND NOWRA

East of Nowra, the Shoalhaven River meanders through dairy country in a system of estuaries and wetlands, finally reaching the sea at Crookhaven Heads.

**Greenwell Point**, on the estuary about 15km east of Nowra, is a quiet, pretty fishing village specialising in fresh oysters. On the way there from Nowra you'll pass the **Jindyandy Mill** (719 Greenwell Point Rd; ☷ 10.30am-5pm Thu-Mon) a convict-built flour mill that is now a craft village. For the famished, the **Butterfactory** ( ☎ 4447 1400; 739 Greenwell Point Rd; ☷ lunch Wed-Sun, dinner Thu-Sat) is a gourmet restaurant set in rolling green paddocks at Pyree.

Further around the inlet there's great **surf** at **Culburra Beach** and **Crookhaven Heads** (Crooky). Also try **Warrain Beach**, which is protected from wind by the headland. There are camping grounds and, for landlubbers, walking tracks to the lighthouse.

On the north side of the estuary, just before Shoalhaven Heads, is **Coolangatta Estate** ( ☎ 4448 7131; www.coolangattaestate.com.au; 1335 Bolong Rd; ☷ 10am-5pm Mon-Thu), a slick winery with a golf course, a good restaurant and accommodation (s/d $100/120) in convict-built buildings. The 2003 semillon is too good to stay bottled for long. Also try nearby **Seven Mile Vineyard** ( ☎ 4448 5466; 84 Coolangatta Rd; www.sevenmilevineyard .com.au; ☷ 11am-5pm Wed-Sun & public holidays).

At **Shoalhaven Heads**, sandbars form a bridge between the river and the sea. There's a motel, caravan park and an excellent **surf** beach here but for a picnic or a swim, keep on trucking north to the **Seven Mile Beach National Park** (admission free), one of the largest stretches of natural coastal dune vegetation. Just off the Sand Track there's a picnic spot with a boardwalk to the beach that stretches all the way to Gerroa. **Surf Camp Australia** ( ☎ 1800 888 732; www.surfcamp .com.au) has overnight and weekend learn-to-surf camps here from $175.

There are camping parks on both sides of the Crooked River at Gerroa, a sleepy little town overlooking the white sand dunes of Seven Mile Beach. If you stop here, don't miss **Seahaven Café** (p325). This road continues to Kiama.

## JERVIS BAY

Despite extensive housing around Huskisson and Vincentia, this spectacular bay retains its clean, white beaches and crystal-clear water (no large rivers flow into it). Dolphins are regularly seen, and whales sometimes drop in on their annual migrations from June to October.

**Beecroft Peninsula** forms the northeastern side of Jervis Bay. Most of the peninsula is navy land, which is off-limits to civilians, but **Currarong**, near Beecroft Head, is a small town with camping and a spectacular walk to **Point Perpendicular Lighthouse**. Contact **Beecroft Ranger Station** ( ☎ 4448 3411) for more info.

## Huskisson
☎ 02 / pop 1600

Huskisson, the oldest town on Jervis Bay, does not get the attention it deserves. It has a handful of excellent eating venues, plenty of adventure-based activity and delightful surrounds that make it a great place to spend a night or two. The main street overlooks a picturesque central boat wharf that juts out over the transparent blue estuary. When the beach is windy, this is the perfect swimming spot. For this reason alone, it's worth stopping by.

---

### PARADISE ALMOST LOST

While you're sitting there squelching your toes in the white sands of Jervis Bay, consider that this pristine scene might have been very different if greed and avarice had had its way. The deep protected waters of the bay were once considered ideal for large ships and, not once but twice in the past 200 years, plans have been hatched to turn Jervis Bay into a bustling port, skirted by a railway line and inundated with docklands and industry. In 1969 the federal government had secret plans for a nuclear power station just a few hundred metres from stunning Murrays Beach (now the car park), while at the same time the NSW government negotiated building a steelworks at Currambene Creek. As recently as 1993 a scheme was devised to relocate an armaments depot to a site on the bay with Sydney naval facilities to follow. While the public outcry has saved the area from such tragedy and the conservation of Jervis Bay has since been recognised with national and marine parks instated, plans are still afoot for a new commercial centre on the wildlife corridor between the Booderee National Park peninsula and the mainland. If you too love this area, ask locally about ways to throw your weight behind its protection.

---

At the end of February, Huskisson hosts the **Shoalhaven Food and Wine Spectacular** (www .shoalhavenfoodandwine.com.au).

### SIGHTS & ACTIVITIES

The **Lady Denman Heritage Complex** ( ☎ 4441 5675; Dent St; www.ladydenman.asn.au; adult/child $8/4; 🕙 10am-4pm) has interesting history on Jervis Bay (see above) and a maritime museum. On the first Saturday of each month it hosts a **growers market**.

South of Huskisson, **Hyams Beach** is a spectacularly white stretch of sand in residential area just off the main road.

For seagoero, **Dolphin Watch Cruises** ( ☎ 1800 246 010; 50 Owen St) has the best reputation for whale- (three hours adult/child $43/28) and dolphin-watching trips (two hours adult/child $20/15). June to November is prime whale time.

**Jervis Bay Kayak Co** ( ☎ 4441 7157; www.jervisbaykay aks.com; Shop 7B, Campbell Court, Vincentia) conducts tours and rents out sea kayaks, starting at $33 for two hours.

### Diving

Jervis Bay is popular with divers, and at least two places in Huskisson offer diving and courses. **Deep 6 Diving** ( ☎ 1300 139 050; www .deep6divingjervisbay.com.au; 64 Owen St) charges $90 for two boat dives, plus equipment hire (about $35 for a full set). You can do a Professional Association of Diving Instructors (PADI) open-water dive course for about $430. **Sea Sports** ( ☎ 4441 5012; www.jbseasports.com.au; 47 Owen St) has similar rates and also runs cruises.

There are some good dives in the bay including the wrecks of TSS *Merimbula* (4m to 13m) and TSS *Wandra* (24m to 26m). The

Arch (10m to 40m) also gets a good rap for its swim-throughs and marine life.

### SLEEPING & EATING

There's quite a lot of guesthouse and motel accommodation in Huskisson and Vincentia (which more or less merge into one), but book ahead on weekends when prices tend to rocket.

**Husky Pub** ( ☎ 4441 5001; Owen St; s/d $50/70) This place has new owners who have maintained the excellent beer-drinking vibe. It has six double pub rooms with shared bathroom facilities, some with fantastic bay views.

**Jervis Bay Guesthouse** ( ☎ 4441 7658; www.jervis bayguesthouse.com.au, 1 Beach St, Huskisson; r with breakfast $145-440; 🗷 ) This two-storey wooden guesthouse has pretty bedrooms with French doors opening onto a wide veranda. Most rooms have beach views and one has a spa.

**Paperbark Camp** ( ☎ 1300 668 167; www.paperbark camp.com.au; 571 Woollamia Rd; d from $270; 🕙 Sep-Jun) Ecotourism at its luxury best. This boutique establishment has five-star accommodation in 12 safari-style tents, pitched amid the flora and fauna. Indulge in an outdoor shower, sleep in a cosy queen-sized bed and wake to the sounds of the bush. The starry nights are free.

**Seagrass Brasserie** ( ☎ 4441 6124; www.seagrass .net.au; 13 Currumbene St; entrees $17, mains $27; 🕙 lunch Fri Sun, dinner Tue-Sun) Special occasions go down well at a place like Seagrass. It has contemporary class (without being too artsy) and a mouth-watering menu that can easily match anything served up in the city. Best to book.

**Jervis Bay Kiosk** ( ☎ 4441 5464; 2/66 Owen St; 🕙 breakfast & lunch) This place has a tranquil view of the water and a breakfast menu less

SOUTH COAST

### VIEWS, PEWS AND THE KITCHEN SINK

Caravans and campervans might be slightly more cumbersome than your average tent but devotees of a home on wheels will not be disappointed by the facilities along the south coast – nor the scenic sites available. Whether you're looking for a secluded spot in a national park or a camping ground with all the mod cons, there are plenty of options for parking by the beach, kicking back and watching the waves roll in. Two of the best basic waterside spots include **Coledale Beach Camping Reserve** ( ☎ 02-4267 4302; Beach Rd, Coledale; 2 person unpowered/powered sites $20/25) and **Pretty Beach** ( ☎ 02-4457 2019; Murramarang National Park, NPWS entry fee $7 per car plus adult/child $5/$3) or, for a little more luxury, check out **Conjola Lakeside Van Park** ( ☎ 02-4456 1407; 1 Norman St, Lake Conjola; 2 person powered sites $25-35); **Tathra Beach Tourist Park** ( ☎ 02-6494 1302; Andy Poole Dr, sites from $22); and **Eden Tourist Park** ( ☎ 02-6496 1139; Aslings Beach Rd; www.edentouristpark.com.au; unpowered/powered sites from $18/21). Keep an eye out for the signs indicating well-placed barbecues and picnic areas dotted along the beaches and headlands. Here, anyone with a home in tow can set the table to dine al fresco on hot, steamy fish and chips or seafood fresh from the local co-op. The views and the best seats in the house are free!

ordinary. Where else could you get a soft-boiled egg served with toast soldiers and chilli jam ($8)? The staff are lots of fun too.

### Booderee National Park

This remarkable national park with a name meaning 'plenty of fish' occupies Jervis Bay's southeastern spit, a stunning area combining heathland, small rainforest pockets, sparkling water, and white sandy beaches plus a Botanic Garden. In 1995 the Aboriginal community won a land claim in the Wreck Bay area so now the federal government and the Wreck Bay Aboriginal Community jointly administer the park. (The ACT originally acquired the land from the NSW government so that the nation's capital had its own port). NPWS passes are not valid. Entry costs $10 per car/motorcycle for 48 hours).

Off Jervis Bay Rd, **Scottish Rocks** and **Murrays Beach** are exceptionally beautiful secluded spots. Further around the point, Caves Beach, Bherwerre and Steamers Head are open ocean beaches with good **surf**.

The **Booderee visitors centre** ( ☎ 02-4443 0977; www.booderee.np.gov.au; Jervis Bay Rd), at the park entrance, has walking-track maps and information on camping at **Green Patch** and **Bristol Point** (camp sites $14-17), and at more basic **Caves Beach** (camp sites $8-10).

### JERVIS BAY TO ULLADULLA

The southern peninsula of Jervis Bay encircles **St Georges Basin**, a large body of water that has access to the sea through narrow Sussex Inlet. The north shore of the basin has succumbed to housing developments reminiscent of the suburban sprawl on the Central Coast.

Further south is pretty **Lake Conjola**, with a quiet town of holiday shacks and a couple of caravan parks that sidle up to the inlet and a fantastic beach. This is a top spot for campervans.

**Milton**, on the highway 6km north of Ulladulla, is this area's original town and it's a pretty place to stop. There are several cafés and a few antique shops on the main street (the Princes Hwy) and it gets pretty busy here on weekends.

### ULLADULLA

☎ 02 / pop 10,500

Situated on the harbour near rocky Warden Head, Ulladulla is neither here nor there. It has excellent beaches and is close to Pigeon House Mountain and Budawang National Park but the town itself doesn't have much to offer. It is, however, the largest town on the highway between Nowra and Batemans Bay and **Mollymook**, a suburb on a lovely surf beach, is a short walk north of the harbour.

Ulladulla's **visitors centre** ( ☎ 4455 1269; www.ulladulla.info; ☼ 10am-6pm Mon-Fri, 9am-5pm Sat) is in the Civic Centre opposite the harbour. The **library** ( ☼ 10am-6pm Mon-Fri, 9am-noon Sat), in the same building, has internet access for $3 per hour.

### Sights & Activities

**One Track For All** is a 2km figure-eight culture track with a series of relief carvings and paintings that tell the story of Aboriginal and non-Aboriginal history in the Shoalhaven area. On the way you'll pass four magnificent lookouts with well-placed resting seats. The track, at the end of Dolphin St, east of the Princes Hwy, is sealed for wheelchairs and prams.

There's a fantastic walk up **Pigeon House Mountain** (below) and worthwhile **surf** at Narrawallee, Mollymook and Collers beaches.

## Sleeping

Standard motels are easy to find in Ulladulla and neighbouring Mollymook.

**Hotel Marlin** ( ☎ 4455 1999; cnr Princes Hwy & Wason St; s/d $30/50) A central place with standard pub rooms and shared bathrooms; handy to the bus stop.

our pick **Ulladulla Guest House** ( ☎ 4455 1796; www .guesthouse.com.au; 39 Burrill St; r from $99; P ⊠ ⊛ ) Don't let the palm trees put you off, this out-of-the-ordinary guesthouse with a prestigious guest list is one of the most welcoming on the coast. It has local and international art lining the walls, a fantastic French restaurant (see right) and hosts that will make you want to stay forever.

### CAMPING

**Ulladulla Tourist Park** ( ☎ 4455 2457; South St; camp sites from $20, cabins from $45) This park is on the headland a few blocks from the town centre (at the end of South St), but it's a bit of a walk to the beach.

## Eating

There are plenty of coffee shops and pasta places on Ulladulla's main street and in the arcades running off it.

**Dao's Thai Kitchen** ( ☎ 4455 1855; 130 Princes Highway; entrees $9; mains $16; ⊠ lunch & dinner) Despite the décor, the food here is excellent. The northern Thai chef specialises in dishes from her hometown. Ask for a little extra heat for an authentic chilli fix.

**Ulladulla Guest House** ( ☎ 4455 1796; www.guest house.com.au; 39 Burrill St; mains $30, ⊠ breakfast daily, dinner Mon & Thu-Sat) The fully licensed restaurant at this guesthouse (see left) serves fine French food and has a classy ambience. On chilly nights you can warm your bones next to the open fire as classical music tinkles in the background.

## Getting There & Away

Buses stop on the highway outside the Marlin Hotel (northbound) or Travelscene (southbound). Ticket agents are **Travelscene** ( ☎ 4455 1388; Shop 3, Ulladulla Plaza, 107 Princes Hwy) and **Harvey World Travel** ( ☎ 4455 5122; Shop 3, Rowen's Arcade).

**Premier Motor Service** ( ☎ 13 34 10) runs south to Eden ($42) and north to Sydney ($31) twice a day. **Priors Scenic Express** ( ☎ 1800 816 234) is a good bus to catch if you want to get off at the smaller places such as Milton, Burrill Lake, Tabourie Lake or Termeil. It continues on to Narooma.

---

### PIGEON HOUSE MOUNTAIN

'Everyone must do it,' said the amiable owner of Ulladulla Guesthouse in his hard-to-pick accent, 'but unfortunately, some people, they drive right past'. It was a small lament, maybe even a throwaway line, but it worked a treat. Climbing **Pigeon House Mountain** (720m) in the far south of Morton National Park might be the kind of upper-thigh workout that isn't called for on holiday but the rewards make any huffing and puffing worthwhile.

The main access road leaves the highway about 8km south of Ulladulla, then it's a rough and rocky 26km drive to the picnic area at the start of the track. The return walk takes three to four hours but plan for longer; the summit is barbaric-yawp territory where the rest of the world rolls out from under your feet in all directions. You could be up there for hours.

The first hour's walk from the car park is a steady climb through wildflowers and black-ash eucalypts. The track then levels out for 1km before another short and steep climb to the rock cliff-face. From here a series of steel ladders lead to the rock platform at the top, dotted with tea tree and Pigeon House ash eucalypts.

On a clear day, Gulaga (Mt Dromedary) sticks its head towards the south and to the northwest is Point Perpendicular. In between, a canopy of stunning national park vegetation spreads out like a blanket, occasionally making creases in the steep gorges carved by the Clyde River and flattening out over the elongated plateaux of Byangee Walls and the Castle.

People with a fear of heights should avoid the final section; and be sure to take water as there is none available.

SOUTH COAST

# FAR SOUTH COAST

The Far South Coast is the least-developed stretch of coast in the state and it has some of the best beaches and forests. The population triples during holiday times, especially in the Eurobodalla area (from Batemans Bay to Narooma), and prices rise accordingly. As well as the beaches and inlets, with swimming, surfing and fishing, there are good walks in the national parks and whale-watching during the migration season (June and July, and September to November). The Sapphire Coast, stretching from Bermagui to Eden, is a popular holiday area centred on Merimbula.

For more information, see the visitors centres in Batemans Bay and Narooma and **NPWS offices** Narooma ( ☎ 02-4476 2888); Merimbula ( ☎ 02-6495 5000).

## MURRAMARANG NATIONAL PARK

This beautiful coastal park covering 12,000 hectares begins about 20km south of Ulladulla and extends almost all the way south to Batemans Bay. It's a haven for surfers and bushwalkers and has three of the best **beachside camping** spots on the south coast. There are numerous walking tracks snaking off from these beach areas and a steep but enjoyable walk up **Durras Mountain** (283m). At the northern end of the park the **Murramarang Aboriginal Area** has a self-guided walking track and interpretative signs explaining the area's exposed middens.

Stunning **Pretty** ( ☎ 02-4457 2019), **Pebbly** ( ☎ 02-4478 6023) and **Depot Beach** ( ☎ 02-4478 6582) camping grounds are idyllic locations close to the surf (Pebbly is the most popular for surfing) and within the grazing territory of kangaroos. It's perfect for a snap-happy moment.

There's a NPWS entry fee of $7 per car plus camping fees if you stay overnight (adult/children $5/$3). The sites, on dirt roads off the Princes Hwy, are well signposted, Pretty Beach being the most accessible. No caravans are allowed at Pebbly Beach.

### Getting There & Away

The Princes Hwy runs parallel to Murramarang, but it's about 10km from the highway to the beaches or the small settlements in and near the park. There's no public transport into the park but **Priors Scenic Express** ( ☎ 1800 816 234) buses stop on the highway at Termeil, East Lynne and Benandarah.

## BATEMANS BAY

☎ 02 / pop 13,000

Don't expect much out of Batemans Bay and you won't be disappointed. This fishing port, which boomed to become one of the South Coast's largest holiday centres, has a lovely estuary and beautiful beaches but the town itself lacks lustre. During summer, it is overrun with holidaying Canberrans who flock here from the landlocked capital to soak up the sun then leave it for dead once the fun's over. Even the locals concede Batemans is best used as a base for exploring the surrounding natural environment.

### Information

The large **visitors centre** ( ☎ 1800 802 528; Princes Hwy; ◷ 9am-5pm) has local art for sale and an internet kiosk. **Total Computer Care** ( ☎ 4472 2745; 10 Citi Centre Arcade, Orient St) has internet access for $3/5 per half/full hour.

### Sights & Activities

On the north side of the Clyde River estuary just across the bridge there are a couple of boat-hire places. **Red Boat Hire** ( ☎ 4472 5649; Wray St; ◷ 7am-7pm) hires out runabouts from $50 for two hours.

Several boats offer **cruises** up the estuary from the ferry wharf just east of the bridge. **Merinda Cruises** ( ☎ 4473 4052) has a three-hour cruise to Nelligen (adult/child $25/12) and you can have lunch on board (fish, chips and salad). There are also sea cruises, during which you might see penguins at the Tollgate Islands Nature Reserve in the bay.

#### BEACHES & SURF

Corrigans Beach is the closest beach to the town centre. South of here is a series of small beaches nibbled into the rocky shore. There are longer beaches along the coast north of the bridge, leading into Murramarang National Park.

Surfers flock to Surf Beach, Malua Bay, the small McKenzies Beach (just south of Malua Bay) and Broulee, which has a small wave when everywhere else is flat. For the experienced, the best surfing in the area is at Pink Rocks (near Broulee) when a north swell is running. Broulee itself has a wide crescent of sand, but there's a strong rip at the northern end.

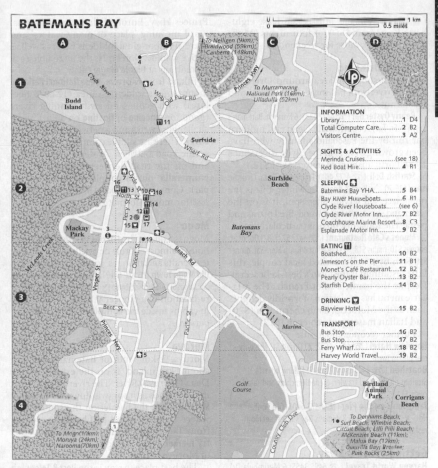

**BATEMANS BAY**

## Sleeping

There are many holiday apartments. Letting agents are the **Professionals** ( ☎ 1800 808 054) and **Ray White Real Estate** ( ☎ 4472 4799).

**Batemans Bay YHA** ( ☎ 4472 4972; Old Princes Hwy; dm $25, d $55) The youth hostel is in the Shady Wil lows Holiday Park just south of the centre. It is clean and tidy with male and female dorms, a TV room and kitchen. Outside there's barbecue action.

**Clyde River Motor Inn** ( ☎ 4472 6444; www.clydemo tel.com.au; 3 Clyde St; s/d $75/79) This central motel close to the river is the best value in town. It's worth paying a tad more for the river rooms. Townhouses are also available.

**Esplanade Motor Inn** ( ☎ 4472 0200; www.esplanade .com; 23 Beach Rd; d from $118) If you're cashed up,

stay here. It's central and the river views kick butt. Seagulls Restaurant has a good reputation for seafood.

## CAMPING

**Coachhouse Marina Resort** ( ☎ 4472 4392; www .coachhouse.com.au; 49 Beach Rd; unpowered/powered sites $20/25, cabins from $40; 🏊 ) A well-equipped family-friendly park at the start of Corrigans Beach.

## HOUSEBOATS

Eight- and 10-berth houseboats are an inspired way to escape the summer crowds and find your own way around the waterways with your mates. On the north side of the river **Bay River Houseboats** ( ☎ 4471 2253; www.bayriverhouse boats.com.au; Wray St) and **Clyde River Houseboats**

( ☎ 4472 6369; www.clyderiverhouseboats) lease eight-berth boats from $550 for four nights (Monday to Friday), more for weekends.

## Eating & Drinking

The main shopping area around Orient St and the riverfront has some decent cafés and restaurants.

**Pearly Oyster Bar** ( ☎ 4472 4233; 6 North St, Bateman's Bay; ❦ Fri-Tue) A sparklingly clean and modern bar run by the Paschalidis family who have been growing oysters in the Clyde River since 1970. Forty unshucked oysters cost $12.

**Starfish Deli** ( ☎ 4472 4880; Promenade Plaza, Clyde St; mains $15-20; ❦ lunch & dinner) In winter, this is the only place still serving after 8pm. It is on the water and serves gourmet wood-fired pizzas and pasta. The Kilpatrick pizza is particularly good.

**Monet's Café Restaurant** ( ☎ 4472 5717; 3/1 Orient St; entrees $10, mains $18; ❦ breakfast & lunch Mon-Sat, dinner Sat) Run by a well-travelled local couple, this little restaurant is the town's best-kept secret. Despite the name, it's not French. The à-la-carte menu has a selection of worldly delights such as the Moroccan lamb chermoula ($20) and Italian mascarpone chicken ($17).

Further recommendations:

**Bayview Hotel** ( ☎ 4472 4522; 20 Orient St) The only real pub in town.

**Boatshed** ( ☎ 4421 2419; Clyde St fishing wharf) Straight off the local trawler: grenadier, chips and salad costs $11.

**Jameson's on the Pier** ( ☎ 4472 6405; Old Punt Rd; ❦ lunch & dinner) Batemans Bay's finest seafood restaurant.

## Getting There & Away

**Harvey World Travel** ( ☎ 6495 3455; 6 Merimbula Dr) handles bus bookings and has timetables in the window. The bus stop is outside the newsagent on Clyde St.

**Premier Motor Service** ( ☎ 13 34 10) runs south to Eden ($35) and north to Sydney ($41) twice a day. **Murrays** ( ☎ 13 22 51) and **Rixon** ( ☎ 4474 4243) bus services stop here on their daily run between Narooma ($23) and Canberra ($24). **Sapphire Coast Express** ( ☎ 1800 812 135) runs from Batemans Bay through to Melbourne twice a week.

## BATEMANS BAY TO NAROOMA

This stretch of coast features the **Eurobodalla National Park** (admission free), an area of many lakes, bays and inlets backed by spotted-gum forests that can be accessed from various roads off the Princes Hwy. Eurobodalla is an Aboriginal word meaning 'place of many waters' and there are Aboriginal middens here, as well as native wildlife. Don't miss the incredible rock formations at **Bingie Bingie Point**.

Inland from Moruya, **Deua National Park** is a mountainous wilderness area (122,033 hectares) with gentle and swift-running rivers (good for **canoeing** or **floating** on a lilo), some challenging walks and a network of limestone caves. There are simple camping areas off the scenic road between Araluen and Moruya and off the road between Braidwood and Numeralla, plus a couple more within the park. Contact the **Narooma NPWS office** ( ☎ 4476 2888) for more information.

## Mogo

Mogo is a quaint strip of old wooden shops and houses almost entirely devoted to Devonshire teas, crafts and antiques. Just off the highway is **Old Mogo Town** ( ☎ 02-474 2123; www.oldmogotown.au; James St; adult/child $14/6; ❦ 10am-5pm), a rambling re-creation of a pioneer village. You can stay in cabins inside the complex ($22 to $105 per person).

## Moruya

Moruya, 25km south of Batemans Bay and about 5km inland, is on the estuary of the Deua (Moruya) River. The river's banks turn into wetlands as it sprawls down to the sea at **Moruya Heads**, the hamlet on the south head, where there's a good **surf beach** and views from Taragy Point. There's a popular country **market** every Saturday, on the south side of Moruya Bridge.

The best place to stay is the **Post & Telegraph B&B** ( ☎ 02-4474 5475; cnr Page & Campbell Sts; r from $90) and at **River** ( ☎ 02-4474 5505; 16b Church St; ❦ lunch & dinner) you can feast your eyes on the Moruya River, not to mention the seafood.

**Rixon** ( ☎ 02-4474 4243) bus service stop here and at Mogo on its daily run between Narooma and Canberra.

## NAROOMA

☎ 02 / pop 6000

Narooma is a seaside holiday town that isn't as developed as Batemans Bay to the north or Merimbula to the south, yet it's one of the more attractive spots on the South Coast. When you're sitting by the water on Riverside Dr, it's hard to imagine why this place is not busier.

The **visitors centre** ( ☎ 1800 240 003/4476 2881; www.naturecoast tourism.com.au; Princes Hwy; ☽ 9am 5pm), incorporating the Lighthouse Museum, is just south of the bridge. All boat charters and tours can be booked here.

Narooma is an access point for Deua, Gulaga and Wadbilliga National Parks, and there's a **NPWS office** ( ☎ 4476 2888; www.national parks.nsw.gov.au; 36 Princes Hwy). There's free internet access at the **library** ( ☎ 4476 1164; Field St; ☽ 9am-5pm Mon-Sat).

## Sights & Activities

Cruise inland up the Wagonga River on the **Wagonga Princess** ( ☎ 4476 2665). A three-hour cruise, including a stop for a bushwalk and billy tea, costs $30/20 for adults/children. **Calm Water Charters** ( ☎ 4476 2483) has a two-hour cruise ($25) that includes coffee and cake at Quarterdeck Marina (see right). There are several **boat hire** places along Riverside Dr, so you can go boating on Wagonga Inlet under your own steam. **Fishing charters** cost about $100 for four hours including all equipment.

Heading north over the bridge, take the first two right turns to **Mills Bay Boardwalk**, part of a 5km wheelchair and pram-friendly walking track where you can spot large schools of fish and stingrays. It follows the water's edge around the inlet to **Bar Beach** where nervous swimmers will appreciate a netted-off area.

A good rainy-day weekend activity is to see a film at the **Narooma Cinema** ( ☎ 4476 2352; 94 Campbell St), an Art Deco picture palace that began showing flicks in 1928.

For **surfing**, Mystery Bay, between Cape Dromedary and Corunna Point, is rocky but good, as is Handkerchief Beach, especially at the north end. Narooma's Bar Beach is best when a southeasterly is blowing. Potato Point is another popular hangout for surfers.

## Montague Island

About 10km offshore from Narooma, this small island was once an important source of food and a cultural site for local Aborigines (who called it Barunguba) and is now a nature reserve. **Little penguins** nest here and the best time to see them is spring. Many other seabirds and hundreds of fur seals make their homes on the island. There's also a historic **lighthouse**. **Narooma Charters** ( ☎ 0407 909 111; adults/children $100/77) operates a daily 30-minute **boat trip** to Montague Island including a NPWS tour. Take the afternoon trip if you want to see

the little penguins. Trips should leave daily in summer but are dependent on numbers and weather conditions so book ahead.

The clear waters around the island are good for **diving**, especially from February to June when you can snorkel with the fur seals. **Island Charters Narooma** ( ☎ 4476 1047; www.islandchartersna rooma.com) offers diving (from $70), snorkelling (from $60) and whale watching (from $55). Attractions in the area include grey nurse sharks, fur seals and the wreck of the SS *Lady Darling*.

## Sleeping

**Narooma Real Estate** ( ☎ 4476 2169), across the road from the visitors centre, deals in holiday accommodation.

**Narooma YHA** ( ☎ 4476 4440; www.yha.com.au; 243 Princes Hwy; dm/s/d $25/40/50; 💻 ) The comfortable, clean motel-style rooms here get a high-five. The owners are good fun and have a courtesy bus for taking guests to and from the pub, winery, wherever.

**Lynch's Hotel** ( ☎ 4476 2001; 135 Wagonga St; s/d $40/70) This old-school place in the heart of town is perfect if you're jumping off the late-night bus. It has lovely rooms and shared kitchen and bathroom facilities. Ask for a balcony room with water views.

**Whale Motor Inn** ( ☎ 4476 2411; www.whalemotorinn .com; 104 Wagonga St; d $115; ☒ ☒ ) This motel, just off the main drag, still offers the best all-round views of Narooma from the ocean to the inlet. It has large, clean rooms with balconies, and a nice restaurant.

### CAMPING

**Surf Beach Holiday Park** ( ☎ 4476 2275; camp sites un-powered/powered from $22/18, d cabins from $50). This small, peaceful place has a prime spot on a beautiful beach. It also caters to golfers who tee-off next door.

## Eating

**Pelicans** ( ☎ 4476 2403; 31 Riverside Dr; ☽ breakfast & lunch Tue-Sun, dinner Fri & Sat Sep-Apr only) Even in winter the sun can settle on this waterside venue that serves a mouth-watering big breakfast ($12) and excellent coffee.

**Quarterdeck Marina** ( ☎ 4476 2723; 13 Riverside Dr; mains $22; ☽ breakfast & lunch, dinner Sat & Sun) Pull up a chair on the great deck overhanging the river and tuck into the good portions of fresh seafood served here. There's usually live music in the evening on weekends.

**Taylors' Boatshed** ( ☎ 4476 2127; Riverside Dr; ☯ lunch & dinner) This fresh fish joint has takeaway out front or join the locals on the rear deck for sit-down fancy fish and chips ($12). Don't forget to BYO bottle.

Other recommendations:

**Narooma Bridge Oysters** ( ☎ 4476 1586, Princes Hwy) Sells fresh seafood straight off the boat. Shucked oysters cost $8 a dozen. Eat them at any of the picnic tables around the water's edge.

**Raw Prawn** ( ☎ 4476 3691; breakfast $9-12, mains $18; ☯ breakfast, lunch & dinner) This bistro, inside O'Brien's Hotel, has solid steaks and an awesome deck.

## Getting There & Away

Bus bookings are handled by **Trax Travel** ( ☎ 4476 2688; 139 Princes Hwy).

**Premier Motor Service** ( ☎ 13 34 10) buses stop in Narooma, outside Lynch's Hotel, on the run between Sydney ($53) and Melbourne ($62). **Murrays** ( ☎ 13 22 51) stops here on its daily run to Canberra ($37) via Batemans Bay ($23).

## AROUND NAROOMA
### Mystery Bay

Near Cape Dromedary, about 12km south of Narooma, this little settlement of new houses has a fine rocky beach (there are sandy beaches nearby) and a big but basic **camping area** ( ☎ 4473 7053; unpowered sites $13-20) in a forest of spotted gums.

### Central Tilba & Around

This is a tiny 19th-century town that has been painted and preened to attract visitors, especially on summer weekends. If it weren't so quaint, it would be labelled a tourist trap. You'll find information and a town guide at **Bates Emporium** at the start of the main street (Bates St). Further along are several craft, antique and gift shops, galleries and food venues including the **ABC Cheese Factory** ( ☎ 4473 7387; ☯ 10am-4.30pm), where you can chow down on cheddar.

For a sleepover, **Green Gables B&B** ( ☎ 4473 7435; 269 Corkhill Dr, Tilba Tilba; d incl breakfast $140), across from Foxglove Spires, is beautifully decorated and has oodles of charm. Relax by the log fire, stroll around the garden and indulge in a gourmet dinner. Also, **Dromedary Hotel** ( ☎ 4473 7223; Bates St, Central Tilba; d with breakfast $30) has a lot of character with corny Aussie jokes posted on the walls and cosy wood heater. The rooms are basic but nice.

Not far from Central Tilba towards Batemans Bay is **Tilba Valley Wines** ( ☎ 4473 7308; www.tilbavalleywines.com; ☯ 10am-5pm Sep-Jul) where Sunday sessions are the go.

The **Tilba Festival**, with lots of music and entertainment, is held at Easter.

From Tilba Tilba the highway swings inland to **Cobargo**, another small town that has changed little since it was built, and where there are craft shops, a pub and motels.

## Getting There & Away

**Premier Motor Service** ( ☎ 13 34 10) buses come through Tilba Tilba on their daily run to Sydney ($54) but not to Melbourne. If you're heading for Melbourne, jump on a bus in Narooma ($62).

If you just want an interesting drive, leave the highway at Tilba Tilba and take the sealed coastal road to Bermagui.

## WADBILLIGA NATIONAL PARK

A rugged, sub-alpine wilderness area that covers around 95,500 hectares, Wadbilliga National Park offers good walking for experienced bushwalkers. One popular track is the Cascades Walk along the 5km **Tuross River Gorge** to the **Tuross Falls**. You can find a camping area on the northwestern side of the park, close to the walk to the falls. Access to the Cascades camping area and the centre of the park can be gained by 4WD only. For more information, contact the **Narooma NPWS office** ( ☎ 02-4476 2888).

**Brogo Wilderness Canoes** ( ☎ 02-6492 7328; www.brogocanoes.com.au) offers canoe and overnight camping packages. The hire office is at the boat ramp, but call ahead so someone can meet you.

## GULAGA NATIONAL PARK

Gulaga National Park, which includes the Gulaga Flora Reserve, a large portion of Gulaga (Mt Dromedary) and the former Wallaga Lake National Park, was recently transferred to the local Aboriginal people. Trees have blocked the views from the summit of Gulaga but there are many sites of Aboriginal significance worth experiencing. For an expert tour visit **Umbarra Cultural Centre** ( ☎ 02-4473 7232; www.umbarra.com.au; ☯ 9am-5pm Mon-Fri, to 4pm Sat & Sun), which is run by the Yuin people from Wallaga Lake Koori community. It is located 3km from the highway on the road to Wallaga Lake.

## BERMAGUI
☎ 02 / pop 1300

Bermagui is a small fishing community centred on pretty Horseshoe Bay. Holidaymakers come here, mainly to fish (there are a handful big-game tournaments from March to May each year), and visitors from neighbouring towns don't mind popping in for fish and chips. It's also a handy base for visits to Wallaga Lake, Mimosa Rocks and Wadbilliga National Parks. The **information centre** ( ☎ 1800 645 808; www.bermagui.net; Lamont St; ⊙ 10am-4pm) is on the main street.

There are several **walks** around Bermagui. You can wander 6km along the coast north to **Camel Rock Beach** and a further 2km around to Wallaga Lake along **Haywards Beach**. The 9km walk from Cuttagee Beach to Bermagui is less enticing as much of the track is along the road.

For a swim, head down the main street, turn right into Scenic Drive and left at **Blue Pool**. This natural rock seawater swimming pool jutting out into the big blue is a local favourite.

Camel Rock and Cuttagee are considered the best **surfing beaches**.

### Sleeping & Eating

There are many holiday houses and apartments. Letting agents include **Fisk & Nagle** ( ☎ 6493 4255; 14 Lamont St).

**Bermagui Beach Hotel** ( ☎ 6493 4206; 10 Lamont St; dm/d from $20/110) This place has been given a jolly good facelift. The double rooms are especially good with balconies and, for a little extra, spa baths. It's also the best place in town for a beer with 10 on tap.

**Bimbimbi House** ( ☎ 6493 4456; www.bimbimbihouse .com.au; 62 Nutleys Creek Rd; r incl breakfast $100-70) This is a gorgeous homestead set in tranquil gardens a 2km stroll from town. The 3-hectare property slopes down to the Bermagui River.

**Morrisons on Lamont** ( ☎ 6493 3165; Lamont St; ⊙ dinner Fri-Tue) A snazzy restaurant on the laid-back main street with seafood delights such as mussels with leak-and-saffron cream sauce ($14) and Wapengo Lake oysters ($10 to $16).

**Mimosa Cottages & Wines** ( ☎ 6494 0163; www .mimosawines.com.au; 2845 Bermagui-Tathra Rd, Bunga; ⊙ 11am-5pm Fri-Mon) This glorious winery is set on a hilltop with views of Gulaga; it's a great place to taste-test a few wines. Accommodation is also available (double rooms $120)

and a restaurant, with a Spanish influence, is in the making.

**Fish co-op** ( ☎ 6493 4239; Lamont St) Aka the butcher shop, this place has fresh seafood for camp cooking.

#### CAMPING

**Zane Grey Park** ( ☎ 6493 4382; Lamont St; camp sites per adult from $17, cabins from $60) This park has a prime position on Dickson's Point overlooking Horseshoe Bay, close to the pub. Prices rise considerably at peak times.

### Getting There & Away

Bermagui is off the highway, so not all buses call in here. **Bega Valley Coaches** ( ☎ 6492 5188) has a weekday 'hail & ride' service between Bermagui and Bega, and **Premier Motor Service** ( ☎ 13 34 10) stops here once a day on its way to Sydney ($55). For trips to Melbourne, catch the bus from Narooma ($62).

Driving north, the quickest way back to the highway is to go past Wallaga Lake; this is a pretty drive. If you have time, take the picturesque **Tathra–Bermagui Rd** south alongside Mimosa Rocks National Park (see below) to Tathra. It's sealed and accesses all the beaches and coastline camp sites.

## MIMOSA ROCKS NATIONAL PARK

Running along 20km of beautiful coastline, Mimosa Rocks (5802 hectares) is an earthly paradise with dense and varied bush, caves, headlands and crystal-clear beaches. Admission is free and there are basic **camp sites** (per adult $7) at **Aragunnu Beach, Picnic Point, Middle** and **Gillards Beaches**. For a swim or sunbake, turn off Tathra–Bermagui Rd onto Nelson Lake Rd, drive 2km to Moon Beach car park, then walk 250m to the beach; white sands await. Contact the **NPWS office** (Narooma ☎ 02-6476 2888; Merimbula ☎ 02-6495 5000) for more information.

**Sapphire Coast Ecotours** ( ☎ 02-6494 0283; www .sapphirecoastecotours.com.au) has fantastic half-day ($60) and overnight walking tours along the northern coast and headlands.

## BEGA
☎ 02 / pop 4400

Bega is the business and commercial hub of the Sapphire Coast and the centre for the rich dairy and cattle country of the southern Monaro Tableland. After the tourist bustle of the coastal or mountain resorts, you'll find Bega very much a laid-back country town.

## Information

The **visitors centre** ( ☎ 6491 7645; Lagoon St; ☺ 9am-5pm) is in the Bega Cheese Factory & Heritage Centre (see below). The **library** ( ☎ 6499 2127; Zingel Pl) has internet access for $4 per half hour.

## Sights & Activities

There are a number of mildly interesting old buildings and a **Pioneer Museum**; the visitors centre has a walking-tour map.

At the **Bega Cheese Factory & Heritage Centre** ( ☎ 6492 1714; Lagoon St; admission free; ☺ 9am-5pm), north across the river, you can watch the cheese-making process, check out the dairy museum and, best of all, taste the cheese. **Grevillea Estate Winery** ( ☎ 6492 3006; Buckajo Rd; ☺ 9am-5pm) is also open for tasting and sales. It's about 2km from the town centre.

## Sleeping

**Bega Valley Backpackers** ( ☎ 6492 3103; Kirkland Cres; dm $20) This place is run down but the linen is clean and the owners couldn't be friendlier. It's north of the centre just over the bridge.

**Central Hotel** ( ☎ 6492 1263; 90 Gipps St; pub s/d $40/50, motel s/d $50/60) This big, converted pub has a bit of character and some permanent residents. The large pub rooms are clean and light, and the motel rooms are set in a leafy garden out back.

**Pickled Pear** ( ☎ 6492 1393; 60 Carp St; s/d incl breakfast from $100) This lovely 1870s house is still the pick of Bega's accommodation. It's near the centre of town and has beautiful rooms with bathrooms. Dinner is available and the owners will pack a picnic hamper on request.

## Eating

**Niagara Café** ( ☎ 6492 1091; 210 Carp St; ☺ breakfast & lunch) On the main street, this no-nonsense café with a comfy couch and TV opens from 7am. It does a great cappuccino and has a blackboard menu to suit most palates.

**Mr Pizza** ( ☎ 6492 2807; cnr Carp & Peden Sts; ☺ from 5pm Tue-Sat) The gourmet pizzas in this quick stop shop are a good fallback position. The Taj Mahal ($16) with tandoori chicken is scrumptious – it even tastes good the next day.

## Getting There & Away

**CountryLink** ( ☎ 13 22 32) has a service from Bega inland to Canberra($39). **Premier Motor Service** ( ☎ 13 34 10) buses between Sydney ($58) and Melbourne ($53) stop here. Buses leave from Gipps St.

A local service, **Deane's** ( ☎ 6495 6452), runs daily between Bega and Merimbula ($10), and Merimbula and Eden ($9). **Bega Valley Coaches** ( ☎ 6492 5188) has a weekday 'hail & ride' service between Bermagui and Bega. On weekdays, **Tathra Bus Service** ( ☎ 6492 1991) leaves for Tathra from the post office at 9.30am (7.45am during school holidays), and from Church St at 2pm and 3.30pm.

## AROUND BEGA

The **Bega Lookout** is approximately 4km north of town on the Princes Hwy. Nearby, **Mumballa Falls** has a picnic area.

**Candelo** is a pleasant old village 26km southwest of Bega. It straggles along both sides of a steep valley and is split by the large, sandy Candelo Creek. The nearby country is cleared but pretty. There are several **craft galleries** and a great craft **market** on the first Sunday of each month. From Candelo it's 20km along a gorgeous road to **Bemboka**, a town perched on the crest in a valley and famed for its pie shop.

From Candelo you can return to the Princes Hwy via **Toothdale**, or continue south to the Bombala road. This route takes you over **Myrtle Mountain**, where there's a picnic area with good views, and through the state forest. The Bombala road leads west to **Wyndham**, a small village just after the intersection with the Candelo road, or east to Pambula and Merimbula.

## TATHRA

☎ 02 / pop 1700

This small town is popular with people from the Bega area in summer. It starts on a headland, where you'll find the post office and the pub as well as access to the historic wharf. Down a steep road and to the north, Tathra follows a long beach towards Mimosa Rocks National Park. There's internet access at Auckland Store ( ☎ 6494 1327; Francis Hollis Dr; per 15 min $3).

Formerly used for steamships, **Tathra wharf** ( ☎ 6494 4062) is a popular place for fishing and whale watching (August to November). The wharf storehouse now houses a small **Maritime Museum** (adult/child $2/1; ☺ 10am-5pm) and rustic café with a flawless view across the water to the beach.

For great views, head for **Cliff Place**. Follow the path that begins near the surf club.

Just south of town on the Bega River, **Hancock's Bridge** picnic spot is set amid stunning white dunes and crystal-clear water; a good place for a picnic.

## Sleeping & Eating

Prices for accommodation in Tathra rise considerably in summer. **Tathra Beach Accommodation Service** ( ☎ 6494 1306) is one of the agents handling holiday letting.

**Tathra Hotel-Motel** ( ☎ 6494 1101; s/d $65/80) This is Tathra's drinking, eating and dancing epicentre (in that order). Some of the decent motel-style rooms have excellent sea views and balconies on which to enjoy them. The pub has entertainment on weekends.

**Wharf Café** ( ☎ 6494 4062; ☾ lunch) In the rustic wooden wharf building, this café does a tasty grilled snapper, chips and salad ($15) and you can't get a table much closer to the big blue.

**our pick** **Pickle Factory** ( ☎ 6494 4132; 35 Andy Poole Dr; ☾ breakfast & lunch) An excellent foodie shop, the kind you'd expect in the big smoke, with damn good coffee, simple but succulent snacks and gourmet produce fit for the fridge back home (or the camp fire). Try the beef and mushy pie with chunky homemade chutney.

**Harbourmaster Restaurant** ( ☎ 6494 1344; 15 Bega St; mains $20; ☾ lunch & dinner Fri-Tue) This pleasant place is on the headland next to the road going down to the beach, in an old house. It has a healthy cocktail list and specialises in seafood.

### CAMPING

**Tathra Beach Tourist Park** ( ☎ 6494 1302; Andy Poole Dr; camp sites per adult from $22). This caravan park is clean and tidy and has a prime position with sites all the way down the beach.

## Getting There & Away

Buses to Bega depart daily; see opposite. Tathra is 18km from the Princes Hwy at Bega. If you're heading north, consider the excellent Tathra–Bermagui Rd, it runs through forest and alongside Mimosa Rocks National Park (see p337). South to Merimbula, you can turn off the Bega road 5km out of Tathra onto Sapphire Coast Dr, which runs past Bournda National Park.

# MERIMBULA

☎ 02 / pop 4560

Merimbula's impressive inlet (or lake) is its central focus and somehow, by focusing on the rocking boat masts and sky-blue water, it's easy to forgive the glaringly new holiday apartments dotting the hillsides.

## Information

The **tourist information centre** ( ☎ 6495 1129; ☾ 9am-5pm Mon-Sat, to 4pm Sun) is on the water front at the bottom of Market St, the main shopping street. It has info on accommodation and can book tours and activities. **Dragnet Internet Café** ( ☎ 6495 2666; 3/11 Merimbula Dr; ☾ Mon-Sat; per hr $5) has internet access.

There's a useful **NPWS office** ( ☎ 6495 5000; cnr Merimbula & Sapphire Coast Drs; ☾ 9am-5pm) with the low-down on bushwalking in the area.

## Sights & Activities

At the wharf on the eastern point is the small **Merimbula Aquarium** ( ☎ 6495 4446; adult/child $9/5; ☾ 10am-5pm). There are good views across the lake from near here and the jetty is a popular little fishing spot.

**Merimbula Divers Lodge** ( ☎ 1800 651 861; www .merimbuladiverslodge.com.au; 15 Park St) has one shallow dive ($40), PADI-certificate courses ($400) and snorkelling trips ($30). The more adventurous can descend into the depths and explore the 1950 wreck of the SS *Empire Gladstone*, which lies intact and upright only 10m down ($99).

There are cruises from the Merimbula marina, opposite the Merimbula Lakeview Hotel (see below), including a dolphin cruise run by **Sapphire Coast Fishing Charters** ( ☎ 6495 1686; adult/child $30/20).

There's a **boat-hire** place at the Merimbula Marina jetty. **Cycle 'n' Surf** ( ☎ 6495 2171; 1B Marine Pde), south of the lake, hires out bikes, boogie boards, surf-skis and fishing tackle.

North of the bridge, just off the causeway, a magnificent 1.75km **boardwalk** takes nature lovers and morning people hopping and skipping around mangroves, oyster farms and melaleucas.

## Sleeping

There are hundreds of motels and holiday apartments, and plenty of campsites. Letting agents for the area include **LJ Hooker** ( ☎ 6495 3300; shop 1 Centrepoint, Market St).

**Wandarrah YHA Lodge** ( ☎ 6495 3503; wanlodge@asitis .com.au; 8 Marine Pde; dm $24-31, d $55-70) This clean place with a good kitchen and hanging out areas is near the surf beach and the bus stop. Late arrivals are catered for if your let the staff know you're coming.

**our pick** **Merimbula Lakeview Hotel** ( ☎ 6495 1202; Market St; s/d $69/79) This waterfront establishment has stylish rooms with all the motel-style trimmings such as tea and coffee. A handful of rooms have good views. Come summertime, they're close to the beer garden, which could be good or bad.

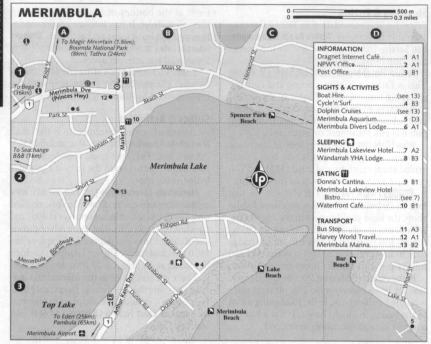

MERIMBULA

**Seachange B&B** ( ☎ 6495 3133; www.sapphirecoast
.com.au/seachange; 49 Imlay St; r with breakfast from $110/135)
This comfortable and modern B&B is 2km out
of town. It has fantastic water views.

## Eating

Merimbula offers quite a wide range of eateries, most of them concentrated in the busy
shopping area.

**Waterfront Café** ( ☎ 6495 2211; cnr Beach & Market
Sts; mains $15-19; ☻ breakfast, lunch & dinner) With
excellent coffee, a mean eggs Florentine ($14)
and a sunny spot by the water, you can't go
wrong with this place. It's next to the information centre.

**Donna's Cantina** ( ☎ 6495 1085; 56 Market St; mains
$18; ☻ lunch & dinner) Donna's is one of the
town's popular haunts. The menu features
imaginative seafood dishes and Spanish-styled
entrées.

**Merimbula Lakeview Hotel Bistro** ( ☎ 6495 1202;
Market St; entrees $15, mains $24; ℗ ) This place has
an upmarket bistro menu with a chilli-mussel
dish worth writing home about. There's an
open fire in winter and the views are pretty
good too.

## Getting There & Away

Travel bookings can be made at **Harvey World
Travel** ( ☎ 6495 3455; 6 Merimbula Dr). Also try **Sapphire Cost Tourism Booking Service** ( ☎ 1800 150 457;
www.sapphirecoast.com.au).

There are daily flights to Melbourne and to
Sydney with **Regional Express Airlines** (Rex; ☎ 13
17 13). The airport is 1km out of town on the
road to Pambula.

**Premier Motor Service** ( ☎ 13 34 10) buses stop
near the lakeside BP in Merimbula on their way
to Sydney ($64) and Melbourne ($53). **CountryLink** ( ☎ 13 22 32) runs a service from Merimbula to Canberra ($46). A local service, **Deane's**
( ☎ 6495 6452), runs between Bega and Merimbula
($10), and Merimbula and Eden ($9).

## AROUND MERIMBULA
### Bournda National Park

Taking in most of the coast from Merimbula
north to Tathra, **Bournda National Park** ($6 per
car) is a 2378-hectare park with some good
beaches, freshwater lagoons and several walking tracks. **Camping** (site per adult $8) is permitted
at Hobart Beach, on the southern shore of the
big **Wallagoot Lagoon**. During the Christmas

and Easter holidays, sites are usually booked out. Contact the **Merimbula NPWS office** ( ☎ 02-6495 5000) for more information.

## Pambula

☎ 02 / pop 1100

Just south of Merimbula, Pambula is a small town that has largely avoided the holidaying hordes of its neighbour. The town itself is not overly interesting but Pambula Beach, 4km east, is great. This tranquil little place is home to hundreds of **kangaroos** that languidly feed in the beachside reserve and hop nonchalantly across the road.

The **Holiday Hub Beach Resort** ( ☎ 1800 677 808; Pambula Beach Rd; unpowered/powered sites $27/32, cabins from $70) is a pristine family friendly park that plays host to the friendly marsupials. Keep your food hidden. Between Pambula and Merimbula, **Wheeler's Restaurant & Oyster Farm** ( ☎ 6495 6089; Arthur Kaine Dr; adult/child $7/3; �9 tours 11am Mon-Sat) has informative tours and tastings. For an oyster fix without fuss, **Brown's Oysters** ( ☎ 6495 6001; Lot 371, Arthur Kaine Dr), just up the road, is a private house with a cool room at the rear where they shuck fresh local oysters on the spot for $9 a dozen.

**Deane's** ( ☎ 6495 6452) buses run between Bega and Eden (via Pambula and Merimbula) daily.

## EDEN

☎ 02 / pop 5000

Eden's tide is turning. The seaside town, once a haven for fishermen and woodchippers, is now making the most of its authentic port setting by jumping on the tourism bandwagon. A stubbie holder and deckchair is about all visitors will need to complement Eden's 1.5km beach and ocean vistas but those keen on exerting more energy will find the surrounding national parks and wilderness areas quite breathtaking.

The **Eden visitors centre** ( ☎ 6496 1953; Mitchell St; �9 9am-5pm Mon-Fri, to 4pm Sat & Sun) is well-stocked with brochures about the area. The **library** ( �9 9am-5pm Mon-Fri, to noon Sat) and the access centre, both in the same building, have internet access for $4 per half-hour.

Eden comes alive at the start of November with the **Whale Festival** (www.edenwhalefestival.com). It features a **mock whale rescue** competition on Asling's Beach.

## Sights & Activities

The **Killer Whale Museum** ( ☎ 6496 2094; 94 Imlay St; adult/child $6/2; �9 9.15am-3.45pm Mon-Sat, 11.15am

3.45pm Sun) is often derided as a little old-hat. You decide. The skeleton of Old Tom, a killer whale and local legend is housed there. On the same theme there's a **maritime heritage walk** brochure available at the visitors centre.

In October and November, **Cat Balou Cruises** ( ☎ 0427 962027; www.catbalou.com.au; Main Wharf ) has whale-spotting cruises (adult/child $65/55). At other times of the year, dolphins, fur seals and seabirds can usually be seen during the shorter bay cruise ($30/17).

For a spot of sea-kayaking, try **Ocean Wilderness** ( ☎ 6496 9066; www.oceanwilderness.com.au), which has sea kayaking day and half-day trips ($125/80) exploring the local area and two-hour whale-watching tours during whale season ($40). Trips depart Cocora Beach.

**Boydtown**, off the highway 10km south of Eden, has relics of Ben Boyd's stillborn empire. The ruins of a church can be seen and the impressive Seahorse Inn still operates (see below).

Plans to open Eden's **Sapphire Coast Marine Discovery Centre** are rolling along. Check its progress at www.edenmarinediscovery.org.au.

## Sleeping

**Great Southern Hotel** ( ☎ 6496 1515; 121 Imlay St; dm $10-65) This is good-value shared pub rooms. By mid-2007 this place plans to offer fully fledged dorm-style backpacker accommodation with similar rates. When it does, BYO linen or pay a bit extra.

**Crown & Anchor Inn** ( ☎ 6496 1017; www.crownandanchoreden.com.au; 239 Imlay St; r incl breakfast from $130) Put your feet up; this historic house (1845) has been beautifully restored and has a whale-watching view from the back patio. Each room is different but all have stylish period furniture (such as four-post beds and claw-foot baths).

**Seahorse Inn** ( ☎ 6496 1361; d from $180) Down at Boydtown, this place overlooks Twofold Bay and is a solid old building, built by Ben Boyd as a guesthouse in 1843. It has been converted into a luxury boutique hotel but it's worth just having a look around. There's also a camping ground.

### CAMPING

**Eden Tourist Park** ( ☎ 6496 1139; Aslings Beach Rd; www.edentouristpark.com.au; unpowered/powered sites from $18/21, cabins from $55) This neat and trim park is in prime position on a spit separating Aslings Beach from Lake Curalo.

---

**LIGHT TO LIGHT WALKING TRACK**

OK, so Boyd's Tower was never an official lighthouse but you get the point. The Light to Light track, stretching 31km between Boyd's Tower and Green Cape Lighthouse, has some of the area's most dramatic coastal landscape. While traversing the full distance can take three days, the sealed roads into **Saltwater Creek** and **Bittangabee** (via Edrom and Green Cape Rds) and the 4WD road (via Edrom Rd) into Leatherjacket Bay make it possible to walk shorter sections. Just follow the track markers with the lighthouse icon in either direction.

Expect to see diverse landscapes and habitats, from folding red rock cliffs, sheltered coves and rugged shorelines to waist-high shrubby heath and imposing native forests. Goannas, eastern grey kangaroos and brushtail possums are plentiful and during autumn and spring you're a chance to see whales and seals.

There are camping spots at Saltwater Creek and Bittangabee Bay and bush camping sites (without facilities) at Mowarry Point, Leatherjacket Bay and Hegarty's Bay. If the maritime feel of the historic **Green Cape Lighthouse cottage** (overnight for 4 to 6 people $175) sounds more comfortable, overnight accommodation is available. Tours also run. **Merimbula NPWS office** ( ☎ 6495 5000) and **Eden visitors centre** ( ☎ 02-6496 1953) have all the info.

---

## Eating

**Disaster Bay Chillies** ( ☎ 6496 4145; www.disasterbaychillies.com) This family-run company has got the business of chillies down pat. The flagship Hot Chilli Wine is made from nine different chillies and is ideal served iced cold with fresh local oysters. It is sold in outlets up the coast.

**Fare n Square Café** ( ☎ 6496 3007; 126 Imlay St; ❤ breakfast & lunch) Come here for decent breakfasts and excellent coffee. The outdoor terrace area is a fine place to watch the world go by.

**Taste of Eden** ( ☎ 6496 1304; Main Wharf; mains $17; ❤ breakfast, lunch & dinner) An atmospheric, tiny café with seafood and an à-la-carte menu.

**Great Southern Hotel** ( ☎ 6496 1515; 121 Imlay St; mains $17; ❤ lunch & dinner) Catch some rays on the huge rear deck and enjoy upmarket bistro food like a steak or chicken parmagiana (mains $17).

## Getting There & Away

**Premier Motor Service** ( ☎ 13 34 10) buses between Melbourne and Sydney ($79) stop opposite the Caltex Service Station. Bus bookings can be made at the visitors centre.

## BEN BOYD NATIONAL PARK

Protecting some relics of Ben Boyd's operations, this national park (9450 hectares), stretching north and south along the coast on either side of Eden, has dramatic coastline, bush and walking territory (see above). The southern access road is the sealed Edrom Rd, off the Princes Hwy 19km south of Eden. Follow this to the turn-offs to historic **Davidson Whaling Station** on Twofold Bay, and **Boyd's Tower**, an impressive structure built with Sydney sandstone.

The northern section of Ben Boyd National Park runs up the coast from Eden; access is from Haycocks Rd off the Princes Hwy 8km north of the town. When a southerly is blowing, sheltered **Barmouth** beach is great for swimming. From **Haycock Point** a walking track leads to a headland overlooking the Pambula River. Another good walk is to the **Pinnacles**, an eroded formation of layered rock; access is from the car park not too far in from the Princes Hwy. Between the two, Quondolo Point has good **surf**.

## NADGEE NATURE RESERVE

Nadgee Nature Reserve is one of Australia's spectacularly wild and remote wilderness areas. Such is the importance of this pristine reserve, general access is only allowed as far as the ranger station near Merrica River, 7km from Newton's Beach. To get a feel for the breathtaking scenery a limited number of visitors can apply for a permit. Most do so to see the **Nadgee Howe Wilderness Walk**, 50km of remote heathlands, windswept beaches and coastal lagoons. The **Merimbula NPWS office** ( ☎ 6495 5000) has all the info.

On Wonboyn Lake at the north end of the reserve, the small settlement of **Wonboyn** has a store selling petrol, a caravanpark and basic supplies. Wonboyn is near access roads into Nadgee, including one down to Wonboyn Beach, a hub for fishermen who come to hook huge flathead and enjoy some of the state's most remote offshore fishing.

**Nadgee by Nature Cottages** ( ☎ 0410 511 458; www .nadgeebynature.com.au; d $165) has three lovely cottages set in serene bushland. It's a good place to get information on walks in the area.

# Australian Capital Territory

The Australian Capital Territory (ACT) was carved out of the Limestone Plains, a region of New South Wales 280km southwest of Sydney and 150km inland from the east coast. Its weathered ranges and quintessential bushland cradle the Australian capital, Canberra, a geometrically designed city housing the symbols and machinery of a nation's aspirations.

Canberra is home to many a national treasure, yet it has also evolved from its bureaucratic origins into a flourishing city of hip cafés, multi-cuisine dining, modish bars and lively festivals. As the nexus of Australian political power it is a city that thrives on networking, business lunches and gossip. Politics, scandals and the latest conspiracy theory are never off the agenda, and power brokers or image breakers can be easily seen or imagined scribbling notes in a Manuka café or a Civic bar.

The city and its suburbs occupy only the top third of the territory. Within the ACT – only 88km north to south and 30km east to west – you can find rustic townships that predate the city and a surprising amount of bushland. Bushwalkers, bird-watchers and connoisseurs of nature will find half the territory is protected as national park or reserve. There's also accessible Aboriginal rock art and splendid camping. For more genteel pursuits there are cool-climate wineries and the meandering Murrumbidgee River to explore. The immediate surrounding region of southeast NSW boasts snowfields, historic towns, more wineries and pristine lakes and rivers and is yet another reason to base yourself in the capital and see the sights.

## HIGHLIGHTS

- Peer at the MPs as they reveal their policies and principles at **Parliament House** (p349)
- Stroll the corridors of creativity in the **National Gallery of Australia** (p350)
- Stand silently for the last post at the **Australian War Memorial** (p351)
- Discover the wilderness on your doorstep in **Namadgi National Park** (p365)
- Discuss life and the universe with a representative of indigenous Australia at the **Tent Embassy** (p351)
- Calculate your weight if you were on Mars and marvel at what lies above at the **Canberra Space Centre** (p363)
- Walk, run, cycle or skate around **Lake Burley Griffin** (p349)
- Negotiate the network of Australiana in the **National Museum of Australia** (p351)

- TELEPHONE CODE: 02     ■ POPULATION: 323,000     ■ AREA: 2360 SQ KM

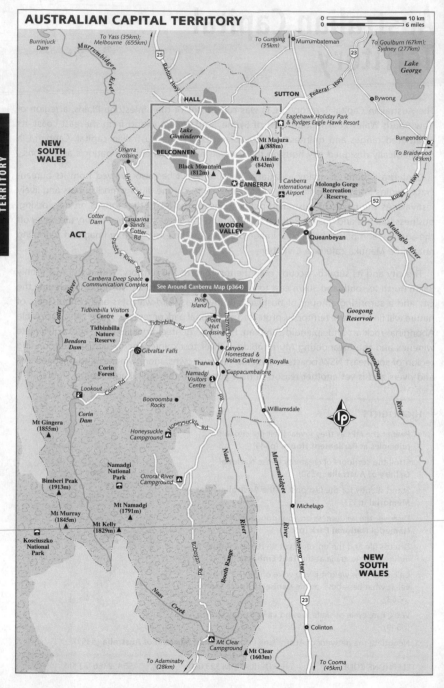

# AUSTRALIAN CAPITAL TERRITORY

0 ——— 10 km
0 ——— 6 miles

Burrinjuck Dam

To Yass (35km); Melbourne (655km)

Murrumbidgee River

To Gunning (35km)

Murrumbateman

To Goulburn (67km); Sydney (277km)

Lake George

Bywong

SUTTON

Federal Hwy

HALL

Eaglehawk Holiday Park & Rydges Eagle Hawk Resort

Bungendore

NEW SOUTH WALES

Lake Ginninderra

BELCONNEN

Uriarra Crossing

Uriarra Rd

Mt Majura (888m)

Black Mountain (812m)

Mt Ainslie (843m)

CANBERRA

Canberra International Airport

Molonglo Gorge Recreation Reserve

To Braidwood (49km)

Kings Hwy

52

Molonglo River

ACT

Cotter Dam

Casuarina Sands

Cotter Rd

Paddy's River Rd

WODEN VALLEY

Queanbeyan

Cotter River

Canberra Deep Space Communication Complex

See Around Canberra Map (p364)

Pine Island

Googong Reservoir

Tidbinbilla Visitors Centre

Tidbinbilla Rd

Point Hut Crossing

Tharwa Dr

Queanbeyan River

Tidbinbilla Nature Reserve

Bendora Dam

Gibraltar Falls

Lanyon Homestead & Nolan Gallery

Tharwa

Royalla

Corin Forest

Conn Rd

Namadgi Visitors Centre

Cuppacumbalong

Lookout

Corin Dam

Booroomba Rocks

Williamsdale

Mt Gingera (1855m)

Honeysuckle Campground

Honeysuckle Rd

Murrumbidgee River

Namadgi National Park

Orroral River Campground

Bimberi Peak (1913m)

Naas River

Michelago

Mt Murray (1845m)

Mt Namadgi (1791m)

Mt Kelly (1829m)

Monaro Hwy

Kosciuszko National Park

Bicboyan Rd

Booth Range

NEW SOUTH WALES

Naas Creek

23

Colinton

Mt Clear Campground

Mt Clear (1603m)

To Adaminaby (28km)

To Cooma (45km)

Barton Hwy

25

Mt Clear

# CANBERRA

☎ 02 / pop 309,800

Canberra is a celebration of what Australians hold dear – their origins, sacrifices, treasures and values. Iconic cultural landmarks such as the National Museum, National Library, War Memorial, Art Gallery, High Court and Parliament House are symbolic and accessible, informative and free and, with few exceptions, replete with café and souvenir shop. Canberra is the hub of the ACT and of a much greater region of southern NSW. It is orderly and unapologetically suburban, but the days when Canberra was an incubator for a uniform public service are long gone, with more than half the workforce now employed in the private sector.

When you have finished exploring the nation's cultural legacies, houses of power and thriving art scene, don't think that is all Canberra has to offer. There are numerous dining and entertainment options and Canberra is a city that thrives outdoors – lakes, rivers, parks, sporting fields, bush tracks and more are easily reached and the envy of larger cities.

## HISTORY

For over 20,000 years the Ngunnawal Aboriginal people made this country their home. The Ngunnawal were nomadic by necessity. The seasonal abundance of foods, such as the yam daisies of the plains and the bogong moths of the high country, precipitated occasional large gatherings of people, and 'Canberra' or 'Kanberra' is believed to be an Aboriginal term for 'meeting place'. In Namadgi National Park (p365) you can see rock art, while other evidence of traditional occupation lies scattered throughout the ACT.

European settlement began in the 1820s, as pastoralists realised potential in the grasslands of the Limestone Plains. Many Ngunnawal people ended up working on expansive sheep stations. Despite years of persecution, introduced diseases, official disregard and massive environmental change, the Ngunnawal have endured and have increased their profile in recent years.

When Australia's separate colonies were federated in 1901 and became states, the decision to build a national capital was written into the constitution. In 1908 the site – diplomatically situated between the arch-rival cities of Sydney and Melbourne – was selected, and in 1911 the Commonwealth government created the Federal Capital Territory (changed to the Australian Capital Territory in 1938). American architect Walter Burley Griffin then beat 136 other entries to win an international competition to design the city.

On 12 March 1913, when the foundation stones of the new capital were being laid, the city was officially baptised. Canberra eventually took over from Melbourne as the seat of national government in 1927, but development of the site was slow and virtually stopped during the Depression – real expansion of the city only got under way after WWII.

## ORIENTATION

Think crop circles in suburbia and you have an aerial picture of this city conceived on an architect's drawing board with the aid of ruler, compass and protractor. Two great road axes, Kings and Commonwealth Aves, converge at the apex of Capital Hill, which, with Constitution Ave, create Walter Burley Griffin's parliamentary triangle. Located within and near the parliamentary triangle are a number of important buildings, including the National Library of Australia, the High Court of Australia, the National Gallery of Australia and Old and New Parliament Houses. Kings and Commonwealth Aves span Canberra's central water feature – Lake Burley Griffin – complete with spout, and all roads end with roundabouts that will have you (or your navigator) spinning.

The main axis starts north of the city when the Federal and Barton Hwys converge into Northbourne Ave, which then runs south through the suburbs of Downer, Dickson and Braddon before entering Civic, the city centre. After circling City Hill this axis road becomes Commonwealth Ave and heads across Lake Burley Griffin to Capital Hill.

Capital Hill is encircled by State Circle and Capital Circle. Depending on which of these you find yourself on (apparently there is more to it than luck) you can peel off northeast along Kings Ave towards the airport and the War Memorial, east along Brisbane Ave to Kingston, southeast along Canberra Ave to Manuka and Queanbeyan, or west along Adelaide Ave to Deakin.

Parkes Way skirts the northern shore of the lake and you have to be careful not to miss the turn offs to the National Museum, Black

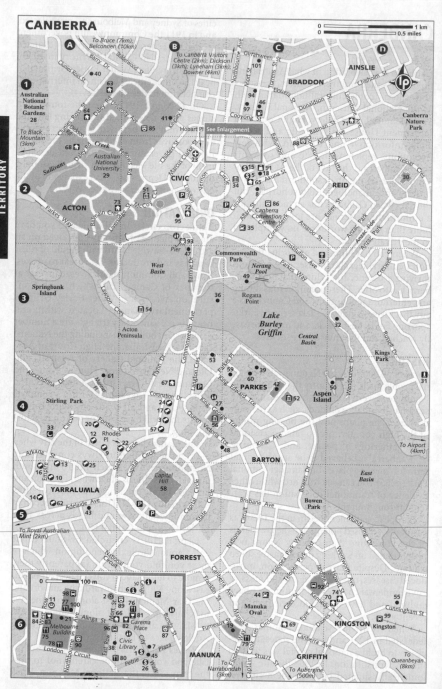

| | | |
|---|---|---|
| **INFORMATION** | | |
| American Express | (see 26) | |
| ANZ Bank | 1 | B6 |
| Bytes Internet Cafe | (see 92) | |
| Cafe Cactus | 2 | A6 |
| Canadian High Commission | 3 | B4 |
| Citizens Advice Bureau ACT | 4 | B6 |
| Commonwealth Bank | 5 | C2 |
| Community Information & Referral Service | 6 | B6 |
| Dymock's | 7 | B6 |
| Electric Shadows Bookshop | 8 | C2 |
| French Embassy | 9 | A4 |
| German Embassy | 10 | A5 |
| GPO | 11 | A6 |
| Indonesian Embassy | 12 | A4 |
| Irish Embassy | 13 | A5 |
| Japanese Embassy | 14 | A5 |
| Map World | (see 98) | |
| National Australia Bank | 15 | C2 |
| National Library Bookshop | (see 53) | |
| Netherlands Embassy | 16 | A5 |
| New Zealand High Commission | 17 | B4 |
| NRMA | 18 | C2 |
| Paperchain Bookstore | 19 | C6 |
| Singapore High Commission | 20 | A4 |
| Smiths Alternative Bookshop | 21 | A6 |
| South African Embassy | 22 | B4 |
| Travelex | (see 91) | |
| Travellers' Medical & Vaccination Centre | 23 | B2 |
| UK High Commission | 24 | B4 |
| US Embassy | 25 | A5 |
| Westpac Bank | 26 | B6 |
| **SIGHTS & ACTIVITIES** | | |
| Aboriginal Tent Embassy | 27 | B4 |
| Australian National Botanic Gardens | 28 | A1 |
| Australian National University | 29 | A2 |
| Australian War Memorial | 30 | D2 |
| Australian-American Memorial | 31 | D4 |
| Blundells' Cottage | 32 | D3 |
| Canberra Mosque | 33 | A4 |
| Canberra Museum & Gallery | 34 | C2 |
| Canberra Olympic Pool | 35 | C2 |
| Captain Cook Memorial Water Jet | 36 | B3 |
| Church of St John the Baptist | 37 | C3 |
| Civic Library | 38 | A6 |
| Commonwealth Place | 39 | C4 |
| CSIRO Discovery | 40 | A1 |
| Drill Hall Gallery | 41 | B1 |
| High Court of Australia | 42 | C4 |
| Lake Burley Griffin Boat Hire | (see 93) | |
| Lodge | 43 | A5 |
| Manuka Swimming Pool | 44 | C6 |
| Merry go round | 45 | B6 |
| Mountain Designs | 46 | C1 |
| Mr Spokes Bike Hire | 47 | B3 |
| National Archives of Australia | 48 | C4 |
| National Capital Exhibition | 49 | C3 |
| National Carillon | 50 | D4 |
| National Film & Sound Archive | 51 | B2 |
| National Gallery of Australia | 52 | C4 |
| National Library of Australia | 53 | B4 |
| National Museum of Australia | 54 | B3 |
| National Portrait Gallery | (see 56) | |
| Old Bus Depot Markets | 55 | D6 |
| Old Parliament House | 56 | B4 |
| Papua New Guinea High Commission | 57 | B4 |
| Parliament House | 58 | B5 |
| Questacon - National Science & Technology Centre | 59 | C4 |
| Reconciliation Place | 60 | C4 |
| St John's Schoolhouse Museum | (see 37) | |
| Southern Cross Yacht Club | 61 | A4 |
| Thai Embassy | 62 | A5 |
| **SLEEPING** | | |
| Bruce Hall | 63 | A1 |
| Burton & Garran Hall | 64 | A1 |
| Canberra YHA Hostel | 65 | C2 |
| City Walk Hotel | 66 | B6 |
| Hyatt Hotel Canberra | 67 | B4 |
| John XXIII College | 68 | A2 |
| Kingston Hotel | 69 | C6 |
| Motel Monaro | 70 | D6 |
| Novotel | (see 98) | |
| Ollims Hotel Canberra | 71 | D1 |
| Pacific International Apartments - Capital Tower | 72 | B2 |
| University House | 73 | A2 |
| Ursula College | (see 68) | |
| Victor Lodge | 74 | D6 |
| **EATING** | | |
| Alanya | (see 19) | |
| Asian Café | 75 | A6 |
| Café in the House | (see 56) | |
| Caffe della Piazza | 76 | B6 |
| Cipriani | (see 92) | |
| First Floor | (see 92) | |
| Food Hall | (see 91) | |
| la pasa | 77 | A6 |
| Legends | (see 19) | |
| Lemon Grass | 78 | A6 |
| Mecca Bah | 79 | C6 |
| My Café | (see 19) | |
| Ruchi | (see 19) | |
| Santa Lucia | (see 92) | |
| Silo | (see 92) | |
| Tosolini's | 80 | B6 |
| **DRINKING** | | |
| Belgian Beer Cafe | (see 92) | |
| Durham Castle Arms | (see 92) | |
| Filthy McFadden's | (see 92) | |
| Hippo Bar | 81 | B6 |
| King O'Malley's | 82 | B6 |
| Kremlin | (see 98) | |
| PJ O'Reilly's | 83 | A6 |
| Wig & Pen | 84 | A6 |
| **ENTERTAINMENT** | | |
| ANU Union Bar | 85 | B1 |
| Canberra Theatre Centre | (see 34) | |
| Casino Canberra | 86 | C2 |
| Club Mombasa | 87 | B6 |
| Electric Shadows Cinema | (see 8) | |
| Gorman House Arts Centre | 88 | C2 |
| Greater Union | 89 | B6 |
| icbm & Meche | 90 | A6 |
| Toast | (see 8) | |
| **SHOPPING** | | |
| Canberra Centre | 91 | C2 |
| Craft ACT | (see 34) | |
| Kingston Shopping Centre | 92 | C6 |
| Manuka Shopping Centre | (see 19) | |
| **TRANSPORT** | | |
| Action Information Kiosk | (see 96) | |
| Acton Park Ferry Terminal | 93 | B2 |
| Avis | 94 | C1 |
| Budget | 95 | B2 |
| Bus Station (Interstate) | (see 98) | |
| Civic Bus Interchange | 96 | A6 |
| Countrylink Travel Centre | (see 98) | |
| Guidepost Travel | (see 98) | |
| Hertz | 97 | C1 |
| Jolimont Centre | 98 | A6 |
| Kingston Train Station | 99 | D6 |
| Qantas | 100 | A6 |
| Thrifty | 101 | C1 |

Mountain, and the Botanic Gardens. The rest of the city is made up of suburban satellites: patchworks of brick and tile arranged around cul de sacs and steadily spreading over the erstwhile sheep paddocks and spawning the occasional town centre.

## Maps

The **NRMA** (Map p346; ☎ 6240 4630; 6 City Walk, Canberra Centre, Civic; 9am-5pm Mon-Fri) has the *Canberra & Southeast* map ($7; free if you belong to an affiliated motoring organisation), which has a detailed map of Canberra, another of the greater suburban area. On the back are maps of the ACT and southeast NSW and Victoria. The Canberra Visitors Centre (p349) stocks UBD's *Canberra* maps ($8), pocket-size city maps ($3), and maps for bushwalking in Namadgi National Park ($4.50). Map World (p348) and the Namadgi Visitor Centre (p365) stock regional topographic maps.

# INFORMATION

## Bookshops

**Dymocks Canberra** (Map p346; ☎ 6257 5057; 177 City Walk, Civic) Large, central bookshop with latest releases.

**Electric Shadows Bookshop** (Map p346; ☎ 6248 8352; City Walk, Civic) This bookshop specialises in books on theatre and film, plus gay and lesbian books and rentable arthouse DVDs.

**Map World** (Map p346; ☎ 6230 4097; Jolimont Centre, 65 Northbourne Ave, Civic) Numerous maps and travel guides.

**National Library Bookshop** (Map p346; ☎ 6262 1424; Parkes Pl, Parkes) Stocks exclusively Australian books, including a superb range of fiction.

**Paperchain Bookstore** (Map p346; ☎ 6295 6723; 34 Franklin St, Manuka) Has a wide-ranging book list.

**Smiths Alternative Bookshop** (Map p346; ☎ 6247 4459; 76 Alinga St, Civic) Sells everything from New Age 'science' to gay and lesbian literature.

## Emergency

**Ambulance** ( ☎ 000, TTY 106)

**Canberra Rape Crisis Centre** ( ☎ 6247 2525, TTY 6247 1657) 24-hour help.

**Fire** ( ☎ 000, TTY 106)

**Lifeline** ( ☎ 13 11 14) 24-hour crisis counselling.

**Police** ( ☎ 000, TTY 106)

## Internet Access

Public libraries, the Canberra Centre (p361; near the information desk), the interstate bus terminal at the Jolimont Centre (p362) and hostels such as the Canberra YHA Hostel (p356) and Victor Lodge (p356), all have public internet access.

**Bytes Internet Cafe** (Map p346; ☎ 6239 7070; 47 Jardine St, Kingston; per hr $8; 9.30am-5pm Mon-Fri; 9.30am-4pm Sat).

**Cafe Cactus** (Map p346; ☎ 6248 0449; 1/7 Mort St, Civic; per hr $10; 7.30am-4pm Mon-Fri) You can get light meals here.

## Medical Services

**Canberra Hospital** (Map p364; ☎ 6244 2222, emergency dept 6244 2611; Yamba Dr, Garran)

**Capital Chemist** (Map p364; ☎ 6248 7050; Sargood St, O'Connor; 9am-11pm)

**Travellers' Medical & Vaccination Centre** (Map p346; ☎ 6257 7156; 5th fl, 8-10 Hobart Pl, Civic; 8.30am-4.30pm Mon-Wed & Fri, to 7pm Thu) Appointment essential.

## Money

Branches of major banks are scattered around the city. Foreign-exchange bureaus include the following.

**American Express** (Map p346; ☎ 1300 139 060; Petrie Plaza, Civic; 9.30am-4pm Mon-Thu, 9.30am-5pm Fri) Located inside the Westpac bank.

**Travelex** (Map p346; ☎ 1800 637 642; Canberra Centre, Bunda St, Civic; 9am-5pm Mon-Fri, 9.30am-12.30pm Sat) Found inside the Harvey World Travel office.

## Post

Pick up poste restante at the **GPO** (Map p346; ☎ 13 13 18; 53-73 Alinga St, Civic). Mail can be addressed: Poste restante Canberra GPO, Canberra City, ACT 2601.

---

### CANBERRA IN...

#### Two days

Breakfast in a **Kingston** (p359) or **Manuka** (p359) café before taking your time ticking off the parliamentary triangle's sights, such as **Parliament House** (opposite) and **Old Parliament House** (p350), which includes the **National Portrait Gallery**. Drop in on the **Aboriginal Tent Embassy** (p351) and allocate several hours to the **National Gallery** (p350). Catch a breath of crisp morning air exploring the lawns of **Commonwealth Place** (opposite) and **Reconciliation Place** (opposite), as well as along the foreshore of **Lake Burley Griffin** (opposite). As the sun sinks from the western sky witness the sombre history and listen to the Last Post at the **Australian War Memorial** (p351).

#### Four days

With four days you can take more time to visit the sights of the parliamentary triangle and perhaps include a visit to the **High Court** (p352), **Questacon** (p352) or the **National Library** (p352). Take a ferry ride to the iconic chaos of the **National Museum** (p351) or talk to the animals at the **National Zoo & Aquarium** (p352). If you have your own transport, you should check out the art and antiques at peaceful **Bungendore** (p365), explore the universe at the **Canberra Space Centre** (p363), or go bush at **Namadgi National Park** (p365).

**WHAT'S IN A NAME?**

The answer is too much in the case of one of the alternative names considered for the national capital 'Sydmeladperbrisho'. Flora and Fauna found endorsement in the whimsically emblematic 'Kangaromu' and the rather stately 'Eucalyptia'. 'Engirscot' was probably a grand inclusive gesture in its day, to be sure; try to imagine the modern equivalent encompassing Australia's multicultural cocktail! 'Woolgold' points to the sort of economic tunnel vision that can still be tapped at Capital Hill, while 'Empire City', 'Democratia', and 'Federatia' fairly burst off the map with swollen pride and infinite vision (if not imagination).

## Tourist Information

**Canberra Visitors Centre** (Map p346; ☎ 1300 554 114, 6205 0044; www.visitcanberra.com.au; 330 Northbourne Ave, Dickson; ❂ 9am-5.30pm Mon-Fri, to 4pm Sat & Sun) Operated by the ACT's peak tourist information body, the Canberra Tourism & Events Corporation.

**Citizens Advice Bureau ACT** (Map p346; ☎ 6248 7988; www.citizensadvice.org.au; New Griffin Centre, Genge St, Civic; ❂ 10am-4pm Mon-Tue & Thu Fri, to 1pm Wed) Provides information on community services and facilities.

## SIGHTS

Canberra's significant edifices, museums and galleries are dotted around Lake Burley Griffin. Wheelchair-bound visitors will find that most sights are fully accessible. Nearly all attractions close on Christmas Day.

Those keen on visiting Questacon (p352), the Australian Institute of Sport (p353) and Cockington Green (p365) should get a **3-in-1 Ticket** (adult/child/concession/family $36.40/19.80/26.10/103) giving access to all three attractions; you can buy it at any of the three sites or at the visitors centre.

Bus No 34 from the Civic bus interchange is handy for many of the city sights. For more detailed information on bus services, see p363.

## Lake Burley Griffin

Named after Canberra's architect, Lake Burley Griffin was created by damming the Molonglo River in 1963 with the 33m-high **Scrivener Dam** (Map p364).

Around the lake's 35km shore are many places of interest. The most visible, built in 1970 for the bicentenary of Cook's landfall, is the **Captain Cook Memorial Water Jet** (Map p346; ❂ 10am-noon & 2-4pm, also 7-9pm during daylight saving), which flings a 6-tonne column of water 147m into the air at 500L a second – and sometimes gives free showers, despite its automatic switch-off in strong winds. At nearby **Regatta Point** there's a skeletal bronze globe on which Cook's great voyages are traced. Also here is the **National Capital Exhibition** (Map p346; ☎ 6257 1068; www.nationalcapital.gov.au/exhibition/index .htm; Barrine Dr; admission free; ❂ 9am-5pm), where the city's history is on display. Just north of here is beautiful **Commonwealth Park** (Map p346), where a series of paths leads you through flower gardens to Nerang Pool.

Further east around the lake is the simple stone-and-slab **Blundells' Cottage** (Map p346; ☎ 6257 1068; Wendouree Dr; adult/child/family $4/2/10; ❂ 11am-4pm), built in 1860 to house workers on the surrounding estate and now a reminder of the area's early farming history.

On Aspen Island, at the far end of Commonwealth Park, is the 50m-high **National Carillon** (Map p346; ☎ 6257 1068; ❂ recitals 12.45-1.35pm Tue & Thu, 2.45-3.35pm Sat & Sun), a gift from Britain on Canberra's 50th anniversary in 1963 and opened seven years later. The tower's 55 bronze bells weigh from 7kg to six tonnes. Bookings are required for Carillon **tours** (adult/child/family $8/4/20; ❂ 12.45pm Mon, Wed & Fri).

On the northern shore fronting Old Parliament House and between the High Court and Questacon is **Reconciliation Place** (Map p346), where artworks represent the nation's commitment to reconciliation between indigenous and non-indigenous Australians. A walkway slices into the well-maintained lawns along Burley Griffin's land axis to link with **Commonwealth Place** (Map p346), a ceremonial venue with an international flag display, a Southern Cross-shaped grove of trees and Speakers Square, the Centenary of Federation Gift from the Canadian government.

Swimming in the lake is not recommended, but it's OK for boating, and the lake shore is great to cycle or walk around. Boats and bikes are available for hire at Acton Park ferry terminal on the northern shore; see p354.

## Parliament House

The striking **Parliament House** (Map p346; ☎ 6277 5399; www.aph.gov.au; admission free; ❂ 9am-5pm) is worth a few hours' exploration (see the boxed text p350).

## DESIGN FOR A NATION

Parliament House is another aspect of Walter Burley Griffin's vision to become reality. Opened in 1988, it took $1.1 billion and eight years to build and replaced the Old Parliament House, which served 11 years longer than its intended temporary 50 years. It was designed by Romaldo Giurgola of Mitchell, Giurgola & Thorp architects, winner of a design competition that attracted 329 entries from 28 countries. Its splendid interior incorporates different combinations of Australian timbers in each main section and more than 3000 original artworks.

The structure was built into the hillside and covered by grass to preserve the site's original landscape. Great swathes of neatly clipped lawn gently rise over the roof where a shiny metallic flagpole soars 81m to hoist a flag the size of a double-decker bus, a monumental, if unintentional, tribute to the Aussie backyard, the galvanised Hill's hoist and a beach towel.

The main axis of Parliament House runs northeast–southwest in a direct line with Old Parliament House, the Australian War Memorial and Mt Ainslie, Burley Griffin's original 'land axis'. Two high, granite-faced walls curve out from the axis to the corners of the building; the House of Representatives (east of the walls) and the Senate (to the west) are linked to the centre by covered walkways.

Enter the building across the 90,000-piece **forecourt mosaic** by Michael Nelson Tjakamarra – the theme of which is 'a meeting place' – representing possum and wallaby Dreaming, and through the white marble **Great Verandah** at the northeastern end of the main axis. In the **foyer**, the grey-green marble columns symbolise a forest, and marquetry wall panels are inlaid with designs of Australian flora.

The first floor overlooks the **Great Hall** and, hanging outside the hall, its 20m-long **tapestry**, inspired by the original Arthur Boyd painting of eucalypt forest. Beyond it is the **Members' Hall**. In the public gallery above the Great Hall is the 16m-long **embroidery**, created by more than 500 members of the Embroiders Guild of Australia. Both works make subtle references to European settlement.

The Great Hall is the centre of the building, with the flagpole above it and passages to chambers on each side. One of only four known copies of the 1297 **Magna Carta** is on display here – so close you could almost touch it, if it wasn't for the gas-filled, glass casing. South of the Members' Hall are the committee rooms and ministers' offices; visitors are welcome to view committee rooms and attend some of the proceedings.

There are free 45-minute guided tours on nonsitting days and 20-minute tours on sitting days (every half-hour from 9am to 4pm daily), but you're welcome to self-navigate and watch parliamentary proceedings from the public galleries. Tickets for question time (2pm on sitting days) in the **House of Representatives** are free but must be booked through the **Sergeant at Arms** ( ☎ 6277 4889); tickets aren't required for the **Senate Chamber**. Visitors can catch a lift to the roof to gaze up at the flag pole or down on the city. You can also explore the rooftop lawns and 23 hectares of landscaped gardens.

### Old Parliament House

The venerable **Old Parliament House** (Map p346; ☎ 6270 8222; www.oph.gov.au; King George Tce, Parkes; adult/concession/family $2/1/5; ⏰ 9am-5pm) was the seat of government from 1927 to 1988 and is a great place to get a whiff of bygone parliamentary activity, be it peering through the spy hole into the prime minister's office, re-acquainting yourself with the 1975 dismissal, silently addressing the House of Representatives, or buying your own Hansard bookend from the gift shop. There are free **guided tours** (45 min; ⏰ 9.30am, 10.15am, 11am, 11.45am, 12.45pm, 1.30pm, 2.15pm, 3pm & 3.45pm), or pick up the *Self-Guided Tour* brochure. It also has a wonderful café (p360).

The building incorporates the mesmerising **National Portrait Gallery** ( ☎ 6270 8210; www .portrait.gov.au), which exhibits painting, photography and new-media portraiture. It has a lakeside annexe at Commonwealth Place (Map p346).

Opposite the main entrance to Old Parliament House is the culturally significant **Aboriginal Tent Embassy** (Map p346).

### National Gallery of Australia

The **National Gallery** (Map p346; ☎ 6240 6502; www .nga.gov.au; Parkes Pl, Parkes; permanent collection admission free; ⏰ 10am-5pm) has a stunning collection of over 100,000 works of art representing four major areas: Aboriginal & Torres Strait Islander, Australian (from colonial to contemporary), Asian, and international. Plus a spectacular new Art of the Indian Subcontinent gallery showcasing one of the largest collections of paintings, bronzes and sculptures outside India. The Australian treasures range from traditional Aboriginal art to Sydney Nolan's Ned Kelly series, and all the Australian greats are well represented.

Sharing gallery space with paintings are sculptures (visit the Sculpture Garden), drawings, photographs, furniture, ceramics, fashion, textiles and silverware. Visiting exhibitions usually attract an admission fee. In addition to regular all-inclusive **guided tours** ( 11am & 2pm), there's also a **tour** ( 11am Thu & Sun) focusing on Aboriginal and Torres Strait Islander art.

## Australian War Memorial

Opened in 1941, the massive **war memorial** (Map p346; 6243 4211; www.awm.gov.au; Treloar Cres, Campbell; admission free; 10am-5pm) looks along Anzac Pde to Old and New Parliament Houses across the lake. The building houses an enormous collection of pictures, dioramas, relics and exhibitions detailing the events, weapons and human toll of wartime; most of the heavy machinery is arrayed within **Anzac Hall**, which features an impressive **sound-and-light show** ( hourly from 10am). Entombed among the mosaics of the Hall of Memory is the **Unknown Australian Soldier**, whose remains were returned from a WWI battlefield in 1993 and who symbolises all Australian war casualties.

There are free 90-minute **guided tours**; alternatively, purchase the *Self-guided Tour* leaflet ($3).

Along **Anzac Pde**, which is Canberra's broad commemorative way, are 11 poignant memorials to various campaigns and campaigners.

## National Museum of Australia

This **museum** (Map p346; 1800 026 132, 6208 5000; www.nma.gov.au; Lawson Cres, Acton Peninsula; admission free; 9am-5pm) is one big abstract Australian storybook. Using creativity, controversy, humour and self-contradiction, the National Museum dismantles national identity, and in the process provokes visitors to come up with ideas of their own. From the skewed angles of the architecture to the use of interactive technology, it's an inspiring collision of aesthetics. There are lots of attendants on hand to help you navigate exhibitions on environmental change, indigenous culture, national icons and more, and you can take one-hour **guided tours** (adult/child/family $7.50/5/20). It can be a bit confusing and it's recommended that you don't miss the introductory 'C' show. While general admission is free, a fee is usually charged to access visiting exhibitions. Pick up a copy of the Calendar of Events to see what special shows and exhibits are on.

---

### THE ABORIGINAL TENT EMBASSY

A smouldering log fire, a lop-sided tent and a wobbly caravan outside Old Parliament House are just too intriguing for the Beijing tourists. A discussion rambles from the British Crown's German ancestry (a bronzed King George stands nearby), to how long the fire has been burning, to a discussion on land rights, and finally a photo with Robert Craigie. 'My photo must be all around the world. We get them all here. They know … everybody comes.' Robert is a Murri from Kamilaroi country, around Moree, NSW. His elder brother Billy was one of the original four 'representatives' who established the 'embassy' and spent that first cold night sheltering under an umbrella. On this sunny almost-spring day, Robert is one of the few left at the Tent Embassy while the area is being rested – the grass and trees are given a chance to rejuvenate the traditional way.

The Tent Embassy was established on Australia Day, 26 January 1972 as a protest against the denial of land rights and self-determination. Through official condemnation and destruction, followed by phoenix-like revival, it quickly became a symbol of resistance and is where the Aboriginal flag first gained prominence. Since then the Tent Embassy has waxed and waned over the decades and the politicians built a bigger house in their backyard and moved away. But this poignant camp always manages to remind the world, especially on Australia/Sovereignty/Invasion Day, that Australia still has much to do in regard to reconciliation, land rights and the fair treatment of its indigenous people. As a living, breathing reality check and education facility, it has no peers. The most recent threat to the embassy is to replace it with yet another static museum/memorial, presumably with a digital visitors counter and café.

Bus No 34 runs here. There's also a free bus on weekends and public holidays, departing regularly from 10.30am from platform 7 in the Civic bus interchange.

## High Court of Australia

The grandiose **High Court** (Map p346; ☎ 6270 6811; www.hcourt.gov.au; Parkes Pl, Parkes; admission free; ☿ 9.45am-4.30pm Mon-Fri, closed public holidays) was dubbed 'Gar's Mahal' when it opened in 1980, a reference to Sir Garfield Barwick, chief justice during the building's construction.

The rarefied heights of the foyer (that's a 24m-high ceiling!) and main courtroom are in keeping with the building's name and position as the highest court in the Australian judicial system. Have a chat to a knowledgeable attendant about judicial life, and check out the murals and paintings adorning the walls. High Court sittings, which usually occur for two weeks each month (except January and July), are open to the public.

## Questacon

The hands-on **National Science & Technology Centre** (aka Questacon; Map p346; ☎ 1800 020 603, 6270 2800; www.questacon.edu.au; adult/child/concession/family $15.50/9/10.50/46; ☿ 9am-5pm) is a child magnet, with its lively, educational and just-plain-fun interactive exhibits on the merits of everyday science and technology. Within the spiral arrangement of galleries, kids can explore the physics of sport, athletics and fun parks, cause tsunamis and take shelter from cyclones and earthquakes. There are also exciting science shows, presentations and puppet shows included in the admission price.

## National Zoo & Aquarium

Nestled behind Scrivener Dam is this engaging **zoo and aquarium** (Map p364; ☎ 6287 8400; www.nationalzoo.com.au; Lady Denman Dr, Yarralumla; adult/child/concession/family $21.50/11.50/17.50/62.50; ☿ 10am-5pm), to which you should definitely devote a few hours. It has a roll call of fascinating animals, ranging from capuchins to sharks, and includes Australia's largest collection of big cats, including tigons (the unnatural result of breeding tigers with lions in captivity, a practice that has thankfully been discontinued). Heavily promoted are the additional tours where you can cuddle a cheetah ($150) or take a **tour** (adult/child from $125/65) behind the scenes to hand-feed a tiger, and much more.

## Australian National Botanic Gardens

Spread over 90 invigorating hectares on Black Mountain's lower slopes are these beautiful **gardens** (Map p346; ☎ 6250 9450; www.anbg.gov .au/anbg; Clunies Ross St, Acton; admission free; ☿ 8.30am-5pm Mar-Dec, to 6pm weekdays & 8pm weekends Jan), devoted to the growth, study and promotion of Australian floral diversity. While enjoying the gardens' tranquillity, take the **Aboriginal Plant Use Walk** (1km, 45 minutes), which passes through the cool **Rainforest Gully**. The **Eucalypt Lawn** is peppered with 600 species of this quintessential Aussie tree.

The **visitors centre** and **bookshop** (☿ 9.30am-4.30pm) is the departure point for free guided **walks** (☿ 11am and 2pm, also 10am summer). Nearby is **Hudsons in the Gardens** (☎ 6248 9680; mains $10-15; ☿ breakfast & lunch), a pleasant café with a verdant aspect.

## Canberra Museum & Gallery

This stylish **museum and gallery** (Map p346; ☎ 6207 3968; www.museumsandgalleries.act.gov.au/museum/index .asp; Civic Sq, London Circuit, Civic; admission free; ☿ 10am-5pm Tue-Fri, noon-5pm Sat & Sun) is ostensibly devoted to Canberra's social history and visual arts. The interesting permanent exhibition, 'Reflecting Canberra', includes a charred dishwasher salvaged from a house destroyed in the 2003 bushfire, while visiting collections have run the aesthetic gamut from traditional Palestinian crafts to Korean sculptors. The museum also holds talks and craft-oriented workshops.

## National Film & Sound Archive

This **archive** (Map p346; ☎ 6248 2000; www.nfsa.afc.gov .au; McCoy Circuit, Acton; admission free; ☿ 9am-5pm Mon-Fri, 10am-5pm Sat & Sun) preserves Australian moving-picture and sound recordings for posterity. Highlights include the absorbing permanent exhibition 'Sights + Sounds of a Nation', 100 years of audio and visual recordings, from Norman Gunston's idiosyncratic interviews to the 1943 Oscar-awarded propaganda flick *Kokoda Front Line*. There are also temporary exhibitions, talks and film screenings.

## National Library of Australia

The **National Library** (Map p346; ☎ 6262 1111; www .nla.gov.au; Parkes Pl, Parkes; admission free; ☿ main reading room 9am-9pm Mon-Thu, to 5pm Fri & Sat, 1.30-5pm Sun) was established in 1901 and has since accumulated over six million items, most of which can be accessed in one of eight reading rooms. Be sure to check out the **Exhibition Gallery** (admission free; ☷9am-5pm) highlighting visual treats collated from the library's diverse collections as well as the artworks dotted around the library and its grounds. Bookings are required for the free customised **guided tours** ( ☎ 6262 1271) or simply join the **Behind-the-Scenes Tour** ( ☷ 12.30pm Thu).

## National Archives of Australia

Canberra's original post office now houses the **National Archives** (Map p346; ☎ 6212 3600; www.naa .gov.au; Queen Victoria Ice, Parkes; admission free; ☷ 9am-5pm), a repository for Commonwealth government records in the form of personal papers, photographs, posters, films, maps and paintings. There are short-term special exhibits, such as Robin Archer's recent 'Unexpected Archives'. But the centrepiece exhibit is the **Federation Gallery** and its original charters, including Australia's 1900 Constitution Act and the 1967 amendment ending constitutional discrimination against Aboriginal people. Records of military service and emigration can be accessed for those keen on exploring their ancestry or unearthing a family secret.

## Royal Australian Mint

To see Australia's biggest money-making operation, visit the **Mint** (Map p364; ☎ 6202 6800; www.ramint.gov.au; Denison St, Deakin; admission free; ☷ 9am-4pm Mon-Fri, 10am-4pm Sat & Sun). It has a gallery showcasing the history of Australian coinage, where you can learn about the 1813 'holey dollar' and its enigmatic offspring, the 'dump'. Also on show are Mint-produced official insignia and Sydney Olympics medals. Plate-glass windows give a view to the production of proof (collectable) coins and circulating coins; note that production ceases over the weekend.

As a souvenir, you can mint your own brand-new $1 coin, complete with a special 'c' mark. And to emphasise that you're in the cradle of capitalism, it'll cost you $2.50.

## Australian National University (ANU)

The attractive, busy grounds of the **ANU** (Map p346; ☎ 6125 5111; www.anu.edu.au) have taken up most of the area between Civic and Black Mountain since 1946 and make for a pleasant wander. Drop into the **Drill Hall Gallery** (Map p346; ☎ 6125 5832; Kingsley St; admission free; ☷ noon-5pm Wed-Sun) to see special exhibitions and paintings from the university's art collection; a per-

manent fixture is Sidney Nolan's *Riverbend*, with its near-phosphorescent hue. While you're here, collect the ANU *Sculpture Walk* brochure and explore the outdoor art.

## Australian Institute of Sport (AIS)

The country's elite and aspiring-elite athletes hone their sporting prowess at the **AIS** (Map p364; ☎ 6214 1444; www.ausport.gov.au/tours; Leverrier Cres, Bruce). The 90-minute **tours** (adult/child/ concession/family $13/7/10/36; ☷ 10am, 11.30am, 1pm & 2.30pm) are led by resident athletes, with information on training routines and diets, displays on Australian champions and the Sydney Olympics, and interactive exhibits where you can publicly humble yourself at basketball, rowing and skiing.

## Lookouts

**Black Mountain** (812m) is topped by the 195m-high **Telstra Tower** (Map p364; ☎ 6219 6111; Black Mountain Dr; adult/child $4.40/1.90; ☷ 9am-10pm), which has a great windblown vista, plus a display on the history of local telecommunications and a revolving restaurant (p360). A 2km bush-lined walking track to the top starts on nearby Frith Rd, while other tracks wander northwest around the other side of the mountain from Belconnen Way and Caswell Dr; you can get a basic walking-tracks map from the tower.

**Mt Ainslie**, just northeast of the city, stands at 843m and is one of the anchors for the Anzac Parade axis. Therefore it has particularly fine views of the city's layout and is best in the morning and at night. It's an easy drive and walking tracks to the mountain start behind the Australian War Memorial and end 4km further on at 888m-high **Mt Majura**.

## Other Attractions

You can only peek through the gates of the prime minister's official residence, the **Lodge** (Map p346; Adelaide Ave, Deakin), and peer across the lawns to the governor general's official residence, **Government House** (Map p364; Dunrossil Dr, Yarralumla) near the **Scrivener Dam lookout** (Map p364; Lady Denman Dr, Yarralumla).

Canberra's 80-odd embassies and high commissions are mostly nondescript houses in Yarralumla, but several are architecturally interesting and periodically open to the public. The **Thai embassy** (Map p346; Empire Circuit, Yarralumla), with its pagoda-style, orange-tiled roof, is reminiscent of Bangkok temples. The **Papua New Guinea high commission** (Map p346;

AUSTRALIAN CAPITAL TERRITORY

☎ 6273 3322; Forster Cres, Yarralumla) resembles a *haus tamberan* (spirit house) from the Sepik region and has a **cultural display** (☺ 9am-1pm & 2-4pm Mon-Fri). A comprehensive list of the diplomatic missions and their addresses is available from the National Capital Exhibition (p349).

At the eastern end of Kings Ave is the 79m-tall **Australian-American Memorial** (Map p346; Kings Ave, Russell), a pillar topped by an eagle that, from a distance, resembles Bugs Bunny's ears. The memorial recognises US support for Australia during WWII.

The **Church of St John the Baptist** (Map p346; Constitution Ave, Reid) was finished in 1845, its stained-glass windows donated by pioneer families. The **St John's Schoolhouse Museum** (Map p346; ☎ 6249 6839; Constitution Ave, Reid; admission by donation; ☺ 10am-noon Wed, 2-4pm Sat & Sun), adjoining the church, houses memorabilia from Canberra's first school.

The **Canberra Bicycle Museum** (Map p364; ☎ 6247 1363; www.canberrabicyclemuseum.com.au; 3 Rosevear Pl; admission by donation; ☺ 10am-4pm Wed, 11am-3pm Sat) has an astonishing collection of old clankers, including a penny farthing and the aptly named Boneshaker. You can make planetary observations at the **Canberra Space Dome & Observatory** (Map p364; ☎ 6248 5333; www.ctuc.asn.au/planetarium; 72 Hawdon Pl, Dickson; adult/child/family $10/6/28; ☺ 7.30 & 8.30pm winter, 7.30 & 9.30pm summer, Tue-Sat); bookings are essential. And you can learn about innovative scientific research taking place in Australia– such as virtual reality, gene technology and climate research at **CSIRO Discovery** (Map p346; ☎ 6246 4646; www.csiro.au; Clunies Ross St, Acton; adult/child/family $6/3/15; ☺ 9am-5pm Mon-Fri).

For other sights just a short drive from Canberra, see p363.

## ACTIVITIES

Thanks to the ACT's lakes and mountains, not to mention a pretty good climate, there are plenty of vitalising activities on offer here.

### Boating

**Lake Burley Griffin Boat Hire** (Map p346; ☎ 6249 6861; Acton Jetty, Civic; ☺ 9am-5pm Mon-Fri, 8am-dusk Sat & Sun, closed May-Aug) has canoe, kayak, surf-ski and paddleboat hire (kayaks from $12 per hour).

### Bushwalking

**Tidbinbilla Nature Reserve** (p365), southwest of the city, has numerous marked tracks.

Another great area for walking is **Namadgi National Park** (p365), which is one end of the difficult, 655km-long Australian Alps Walking Track; the other end is Walhalla in Victoria.

Local bushwalking maps and guides are available at **Map World** (Map p346; ☎ 6230 4097; Jolimont Centre, 65 Northbourne Ave, Civic) and **Mountain Designs** (Map p346; ☎ 6247 7488; 6 Lonsdale St, Braddon). The *Namadgi National Park* map ($4.50), available from the Canberra and Namadgi visitors centres, details 22 walks in the area.

### Cycling

Canberra has one of the most extensive cycle-path networks of any Australian city, with dedicated routes making it almost possible to tour the city without touching a road. One popular track circles the lake, while others shadow the Murrumbidgee River. The visitors centre sells the *Canberra Cycleways* map ($6) and the *Canberra & Queanbeyan Cycling & Walking Map* ($8), the latter published by **Pedal Power ACT** (www.pedalpower.org.au) for super-keen recreational cyclists.

**Mr Spokes Bike Hire** (Map p346; ☎ 6257 1188; Barrine Dr, Civic; ☺ 9am-5pm Wed-Sun, daily during school holidays) is located near the Acton Park ferry terminal. Bike hire per hour/half-/full-day costs $12/30/40. Canberra YHA Hostel (p356) and Victor Lodge (p356) also rent bikes and **Row'n'Ride** (☎ 0410-547 838) delivers bikes (hired per day/week $40/95) to your door. As well as providing bike hire ($40 per day), **Brindabella Bike Tours** (☎ 6242 6276, 0407-426 276) naturally enough runs cycling tours (see p356).

### Swimming

Canberra's swimming pools include the **Canberra International Sports & Aquatics Centre** (Map p364; ☎ 6251 7888; www.clubgroup.com.au/home; 100 Eastern Valley Way, Bruce; adult/child $4.80/3.50; ☺ 6am-9pm Mon-Fri, 7am-7pm Sat & Sun). **Canberra Olympic Pool** (Map p346; ☎ 6248 6799; Allara St, Civic; adult/child $4.70/3; ☺ 6am-8.30pm Mon-Thu, to 7.50pm Fri, 7am-6pm Sat, 8am-6pm Sun) and the National Trust–listed 75-year-old **Manuka Swimming Pool** (Map p346; ☎ 6295 1349; Manuka Circle, Manuka; adult/child $4/3; ☺ 6.30am-7pm Mon-Fri, 8am-7pm Sat & Sun Nov-Mar, usually closed Apr-Oct).

See Murrumbidgee River Corridor (p363) for more information on inviting waterholes around the city.

# WALKING TOUR
## Parliamentary Precinct Walk

Canberra is widely spread, but many of its major attractions are in or near the parliamentary triangle defined by Lake Burley Griffin, Commonwealth Ave and Kings Ave.

The focus of the triangle is **Parliament House** (1; p349) on Capital Hill. Heading north from here along Commonwealth Ave towards the lake, you'll pass the Canadian, New Zealand and UK **high commissions** on your left. Turn right (east) at Coronation Dr to King George Tce and **Old Parliament House** (2; p350), which houses the **National Portrait Gallery**. Opposite the main entrance to Old Parliament House is the **Aboriginal Tent Embassy (3)**.

Head southeast along King George Tce and turn left at Parkes Pl, across King Edward Tce, to the grand **High Court of Australia** (4; p352), with its ornamental watercourse burbling alongside the path to the entrance. Next door, across Parkes Pl, is the wonderful **National Gallery of Australia** (5; p350), where you can imbibe caffeine as well as culture.

Follow Parkes Pl down to shores of **Lake Burley Griffin** (6; p349) where you'll see and perhaps hear the **National Carillon** (7; p349) on Aspen Island. Turn left towards **Commonwealth**

**Place** (8; p349), where you can examine famous heads at the annexe of the **National Portrait Gallery** (9; p350) and explore indigenous issues through art at nearby **Reconciliation Place** (10; p349).

Cross diagonally (northwest) over the lawns to **Questacon** (11; p352), Canberra's interactive science museum. From here, cross the Parkes Pl (northwest) to arrive at the **National Library of Australia** (12; p352). Head back up Parkes Pl to Coronation Dr, cross the busy Commonwealth Ave and head north to the Art Nouveau classic **Hyatt Hotel** (13; p358) for a well-earned refreshment.

# CANBERRA FOR CHILDREN

Keeping your children occupied in Canberra is easy. There's lots of free stuff and outdoor activities, but some of the big-ticket attractions have big-ticket prices and strategically placed souvenir shops. Also watch out for the family-ticket small print where more than two kids is considered a rort.

The visitors centre has the *Kidfriendly* brochure (www.kidfriendly.com.au), a *Parks & Playgrounds* leaflet and a map of skate parks.

For the stroller-bound head for the (free) **Australian National Botanic Gardens** (p352), where hills, fresh air and exercise, and a café will keep you happy and them happy or, even better, asleep. For more demanding budding Attenboroughs you will have to fork out for the tooth and claw distractions of the **National Zoo & Aquarium** (p352), or drape them in a python at the **Australian Reptile Centre** (p365). The littlest littlies will appreciate a spin on Civic's landmark **merry-go-round** (Map p346).

For hands-on quirky science and lots of noise visit **Questacon** (p352). Another place with a scientific bent is **CSIRO Discovery** (p353), where you can don a lab coat and come to grips with virtual reality or a stick insect. Budding capitalists can mint their own money at the **Royal Australian Mint** (p353).

Miniature steam-train rides around a miniature village can be had at **Cockington Green Gardens** (p365). There's also a plethora of museums custom-built for curiosity and active imaginations, among them the **National Dinosaur Museum** (p365) and the **National Museum of Australia** (p351) where you will probably be able to lose them, if not yourself, for a while.

Energy levels can be further accommodated by a swim at a Canberra **pool** (opposite) or **waterhole** (p363), or by hiring **bikes** (opposite).

---

> **WALK FACTS**
>
> **Start/Finish** Capital Hill
> **Distance** 6km
> **Duration** 2-3 hours

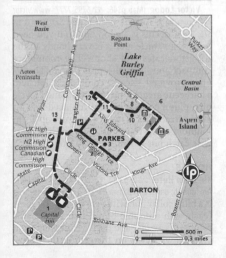

## TOURS

**Aquila Helicopters** ( ☎ 0412 066 766; www.aquilaheli copters.com.au; Canberra International Airport; flights from $70) For aerial views.

**Balloon Aloft** ( ☎ 6285 1540; www.balloon.canberra.net .au; adult/child from $230/160) For quieter aerial views.

**Brindabella Bike Tours** ( ☎ 6242 6276, 0407-426 276; www.brindabellabiketours.com; half/full day tours $55/95) Bikes, equipment and refreshments provided. Half-day Canberra sightseeing or full-day wilderness touring. Complimentary pick-up and drop-off.

**Canberra Day Tours** ( ☎ 0418 455099; www.canberra daytours.com.au) Shuttles you around various capital sites all day for $40/35 adult/child, including entry fees. This hop-on hop-off service is called the *Red Explorer* bus and there are five services kicking off from the Melbourne Building, Northbourne Ave. The first service leaves at 9.30am, the last at 3pm. Check the website or pick up a brochure at the visitors centre for a timetable.

**Go Bush Tours** ( ☎ 6231 3023; www.gobushtours .au) Reputable tailored excursions around Canberra, including a circuit of city lookouts (adult/concession from $40/35) and a day-long exploration of Namadgi National Park (adult/con cession $120/80) They have a wheelchair-accessible vehicle.

**Southern Cross Yacht Club** ( ☎ 6273 1784; www .cscc.com.au; 1 Mariner Pl, Yarralumla; adult/child $15/9) Provides a sightseeing cruise aboard the MV *Southern Cross* departing 3pm daily.

**SS Maid Marion** ( ☎ 0418-828 357; adult/child $12/5) Operates one-hour cruises that pick-up/drop-off at lakeside locales such as Regatta Point ferry terminal, the National Library and the National Museum.

## FESTIVALS & EVENTS

For a comprehensive listing of Canberra's festi val calendar see www.visitcanberra.com.au.

### January

**Summernats Car Festival** (www.summernats.com.au) Hot rods and custom cars rev up at Exhibition Park.

**Australia Day Live** (www.australiadaylive.gov.au) The annual 25 January live concert on the lawns of Federal Par liament featuring the hottest names in Australian music.

### February

**National Multicultural Festival** (www.multicultural festival.com.au) Celebrated over 10 days, with most events in Commonwealth Park.

**Royal Canberra Show** (www.rncas.org.au/showweb site/main.html)

### March

**Celebrate Canberra** (www.celebratecanberra.com) The city's extended birthday party, which kicks off with a day-long food, drinks and arts feast.

### March/April

**National Folk Festival** (www.folkfestival.asn.au) One of the country's largest folk festivals.

### June

**National Capital DanceSport Championships** Competition ballroom dancing at its glitziest best.

### September/October

**Floriade** (www.floriadeaustralia.com) A celebration of Canberra's spectacular spring flowers.

## SLEEPING

Most hotels and motels are strung along Northbourne Ave or hidden in northern sub urbs like Ainslie, Braddon, O'Connor and Downer. The other main accommodation area lies south around Capital Hill, particularly in the politician-favoured domains of Kingston and Barton. When parliament is sitting it pays to book ahead. Inexpensive motel accommo dation can be found in Queanbeyan (p365), 12km southeast of Canberra.

### Budget

#### HOSTELS

**Canberra YHA Hostel** (Map p346; ☎ 6248 9155; www .yha.com.au; 7 Akuna St, Civic; dm $24-27, d/f $70/100; 🔀 🖾 🐾 ) This bright, well-run hostel has an impressive list of services including a pool, 24-hour reception, a bar and self-catering kitchen and cable TV. It remains fond of backpackers, but has all the facilities (except parking) to attract families seeking central, reasonably priced rooms.

**Victor Lodge** (Map p346; ☎ 6295 7777; www.victor lodge.com.au; 29 Dawes St, Kingston; dm/s $27/59, d & tw $76; 🅿 🖾 ) This is a good option if you need to park a vehicle and it is very handy to the Kingston cafés and shops. The rooms are compact and the bathrooms shared. There's linen provided, use of a commercial kitchen, a barbecue area, filling breakfasts and bicycle hire, plus a helping hand if you need info on local attractions. They'll pick you up from Jolimont or the train station if need be; other wise catch bus No 38, 39 or 80 from Civic.

#### HOTELS

**Kingston Hotel** (Map p346; ☎ 6295 0123; 73 Canberra Ave, Griffith; dm $20, bed linen $5; 🅿 ) The Kingston is a blue-collar pub with very basic pub rooms (each with a double bunk) that share bath rooms. It's a noisy and lively venue where you can throw a steak on the grill in the bistro, wrestle a poker machine or join the crowd at the bar.

**City Walk Hotel** (Map p346; ☎ 1800 600 124, 6257 0124; www.citywalkhotel.com.au; 2 Mort St, Civic; dm $28, s $55-85, d $70-95, f $110) This five-storey budget hotel is smack in the middle of Civic and the compact rooms are pretty good shape thanks to the smoking ban. The more expensive rooms have private bathrooms.

### HALLS OF RESIDENCE

Some of the ANU's pleasant halls of residence rent out rooms from late November to late February during university holidays. Most offer similar facilities and room prices start from around $50 (up to $15 more for B&B).

**Bruce Hall** (Map p346; ☎ 6267 4000) and **Burton & Garran Hall** (Map p346; ☎ 6267 4333) are at the northern end of Daley Rd. The affiliated **Ursula College** (Map p346; ☎ 6279 4303) and **John XXIII College** (Map p346; ☎ 6279 4905) lie to the south, opposite Sullivans Creek. Civic is a brisk 15-minute walk across campus.

### CAMPING & CARAVAN PARKS

**Canberra Motor Village** (Map p364; ☎ 6247 5466; canmotorvillage@ozemail.com.au; Kunzea St, O'Connor; camp site $16-22, caravan site $30, d $65-132; ℗ 🐾 ) Attractively positioned in a peaceful, bush hillside setting 6km northwest of Civic, this place has an abundance of amenities, motel rooms and self-contained cabins in various sizes. Note no pets allowed.

**Canberra Carotel** (Map p364; ☎ 6241 1377; info@carotel.com.au; Federal Hwy, Watson; camp site $18, caravan site $24, d $65-180; ℗ 🐾 🖵 ) This is a large caravan park and motel complex on the northern outskirts of town. The complex looks a little ordinary on its 22 acres with not enough trees, but the reception/shop is friendly and the cabins are good value, especially for larger families and groups.

**Eaglehawk Holiday Park** (Map p344; ☎ 6241 6411; www.eaglehawk.contact.com.au; Federal Hwy, Sutton; camp/caravan site $18/25, s & d $80-135, f $90-145; ℗ 🖵 ) This friendly highwayside complex is only 12km north of the centre, just over the NSW border. It has plenty of sheltered midrange accommodation and recreation facilities and is pet friendly. Meals are available at the pub next door.

## Midrange

The **Canberra visitors centre** (Map p346; ☎ 1300 554 114, 6205 0044; www.visitcanberra.com.au; 330 Northbourne Ave, Dickson; 🕙 9am-5.30pm Mon-Fri, 9am-4pm Sat & Sun) can often provide a midrange or top-end room cheaper than standby rates and the rack rates mentioned here.

**our pick** **Blue & White Lodge** (Map p364; ☎ 6248 0498; blueandwhitelodge@bigpond.com; 524 Northbourne Ave, Downer; s $55-88, d $90-95, f $110 130; ℗ 🐾 ) The Grecian pillars and name hint at the friendly Mediterranean reception and squeaky clean accommodation that greets guests of this recommended B&B. The comfortable rooms, some share bathrooms, are neat as a pin and come with a delicious cooked breakfast (or you can elect for a room-only rate). The owners of Blue & White Lodge also manage Canberran Lodge (Map p364; 528 Northbourne Ave, Downer), a similarly styled place, with parking and air-conditioning, where all the rooms are en suite, two doors down. Direct inquiries to Blue & White Lodge where you will also find your breakfast dining room.

**Northbourne Lodge** (Map p364; ☎ 6257 2599; 522 Northbourne Ave, Downer; s/d $70/90; ℗ 🐾 ) This stylish, adobe-washed B&B provides good-value, accommodation with private bathrooms and a choice of breakfast ($10) – English, Continental and Asian. The owner has a wealth of ideas for what to do in Canberra.

**Motel Monaro** (Map p346; ☎ 6295 2111; www.best western.com.au/motelmonaro; 27 Dawes St, Kingston; s/d from $105/116; ℗ 🐾 🖵 ) This well-maintained motel is on a quiet street a short stroll away from the coffee-scented Kingston shopping centre. It is run by the same convivial folk who manage Victor Lodge (opposite) next door. It has a couple of large rooms that are ideal for groups. Book ahead when parliament is sitting.

**Rydges Eagle Hawk Resort** (Map p344; ☎ 1800 651 543, 6241 6033; www.rydges.com/eaglehawk; Federal Hwy, Sutton; s & d from $100, f $145; ℗ 🐾 🖵 ) This well-appointed conference facility is just over the border in NSW, about 10km from the city. It boasts an expansive block of bushland, a pool and tennis courts, and welcomes families.

**Tall Trees Motel** (Map p364; ☎ 6247 9200; www.bestwestern.com.au/talltrees; 21 Stephen St, Ainslie; d $100-125; ℗ 🐾 ) The trees are tall and the quiet, leafy gardens help make this a good choice for light sleepers. The rooms are spacious, have garden outlooks and yet you are still only minutes from the city.

**Olims Hotel Canberra** (Map p346; ☎ 1800 475 337, 6243 0000; www.olimshotel.com; cnr Ainslie & Limestone Aves, Braddon; d $105-145; ℗ 🐾 🖵 ) This 1927 National Trust heritage-listed building and its later refurbishments look a little worse for wear on the outside but the well-appointed rooms surround a nice, terraced courtyard garden. There are standard rooms, superior rooms and 1st-floor, self-contained 'loft' rooms with balconies looking over the inner garden. The rooms where smoking is allowed, with their sealed in corridors, are certainly not a suitable option for non-smokers.

**Miranda Lodge** (Map p364; ☎ 6249 8038; www.miranda lodge.com.au; 534 Northbourne Ave, Downer; s/d $100/120; P ⊠) This motel-style lodge has clean-cut rooms in a variety of sizes and puts a full cooked breakfast under your bleary morning eyes. The owners of Miranda Lodge also run the equally priced Parkview Lodge (Map p364; 526 Northbourne Ave, Downer) nearby; direct inquiries to Miranda Lodge.

**University House** (Map p346; ☎ 6125 5211; www.anu .edu.au/unihouse; 1 Balmain Cres, Acton; s $75-130, d $125-180; P) This 1950s-era building, with furniture to match, resides in the bushy grounds of ANU. The spacious rooms can be hired with or without breakfast and come with a small balcony from where you can watch attendees of academic conferences come and go. It also has a pleasant courtyard in which to let your thoughts wander and a good selection of wine in the cellar bottle shop.

### Top End

**Novotel** (Map p346; ☎ 1300 656 565, 6245 5000; www .novotelcanberra.com.au; 65 Northbourne Ave, Civic; s & d $150-410; P ⊠ ❑ ☎) The 197-room Novotel occupies prime central real estate just a few minutes' stroll from restaurants and shops. The four-star mod-cons include in-room data points, a business centre, spa, gym and a pool. The operators have thought of pretty much everything, down to the daily weather reports posted in the lifts.

**Pacific International Apartments – Capital Tower** (Map p346; ☎ 1800 224 584, 6276 3444; www.pacificinthotels .com; 2 Marcus Clarke St, Civic; apt from $155; P ⊠ ☎ ❑) Rooms on the southern side of this apartment complex face the soporific waters of Lake Burley Griffin and attract a slightly higher tariff than city-side rooms. The majority of apartments have two or three bedrooms and can fit up to six people. There's no restaurant, but limited room service is available (mains $10 to $15).

**Hyatt Hotel Canberra** (Map p346; ☎ 6270 1234; www .canberra.park.hyatt.com; Commonwealth Ave, Yarralumla; r from $325; P ⊠ ☎) This beautifully restored, luxurious, Art-Deco hotel boasts an impressive spa, gym and pool, a cigar bar, restaurant, tea lounge and round-the-clock room service, making it Canberra's only five-star accommodation. Try for a room with a view of the lake, and ask about the various B&B packages.

## EATING

Canberra's dining scene is mainly concentrated in the city centre (Civic), in the trendy enclaves of Manuka and Kingston, and in the northern suburb of Dickson where Asian cuisine reigns supreme. Most of the city's major sights have a decent café or restaurant attached, some with lake views.

### Civic

Within and around Civic you'll find everything from burger joints to no-fuss Italian restaurants and trendy Asian eateries. Fast food is on the menu at the Canberra Centre's **food hall** (Map p346; Bunda St; meals $6-12; ☯ breakfast, lunch & dinner), including sushi, kebabs, burgers, laksa, gourmet rolls and smoothies.

**la pasa** (Map p346; ☎ 6248 6288; Shop 1 Alinga St; mains $11-17; ☯ lunch & dinner) This Singaporean beauty woks up superb Malaysian meals including a variety of fiery laksas, chilli prawns, and beef rendang. There are several vegetarian options and good-value lunch boxes for $7.

**Caffe della Piazza** (Map p346; ☎ 6248 9711; 19 Garema Pl; mains $14-22; ☯ lunch & dinner) With plenty of outdoor seating, a commendable wine list, and generous serves of traditional pasta this Italian institution attracts a appreciative lunchtime crowd.

**Lemon Grass** (Map p346; ☎ 6247 2779; 65 London Circuit; mains $14-18; ☯ lunch Mon-Fri, dinner Mon-Sat) Situated in the delightful Melbourne building, this dependable Thai institution offers a long list of vegetarian, stir-fry, curry and seafood dishes. If you're a fan of king prawns order the *goong gratiam* and pepper with steamed vegetables.

**Asian Café** (Map p346; ☎ 6262 6233; 32 West Row; mains $9-20; ☯ lunch & dinner) Chinese and Malaysian standards such as roast duck and laksa are professionally dished out in this busy and brightly coloured café. Takeaway is available if you just can't sit still.

**Tosolini's** (Map p346; ☎ 6247 4317; cnr London Circuit & East Row; mains $15-28; lunch & dinner Mon-Fri, dinner Sat) Tosolini's has predominantly rich, meaty meals, such as the venison pie with winter vegetables, though the menu changes with the seasons and there are several salads and a few vegetarian options available.

## Manuka

Southeast of Capital Hill is the multi-cuisine culture of Manuka shopping centre, an upmarket hub for diplomats and other suits. Try French, Spanish, Turkish, Italian, Lebanese, Vietnamese, Indonesian, and more, in the local eateries.

**Ruchi** (Map p346; ☎ 6295 7122; Style Arcade, Franklin St; mains $7-15; ☻ lunch Tue-Fri & Sun, dinner Tue-Sat) Ruchi specialises in South Indian cuisine and has a comprehensive menu of veg and nonveg dishes from Goan vindaloos and Keralan fish curries to lamb Madras. Bring a group of friends and take an inexpensive epicurean excursion of the other Deep South. There's a popular lunch buffet on Sunday ($16.50).

**My Café** (Map p346; ☎ 6295 6632; Franklin St; mains $10-20; ☻ breakfast, lunch & dinner) This small licensed café serving bruschettas, bagels and burgers attracts a breakfast crowd keen to bring their office wherever they go. With sunny sidewalk tables it is also popular for lingering lunches and with espresso junkies throughout the day.

**Alanya** (Map p346; ☎ 6295 9678; Style Arcade, Franklin St; mains $15-25; ☻ lunch Tue-Fri, dinner Tue-Sat) This long-standing Turkish restaurant has been feeding its fans for over 20 years with authentic delights. There are plenty of banquet options (including vegetarian) and mains like the excellent *hünkâr beğendi* (diced lamb on a bed of eggplant).

**Mecca Bah** (Map p346; ☎ 6260 6700; 25-29 Manuka Tce; mains $15-20; ☻ lunch & dinner) Satisfy the biggest hunger with the dips and bread, tagines, grills and wood-fired Turkish pizzas of this stylish Middle Eastern restaurant.

**Legends** (Map p346; ☎ 6295 3966; Franklin St; mains $20-30; ☻ lunch Mon-Fri, dinner Mon-Sat) This lively Spanish restaurant is upstairs in the Capital Cinema Centre. House specialities include paella (a vegetarian version is available) and *bacalao* (salted cod), and there are lots of delicious tapas (from $9) to nibble. There's also the odd bit of live flamenco guitar most nights.

## Kingston

Kingston's cafés, bars and restaurants surround the leafy Green Square and continue around the perimeter of the shopping centre.

**Cipriani** (Map p346; ☎ 6295 0777; 27 Kennedy St; mains $11-28; ☻ lunch & dinner) The casual elegance, attentive service, smooth lines and warm Tuscan tones only hint at the dining delight that is Cipriani. Specialities include homemade sausages, such as the delicious chicken, rocket and ricotta salsicce, and the traditional Italian pork sausage served with a roasted capsicum relish or creamy mashed potato. It also has a mouthwatering range of pizzas and an extensive wine list with quality wines available by the glass.

**Silo** (Map p346; ☎ 6260 6060; 36 Giles St; mains $14-20; ☻ breakfast & lunch Tue-Sat) This accomplished bakery/café can be standing room only during the breakfast and lunch rushes. Besides a fine range of breads and breakfast standards like eggs Florentine, it offers gourmet pizzas and exquisite flans and tarts.

**First Floor** (Map p346; ☎ 6260 6311; Green Sq; mains $18-30; ☻ lunch Mon-Fri, dinner Mon-Sat) Overlooking Green Square is this fine-dining establishment with minimalist décor, where the seasonal Mod Oz menus run the gamut from fish and chips to stir-fries and pasta. The desserts are truly decadent and you can sip wines from around Australia.

**Santa Lucia** (Map p346; ☎ 6295 1813; 21 Kennedy St; mains $20-25; ☻ lunch Mon-Fri, dinner Mon-Sat) Canberra's first Italian restaurant is three decades old and still going strong. Generous pasta dishes with rich sauces are delivered to the patent red-and-white-checked tablecloths, and there are kids' meals for $10 to $12.

## Dickson

Dickson's eclectic shopping precinct is dominated by an Asian smorgasbord where Chinese, Thai, Laotian, Vietnamese, Korean, Japanese, Indian, Turkish and Malaysian restaurants compete with such odd bedfellows as McDonald's and an Irish pub.

**Sfoglia** (Map p364; ☎ 6262 5538; Woolley St; mains $6-12; ☻ breakfast & lunch) A delightful patisserie and café where you can find a hearty cooked breakfast and strong coffee to kickstart your day or a healthy focaccia to give you a lunchtime boost.

**Âu Lac** (Map p364; ☎ 6262 8922; 39 Woolley St; mains $9-12; ☻ lunch Tue-Sun, dinner daily) This simple Vietnamese vegetarian restaurant employs soya bean as a culinary chameleon, making it pretend to be a beef curry, fried fish or honey-roast chicken. The meals are tasty and the service is quick, and there's a value lunch box special for $7.

**Kingsland Vegetarian Restaurant** (Map p364; ☎ 6262 9350; Shop 5, Dickson Plaza; mains $8-15; ☻ lunch

AUSTRALIAN CAPITAL TERRITORY

& dinner Wed-Mon, dinner Sat) Another popular vegetarian restaurant where the Asian dishes make use of soy substitute to look like various meats. It is located off Woolley St.

**Dickson Asian Noodle House** (Map p364; ☎ 6247 6380; 29 Woolley St; mains $11-14; ☒ lunch & dinner) This perennially popular Laotian and Thai café is usually booked up towards the end of the week, though thankfully there's always takeaway. Within minutes of ordering, eat your fill of wok-fried, Hokkien-style or soup-laden noodles. Pick of the menu is the addictive combination laksa.

## Elsewhere

Other recommended eateries:

**Bernadette's Café & Restaurant** (Map p364; ☎ 6248 5018; Wakefield Gardens, Ainslie; mains $8-17; ☒ lunch & dinner Tue-Sat) A good veg option with burgers, pizzas and soups.

**Café in the House** (Map p346; ☎ 6270 8156; Old Parliament House, King George Tce, Parkes; mains $10-25; ☒ lunch Sun-Mon & dinner Fri) Enjoy white linen service in the delightful surrounds of Old Parliament House (p350).

**Meeting Place** (Map p364; ☎ 6230 2657; Kamberra Wine Company, cnr Northbourne Ave & Flemington Rd, Lyneham; mains $25-30; ☒ lunch Sun-Sat & dinner Thu-Sat) A delightful lunch spot in the well-tended grounds of the winery.

**Tower Restaurant** (Map p364; ☎ 6248 6162; Telstra Tower, Black Mountain Dr; mains $30-35; ☒ lunch & dinner) Canberra's only revolving restaurant.

## DRINKING

Pubs and bars are mostly concentrated in Civic, but some good establishments have also set themselves up in the northern suburbs of Dickson and O'Connor, and across the lake in Kingston.

**Wig & Pen** (Map p346; ☎ 6248 0171; cnr Alinga St & West Row, Civic) This little brewery pub has its two-room interior packed out on Friday nights by thirsty office workers who also enjoy the hearty pub meals ($10 to $12). It produces several styles of beer, including real English ale.

**Belgian Beer Cafe** (Map p346; ☎ 6260 6511; 29 Jardine St, Kingston) With 33 bottled Belgian beers and five on tap, such as the ever popular Stella Artois, this is the place to quench a thirst and educate a palate.

**Trinity Bar** (Map p364; ☎ 6262 5010; 28 Challis St, Dickson) Sleek, DJ-equipped Trinity has fine vodkas, martinis and cocktails to sample, plus beer pulled from ceiling-hung taps. Look for

the deep-red lighting and the tri-stripe symbol on the wall – the only signs directing strangers to this out-of-the way haunt.

**Kremlin** (Map p346; ☎ 6257 7779; 61 Northbourne Ave, Civic) This ultra cool but friendly bar soothes the soul with occasional live strings, a breathable atmosphere and subdued lighting.

**All Bar Nun** (Map p364; ☎ 6257 9191; MacPherson St, O'Connor) This popular bar languishing comfortably in suburbia has a diminutive interior tailor-made for crowded carousing, and tables appealingly sprawled all over the sidewalk. It also has a decent selection of snacks and light meals.

**Hippo Bar** (Map p346; ☎ 6257 9090; 17 Garema Pl, Civic) Chilled-out Hippo is indeed hip and appropriately cosy for a lounge-bar. The red poufs are accosted by a young crowd of cocktail slurpers and heavy smokers, who also file in for Wednesday-night jazz.

**King O'Malley's** (Map p346; ☎ 6257 0111; 131 City Walk, Civic) This Irish theme park is notable for its labyrinthine interior and the fact that its name literally takes the piss out of the teetotaller bureaucrat who kept Canberra 'dry' from its foundation until 1928.

For more of the same, head across Northbourne Ave to **PJ O'Reilly's** (Map p346; ☎ 6230 4752; Melbourne Bldg, cnr Alinga St & West Row, Civic), which is endearingly referred to by the locals as Plastic McPaddy's.

The **Durham Castle Arms** (Map p346; ☎ 6295 1769; Green Sq, Kingston) is a cosy village pub wannabe in the middle of café-filled Kingston, but those who prefer Guinness to an espresso don't mind. Next door is **Filthy McFadden's** (Map p346; ☎ 6239 5303; 62 Jardine St, Kingston), another of Canberra's Guinness-drenched drinking dens.

## ENTERTAINMENT

Canberra has always been curiously good at nurturing its talented musicians, and they pop up around town. You'll find entertainment listings in Thursday's *Canberra Times* and in the free monthly street mag *bma*. **Ticketek** ( ☎ 6219 6666; www.ticketek.com.au; Akuna St, Civic) sells tickets to all major events.

### Casino

At the southern end of City Walk is **Casino Canberra** (Map p346; ☎ 6257 7074; www.casinocanberra.com .au; 21 Binara St, Civic; ☒ noon-6am; P ) where you can 'play to win', though there's no money-back guarantee if you lose. The only dress requirement is that you look 'neat and tidy'.

## Cinemas

**Electric Shadows** (Map p346; ☎ 6247 5060; City Walk, Civic; adult/child/concession $15/9/8) A well-established cinema that prefers the artful approach to a blockbuster rampage. Matinee sessions (pre-5pm) cost adults only $9 and on Wednesday all tickets are $8. Note that the cinema was planning to move into a new building across City Walk at the time of research.

**Greater Union** (Map p346; ☎ 6247 5522; www.greater union.com.au; 6 Mort St, Civic; adult/child $15/11) This venue screens mainstream releases. Other multiplex cinemas can be found within Canberra's various suburban shopping malls.

## Live Music

Many pubs have free live music. Those belonging to the pro-forma Irish collective usually have bands three or four nights a week (free).

**ANU Union Bar** (Map p346; ☎ 6125 2446; www.anu union.com.au; Union Court, Acton; admission $5-15; ☺ gigs usually 8pm) The Uni Bar is the mainstay of Canberra's live-music scene, with the sounds of bands reverberating around its walls up to three times a week during semester. Big touring acts often play in the high-ceilinged Refectory.

**Tilley's Devine Café Gallery** (Map p364; ☎ 6249 1543; cnr Wattle & Brigalow Sts, Lyneham; usually $20-30) People of all ages breeze in and out of Tilley's cool, smoke-free interior, with its scuffed furniture, dark booths and eclectic menu of local and international musicians and comedians. It also does poetry nights, writers sessions and great cooked breakfasts.

**Toast** (Map p346; ☎ 6230 0003; City Walk, Civic; usually $5-10) Located upstairs behind (well behind) the Electric Shadows cinema is this gritty little bar which has live music (solo acoustic, bands, CD launches) at week's end. Decked out with pinball games and a pair of pool tables, it attracts a lively young crowd.

**Hippo Bar** (Map p346; ☎ 6257 9090; 17 Garema Pl; usually $5-10; ☺ gigs from 9pm Wed) This is another good place for emerging live music. You can hear jazz and turntable sounds.

## Nightclubs

**icbm & Meche** (Map p346; ☎ 6248 0102; 50 Northbourne Ave, Civic; Meche Sat, $10-12; ☺ icbm 7pm-late daily, Meche midnight-3am Wed-Sat) Young drinking crowds attend this clubbing complex, with the music-blasted bar icbm downstairs and the dancehall Meche upstairs. Hosting the odd international

DJ the complex diversifies with Wednesday comedy nights.

**Club Mombasa** (Map p346; ☎ 0419-609 106; www .clubmombasa.com.au; 128 Bunda St, Civic; events $5-10; ☺ 8pm-late Wed-Sun) The energetic patrons of Club Mombasa spend their evenings counting the beat to African and Latin rhythms, reggae, hip-hop, funk and drum 'n' bass.

## Performing Arts

**Canberra Theatre Centre** (Map p346; ☎ box office 1800 802 025, 6275 2700; www.canberratheatre.org.au; Civic Sq, London Circuit, Civic; ☺ box office 9am-5.30pm Mon-Sat) There are many dramatic goings-on within this highly cultured centre, from Shakespeare to Circus Oz and indigenous dance troupes. Information and tickets are supplied by Canberra Ticketing, in the adjacent North Building.

**Gorman House Arts Centre** (Map p346; ☎ 6249 7377; Ainslie Ave, Braddon) Gorman House hosts various theatre and dance companies that stage their own self-hatched productions, including the innovative moves of the Australian Choreographic Centre ( ☎ 6247 3103).

## Spectator Sports

The Canberra Raiders are the home-town rugby league side and during the league season (March to September) they play regularly at **Canberra Stadium** (Map p364; ☎ 6256 6700; www .canberrastadium.com; Battye St, Bruce; P ). Also laying tackles at Canberra Stadium are the Brumbies rugby union team, who play in the international Super 14 competition (February to May). You can catch the highly rated women's basketball team, the Canberra Capitals, in action (October to February) at **Southern Cross Stadium** (Map p364; ☎ tickets 6253 3066; cnr Cowlishaw St & Athllon Dr, Greenway; P ), while their compatriots the AIS play at the **AIS Training Hall** (Map p364; ☎ 6214 1201; Leverrier Cres, Bruce; P ).

## SHOPPING

There are a variety of creative gifts and interesting souvenirs from galleries and shops associated with the major sights. For Aboriginal Art see Gold Creek Village (p365), and for antiques and craft see Bungendore (p365).

**Canberra Centre** (Map p346; ☎ 6247 5611; Bunda St, Civic) The city's biggest shopping centre boasts numerous speciality stores, including fashion boutiques, food emporiums and jewellery shops and several chain stores. The ground-floor information desk can help with wheelchair and stroller hire. More well-browsed shops line adjacent stretches of the pedestrianised City Walk.

**Craft ACT** (Map p346; ☎ 6262 9333; www.craftact .org.au; 1st fl, North Bldg, Civic Sq, Civic) There are some wonderful exhibitions of contemporary work here, with cutting-edge designs in the form of bags, bowls, pendants and prints.

**Old Bus Depot Markets** (Map p346; ☎ 6292 8391; www.obdm.com.au; Wentworth Ave, Kingston; ☯ 10am-4pm Sun) This popular indoor market specialises in hand-crafted goods and regional edibles, including the output of the Canberra district's 20-plus wineries.

**Gorman House Arts Centre Markets** (Map p346; ☎ 6249 7377; Ainslie Ave, Braddon; ☯ 10am-4pm Sat) Art, craft and bric-a-brac and the odd burst of entertainment liven up the courtyards of this heritage precinct.

**Kamberra Wine Company** (Map p364; ☎ 6262 2333; www.kamberra.com.au; cnr Northbourne Ave & Flemington Rd, Lyneham; ☯ 10am-5pm) A winery and part-time gallery, this complex showcases the district's fine cool-climate wines and has a café and restaurant for further ingestion treats.

## GETTING THERE & AWAY
### Air
**Canberra airport** (Map p344; ☎ 6275 2236) is chiefly serviced by **Qantas** (Map p346; ☎ 13 13 13, TTY 1800 652 660; www.qantas.com.au; Jolimont Centre, Northbourne Ave, Civic) and **Virgin Blue** (☎ 13 67 89; www.virginblue .com.au) with (usually) direct flights to Adelaide (one way, 1½ hours), Brisbane (one way, 1½ hours), Sydney (one way, 45 minutes) and Melbourne (from $180 one way, one hour).

**Brindabella Airlines** (☎ 1300 668 824; www.brinda bellaairlines.com.au) flies between Canberra, Albury Wodonga and Newcastle.

### Bus
The **Interstate Bus Terminal** (Map p346; Northbourne Ave, Civic) is at the Jolimont Centre, which has lockers, showers, internet access and free phone lines to the visitors centre and budget accommodation. In the centre, facing Northbourne Ave, is **Guidepost Travel** (☎ 6249 6006; 65 Northbourne Ave, Civic), who handles **CountryLink** (www.countrylink.info) train/coach tickets and books seats on most bus services.

**Greyhound Australia** (☎ 13 14 99; www.greyhound .com.au; Jolimont Centre office ☯ 6am-9.30pm) has frequent services to Sydney (adult/concession $36/26, four to five hours) and also runs to/from Adelaide ($135/110, 18 hours) and Mel-

bourne ($80/65, nine hours). In winter there are services to Cooma, Jindabyne and Thredbo.

**Murrays** (☎ 13 22 51; www.murrays.com.au; ☯ Jolimont Centre counter 7am-7pm) has daily express services running to Sydney (adult/child $36/29, 3¼ hours) and also runs to Batemans Bay ($24/12, 2½ hours), Narooma ($36/18, 4½ hours) and Wollongong ($31/19, 3½ hours). In winter Murrays run services to Thredbo and Perisher Blue.

**Transborder** (☎ 6241 0033; www.transborder.com .au) runs daily to Yass (adult/child $14/7, 50 minutes). Its 'Alpinexpress' service runs to Thredbo ($64/32, three hours) via Jindabyne ($45/36, 2½ hours) daily.

### Car & Motorcycle
The Hume Hwy links Sydney and Melbourne, passing about 50km north of Canberra. The Federal Hwy runs north to connect with the Hume near Goulburn (for Sydney) and the Barton Hwy meets the Hume near Yass (for Melbourne). To the south, the Monaro Hwy connects Canberra with Cooma.

Rental car prices start at around $45 a day. Major companies with Canberra city offices (and desks at the airport):

**Avis** (Map p346; ☎ 13 63 33, 6249 6088; 17 Lonsdale St, Braddon)

**Budget** (Map p346; ☎ 1300 362 848, 6257 2200; Rydges Lakeside Hotel, 1 London Circuit, Civic)

**Hertz** (Map p346; ☎ 13 30 39, 6257 4877; 32 Mort St, Braddon)

**Thrifty** (Map p346; ☎ 13 61 39, 6247 7422; 29 Lonsdale St, Braddon)

Another option is **Rumbles** (Map p364; ☎ 6280 7444; 11 Paragon Mall, Gladstone St, Fyshwick).

### Train
**Kingston train station** (Map p346; Wentworth Ave) is the city's rail terminus. You can book trains and connecting buses inside the station at the **CountryLink travel centre** (☎ 13 22 32, 6295 1198; ☯ 6am-5pm Mon-Sat, 10.30am-5.30pm Sun) and at **Guidepost Travel** (Map p346; ☎ 6249 6006; 65 Northbourne Ave, Civic).

CountryLink trains run to/from Sydney (adult/child $54/27, four hours, three daily). There's no direct train to Melbourne, but a CountryLink coach to Cootamundra links with the train to Melbourne ($102/51, nine hours, one daily); the service leaves Jolimont at 10am. A daily **V/Line** (☎ 13 61 96; www.vline .com.au) Canberra Link service involves a train between Melbourne and Albury-Wodonga, then a connecting bus to Canberra ($63/41, 8½ hours, one daily). A longer but more scenic bus/train service to Melbourne is the V/Line Capital Link ($63/41, 10½ hours) running every Tuesday, Friday and Sunday via Cooma and the East Gippsland forests to Sale, where you board the Melbourne-bound train. Return trips are run on Monday, Thursday and Saturday.

## GETTING AROUND
### To/From the Airport
Canberra airport is 8km southeast of the city. Taxi fares to the city average $20. **Deane's Buslines** ( ☎ 6299 3722) operates the AirLiner bus ($7, 20 minutes, 11 times daily weekdays), which runs between the airport and the Civic bus interchange (bay 6).

### Bus
Canberra's public transport provider is the **ACT Internal Omnibus Network** (Action; ☎ 13 17 10, 6207 7611; www.action.act.gov.au). The main Civic bus interchange is along Alinga St, East Row and Mort St in Civic. Visit the **information kiosk** (Map p346; East Row, Civic; ⏱ 7.15am-5pm Mon-Fri) for free route maps and timetables.

You can purchase single-trip tickets (adult/concession $3/1.50), but a better bet for most visitors is a daily ticket (adult/concession $6.60/3.30). Tickets can be purchased in advance from Action agents (including the visitors centre and some newsagents), or buy them direct from the driver.

### Car & Motorcycle
Canberra's road system is as circuitous as a politician's answer to a straight question. That said, the wide and relatively uncluttered main roads make driving easy, even at so-called 'peak-hour' times. A map is essential.

### Taxi
Call **Canberra Cabs** ( ☎ 13 22 27). One of the main taxi ranks is on Bunda St, outside the cinemas.

# AROUND CANBERRA

For information and maps on attractions around Canberra, including the unspoiled bushland just outside the outer urban limits, head to the visitors centre (p349).

## SOUTH & WEST OF THE CITY – THE WILD SIDE
### Murrumbidgee River Corridor
About 66km of the **Murrumbidgee River** flows through the ACT, and along with major tributaries of the **Molonglo** and **Cotter Rivers**, it provides great riverside picnic locations and swimming spots. Pick up a map and brochure at the visitors centre and explore the waters of **Uriarra Crossing**, 24km northwest of the city, on the Murrumbidgee near its meeting with the Molonglo River; **Casuarina Sands**, 19km west of the city at the meeting of the Cotter and Murrumbidgee Rivers; **Kambah Pool Reserve**, another 14km upstream on the Murrumbidgee; **Cotter Dam**, 23km west of the city on the Cotter River and with a camping ground; **Pine Island** and **Point Hut Crossing**, upstream of Kambah Pool Reserve on the Murrumbidgee; and **Gibraltar Falls**, roughly 45km southwest of the city.

On the banks of the Murrumbidgee, 20km south of Canberra, is the beautiful **Lanyon Homestead** ( ☎ 6237 5136; Tharwa Dr; adult/concession/family $7/5/15; ⏱ 10am-4pm Tue-Sun). Also on-site but in a separate building is the **Nolan Gallery** ( ☎ 6235 5688; adult/concession/family $3/2/6; ⏱ 10am-4pm Tue-Sun), containing paintings by celebrated Australian artist Sidney Nolan, including his famous Ned Kelly art. You can buy a **combined ticket** (adult/concession/family $9/7/20) to both homestead and gallery.

Near Tharwa is **Cuppacumbalong** ( ☎ 6237 5116; Naas Rd; ⏱ 11am-5pm Wed-Sun & public holidays), a 1922 homestead and heritage garden reincarnated as a quality Australian craftware studio and gallery.

### Space Observatories
The ANU's **Mt Stromlo Observatory** ( ☎ 6201 7800; www.mso.anu.edu.au; Mt Stromlo Rd, Stromlo; admission free; ⏱ 10am-5pm Wed-Sun) was virtually destroyed by the bushfires of January 2003. All but one of the optical telescopes were completely destroyed and the burnt-out domes make for a rather spooky, sci-fi attraction. Huge optical telescopes are dinosaurs in the space exploration field so they won't be replaced. There's an interesting education centre, a meteorite you can stick a magnet on and a breezy café.

The **Canberra Space Centre** ( ☎ 6201 7880; www.cdscc.nasa.gov; off Paddy's River Rd; admission free; ⏱ 9am-5pm) resides in grounds of the Canberra Deep Space Communication Complex, 40km southwest of the city. Pride of place goes to Deep

AUSTRALIAN CAPITAL TERRITORY

# AROUND CANBERRA

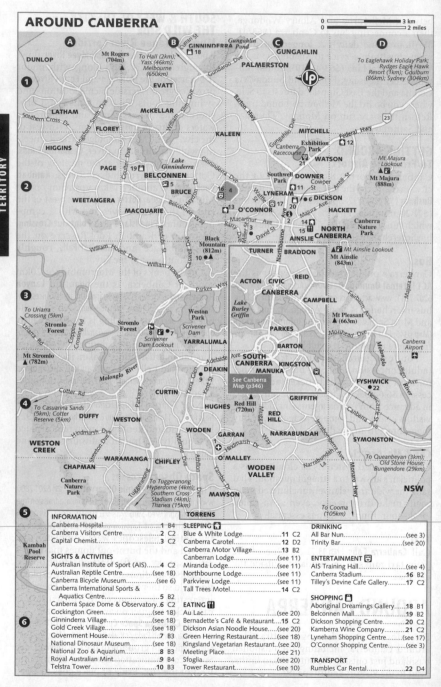

Space Station 43, a 70m-diameter dish that has communicated with the likes of Voyager 1 and 2, Galileo and various Mars probes. There are displays of spacecraft and deep-space tracking technology, plus a piece of lunar basalt scooped up by Apollo XI in 1969. A theatrette continuously screens short films on space exploration and the **Moon Rock Café** ( ☎ 6281 2190) serves drinks and lunches.

## Tidbinbilla & Namadgi

**Tidbinbilla Nature Reserve** ( ☎ 6205 1233; www.environment.act.gov.au; off Paddy's River Rd), is just 45km southwest of the city, and is threaded with bushwalking tracks. There are kangaroos and emus and this is a great spot to view platypus and lyrebirds at dusk. Call for information on ranger-guided activities on weekends and school holidays.

**Corin Forest** ( ☎ 6235 7333; www.corin.com.au; Corin Rd), roughly 50km southwest of the city is a mountain recreation facility surrounded by Tidbinbilla Reserve. There's a 1.2km bobsled track and a flying fox, both open year-round; a water-slide in summer; and a 'snowplay' area in winter. See the website for prices and special packages.

**Namadgi National Park** (www.environment.act.gov.au) includes eight peaks higher than 1700m and offers excellent opportunities for bushwalking, mountain biking, fishing, horseriding and viewing Aboriginal rock art. For more information, visit the **Namadgi Visitor Centre** ( ☎ 6207 2900; Naas Rd, Tharwa; ☼ 9am-4pm Mon-Fri, 9am-4.30pm Sat & Sun), 2km south of the Tharwa township. There is **camping** (unpowered sites per person $3-5) available at Honeysuckle Creek, Mt Clear and Orroral River; bookings must be made through the Namadgi Visitor Centre.

# NORTH & EAST OF THE CITY
## Gold Creek Village

The attractions at **Gold Creek Village** ( ☎ 6253 9780; Gold Creek Rd, Barton Hwy, Nicholls; admission free; ☼ 10am 5pm) are a combination of colonial kitsch and genuinely interesting exhibits that will keep the kids occupied.

The forlorn, touristy **Ginninderra Village** (admission free; ☼ 10am-5pm) was sporting a few 'For Lease' signs when we visited. Kids will find the big bones at the **National Dinosaur Museum** ( ☎ 6230 2655; www.nationaldinosaurmuseum.com.au; adult/child/family $9.50/6.50/30; ☼ 10am-5pm) more their style.

The **Australian Reptile Centre** ( ☎ 6253 8533; adult/child/concession/family $7.50/5/6/26; ☼ 10am-5pm) is a fascinating showcase of reptilian life. Behind glass are tree skinks and scrub pythons, plus the world's four deadliest land snakes. Encourage the kids to be cuddled by one of their harmless brethren – a slippery python.

**Cockington Green** ( ☎ 6230 2273; www.cockington-green.com.au; adult/child/family $15/8/40; ☼ 9.30am-5pm), an immaculately groomed, too-quaint-for-its-own-good English village in miniature coupled with miniature steam-train rides.

Nearby is the **Aboriginal Dreamings Gallery** (Map p364; ☎ 6230 2922; 19 O'Hanlon Pl, Nicholls) with an excellent selection of Aboriginal artworks that includes didgeridoos and bark paintings, with certificates of authenticity provided where possible.

## Queanbeyan & Bungendore

The NSW towns of Queanbeyan and Bungendore lie just over the border and are intrinsically linked with the national capital. Queanbeyan is a thriving country town that provides inexpensive motel accommodation only 12km from the centre of Canberra. Try the **Mid City Motor Inn** ( ☎ 02-6297 7366; 215 Crawford St, Queanbeyan; s/d $64/79; P ✷ ) if you run out of options in Canberra.

Bungendore is a very attractive village 35km east of Canberra, which bustles on weekends but sleeps during the week. There are galleries and antique stores aplenty to keep the cardigan crowd amused and bemused, but the highlight would have to be the **Bungendore Wood Works Gallery** ( ☎ 02-6238 1682; cnr Malbon & Ellendon Sts, Bungendore; s/d $64/79; P ✷ ). As well as showcasing superb work crafted from Australian timber there are changing exhibits of contemporary Australian artists.

The best place to stay in the region is the **Old Stone House** ( ☎ 6238 1888; stnhsebb@tpg.com.au; 41 Molonglo St, Bungendore; s/d $130/190; P ✷ ) a charismatic 1867 granite-block house offering B&B in four antique-furnished rooms.

DIRECTORY

# Directory

## CONTENTS

## ACCOMMODATION

It's not difficult to get a good night's sleep in New South Wales (NSW), which offers everything from the tent-pegged confines of camping grounds and the communal spaces of hostels to gourmet breakfasts in guesthouses and at-your-fingertip resorts, plus the gamut of hotel and motel lodgings.

The accommodation listings in this book are in order of price, starting with budget, then midrange, and finishing with top-end categories. Prices quoted are for high season and we generally treat any place that charges up to $50 per single or $100 per double as budget accommodation. Midrange facilities are usually in the range of $100 to $180 per

double per night. The top-end tag is applied to places charging more than $180 per double. Sydney is generally more expensive than the rest of the state, particularly for anything other than a hostel. Midrange options there can cost up to $200 per double and the sky's the limit for top-end hotels. Conversely, in the regions out west, particularly Back o' Bourke, the Central West and The Riverina, you'll be able to get a decent midrange room for $60.

In most areas you'll find seasonal price variations. Over summer (December to February) and at other peak times, particularly school and public holidays, prices are usually at their highest, whereas outside these times useful discounts and lower walk-in rates can be found.

The weekend escape is a notion that figures prominently in the Australian psyche, meaning accommodation from Friday night through Sunday can be in greater demand (and pricier) in major holiday areas. High-season prices are quoted in this guidebook unless otherwise indicated. For more information on climatic seasons and holiday periods, see p15.

### B&Bs

The local bed and breakfast (B&B) or guest-house birth rate is climbing rapidly, and the options are diverse. In areas that attract weekenders – quaint historic towns, wine regions and accessible forest regions such as the Blue Mountains – B&Bs are often up-market and will charge premium rates if you want to stay between Friday and Sunday in high season (assuming you can even get in). Tariffs are typically in the $80 to $150 (per double) bracket.

---

**BOOK ACCOMMODATION ONLINE**

For more accommodation reviews and recommendations by Lonely Planet authors, check out the online booking service at www.lonelyplanet.com. You'll find the true, insider lowdown on the best places to stay. Reviews are thorough and independent. Best of all, you can book online.

## PRACTICALITIES

- The *Sydney Morning Herald, Daily Telegraph* and the national *Australian* and *Financial Review* are newspapers available throughout NSW. The *Bulletin* is one of Australia's best current affairs magazines, with features, editorials, travel, technology and more. *Australian Geographic* produces a quarterly magazine to illuminate the environment's issues and diversity. *Australian Gourmet Traveller* focuses on Australian food, wine and restaurants with a travel bent. The bi-monthly *Australian Traveller* is a relatively new kid on the magazine stand, but it's chunky and informative about all things travel in Oz.

- Nationwide there are three commercial TV networks – Seven, Nine and Ten – which screen mostly Australian and US content. The government-sponsored ABC and SBS are far more multicultural. The ABC also provides a number of nationwide radio stations, and has excellent coverage in rural Australia where commercial stations are lacking.

- Videos use the PAL system and DVDs use the PAL-B system.

- For weights and measures, the metric system is used.

- Power plugs have two angled pins; the electricity supply is 220-240V AC, 50Hz.

---

Local tourist offices can usually give you a list of places. Online sources:

**australianbandb.com.au** (www.australianbandb.com.au) Information and booking site for B&B accommodation.

**babs.com.au** (www.babs.com.au) Information and booking site for B&B and self-contained accommodation.

**OZBedandBreakfast.com** (www.ozbedandbreakfast.com) Comprehensive listing of B&Bs throughout Australia. Good site for specials.

## Camping & Caravan Parks

Pitching a tent is not only the cheapest way to travel, but also the most sustainable. Camping and caravanning are exceedingly popular in Australia, and parks with excellent facilities are prolific. The nightly cost of an unpowered site for two people is usually somewhere between $13 and $25. Camping in the bush is a highlight of travelling in Australia. In places like the outback you often won't even need a tent, and the nights spent around a camp fire under the stars are unforgettable. Stays at designated camp sites in national parks normally cost between $3 and $8 per person. When it comes to urban camping, remember that most city camping grounds are miles away from the centre of town, especially in Sydney.

Most caravan parks are good value, with almost all equipped with hot showers, flushing toilets, laundry facilities and, occasionally, a pool. Many have old on-site caravans for rent, but these are largely being replaced by on-site cabins. Cabin sizes and facilities vary, but expect to pay $60 to $100 per night for a cabin with a kitchenette for two people.

Useful websites:

**Big 4 Holiday Parks** (www.big4.com.au) Lists caravan and camping sites throughout Australia.

**Caravan and Camping Network** (www.caravancampingnetwork.com.au) Online booking system for caravan and camping parks.

## Farmstays

A decent number of the country's farms offer a bed for a night. A couple of remote outback stations also allow you to stay in homestead rooms or shearers' quarters and try activities such as horse riding. Check out **Australian Farmstays** (www.australiafarmstay.com.au) for your options. You can also get your hands dirty in organic dirt with **Willing Workers on Organic Farms** ( ☎ 03-5155 0218; www.wwoof.com.au).

## Hostels

Backpacker hostels line the New South Wales coast, particularly in major tourist centres. Highly social affairs, they're generally overflowing with 18- to 30-year-olds, but some are reinventing themselves as 'inns' or 'guesthouses' to attract other travellers who simply want to sleep for cheap.

Typically a dorm bed costs $19 to $26 per night and a double (usually without bathroom) $60. NSW also has dozens of hostels that are part of the Youth Hostels Association (YHA; ☎ 02-9261 1111; www.yha.com.au), which is part of the **International Youth Hostel Federation** (IYHF; www.hihostels.com), also known as Hostelling International (HI). For a discounted YHA rate, international travellers should purchase

---

**ECO-FRIENDLY TRAVEL**

Choosing eco-friendly tours and accommodation is one of the best ways you can limit your impact on the environment while you travel. Obvious choices include the hostel using energy-efficient methods; the cottage industry that gives back to its community; the small group tour over big coach companies. But the distinction between well-meaning and well-marketed can be blurry in other instances. The following initiatives have come up with guidelines that should steer you in the right direction.

- Look for operators sporting the eco-tick assurance, determined by Ecotourism Australia. See www.ecotourism.org.au for their eco-certification program.

- Green Globe 21 is a benchmarking certification scheme for all sectors in the tourism industry, working towards a standard for companies and communities. See greenglobe21.com.

- Sustainable Travel International has developed an eco-certification program. See www.sustainabletravelinternational.org.

- The Green Building Council of Australia has a greenstar rating for buildings (examining design and construction). See www.gbcaus.org.

---

an HI card in their country of residence, or from a major local YHA hostel at a cost of $37 for 12 months. Australian residents can become full YHA members for $52/85 for one/two years.

More useful international hostel organisations include the following:

**Nomads Backpackers** ( ☎ 02-9299 7710; www.nomadsworld.com; 89 York St, Sydney) Membership ($34 for 12 months) entitles you to numerous discounts.

**VIP Backpacker Resorts** ( ☎ 07-3395 6111; www.vipbackpackers.com; 3/41 Steele Pl, Morningside, Qld 4170) 12-month membership is $43 and entitles you to many discounts.

## Hotels & Motels

Except for pubs (right), hotels in cities or places visited by lots of tourists are generally of the business or luxury variety, where you get a generically comfortable room in a multistorey block. These places tend to have a pool and restaurant/café.

For comfortable midrange accommodation that's available all over NSW, motels (or motor inns) are the places to stay in. Most motels are modern, low-rise and have similar facilities (tea and coffee, fridge, TV, air-con, bathroom), but the price will indicate the standard. You'll mostly pay between $60 and $130 for a room.

Useful booking agencies that can save you some dosh:

**Lastminute.com** (www.au.lastminute.com) British site offering special deals on travel and entertainment. Good for international travellers heading to Australia.

**Quickbeds.com** (www.quickbeds.com.au) Booking site for accommodation with some great deals.

**Wotif.com** (www.wotif.com.au) Booking site for discounted accommodation.

## Pubs

In country towns, pubs are invariably found in the town centre. Many were built during boom times, so they're often among the largest and most extravagant buildings in town. In tourist areas some have been restored as heritage buildings, but generally the rooms remain small and old-fashioned, with a long amble down the hall to the bathroom. You can sometimes rent a single room at a country pub for not too much more than a hostel dorm, but if you're a light sleeper, never (ever) book a room above the bar.

Standard pubs have singles/doubles with shared facilities starting from around $40/55. Few have a separate reception area – just ask in the bar if there are rooms available.

## Rental Accommodation

Self-contained holiday flats are another mainstay on the NSW landscape. They range from simple, studio-like rooms with a small kitchenette to two-bedroom apartments with full laundries and state-of-the-art entertainment systems. They are great value for multinight stays.

If you're interested in a shared flat or house for a long-term stay, delve into the classified advertisements sections of the daily newspapers; Wednesday and Saturday are usually the best days. Noticeboards in universities, hostels, bookshops and cafés are also good to check out.

Useful websites:

**Domain.com.au** (www.domain.com.au) Holiday and long-term rentals.

**Flatmate Finders** (www.flatmatefinders.com.au) Great site for long-term share accommodation in Sydney.

**Sleeping with the Enemy** (www.sleepingwiththe enemy.com) Another good site for long-term share accommodation in Sydney.

## ACTIVITIES

NSW offers abundant activities; see the New South Wales Outdoor chapter (p40) for greater detail on featured activities.

### Aerial Pursuits

Skydiving, paragliding and hang-gliding enthusiasts can launch themselves from up high in Wollongong (p321) and Manilla (p227), which has some of the best conditions in the world for paragliding. In the Southeast, there's powered hang-gliding on offer in Tumut (p309), and on the North Coast, gliding, hang-gliding and skydiving are all the rage in Byron Bay (p189).

### Diving

Sydney has many good spots for shore dives (p64), including Gordons Bay, Shark Point, and Ship Rock. Popular boat dive sites are Wedding Cake Island, Sydney Heads and off Royal National Park. Elsewhere in NSW, the waters around Jervis Bay (p329), and Merimbula's wreck of the Empire Gladstone (p339) are among the more popular.

On the North Coast, there is good diving in Port Stephens (p150), the Solitary Islands Marine Park (p179) and the Julian Rocks Marine Reserve off Byron Bay (p189).

Diving outfits typically offer four-day dive courses from the Professional Association of Diving Instructors (PADI; www.padi.com) from around $350.

### Fishing

Fishing is a way of life for many coastal towns in NSW, but you'll generally need to have your own gear with you. Boat hire is easy to find in fishing towns such as Yamba (p182), Ballina (p185) and Tweed Heads (p194).

On the South Coast popular fishing haunts include Batemans Bay (p332), Narooma (p334), Bermagui (p337) and Merimbula (p339).

There's fabulous lake fishing in the Monaro Tablelands' Lake Eucumbene (p305) and Jindabyne (p307).

The Namoi River and Lake Keepit near Manilla (p226) in New England are touted as some of the best fishing spots in the state.

The **NSW Department of Primary Industries** (www.dpi.nsw.gov.au) publishes the helpful *Saltwater Recreational Fishing in NSW* brochure, which details fishing rules and regulations for the coast.

### Mountain Biking & Cycling

NSW is a pedal-pusher's utopia and it's not uncommon to see mountain bikers carting their whole kit and caboodle about on multiweek rides. City-cyclers will appreciate the excellent network of paths in Canberra (p354). But the best cycling is done off-road on a mountain bike. The national parks around Sydney (p109) and the Blue Mountains (p119) offer stunning challenges. In the southeast, mountain biking is a warm-weather favourite in Thredbo (p300), and new tracks are being laid in Tumut State Forest (p309). See Mountain-Biking & Cycling in the New South Wales Outdoor chapter (p42) and the Bicycle section of the Transport chapter (p387) for more destinations and information.

### Swimming

See the relevant regional chapters for coverage of NSW beaches and how to get to them.

### Trekking

There are countless bushwalking and trekking opportunities in NSW. Major walks for experienced hikers include the Royal National Park's 28km Coastal Walking Trail (p109) and the 21km glacial lakes walk in Kosciuszko National Park (p295). Reeeeally keen walkers can indulge in the 250km Great North Walk (p138) from Sydney to Newcastle, or the 440km Hume and Hovell Walking Track (p309) between Yass and Albury.

Most folk will be happy with the shorter tracks that cover anything from 500m to 7km in the state's prolific national parks. See Bushwalking in the NSW Outdoors chapter (p40) for more destinations.

## BUSINESS HOURS

Most shops and businesses open around 9am, and close at 5pm or 6pm Monday to Friday and at either noon or 5pm on Saturday. Sunday trading is increasingly common, and you'll encounter it in popular tourist haunts. In larger towns there is usually late-night shopping till 9pm on Thursday and/or Friday. Supermarkets are generally open from 7am until at least 8pm and sometimes 24 hours. You'll also find milk bars (general stores) and convenience stores often open until late.

Banks are normally open from 9.30am to 4pm Monday to Thursday, and until 5pm on Friday. Post offices are open from 9am to 5pm Monday to Friday, but you can also buy stamps on Saturday morning at post office agencies (operated from newsagencies) and from Australia Post shops in the major cities.

Restaurants typically open at noon for lunch and between 6pm and 7pm for dinner. Restaurants stay open until at least 9pm, but tend to serve food until later in the evening on Friday and Saturday. That said, the main restaurant strips in large cities keep longer hours throughout the week. Cafés tend to be all-day affairs that either close around 5pm or continue their business into the night. Pubs usually serve food from noon to 2pm and from 6pm to 8pm. Pubs and bars often open for drinking at lunchtime and continue well into the evening, particularly from Thursday to Saturday.

# CHILDREN
## Practicalities

All cities and most major towns have centrally located public rooms where parents can go to nurse their baby or change nappies; check with the local tourist office or city council for details. Most Australians have a relaxed attitude about breast-feeding or nappy changing in public.

Many hotels, motels and the better-equipped caravan parks have playgrounds and swimming pools, and can supply cots and baby baths. B&Bs, on the other hand, often market themselves as sanctuaries from all things child-related. Many restaurants, and pubs in particular, have kids meals, or will provide small serves from the main menu. Some also supply highchairs.

To find licensed child-care agencies, check under Baby Sitters and Child Care Centres in the *Yellow Pages* telephone book (or on www.yellowpages.com.au), or phone the local council for a list. Licensed centres are subject to government regulation and usually adhere to high standards.

Child concessions (and family rates) often apply for such things as accommodation,

tours, admission fees, and air, bus and train transport, with some discounts as high as 50% of the adult rate. Accommodation concessions generally apply to children under 12 years sharing the same room as adults. On the major airlines, infants travel free provided they don't occupy a seat – child fares usually apply between the ages of two and 11 years.

Medical services and facilities in NSW are of a high standard, and items such as baby-food formula and disposable nappies are widely available in urban centres. Major hire-car companies will supply and fit booster seats for you for an additional fee. Lonely Planet's *Travel with Children* contains plenty of useful information.

## Sights & Activities

There's no shortage of active, interesting or amusing things for children to focus on in NSW. Every town or city has at least some parkland, or you could head into the countryside for wide-open spaces, bushland or rainforests. Some companies specifically tailor outdoor pursuits for kids, like Kidz Klub in Byron Bay (p187). Similarly the free kids program at the Newcastle Region Art Gallery (p144) and the Red Art Shed at the Moree Plains Gallery (p255) hold weekly kids art classes.

Some surf schools in Byron Bay run camps specifically for kids during school holidays (see p189).

Plenty of museums, zoos, aquariums, interactive technology centres and pioneer villages have historical, natural or science-based exhibits to get kids thinking. For tips on occupying kids in Sydney and Canberra, see p67 and p355 respectively.

# CLIMATE CHARTS

The Australian summer starts in December, autumn in March, winter in June and spring in September. The climate in NSW varies depending on the location, but the rule of thumb is that the further north you go, the warmer and more humid it'll be. It's also hotter and drier the further west you go. See When to Go (p15) in the Getting Started chapter for more information.

# CUSTOMS & QUARANTINE

For comprehensive information on customs regulations, contact the **Australian Customs Service** ( ☎ 1300 363 263; www.customs.gov.au).

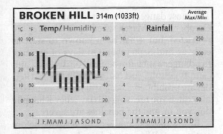

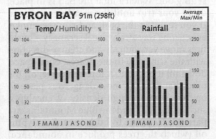

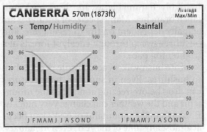

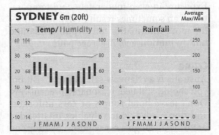

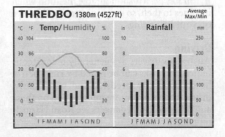

When entering Australia you can bring most articles in free of duty, provided that customs is satisfied they are for personal use and that you'll be taking them with you when you leave. There's a duty-free quota per person of 2.25L of alcohol, 250 cigarettes and dutiable goods up to the value of $900.

When arriving or departing the country, you will need to declare all animal and plant material (wooden spoons, straw hats, the lot) and show them to a quarantine officer. The authorities are naturally keen to protect Australia's unique environment and important agricultural industries by preventing weeds, pests or diseases getting into the country. Food is also prohibited, particularly meat, cheese, fruit, vegetables and flowers; plus, there are restrictions on taking fruit and vegetables between states (see boxed text, p396).

You also need to declare currency in excess of $10,000 (including foreign currency) and all medicines. Before declaring firearms and ammunition (which is mandatory) you must obtain a Restricted Goods Permit from Australian Customs.

Unless you want to undertake a first-hand investigation of conditions in Australian jails, don't bring illegal drugs in with you. Customs authorities are adept at searching for these and those cute sniffer beagles are a permanent fixture in arrival and baggage halls.

Australia takes quarantine very seriously. All luggage is screened or X-rayed – if you fail to declare quarantine items on arrival and are caught, you risk an on-the-spot fine or prosecution which may result in fines and up to 10 years imprisonment. For more information on quarantine regulations contact the **Australian Quarantine & Inspection Service** (AQIS; www.aqis.gov.au).

## DANGERS & ANNOYANCES
For emergencies, dial ☎ 000.

### Animal Hazards
Australia's profusion of dangerous creatures is legendary, and although it does have an abundance of poisonous snakes, spiders and politicians, the chances of actually encountering any in NSW (with the exception of Canberra with its politicians) is extremely low. Hospitals have antivenin on hand for all common snake and spider bites, but it helps to know what it was that bit you. In the case of politics the only course of action is to suck firmly on an egg.

**DIRECTORY**

Australia has also had its share of shark attacks, although again it's worth noting that a) it *is* an island and more importantly b) there have only been three fatal shark attacks in NSW since 1970. Beaches in greater Sydney, Wollongong, Newcastle and the central coast, covering some 200km of coast, have contentious shark nets set at least 13 days per month, which have sadly resulted in the death of thousands of marine creatures.

### INSECTS

For four to six months of the year you'll have to cope with those two banes of the Australian outdoors: the fly and the mosquito (mozzie). Flies aren't too bad in the cities but they start getting out of hand in the outback and some coastal areas.

Mozzies are a problem in summer, especially near wetlands in tropical areas, and some species are carriers of viral infections; see p402. Try to keep your arms and legs covered as soon as the sun goes down and make liberal use of insect repellent.

### SNAKES

There are many venomous snakes in the Australian bush, the most common being the brown and tiger snakes, but few are aggressive. Unless you're interfering with one, or have the misfortune to stand on one, it's extremely unlikely that you'll be bitten. The golden rule if you see a snake is to make like the Beatles and *let it be*.

For information on treating snake bites, see p401.

### SPIDERS

The deadly funnel-web spider is found in NSW (including Sydney) and its bite is treated in the same way as a snake bite. It has an especially nasty set of fangs. Another eight-legged critter to stay away from is the black one with a distinctive red stripe on its body, called the redback spider; for bites, apply ice and seek medical attention. For more on spider bites, see p401.

## Bushfires & Blizzards

As has been dramatically illustrated in recent times, bushfires are a regular occurrence in NSW. Don't be the mug who starts one. In hot, dry and windy weather, be extremely careful with any naked flame – cigarette butts thrown out of car windows have started many a fire.

The most dangerous season is usually from 1 October to 31 March when open-air fires are restricted, but it has been known to start as early as mid-September. On days of extreme fire danger a total fire ban will be declared and campfires, solid-fuel barbecues, ovens and kettles are prohibited. Locals will not be amused if they catch you breaking this law; they'll happily dob you in, and the penalties are severe.

Bushwalkers should seek local advice before setting out. When a total fire ban is in place, delay your trip until the weather improves. If you're out in the bush and you see smoke, even a long way away, take it seriously – bushfires move very quickly and change direction with the wind. Go to the nearest open space, downhill if possible. A forested ridge, on the other hand, is the most dangerous place to be. Areas with a high density of eucalypts, such as the ACT and the Blue Mountains, are particularly prone to bush fires. Eucalyptus oil (which the trees produce in abundance) is highly flammable as are dead bark and fallen branches. Many species of eucalypts are actually dependent on fire to regenerate, and bushfires sweep through eucalypt forests at a frightening pace.

More bushwalkers actually die of cold than in bushfires. Even in summer, temperatures can drop below freezing at night in the mountains and the weather can change very quickly. Blizzards in the mountains of NSW can occur at almost any time of the year, even in January. Exposure in even moderately cool temperatures can sometimes result in hypothermia – for more information on hypothermia and how to minimise its risks, see p401.

## Crime

Australia is a relatively safe place to visit but you should still take reasonable precautions. Don't leave hotel rooms or cars unlocked, and don't leave your valuables unattended or visible through a car window. Sydney and Byron Bay get a dishonourable mention when it comes to theft, so keep an extra-vigilant eye on your belongings.

## Driving

Australian drivers are generally a courteous bunch, but risks can be posed by rural petrol heads, inner-city speedsters and, particularly, drunk drivers. For more information on these and other potential dangers see Road Hazards on p394.

---

**BETWEEN THE FLAGS**

On any popular ocean beach in Australia during summer you'll probably find a pair of poles stuck in the sand about 200m apart, each with a red-and-yellow flag on them. They signify that the area of the beach between the flags is patrolled by surf lifeguards. It also means that the area outside the flags may not be safe for swimming because of undertows and currents. If you swim between the flags, help should arrive quickly if you get into trouble; raise your arm (and yell!) if you need help. Outside the flags and on unpatrolled beaches you are, more or less, on your own.

Australia has a strong tradition of surf life-saving, with regular carnivals in which super-fit athletes compete in a series of events such as swimming, surf kayaking and running. The most well-known competition is the Iron Man series. There are surf life-saving clubs all along the east coast and most of the lifeguards are volunteer members.

---

## Swimming

Popular beaches are patrolled by surf life-savers, and patrolled areas are marked by flags (for details see the boxed text, above). Even so, surf beaches can be dangerous places to swim if you aren't used to the conditions. Undertows (or 'rips') are the main problem. If you find yourself being carried out by a rip, the important thing to do is just keep afloat; don't panic or try to swim against the rip, which will exhaust you. In most cases the current stops within a couple of hundred metres of the shore and you can then swim parallel to the shore for a short way to get out of the rip and make your way back to land.

## DISCOUNT CARDS
### Senior Cards

Senior travellers with some form of identification are often eligible for concession prices. Overseas pensioners are entitled to discounts of at least 10% on most express bus fares with Greyhound. Travellers over 60 years of age (both Australian residents and visitors) will simply need to present current age-proving identification to be eligible for discounts on full economy airfares.

### Student & Youth Cards

The **International Student Travel Confederation** (ISTC; www.istc.org) is an international collective of specialist student travel organisations. It's also the body behind the internationally recognised International Student Identity Card (ISIC), which is only issued to full time students aged 12 years and over, and gives the bearer discounts on accommodation, transport and admission to various attractions. The ISTC also produces the International Youth Travel Card (IYTC or Go25), which is issued to people who are between 12 and 26

years of age and not full-time students, and has benefits equivalent to the ISIC. A similar ISTC brainchild is the International Teacher Identity Card (ITIC), available to teaching professionals. All three cards are chiefly available from student travel companies.

## EMBASSIES & CONSULATES
### Australian Embassies & Consulates

The website of the **Department of Foreign Affairs & Trade** (www.dfat.gov.au) provides a full listing of all Australian diplomatic missions overseas.

**Canada** Ottawa ( ☎ 613-236 0841; www.ahc-ottawa.org; Suite 710, 50 O'Connor St, Ottawa, Ontario K1P 6L2) Also in Vancouver and Toronto.

**France** Paris ( ☎ 01-4059 3300; www.france.embassy .gov.au; 4 Rue Jean Rey, 75724 Paris Cedex 15)

**Germany** Berlin ( ☎ 030-880088-0; www.germany .embassy.gov.au; Wallstrasse 76-79 Berlin 10179) Also in Frankfurt.

**Ireland** Dublin ( ☎ 01-664 5300; www.ireland.embassy .gov.au; 7th fl, Fitzwilton House, Wilton Terrace, Dublin 2)

**Japan** Tokyo ( ☎ 03-5232 4111; www.australia.or.jp; 2-1-14 Mita, Minato-Ku, Tokyo 108-8361) Also in Osaka, Nagoya and Fukuoka City.

**Netherlands** The Hague ( ☎ 070-310 8200; www.aus tralian-embassy.nl; Carnegielaan 4, The Hague 2517 KH)

**New Zealand** Auckland ( ☎ 09-921 8800; Level 7, Price Waterhouse Coopers Bldg, 186-194 Quay St, Auckland), Wellington ( ☎ 04-473 6411; www.newzealand.embassy .gov.au; 72-78 Hobson St, Thorndon, Wellington)

**Singapore** Singapore ( ☎ 6836 4100; www.singapore .embassy.gov.au; 25 Napier Rd, Singapore 258507)

**South Africa** Pretoria ( ☎ 12-423 6000; www.australia .co.za; 292 Orient Street, Arcadia, Pretoria 0083)

**UK** London ( ☎ 020-7379 4334; www.australia.org.uk; Australia House, The Strand, London WC2B 4LA) Also in Edinburgh.

**USA** Washington DC ( ☎ 202-797 3000; www.austemb .org; 1601 Massachusetts Ave NW, Washington DC 20036) Also in Los Angeles, New York and other major cities.

## Embassies & Consulates in Australia

The principal diplomatic representations to Australia are in Canberra.

**Canada** Canberra (Map p346; ☎ 02-6270 4000; www .dfait-maeci.gc.ca/australia; Commonwealth Ave, Canberra, ACT 2600); Sydney ( ☎ 02-9364 3000; Level 5/111 Harrington St, Sydney, NSW 2000)

**France** Canberra (Map p346; ☎ 02-6216 0100; www .ambafrance-au.org; 6 Perth Ave, Yarralumla, ACT 2600); Sydney ( ☎ 02-9261 5779; Level 26, St Martins Tower, 31 Market St, Sydney, NSW 2000)

**Germany** Canberra (Map p346; ☎ 02-6270 1911; www .germanembassy.org.au; 119 Empire Circuit, Yarralumla, ACT 2600); Sydney ( ☎ 02-9328 7733; 13 Trelawney St, Woollahra, NSW 2025)

**Ireland** Canberra (Map p346; ☎ 02-6273 3022; irish emb@cyberone.com.au; 20 Arkana St, Yarralumla, ACT 2600); Sydney ( ☎ 02-9231 6999; Level 30, 400 George St, Sydney, NSW 2000)

**Japan** Canberra (Map p346; ☎ 02-6273 3244; www .japan.org.au; 112 Empire Circuit, Yarralumla, ACT 2600); Sydney ( ☎ 02-9231 3455; Level 34, Colonial Centre, 52 Martin Pl, Sydney, NSW 2000)

**Netherlands** Canberra (Map p346; ☎ 02-6220 9400; www.netherlands.org.au; 120 Empire Circuit, Yarralumla, ACT 2600); Sydney ( ☎ 02-9387 6644; Level 23, Tower 2, 101 Grafton St, Bondi Junction, NSW 2022)

**New Zealand** Canberra (Map p346; ☎ 02-6270 4211; www.nzembassy.com; Commonwealth Ave, Canberra, ACT 2600); Sydney ( ☎ 02-8256 2000; Level 10, 55 Hunter St, Sydney, NSW 2000)

**Singapore** Canberra (Map p346; ☎ 02-6271 2000; www .mfa.gov.sg/canberra; 17 Forster Cres, Yarralumla, ACT 2600)

**South Africa** Canberra (Map p346; ☎ 02-6272 7300; www.sahc.org.au; cnr Rhodes Pl & State Circle, Yarralumla, Canberra, ACT 2600)

**UK** Canberra (Map p346; ☎ 02-6270 6666; www.britaus .net; Commonwealth Ave, Yarralumla, ACT 2600); Sydney ( ☎ 02-9247 7521; 16th fl, 1 Macquarie Pl, Sydney Cove, NSW 2000)

**USA** Canberra (Map p346; ☎ 02-6214 5600; http://us embassy-australia.state.gov; Moonah Pl, Yarralumla, ACT 2600); Sydney ( ☎ 02-9373 9200; Level 10, 19-29 Martin Pl, Sydney, NSW 2000)

## FESTIVALS & EVENTS

Some of the most enjoyable Australian festivals are also the most typically Australian – like the surf life-saving competitions on beaches all around the country during summer; or outback race meetings, which draw together isolated communities. There are also some big city-based street festivals, sporting events and arts festivals that showcase comedy, music and dance, and some important commemorative get-togethers.

Details of festivals and events that are grounded in a single place – be it a city, town, valley or reserve – are provided throughout the chapters of this book. But the following events occur throughout a particular region, or the state, or even around the country.

### January

**Big Day Out** (www.bigdayout.com) This huge open-air music concert tours Sydney and attracts big-name international acts and dozens of local bands and DJs.

**Australia Day** This national holiday, commemorating the arrival of the First Fleet in 1788, is observed on 26 January.

**Summernats Car Festival** (www.summernats.com.au) Revheads from around the country gather in Canberra.

**Survival Festival** The Aboriginal version of Australia Day, also held on 26 January, is marked by Koori music, dance, and arts and crafts displays in Sydney.

**Australasian Country Music Festival** (www.country .com.au) Held in Tamworth on the Australia Day long weekend, this festival showcases the country's top country and western artists.

### February/March

**Gay & Lesbian Mardi Gras** (www.mardigras.org.au) The most colourful event on the Sydney social calendar culminates in a spectacular parade along Oxford St.

**National Multicultural Festival** (www.multicultural festival.com.au) Celebrated over 10 days in Canberra.

**Tropfest** (www.tropfest.com.au) The world's largest short-film festival, held in Sydney but broadcast throughout the country.

### March

**Surfest** (www.surfest.com) Australia's longest-running professional surf carnival is held at Newcastle Beach.

**Royal Easter Show** (www.eastershow.com.au) Livestock contests and rodeos are held in Sydney.

**National Folk Festival** (www.folkfestival.asn.au) One of the country's largest folk festivals, held in Canberra.

### April

**East Coast International Blues & Roots Music Festival** (www.bluesfest.com.au) Held over Easter in Byron Bay, this international jam attracts high-calibre performers and around 10,000 visitors.

### May

**Sorry Day** (www.journeyofhealing.com) On 26 May each year, the anniversary of the tabling in 1997 of the *Bringing Them Home* report, concerned Australians acknowledge the continuing pain and suffering of indigenous people affected by Australia's one-time child-removal practices and policies. Events are held in most cities countrywide.

**July**
**Naidoc Week** (www.naidoc.org.au) Communities across Australia celebrate the National Aboriginal and Islander Day of Celebration.
**Splendour in the Grass** (www.splendourinthegrass .com) Huge indie music festival in Byron Bay.

**September**
**Mudgee Wine Festival** (www.mudgeewines.com.au) Sample Mudgee's finest wine and welcome in the spring at this yearly festival.
**Wagga Wagga Jazz Festival** (www.waggajazz.org.au) Well-regarded international jazz festival.

**October**
**Bathurst 1000** Motor-racing enthusiasts flock to Bathurst for the annual 1000km touring-car race on the superb Mt Panorama circuit.
**Jazz in the Vines** (www.jazzinthevines.com.au) Food, wine and jazz in the Hunter Valley.

**November**
**Melbourne Cup** On the first Tuesday in November, Australia's premier horse race is run in Melbourne. Many country towns in NSW schedule racing events to coincide with it.

**December & January**
**Sydney to Hobart Yacht Race** (www.rolexsydney hobart.com) One of the world's most gruelling ocean races, starting on 26 December every year.

## FOOD
Visitors to NSW enjoy the range and wealth of food available in the state's restaurants, markets, delicatessens (delis) and cafés. In urban and tourist hubs such as Sydney, Canberra, Byron Bay and Newcastle, you'll find excellent fare and plenty of fresh seafood. Many small towns also pride themselves on their gastronomic ability, but in others you'll be dining on simple pub grub and sandwiches. In general, however, the dining is fine, owing to the abundance of reasonably priced fresh produce. Also, many people from different cultures have made their home here, bringing with them a huge range of ethnic cuisines that are now part of the country's culinary repertoire.

Eating listings in this book are in order of price, from cheapest to most expensive. Quality restaurants charge from $25 to $40

for a main meal. Best value are modern cafés, ethnic restaurants (mains under $20), and pub bistros, where you can get a good meal in casual surroundings for under $20.

For general opening hours, breakfast is normally served between 6am and 11am, lunch starts around noon till about 3pm and dinner usually starts after 6pm. But note that in rural areas, the kitchen may close by 8pm.

It's customary to tip in restaurants and upmarket cafés if the service warrants it – a gratuity of between 5% to 15% of the bill is the norm.

See p45 for full details on NSW's specialities and modern Australian (Mod Oz) cuisine.

Diners who enjoy a pre- or post-digestive puff will need to go outside, as smoking has been made illegal in most enclosed public places in all Australian states and territories, including indoor cafés, restaurants and (sometimes only at mealtime) pub dining areas.

## GAY & LESBIAN TRAVELLERS
Australia is a popular destination for gay and lesbian travellers, with the so-called 'pink tourism' appeal of Sydney especially big, thanks largely to the city's annual, high-profile and spectacular Sydney Gay & Lesbian Mardi Gras.

In Sydney and along the east coast, there are tour operators, travel agents, resorts and other accommodation places that are either exclusively gay and lesbian, or make a point of welcoming gays. See p71 for more information.

In NSW, certain areas are the focus of the gay and lesbian communities, among them Oxford St and King's Cross in Sydney, the Blue Mountains, Hunter Valley and the South Coast.

In general Australians are open-minded about homosexuality, but the further into the country you get, the more likely you are to run into overt homophobia. Homosexual acts are legal in all states but the age of consent between males varies – in the Australian Capital Territory (ACT) and NSW it's 16 years.

### Publications & Contacts
All major cities have gay newspapers, which are available from gay and lesbian venues, and from newsagents in popular gay and lesbian residential areas.

The website of **Gay & Lesbian Tourism Australia** (GALTA; www.galta.com.au) is a good place to look for general information, though you need to become a member to receive the full benefits. **Beyond the Blue** ( ☎ 02-8399 0070; 685-687 South Dowling St, Surry Hills, NSW 2010) is a tour operator catering to gay and lesbian travellers.

Other helpful websites:

**Gay Australia** (www.gayaustralia.com.au)
**Pinkboard** (www.pinkboard.com.au) Sydney-based.

## HOLIDAYS
### Public Holidays

The following is a list of the main national and state public holidays. As the timing can vary from state to state, check locally for precise dates.

### National
**New Year's Day** 1 January
**Australia Day** 26 January
**Easter** (Good Friday to Easter Monday inclusive) March/ April
**Anzac Day** 25 April
**Queen's Birthday** (except WA) Second Monday in June
**Queen's Birthday** (WA) Last Monday in September
**Christmas Day** 25 December
**Boxing Day** 26 December

### Australian Capital Territory
**Canberra Day** March
**Bank Holiday** First Monday in August
**Labour Day** First Monday in October

### New South Wales
**Bank Holiday** First Monday in August
**Labour Day** First Monday in October

### School Holidays

The Christmas holiday season, from mid-December to late January, is part of the summer school holidays – it's the time you are most likely to find transport and accommodation booked out, and long, restless queues at tourist attractions. There are three shorter school holiday periods during the year. They fall roughly from early to mid-April, late June to mid-July, and late September to early October.

## INSURANCE

Don't underestimate the importance of a good travel-insurance policy that covers theft, loss and medical problems – nothing is guaranteed to ruin your holiday plans quicker than an accident or having that brand-new digital camera stolen. There is a wide variety of policies available, so compare the small print.

Some policies specifically exclude designated 'dangerous activities' such as scuba diving, skiing and even bushwalking. If you plan on doing any of these things, make sure the policy you choose fully covers you for your activity of choice.

You may prefer a policy that pays doctors or hospitals directly, rather than your having to pay on the spot and claim later. If you have to claim later make sure you keep all documentation. Some policies ask you to call back (reverse charges or collect) to a centre in your home country where an immediate assessment of your problem is made. Check that the policy covers ambulances and emergency medical evacuations by air. Worldwide coverage for travellers from over 44 countries is available online at www.lonelyplanet.com /travel_services.

See also Insurance (p398) in the Health chapter. For information on insurance matters relating to cars that are bought or rented, see p391.

## INTERNET ACCESS

Email and internet access is easy to find in NSW. You'll find internet cafés in cities, sizable towns and pretty much anywhere that travellers congregate. The average rate is about $6 an hour, usually with a minimum of 10 minutes' access, although fierce competition in Sydney keeps the cost lower there. Most youth hostels and backpacker places can hook you up, as can many hotels and caravan parks.

Most public libraries have internet access, but generally there are a limited number of terminals and these are provided for research needs, not for travellers to check their emails. Furthermore many libraries require you to join and make a terminal booking, so an internet café is generally easier.

If you're carrying your own laptop, hooking up to the internet is as simple as plugging it into the phone line in your room. You'll need to have a dial-up account with an Internet Service Provider, and ensure that the access number is the cost of a local call throughout NSW (this is fairly common for Australian ISPs). A useful tip is to put 0 (zero), in front of your dial-up number to enable your modem to dial an outside line.

Australia primarily uses the RJ-45 telephone plugs although you may see Telstra EXI-160 four-pin plugs – electronics shops such as Dick Smith sell adaptors.

In this book, this symbol ▣ denotes internet access is available at the respective sleeping or eating option. For useful websites about NSW see p16.

## LEGAL MATTERS

Most travellers to NSW will have no contact with the Australian police or any other part of the legal system. Those that do are most likely to experience it while driving.

There is a significant police presence on the country's roads, with the power to stop your car and ask to see your licence (you're required to carry it), check your vehicle for roadworthiness, and also to insist that you take a breath test to check your blood alcohol level – needless to say, drink-driving offences are taken very seriously here.

First offenders caught with small amounts of illegal drugs are likely to receive a fine rather than go to jail, but nonetheless the recording of a conviction against you may affect your visa status.

If you are arrested, it's your right to telephone a friend, relative or lawyer before any formal questioning begins. Legal aid is available only in serious cases and only to the truly needy (for links to Legal Aid offices see www .nla.aust.net.au). However, many solicitors do not charge for an initial consultation.

The legal driving age is 17 and the drinking age is 18.

## MAPS

Good-quality road and topographical maps are plentiful in Australia. The NRMA (p390) is a dependable source of road maps especially for rural NSW. Many newsagencies and bookshops sell good maps for surrounding areas. Local tourist offices usually supply free maps, though the quality varies.

Authors on this book got off the beaten track and scrutinised their maps. Lonely Planet also produces a handy fold-out city map of Sydney.

For bushwalking and other outdoor activities for which large-scale maps are essential, browse the topographic sheets put out by **Geoscience Australia** ( ☎ 1800 800 173, 02-6249 9111; www.ga.gov.au; cnr Jerrabomberra Ave & Hindmarsh Dr, Symonston, ACT 2609).

## MONEY

Changing foreign currency or travellers cheques is usually no problem at banks throughout NSW. Exchange rates are listed in the Quick Reference at the front of this book.

In this book, unless otherwise stated, all prices given in dollars refer to Australian dollars. For an idea of the money required to travel in NSW, see p15.

### ATMs & Eftpos

ATMs are common in NSW and are linked to international networks. They are an excellent way to procure local currency and avoid the hassle of carrying travellers cheques or large sums of cash.

Eftpos (Electronic Funds Transfer at Point of Sale) enables you to use your bank card to pay for services or purchases directly, and to withdraw money. Australians use the service liberally and it's available just about anywhere, from the supermarket to the pub. Some places demand a $10 minimum purchase.

### Cash

Australia's currency is the Australian dollar, made up of 100 cents. There are 5c, 10c, 20c, 50c, $1 and $2 coins, and $5, $10, $20, $50 and $100 notes. Although the smallest coin in circulation is 5c, prices are often still marked in single cents and then rounded to the nearest 5c when you come to pay.

### Credit Cards

MasterCard and Visa are widely accepted. American Express is limited more to major towns and destinations.

The most flexible option is to carry both a credit card and an ATM or debit card.

### Taxes & Refunds

The Goods and Services Tax (GST) is a flat 10% tax on all goods and services – accommodation, eating out, transport, electrical, books, furniture, clothing and so on. There are, however, some exceptions, such as basic foods (milk, bread, fruits and vegetables etc). By law the tax is included in the quoted or shelf prices, so all prices in this book are GST-inclusive.

If you purchase new or second-hand goods with a total minimum value of $300 from any one supplier no more than 30 days before you leave Australia, you are entitled under the Tourist

DIRECTORY

Refund Scheme (TRS) to a refund of any GST paid. The scheme only applies to goods you take with you as hand luggage, or wear, onto the plane or ship. Also note that the refund is valid for goods bought from more than one supplier, but only if at least $300 is spent in each. For more details, contact the **Australian Customs Service** ( ☎ 1300 363 263; www.customs.gov.au).

## PHOTOGRAPHY & VIDEO

Digital cameras, memory sticks and batteries are sold prolifically in Sydney. Electronic stores like Dick Smith will stock everything you need, as will the larger departments stores. The availability of batteries and memory sticks outside of Sydney and Newcastle is far diminished so if you're planning to get trigger happy it's best to stock up in the cities. Many internet cafés, camera stores and large stationers like **Officeworks** (www.officeworks.com.au) have facilities that enable you to produce prints directly from your memory stick or to burn CDs.

Film and slide film are still widely available and developing standards are high. You can get your shots processed at any camera store and just about any chemist. Video cassettes are widely available at camera and electronics stores.

As in any country, politeness goes a long way when taking photographs; ask before taking pictures of people. Aborigines generally do not like to have their photographs taken, even from a distance.

Useful Lonely Planet titles for the budding photographer include *Urban Travel Photography, Wildlife Travel Photography,* and *Landscape Photography.*

## POST

Australia's postal services are efficient and fairly cheap. It costs 50c to send a standard letter or postcard within the country. **Australia Post** (www.auspost.com.au) has two regions for international destinations: Asia-Pacific and Rest of the World; airmail letters up to 50g cost $1.10/1.65, respectively. The cost of a postcard (up to 20g) is $1 and an aerogram to any country is 85c. There are five international parcel zones and rates vary by distance and class of service.

All post offices will hold mail for visitors, and some city GPOs (main or general post offices) have very busy poste restante sections. You need to provide some form of identification (such as a passport) to collect mail.

See p369 for post office opening times.

## SOLO TRAVELLERS

Solo travellers are a common sight throughout Australia and there is certainly no stigma attached to lone visitors. But in some places there can be an expectation that the visitor should engage in some way with the locals, particularly in rural pubs where keeping to yourself can prove harder than it sounds. Women travelling on their own should exercise caution when in less-populated areas, and will find that guys can get annoyingly attentive in drinking establishments. See also Women Travellers (p380).

## TELEPHONE

There are a number of providers offering various services. The two main players are the mostly government-owned **Telstra** (www.telstra.com.au) and the fully private **Optus** (www.optus.com.au). Both are also major players in the mobile (cell) phone market, along with **Vodafone** (www.vodafone.com.au).

### Information & Toll-Free Calls

Numbers starting with ☎ 190 are usually recorded information services, costing anything from 35c to $5 or more per minute (more from mobiles and payphones). To make a reverse-charge (collect) call from any public or private phone, just dial ☎ 1800-REVERSE (738 3773), or ☎ 12 550.

Toll-free numbers (prefix ☎ 1800) can be called free of charge from anywhere in the country, though they may not be accessible from certain areas or from mobile phones. Calls to numbers beginning with ☎ 13 or ☎ 1300 are charged at the rate of a local call; the numbers can usually be dialled Australiawide, but may be applicable only to a specific state or STD district. Telephone numbers beginning with ☎ 1800, ☎ 13 or ☎ 1300 cannot be dialled from outside Australia.

### International Calls

Most pay phones allow ISD (International Subscriber Dialling) calls, the cost and international dialling code of which will vary depending on which provider you're using. International calls from Australia are very cheap and subject to specials that reduce the rates even more, so it's worth shopping around – look in the *Yellow Pages* telephone book (or on www.yellowpages.com.au) for a list of providers.

The **Country Direct service** ( ☎ 1800 801 800) connects callers in Australia with operators in nearly 60 countries to make reverse-charge (collect) or credit-card calls.

When calling overseas you need to dial the international access code from Australia ( ☎ 0011 or ☎ 0018), the country code and the area code (without the initial 0). So for a London number you'd dial ☎ 0011-44-20, then the number. Also, certain operators will have you dial a special code to access their service.

Following is a list of some country codes:

| Country | International country code |
| --- | --- |
| France | ☎ 33 |
| Germany | ☎ 49 |
| Japan | ☎ 81 |
| Netherlands | ☎ 31 |
| New Zealand | ☎ 64 |
| UK | ☎ 44 |
| USA & Canada | ☎ 1 |

If dialling Australia from overseas, the country code is ☎ 61 and you need to drop the 0 (zero) in the state/territory area codes; from the '02' for NSW and ACT, for example. Similarly, if dialling an Australian mobile phone from overseas dial ☎ 61 and drop the initial 0 of the mobile number.

## Local Calls

Calls from private phones cost 15c to 25c; local calls from public phones cost 50c – both with unlimited talk time. Calls to mobile phones cost more and are timed.

## Long-Distance Calls & Area Codes

For long-distance calls, Australia uses four STD (Subscriber Trunk Dialling) area codes. STD calls can be made from virtually any public phone and are cheaper during off-peak hours, which are roughly between 7pm and 7am weeknights, and from 7pm Friday to 7am Monday. Broadly, the main area codes are as follows:

| State/territory | Area code |
| --- | --- |
| ACT | ☎ 02 |
| NSW | ☎ 02 |
| NT | ☎ 08 |
| QLD | ☎ 07 |
| SA | ☎ 08 |
| TAS | ☎ 03 |
| VIC | ☎ 03 |
| WA | ☎ 08 |

In some border areas, NSW uses each of the four neighbouring codes

## Mobile (Cell) Phones

Local numbers with the prefixes ☎ 04xx or ☎ 04xxx belong to mobile phones. Australia's two mobile networks – digital GSM and digital CDMA – service more than 90% of the population but leave vast tracts of the country uncovered. Sydney, Canberra and the coast get good reception, but elsewhere (apart from major towns) it's haphazard or nonexistent. In northwest, central west and far west NSW CDMA is the most common network.

Australia's digital network is compatible with GSM 900 and 1800 (used in Europe), but generally not with the systems used in the USA or Japan. It's easy and cheap enough to get connected short-term, though, as the main service providers (such as Telstra, Optus, Vodafone, Virgin and 3) all have prepaid mobile systems.

## Phonecards

A wide range of phonecards is available from newsagents and post offices for a fixed dollar value (usually $10, $20, $30 etc), and can be used with any public or private phone by dialling a toll-free access number and then the PIN number on the card. Once again it's well worth shopping around, as call rates vary from company to company. Some public phones also accept credit cards.

## TIME

Australia is divided into three time zones. NSW and the ACT are on Eastern Standard Time (GMT/UTC plus 10 hours). There are minor exceptions – for instance, Broken Hill is on Central time (GMT/UTC plus 9½ hours). When it's noon in Sydney, the time in London is 3am (April to October) or 1am (November to March).

For more on international timing, see www.timeanddate.com/worldclock.

Daylight saving – for which clocks are put forward an hour – operates in NSW during the warmer months (October to March).

## TOILETS

One of the pleasures of travelling in a 'first world' country is the abundance of clean and free public toilets. These can be found in shopping centres, parks and just about any other public space in NSW.

## TOURIST INFORMATION

Australia's and NSW's highly self-conscious tourism infrastructure means that when looking for information you can easily end up being buried neck-deep in brochures, booklets, maps and leaflets, or get utterly swamped with detail during an online surf.

The **Australian Tourist Commission** (www.australia .com) is the national government tourist body, and has a good website for pre-trip research.

**Tourism New South Wales** ( ☎ 02-9931 1111; www .visitnsw.com.au) is the state's tourism body and offers no end of information, touring ideas and contacts.

### Local Tourist Offices

Almost every town in NSW seems to maintain a tourist office of some type and in many cases they are very good, with friendly staff (often volunteers) providing local information. If you're going to book accommodation or tours from local offices, bear in mind that they often only promote businesses that are paying members of the local tourist association. Details of local tourism offices are given in the relevant city and town sections throughout this book.

## TRAVELLERS WITH DISABILITIES

Disability awareness in Australia is pretty high and getting higher. Legislation requires that new accommodation meet accessibility standards, and discrimination by tourism operators is illegal. Many of Australia's key attractions provide access for those with limited mobility, and a number of sites have also begun addressing the needs of visitors with visual or aural impairments; contact attractions in advance to confirm the facilities available. Tour operators with wheelchair-accessible vehicles operate from most capital cities.

## VISAS

All visitors to Australia need a visa – only New Zealand nationals are exempt, and even they receive a 'special category' visa on arrival. Visa application forms are available from Australian diplomatic missions overseas, travel agents or the website of the **Department of Immigration & Multicultural Affairs** ( ☎ 13 18 81; www.immi.gov.au). There are several types of visas, as follows.

### Electronic Travel Authority (ETA)

Many visitors can get an ETA, valid for three months of travel in Australia, through any overseas airline or travel agent registered with the International Air Transport Association (IATA). They make the application directly when you buy a ticket and issue the ETA, which replaces the usual visa stamped in your passport. It's common practice for travel agents to charge a fee, in the vicinity of US$25, for issuing an ETA. This system is available to passport holders of some 33 countries, including the UK, USA and Canada, most European countries, Malaysia, Singapore, Japan and Korea.

You can also make an online ETA application at www.eta.immi.gov.au, where no fees apply.

### Tourist Visas

Short-term tourist visas have largely been replaced by the Electronic Travel Authority (ETA, see left). However, if you are from a country not covered by the ETA, or you want to stay longer than three months, you'll need to apply for a visa. Standard Tourist visas (which cost $75) allow one (in some cases multiple) entry and stays of up to three months, and are valid for use within 12 months of issue.

### Visa Extensions

Visitors are allowed a maximum stay of 12 months, including extensions. Visa extensions are made through the Department of Immigration & Multicultural & Indigenous Affairs and it's best to apply at least two or three weeks before your visa expires. The application fee is $205 – it's nonrefundable, even if your application is rejected.

### Working Holiday-Maker (WHM) Visas

Visitors between the ages of 18 and 30 from Belgium, Canada, Denmark, France, Germany, Hong Kong, Republic of Ireland, Italy, Japan, Netherlands, Sweden, and the UK among others are eligible for a WHM visa, which allows you to visit for up to 12 months and gain casual employment.

## WOMEN TRAVELLERS

NSW is generally a safe place for women travellers, although the usual sensible precautions apply. It's best to avoid walking alone late at night in any of the major cities and towns. And if you're out on the town, always keep enough money aside for a taxi back to your accommodation. The same

## NSW FOR TRAVELLERS WITH DISABILITIES

### Information

Reliable information is the key ingredient for travellers with disabilities and the best source is the **National Information Communication & Awareness Network** (Nican; ☎ /TTY 1800 806 769, 02-6241 1220; www.nican.com.au; Unit 5, 48 Brookes St, Mitchell, ACT 2911). It's an Australia-wide directory providing information on access issues, accessible accommodation, sporting and recreational activities, transport and specialist tour operators.

The website of the **Australian Tourist Commission** (www.australia.com) publishes detailed, downloadable information for people with disabilities, including travel and transport tips and contact addresses of organisations in each state.

The publication **Easy Access Australia** (www.easyaccessaustralia.com.au) is available from various bookstores and provides details on easily accessible transport, accommodation and attraction options.

A comprehensive website covering public toilets nationwide lists every one that has disability access. For more information, visit www.toiletmap.gov.au.

**Blind Citizens Australia** ( ☎ 1800 033 660, 03-9372 6400, TTY 03-9376 9275; www.bca.org.au) provides useful information for the visually impaired.

The **Paraplegic & Quadriplegic Association of NSW** ( ☎ 02-8741 5600; www.paraquad.org.au) provides some information about accommodation and care.

### Air

Accepted only by Qantas, **Community Fares** ( ☎ 13 13 13, TTY 1800 652 660; www.qantas.com.au) entitles a disabled person and the carer travelling with them to a 10% discount on full economy fares; call Nican (see earlier in this box) for eligibility and an application form. Guide dogs travel for free on **Qantas** ( ☎ 13 13 13; www.qantas.com.au), **Jetstar** ( ☎ 13 15 38; www.jetstar.com.au) and **Virgin Blue** ( ☎ 13 67 89; www.virginblue.com.au) and their affiliated carriers. All of Australia's major airports have dedicated parking spaces, wheelchair access to terminals, accessible toilets, and skychairs to convey passengers onto planes via airbridges.

### Car Hire

Avis and Hertz offer hire cars with hand controls at no extra charge for pick-up at capital cities and the major airports, but advance notice is required.

The international wheelchair symbol (blue on a white background) for parking in allocated bays is recognised.

### Taxi

Most taxi companies in major cities and towns have modified vehicles that will take wheelchairs.

### Train

In NSW, **CountryLink** ( ☎ 13 22 32; www.countrylink.info) has XPT trains that have at least one carriage (usually the buffet car) with a seat removed for a wheelchair, and an accessible toilet. In Sydney some, but not all, rail stations are accessible. **CityRail** ( ☎ 13 15 00; www.cityrail.info) has details.

---

applies to outback and rural towns where there are often a lot of unlit, semideserted streets between you and your temporary home. When the pubs and bars close and there are inebriated people roaming around, it's not a great time to be out and about. Lone women should also be wary of staying in basic pub accommodation unless it looks safe and well managed.

Sexual harassment is an ongoing problem, be it via an aggressive urban male or a rural bloke living a less-than-enlightened pro-forma bush existence. Stereotypically, the further you get from 'civilisation' (ie the

## SEASONAL WORK

Working holiday makers will find an abundance of hospitality, temporary and other short-term work in Sydney. The NSW ski fields are also good prospects for seasonal work, particularly around Thredbo (p298), although you'll need to apply early as jobs are extremely popular. There is plenty of cotton work in Narrabri (p253) and Moree (p254), and grape picking in the Hunter Valley (p149). Fruit picking is all the go near Tenterfield (p224), around Braidwood (p304), Batlow (p310) and Tumbarumba (p310).

Employment websites:

**Career One** (www.careerone.com)
**Face2Face Fundraising** (www.face2facefundraising.com.au) Fundraising jobs for charities and not-for-profits.
**Good Cause** (www.goodcause.com.au) More fundraising jobs for charities and not-for-profits.
**Harvest Trail** (www.jobsearch.gov.au/harvesttrail) Harvest jobs around Australia.
**Seek** (www.seek.com)

big cities), the less enlightened your average Aussie male is probably going to be about women's issues. Having said that, many women travellers say that they have met the friendliest, most down-to-earth blokes in outback pubs and remote roadhouse stops. And cities still have to put up with their unfortunate share of 'ocker' males who regard a bit of sexual harassment as a right, and chauvinism as a desirable trait.

Lone female hitchers are tempting fate – hitching with a male companion is safer and not hitching at all is common sense.

## VOLUNTEERING

Volunteering is extremely popular in Australia with locals as well as travellers and can be the most rewarding feature of your trip. Opportunities range from writing research papers for your favourite social cause to planting trees. It's even possible to base your trip around a volunteer project – organisations like the **Earthwatch Institute** (www.earthwatch.org) offer volunteer 'expeditions' that focus on conservation and wildlife. **Conservation Volunteers Australia** ( ☎ 1800 032 501; www.conservationvolunteers.com.au) has a nature holiday section, including programs on the south coast. **STA** (www.statravel.co.uk) is another great resource for international travellers seeking volunteer holiday opportunities in Australia.

Good volunteering websites:

**Go Volunteer** (www.govolunteer.com.au) National website listing volunteer opportunities.
**i-to-i** (www.i-to-i.com) Conservation-based volunteer holidays in Australia.
**Responsible Travel** (www.responsibletravel.com) Volunteer travel opportunities.
**Volunteering Australia** (www.volunteeringaustralia.org) Support, advice and volunteer training.

# Transport

## CONTENTS

# GETTING THERE & AWAY

They don't call Australia the land 'down under' for nothing. It's a long way from just about everywhere, and getting here usually means a long-haul flight. That 'over the horizon' feeling doesn't stop once you're here either – even in just one state like New South Wales (NSW), the distances between key towns can be vast, requiring a minimum of a day or two of highway cruising or dirt-road jostling to traverse.

Flights, tours and rail tickets can be booked online at www.lonelyplanet.com/travel _services.

## ENTERING THE COUNTRY

Entering Australia is a straightforward process and you shouldn't encounter any problems as long as you have a valid visa (p380). There are no restrictions when it comes to citizens of foreign countries entering Australia.

## AIR

There are many competing airlines and a wide variety of air fares to choose from if you're flying in from Asia, Europe or North America, but you'll still pay a lot for a flight. Because of Australia's size and diverse climate, any time of the year can prove busy for inbound tourists – if you plan to fly at a particularly popular period (Christmas is a notoriously difficult time to get into Sydney) or on a particularly popular route (such as Hong Kong, Bangkok or Singapore to Sydney), make your arrangements well ahead.

Disembarking in Australia is generally a straightforward affair, with only the usual customs declarations and the fight to be first to the luggage carousel to endure.

Recent global instability, thanks (or rather, no thanks) to terrorism and war-fever, has meant conspicuously increased security in Australian airports, both in domestic and international terminals, and you may find customs procedures now more time consuming. This is especially true in Sydney, where the immigration lines can seem endless.

For more information on customs and quarantine, see p370.

### Airports & Airlines

Australia has a number of international gateways, with Sydney being the busiest. Sydney's **Kingsford Smith Airport** (code SYD; ☎ 02-9667 9111; www.sydneyairport.com.au) is 10km south of the city centre, in Mascot.

Australia's overseas carrier is Qantas. Viewed as one of the world's safest airlines, it flies chiefly to Europe, North America, Asia and the Pacific. A low-fare subsidiary of Qantas, Jetstar, has a growing list of nonstop flights to international destinations.

---

**THINGS CHANGE...**

The information in this chapter is particularly vulnerable to change. Check directly with the airline or a travel agent to make sure you understand how a fare (and ticket you may buy) works and be aware of the security requirements for international travel. Shop carefully. The details given in this chapter should be regarded as pointers and are not a substitute for your own careful, up-to-date research.

---

**TRANSPORT**

**TRANSPORT**

Airlines that visit Sydney include the following. (Note, all phone numbers mentioned here are for dialling from within Sydney.)
**Air Canada** (airline code AC; ☎ 1300 655 757, 02-8248 5757; www.aircanada.ca)
**Air New Zealand** (airline code NZ; ☎ 13 24 76, 02-8235 9999; www.airnz.com.au)
**British Airways** (airline code BA; ☎ 1300 767 177; www.britishairways.com.au)
**Cathay Pacific** (airline code CX; ☎ 13 17 47, 02-9667 3816; www.cathaypacific.com.au)
**Emirates** (airline code EK; ☎ 1300 303 777, 02-9290 9776; www.emirates.com)
**Garuda Indonesia** (airline code GA; ☎ 1300 365 330; www.garuda-indonesia.com)
**Gulf Air** (airline code GF; ☎ 1300 366 337; www.gulfairco.com)
**Japan Airlines** (airline code JL; ☎ 02-9272 1111; www.jal.com)
**KLM** (airline code KL; ☎ 1300 392 192; www.klm.com)
**Lufthansa** (airline code LH; ☎ 1300 655 727; www.lufthansa-australia.com)
**Malaysia Airlines** (airline code MH; ☎ 13 26 27, 02-9364 3500; www.malaysiaairlines.com.au)
**Pacific Blue** (airline code DJ; ☎ 13 16 45; www.flypacificblue.com)
**Qantas** (airline code QF; ☎ 13 13 13; www.qantas.com.au)
**Singapore Airlines** (airline code SQ; ☎ 13 10 11, 02-9350 0100; www.singaporeair.com.au)
**South African Airways** (airline code SA; ☎ 02-9286 8960; ww3.flysaa.com)
**Thai Airways International** (airline code TG; ☎ 1300 651 960; www.thaiairways.com.au)
**United Airlines** (airline code UA; ☎ 13 17 77; www.unitedairlines.com.au)
**Virgin Atlantic** (airline code VS; ☎ 1300 727 340; www.virgin-atlantic.com)

## Tickets

The internet is a vital resource for checking airline prices and many offer great deals on both economy and business-class tickets.

Automated online ticket sales work well if you're doing a simple one-way or return trip on specified dates, but are no substitute for a travel agent for advice and the low-down on avoiding stopovers.

For online bookings, try the following:
**Cheap Flights** (www.cheapflights.com, www.cheapflights.co.uk) Informative site with specials, airline information and flight searches covering the USA and UK.
**Expedia** (www.expedia.msn.com)
**Flight Centre International** (www.flightcentre.com) Respected operator handling direct flights, with sites for Australia, New Zealand, the UK, the USA and Canada.
**Opodo** (www.opodo.com) Excellent pan-European travel site offering fares from European countries.
**Roundtheworld.com** (www.roundtheworldflights.com) Allows you to build your own RTW trips with up to six stops.

---

### CLIMATE CHANGE & TRAVEL

Climate change is a serious threat to the ecosystems that humans rely upon, and air travel is the fastest-growing contributor to the problem. Lonely Planet regards travel, overall, as a global benefit, but believes we all have a responsibility to limit our personal impact on global warming.

#### Flying & Climate Change

Pretty much every form of motor transport generates $CO_2$ (the main cause of human-induced climate change) but planes are far and away the worst offenders, not just because of the sheer distances they allow us to travel, but because they release greenhouse gases high into the atmosphere. The statistics are frightening: two people taking a return flight between Europe and the US will contribute as much to climate change as an average household's gas and electricity consumption over a whole year.

#### Carbon Offset Schemes

Climatecare.org and other websites use 'carbon calculators' that allow travellers to offset the greenhouse gases they are responsible for with contributions to energy-saving projects and other climate-friendly initiatives in the developing world – including projects in India, Honduras, Kazakhstan and Uganda.

Lonely Planet, together with Rough Guides and other concerned partners in the travel industry, supports the carbon offset scheme run by climatecare.org. Lonely Planet offsets all of its staff and author travel.

For more information check out our website: lonelyplanet.com.

## ECONOMY-CLASS SYNDROME

Deep vein thrombosis (DVT) is a relatively rare but potentially serious condition that may develop when flying. DVT is the formation of a blood clot, usually in the legs, caused by sitting in cramped conditions for an extended period. It can be fatal if the clot moves to the heart or lungs.

The term 'Economy-Class Syndrome' is a bit of a misnomer since it can happen in any class, and indeed any situation. Awareness of the link between DVT and flying economy class heightened a few years ago when an Australian passenger died at Heathrow airport after a long-haul flight. Many passengers have since come forward to say they experienced blood clotting during or after flying.

You can't really avoid the flight to Australia, but you can get up and walk around during the flight, factor in stopovers rather than taking a direct flight, and see your doctor prior to flying if you feel you may be at risk. The elderly and overweight are most at risk of DVT complications.

**STA** (www.statravel.com) Linked to worldwide STA sites.

**Travel.com** (www.travel.com) Fares from the US.

**Travelocity** (www.travelocity.com) Good US site.

**Travel Online** (www.travelonline.co.nz) Good place to check worldwide flights from New Zealand.

**Zuji** (www.zuji.com) Excellent site for fares from the Asia Pacific region.

### From Asia

Most Asian countries offer fairly competitive air-fare deals, with Bangkok, Singapore and Hong Kong being the best places to shop around for discount tickets.

Flights between Hong Kong and Australia are notoriously heavily booked. Flights to/from Bangkok and Singapore are often part of the longer Europe-to-Australia route so they are also sometimes full. The moral of the story is to plan your preferred itinerary well in advance.

Some local agents:

**No 1 Travel** ( ☎ 03-3205 6073; www.no1-travel.com) In Japan.

**STA Travel** Bangkok ( ☎ 02-236 0262; www.statravel .co.th); Singapore ( ☎ 65-6737 7188; www.statravel.com .sg); Tokyo ( ☎ 03-5391 2922; www.statravel.co.jp)

### From Canada

The air routes from Canada are similar to those from mainland USA, with most Toronto and Vancouver flights stopping in one US city such as Los Angeles or Honolulu before heading on to Australia.

Canadian discount air-ticket sellers are known as consolidators (although you won't see a sign on the door saying 'Consolidator') and their air fares tend to be a little higher than those sold in the USA.

Useful agencies:

**Pacesetter Travel** ( ☎ 1800 387 8827; www.paceset tertravel.com)

**Travel Cuts** ( ☎ 1800 246 8762; www.travelcuts.com) Canada's national student travel agency.

### From Continental Europe

From the major destinations in Europe, most flights travel via one of the Asian capitals. Some flights are also routed through London before arriving in Australia via Singapore, Bangkok, Hong Kong or Kuala Lumpur.

Useful agencies:

**Adventure Travel** (www.adventure-holidays.com) German agency specialising in Australian travel.

**BarronTravel** ( ☎ 020-625 8600; www.barron.nl) Dutch agency specialising in Australian travel.

**Holland International** (www.hollandinternational.nl) Good Dutch agency.

**OTU Voyages** ( ☎ 01 55 82 32 32; www.otu.fr) French network of student travel agencies; supplies discount tickets to travellers of all ages.

**Nouvelles Frontières** ( ☎ 0825 000 747; www.nouv elles-frontieres.fr)

**Usit Connect Voyages** ( ☎ 0825 082 525; www.usit connections.fr) French Student/youth specialists.

**Voyageurs du Monde** (www.vdm.com)

**Wereldcontact** ( ☎ 0343 530 530; www.wereldcontact .nl) Dutch agency.

### From New Zealand

Air New Zealand and Qantas operate a network of flights linking Auckland, Wellington and Christchurch in New Zealand with Sydney. Also look for foreign carriers like Emirates, which offers some reasonable fares.

Other trans-Tasman options:

**Air New Zealand** ( ☎ 0800 737 000; www.airnew zealand.co.nz)

**Go Holidays** (www.goholidays.co.nz) Specialists for Australian travel.

**House of Travel** (www.houseoftravel.co.nz) Nation-wide travel agency.

**Travel Online** ( ☎ 0800 000 747; www.travelonline.co.nz)

**Freedom Air** ( ☎ 0800 600 500; www.freedomair.com) An Air New Zealand subsidiary that operates direct flights and offers excellent rates year-round.

## From the UK & Ireland

There are two routes from the UK: the western route via the USA and the Pacific, and the eastern route via the Middle East and Asia; flights are usually cheaper and more frequent on the latter. Some of the best deals around are with Emirates, Gulf Air, Malaysia Airlines, Japan Airlines and Thai Airways International. Unless there are special deals on offer, British Airways, Singapore Airlines and Qantas generally have higher fares but may offer a more direct route.

Airline ticket discounters are known as bucket shops in the UK, and many advertise in the travel pages of the free magazine *TNT*.

**Austravel** ( ☎ 0870 166 2020; www.austravel.net)

**Bridge the World** ( ☎ 0870 444 7474)

**Ebookers** ( ☎ 0870 814 0000; www.ebookers.com)

**Oz Flights** ( ☎ 0870 747 11 747; www.ozflights.co.uk)

**Trailfinders** ( ☎ 0845 058 5858; www.trailfinders.co.uk)

**Travel Bag** ( ☎ 0870 814 4441; www.travelbag.co.uk)

## From the USA

Airlines directly connecting Australia non-stop across the Pacific with Los Angeles or San Francisco include Qantas, Air New Zealand and United Airlines. There are also numerous airlines offering flights via Asia, with stopover possibilities including Tokyo, Kuala Lumpur, Bangkok, Hong Kong and Singapore; and via the Pacific with stopover possibilities like Nadi (Fiji), Rarotonga (Cook Islands), Tahiti (French Polynesia) and Auckland (NZ).

As in Canada, discount travel agents in the USA are known as consolidators. San Francisco is the ticket-consolidator capital of America.

Useful agencies:

**Air Brokers International** ( ☎ 1800 883 3273; www .airbrokers.com) Good for RTW fares including Australian stops.

**Airtreks** ( ☎ 1877 247 8735; www.airtreks.com)

**STA Travel** ( ☎ 1800 781 4040; www.statravel.com)

## LAND

See the Getting Around section for bus (p388) and train (p396) services between NSW and other parts of Australia.

### Border Crossings

There are three main road routes to/from NSW and the rest of Australia.

**East Coast North** The Pacific Hwy follows the East Coast north into Queensland and on to Brisbane.

**East Coast South** The Princes Hwy (Hwy 1) follows the East Coast south into Victoria and on to Melbourne.

**Inland** The Hume Fwy/Hwy (Hwy 31) is the shortest route to Melbourne from Sydney and links with Wagga Wagga and Canberra.

There are numerous other options, including remote tracks right across the outback.

See the Getting Around section (below) for road rules and other considerations such as quarantine rules for driving to NSW.

## SEA

International cruise lines are increasingly serving Sydney. **Princess Cruises** (www.princess.com) operates routes around Australia and New Zealand. However these voyages are mainly geared for travellers starting and ending their trips in the same city, such as Sydney. You'll have to look around for options that let you go one way.

Another option is travel by freighter. These huge container ships circumnavigate the globe and it is possible to book trips from both the US and UK to Sydney. However, note that ports of call may be remote container ports lacking in charm, and life aboard ship will be the exact opposite of the boozy excesses promised by cruise lines.

For details, try www.freighterworld.com and www.strandtravel.co.uk.

# GETTING AROUND

## AIR

Australia is so vast that flying is common between the far-flung cities. The industry is safe and increased competition over the last 10 years has seen fares plummet. Within NSW there are numerous routes you can take to cut your travel time. All domestic flights are nonsmoking.

### Airlines in Australia

Qantas, Virgin Blue and Jetstar are the main competitors in the domestic market. In general they stick to the larger hubs, but small towns in NSW are also served by subsidiaries and affiliates, particularly QantasLink and Regional Express.

Regional airlines:

**Brindabella Airlines** ( ☎ 1300 668 824, www.brinda
bellaairlines.com.au)

**Jetstar** ( ☎ 13 15 38; www.jetstar.com.au) The budget
wing of Qantas.

**Qantas** ( ☎ 13 13 13; www.qantas.com.au)

**QantasLink** ( ☎ 13 13 13; www.qantas.com.au)

**Regional Express** (Rex; ☎ 13 17 13; www.regionalex
press.com.au) Flies to rural destinations in NSW.

**Virgin Blue** ( ☎ 13 67 89; www.virginblue.com.au)
Highly competitive.

## Air Passes

With discounting being the norm these days,
air passes are not great value, but international travellers on a tight itinerary might
benefit from a Qantas **Boomerang Pass**, which
involves buying at least two sectors (priced
from $160 to $360 depending on the distance)
in conjunction with your international ticket.
Qantas also offers an **Aussie AirPass** (US$999
from Los Angeles or CA$1399 from Vancou-
ver) which includes your round trip from
Los Angeles or Vancouver plus three flights
within Australia.

Regional Express has a **Rex Backpacker**
scheme, where international visitors pay
$500/$950 for one month/two months of unlimited travel on the airline – standby fares
only. You'd need to fit in four or five flights in
a month in NSW to make this worthwhile.

## BICYCLE

Australia has much to offer cyclists, from
leisurely bike paths winding through most
major cities (Canberra has one of the most
extensive networks) to thousands of kilometres of good country roads where you can
wear out your chain wheels. Mountainous is
not an adjective that applies to this country;
instead, there's lots of flat countryside and
gently rolling hills.

Bicycle helmets are compulsory in NSW,
as are white front lights and red rear lights
for riding at night.

If bringing your own bike, check with your
airline for costs and the degree of dismantling
and packing required. Within Australia, bus
companies require that you dismantle your
bike, and some don't guarantee that the bike
will travel on the same bus as you. On trains,
supervise the loading and, if possible, tie your
bike upright. Check for possible restrictions:
most intercity trains will only carry two to
three boxed bikes per service.

Much of NSW was settled on the principle
of not having more than a day's horse ride
between pubs, so it's possible to plan even
ultralong routes and still get a shower at the
end of each day. Most riders carry camping
equipment, but on the east coast at least, it's
feasible to travel from town to town staying
in hostels, hotels or caravan parks.

You can get by with standard road maps,
but as you'll probably want to avoid both the
highways and the low-grade unsealed roads,
the government series is best. The 1:250,000
scale is the most suitable, though you'll need
a lot of maps if you're going far. The next
scale up, 1:1,000,000, is adequate and is widely
available in speciality map shops.

Carry plenty of water to avoid becoming
dehydrated. Cycling in the summer heat can
be made more endurable by wearing a helmet
with a peak (or a cap under your helmet),
using plenty of sunscreen, not cycling in the
middle of the day, and drinking lots of water
(not soft drinks). It can get very cold in the
mountains, so pack appropriate clothing.

Outback travel needs to be properly
planned, with the availability of drinking
water the main concern – those isolated water
sources (bores, tanks, creeks and the like)
shown on your map may be dry or the water
may be undrinkable, so you can't depend entirely on them. Also make sure you've got the
necessary spare parts and bike-repair knowledge. Check with locals if you're heading into
remote areas, and let someone know where
you're headed before setting off.

For suggestions on where to cycle in NSW
see the Directory (p369) and New South
Wales Outdoors (p42).

## Hire

The rates charged by most outfits for renting
road or mountain bikes (not including the
discounted fees offered by budget accommodation places to their guests) are anywhere
between $8 to $12 per hour and $20 to $50 per
day. Security deposits can range from $50 to
$200, depending on the rental period.

## Purchase

If you want to tour NSW by bike then renting
isn't an option – you'll need to buy a set of
wheels. For a new road cycle or mountain bike
that won't leave a trail of worn-out or busted
metal parts once it leaves the city limits, your
starting point (and we mean your absolute

**TRANSPORT**

bottom-level starting point) is $400 to $500. To set yourself up with a new bike, plus all the requisite on-the-road equipment such as panniers, helmet etc, your starting point becomes $1500 to $2000. Second-hand bikes are worth checking out in the cities, as are the post-Christmas sales and mid-year stocktakes, which is when newish bicycles can be heavily discounted.

Your best bet for re-selling your bike is the **Trading Post** ( ☎ 1300 138 016; www.tradingpost.com.au), which is distributed in newspaper form in urban centres around Australia, and which also has a busy online trading site. Also check the classifieds section at the website of **Bicycling Australia** (www.bicyclingaustralia.com).

## BOAT

There's a hell of a lot of water around Australia but unless you're fortunate enough to hook up with a yacht, it's not a feasible way of getting around.

## BUS

New South Wales has an extensive, reliable and relatively cheap bus network. Bear in mind that distances can be vast, and if you're covering a lot of ground in one go (eg Sydney to Byron Bay), you may be better off booking a cheap flight. Most buses are equipped with air-con, toilets and videos, and all are smoke-free zones. The smallest towns eschew formal bus terminals for a single drop-off/pick-up point, usually outside a post office, newsagent or shop.

The two main companies servicing the New South Wales coast are **Greyhound** ( ☎ 13 14 99; www.greyhound.com.au) and **Premier Motor Service** ( ☎ 13 34 10; www.premierms.com.au). Fares and stops for both companies are interchangeable, although Greyhound is often ever so slightly more expensive. Greyhound fares can be purchased online and are roughly 5% cheaper than over-the-counter tickets.

**CountryLink** ( ☎ 13 22 32; www.countrylink.info) replaced many of its trains with buses after closing numerous train lines in recent years.

Smaller regional operators running key routes or covering a lot of ground are listed as follows:

**Fearnes Coaches** ( ☎ 1800 029 918; www.fearnes.com
.au) Runs between Sydney, Canberra and Wagga Wagga.
**Firefly Express** ( ☎ 1800 631 164; www.fireflyexpress
.com.au) Runs between Sydney, Melbourne and Adelaide.
**Murrays Coaches** ( ☎ 13 22 51; www.murrays.com.au)
Runs between Sydney and Canberra.

**Port Stephens Coaches** ( ☎ 02-4982 2940; www.ps coaches.com.au) Runs between Sydney and Port Stephens and Newcastle.
**Transborder** ( ☎ 02-6241 0033; www.transborder
.com.au)

### Bus Passes

Greyhound offers a profusion of bus passes around Australia, but the following are useful for travel in NSW. There's a 10% discount for members of YHA/HI, VIP, Nomads and Roam Free.

The **Explorer Pass** gives you from one to 12 months to cover a set route – there are 24 in all and the validity period depends on distance. You can't backtrack but if you can find a route that suits you it generally works out cheaper than booking individual sections. The Explorer Central Coaster Pass covers the east coast north of Sydney to Brisbane and costs $175.

The easiest and simplest pass is the **Aussie Kilometre Pass**, which gives you a specified amount of travel, starting at 2000km ($340) and going up in increments of 1000km to a maximum of 20,000km ($2450). The pass is valid for 12 months and you can travel where and in what direction you like, and stop as many times as you like.

**Premier Motor Services** also offer a Sydney to Brisbane pass with either one stop ($90) or unlimited stops ($130).

### Backpacker Buses

While the companies offering transport options for budget travellers in various parts of Australia are pretty much organised-tour operators, they do also get you from A to B (sometimes with hop-on hop-off services) and so can be a cost-effective alternative to the big bus companies. The buses are usually smaller, you'll meet lots of other travellers, and the drivers sometimes double as tour guides; conversely, some travellers find the tour-group mentality and inherent limitations don't suit them. Discounts for card-carrying students and members of hostel organisations are regularly available.

**Autopia Tours** ( ☎ 1800 000 507, 03-9419 8878; www
.autopiatours.com.au) has a four-day Melbourne to Sydney tour via the Snowy Mountains, Canberra and the Blue Mountains, including breakfast, lunch and accommodation ($400).

**Oz Experience** ( ☎ 1300 300 028; www.ozexperience
.com) is a hop-on hop-off service you'll either

## ROAD DISTANCES (KM)

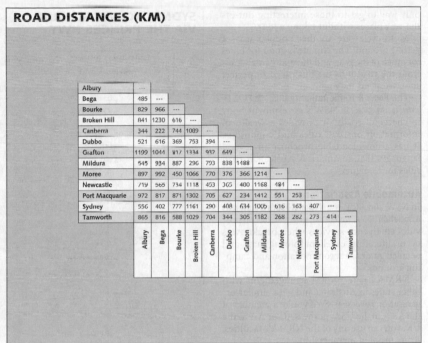

| | Albury | Bega | Bourke | Broken Hill | Canberra | Dubbo | Grafton | Mildura | Moree | Newcastle | Port Macquarie | Sydney | Tamworth |
|---|---|---|---|---|---|---|---|---|---|---|---|---|---|
| Albury | --- | | | | | | | | | | | | |
| Bega | 485 | --- | | | | | | | | | | | |
| Bourke | 829 | 966 | --- | | | | | | | | | | |
| Broken Hill | 841 | 1230 | 616 | --- | | | | | | | | | |
| Canberra | 344 | 222 | 744 | 1089 | --- | | | | | | | | |
| Dubbo | 521 | 616 | 369 | 753 | 394 | --- | | | | | | | |
| Grafton | 1199 | 1044 | 817 | 1334 | 932 | 649 | --- | | | | | | |
| Mildura | 545 | 934 | 887 | 296 | 793 | 838 | 1488 | --- | | | | | |
| Moree | 897 | 992 | 450 | 1066 | 770 | 376 | 366 | 1214 | --- | | | | |
| Newcastle | 719 | 565 | 734 | 1118 | 453 | 365 | 400 | 1168 | 484 | --- | | | |
| Port Macquarie | 972 | 817 | 871 | 1302 | 705 | 627 | 234 | 1412 | 551 | 253 | --- | | |
| Sydney | 556 | 402 | 777 | 1161 | 290 | 408 | 634 | 1005 | 616 | 163 | 407 | --- | |
| Tamworth | 865 | 816 | 588 | 1029 | 704 | 344 | 305 | 1182 | 268 | 282 | 273 | 414 | --- |

**TRANSPORT**

love or hate. Many travellers complain they can't get a seat on the bus of their choice and are left on stand-by lists for days, or summarise it as a party bus for younger travellers, while others rave about it as a highly social experience. The country's biggest backpacker bus network, it covers central and eastern Australia. Travel is one-directional and passes are valid for six months with unlimited stops. Passes include some accommodation, meals and activities; a Sydney–Darwin pass via Melbourne, Adelaide and Alice Springs is $1895; Sydney–Cairns is $795; Sydney–Brisbane is $380.

### Classes
There are no separate classes on buses, and the vehicles of the different companies all look pretty similar and are equipped with air-con, toilets and videos. Smoking isn't permitted on Australian buses.

### Costs
Following are the average, non-discounted, one-way bus fares on some well-travelled routes through NSW.

| Destination | Adult/child/concession |
|---|---|
| Sydney-Brisbane | $111/91/103 |
| Sydney-Canberra | $36/26/26 |
| Sydney-Melbourne | $71/58/65 |

### Reservations
Over summer, school holidays and public holidays, you should book well ahead on the more popular routes, including intercity and east-coast services. At other times you should have few problems getting on to your preferred service. But if your long-term travel plans rely on catching a particular bus, book at least a day or two ahead just to be safe.

You should make a reservation at least one day in advance if you are planning to use a Greyhound pass.

## CAR & MOTORCYCLE
NSW ranges from the built-up east coast to the sparsely populated interior where public transport is often neither comprehensive nor convenient, and sometimes nonexistent. Many travellers find that the best way to see the place is to buy a car, and it's certainly the

only way to get to those interesting out-of-the-way places without taking a tour.

Motorcycles are another popular way of getting around. The climate is good for bikes for much of the year, and the many small trails from the road into the bush lead to perfect spots to spend the night.

The **Roads & Traffic Authority** (RTA; ☎ 13 22 13; www.rta.nsw.gov.au) is NSW's government body in charge of roads. It provides a wealth of information on road rules and conditions. It has a downloadable brochure in several languages that summarises Australian road rules for foreigners.

## Automobile Associations

In NSW and ACT, the **National Roads & Motorists Association** (NRMA; ☎ 13 11 22; www.nrma.com.au) provides emergency services when breakdowns occur, literature, excellent touring maps and detailed guides to accommodation and camping grounds.

NRMA has reciprocal arrangements with other states in Australia and with similar organisations overseas. So if you're a member of the AAA in the USA, or the RAC or AA in the UK, you can use any of the NRMA's facilities. Bring proof of membership.

## Bringing Your Own Vehicle

Bringing your own motorcycle into Australia will entail an expensive shipping exercise, valid registration in the country of origin and a *Carnet De Passages en Douanes*. This is an internationally recognised customs document that allows the holder to import their vehicle without paying customs duty or taxes. To get one, apply to a motoring organisation/association in your home country. You'll also need a rider's licence and a helmet. The long, open roads are really made for large-capacity machines above 750cc, which Australians prefer once they outgrow their 250cc learner restrictions.

## Driving Licence

You can use your own home-country's driving licence in NSW, as long as it's in English and has your photograph for identification. If it's not in English then a) we're very impressed that you're reading this and b) you need an English translation or an **International Driving Permit** (IDP), which must be supported by your home licence. It's easy enough to get an IDP – just go to your home country's automobile association and they issue it on the spot. The permits are valid for 12 months.

## Fuel & Spare Parts

Fuel (super, diesel and unleaded) is available from service stations sporting the well-known international brand names. LPG (gas) is not always stocked at more remote roadhouses – if you're on gas, it's safer to have dual fuel capacity. Prices vary from place to place and from price war to price war, but basically fuel is heavily taxed and prices continue to climb. At the time of writing, unleaded petrol hovered around $1.45 per litre. Once you get out into the country, prices soar as high as $1.60. Note that in rural NSW petrol stations may be 150km or more apart.

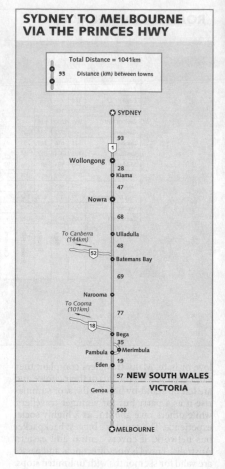

**SYDNEY TO MELBOURNE VIA THE PRINCES HWY**

Total Distance = 1041km

93 · Distance (km) between towns

○ SYDNEY

93

Wollongong ○

28 · Kiama

47

Nowra ○

68

To Canberra (144km) · ○ Ulladulla

48

Batemans Bay

69

Narooma ○

To Cooma (101km)

77

○ Bega

35

Pambula ○ · Merimbula

19

Eden ○

57 · **NEW SOUTH WALES**

Genoa ○ · **VICTORIA**

500

○ MELBOURNE

The further you get from the cities, the better it is to be in a Holden or a Ford – if you're in an older vehicle that's likely to require a replacement part, life is much simpler if it's a make for which spare parts are more readily available. See also Road Conditions (p393).

## Hire

Competition between car-rental companies in Australia is pretty fierce, so rates tend to be variable and lots of special deals come and go. The main thing to remember when assessing your options is distance – if you want to travel far, you need unlimited kilometres.

As well as the big firms, there are a vast number of local firms, or firms with outlets in a limited number of locations. These are almost always cheaper than the big operators – sometimes half the price – but cheap car hire can often come with serious restrictions.

The major companies offer a choice: either unlimited kilometres, or 100km or so a day free, plus so many cents per kilometre over this. Daily rates in cities or on the east coast are typically about $60 to $65 a day for a small car, about $70 to $80 a day for a medium car, or $90 to $120 a day for a big car. Insurance is extra, and can often be more than the cost of the rental itself. You must be at least 21 years old to hire from most firms – if you're under 25 you may only be able to hire a small car or have to pay a surcharge. It's much cheaper if you rent for a week or more and there are often low-season and weekend discounts. Credit cards are the usual payment method.

Major companies all have offices or agents in Sydney and some smaller towns.

**Avis** ( ☎ 13 63 33; www.avis.com.au)
**Budget** ( ☎ 13 27 27; www.budget.com.au)
**Europcar** ( ☎ 1300 131 390; www.europcar.com.au)
**Hertz** ( ☎ 13 30 39; www.hertz.com.au)
**Thrifty** ( ☎ 1300 367 227; www.thrifty.com.au)

### 4WD & CAMPERVAN HIRE

Renting a 4WD enables you to get right off the beaten track and out to some of the natural wonders that most travellers miss. Something small like a Suzuki Vitara or Toyota Rav4 costs around $100 per day. For a Toyota Landcruiser you'll spend at least $160, which should include some free kilometres (typically 100km to 200km per day, sometimes unlimited).

Check insurance conditions carefully, especially the excess amount, as it can be onerous – $5000 is common, although this can be

reduced to around $1000 (or even to nil) on payment of an additional daily charge (around $50). Even for a 4WD, the insurance offered by most companies does not cover damage caused when travelling 'off-road', which basically means anything that is not a maintained bitumen or dirt road. Hertz, Budget and Avis have 4WD rentals.

**Britz Rentals** ( ☎ 1800 331 454, 02-9667 0402; www .britz.com) hires fully equipped 4WDs fitted out as campervans. The high-season costs start from around $165 (two-berth) or $210 (four-berth) per day for a minimum hire of five days (with unlimited kilometres), but the price climbs from there; to reduce the insurance excess from $5000 to zero costs an extra $50 per day.

**Wicked Campers** ( ☎ 1800 246 869; www.wickedcamp ers.com.au) has an office in Sydney (see p105) and rents out spectacularly painted vehicles with a spot to sleep in the back.

## Insurance

In Australia, third-party personal injury insurance is always included in the vehicle registration cost, ensuring that every registered vehicle carries at least the minimum

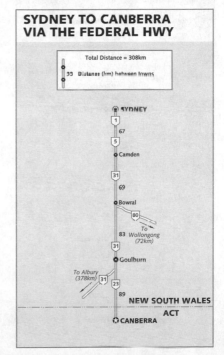

**SYDNEY TO CANBERRA VIA THE FEDERAL HWY**

Total Distance = 308km

33 Distance (km) between towns

SYDNEY

67

Camden

69

Bowral

To Wollongong (72km)

Goulburn

To Albury (378km)

NEW SOUTH WALES

ACT

CANBERRA

TRANSPORT

TRANSPORT

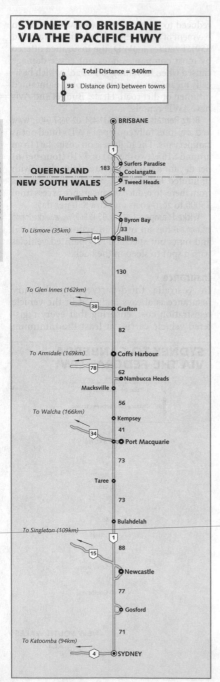

## SYDNEY TO BRISBANE VIA THE PACIFIC HWY

Total Distance = 940km

93 Distance (km) between towns

BRISBANE

1

QUEENSLAND 183 Surfers Paradise
Coolangatta
NEW SOUTH WALES Tweed Heads
24
Murwillumbah

7
Byron Bay
33
To Lismore (35km) 44 Ballina

130

To Glen Innes (162km) 38 Grafton

82

To Armidale (169km) Coffs Harbour
62
78 Nambucca Heads
Macksville

56
To Walcha (166km) Kempsey
41
34 Port Macquarie

73

Taree

73

Bulahdelah
To Singleton (109km) 1
88
15
Newcastle

77

Gosford

71
To Katoomba (94km)
4 SYDNEY

insurance. You'd be wise to extend that minimum to at least third-party property insurance as well – minor collisions with other vehicles can be amazingly expensive.

When it comes to hire cars, know exactly what your liability is in the event of an accident. Rather than risk paying out thousands of dollars if you do have an accident, you can take out your own comprehensive insurance on the car, or (the usual option) pay an additional daily amount to the rental company for an 'insurance excess reduction' policy. This brings the amount of excess you must pay in the event of an accident down from between $2000 and $5000 to nil.

Be aware that if you travel off bitumen/dirt roads onto bush tracks you will not be covered by insurance even if you have a 4WD – in other words, if you have an accident you'll be liable for all the costs involved. Also, most companies' insurance won't cover the cost of damage to glass (including the windscreen) or tyres. Always read the small print.

### Outback Travel

In western NSW there are plenty of roads and trails that bring new meaning to the phrase 'off the beaten track'.

While you may not need 4WD or fancy expedition equipment to tackle most of these roads, you do need to be carefully prepared for the loneliness and lack of facilities. Vehicles should be in good condition and have reasonable ground clearance. Always carry a tow rope so that some passing good Samaritan can pull your broken-down car to the next garage.

When travelling to very remote areas, such as the central deserts, you need to carry a high-frequency (HF) radio transceiver, equipped to pick up the relevant Royal Flying Doctor Service bases, and a CB radio. A satellite phone and Global Positioning System (GPS) finder can also be handy. Of course, all this equipment comes at a cost, but travellers have perished in the Australian desert after breaking down. Mobile phones only work in a couple of large outback towns so are basically useless.

Always carry plenty of water. In warm weather allow 5L per person per day and an extra amount for the radiator, carried in several containers.

It's wise not to attempt the tougher routes during the hottest part of the year (October to April inclusive) – apart from the risk of heat exhaustion, simple mishaps can easily lead to tragedy at this time. Conversely, you can't go anywhere on dirt roads in the outback if it's been raining. The roads are closed and fines for using them are hefty (see also p264). Get local advice before heading off into the middle of nowhere. For more information regarding NSW's climate see p370.

If you do run into trouble in the back of beyond, don't wander off – stay with your car. From the air, it's easier to spot a car than a human being, and you wouldn't be able to carry a heavy load of water very far anyway. Police suggest that you carry two spare tyres (for added safety) and, if stranded, try to set fire to one of them (let the air out first) – the pall of smoke will be seen for miles.

Of course, before you set out, let family, friends or your car-hire company know where you're going and when you intend to be back.

## Purchase

When it comes to buying or selling a car, every state has its own regulations, particularly in regard to registration (rego). In NSW safety checks are compulsory every year when you renew the registration. Stamp duty has to be paid when you buy a car and, as this is based on the purchase price, it's not unknown for buyer and seller to agree privately to understate the price.

Note that it's much easier to sell a car in the same state that it's registered in, otherwise you (or the buyer) must re-register it in the new state, and that's a hassle.

The best place to buy a car is Sydney – see p105 for more information.

### BUY-BACK DEALS

One way of getting around the hassles of buying and selling a vehicle privately is to enter into a buy-back arrangement with a car or motorcycle dealer. However, dealers may find ways of knocking down the price when you return the vehicle (even if the price was agreed to in writing), often by pointing out expensive repairs that allegedly will be required to gain the dreaded roadworthiness certificate needed to transfer the registration.

A company that specialises in buy-back arrangements on cars and campervans is **Travellers Auto Barn** ( ☎ 1800 674 374; www.travellers-autobarn .com.au), which has offices in Sydney and offers a range of vehicles.

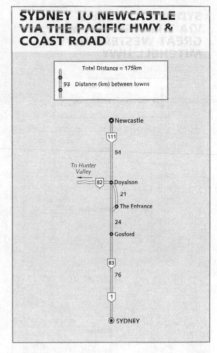

**SYDNEY TO NEWCASTLE VIA THE PACIFIC HWY & COAST ROAD**

Total Distance = 175km

93  Distance (km) between towns

Newcastle
111
54
To Hunter Valley
82  Doyalson
21
The Entrance
24
Gosford
83
76
1
SYDNEY

Buy-back arrangements are also possible with large motorcycle dealers in major cities. They're usually keen to do business, and basic negotiating skills allied with a wad of cash (say, $8000) should secure an excellent second hand road bike with a written guarantee that they'll buy it back, if it's in good condition, minus around $2000. **Better Bikes** ( ☎ 02-9718 6668; www.betterbikes.com.au; 605 Canterbury Rd, Belmore) is a Sydney dealer that offers buy-back deals.

## Road Conditions

NSW has few multilane highways. There are stretches of divided road (four or six lanes) in some particularly busy areas of Sydney although even here you will find yourself on coagulated local streets more often than you would like. Elsewhere the major roads are sealed two- or three-laners.

You don't have to get far off the beaten track to find dirt roads. In fact, anybody who sets out to see the country in reasonable detail should expect some dirt-road travelling. And if you seriously want to explore more remote parts, you'd better plan on having a

TRANSPORT

**TRANSPORT**

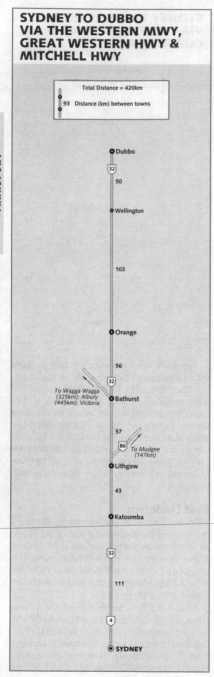

## SYDNEY TO DUBBO VIA THE WESTERN MWY, GREAT WESTERN HWY & MITCHELL HWY

Total Distance = 420km

93 Distance (km) between towns

● Dubbo

[32]

50

● Wellington

103

● Orange

56

[32]

To Wagga Wagga
(325km); Albury
(445km); Victoria

● Bathurst

57

[86]  To Mudgee
(147km)

● Lithgow

43

● Katoomba

[32]

111

[4]

◉ SYDNEY

4WD and a winch. A few basic spare parts, such as fan belts and radiator hoses, are worth carrying if you're travelling to places where traffic is light and garages are few and far between.

Motorcyclists should beware of dehydration in the dry, hot air – carry at least 5L of water on remote roads in central Australia and drink plenty of it, even if you don't feel thirsty. It's worth carrying some spares and tools even if you don't know how to use them, because someone else often does. Carry a workshop manual for your bike and spare elastic (octopus) straps for securing your gear.

The RTA (p390) can provide up-to-date road condition information.

### Road Hazards

The roadkill that you unfortunately see a lot of in the outback is mostly from cars and trucks hitting animals during the night. Many Australians avoid travelling altogether once the sun drops because of the risks posed by animals on the roads.

Kangaroos are common hazards on country roads, as are cows and sheep in the unfenced outback – hitting an animal of this size can make a real mess of your car. Kangaroos are most active around dawn and dusk. They often travel in groups, so if you see one hopping across the road in front of you, slow right down, as its friends may be just behind it.

If you're travelling at night and a large animal appears in front of you, hit the brakes, dip your lights (so you don't continue to dazzle and confuse it) and only swerve if it's safe to do so – numerous travellers have been killed in accidents caused by swerving to miss animals.

A not-so-obvious hazard is driver fatigue. Driving long distances (particularly in hot weather) can be so tiring that you might fall asleep at the wheel – it's not uncommon and the consequences can be unthinkable. So on a long haul, stop and rest every two hours or so – do some exercise, change drivers or have a coffee.

### Road Rules

Driving in NSW holds few real surprises, other than the odd animal caught in your headlights. Australians drive on the left-hand side of the road and all cars are right-hand drive. An important road rule is 'give way

## OUTBACK ROAD SHOW

On many outback highways you'll see thundering road trains – huge trucks (a prime mover, plus two or three trailers) up to 50m long. These things don't move over for anyone and it's like something out of a *Mad Max* movie to have one bearing down on you at 120km/h. When you see a road train approaching on a narrow bitumen road, slow down and pull over – If It has to put its wheels off the road to pass you, the resulting shower of stones will almost certainly smash your windscreen. When trying to overtake one, make sure you have plenty of room to complete the manoeuvre (allow about a kilometre). Road trains throw up a lot of dust on dirt roads, so if you see one coming it's best to pull over and stop until it has gone past.

And while you're on outback roads, don't forget the standard bush wave to oncoming drivers – It's simply a matter of lifting the index finger off the steering wheel to acknowledge your fellow motorist.

to the right' – if an intersection is unmarked (unusual), you must give way to vehicles entering the intersection from your right.

The general speed limit in built-up areas is 60km/h, although this has been reduced to 50km/h on residential streets in most states; keep an eye out for signs. Near schools, the limit is 40km/h in the morning and afternoon. On the open highway it's usually 100km/h or 110km/h. The police have speed radar guns and cameras and are fond of using them in strategically concealed locations.

Oncoming drivers who flash their lights at you may be giving you a friendly warning of a speed camera ahead – or they may be telling you that your headlights are not on. Whatever, it's polite to wave back if someone does this. Try not to get caught doing It yourself, since it's illegal.

All new cars in Australia have seat belts back and front and it's the law to wear yours – you're likely to get a fine if you don't. Small children must be belted into an approved safety seat.

Drink-driving is a real problem, especially in country areas. Serious attempts to reduce the resulting road toll are ongoing and random breath-tests are not uncommon in built-up areas. If you're caught with a blood-alcohol level of over 0.05% be prepared for a big fine and the loss of your licence.

The RTA (p390) provides a downloadable brochure in several languages that summarises Australian road rules for foreigners.

### PARKING
One of the big problems with driving around Sydney (or popular tourist towns like Byron Bay) is finding somewhere to park. Even if you do find a spot, there's likely to be a time

restriction, meter (or ticket machine) or both. It's one of the great rorts in Australia that by overstaying your welcome (even by five minutes) in a space that may cost only a few dollars to park in, local councils are prepared to fine you anywhere from $50 to $120. Also note that if you park in a 'clearway' your car will be towed away or clamped – look for signs. In Sydney there are large multistorey car parks where you can park all day for between $15 and $30.

Many towns in NSW have a peculiar form of reverse-angle parking, a recipe for disaster if ever there was one. If in doubt, park your car in the same direction and at the same angle as other cars.

### HITCHING
Hitching is never entirely safe in any country in the world, and we don't recommend it. Travellers who decide to hitch should understand that they are taking a potentially serious risk. People who do choose to hitch will be safer if they travel in pairs and let someone know where they are planning to go.

In Australia, the hitching signal can be a thumbs up, but a downward-pointed finger is more widely understood.

### LOCAL TRANSPORT
#### Bus & Train
Sydney has a good public transport network. The **Transport Infoline** ( ☎ 13 15 00; www.131500.com .au) provides schedule and service information. In Canberra, Wollongong and Newcastle, it's also possible to get around by public transport. Anywhere else, it becomes a bit problematic. There are buses in cities such as Wagga Wagga, Nowra and Dubbo, but they're fairly infrequent.

TRANSPORT

## Taxi

Sydney has a lot of taxis, but you won't see many plying for trade on the streets of country towns. That doesn't mean they aren't there – even small towns often have at least one taxi and you can find the number in a local phone book or at the tourist office.

Taxi fares vary through the state, but shouldn't differ much from Sydney. In most towns you should be able to call a taxi service by dialling ☎ 13 10 08.

## TRAIN

Rail travel in Australia is something you do because you really want to – not because it's cheaper or more convenient, and certainly not because it's fast. That said, trains are more comfortable than buses, and on some of Australia's long-distance train journeys the romance of the rails is alive and kicking. The *Indian Pacific* across the Nullarbor Plain between Sydney and Perth is one of Australia's great rail journeys. For details on this journey contact **Great Southern Railways** ( ☎ 13 21 47; www.gsr.com.au).

Rail services in NSW are run by the government's **CountryLink** ( ☎ 13 22 32; www.countrylink .info) which serves a variety of destinations with trains and connecting buses. Some services include destinations in Victoria and Queensland. Fairly fast trains known as XPTs serve Canberra (four hours), Wagga Wagga (six hours), Melbourne (10 hours) and Brisbane (14 hours).

Many other routes are served such as those to Byron Bay (13 hours), Broken Hill (13 hours) and Moree (seven hours) but these trains can run quite slowly, and often only once a day or less.

CountryLink trains are air-conditioned and comfortable. There are usually two classes of service – first and economy – with the former offering more room and nicer seats. Food and drink are available for purchase. There are Sydney to Brisbane and Melbourne night trains, which include sleepers with twin compartments.

**CityRail** ( ☎ 13 15 00; www.cityrail.info), the Sydney metropolitan service, runs frequent commuter-style trains south through Wollongong to Bomaderry; west through the Blue Mountains to Katoomba and Lithgow; north to Newcastle; and southwest through the Southern Highlands to Goulburn. Some services duplicate the near-Sydney portions of CountryLink services, but they're slower and much cheaper, especially if you buy a day-return ticket. Off-peak return fares are available after 9am on weekdays and all day on weekends.

### Costs

Children can travel for reduced fares; advance purchase fares will save you 30% to 50%. First class costs about 40% more than economy.

Some standard one-way adult economy fares on CountryLink trains:

| Destination | Fare |
| --- | --- |
| Sydney-Brisbane | $100 |
| Sydney-Broken Hill | $110 |
| Sydney-Canberra | $55 |
| Sydney-Melbourne | $100 |
| Sydney-Moree | $80 |
| Sydney-Wagga Wagga | $70 |

### Reservations

As the CountryLink booking system is computerised, most stations can make a booking for most journeys. For reservations telephone ☎ 13 22 32 during office hours; this will connect you to the nearest main-line station.

You can't book seats on CityRail trains.

## Train Passes

The **Great Southern Railways Pass** (☎ 13 21 47), which is only available to passport-equipped non-Australian residents, allows unlimited travel on the national rail network for a period of six months. The pass costs a meagre $690/590 per adult/concession (meagre when you consider the amount of ground you could cover over the life of the pass), but note that you'll be travelling in a 'Daynighter' reclining seat, and not a cabin. You need to pre-book all seats at least 24 hours in advance.

**CountryLink** offers several travel passes. The **East Coast Discovery Pass** allows one-way economy travel from Melbourne through NSW and Sydney and on to Brisbane and Cairns (in either direction) with unlimited stopovers, and is valid for six months – the full trip costs $470, while segments from Sydney to Brisbane and Sydney to Melbourne cost $110. Available to overseas visitors with valid passports only is the **Backtracker Rail Pass**, which allows travel on the entire CountryLink network and comes in four versions: a 14-day/1-/3-/6-month pass costing $235/275/300/420 respectively.

**CityRail** (☎ 13 15 00; www.cityrail.info) offers the **DayTripper Pass** (adult/child $16/8) good on trains, buses and ferries throughout Sydney and its suburbs. The **Blue Mountains ExplorerLink** (adult/child $45/17) includes a day-return ticket to Katoomba and all-day access to the Explorer Bus that visits 27 attractions in the Blue Mountains.

TRANSPORT

# Health Dr David Millar

Australia is a remarkably healthy country in which to travel, considering that such a large portion of it lies in the tropics. Tropical diseases such as malaria and yellow fever are unknown, diseases of insanitation such as cholera and typhoid are unheard of, and, thanks to Australia's isolation and quarantine standards, even some animal diseases such as rabies and foot-and-mouth disease have yet to be recorded.

Few travellers to NSW should experience anything worse than an upset stomach or a bad hangover, and if you do fall ill, the standard of hospitals and health care is high.

# BEFORE YOU GO

Since most vaccines don't produce immunity until at least two weeks after they're given, visit a physician four to eight weeks before departure. Ask your doctor for an International Certificate of Vaccination (otherwise known as the yellow booklet), which will list all the vaccinations you've received. This is mandatory for countries that require proof of yellow-fever vaccination upon entry (sometimes required in Australia, see this page), but it's a good idea to carry it wherever you travel.

Bring medications in their original, clearly labelled containers. A signed and dated letter from your physician describing your medical conditions and medications, including generic names, is also a good idea. If carrying syringes or needles, be sure to have a physician's letter documenting their medical necessity.

If your health insurance doesn't cover you for medical expenses abroad, consider getting extra insurance; check www.lonelyplanet.com for more information. Find out in advance if your insurance plan will make payments directly to providers or reimburse you later for overseas health expenditures. See opposite for details of health care in NSW.

## INSURANCE

Health insurance is essential for all travellers. While health care in NSW is of a high standard and not overly expensive by international standards, considerable costs can build up and repatriation is extremely expensive. If you are unsure whether your existing insurance will cover you check www.lonelyplanet.com for more information.

## RECOMMENDED VACCINATIONS

Proof of yellow-fever vaccination is required only from travellers entering Australia within six days of having stayed overnight or longer in a yellow-fever-infected country. For a full list of these countries visit the website of the **World Health Organization** (WHO; www.who.int/wer/) or that of the **Centers for Disease Control and Prevention** (www.cdc.gov/travel/blusheet.htm).

If you're really worried about your health when travelling there are a few vaccinations you could consider for NSW. The WHO recommends that all travellers should be covered for diphtheria, tetanus, measles, mumps, rubella, chickenpox and polio, as well as hepatitis B, regardless of their destination. Planning to travel is a great time to ensure that all routine vaccination cover is complete. The consequences of these diseases can be severe and while Australia has high levels of childhood vaccination coverage, outbreaks of these diseases do occur.

## MEDICAL CHECKLIST

- antibiotics
- antidiarrhoeal drugs (eg loperamide)
- acetaminophen/paracetamol or aspirin
- anti-inflammatory drugs (eg ibuprofen)

- antihistamines (for hay fever and allergic reactions)
- antibacterial ointment for cuts and abrasions
- steroid cream or cortisone (for poison ivy and other allergic rashes)
- bandages, gauze, gauze rolls
- adhesive or paper tape
- scissors, safety pins, tweezers
- thermometer
- pocketknife
- DEET-containing insect repellent for the skin
- permethrin-containing insect spray for clothing, tents and bed nets
- sun block
- oral rehydration salts
- iodine tablets or water filter (for water purification)

## INTERNET RESOURCES

There is a wealth of travel health advice on the internet. For further information, the **Lonely Planet website** (www.lonelyplanet.com) is a good place to start. The **WHO** (www.who.int/ith/) publishes a superb book called *International Travel & Health,* which is revised annually and is available online at no cost. Another website of general interest is **MD Travel Health** (www.mdtravelhealth.com), which provides complete travel health recommendations for every country and is updated daily.

## FURTHER READING

Lonely Planet's *Healthy Travel Australia, New Zealand & the Pacific* is a handy, pocket-sized guide packed with useful information including pretrip planning, emergency first aid, immunisation and disease information and what to do if you get sick on the road. *Travel with Children* from Lonely Planet also includes advice on travel health for younger children.

# IN TRANSIT

## DEEP VEIN THROMBOSIS (DVT)

Blood clots may form in the legs (deep vein thrombosis) during plane flights, chiefly because of prolonged immobility. The longer the flight, the greater the risk. Though most blood clots are reabsorbed uneventfully, some may break off and travel through the blood vessels to the lungs, where they could cause life-threatening complications.

---

**TRAVEL-HEALTH WEBSITES**

It's usually a good idea to consult your government's travel-health website before departure, if one is available:
**Australia** www.dfat.gov.au/travel
**Canada** www.travelhealth.gc.ca
**United Kingdom** www.doh.gov.uk/traveladvice
**United States** www.cdc.gov/travel

---

The chief symptom of deep vein thrombosis is swelling or pain of the foot, ankle or calf, usually – but not always – on just one side. When a blood clot travels to the lungs, it may cause chest pain and breathing difficulties. Travellers with any of these symptoms should immediately seek medical attention.

To prevent the development of deep vein thrombosis on long flights, you should walk about the cabin, perform isometric compressions of the leg muscles (ie flex the leg muscles while sitting), drink plenty of fluids and avoid alcohol and tobacco.

## JET LAG & MOTION SICKNESS

Jet lag is common when crossing more than five time zones, resulting in insomnia, fatigue, malaise or nausea. To avoid jet lag try drinking plenty of nonalcoholic fluids and eating light meals. Upon arrival, get exposure to natural sunlight and readjust your schedule (for meals, sleep etc) as soon as possible.

Antihistamines such as dimenhydrinate and meclizine are usually the first choice for treating motion sickness. Their main side effect is drowsiness. A herbal alternative is ginger, which works like a charm for some people.

# IN NEW SOUTH WALES

## AVAILABILITY & COST OF HEALTH CARE

Australia has an excellent health-care system. It is a mixture of privately run medical clinics and hospitals, and a system of public hospitals funded by the government. The Medicare system covers Australian residents for some health-care costs. Visitors from countries with which Australia has a reciprocal health-care agreement (New Zealand, the UK, the Netherlands, Sweden, Finland, Italy, Malta and Ireland) are eligible for benefits to the extent specified under the Medicare programme. If you are from one of these countries, check the details before departure. In general, the agreements provide for any episode of ill-health that requires prompt medical attention. For further details visit www.health.gov.au/pubs /mbs/mbs3/medicare.htm.

There are excellent, specialised public-health facilities for women and children in Sydney.

Over-the-counter medications are available at privately owned chemists throughout NSW. These include painkillers, antihistamines for allergies and skin-care products.

You may find that medications readily available over the counter in some countries are only available in Australia by prescription. These include the oral contraceptive pill, most medications for asthma and all antibiotics. If you take medication on a regular basis bring an adequate supply and ensure you have details of the generic name as brand names may differ between countries.

In NSW it is possible to get to remote locations where there may well be a significant delay in emergency services reaching you in the event of serious accident or illness – do not underestimate the vastness between most major outback towns. An increased level of self-reliance and preparation is essential; consider taking a wilderness first-aid course, such as those offered at the **Wilderness Medicine Institute** (www.wmi.net.au); take a comprehensive first-aid kit that is appropriate for the activities planned; and ensure that you have adequate means of communication. NSW has extensive mobile phone coverage, but additional radio communications are important for remote areas. The Royal Flying Doctor Service provides an important backup for remote communities.

## INFECTIOUS DISEASES
### Bat lyssavirus
Related to rabies and has caused some deaths. The risk is greatest for animal handlers and vets. Rabies vaccine is effective, but the risk to travellers is very low.

### Giardiasis
Widespread in the waterways around Australia. Drinking untreated water from streams and lakes is not recommended. Water filters and boiling or treating water with iodine are effective in preventing the disease. Symp-

toms consist of intermittent bad-smelling diarrhoea, abdominal bloating and wind. Effective treatment is available (tinidazole or metronidazole).

### Meningococcal Disease
Occurs worldwide and is a risk with prolonged use of dormitory-style accommodation. A vaccine exists for some types of this disease, namely meningococcal A, C, Y and W. No vaccine is presently available for the viral type of meningitis.

### Ross River Fever
Widespread throughout Australia. The virus is spread by mosquitoes living in marshy areas. In addition to fever the disease causes headache, joint and muscular pain and a rash, before resolving after five to seven days.

### Sexually Transmitted Diseases
Occurs at rates similar to most other Western countries. The most common symptoms are pain while passing urine and a discharge. Infection can be present without symptoms so seek medical screening after any unprotected sex with a new partner. Throughout the country, you'll find sexual health clinics in all of the major hospitals. Always use a condom with any new sexual partner. Condoms are readily available in chemists and through vending machines in many public places, including toilets.

## ENVIRONMENTAL HAZARDS
### Bites & Stings
#### MARINE ANIMALS
Marine spikes, such as those found on sea urchins, stonefish, scorpion fish, catfish and stingrays, can cause severe local pain or worse. If this occurs, immediately immerse the affected area in hot water (as hot as can be tolerated). Keep topping up with hot water until the pain subsides and medical care can be reached. Marine stings from jellyfish such as box jellyfish also occur in Australia's tropical waters, particularly during the wet season (October to April). The box jellyfish has an incredibly potent sting and has been known to cause fatalities. Warning signs exist at affected beaches, and stinger nets are in place at the more popular beaches. Never dive into water until you have first checked if it is safe with local beach life-saving representatives. 'Stinger suits' (full-body Lycra swimsuits) prevent

stinging, as do wetsuits. If you are stung, first aid consists of washing the skin with vinegar to prevent further discharge of any remaining stinging cells, followed by rapid transfer to a hospital; antivenom is widely available.

## SHARKS

Despite extensive media coverage, the risk of shark attack in Australian waters is no greater than in other countries with extensive coastlines. The risk of an attack from sharks on scuba divers in NSW is low. Check with local surf life-saving groups about local risks.

## SNAKES

Australian snakes have a fearful reputation that is justified in terms of the potency of their venom, but unjustified in terms of the actual risk to travellers and locals. Snakes are usually quite timid in nature and in most instances will move away if disturbed. They are endowed with only small fangs, making it easy to prevent bites to the lower limbs (where 80% of bites occur) by wearing protective clothing (such as gaiters) around the ankles when bushwalking. The bite marks are small and preventing the spread of toxic venom can be achieved by applying pressure to the wound and immobilising the area with a splint or sling before seeking medical attention. Application of an elastic bandage (you can improvise with a T-shirt) wrapped firmly – but not tight enough to cut off the circulation – around the entire limb, along with immobilisation, is a life-saving first-aid measure.

## SPIDERS

Australia has a number of poisonous spiders although the Sydney funnel-web is the only one to have caused a single death in the last 50 years. Redback spiders are found throughout NSW. Bites cause increasing pain at the site followed by profuse sweating and generalised symptoms. First aid includes application of ice or cold packs to the bite and transfer to hospital.

White-tailed (brown recluse) spider bites may cause an ulcer that is very difficult to heal. Clean the wound thoroughly and seek medical assistance.

## Heat Illness

Very hot weather is experienced year-round in some parts of NSW. When arriving from a temperate or cold climate, remember that it takes two weeks for acclimatisation to occur. Before the body is acclimatised an excessive amount of salt is lost by perspiring, so increasing the salt in your diet is essential.

Heat exhaustion occurs when fluid intake does not keep up with fluid loss. Symptoms include dizziness, fainting, fatigue, nausea or vomiting. On observation the skin is usually pale, cool and clammy. Treatment consists of rest in a cool, shady place and fluid replacement with water or diluted sports drinks.

Heatstroke is a severe form of heat illness that occurs after fluid depletion or extreme heat challenge from heavy exercise. This is a true medical emergency with heating of the brain leading to disorientation, hallucinations and seizures. Prevention is by maintaining an adequate fluid intake to ensure the continued passage of clear and copious urine, especially during physical exertion.

A number of unprepared travellers die from dehydration each year in outback Australia. This can be prevented by following these simple rules:

- Carry sufficient water for any trip, including extra in case of breakdown.
- Always let someone, such as the local police, know where you are going and when you expect to arrive.
- Carry communications equipment of some form.
- In nearly all cases it is better to stay with the vehicle rather than walking for help.

## Hypothermia

Hypothermia is a significant risk, especially during the winter months in the southern alpine region of NSW. Despite the absence of high mountain ranges, strong winds produce a high chill factor that can result in hypothermia in even moderately cool temperatures. Early signs include the inability to perform fine movements (such as doing up buttons), shivering and a bad case of the 'umbles' (fumbles, mumbles, grumbles, stumbles). The key elements of treatment include changing the environment to one where heat loss is minimised, changing out of any wet clothing, adding dry clothes with wind and waterproof layers, adding insulation and providing fuel (water and carbohydrate) to allow shivering, which builds the internal temperature. In severe hypothermia, shivering actually stops – this is a medical emergency

HEALTH

requiring rapid evacuation in addition to the above measures.

## Insect-Borne Illness

Various insects can be a source of irritation. Protection from mosquitoes, sandflies, ticks and leeches can be achieved by a combination of the following strategies:

- Wearing loose, long-sleeved clothing.
- Application of 30% DEET on all exposed skin, repeating application every three to four hours.
- Impregnation of clothing with permethrin (an insecticide that kills insects but is completely safe for humans).

## Surf Beaches & Drowning

NSW has some exceptional surf beaches. Beaches vary enormously in the slope of the underlying bottom, resulting in varying power of the surf. Check with local surf life-saving organisations before entering the surf, and be aware of your own limitations and expertise.

## Ultraviolet Light Exposure

Australia has one of the highest rates of skin cancer in the world. Monitor exposure to direct sunlight closely. UV exposure is greatest between 10am and 4pm so avoid skin exposure during these times. Always use 30+ sunscreen, applied 30 minutes before exposure, and repeat regularly to minimise sun damage.

## Water-Borne Illness

Tap water is universally safe in NSW. Increasing numbers of streams and rivers and lakes, however, are being contaminated by bugs that cause diarrhoea, making water purification essential. The simplest way of purifying water is to boil it thoroughly. Consider purchasing a water filter. It's very important when buying a filter to read the specifications, so that you know exactly what it removes from the water and what it doesn't. Simple filtering will not remove all dangerous organisms, so if you cannot boil water it should be treated chemically. Chlorine tablets will kill many pathogens, but not some parasites such as giardia and amoebic cysts. Iodine is more effective in purifying water and is available in tablet form. Follow the directions carefully and remember that too much iodine can be harmful.

# Glossary

**ACT** – Australian Capital Territory
**arvo** – afternoon

**back o' Bourke** – back of beyond; middle of nowhere
**barbie** – barbecue
**beaut, beauty** – great; fantastic
**bikies** – motorcyclists
**billabong** – waterhole in a riverbed formed by waters receding in the dry season
**billy** – tin container used to boil water in the *bush*
**bitumen** – surfaced road
**black stump** – where the *back o' Bourke* begins
**bloke** – man
**blokey** – exhibiting characteristics considered typically masculine
**blow flies** – large flies
**blowies** – see *blow flies*
**blue** – argument or fight ('have a blue')
**body board** – half-sized surfboard
**bogan** – young, unsophisticated person
**boogie board** – small flat board for body surfing
**booze bus** – police van used for breath-testing for alcohol
**bottle shop** – liquor shop; off-licence
**brekky** – breakfast
**bush, the** – country; anywhere away from the city
**bush tucker** – native foods
**bushie** – a person who lives in the bush
**bushwalking** – hiking
**BYO** – bring your own; a restaurant license that permits customers to drink alcohol they have purchased elsewhere

**cask wine** – wine packaged in a plastic bladder surrounded by a cardboard box (a great Australian invention)
**chocka** – completely full; from 'chock-a-block'
**chook** – chicken
**chuck a U-ey** – make a U-turn; turn a car around within a road
**corroboree** – Aboriginal festival or gathering for ceremonial or spiritual reasons
**cozzie** – swimming costume
**crook** – ill or substandard
**cuppa** – as in cuppa tea, an outback institution, especially when combined with a yarn

**dag** – dirty lump of wool at back end of a sheep; also an affectionate or mildly abusive term for a socially inept person
**didgeridoo** – wind instrument made from a hollow piece of wood, traditionally played by Aboriginal men

**dinkum** – honest or genuine; *true blue*
**dob in** – to inform on someone
**donga** – small, transportable building widely used in the *outback*
**Dreamtime** – complex concept that forms the basis of Aboriginal spirituality, incorporating the creation of the world and the spiritual energies operating around us; 'Dreaming' is often the preferred term as it avoids the association with time
**drongo** – worthless or stupid person
**dunny** – outdoor lavatory

**earbash** – to talk nonstop
**Esky** – large insulated box for keeping food and drinks cold

**fair dinkum** – see *dinkum*
**flog** – sell; steal
**fossick** – hunt for gems or semiprecious stones

**galah** – noisy parrot, thus noisy idiot
**game** – brave ('game as Ned Kelly')
**g'day** – good day; traditional Australian greeting
**goon** – cheap wine, usually from a cask (see cask wine)
**grazier** – sheep or cattle farmer operating on a large scale
**grouse** – very good

**homestead** – residence of a *station* owner or manager
**how are ya?** – standard greeting (expected answer: 'Good, thanks, how are you?')

**iffy** – dodgy, questionable

**jackaroo** – male trainee on an *outback station*
**jillaroo** – female trainee on an *outback station*

**kali** – jumbo-sized boomerang
**kick the bucket** – to die
**knackered** – broken, tired
**Kombi** – a classic (hippies') type of van made by Volkswagon

**lair** – layabout; ruffian
**larrikin** – hooligan; mischievous youth
**lay-by** – to put a deposit on an article so the shop will hold it for you
**lob in** – drop in (to see someone)
**lollies** – sweets, candy
**loo** – toilet

**mate** – general term of familiarity, whether you know the person or not

**milk bar** – small shop selling milk and other basic provisions

**Mod Oz** – modern Australian cuisine influenced by a wide range of foreign cuisines, but with a definite local flavour

**mozzies** – mosquitoes

**mug** – foolish or gullible person

**no worries!** – no problems; that's OK!

**ocker** – uncultivated or boorish Australian; a derider

**outback** – remote part of the *bush; back o' Bourke*

**PADI** – Professional Association of Diving Instructors

**piss** – beer; see also *take the piss*

**piss up** – boozy party

**pissed** – drunk

**pissed off** – annoyed

**plonk** – cheap wine

**pokies** – poker machines

**Pom** – English person

**reckon!** – you bet! Absolutely!

**rego** – (car) registration

**rellie** – (family) relative

**rip** – a strong ocean current or undertow

**road train** – semitrailer truck towing several trailers

**root** – to have sexual intercourse

**rubbish** – to deride or tease

**sanger** – sandwich

**sarni** – sandwich

**schooner** – large beer glass

**sealed road** – bitumen road

**session** – lengthy period of heavy drinking

**shark biscuit** – inexperienced surfer

**sheila** – woman

**she'll be right** – no problems; no worries

**shellacking** – comprehensive defeat

**shout** – to buy a round of drinks ('Your shout!')

**sickie** – day off work ill (or malingering)

**station** – large farm

**stickybeak** – nosy person

**stroppy** – bad-tempered

**stubby** – 375ml bottle of beer

**swag** – canvas-covered bed roll used in the *outback*; also a large amount

**take the piss** – deliberately tell someone an untruth, often as social sport; see also *piss*

**tea** – evening meal

**true blue** – honest or genuine; *dinkum*

**tucker** – food

**unsealed road** – dirt road

**ute** – utility; a pick-up truck

**walkabout** – lengthy walk away from it all

**whinge** – to complain or moan

**wobbly** – disturbing, unpredictable behaviour ('throw or chuck a wobbly')

**woomera** – stick used by Aborigines to propel spears

**yabbie** – small freshwater crayfish

**yobbo** – uncouth, aggressive person

# Behind the Scenes

## THIS BOOK

This is the 5th edition of *New South Wales* and the first time 'Sydney' appears in the title (phew, now we all know where we're talking about!). The previous edition was coordinated by Ryan Ver Berkmoes, ably assisted by Sally O'Brien, Miriam Raphael, Paul Smitz, Rick Starey, Justine Vaisutis and Lucas Vidgen. The Culture and Food & Drink chapters were originally informed by Matthew Evans and Verity Campbell. This time around, Justine stepped up to the plate to coordinate the title, with authors Charles Rawlings-Way, Lindsay Brown, Jocelyn Harewood, Penny Watson and Wendy Kramer doing the hard yards from the Blue Mountains to the back o' Bourke. Historian Michael Cathcart wrote the History chapter and Australia's leading environmental scientist and writer on climate change, Tim Flannery, contributed to the Environment chapter. This guidebook was commissioned in Lonely Planet's Melbourne office, and produced by the following:

**Commissioning Editor** Meg Worby
**Coordinating Editor** Nigel Chin
**Coordinating Cartographer** Jacqueline Nguyen
**Coordinating Layout Designer** Cara Smith
**Managing Editor** Suzannah Shwer
**Managing Cartographer** Julie Sheridan
**Assisting Editors** Elisa Arduca, Jackey Coyle, Melissa Faulkner, Jocelyn Harewood, Liani Solari, Simon Williamson
**Assisting Cartographers** Ross Butler, Marion Byass, Daniel Fennessy, Josh Geoghegan, Corey Hutchison, Amanda Sierp, Sarah Sloane
**Cover Designer** Pepi Bluck

**Colour Designer** Steven Cann
**Project Manager** Kate McLeod

**Thanks to** Sally Darmody, Laura Gibb, Liz Heynes, Geoff Howard, Simone McNamara, Stephanie Ong, Trent Paton, Dianne Schallmeiner, Kate Whitfield, Celia Wood

## THANKS
### JUSTINE VAISUTIS

Many people deserve thanks for putting up with me in general, but for this book additional gratitude goes to Charles, Wendy, Jocelyn, Penny and Lindsay for their outstanding work and assistance. In-house, thanks to Meg Worby, Julie Sheridan, Corie Waddell, Suzannah Shwer, Nigel Chin and Jacqueline Nguyen. Thanks to my ACF crew. Cheers to Kate, Dame and Mark (and Luke and Heidi) for the Byron Bucks Do. For my NSW childhood and the travel bug much love to Mum, Dad and Bill. For giggles, dinners and inspiration thanks to Aidy. And to Simon Sellars for secret languages, nummits and all things bug.

### JOCELYN HAREWOOD

Thank you so much to big brother Ern for joining me for much of the journey, and wonderful friend Anne, who kept her eyes peeled for kangaroos and feral goats as we burnt up the outback highways To Allan and Linda Duffy, thanks heaps for your hospitality and especially for sharing your vast understanding and knowledge of Broken Hill's culture and history. Thanks too to all the helpful staff at visitors centres right across NSW who provided great information and a constant

---

### THE LONELY PLANET STORY

The story begins with a classic travel adventure: Tony and Maureen Wheeler's 1972 journey across Europe and Asia to Australia. There was no useful information about the overland trail then, so Tony and Maureen published the first Lonely Planet guidebook to meet a growing need.

From a kitchen table, Lonely Planet has grown to become the largest independent travel publisher in the world, with offices in Melbourne (Australia), Oakland (USA) and London (UK). Today Lonely Planet guidebooks cover the globe. There is an ever-growing list of books and information in a variety of media. Some things haven't changed. The main aim is still to make it possible for adventurous travellers to get out there – to explore and better understand the world.

At Lonely Planet we believe travellers can make a positive contribution to the countries they visit – if they respect their host communities and spend their money wisely. Every year 5% of company profit is donated to charities around the world.

**BEHIND THE SCENES**

input of enthusiasm to keep my energy levels topped up. To the team at LP and Justine Vaisutis, thanks for everything. And especially thanks to everyone living and working across these great regions whose enjoyment of the vast spaces and optimism in the face of the challenges is totally contagious.

## WENDY KRAMER

Thank you to all my mates for the support and encouragement I unfailingly receive, particularly my three best buds, Duck, Lexy, and the most beautiful selfless woman in the world, Katie Ormonde. Thank you to my family for being my family. *Seinfeld* versus *Everybody Loves Raymond*...we give them both a run for their money. And Justine, you have been my rock during write-up (the ultimate compliment coming from a geologist). Although at times I may linger on the edge, it was your reassurance and guidance that stopped me from toppling over.

## CHARLES RAWLINGS-WAY

Thanks to the following folks for their input, generosity, friendship and distraction during the creation of this book: Megan Worby, Mona & Olivia Rawlings-Way, Warren & Nathan Jones, Jay Chinchen, Lauren Walter, Jenny Blake, Rodney & Sandra Renshaw, Rod & Cathy Connelly, Justine Vaisutis and the in-house LP staff who schmoozed this book through production.

More than ever, thank you my darling Meg for your eternal patience, bottomless wit and unparalleled glamour.

## PENNY WATSON

To my friends and family with the following surnames: Clarkin, Gorman, Jacobs, King, McKenzie, McHarg, McPhee, Smiedt, Watson and Williams. Thanks for your spare rooms, washing machines, shampoo, conditioner, wi-fi and excellent sense of humour during my research and write-up. You're all rather 'unique'.

While on the road, the tip-offs and hospitality from Irena & Jeremy Hutchings, Kierrin McKnight, Andrew & Elizabeth Nowosad, Greg Soster, Steve Melchior and Daniel Joseph McConell were invaluable. So, too, was the information from many of the NSW visitors centres I visited.

Lastly, *muchas muchas gracias* to my lovable travelling companion Pippito Luigi who popped the question on top of Pigeon House Mountain. How could a girl say 'no'?

## OUR READERS

**Many thanks to the travellers who used the last edition and wrote to us with helpful hints, useful advice and interesting anecdotes:**

Alan Affleck, Adam Baumgartner, Elizabeth Cage, Gregory Carroll, Marion Coolen, Louisa Curtis, Eric Dalton, Sue Dodds, PA Elliot, Mark Febery, Kathleen Fechner, Rosie Freeman, Scott Graham, Duncan Heining, Marc Jarnet, Kristi Jordan, Esther Killat, Malcolm Knowles, Jasmine Lange, Hanna Lempola, Kate Matthews, Celine Mckeown, Debra Metcalf-Harrison, Aaron Michie, Arlene Miller, Don Miller, Mariana Nerger, Julia Neumann, Margaret O'Connell, Rhys Owen, Virginnia & Robert Powles, Erin Prior, Liam Putnis, Jane Quick, Caroline Raftery, Jean Relph, Baerbel Richter, John Spencer, Diana Stewart, Kathy Tildsley, Amanda Townsend, Betty Wood

### SEND US YOUR FEEDBACK

We love to hear from travellers – your comments keep us on our toes and help make our books better. Our well-travelled team reads every word on what you loved or loathed about this book. Although we cannot reply individually to postal submissions, we always guarantee that your feedback goes straight to the appropriate authors, in time for the next edition. Each person who sends us information is thanked in the next edition – and the most useful submissions are rewarded with a free book.

To send us your updates – and find out about Lonely Planet events, newsletters and travel news – visit our award-winning website: **www.lonelyplanet.com/contact**.

Note: we may edit, reproduce and incorporate your comments in Lonely Planet products such as guidebooks, websites and digital products, so let us know if you don't want your comments reproduced or your name acknowledged. For a copy of our privacy policy visit www.lonelyplanet.com/privacy.

# Index

**000** Map pages
**000** Photograph pages

**000** Map pages
000 Photograph pages

424

## MAP LEGEND

### ROUTES

Tollway
Freeway
Primary
Secondary
Tertiary
Lane
Under Construction
Unsealed Road
One-Way Street

Mall/Steps
Tunnel
Pedestrian Overpass
Walking Tour
Walking Tour Detour
Walking Trail
Walking Path
Track

### TRANSPORT

Ferry
Monorail
Bus Route

Rail
Rail (Underground)
Tram

### HYDROGRAPHY

River, Creek
Intermittent River
Swamp
Mangrove
Reef

Canal
Water
Lake (Dry)
Lake (Salt)
Mudflats

### BOUNDARIES

International
State, Provincial
Marine Park

Regional, Suburb
Ancient Wall
Cliff

### AREA FEATURES

Airport
Area of Interest
Beach, Desert
Building
Campus
Cemetery, Christian
Cemetery, Other
Forest

Land
Mall
Market
Park
Reservation
Rocks
Sports
Urban

### POPULATION

◎ **CAPITAL (NATIONAL)**
● **Large City**
● Small City

◉ CAPITAL (STATE)
◉ Medium City
● Town, Village

### SYMBOLS

**Sights/Activities**
Beach
Canoeing, Kayaking
Castle, Fortress
Christian
Diving, Snorkeling
Islamic
Jewish
Monument
Museum, Gallery
Picnic Area
Point of Interest
Pool
Ruin
Skiing
Surfing, Surf Beach
Windsurfing
Winery, Vineyard
Zoo, Bird Sanctuary

**Eating**
Eating

**Drinking**
Drinking
Café

**Entertainment**
Entertainment

**Shopping**
Shopping

**Sleeping**
Sleeping
Camping

**Transport**
Airport, Airfield
Bus Station
Cycling, Bicycle Path
General Transport
Taxi Rank
Trail Head

**Information**
Bank, ATM
Embassy/Consulate
Hospital, Medical
Information
Internet Facilities
Parking Area
Petrol Station
Police Station
Post Office, GPO
Telephone
Toilets

**Geographic**
Lighthouse
Lookout
Mountain, Volcano
National Park
River Flow
Waterfall

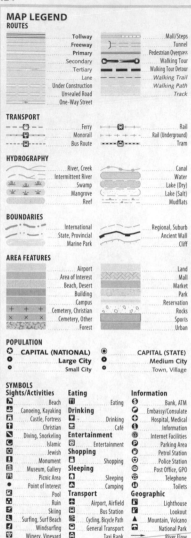

## LONELY PLANET OFFICES

### Australia
Head Office
Locked Bag 1, Footscray, Victoria 3011
☎ 03 8379 8000, fax 03 8379 8111
talk2us@lonelyplanet.com.au

### USA
150 Linden St, Oakland, CA 94607
☎ 510 893 8555, toll free 800 275 8555
fax 510 893 8572
info@lonelyplanet.com

### UK
72–82 Rosebery Ave,
Clerkenwell, London EC1R 4RW
☎ 020 7841 9000, fax 020 7841 9001
go@lonelyplanet.co.uk

**Published by Lonely Planet Publications Pty Ltd**
ABN 36 005 607 983

© Lonely Planet Publications Pty Ltd 2007

© photographers as indicated 2007

Cover photograph: Swimming competition at Bondi Beach, Oliver Strewe/Lonely Planet Images. Many of the images in this guide are available for licensing from Lonely Planet Images: www.lonelyplanetimages.com.

Printed through The Bookmaker International Ltd.
Printed in China.